THE CONCORDIA
BIBLE DICTIONARY

By

ERWIN L. LUEKER

CONCORDIA PUBLISHING HOUSE

ST. LOUIS, MISSOURI

1963

Concordia Publishing House, St. Louis, Missouri 63118

© 1963 Concordia Publishing House

Library of Congress Catalog Card No. 63-2622

MANUFACTURED IN THE UNITED STATES OF AMERICA

PREFACE

This concise Bible dictionary is designed to be used with the King James Version, the British Revised Version (readings often the same in the American Standard Version), and the Revised Standard Version. Cross references facilitate unified treatment of the readings of these versions. It may in a more limited way be used with independent translations. The listing of variants is also helpful for insights into meanings of concepts and names.

The number of entries was made as complete as feasible; hence, variants and material from the Apocrypha (frequently related to canonical material) are included. Articles, possessive pronouns, copulatives, etc., are often omitted in the abbreviated style.

The meaning of proper names is given after the pronunciation when such meaning has been established by scholars as certain or probable. In some instances a different meaning was urged by some scholars with almost equal plausibility.

The preparation of even a concise dictionary increases appreciation of the time devoted by scholars to the study and elucidation of the Sacred Scriptures. Lexicons, concordances, translations, commentaries, reference works, and articles in journals by American, British, German, French, and other European scholars were continually consulted. This applies also to such dictionaries as Wm. Smith, *Dictionary of the Bible* (Hurd and Houghton); J. D. Davis, *A Dictionary of the Bible* (Westminster); Miller-Miller, *Harper's Bible Dictionary* (Harper); M. F. Unger, *Bible Dictionary* (Moody); J. Hastings, *A Dictionary of the Bible* (Scribner's); J. Orr, *The International Standard Bible Encyclopaedia* (Howard-Severance), revised by Kyle (Eerdmans); F. Rienecker, *Lexikon zur Bibel* (Brockhaus); T. Schlatter, *Calwer Bibellexikon* (Calwer).

Several entries are revised summaries made by the author on the basis of material published by the late A. W. Klinck. This is indicated at the end of the article.

On the basis of a sample printing, colleagues at Concordia Seminary, St. Louis, and Concordia Seminary, Springfield, gave the author helpful suggestions. Such suggestions were also received from professors at divinity schools, seminaries, and colleges in the United States and from executives, pastors, and teachers. Luther A. Weigle sent lists of comparative readings to the author.

The dictionary was prepared under the auspices of the Literature Board of The Lutheran Church — Missouri Synod. Otto A. Dorn and Elmer E. Foelber gave the author suggestions regarding form and content.

Erich B. Allwardt critically read the entire manuscript, indicated necessary corrections and additions, suggested changes in form, and assisted in the collation of variants.

ERWIN L. LUEKER

iii

ABBREVIATIONS AND SYMBOLS

AD: after Christ
b: born
BC: before Christ
c: approximately; century
cf: see; compare
comp: compare
d: died
E: East(ern)
e g: for example
et al: and others
etc: and so forth
exc: except
ft: foot; feet
G: Greek
gal(s): gallon(s)
H: Hebrew
i e: namely; that is
in: inch(es)
KJ: King James Version
L: Latin
LXX: Septuagint (Greek translation of Old Testament)
mi: mile(s)
mt: mount; mountain(s)
N: North(ern)
NT: New Testament
OT: Old Testament
oz: ounce(s)
pt(s): pint(s)
r: river
RSV: Revised Standard Version
RV: Revised Version (British). Readings thus designated are often also in the American Standard Version (ASV)
qt(s): quart(s)
S: South(ern)
sq: square
W: West(ern)
yr(s): year(s)
listed: This word is used to describe proper nouns found in lists of names in the Apocry-

pha, but not in corresponding Old or New Testament lists
[ ]: variant(s) enclosed in brackets refer only to the immediately preceding reference. Variants following a period (.) refer to all the references in the preceding series

Old Testament

Gn: Genesis
Ex: Exodus
Lv: Leviticus
Nm: Numbers
Dt: Deuteronomy
Jos: Joshua
Ju: Judges
Ru: Ruth
1 Sm: First Samuel
2 Sm: Second Samuel
1 K: First Kings
2 K: Second Kings
1 Ch: First Chronicles
2 Ch: Second Chronicles
Ez: Ezra
Neh: Nehemiah
Est: Esther
Jb: Job
Ps: Psalms
Pr: Proverbs
Ec: Ecclesiastes
SS: Song of Solomon
Is: Isaiah
Jer: Jeremiah
Lm: Lamentations
Eze: Ezekiel
Dn: Daniel
Hos: Hosea
Jl: Joel
Am: Amos
Ob: Obadiah
Jon: Jonah
Mi: Micah
Nah: Nahum
Hab: Habakkuk
Zph: Zephaniah
Hg: Haggai
Zch: Zechariah
Ml: Malachi

New Testament

Mt: Matthew
Mk: Mark
Lk: Luke
Jn: John
Acts
Ro: Romans
1 Co: First Corinthians
2 Co: Second Corinthians
Gl: Galatians
Eph: Ephesians
Ph: Philippians
Cl: Colossians
1 Th: First Thessalonians
2 Th: Second Thessalonians
1 Ti: First Timothy
2 Ti: Second Timothy
Tts: Titus
Phmn: Philemon
Heb: Hebrews
Ja: James
1 Ptr: First Peter
2 Ptr: Second Peter
1 Jn: First John
2 Jn: Second John
3 Jn: Third John
Jude
Rv: Revelation

Apocrypha

1 Esd: First Esdras
2 Esd: Second Esdras
Tob: Tobit
Jdth: Judith
Ap Est: additions to Esther
Wis: Wisdom of Solomon
Sir: Ecclesiasticus, or the Wisdom of Jesus the Son of Sirach
Bar: Baruch
L Jer: Letter of Jeremiah
Ap Dn: additions to Daniel (the Prayer of Azariah and the Song of the Three Young Men)
Sus: Susanna
Bel: Bel and the Dragon
Man: The Prayer of Manasseh
1 Mac: First Maccabees
2 Mac: Second Maccabees

TRANSLITERATION OF HEBREW

': 'aleph
b, bh: beth
g, gh: gimel
d, dh: daleth
h: he
w: wau
z: zayin
ḥ: cheth
ṭ: teth
y: yod

k, kh: kaph
l: lamedh
m: mem
n: nun
s: samekh
': 'ayin
p, ph: pe
ts: tsade
q: qof

r: resh
ṣ: sin
sh: shin
t, th: tau
a, e, i, o, u transliterate long and short Hebrew vowels
: transliterates the vocal shewa

KEY TO PRONUNCIATION

ā: late
â: chaotic
â: fare
ă: add
ä: father
à: mask
ȧ: account
ȧ: sofa
ē: eve
ê: evade
ĕ: end
ē: maker
ĕ: silent
ḛ: here
ī: ice
ĭ: till
i: charity

ō: old
ô: obey
ô: lord
ǒ: dog
ŏ: odd
o: connect
ōō: food
ŏŏ: foot
ū: cube
ú: unite
û: burn
ŭ: but
u: circus
dụ: verdure
th: then
tụ: nature

In each instance an acceptable pronunciation is given which may not be the only correct one.

A

Aalar (ā'á-lär). See *Allar*.

Aaron (âr'un, *of uncertain meaning*). Moses' spokesman and assistant (Ex 4: 14-17; 7); 1st head of Hebrew priesthood. B in Egypt, son of Amram and Jochebed, both Levites (Ex 6:20); brother of Moses (Ex 6:20) and Miriam (Nm 26:59; 1 Ch 6:3); married Elisheba (daughter of Amminadab), who bore Nadab, Abihu, Eleazar, Ithamar (Ex 6: 23); d at 123 on Mt Hor; buried there (Nm 20:22-29).

Aaron was praised for his eloquence (Ex 4:14); regarded coleader with Moses (Ex 7). Helped Hur hold up Moses' hands during battle with Amalekites (Ex 17:12). When Moses tarried on Sinai, Aaron made golden calf (Ex 32). Aaron and Miriam taunted Moses because of his Cushite (KJ: Ethiopian) wife (Nm 12:1). Authority of Aaron vindicated through miracle of rod (Nm 17). Aaron and Moses doubted at Meribah (Nm 20:12).

Moses anointed Aaron and four sons to priesthood, higher order than Levites (Nm 3:1-3). As "holiest of men," Aaron and descendants received offerings from Israelites (Nm 18:8-14). God was his Portion, hence he received no inheritance in Canaan (Nm 18:20). Priestly adornments (breastplate [RSV: breastpiece], ephod, robe, coat, mitre [RSV: turban], girdle) made for Aaron (Ex 28; 39:1-31). Succeeded by Eleazar (Nm 20:28).

Aaronites (âr'un-īts). Priestly descendants of Aaron (KJ: 1 Ch 12:27; 27:17).

Aaron's rod. Proved Aaron's authority by budding; placed before Ark of Testimony (Nm 17; see Heb 9:4).

Ab (ăb). See *time*.

Abacuc (ăb'á-kŭk). See *Habakkuk*.

Abaddon (á-băd'un, destruction, destroyer. KJ: Rv 9:11. RV: Jb 26:6; Pr 15:11; 27: 20; Rv 9:11. RSV: Jb 26:6; 28:22; 31:12; Ps 88:11; Pr 15:11; 27:20; Rv 9:11. KJ, RV translate "destruction" when they do not use Hebrew word). 1. Destruction, ruin (Jb 31:12). 2. Place of ruin for the lost, linked with grave (Ps 88:11) and Sheol (Jb 26:6; Pr 15:11; 27:20). 3. Personified as the Destroyer and linked with Death personified (Jb 28:22). 4. Apollyon, king of bottomless pit (Rv 9:11).

Abadias (ăb-á-dī'ás). See *Obadiah 10*.

Abagtha (á-băg'thá). Chamberlain of Ahasuerus (Est 1:10).

Abana, Abanah (ăb'á-ná). "River of Damascus" in Syria (2 K 5:12). Identified with Greek Chrysorrhoas, modern Barada.

Abarim (ăb'á-rĭm, regions beyond). Region E of Jordan and S of Bashan; its mountains overlook Jordan and Dead Sea (Dt 32:49; Jer 22:20 [KJ: the passages]).

abase. To humble or make low. The proud and wicked are to be abased (Jb 40:11; Eze 21:26). God abases the proud (Jb 22:29; Ps 44:9; Dn 4:37). In NT, RV, RSV translate "humble" where KJ has "abase," except in Ph 4:12.

Abba (ăb'á, *Aramaic*, father). Used to express filial address to God (Mk 14:36; Ro 8:15; Gl 4:6). H *ab* (*abi*) used in composition of proper names.

Abda (ăb'dá, servant). 1. Adoniram's father (1 K 4:6). 2. See *Obadiah 5*.

Abdeel (ăb'dē-ĕl, servant of God). Shelemiah's father (Jer 36:26).

Abdi (ăb'dī, servant of). 1. Merarite Levite; son of Malluch (1 Ch 6:44; 2 Ch 29:12). 2. Divorced foreign wife (Ez 10:26; 1 Esd 9:27 [RV: Oabdius; KJ omits]).

Abdias (ăb-dī'ás). See *Obadiah 12*.

Abdiel (ăb'dī-ĕl, servant of God). Gadite chief of Bashan; father of Ahi; son of Guni (1 Ch 5:15).

Abdon (ăb'dŏn, servile). 1. Judge of Israel for 8 years; Ephraimite; son of Hillel (Ju 12:13-15). 2. Benjaminite; son of Shashak (1 Ch 8:23). 3. Benjaminite; ancestor of Saul; son of Jehiel (1 Ch 8:30; 9:35, 36). 4. See *Achbor 2*. 5. Levitical city in Asher (Jos 21:30; 1 Ch 6:74).

Abednego (á-bĕd'nē-gō, servant of Nego, or Nebo). Babylonian name given to Azariah (Dn 1:7; 3).

Abel (ā'bel, son? vapor?). 2d son of Adam and Eve; keeper of sheep; murdered by Cain, his jealous, rejected brother (Gn 4: 1-16). Abel, a righteous man (Mt 23:35; 1 Jn 3:12), by faith offered more acceptable sacrifice than Cain (Heb 11:4).

Abel (ā'bel, meadow). Prefix for names of towns and places (Gn 50:10, 11; Nm 33: 49; Ju 7:22; 2 Sm 20:14, 15). [Abel in 1 Sm 6:18 should probably read "stone" (H *'eben*), as RV, RSV.]

Abel-beth-maacah (ā'bel-bĕth-mā'á-ká, meadow of house of oppression. KJ: -maachah). Abel of Beth-maacah in 2 Sm 20:14 [KJ, RV: Abel and Beth-maac(h)ah], 15. Abel in 2 Sm 20:18). Town in N Palestine known for its prudence and adherence to custom; attacked by Joab (2 Sm 20:14, 15), Ben-hadad (1 K 15:20), Tiglath-pileser (2 K 15:29).

Abel-cheramim, Abel-keramim (ā'bel-kĕr'á-mīm, meadow of vineyards. KJ: plain of vineyards). Place E of Jordan, probably near Rabbath Ammon (Ju 11:33).

Abel-maim (ā'bel-mā'ĭm, meadow of waters). Perhaps a name for Abel-bethmaacah (2 Ch 16:4).

Abel-meholah (ā'bel-mē-hō'lá, meadow of the dance). Town (Tell el-Maqlub) near Jordan, N of Jabesh-gilead; birthplace of Elisha (1 K 19:16). Enemies routed by Gideon fled to it (Ju 7:22).

Abel-mizraim (ā'bel-mĭz'rá-ĭm, meadow, or mourning, of Egypt). Name given threshing floor of Atad because of comment of Canaanites when Jacob's sons mourned their father (Gn 50:11).

Abel-shittim (ā'bel-shĭt'ĭm, meadow of acacias. Shittim in Nm 25:1; Jos 2:1). Place in Plains of Moab near Jordan; final camping place of Israelites before entering Canaan (Nm 33:49).

Abez (ā'bĕz, whiteness; tin. RV, RSV: Ebez). Town of Issachar (Jos 19:20).

abhorrence (ăb-hôr'ens). Aversion, act of shrinking or withdrawing from. Believers abhor abominable things (Dt 7:26) and sins (Ps 119:163). Wicked abhor righteous (Am 5:10) and God's statutes (Lv 26:43). God abhors idolaters and transgressors (Lv 26:30).

Abi (ā′bī, progenitor. Abijah in 2 Ch 29:1). Mother of Hezekiah; daughter of Zechariah (2 K 18:2).

Abia, Abiah (á-bī′á). See *Abijah*.

Abi-albon (ā′bī-ăl′bon, father is strength. Possibly textual variant for Abiel in 1 Ch 11:32). One of David's mighty men (2 Sm 23:31).

Abiasaph (á-bī′á-săf, my father has gathered. Ebiasaph in 1 Ch 6:23, 37; 9:19). Levite; son of Korah; head of family (Ex 6:24).

Abiathar (á-bī′á-thär, father of abundance). Son of Ahimelech; only son to escape vengeance of Saul; protected by David, whose consultant he became; brought ark to Jerusalem with Zadok; with Joab supported Adonijah as David's successor; banished by Solomon (1 Sm 22:20-23; 30; 2 Sm 8; 15:24-35; 17—20; 1 K 1:7, 19, 25, 42; 2:22-27; 4:4; 1 Ch 15:11; 18:16; 24:6; 27:34; Mk 2:26).

Abib (ā′bĭb). See *time*.

Abida (á-bī′dá, father has knowledge). Son of Midian (Gn 25:4 [KJ: Abidah]; 1 Ch 1:33).

Abidan (á-bī′dăn, father is judge). Son of Gideoni; outstanding prince of Benjamin (Nm 1:11; 2:22; 7:60, 65; 10:24).

abide. 1. To await (as RSV: Acts 20:23). 2. To endure (as RSV: Jer 10:10). 3. To stay (as RSV: Lk 24:29). 4. To dwell (as RV, RSV: Ps 61:4). 5. To have fellowship with God (Jn 15:4-11). 6. To last, endure (e. g., faith, hope, love: 1 Co 13:13; Word: 1 Ptr 1:23; believers and their heritage: Ps 37:18, 20).

Abiel (ā′bī-ĕl, God is my father). 1. Father of Kish; grandfather of Saul and Abner (1 Sm 9:1). 2. See *Abi-albon*.

Abiezer (ā-bī-ē′zēr, father is help). 1. Son of Gilead (Nm 26:30. KJ: Jeezer. RV, RSV: Iezer); head of clan in Manasseh of which Gideon was member (Jos 17:2; Ju 6:15; 1 Ch 7:18). 2. One of David's chief men (2 Sm 23:27) and military officers (1 Ch 27:12).

Abiezrite (ā-bī-ĕz′rīt). Member of Abiezer clan (Ju 6:11; see Nm 26:30 [KJ: Jeezer-ite. RV, RSV: Iezerite]).

Abigail (ăb′ĭ-gāl, father is exultation). 1. Beautiful, wise wife of Nabal of Carmel and, after his death, of David; brought an appeasement gift to David after her husband refused to reward David for protection given his shearers and flocks (1 Sm 25); captured by Amalekites and rescued by David (1 Sm 30). 2. Sister of David; married Jether, an Ishmaelite; mother of Amasa (2 Sm 17:25 [RV, RSV: Abigal]; 1 Ch 2:16, 17).

Abigal (ăb′ĭ-găl). See *Abigail 2*.

Abihail (ăb′ĭ-hāl, father is strong). 1. Father of Zuriel (Nm 3:35). 2. Abishur's wife (1 Ch 2:29). 3. Eliab's daughter (niece of David), Mahalath's mother (RV, RSV), Rehoboam's wife (2 Ch 11:18). 4. Gadite in Gilead (1 Ch 5:14). 5. Esther's father (Est 2:15; 9:29).

Abihu (á-bī′hū, father is he). Aaron's son (Nm 3:2; Ex 6:23); ascended Sinai with Moses (Ex 24:1, 9); priest (Ex 28:1); consumed for offering strange fire (Lv 10:1, 2; Nm 3:4; 26:61; 1 Ch 24:2).

Abihud (á-bī′hŭd, father is renown?) Benjamin's grandson; Bela's son (1 Ch 8:3).

Abijah (á-bī′ja, LORD is father. RSV: Abijah throughout. KJ: Abia in 1 Ch 3:10; Mt 1:7; Lk 1:5. KJ, RV: Abiah in 1 Ch 2:24 [RSV: his father]; 6:28. KJ: Abiah in 1 Sm 8:2; 1 Ch 7:8). 1. King of Judah (also called Abijam); wicked; son of Rehoboam and Maacah; warred against

Jeroboam I (1 K 15; 2 Ch 12; 13). 2. Son of Jeroboam I (1 K 14). 3. 2d son of Samuel; his corrupt administration led elders to ask for king (1 Sm 8:2). 4. Descendant of Eleazar (1 Ch 24:10; Neh 12:17); gave his name to 8th course of priests, to which Zacharias belonged (Lk 1:5). 5. Ahaz' wife; Hezekiah's mother (2 Ch 29:1). 6. Wife of Hezron (1 Ch 2:24). 7. Benjaminite (1 Ch 7:8). 8. Priest (Neh 10:7).

Abijam (á-bī′jăm). See *Abijah 1*.

Abilene (ăb-ĭ-lē′nē, land of meadows). Syrian tetrarchy near Anti-Lebanon, watered by Barada River; governed by Lysanias in time of Christ (Lk 3:1).

Abimael (á-bĭm′á-ĕl, father is God?). Descendant of Joktan; father of Arabic tribe of Mali (Gn 10:28; 1 Ch 1:22).

Abimelech (á-bĭm′e-lĕk, father is Melech [Molech]). 1. King of Gerar; made covenant with Abraham (Gn 20; 21:22-34). 2. King of Gerar; made covenant with Isaac (Gn 26:1-33); possibly same as 1. 3. Gideon's son by concubine (Ju 8:31; 9; 2 Sm 11:21). 4. Abiathar's son (1 Ch 18:16. RSV: Ahimelech, as in 2 Sm 8:17). 5. Applied to Achish (1 Sm 21:10; Ps 34 title), hence probably throne name of Philistine kings.

Abinadab (á-bĭn′á-dăb, father is noble). 1. Levite of Kiriath-jearim; kept ark from time of its return by Philistines until David moved it (1 Sm 7:1, 2; 1 Ch 13:7). 2. 2d son of Jesse (1 Sm 16:8; 17:13). 3. Saul's son; slain at Gilboa (1 Sm 31:2). 4. KJ: son of Abinadab (1 K 4:11. RV, RSV: Ben-abinadab).

Abinoam (á-bĭn′ō-ăm, father is pleasantness). Barak's father (Ju 4:6; 5:1, 12).

Abiram, Abiron (á-bī′răm, á-bī′ron, exalted one is father). 1. Reubenite; conspired with Korah (Nm 16; Sir 45:18 [KJ: Abiron]). 2. Son of Hiel (1 K 16:34).

Abisei (ăb-ĭ-sē′ī). See *Abishua 2*.

Abishag (ăb-ĭ-shăg, father is wanderer). Fair Shunammite maiden brought to David in his old age (1 K 1:1-4). When Adonijah later requested her as wife, Solomon had him slain (1 K 2:13-25).

Abishai (á-bĭsh′á-ī, father is Jesse?). Joab's brother; son of Zeruiah (1 Ch 2:16); desired to kill sleeping Saul (1 Sm 26:6); fought with David's men against Abner (2 Sm 2:18); participated in murder of Abner (2 Sm 3:30); coleader of David's army (2 Sm 10:14; 18:2); rescued David from giant Ishbi-benob (2 Sm 21:16, 17).

Abishalom (á-bĭsh′á-lom, father is peace). Probably variant spelling for Absalom, son of David (1 K 15:2, 10).

Abishua (á-bĭsh′ū-á, father is help?). 1. Benjaminite, son of Bela (1 Ch 8:4). 2. Son of Phinehas (1 Ch 6:4, 5, 50; Ez 7:5; 1 Esd 8:2 [KJ: Abisum. RV: Abisue]; 2 Esd 1:2 [KJ: Abisei. RV: Abissei]).

Abishur (á-bī′shēr, father is wall). Jerahmeelite; son of Shammai (1 Ch 2: 28, 29).

Abissei, Abisue, Abisum (ăb-ĭ-sē′ī, á-bĭs′ū-ē, á-bī′sum). See *Abishua 2*.

Abital (á-bī′tăl, father is dew). Wife of David (2 Sm 3:4; 1 Ch 3:3).

Abitub (á-bī′tŭb, father is goodness). Benjaminite; son of Shaharaim (1 Ch 8:8-11).

Abiud (á-bī′ud). Ancestor of Jesus (Mt 1:13; missing in 1 Ch 3:19).

ablutions. Ceremonial washings (Heb 6:2 [KJ, RV: baptisms]; 9:10 [KJ, RV: washings]).

Abner (ăb′nēr, father is light). Son of Ner; commander of cousin Saul's forces (1 Sm

14:50, 51; 17:57; 26:5-14); made Ishbosheth, Saul's son, king of Israel at Mahanaim but was defeated by David's men (2 Sm 2:8); killed by Joab and Abishai (2 Sm 3:26-30). Mourned as "a prince and a great man" (2 Sm 3:31-39).

abomination (a-bŏm-i-nā'shŭn). KJ, RV, RSV use this word (with variations) to translate four Hebrew words: to'ebah (loathsome things, esp. religiously, Gn 43:32; Dt 7:25); piggul (stale sacrificial flesh, Lv 7:18; 19:7); sheqets (flesh of prohibited animals, Lv 7:21); shiqquts (used of objects of idolatry, Dt 29:17; Hos 9:10). Detestable thing (animals, persons, acts, idolatry, etc.).

Abomination of Desolation. Mention in Dn 9:27; 11:31; 12:11 is possibly reference to desecration of sanctuary by Antiochus Epiphanes and idol on the altar (1 Mac 1:54) on which sacrifices were offered to Olympian Zeus. This prophecy not exhausted by this fulfillment but belongs to Messianic times. Christ reiterated prophecy (Mt 24:15, 16; Mk 13:14), referring, perhaps, to statue of Caligula in temple. Figuratively applied to neglect of Gospel and to externalism in church.

Abraham (ā'brȧ-hăm, father of a multitude), **Abram** (ā'brăm, exalted father. Name in vogue in Babylonia). Founder of Hebrew nation. Son of Terah; brother of Nahor and Haran. His family, descendants of Shem, lived in Ur of Chaldees. After Haran's death, Terah emigrated to Haran in Mesopotamia with Abram, Abram's wife Sarai, and Haran's son Lot (Gn 11).

In Haran God told Abram to leave his country, kindred, and paternal home for land God would show him; promised to make of him great nation and bless all families of earth in him. Abram, then 75 yrs old, went to Canaan with Sarai and Lot. Abram pitched tent at oak (KJ: plain) of Moreh, where God promised him land and Abram built altar E of Bethel. Famine drove him to Egypt, where Pharaoh took beautiful Sarai into his house after Abram caused her to say she was Abram's sister. Plagues caused Pharaoh to discover deception and dismiss Abram (Gn 12).

Abram with great possessions left Egypt together with Lot and returned to altar near Bethel. Strife between herdsmen of Abram and Lot led to separation; Abram gave Lot choice of land, and Lot chose Jordan plain and pitched tent as far as Sodom. God repeated promise to Abram, who moved to Mamre (Gn 13).

When four kings defeated five of territory where Lot lived and took Lot captive, Abram pursued enemies, recovered spoils, rescued Lot. Thereupon Abram received blessing of Melchizedek, king of Salem (Gn 14).

Promise of Canaan as inheritance confirmed by covenant (Gn 15). Ishmael, son of Hagar, b to Abram (Gn 16). God changed his name to Abraham, promised that His everlasting covenant would be fulfilled in Isaac, and added sign of circumcision (Gn 17). God appeared to Abraham at Mamre; Sarah rebuked for laughter. Abraham pleaded for Sodom (Gn 18). Abraham went to Gerar, denied his wife, who was taken by Abimelech; God revealed deceit in dream, and Sarah was restored (Gn 20).

Isaac born; Hagar and Ishmael cast out (Gn 21). God tested Abraham's faith through command to sacrifice Isaac (Gn 22). Abraham sent servant to get wife

for Isaac (Gn 24). Abraham d at 175, buried in cave of Machpelah (Gn 25).

God called Abraham, who later is called friend of God, from a family that served idols (Jos 24:2). God took initiative in covenants in which God binds Himself to give without receiving anything in return. Circumcision (Ro 4:11) is sign of covenant.

By faith Abraham was just, as God wanted him to be, thus becoming the father of believers (Ro 4; Gl 3). This faith showed itself in works (Ja 2:21). In Christ, Abraham's seed, all nations of earth are blessed (Gl 3:16). Believers are spiritual heirs and sons of Abraham (Ro 4:13, 14; Gl 3:29). Covenant with Abraham not disannulled by that of Sinai (by which men are obligated) but remains for all ages (Gl 3:17, 18).

Abraham's bosom. Term used for everlasting life by Jews (4 Mac 13:17) and Christ (Lk 13:28; 16:22).

Abron (ăb'rŭn). Brook, probably in Cilicia (Jdth 2:24. KJ, RV: Arbonai).

Abronah (ȧ-brō'nȧ, station. KJ: Ebronah). Station of Israel in wilderness (Nm 33: 34, 35).

Absalom (ăb'sȧ-lom, father is peace). 1. Son of David by Maacah (2 Sm 3:3). Noted for his beauty (2 Sm 14:25). Killed Amnon, his half brother, to avenge Tamar; fled to Geshur, where he stayed 3 yrs (2 Sm 13; 14). Conspired to seize throne from David and gathered malcontents around himself. Wise counsel of Ahithophel thwarted by Hushai; David's forces defeated Absalom. Joab killed Absalom with three darts while his hair was entangled in tree. David grieved for his son (2 Sm 15—18). See Abishalom. 2. Father of Mattathias, captain of Jonathan Maccabaeus (1 Mac 11:70). 3. Envoy of Jews (2 Mac 11:17).

abstinence (ăb'sti-nens). Examples of abstinence in OT are: from blood (Lv 3:17), certain meats (Lv 11), parts sacred to altar (Lv 3:9-17), meats consecrated to idols (Ex 34:15), special (Lv 9:10; Nm 6:5). Abstinence also enjoined under special circumstances (Ju 13:4; Nm 6:3; Jer 35:6; Lk 1:15). NT gives liberty according to dictates of conscience and love in matters not commanded or forbidden (Ro 14:1-3; 1 Co 8; Acts 15) and opposes legalistic sects (1 Ti 4:3, 4; Col 2:16).

Abubus (ȧ-bū'bus). Father of Ptolemy (1 Mac 16:11-15).

abuse, abuser. 1. Defile or ravish (Ju 19:25; 1 Co 6:9 [RSV: homosexuals]). 2. Insult or dishonor (Pr 9:7; 22:10; Lk 6:28 [KJ, RV: despitefully use]). 3. Use to the full (1 Co 9:18 [RSV: making full use]).

abyss. In classical Greek the adjective means "bottomless" (e. g., Tartarus, sea of trouble, abyss of Pluto). In LXX it translates t:hom, m:tsulah, tsulah, and rahabah. NT: seat and prison of Satan and source of evil. RV: abyss. KJ: deep (Lk 8:31; Ro 10:7), bottomless pit (Rv 9: 1-11; 11:7; 17:8; 20:1, 3). RSV: abyss (Lk 8:31; Ro 10:7), bottomless pit (Rv).

acacia (ȧ-kā'shȧ). See shittah.

Acatan (ăk'ȧ-tăn). See Hakkatan.

Accaba (ăk'ȧ-bȧ). See Hagab.

Accad (ăk'ăd). Town founded by Nimrod (Gn 10:10), perhaps Agade on Euphrates SW of Baghdad. Also district in N Mesopotamia; center of Assyrian rule.

Accaron (ăk'ȧ-rŏn). See Ekron.

Accho, Acco (ăk'ō, curve). Town and bay on Mediterranean, 25 mi S of Tyre. As-

signed to Asher but could not be captured (Ju 1:31). Name changed to Ptolemais c 100 BC (Acts 21:7). Crusaders and Arabs fought for possession of it. Modern Acre.
accomplish. 1. Bring to successful conclusion (KJ: Ps 64:6; RSV: Acts 20:24). 2. Finish period of time (KJ: Jer 25:12; Lk 2:6). 3. Bring God's wrath to completeness (KJ: Eze 6:12; RSV: Dn 11:36). 4. Bring Christ's work to completion (Lk 12:50; 18:31).
Accos (ăk'ŏs). Eupolemos' grandfather (1 Mac 8:17).
account (n.). 1. "On account of": because of (RSV: Gn 12:13). 2. Record, listing (RSV: 1 K 9:15).
account (v.). 1. Consider, regard (Dt 2:20 [RSV: known]; Ro 8:36 [RSV: regarded]). 2. Impute, reckon (Gl 3:6 [RV, RSV: reckoned]). 3. Repute (Mk 10:42 [RSV: supposed to]).
Accoz (ăk'ŏz). See *Hakkoz* 2.
accursed. Separated for God or from God. KJ translates H *herem* with this word. RV, RSV: devoted (Jos 6:17, 18; 7:1; 22:20; 1 Ch 2:7). Word refers to thing set apart for God. KJ, RSV also translate *anathema* "accursed" in Ro 9:3; 1 Co 12:3; Gl 1:8, 9 (RV transliterates). See *anathema*.
Aceldama (á-sĕl'dá-má). See *Akeldama*.
Achaia (á-kā'yá). Roman province, formerly N part of Peloponnesus, after 140 BC all of Greece S of Macedonia (Acts 18: 12, 27; 19:21; Ro 15:26; 1 Co 16:15; 2 Co 1:1; 9:2; 11:10; 1 Th 1:7, 8).
Achaicus (á-kā'i-kus, of Achaia). Christian who came to Paul at Ephesus from Corinth (1 Co 16:17).
Achan, Achar (ā'kăn, ā'kär, trouble). Judahite who stole spoils at Jericho and was stoned in Valley of Achor (Jos 7; 22:20. Achar in 1 Ch 2:7).
Achaz (ā'kăz). See *Ahaz*.
Achbor (ăk'bôr, mouse). 1. Edomite (Gn 36:38). 2. Son of Micaiah; officer of Josiah (2 K 22:12-20; Jer 26:22; 36:12. Abdon in 2 Ch 34:20).
Achiacharus (á-kī-ăk'á-rus). Nephew of Tobit; governor under Esarhaddon (Tob 1:21. RSV: Ahikar).
Achias (á-kī'ás). Ancestor of Ezra (2 Esd 1:2. RSV: Ahijah).
Achim (ā'kim, LORD will establish). Ancestor of Jesus (Mt 1:14).
Achior (ā'kĭ-ôr). 1. In LXX (Nm 34:27) for Ahihud. 2. General of Ammonites; favorable to Jews (Jdth 5:5-24).
Achipha (ăk'ĭ-fá). See *Hakupha*.
Achish (ā'kĭsh). Son of Maacah, king of Gath, to whom David fled from Saul (1 Sm 21:10-15; 27; 28:1, 2; 29; 1 K 2:39).
Achitob, Achitub (ăk'ĭ-tŏb, ăk'ĭ-tŭb). See *Ahitub* 2.
Achmetha (ăk'mĕ-thá. RSV: Ecbatana). Capital of Media; summer residence of Persian kings. Decree of Cyrus permitting Jews to build temple was found there (Ez 6:2). Identified with Ecbatana (Jdth 1:1-4).
Achor (ā'kôr, trouble). Valley S of Jericho (Jos 15:7) where Achan was stoned (Jos 7:24-26; Is 65:10; Hos 2:15); identified with el-Buqei'a.
Achsah (ăk'sá, anklet). Daughter of Caleb; given to Othniel for capturing Kiriath-sepher (Jos 15:16-19; Ju 1:12-15; 1 Ch 2:49 [KJ: Achsa]).
Achshaph (ăk'shăf, fascination). 1. Town in Upper Galilee (El-Kesaf?; Jos 11:1; 12:20). 2. City of Asher near Acre (Jos 19:25).

Achzib (ăk'zĭb, deceitful). 1. Town of Asher (Ez-Zib) between Acre and Tyre (Jos 19:29; Ju 1:31). 2. Town in lowland of Judah (Jos 15:44; Mi 1:14). Chezib in Gn 38:5. Cozeba (KJ: Chozeba) in 1 Ch 4:22.
Acipha (ăs'ĭ-fá). See *Hakupha*.
Acitho (ăs'ĭ-thō). See *Ahitub* 4.
acknowledge. 1. Admit, confess (Jer 14:20). 2. Confess in thought and action that someone is something, e. g., that God is our Lord (Ro 1:28). KJ, RV frequently have "confess" where RSV has "acknowledge."
acquit. 1. Act like (1 Sm 4:9). 2. Release or free from (Jb 10:14).
acquittal. Forgiveness (Ro 5:18). KJ, RV: free gift . . . to justification.
Acraba (ăk'rá-bá). See *Ekrebel*.
Acrabbim (á-krăb'ĭm). See *Akrabbim*.
Acts, Book of. 5th book of NT; traditionally ascribed to Luke. Traces establishment of church to Holy Spirit and deals primarily with mission activities first of Peter, then of Paul. Outline: 1. The Church in Jerusalem (1:1—8:3). 2. The Church in Judea and Samaria and Some Regions Beyond (8:4—12:24). 3. The Church Extended to Jews and Gentiles of the West (12:25—28:31). See *Peter; Paul.*
Acua (á-kū'á). See *Akkub* 3.
Acub (ā'kŭb). See *Bakbuk*.
Acud (ā'kŭd). See *Akkub* 3.
Adadah (ăd'á-dá; á-dā'dá). City in the Negeb of Judah (Jos 15:22).
Adah (ā'dá, ornament). 1. One of Lamech's wives (Gn 4:19, 20). 2. One of Esau's wives; daughter of Elon, the Hittite (Gn 36:2, 4). Basemath in Gn 26:34.
Adaiah (á-dā'yá, LORD has adorned). 1. Father of Josiah's mother (2 K 22:1). 2. Gershonite Levite (1 Ch 6:41). Iddo in 1 Ch 6:21. 3. Son of Jeroham; a priest (1 Ch 9:12; Neh 11:12). 4. Benjaminite, son of Shimei (1 Ch 8:21). 5. 6. Two men of families called Bani who put away their strange wives (Ez 10:29 [KJ, RV: Jedeus in 1 Esd 9:30], 39). 7. Father of Maaseiah (2 Ch 23:1). 8. Descendant of Judah by Perez (Neh. 11:5).
Adalia (á-dā'lĭ-á). Son of Haman (Est 9:8).
Adam (ăd'ăm, human being; man. 1. 1st human being. God created Adam in His own image, gave him dominion over animals and other creatures, and placed him in Garden of Eden. Man was created male and female, commanded to be fruitful and subdue the earth. Adam and Eve transgressed God's command and were expelled from Eden. Adam died at 930 (Gn 1—5). Paul makes the first man, Adam, the source of sin and death and the second man, Christ, the source of life and righteousness (Ro 5:12-21; 1 Co 15: 22, 45; Eph 4:22-24; Cl 3:9, 10). 2. City in Jordan valley (Jos 3:16).
Adamah (ăd'á-má, soil). Fortified city of Naphtali, 5 mi SW of Tiberias (Jos 19:36).
adamant (ăd'á-mănt). Mineral or hard metal. Translated "adamant" (Eze 3:9) or "diamond" (Jer 17:1). Symbol of hardness (Zch 7:12).
Adami (ăd'á-mī. RV, RSV: Adami-nekeb [Adami of the pass]). Border town of Naphtali (Jos 19:33).
Adami-nekeb (-nĕ'kĕb). See *Adami.*
Adar (á-där'). See *Addar 1; time.*
Adasa (ăd'á-sá). Town near Beth-horon (1 Mac 7:40, 45).
Adbeel (ăd'bĕ-ĕl). Son of Ishmael (Gn 25:13; 1 Ch 1:29).

Addan (ăd'ăn. Addon in Neh 7:61). Place in Babylonia from which people who could not prove Hebrew ancestry returned to Jerusalem (Ez 2:59).
Addar (ăd'är). 1. Border town of Judah Jos 15:3. KJ: Adar). Hazar-addar (village of Addar) in Nm 34:4. 2. Benjaminite (1 Ch 8:3). Ard in Gn 46:21; Nm 26:40.
adder. See cockatrice; serpent.
Addi (ăd'ī). 1. Ancestor of Christ (Lk 3:28). 2. See Pahath-moab.
Addo (ăd'ō). See Iddo 6.
Addon (ăd'ŏn). See Addan.
Addus (ăd'us). 1. Son of servant of Solomon (1 Esd 5:34). 2. Variant for Jaddus, a priest (1 Esd 5:38. RV, RSV: Jaddus).
Ader (ā'dēr). See Eder 4.
adiaphora (ăd-ĭ-ăf'ō-rá). Ecclesiastical term applied to matters neither commanded nor forbidden in Scripture and which require discretion (1 Co 6:12; 8; 10:23; Ro 14:3, 6; Cl 2:16, 17). NT places Levitical observances and some human ordinances in this class (Mt 23:8-10; Lk 22:26; Rv 5:10; 1 Ptr 2:8). See also liberty.
Adida (ăd'ĭ-dá). See Hadid.
Adiel (ā'dĭ-ĕl, ornament of God). 1. Simeonite (1 Ch 4:36). 2. Priest (1 Ch 9:12). 3. Father of Azmaveth (1 Ch 27:25).
Adin (ā'dĭn, luxurious?). Founder of a family which returned from Babylonian captivity (Ez 2:15; 8:6; Neh 10:16; 1 Esd 5:14 [RV: Adinu]; 8:32).
Adina (ăd'ĭ-ná, luxurious). Officer of David (1 Ch 11:42).
Adino (ăd'ĭ-nō). See Josheb-basshebeth.
Adinu (ăd'ĭ-nū). See Adin.
Adinus (ăd'ĭ-nus). See Jamin 3.
Adithaim (ăd-ĭ-thā'ĭm, double booty). Town of Judah in Shephelah (Jos 15:36)
adjuration (ăj-ōō-rā'shun). Act whereby a person imposes upon another the obligation of speaking under oath (Jos 6:26; 1 Sm 14:24; 1 K 22:16; 2 Ch 18:15; Mt 26: 63; Acts 19:13).
Adlai (ăd'lá-ī). Father of Shaphat, a herdsman (1 Ch 27:29).
Admah (ăd'má, redlands). City destroyed with Sodom (Gn 10:19; 14:2, 8; 19:25, 28, 29; Dt 29:23; Hos 11:8).
Admatha (ăd'má-thá). One of 7 princes of Persia (Est 1:14).
Admin (ăd'-mĭn). RV margin and RSV insert in Lk 3:33 on basis of some G mss.
administration (ăd-mĭn-ĭs-trā'shun). KJ: service, performance of service (1 Co 12:5; 2 Co 9:2. RV: ministration). RSV: management, application (1 Sm 7:17; 2 Sm 8:15; 1 Ch 18:14; 1 Co 12:28; 2 Co 8:20).
admonition (ăd-mō-nĭsh'un). Duty of admonition repeatedly enjoined (2 Ch 19:10; Eze 3:18; Mt 18:15-17; Ro 15:14; 1 Co 4: 14; 1 Th 5:14) and demonstrated (2 Sm 12:1-23; Mt 23:37-39) in the Scriptures.
Adna (ăd'ná, pleasure). 1. Priest after exile (Neh 12:15). 2. Divorced foreign wife (Ez 10:30). Naathus in 1 Esd 9:31.
Adnah (ăd'ná, pleasure). 1. Came to David at Ziklag (1 Ch 12:20). 2. Jehoshaphat's commander (2 Ch 17:14).
Adonai (ăd-ō-nā'ī, my lord). Hebrews spoke this word where ineffable Jahveh occurred. JHVH (YHWH) pointed with its vowels (Jehovah).
Adoni-bezek (á-dō'nī-bĕ'zĕk, my lord is Bezek). Captured and mutilated by Judah after battle of Bezek (Ju 1:4-7).
Adonijah (ăd-ō-nī'já, LORD is my lord). 1. Fourth son of David; supported by Joab and Abiathar, proclaimed himself king.

David, however, proclaimed Solomon king, who first pardoned but later executed Adonijah (1 K 1—2; 1 Ch 23:1; 28:5). 2. Levite (2 Ch 17:8). 3. See Adonikam.
Adonikam (ăd-ō-nī'kăm, my lord has arisen). Founder of family which returned after exile (Ez 2:13; Neh 7:18). Adonijah in Neh 10:16.
Adoniram (ăd-ō-nī'răm, my lord is high). In charge of forced labor under David and Solomon (1 K 4:6; 5:14; Adoram in 2 Sm 20:24). Killed by ten tribes when sent by Rehoboam to deal with them (1 K 12: 18; Hadoram in 2 Ch 10:18).
Adoni-zedek (á-dō'nī-zē'dĕk, my lord is righteousness). Amorite; king of Jerusalem; fought Joshua with 4 other kings at Gibeon; captured and slain (Jos 10:1-27).
adoption. 1. Reception into family as child (Ex 2:10; Est 2:7). 2. Reception into family of God (Ro 8:14-17), which is true Israel (Ro 9), through faith in Christ (Gl 3:26-28), as testified by Spirit (Gl 4:6, 7). RSV: "sonship" in Ro 8:15; 9:4.
Ador, Adora, Adoraim (ā'dôr, á-dō'rá, ăd-ō-rā'ĭm, two hills?). City fortified by Rehoboam (2 Ch 11:9). Adora in 1 Mac 13:20. Modern Dura.
Adoram (á-dō'răm). See Adoniram.
Adoration. Attitude of awe and reverence for God and expression of that attitude in words and actions. Does not occur in KJ, RV, or RSV.
adorn, adornment. 1. Christian life is adornment for doctrine (Tts 2:10). 2. Virtues are God-pleasing adornments (1 Ptr 3: 3-12). 3. Church is adorned for Christ, her husband (Rv 21:2). 4. New Jerusalem is resplendent in adornment (Rv 21:19).
Adrammelech (á-drăm'e-lĕk). 1. Deity of Sepharvites, to whom children were sacrificed in Samaria (2 K 17:31). 2. Son and murderer of Sennacherib (2 K 19:37; Is. 37:38).
Adramyttium (ăd-rá-mĭt'ĭ-um). Harbor city of Mysia at base of Mt Ida (Acts 27:2).
Adria (ā'drĭ-á). Ionian Gulf and Sea between Crete and Sicily (Acts 27:27).
Adriel (ā'drĭ-el, flock of God). Meholathite; married Saul's daughter Merab (1 Sm 18:19; 2 Sm 21:8).
Aduel (á-dū'el). Ancestor of Tobit (Tob 1:1).
Adullam (á-dŭl'am). Canaanite city (Tell esh Sheikl Madhkur) SW of Jerusalem; allotted to Judah (Jos 12:15; 2 Ch 11:7); repeopled after exile (Neh 11:30; Mi 1:15; 2 Mac 12:38 [KJ: Odollam]); cave there was David's hiding place (1 Sm 22:1; 2 Sm 23:13; 1 Ch 11:15).
adultery. OT, act whereby a man adulterates a woman, that is, has illicit intercourse with wife of another (Dt 22:22-24). NT, violation of marriage contract by either of parties by illicit relations with third party (Mt 19:3-9). Christ interpreted 6th commandment as forbidding all kinds of unchastity in deed or thought (Ex 20:14; Mt 5:28). Mosaic law punished adultery with death (Lv 20:10; Jn 8:5), and NT lists adultery among open sins of flesh (Gl 5:19). In symbolical language of OT adultery is apostasy from God (Jer 3:9; Eze 23:36-49).
Adummim (á-dŭm'ĭm, red objects). Pass between Jerusalem and Jericho (Jos 15:7; 18:17 Cf Lk 10:30).
Advent of Christ. 1. Coming of Christ in flesh (Zch 9:9; Mt 21:4). 2. Spiritual coming of Christ into hearts of men and

His presence in church (Jn 14:18, 23).
3. Christ's return to judgment (Mt 24:30).
See also *Parousia*.

adversary (ăd'vĕr-sĕr-ĭ). 1. Political or personal enemy (Ju 2:3; Ez 4:1 et al). 2. Enemy of God and His people, esp the devil (1 Ti 5:14; 1 Ptr 5:8).

advocate (ăd'vō-kăt). One who pleads cause of another (1 Jn 2:1). Same word translated Comforter (Jn 14:16. RSV: Counselor).

Aedias (ā-ē-dī'ăs). See *Elijah 4*.

Aeneas (ē-nē'ăs). Paralytic at Lydda healed by Peter (Acts 9:32-35).

Aenon (ē'nŏn). Place W of Jordan, near Salim, where John baptized (Jn 3:23).

aeon. See *time 1*.

Aesora (ē-sō'rȧ). See *Esora*.

affinity. Relation by marriage (1 K 3:1. RSV: marriage alliance).

Agaba (ăg'ȧ-bȧ). See *Hagab*.

Agabus (ag'ȧ-bŭs). Prophet at Antioch (Acts 11:28; 21:10).

Agag (ā'găg, flame). 1. Title or name of kings of Amalekites (Ex 17:14; Nm 24:7; Dt 25:17). 2. King of Amalekites, whom Samuel killed at Gilgal (1 Sm 15).

Agagite (ăg'ȧ-gīt). Appellation of Haman (Est 3:1, 10; 8:3, 5; 9:24).

agape (ăg'ȧ-pē). See *love; love feasts*.

Agar (ā'gär). See *Hagar*.

agate (ăg'ĭt). Precious stone composed of various kinds of quartz. One of stones in high priest's breastplate (Ex 28:19; 39:12; Is 54:12; Eze 27:16; Rv 21:19 [RSV. KJ: chalcedony]). See also *ruby 2*.

aged. Old age regarded as token of God's favor (Jb 5:26; Zch 8:4). Aged venerated for wisdom (Jb 15:10; 32:4), and young were commanded to honor them (Lv 19:32).

Agee (ā'gē, fugitive?). Hararite; father of Shammah, one of David's mighty men (2 Sm 23:11).

Aggaba (ăg'ȧ-bȧ). See *Hagaba*.

Aggaeus, Aggeus (ă-gē'ŭs). See *Haggai*.

Agia (ā'gĭ-ȧ). 1. See *Hattil*. 2. Wife of Jaddus (1 Esd 5:38. KJ: Augia).

Agora (ăg'ō-rȧ). Market place (Acts 17:17) and forum in Athens, Ephesus, and other cities.

Agrapha (ăg'rȧ-fȧ, unwritten). Sayings of Jesus not recorded in Gospels (Jn 21:25; Acts 20:35; codex B on Lk 6:4).

agriculture. 1. After conquest, Joshua assigned each tribe a province, each household a small section of land to be its inheritance forever (Jos 13; 14). Family plot was improved from generation to generation by removing boulders, cultivating carefully, building up fertile terraces (Is 5:1, 2).
2. After first fall rain, ground was cultivated by hand with shovel and mattock, or plow drawn by donkey, cow, or ox. Plow was heavy forked branch of tree or branches bound and pegged together so that one long end became the tongue, a shorter one the plowshare (which might be shod with stone or iron), and another the guiding handle. After plow had torn up ground, large lumps were broken up with mattock and raked fine with harrow (bundle of brushwood, or wooden platform shod with stones or iron spikes).
3. Farmer sowed grain by hand, taking it from basket or from fold of his garment. After sowing ground he harrowed it again or drove his animals back and forth to trample seed in.
4. Ripe grain was cut with sickle. Some early sickles were made of lower jawbone

of ass or cow. Parallel with these primitive instruments, and crowding them out, were modern-looking sickles of bronze or iron set in wooden handles.
5. After reaper cut grain, he raked it up, tied it into bundles with its own straw. Fallen or missed grain he left for poor gleaners (Ru 2:2, 3). From field to threshing floor he transported grain on rack fixed to cart or bound on back of donkey, or even carried on litterlike frame by two men.
6. Threshing floor was roughly circular plot of clay or limestone rock carefully patched and leveled. Workers opened bundles and spread them about a foot deep over this area. Unmuzzled (Dt 25:4) cows, calves, sheep, and donkeys trampled grain out of straw. Primitive threshing sled or wooden flails also used. Grain was winnowed by tossing straw and grain into the air with wooden shovel or fork and cleansed with sieve. Grain was then washed, dried, stored in vermin-proof jars.
Processes of agriculture are applied to spiritual realm (e. g., Mt 3:12; 9:37, 38; 13:18, 39; Jn 4:35; Gal 6:7). (Klinck)

Agrippa (ȧ-grĭp'ȧ). See *Herod*.

ague (ā'gū). See *disease*.

Agur (ā'gŭr, assembler?). Author of Pr 30 (v 1).

Ahab (ā'hăb, father's brother). 1. 7th king of Israel; son and successor of Omri (1 K 16:29); married Jezebel of Tyre, who introduced worship of Baal and Astarte (1 K 16:31, 32) and killed Jehovah's prophets (1 K 18:4); opposed by Elijah, who at Mt Carmel showed prophets of Baal to be false (1 K 18:17-46); had Naboth killed through connivance of Jezebel and took his vineyard (1 K 21); killed by arrow; dogs licked his blood (1 K 22:33-38). Did more to provoke the Lord than all Israelite kings before him (1 K 16:33). Items concerning Ahab excavated. 2. A lying prophet (Jer 29: 21-23).

Aharah (ȧ-hăr'ȧ. Ehi in Gn 46:21. Ahiram in Nm 26:38. Aher in 1 Ch 7:12). Son of Benjamin (1 Ch 8:1).

Aharhel (ȧ-här'hĕl). Son of Harum, founder of family of Judah (1 Ch 4:8).

Ahasai (ȧ-hā'sī). See *Ahzai*.

Ahasbai (ȧ-hăs'bī). See *Ur 2*.

Ahasuerus (ȧ-hăz-ū-ē'rŭs). 1. Father of Darius the Mede (Dn 9:1). 2. Persian king who married Esther (Es 1:2, 19; 2: 16, 17). Hebrew name in Esther corresponds to Aramaic and Babylonian spelling of Xerxes, with whom Ahasuerus is identified.

Ahava (ȧ-hā'vȧ). River in Babylonia on whose banks Ezra assembled Jews who proposed to return to Jerusalem (Ez 8: 15-32). Theras in 1 Esd 8:41.

Ahaz (ā'hăz, possessor). KJ in NT: Achaz). 1. 12th king of Judah; son and successor of Jotham; idolatrous; became vassal of Assyria (2 K 16; 2 Ch 28); died dishonored (2 K 23:12). Isaiah, Hosea, and Micah prophesied during his reign (cf Is 7). 2. Son of Micah (1 Ch 8:35, 36; 9:42).

Ahaziah (ā-hȧ-zī'ȧ, LORD has grasped). 1. 8th king of Israel; son and successor of Ahab; followed cult of Baal-zebub; denounced by Elijah (1 K 22; 2 K 1; 2 Ch 20). 2. 6th king of Judah; son and successor of Jehoram; wicked (2 K 8, 9; 2 Ch 22 [KJ, RV: Azariah in v. 6]). Jehoahaz in 2 Ch 21:17; 25:23 (RSV: Ahaziah).

Ahban (ä'băn, brother of intelligent one). Son of Abishur, Jerahmeelite (1 Ch 2:29).

Aher (ä'hĕr). See *Aharah*.

Ahi (ä'hī, brotherly). 1. Chief of Gadites (1 Ch 5:15). 2. Shamer's son (1 Ch 7:34).

Ahiah (á-hī'á). See *Ahijah 1, 2, 3, 9.*

Ahiam (á-hī'ăm). One of David's heroes (2 Sm 23:33; 1 Ch 11:35).

Ahian (á-hī'án, brotherly). Manassite (1 Ch 7:19).

Ahiezer (ä-hī-ē'zĕr, brother is help). 1. Son of Ammishaddai; head of tribe of Dan (Nm 1:12; 2:25; 7:66, 71; 10:25). 2. Gibeahite; joined David at Ziklag (1 Ch 12:3).

Ahihud (á-hī'hŭd, brother is majesty). 1. Prince of tribe of Asher; overseer in partition of Canaan (Nm 34:27). 2. Benjaminite (1 Ch 8:7).

Ahijah (á-hī'já, brother of LORD). 1. Son of Ahitub; high priest at Gibeah (1 Sm 14:3, 18. KJ: Ahiah). 2. Benjaminite (1 Ch 8:7. KJ: Ahiah). 3. Scribe of Solomon (1 K 4:3. KJ: Ahiah). 4. Prophet of Shiloh (1 K 14:2); addressed prophecies to Jeroboam (1 K 11:29-39) and Jeroboam's wife (1 K 14:6-16). Record of events in the "prophecy of Ahijah the Shilonite" referred to in 2 Ch 9:29. 5. Father of Baasha (1 K 15:27). 6. Son of Jerahmeel (1 Ch 2:25). 7. One of David's heroes (1 Ch 11:36). Eliam in 2 Sm 23:34. 8. Levite; placed by David in charge of treasures of house of God and dedicated things (1 Ch 26:20). 9. Signed covenant of Nehemiah (Neh 10:26. RV, RSV: Ahiah). 10. See *Achias*.

Ahikam . (á-hī'kăm, brother has arisen) Prince of Judah (2 K 22:12); protected Jeremiah (Jer 26:24); father of Gedaliah (Jer 39:14; 40; 41; 43).

Ahikar (á-hī'kär). See *Achiacharus; Manasses 1.*

Ahilud (á-hī'lŭd, perh brother by birth). Father of Jehoshaphat, the recorder (2 Sm 8:16; 20:24; 1 K 4:3; 1 Ch 18:15), and of Baana, the purveyor (1 K 4:12).

Ahimaaz (á-hĭm'á-ăz, brother is anger). 1. Father of Ahinoam, Saul's wife (1 Sm 14:50). 2. High priest, son of Zadok; loyal to David during Absalom's rebellion (2 Sm 15:27-36; 17; 18; 1 K 4:15; 1 Ch 6:8, 9, 53).

Ahiman (á-hī'măn, brother is gift). 1. One of Anakim of Hebron (Nm 13: 22, 28; Jos 11:21; Ju 1:10, 20). 2. Levite gatekeeper (1 Ch 9:17).

Ahimelech (á-hĭm'e-lĕk, brother of Melek [Molech]). 1. Priest at Nob; gave David hallowed bread; slain by Saul (1 Sm 21, 22). 2. Hittite friend of David (1 Sm 26:6). 3. See *Abimelech 4.*

Ahimoth (á-hī'mŏth, brother is death. Mahath in 1 Ch 6:35). Levite (1 Ch 6:25).

Ahinadab (á-hĭn'á-dăb, brother is liberal). Solomon's purveyor (1 K 4:14).

Ahinoam (á-hĭn'ō-ăm, brother is grace). 1. Saul's wife (1 Sm 14:50). 2. David's wife (1 Sm 25:43; 27:3; 30:5; 2 Sm 2:2; 3:2; 1 Ch 3:1).

Ahio (á-hī'ō, brotherly). 1. Helped drive cart on which ark was removed from his father Abinadab's house (2 Sm 6:3, 4; 1 Ch 13:7). 2. Benjaminite (1 Ch 8:14). 3. Son of Jehiel (1 Ch 8:31; 9:37).

Ahira (á-hī'rá, brother is evil). Chief of Naphtali (Nm 1:15; 2:29; 7:78, 83; 10:27).

Ahiram (á-hī'răm, brother is lofty). See *Aharah*.

Ahisamach (á-hĭs'á-măk, brother has supported). Danite; father of Oholiab, tabernacle architect (Ex 31:6; 35:34; 38:23).

Ahishahar (á-hīsh'á-här, brother is dawn). Benjaminite warrior (1 Ch 7:10).

Ahishar (á-hī'shär, brother has sung). Supervisor of Solomon's household (1 K 4:6).

Ahithophel (á-hĭth'ō-fĕl, brother is folly). Wise councilor of David; joined Absalom; council overthrown by Hushai; killed himself (2 Sm 15:12, 31; 16:23; 17; 23:34; 1 Ch 27:33).

Ahitob (á-hī'tŏb). See *Ahitub 2.*

Ahitub (á-hī'tŭb, brother is goodness). 1. Son of Phinehas; father of Ahimelech (1 Sm 14:3; 22:9-20). 2. Father of Zadok (2 Sm 8:17; 1 Ch 6:7, 8; 18:16). 3. Ancestor of a later Zadok (1 Ch 6:11, 12; Neh 11:11). KJ: Achitob (RV: Ahitob) in 1 Esd 8:2; 2 Esd 1:1. 4. Ancestor of Judith (Jdth 8:1. KJ: Acitho).

Ahlab (ä'lăb). City of Asher (Ju 1:31).

Ahlai (ä'lī, oh that!). Daughter of Sheshan (1 Ch 2:31-36), perh ancestress of Zabad (1 Ch 11:41).

Ahoah (á-hō'á, heat). Benjaminite (1 Ch 8:4).

Ahohite (á-hō'hīt). Descendant of Ahoah (2 Sm 23:28; 1 Ch 11:12, 29; 27:4).

Aholah (á-hō'lá). See *Oholah*.

Aholiab (á-hō'lĭ-ăb). See *Oholiab*.

Aholibah (á-hŏl'ĭ-bá). See *Oholibah*.

Aholibamah (á-hŏl-ĭ-bä'má). 1. See *Judith 1.* 2. See *Oholibamah 2.*

Ahumai (á-hū'mī, swarthy?). Descendant of Judah (1 Ch 4:2).

Ahuzzam, Ahuzzam (á-hū'zăm, á-hŭz'ăm, possessor). Man of Judah (1 Ch 4:6).

Ahuzzath (á-hŭz'ăth, possession). Adviser (KJ, RV: friend) of Abimelech (Gn 26:26).

Ahzai (ä'zī, holder. Jahzerah in 1 Ch 9:12). Priest (Neh 11:13 [KJ: Ahasai]).

Ai (ä'ī, ruin. KJ: Hai in Gn; Aija in Neh 11:31; Aiath in Is 10:28). City (et-Tell) 1½ mi from Bethel; excavated 1933—35 (Gn 12:8; 13:3; Jos 7; 8; 9:3; 10: 1, 2; 12:9; Ez 2:28; Neh 7:32; Jer 49:3).

Aiah (á-ī'á, bird of prey). 1. Son of Zibeon (Gn 36:24 [KJ: Ajah]; 1 Ch 1:40). 2. Father of Rizpah (2 Sm 3:7; 21:8, 10, 11).

Aiath, Aija (ä-ī'äth, á-ī'já). See *Ai.*

Aijalon (ä'já-lŏn, deer field). 1. Town (Yalo) in Dan (Jos 10:12 [KJ: Ajalon]; 19:42 [KJ: Ajalon]; 21:24; Ju 1:35; 1 Sm 14:31; 1 Ch 6:69; 8:13; 2 Ch 11:10; 28:18 [KJ: Ajalon]). 2. City in Zebulun (Ju 12:12).

Aijeleth Shahar (ä'je-lĕth shä'här. RV: Aijeleth hash-Shahar; RSV: The Hind of the Dawn). Probably tune to be used for Ps 22.

Ain (ä'ĭn, eye). 1. Place near Riblah (Nm 34:11). 2. Levitical town in Judah near Rimmon (Jos 15:32; 1 Ch 4:32) assigned to Simeon (Jos 19:7 [RSV: En-rimmon]); identified with Bir Khuweilfeh. 3. See *Ashan.* 4. Ain Fashka, cave where first Dead Sea scrolls were found.

Airus (ä-ī'rus). See *Reaiah 3.*

Ajah (ä'já). See *Aiah.*

Ajalon (ăj'á-lŏn). See *Aijalon.*

Akan (ä'kăn). See *Jaakan.*

Akatan (ăk'á-tăn). See *Hakkatan.*

Akeldama (á-kĕl'dá-má, field of blood. KJ: Aceldama). Potter's field, purchased with 30 pieces of silver thrown into temple by Judas (Acts 1:19). Probably on S slope of Hinnom.

Akkos (ăk'ŏz). See *Hakkoz 2.*

Akkub (ăk'ŭb). 1. Descendant of Shecaniah (1 Ch 3:21, 24). 2. Founder of family of porters (RSV: gatekeepers) of temple (1 Ch 9:17; Ez 2:42; Neh 11:19; 12:25; 1 Esd 5:28 [KJ: Dacobi; RV: Dacubi]). 3. Family of Nethinim (Ez 2:45; 1 Esd 5:30 [KJ: Acua; RV: Acud]). **4.** Levite (Neh 8:7; 1 Esd 9:48 [KJ, RV: Jacubus]).

Akrabattine (ăk-rá-bă-tī'nē. KJ: Arabattine; RSV: Akrabbatene). Probably Akkrabbim (1 Mac 5:3).

Akrabbim (ăk-răb'ĭm, scorpion). Range forming a S boundry between Judah and Edom (Nm 34:4; Jos 15:3 [KJ: Maalehacrabbim]; Ju 1:36).

alabaster. White or cream-colored mineral (carbonate of lime), easy to carve; resembled marble (SS 5:15; Mt 26:7; Mk 14:3; Lk 7:37). RSV: mother-of-pearl in Est 1:6 (KJ: white marble; RV: yellow marble).

Alameth (ăl'á-mĕth). See *Alemeth*.

Alammelech (á-lăm'e-lĕk). See *Allammelech*.

Alamoth (ăl'á-mŏth, according to maidens). Probably music for treble or soprano voices (1 Ch 15:20; Ps 46).

Alcimus (ăl'sĭ-mus, valiant). High priest (1 Mac 7:21).

Alema (ăl'ē-má). City of Gilead (1 Mac 5: 26).

Alemeth (ăl'ē-mĕth, covert). **1.** Benjaminite (1 Ch 7:8. KJ: Alameth). **2.** Descendant of Saul (1 Ch 8:36; 9:42). **3.** City of priests in Benjamin (1 Ch 6:60. RV: Allemeth). Almon in Jos 21:18.

aleph (ä'lĕf). First letter of H alphabet.

Alexander (ăl-ĕg-zăn'dēr). **1.** "The Great" (356—323 BC); king of Macedonia; propagated Greek culture in Asia and Egypt. **2.** Son of Antiochus IV (1 Mac 10; 11). **3.** Son of Simon of Cyrene (Mk 15:21). **4.** Relative of Annas (Acts 4:6). **5.** Jew at Ephesus attempted to quiet riot of silversmiths (Acts 19:33). **6.** Ephesian; censured by Paul (1 Ti 1:20); perh the coppersmith (2 Ti 4:14).

Alexander Jannaeus (jăn'ē-us). See *Maccabees*.

Alexandra (ăl-ĕg-zăn'drá). See *Maccabees*.

Alexandria (ăl-ĕg-zăn'-drĭ-á). Egyptian city founded by Alexander the Great (332 BC); center of Greek culture; noted for its libraries, architecture, and commerce; many Greek-speaking Jews lived there; translation of LXX began there in 3d century, completed 50 BC; Christian center; noted for scholarship and textual criticism. (Acts 6:9; 27:6; 28:11)

algum. Probably hard, fine-grained red sandalwood used for furniture, harp frames, etc (2 Ch 2:8; 9:10, 11). Almug in 1 K 10:11, 12.

Aliah (á-lī'á, high. Alvah in Gn 36:40. Duke (RSV: chief) of Edom (1 Ch 1:51).

Alian (ăl'ĭ-án, high. Alvan in Gn 36:23). Horite (1 Ch 1:40).

Allammelech (á-lăm'e-lĕk, king's oak. KJ: Alammelech). Village of Asher (Jos 19: 26).

Allar (ăl'ăr. KJ: Aalar). Town in Babylonia (1 Esd 5:36. RSV: Immer as in Ez 2:59; Neh 7:61).

allegiance (á-lē'jăns). Loyalty to kings (1 Ch 12:29 [KJ: ward]; 29:24 [KJ, RV: submitted] and God (Is 19:18 [KJ, RV omit]).

allegory. Figure of speech whereby that seen or heard represents something similar to it. Verb occurs once in NT (Gl 4:24). Figure is used, e. g., "vine" (Jn 15). Word used in translation (RSV: Eze 17:2; 20:49; 24:3; Rv 11:8).

Alleluia (ăl-ē-lū'yá). See *Hallelujah*.

Allemeth (ăl'ē-mĕth). See *Alemeth 3*.

Allom (ăl'om). See *Allon 3*.

Allon (ăl'on, oak). **1.** Ancestor of Ziza (1 Ch 4:37). **2.** KJ, incorrectly, place in Naphtali (RV, RSV: oak. Jos 19:33). **3.** Name for Ami (1 Esd 5:34. KJ: Allom; RSV: Ami).

Allon-bachuth, Allon-bacuth (ăl'on-băk'uth, oak of weeping). Oak under which Deborah was buried (Gn 35:8).

almighty See *omnipotence*.

Almodad (ăl-mō'dăd, immeasurable). Shemites who settled in Arabia (Gn 10:26; 1 Ch 1:20).

Almon (ăl'mon). See *Alemeth 3*.

almond (ä'mund). Nut tree (*Amygdalus communis*), resembling peach in appearance (Gn 30:37 [KJ: hazel]; 43:11; Ex 25:33, 34; 37:19; Nu 17:8; Ec 12:5; Jer 1:11). See *orchard 5*.

Almon-diblathaim (ăl'mon-dĭb'lá-thā-ĭm). Stopping place of Israel (Nm 33:46, 47); perh Beth-diblathaim.

alms. Gifts, freely given, to needy. Commanded (Dt 15:11; Lv 19:9; Ru 2:2). Later prominent religious duty (Ps 112:9; 19:17; Sir 29:12; Tob 4:7-11). Alms emphasized by Christ (Mt 25:35, 36; Mk 9: 41) and apostles (Acts 6:1-6; Ro 15:25-27; 1 Co 16:1-4; 2 Co 9:7-9). Alms receptacles stood in temple (Mk 12:41).

almug. See *algum*.

Alnathan (ăl'ná-thăn). See *Elnathan 2*.

aloes. Probably the eaglewood (*Aquilaria agallocha*) of India, whose resin and oil were prized for fragrance (Nm 24:6; Ps 45:8; Pr 7:17; SS 4:14; Jn 19:39).

Aloth (ā'lŏth). See *Bealoth*.

alpha (ăl'fá). First letter of G alphabet. With omega (last letter) it means beginning and end (Rv 1:8, 11; 21:6; 22:13. See Is 41:4; 44:6).

alphabet. Letters used in writing and printing. Pictograms (picture writing) have been found in Palestine from 4th millennium BC; hieroglyphics from end of 3d millennium; Serabic alphabet, e g, that found at Sarâbit al-Khâdim in Sinaitic peninsula (early example of Semitic writing) from between 1850 and 1500 B. C. H alphabet in KJ, Ps 119. Alphabet of Moabite stone resembles OT Hebrew. See also *writing*.

Alphaeus (ăl-fē'us, transient?). **1.** Father of James (the Less) and Moses (Mt 10:3; Mk 3:18; Mk 15:40). **2.** Father of Matthew Mt 9:9; Mk 2:14).

Altaneus (ăl-tá-nē'us). See *Mattenai 2, 3*.

altar (high). Elevation usually of earth or stone (Ex 20:24-26). According to ancient OT principle, altar was erected wherever the LORD manifested Himself (Gn 8:20; 12:7; 26:25; 35:1). Tabernacle had two altars: 1. Altar of burnt offering (brazen; Ex 27:1, 2). All sacrifices were offered at this altar and reminded Israel that it had access to God only through atonement. **2.** Altar of incense (golden; Ex 30:1-10) symbolized adoration.

Al-taschith, Al-tashheth (ăl-tăs'kĭth, ăl-tăsh'hĕth. RSV: Do Not Destroy). Perh name of a melody (Ps 57; 58; 59; 75).

Alush (ā'lŭsh). Encampment of Israel between Egypt and Sinai (Nm 33:13, 14).

Alvah (ăl'vá). See *Aliah*.

Alvan (ăl'văn). See *Alian*.

Amad (ā'măd, station). Village of Asher (Jos 19:26).

Amadatha, Amadathus (á-măd'á-thá, -thus). See *Hammedatha*.

Amal (ā'măl, labor). Asherite (1 Ch 7:35).

Amalek (ăm'á-lĕk). Son of Eliphaz; Esau's grandson (Gn 36:12; 1 Ch 1:36).

Amalekites (ăm'á-lĕk-īts). Descendants of Esau (Gn 36:12), lived S of Canaan in Sinai Peninsula (Negeb), penetrated N into Arabah. Called "first of nations" (Nm 24:20). Traditional enemies of Israel (Ps 83:7). Smitten by Gideon (Ju 7), Saul (1 Sm 15), David (1 Sm 30:18).

Amam (ā'măm). Village of Judah (Jos 15:26).

Aman (ā'măn). See *Haman*.

Amana (á-mä'ná). Mountains of Anti-Lebanon (SS 4:8).

Amariah (ăm-á-rī'á, LORD has promised). 1. Father of Ahitub (1 Ch 6:7). 2. Son of Azariah (1 Ch 6:11; Ez 7:3). KJ, RV: Amarias in 1 Esd 8:2; 2 Esd 1:2. 3. Chief of priests who returned from captivity (Neh 12:2, 7, 13). Possibly same as in Neh 10:3. 4. Levite (2 Ch 31:14, 15). 5. Divorced foreign wife (Ez 10:42; 1 Esd 9:34 [KJ: Zambis; RV: Zambri]). 6. Judahite (Neh 11:4). 7. Ancestor of Zephaniah (Zph 1:1). 8. Chief priest of Jehoshaphat's time (2 Ch 19:11). 9. Levite (1 Ch 23:19; 24:23).

Amarias (ăm-á-rī'ăs). See *Amariah* 2.

Amasa (ăm'á-sá, burden). 1. David's nephew (1 Ch 2:17), Joab's cousin (2 Sm 17:25); captain of Absalom's army; forgiven by David and made commander in chief; killed by Joab (2 Sm 19:13; 20: 4-13). 2. Prince of Ephraim (2 Ch 28:12).

Amasai (á-măs'â-ī, burdensome). 1. Levite (1 Ch 6:35; perh different from 1 Ch 6:25). 2. Chief of David (1 Ch 12:18). 3. Priest, trumpeter (1 Ch 15:24).

Amashai, Amashsai (á-măsh'â-ī, á-măsh'sâ-ī, burdensome). Priest (Neh 11:13).

Amasiah (ăm-á-sī'á, LORD has borne). Captain of Jehoshaphat (2 Ch 17:16).

Amatheis (ăm-á-thē'ĭs). See *Athlai*.

Amathis (ăm'á-thĭs). See *Hamath* 2.

Amaw (ā'mô). Land on N Euphrates; includes Pethor (Nm 22:5. KJ, RV: of his people).

Amaziah (ăm-á-zī'á, LORD is mighty). 1. Son of Joash; king of Judah after Joash's assassination; avenged father; defeated Edomites; rebuked for idolatry; defeated by Jehoash and murdered at Lachish (2 K 12:21; 14; 15; 2 Ch 24:27; 25; 26). 2. Simeonite (1 Ch 4:34). 3. Merarite Levite (1 Ch 6:45). 4. Priest; opposed Amos (Am 7:10-17).

ambassador. Messenger of potentate (Is 18:2; Eze 17:15). Paul called himself ambassador of Christ (2 Co 5:20; Eph 6:20; Phmn 9). RSV often "envoy" where KJ, RV have "ambassador" (2 Ch 32:31; 35:21; Is 30:4; 33:7; 57:9).

amber (RV margin: electrum; RSV: gleaming bronze). Substance which has glowing yellow color (Eze 1:4, 27; 8:2).

amen (ā'mĕn'; in singing: ä'mĕn', true). 1. Name of Jesus emphasizing that He is Truth (Rv 3:14). 2. "So be it" indicates confirmation (Nm 5:22; Dt 27:15-26; Mt 6:13; 1 Co 14:16). God's promises are Amen (2 Co 1:20).

amethyst (ăm'ê-thĭst). Bluish-violet, clear quartz. Stone in high priest's breastplate. Foundation stone of New Jerusalem (Ex 28:19; 39:12; Rv 21:20).

Ami (ā'mī). Amon in Neh 7:59. Head of family returned from captivity (Ez 2:57).

Aminadab (á-mĭn'á-dăb). See *Amminadab*.

Amittai (á-mĭt'ī, truthful). Father of Jonah (2 K 14:25; Jon 1:1).

Ammah (ăm'á). Hill near Giah (2 Sm 2:24).

Ammi (ăm'ī). "My people" (Hos 2:1. RSV: My people). See 1 Ptr 2:10; Ro 9:25, 26. See also *Lo-ammi*.

Ammidioi (á-mĭd'ĭ-oi. RSV: Ammidians). Returned captives (1 Esd 5:20).

Ammiel (ăm'ĭ-ĕl, kinsman is God). 1. Spy of Dan (Nm 13:12). 2. Father of Machir (2 Sm 9:4, 5). 3. See *Eliam 1*. 4. Doorkeeper of temple (1 Ch 26:5).

Ammihud (á-mī'hŭd, my people is glory). 1. Ephraimite; father of Elishama (Nm 1:10; 1 Ch 7:26). 2. Simeonite; father of Shemuel (Nm 34:20). 3. Naphtalite; father of Pedahel (Nm 34:28). 4. Father of Talmai, king of Geshur (2 Sm 13:37. RV: Ammihur). 5. Judahite; father of Uthai (1 Ch 9:4).

Ammihur (ăm'ĭ-hûr). See *Ammihud* 4.

Amminadab (á-mĭn'á-dăb, kinsman is noble. KJ in NT: Aminadab). 1. Man of Judah, father-in-law of Aaron, ancestor of David (Ex 6:23; Nm 1:7; 1 Ch 2:10; Ru 4:19; Mt 1:4; Lk 3:33). 2. Kohathite; house of Uzziel (1 Ch 15:10, 11). 3. See *Izhar 1*.

Amminadib (á-mĭn'á-dĭb). Perh not proper noun (SS 6:12. RSV: my prince).

Ammishaddai (ăm-ĭ-shăd'ī, people of the Almighty). Danite, father of Ahiezer Nm 1:12; 2:25; 7:66; 7:71; 10:25).

Ammizabad (á-mĭz'á-băd, people has given). Leader in David's army (1 Ch 27:6).

Ammon (ăm'on). Name for Ben-ammi, ancestor of Ammonites (Gn 19:38; Dt 2:19).

Ammonites (ăm'on-īts). Dwellers E of Dead Sea and Jordan; capital city: Rabbah-Ammon (Dt 3:11. Modern Amman). Saul defeated them (1 Sm 11); David took their capital (2 Sm 12:26-31). Inveterate, idolatrous, cruel enemies of Israel (Dt 23: 3-6; Ju 3:13; 1 Sm 11:1-11; Am 1:13; Neh 4:3-9; Jer 49:1-6; Eze 25:1-7).

Amnon (ăm'nŏn, faithful). 1. Son of David; forced his half-sister Tamar; killed by Absalom (2 Sm 13). 2. Son of Shimon (1 Ch 4:20).

Amok (ā'mŏk, deep). Chief priest; returned from captivity (Neh 12:7, 20).

Amon (ā'mon, skilled workman). 1. Governor of Samaria under Ahab (1 K 22:26; 2 Ch 18:25). 2. 15th king of Judah; son and successor of Manasseh; idolatrous; murdered by his servants (2 K 21:19-26; 2 Ch 33:21-25). 3. See *Ami*.

Amon (ā'mon). Ancient Egyptian city of Thebes, center of worship of sun-god Amon (Amen, Amun-Re. Jer 46:25 [KJ: No]; Nah 3:8 [KJ: No; RSV: Thebes]).

Amorites (ăm'ō-rīts). Powerful nation of Canaan (Gn 10:16; 14:7; Jos 5:1; 10:6); occupied both sides of Jordan (Nm 21: 26-31; Jos 13:15-21); Samuel had peace with them (1 Sm 7:14); Solomon made them bond servants (1 K 9:20, 21).

Amos (ā'mos, burden). 1. Shepherd of Tekoah; prophet during reign of Uzziah and Jeroboam II. Book emphasizes judgment of God. Outline: 1. Indictment of Foreign Nations, Judah, and Israel (1, 2). 2. Exhortations and Threats (3—6). 3. Visions (7—9). 2. Ancestor of Jesus (Lk 3:25).

Amoz (ā'mŏz, strong). Isaiah's father (Is 1:1).

Amphipolis (ăm-fĭp'ō-lĭs, city surrounded). City of Macedonia on Strymon River (Acts 17:1).

Amplias, Ampliatus (ăm'plĭ-ăs, ăm'plĭ-ā'tus, enlarger). Friend of Paul at Rome (Ro 16:8).

Amram (ăm'răm, high people). 1. Father of Moses and Aaron (Ex 6:20). 2. Divorced foreign wife (Ez 10:34; 1 Esd 9:34 [KJ: Omaerus. RV: Ismaerus]). 3. See *Hemdan*.

Amramites (ăm'răm-īts). Descendants of Amram (Nm 3:27; 1 Ch 26:23).

Amraphel (ăm'rȧ-fĕl). King of Shinar; fought Sodom (Gn 14).

amulets. Charm worn as protection against sickness, accident, sorcery, and evil spirits (Is 3:20. KJ: earrings).

Amzi (ăm'zī). 1. Merarite; ancestor of Ethan (1 Ch 6:46). 2. Father of Pelaliah (Neh 11:12).

Anab (ā'năb, grapes). Town of Judah, 13 mi SW of Hebron (Jos 11:21; 15:50).

Anael (ăn'ȧ-ĕl). Tobit's brother (Tob 1:21).

Anah (ā'nȧ, answer). 1. Daughter (RSV: son) of Zibeon; mother (or father) of Oholibamah (Gn 36:2, 14, 18, 25). LXX, Syriac, Samaritan OT have "son"; then same in Gen 36:24. 2. Horite duke (Gn 36:20, 29; 1 Ch 1:38). Possibly same as 1.

Anaharath (ȧn-ā'hȧ-răth, gorge). Town of Issachar (Jos 19:19). Perh modern en-Na'ûrah, 5 mi NE of Jezreel.

Anaiah (ȧ-nī'ȧ, LORD has answered). One who stood by Ezra as he read Law (Neh 8:4; 1 Esd 9:43 [KJ, RV: Ananias]); signed covenant (Neh 10:22).

Anak (ā'năk). Collective name of Anakim. See giants 3.

Anakim (ăn'ȧ-kĭm). See giants 3.

analogy of faith. Harmony of Scripture teachings. Hence rule that interpretation of each passage should harmonize with sum total of Scriptural teaching (Ro 12:6).

Anamim (ăn'ȧ-mĭm). Unknown Egyptian tribe (Gn 10:13; 1 Ch 1:11).

Anammelech (ȧ-năm'e-lĕk). Babylonian god brought to Samaria by Sepharvites (2 K 17:31).

Anan (ā'năn). 1. Co-covenanter with Nehemiah (Neh 10:26). 2. See Hanan 4.

Anani (ȧ-nā'nī). Descendant of David (1 Ch 3:24).

Ananiah (ȧn-ȧ-nī'ȧ, LORD has covered). 1. Grandfather of Azariah (Neh 3:23). 2. Town near Jerusalem (Neh 11:32).

Ananias (ăn-ȧ-nī'ăs, LORD has covered). 1. Member of church in Jerusalem; died suddenly after conspiring with wife to deceive and defraud the church (Acts 5: 1-6). 2. Disciple at Damascus sent to restore Paul's sight (Acts 9:10-20; 22:12). 3. High priest (Acts 23:1-5; 24:1). 4. Listed in 1 Esd 5:16 (RV: Annis; RSV: Annias). 5. See Hanani 4. 6. See Hananiah 9. 7. See Anaiah. 8. See Hanan 5. 9. "The Great," kinsman of Tobit (Tob 5:12, 13). 10. Ancestor of Judith (Jdth 8:1).

Ananiel (ȧ-năn'ĭ-ĕl). Ancestor of Tobit (Tob 1:1).

Anasib (ăn'ȧ-sĭb). See Sanasib.

Anath (ā'năth, answer). Father of Shamgar (Ju 3:31; 5:6).

anathema (ȧ-năth'ē-mȧ). LXX usually uses this word to translate H herem, which designates vow by which persons or things are devoted to God. Inanimate thing fell to priests (Nm 18:12-14), living thing must be slain (Lv 27:28, 29). Later, anathema removed person from group (Ez 10:8). NT: solemn curse which implies separation (RV: Ro 9:3; 1 Co 12:3 [KJ margin]; Gl 1:8, 9). KJ, RSV usually translate accursed in NT.

anathema maranatha (ȧ-năth'ē-mȧ măr-ȧ-năth'ȧ). Accursed person (KJ: 1 Co 16:22. RV, RSV regard Maranatha as separate sentence: Let God come!).

Anathoth (ăn'ȧ-thŏth, answers). 1. Descendant of Benjamin (1 Ch 7:8). 2. Signed covenant with Nehemiah (Neh 10:19). 3. Levitical city in Benjamin; noted as birthplace of Jeremiah (Jos 21: 18; Jer 1:1; 11:21-23; 29:27); identified with modern 'Anata.

Anathothite (ăn'ȧ-thŏth-īt). See Anethothite.

ancestor (RSV: Jos 19:47; Ju 18:29; Heb 7:10). See also father 2; 3.

anchor. 1. Ship's anchor (Acts 27:29-40). 2. Spiritual support in time of trial (Hb 6:19).

Ancient of Days. Name applied to LORD by Daniel (7:9-22) to inspire veneration and convey majesty.

Andrew (ăn'drōō, manly). Native of Bethsaida (Jn 1:44); fisherman; brother of Simon Peter (Mt 4:18; Mk 1:16-18); disciple of John the Baptist, who directed him to Jesus (Jn 1:35-42); later became permanent disciple (Mt 4:18, 19; Mk 1: 16, 17) and apostle (Mt 10:2; Mk 3:18; Lk 6:14; Acts 1:13). Andrew brought Peter to Jesus (Jn 1:41); called Jesus' attention to lad with loaves and fishes (Jn 6:8); introduced Greeks to Jesus (Jn 12:20-22); inquired regarding destruction of temple (Mk 13:3, 4). According to tradition, crucified in Achaia on cross shaped like an X (crux decussata) on Nov. 30.

Andronicus (ăn-drŏ-nī'kus, man conqueror). 1. Friend and fellow prisoner of Paul (Ro 16:7). 2. Viceroy of Antiochus (2 Mac 4:31-38). 3. Officer of Antiochus at Garizim (2 Mac 5:23).

Anem (ā'nĕm). En-gannim in Jos 21:29). Levitical city in Issachar (1 Ch 6:73).

Aner (ā'nĕr). 1. Amorite chief; confederate of Abraham (Gn 14:13-24). 2. Levitical city in Manasseh, W of Jordan (1 Ch 6:70). Probably same as Taanach.

Anethothite, Anetothite, Antothite (ăn'ē-thŏth-īt, ăn'ē-tŏth-īt, ăn'toth-īt. RV: Anthothite; RSV: of Anathoth). Inhabitant of Anathoth (2 Sm 23:27; 1 Ch 11:28; 12:3; 27:12).

angels (messengers). 1. Unseen, spiritual (Mt 22: 30; Heb 1:14), holy (Ps 89:5, 7) celestial beings who continually do God's bidding (Ps 104:4; Mt 4:6; Heb 2:7). They protect and serve those who fear God (Gn 28:12; 48:16; 2 K 6:17; Ps 34:7; Is 63:9); differ in rank and dignity (Dn 10:13, 21; Lk 1: 19, 26; Ro 8:38; Eph 1:21. 2. An angel of the LORD may be an angel which executes God's will (1 K 19:5, 7); yet there is frequent mention of "the angel of the LORD," a distinct person and yet of essence of the LORD (Gn 16:10, 13; 18:2-4, 13, 14, 33), who revealed God (Gn 32:30), has the LORD's name (Ex 23:21) and presence (Ex 32:14), and is therefore identified with preincarnate Son. 3. Evil angels are fallen spirits (2 Ptr 2:4). See demon; Satan. 4. The "angels of the seven churches" are representatives of the churches, possibly pastors (Rv 1:20; 2:1, 8, 12, 18; 3:1, 7, 14). 5. John the Baptist called messenger (G angelos) sent before Christ (Mt 11:10; Mk 1:2; Lk 7:27).

anger. See wrath.

Aniam (ȧ-nī'ăm, sighing of people). Manassite (1 Ch 7:19.

Anim (ā'nĭm, fountains). City of Judah, 10 mi SW of Hebron (Jos 15:50).

anise. See dill.

ankle chain. RV in Nm 31:50; Is 3:20. KJ: chains and ornaments of the legs; RSV: armlets.

anklet. Ornamental metallic or glass ring for ankles (Is. 3:18. KJ: tinkling ornaments about the feet).

Anna (ăn'ȧ, grace). 1. Prophetess; thanked God at presentation of Jesus (Lk 2:36-38). 2. Tobit's wife (Tob 1:9).

Annaas (ăn'ȧ-ăs). See Hassenah.

Annan (ăn'ăn). See Harim 3.

Annas (ăn′ăs, merciful). 1. High priest at Jerusalem; father-in-law of Caiaphas (Lk 3:2; Jn 18:13); appointed by Quirinius, A. D. 7; deposed by Valerius Gratus c A. D. 15 (Josephus, Ant XVIII, ii, 1, 2). Regarded as virtual high priest during time when sons and Caiaphas held office (Jn 18:13; Acts 4:6). 2. See *Harim 3.*

Annias, Annis (ă-nī′ăs, ăn′is). See *Ananias 4.*

Anniuth, Annus (ăn′ĭ-ŭth, ăn′ŭs). See *Bani 7.*

Annunus, Annuus (ăn′u-nus, ăn′ū-nus). Listed in 1 Esd 8:48.

anoint. To apply oil to person or thing as: 1. Part of toilet (Ru 3:3); expression of joy (Ps 23:5; 45:7; cf Ps 92:10). 2. Civility to guests (Lk 7:46). 3. Act of consecration (Gn 28:18; Ex 30:23-36); induction to priestly (Ex 40:15) or kingly (1 Sm 9:16) office. 4. Act of healing (Ja 5:14). 5. Christ anointed with Holy Ghost (Lk 4:18; Acts 4:27; 10:38; Ps 45:7; Is 61:1). Common custom of Egyptians, Hebrews, Greeks, Romans.

Anos (ā′nŏs). See *Venaiah.*

ant. Cited as example of diligence (Pr 6: 6-8) and wisdom (Pr 30:24, 25).

antelope. Animal ceremonially fit for food (Dt 14:5; Is 51:20. KJ: wild ox; wild bull).

Anthothijah (ăn-thŏ-thī′já, answers of LORD. KJ: Antothijah). Benjaminite (1 Ch 8:24).

antichrist (ăn′tĭ-krist, against Christ). Enemy of Christ and usurper of His prerogatives. In NT John alone uses the word (1 Jn 2:18, 22; 4:3; 2 Jn 7). Other passages in Scriptures (Dn 7; 8; 11:31-35; 2 Th 2:3-12; Rv 10; 13; 17; 18) were applied to *the* Antichrist early in history of church.

Antigonus (ăn-tĭg′ō-nus). See *Maccabees.*

Anti-Lebanon (ăn′tĭ-lĕb′á-nun). See *Lebanon.*

antilegomena (ăn-tĭ-lē-gŏm′ē-ná). Books of NT which were not received as canonical by church everywhere until latter part of 4th century (James, Jude, 2 and 3 John, 2 Peter, Hebrews, Apocalypse).

Antioch (ăn′tĭ-ŏk, from Antiochus, Syrian king). 1. City in Syria on S bank of Orontes; founded c 300 BC by Seleucus Nicator; Pompey made it seat of legate of Syria (64 BC) and free city. Barnabas and Paul worked there. Followers of Jesus there called Christians (Acts 11: 19-26; 13:1-3; 14:26; 15; 18:22; Gl 2:11). Modern Antakid. 2. City in Pisidia also founded by Seleucus Nicator (Acts 13: 14-52; 14:21).

Antiochus (ăn-tĭ′ō-kus, opponent). 1. Father of Numenius, messenger of Jonathan to Romans (1 Mac 12:16; 14:22). 2. Antiochus III, the Great, king of Syria, 223—187 BC (Dn 11:14-19). 3. Antiochus IV, Epiphanes, 175—164 BC, intolerant and energetic (1 Mac 1:10). 4. Antiochus V, Eupator, 164—163 BC (1 Mac 6:17-63). 5. Antiochus VI (1 Mac 11:39, 40; 13: 31, 32). 6. Antiochus VII, 138—128 BC (1 Mac 15).

Antipas (ăn′tĭ-păs, like father). 1. Martyr of Pergamos (Rv 2:13), traditionally, bishop burned in brazen bull under Domitian. 2. Herod Antipas.

Antipater (ăn-tĭp′-á-tēr, like father). 1. Jew, son of Jason, ambassador of Jonathan (1 Mac 12:16; 14:22; Ant XIII, v, 8). 2. Father of Herod the Great (Ant XIV, vii, 3).

Antipatris (ăn-tĭp′á-trĭs). City built by Herod the Great between Caesarea and Jerusalem (Ras-el-Ain) and named after Herod's father. Paul prisoner there (Acts 23:31).

antitype. Perfect thing of which the type is image (1 Ptr 3:21; RV margin. KJ: figure. RV: likeness. RSV: which corresponds).

Antonia (ăn-tō′nĭ-á). Fortress, NW side of temple, built by Herod the Great. Garrisoned by Roman soldiers who watched temple area (see Acts 21:31-40; 22; 23).

Antothijah (ăn-tō-thī′já). See *Anthothijah.*

Antothite (ăn′toth-īt). See *Anethothite.*

Anub (ā′nŭb). Son of Koz of tribe of Judah (1 Ch 4:8).

Anus (ā′nus). See *Bani 7.*

anvil. See *trade 7.*

anxiety. See *care.*

Apame (á-pā′mē). Daughter of Bartacus (1 Esd 4:29).

Apelles (á-pĕl′ēz, called). Friend of Paul (Ro 16:10).

ape. Imported by navies of Solomon and Hiram (1 K 10:22; 2 Ch 9:21).

Aphaerema, Aphairema (á-fī′rē-má. KJ: Apherema). District taken from Samaria, annexed to Judea by Demetrius Nicator (1 Mac 11:34). Perhaps variant for Ephraim (Ju 11:54).

Apharsachites, Apharsathchites (á-fär′să-kĭts, ăf-är-săth′kĭts. RSV: governors). Colonists in Samaria (Ez 4:9; 5:6).

Aphek (ā′fĕk, fortress). 1. Town of Sharon (Jos 12:18) where Philistines encamped before battle at Ebenezer (1 Sm 4:1). Modern Ras el-′Ain. 2. City commonly identified with Afqa, 23 mi N of Beirut (Jos 13:4). 3. Asherite city (Jos 19:30). Aphik in Ju 1:31. Probably same as 2. 4. Town 4 mi E of Sea of Galilee (1 K 20:26, 30; 2 K 13:17). 5. Town near Jezreel (1 Sm 28:4; 29:1, 11; 31:3). Probably same as 1.

Aphekah (á-fē′ká, fortress). City in Judah (Jos 15:53).

Apherema (á-fĕr′ē-má). See *Aphaerema.*

Apherra (á-fĕr′á). Listed in 1 Esd 5:34.

Aphiah (á-fī′á, refreshed). Ancestor of Saul (1 Sm 9:1).

Aphik (ā′fĭk). See *Aphek 3.*

Aphrah (ăf′rá). See *Beth-le-aphrah.*

Aphses (ăf′sēz). See *Happizzez.*

apocalypse (á-pŏk′á-lĭps, uncover). Greek name for Revelation.

apocalyptic literature. Scriptural writings (e. g., Daniel, Revelation) which reveal events of last times, judgment, and hereafter. Also noncanonical literature which flourished in late Judaism and early Christianity (e. g., Enoch, Baruch, Apocalypse of Peter, Ascension of Isaiah, Assumption of Moses, Book of Jubilees, Shepherd of Hermas).

Apocrypha (á-pŏk′rĭ-fá, hidden). Term in patristic literature for writings that were esoteric or obscure and books whose authorship was unknown; gradually came to be used synonymously with H *sepharim hitsonim* (books outside the canon). In Reformation period apocrypha were uncanonical books in Vulgate (1 and 2 Esdras, Additions to Esther, Song of the Three Children, History of Susannah, Bel and the Dragon, Prayer of Manasses, Baruch, Epistle of Jeremiah, Tobit, Judith, 1 and 2 Maccabees, Ecclesiasticus [Sirach], Wisdom of Solomon). Other "outside books" of Jews and Christians were then designated as "pseudepigrapha." For NT period "apocrypha" and "pseudepigrapha" are usually used interchangeably.

Apollonia (ăp-o-lō'nĭ-á, belonging to Apollo). City in Macedonia (Acts 17:1).
Apollonius (ăp-o-lō'nĭ-us, belonging to Apollo). **1.** Son of Thrasaeus; governor of Coelesyria (2 Mac 3:5). **2.** Son of 1; governor of Coelesyria (1 Mac 10:69-85). **3.** Son of Menestheus; official of Antiochus Epiphanes and governor of Samaria (1 Mac 3:10, 11; 2 Mac 4:21; 5: 24-27). **4.** Son of Gennaeus; governor of a toparchy in Palestine under Antiochus Eupator (2 Mac 12:2).
Apollophanes (ăp-o-lŏf'á-nēz). Syrian general (2 Mac 10:37).
Apollos (á-pŏl'os, belonging to Apollo). Learned Jew; Alexandrian by birth; adhered to John's baptism; instructed by Aquila and Priscilla; eloquent preacher; friend of Paul (Acts 18:24-28; 1 Co 1:12; 3:4-22; 4:6; 16:12; Tts 3:13).
Apollyon (á-pŏl'yun, destroyer). See *Abaddon 4.*
apostasy (á-pŏs'tá-sĭ). Forsaking the Lord (Jer 2:19; 5:6. AV: forsake, backslide) or departing from the faith (Hb 6:6. KJ: fall away). There are many warnings against apostasy, i. e., departure from known truth (Hb 6:1-8; 10:26-29; 2 Ptr 2:15-21). Apostate not to be confused with errorist or heretic.
apostle (one sent forth). **1.** Official name of 12 disciples: Simon Peter (Cephas, Bar-jona), Andrew, John, Philip, James, Bartholomew (perh same as Nathanael), Thomas (Didymus), Matthew (Levi), Simon Zelotes, Jude (Lebbaeus, Thaddeus), James the Less, Judas Iscariot (Mt 10). Matthias took place of Judas Iscariot (Acts 1:15-26). Paul called to be apostle on way to Damascus (Acts 9; 1 Co 1:1; 2 Co 10—12). Apostles personally acquainted with Jesus (Acts 1: 21, 22). Apostles established Christian church (Mk 16:20; Acts); through their verbal and written testimony are foundation of church (Eph 2:20). **2.** Anyone commissioned to preach Gospel (Ro 10: 13-15; 2 Co 8:23; Ph 2:25). **3.** Christ (Heb 3:1).
apothecary (á-pŏth'ê-kĕr-ĭ, *raqah*, to perfume). Person who mixed ointments (Ex 30:25, 35; Neh 3:8. RSV: perfumer). Bezaleel compounded anointing oil (Ex 31:11; 37:29). Perfumers prepared burial spices (2 Ch 16:14) and, according to excavations, medicinal herbs.
Appaim (ăp'á-ĭm, nostrils). Son of Nabad (1 Ch 2:30, 31).
apparel. See *dress.*
appeal. In ancient Israel appeals were made to head of tribe (Gn 38:24). Moses appointed judges who handled appeals before directed to himself (Ex 18:13, 26). Later supreme decisions were made at sanctuaries (Dt 17:8-11). Judges and kings handled appeals (Ju 4:5; 2 Sm 15:3). Jehoshaphat and Ezra established courts (2 Ch 19:8; Ez 7:25). Later Sanhedrin became highest court of Jews. Every Roman citizen could appeal to emperor (Acts 25:11, 12).
appendage (á-pĕn'dĭj). See *caul 2.*
Apphia (ăf'ĭ-á). Woman at Colosse, traditionally, wife of Philemon (Phmn 2).
Apphus (ăf'us). Surname of Jonathan Maccabaeus (1 Mac 2:5).
Appii Forum (ăp'ĭ-ī fō'rum. RV: Market of Appius. RSV: Forum of Appius). Town about 40 mi from Rome on Appian Way (Acts 28:15).
apple. Popular fruit in Palestine (Pr 25:11; SS 2:3, 5; 7:8; 8:5; Jl 1:12). See *orchard.*

Aqaba, Gulf of (ŭ'kŏ-bá). NE arm of Red Sea, where Ezion-geber, Solomon's seaport, was located (see 1 K 9:26).
Aquila (ăk'wĭ-lá, eagle). Jew born in Pontus; tentmaker by trade; prominent coworker (with wife Priscilla) of Paul (Acts 18:1-3, 18, 19, 26; Ro 16:3; 1 Co 16:19; 2 Ti 4:19).
Ar (är, city). Prominent city of Moab Nm 21:28; Dt 2:9, 18, 29; Is 15:1).
Ara (ā'rá, lion). Asherite (1 Ch 7:38).
Arab (ā'răb, ambush). City of Judah (Jos 15:52).
Arabah (ăr'á-bá, desert. KJ: plain, *exc* Jos 18:18 and as noted). Name applied to valley between Dead Sea and Gulf of Aqaba (Dt 1:1, 7; 11:30 [KJ: champaign]; Jos 3:16; 1 Sm 23:24; 2 Sm 2:29; 2 K 14:25; Jer 39:4; Eze 47:8 [KJ: desert]; Am 6:14 [KJ: wilderness]).
Arabattine (ăr-á-bă-tī'nē). See *Akrabbatine.*
Arabia (á-rā'bĭ-á, desert). Originally, N portions of peninsula between Red Sea and Persian Gulf (Is 21:13; Jer 25:24; Eze 27:21). Later, entire peninsula (Neh 2:19; 6:1; Acts 2:11; Gl 1:17; 4:25).
Arad (ā'răd, fugitive). **1.** Benjaminite (1 Ch 8:15). **2.** Canaanite city (Tell Arad), 20 mi S of Hebron; conquered by Joshua (Nm 21:1; 33:40; Jos 12:14; Ju 1:16). KJ (incorrectly): King Arad in Nm 21:1; 33:40).
Aradus (ăr'á-dus). See *Arvad.*
Arah (ā'rá). **1.** Asherite (1 Ch 7:39). **2.** Head of family which returned from captivity (Ez 2:5; Neh 7:10; 1 Esd 5:10 [KJ, RV: Ares]). Possibly same in Neh 6:18.
Aram (ā'răm). **1.** Descendant of Shem (Gn 10:22, 23; 1 Ch 1:17). **2.** Grandson of Nahor (Gn 22:21). **3.** Asherite (1 Ch 7:34). **4.** See *Ram 1.* **5.** Aramaean people (Syrians) spread from Lebanon Mts to beyond Euphrates and from Taurus Mts to S of Damascus. Several divisions mentioned in OT: Aram-Naharaim (KJ: Syrians . . . beyond the river; RSV: Syrians . . . beyond the Euphrates. 2 Sm 10:16), home of patriarchs; Aram-Damascus (KJ, RSV: Syrians of Damascus. 2 Sm 8:5); Aram-Zobah (Syrians of Zobah. 2 Sm 10:6), named after kingdom of Zobah (1 Sm 14:47); Aram-Maacah (1 Ch 19:6). H Aram often translated with Syria.
Aramaic (ăr-á-mā'ĭk). Semitic language in Aram (incorrectly called Chaldee on basis of Dn 2:4—7:28), which spread to all of SW Asia. Aramaic inscriptions are extant from 850 BC. Following portions of OT are in Aramaic: Dn 2:4—7:28; Ez 4:8—6:18; 7:12-26; Jer 10:11. Jesus spoke Aramaic.
Aran (ā'răn). Horite (Gn 36:28).
Ararat (ăr'á-răt, H for Accadian *Urartu*). Name applied to Armenia (2 K 19:37 [KJ: Armenia]; Is 37:38 [KJ: Armenia]; Jer 51:27) and to its mountain range, especially two peaks 14,000 and 10,000 ft high (Gn 8:4). Armenia extends from Black Sea to Caspian Sea and from Caucasus to Taurus Mts. KJ: Ararath in Tob 1:21.
Ararite (ăr'á-rīt). See *Hararite.*
Arathes (á-rā'thēz). King of Cappadocia, 162—131 BC (1 Mac 15:22. AV: Ariarathes; RSV: Ariarthes).
Araunah (á-rô'ná). Ornan in 1 Ch 21: 15:28; 2 Ch 3:1. Jebusite who sold threshing floor on Mt Moriah to David (2 Sm 24:16-24).

Arba (är'bá). Giant; ancestor of Anak (Jos 14:15; 15:13; 21:11).

Arbah (är'bá). See *Kiriath-arba*.

Arbathite (är'ba-thīt). Native of Beth-arabah (2 Sm 23:31; 1 Ch 11:32).

Arbatta, Arbattis (är-băt'á, är-băt'ĭs). Place near Galilee (1 Mac 5:23).

Arbela (är-bē'lá). Town in Galilee (1 Mac 9:2). Perh Beth-arbel.

Arbite (är'bīt). Native of Arab (2 Sm 23:35).

Arbonai (är-bō'nä-ī). See *Abron*.

arch. Architectural term of KJ, RV. RSV: vestibule (Eze 40:16, 22, 26, 29).

archaeology (är-kē-ŏl'ō-jĭ). Study of material remains of past. Biblical archaeology is concerned with Palestine, ancient countries with which Hebrews came into contact, and countries to which early Christianity was brought. Modern archaeology is usually traced to Napoleon's expedition to Egypt, on which about 100 scholars accompanied him to study monuments (1798) C. J. Rich of East India Company in Baghdad made first excavations in Mesopotamia. Edward Robinson of Union Theological Seminary, New York, made extensive observations in Palestine (1838, 1852). From these beginnings Biblical archaeology developed. Earlier excavators (1800—1890) were primarily concerned with finding objects of interest. Scientific aspects of archaeology, however, soon developed (1890 to 1915). Results used in Bible dictionaries.

archangel (ärk'ān'jel). Chief angel (1 Th 4:16; Jude 9). See *angels 1*.

Archelaus (är-kē-lā'us). See *Herod 2*.

archery. Bow and arrow were ancient weapons. Benjaminites (1 Ch 8:40; 2 Ch 14:8; 17:17), Philistines (1 Sm 31:3), Medes (Is 13:18), and Elamites (Jer 49:35) were famous archers. "Arrow" used figuratively for calamity (Jb 6:4), wicked tongue (Jer 9:8; Ps 64:3), danger (Ps 91:5), power (Ps 45:5; 127:4). "Bow" also used figuratively (Ps 7:12; 64:3; 78:57). Quiver: case for arrows (Gn 27:3; Jb 39:23).

Archevites (är'kē-vīts). Inhabitants of Erech (Ez 4:9).

Archi (är'kī). KJ for Archite (Jos 16:2).

Archippus (är-kĭp'us, *master of horse*). Christian at Colosse (Cl 4:17; Phmn 2).

architecture (är'kĭ-těk-tŭr). For early architecture see *homes*. Little emphasis on architecture before time of kings. David built house trimmed with cedar (2 Sm 7:2); Solomon built palaces for himself and harem (1 K 7). Palaces of later kings more ornate, decorated with ivory (Am 3:15). Temple, city gates, pillars, etc., offered further opportunity for architectural achievement. Splendor of Jerusalem under Herod was admired by disciples of Jesus (Mk 13:1).

Archites (är'kīts). Clan whose possessions were on S boundary of Ephraim (Jos 16:2; 2 Sm 15:32; 16:16; 17:5, 14; 1 Ch 27:33).

archives. Place for storing documents (Ez 5:17 [KJ, RV: treasure house]; 6:1 [KJ: house of the rolls]).

Arcturus (ärk-tū'rus). Constellation Ursa Major, or "Great Bear" (Jb 9:9; 38:32. RV, RSV: the Bear).

Ard (ärd). Grandson of Benjamin (Gn 46: 21 [son]; Nm 26:40). See *Addar 2*.

Ardat, Ardath (är'dăt, är'dăth). Field (2 Esd 9:26).

Ardites (är'dīts). Descendants of Ard (Nm 26:40).

Ardon (är'dŏn). Son of Caleb (1 Ch 2:18).

Areli (á-rē'lī). Son of Gad (Gn 46:16; Nm 26:17).

Areopagite (ăr-ē-ŏp'á-jīt). Member of the court, primarily religious, which met on Areopagus (Mars' Hill) in Athens (Acts 17:34).

Areopagus (ăr-ē-ŏp'á-gus). Hill of Ares (Greek god of war), or Mars' Hill, where court met which in Paul's day was primarily concerned with education and religion (Acts 17:19-34).

Ares (ā'rēz). See *Arah 2*.

Aretas (ăr'ē-tăs, excellence); 1. Arab chief (2 Mac 5:8). 2. Father-in-law of Herod Antipas (2 Co 11:32).

Areus (á-rē'us). See *Arius*.

Argob (är'gŏb). Tableland in Bashan (Dt 3:4; 1 K 4:13); later called Trachonitis (Lk 3:1). Compare KJ and RSV on 2 K 15:25.

Ariarathes, Ariarthes (ăr-ĭ-á-rä'thēz, ăr-ĭ-är'thēz). See *Arathes*.

Aridai (á-rĭd'ä-ī). Haman's son (Est 9:9).

Aridatha (á-rĭd'á-thá). Haman's son (Est 9:8).

Arieh (á-rī'ē, lion). Either a person involved in assassination of Pekahiah by Pekah (KJ, RV) or a place in RSV. 2 K 15: 25).

Ariel (âr'ĭ-ĕl, lion of God). 1. Leader under Ezra (Ez 8:16). Iduel in 1 Esd 8:43. 2. Figurative name for Jerusalem (Is 29: 1-10).

Ariels (KJ: lionlike men. RV: sons of Ariel). Meaning unknown (2 Sm 23:20; 1 Ch 11:22).

Arimathaea, Arimathea (ăr-ĭ-má-thē'á, height). Home of the Joseph who buried Jesus (Mt 27:57; Mk 15:43; Lk 23:51; Jn 19:38). Possibly same as Ramathaim-zophim (Ramah 5) in OT.

Arioch (är'ĭ-ŏk, servant of moon-god). 1. King of Ellasar (Gn 14: 1, 9). 2. Captain under Nebuchadnezzar (Dn 2:14). 3. King of Elymeans (Jdth 1:6).

Arisai (á-rĭs'ä-ī). Haman's son (Est 9:9).

Aristarchus (ăr-ĭs-tär'kus, best ruler). Thessalonian companion of Paul on some of his journeys (Acts 19:29; 20:4; 27:2) and fellow prisoner (Phmn 24; Cl 4:10).

Aristobulus (á-rĭs-tō-bū'lus, best counselor). 1. Christian at Rome (Rm 16:10). 2. Priest of Egyptian Jews (2 Mac 1:10).

Arius (á-rī'us. KJ: Areus). Lacedaemonian king (1 Mac 12:19-23). See *Onias*.

ark (chest). 1. Vessel of gopherwood (300 by 50 by 20 cubits) in which Noah, Noah's family, and animals were saved during flood (Gn 6—8). 2. Vessel (RSV: basket) in which infant Moses was placed (Ex 2:3-10). 3. Chest of acacia wood (2½ by 1½ by 1½ cubits), lined and covered with gold, whose lid was the mercy seat on either end of which were cherubs. Poles passed through golden rings for carrying (Ex 25:10-22). Contained stone tablets of Law (Ex 25:21; 31:18), book of Law (Dt 31:26), manna (Ex 16:33), Aaron's rod (Nm 17:10; Heb 9:4). Carried into Palestine (Jos 3:11-17), brought to Shiloh (1 Sm 3:3), captured by Philistines (1 Sm 4), returned to Beth-shemesh (1 Sm 6:12-20), removed to Kiriath-jearim (1 Sm 7:1, 2), taken to Jerusalem by David (2 Sm 6:12-23), and placed in Holy of Holies in Solomon's temple (1 K 8:1-9). Also called ark of testimony (Ex 25:16, 22) and ark of God (1 Sm 3:3).

Arkite (är'kīt). One of tribe descended from Canaan; inhabited Arka (Gn 10:17; 1 Ch 1:15).

Armageddon (är-mȧ-gĕd'un, hill of Megiddo. RV: Har-Magedon). Hill on S rim of Esdraelon, battlefield of Palestine, where Barak defeated Canaanites (Ju 5: 19), Gideon, the Midianites (Ju 7), and where Ahaziah (2 K 9:27) and Josiah (2 K 23:29) were killed. "Armageddon" became typical battlefield between good and evil (Rv 16:16).

Armenia (är-mē'nĭ-ȧ). See *Ararat*.

armlet. Ornament worn on arm higher than wrist (Ex 35:22 [KJ: tablets]; Nm 31:50 [KJ: chains; RV: ankle chains]; 2 Sm 1: 10 [KJ, RV: bracelet]; Is 3:20 [KJ: ornaments of legs; RV: ankle chains]).

Armoni (är-mō'nī, of the palace). Son of Saul (2 Sm 21:8).

armor, arms. Hebrew offensive weapons: sword (1 Sm 13:19); spear (2 Sm 2:23); javelin (1 Sm 17:6. KJ: target); dart (Jb 41:26); bow and arrow (see *archery*); sling (2 K 3:25); hammer, battle axe, mace, or maul (Jer 51:20); engines (2 Ch 26:15); battering rams (Eze 4:2). Hebrew defensive weapons: shield (1 Ch 12:24); buckler (1 Ch 5:18. Bucklers smaller than shields. Both of various sizes and shapes); helmet (1 Sm 17:38); breastplate (Is 59:17); coat of mail (1 Sm 17:5); greaves and war boots (1 Sm 17:6; Is 9:5); girdle (Is 5:27).

armor-bearer. Adjutant who carried armor, guarded, and otherwise assisted officer (Ju 9:54; 1 Sm 14:7; 31:4).

armory. Depository for weapons (Neh 3:19; SS 4:4 [RSV: arsenal]; Is 39:2; Jer 50: 25).

army. Children of Israel marched in wilderness according to tribes (Nm 1; 2). Males (except Levites) at age 20 subject to military duty (Nm 1; 2). Fighting men were gathered for war by inspectors (Dt 20:1-9; 24:5; 2 K 25:19). Tribes formed army divisions, subdivided into hundreds and thousands, with respective captains (Nm 31:14), and families (Nm 2:34). Armies were militia. Kings had bodyguards (1 Sm 13:2) and later standing armies of mercenaries (2 Ch 25:6). "Captain of the host" headed the army (1 Sm 14:50. RSV: commander). Army originally consisted of infantry (1 Sm 4:10); later horsemen and chariots were added (2 Sm 8:4; 1 K 10:26, 28, 29).

Roman army was composed of legions divided into cohorts. Cohort divided into three maniples; maniple into two centuries (Acts 10:1; 21:31; Mt 8:5; 27:54).

Arna (är'nȧ). See *Zerahiah 1*.

Arnan (är'năn). Descendant of Solomon through Zerubbabel (1 Ch 3:21).

Arni (är'nī). See *Ram 1*.

Arnon (är'nŏn). River flowing from E of Jordan into Dead Sea; boundary between Amorites and Moabites (Nm 21:13; Ju 11: 18); later, between Israel and Moabites (Dt 2:24; Jos 12:1).

Arod (ā'rŏd. Aradi in Gn 46:16). Son of Gad; forefather of Arodites (Nm 26:17).

Aroer (ȧ-rō'ẽr, naked). 1. Reubenite town on Arnon (Dt 2:36; Jos 12:1-2; Ju 11: 26); later fell back to Moab (Jer 48:19, 20). Modern 'Ara'ir. 2. Town of Gad (Nm 32:34; Jos 13:25; Ju 11:33; 2 Sm 24:5). 3. Town 12 mi SE of Beersheba (1 Sm 30:26-28).

Aroerite (ȧ-rō'ẽr-īt). Hothan (1 Ch 11:44).

Arom (ā'rŏm). See *Hashum 1*.

Arpachshad (är-păk'shăd. KJ: Arphaxad). 1. Son of Shem; ancestor of Abraham (Gn 10:22, 24; 11:10-13; 1 Ch 1:17, 18). 2. King of Medes (Jdth 1).

Arpad, Arphad (är'păd, är'făd. KJ: Arphad in Is 36:19; 37:13). City near Hamath (2 K 18:34; 19:13; Is 10:9; Jer 49:23).

Arphaxad (är-făk'săd). See *Arpachshad*.

arrows. See *archery*.

Arsaces (är'sȧ-sēz). Mithridates I, king of Persia and Media, c 174—136 BC (1 Mac 14:1-3; 15:22).

arsenal. See *armory*.

Arsiphurith (är-sĭ-fū'rĭth). See *Hariph 1*.

Artaxerxes (är-tăg-zûrk'sēz). 1. Persian king (probably Smerdis), who stopped rebuilding of temple (Ez 4:7, 23, 24). 2. Persian king (Longimanus, 465—425 BC) who sent Ezra to Jerusalem (Ez 7), also befriended Nehemiah (Neh 2:1-8).

Artemas (är'tē-mȧs, gift of Artemis). Friend of Paul (Tts 3:12).

Artemis (är'tē-mĭs. KJ, RV: Diana). Greek goddess (Roman Diana) of moon, woods, and fields. Huntress and symbol of chastity. Artemis at Ephesus was combination of Artemis and Ashtoreth (Acts 19:24 to 28).

artillery. See *armor, arms*.

arts, secret. See *enchantment; magic*.

Arubboth, Aruboth (ȧ-rŭb'oth, ȧ-rōō'bōth). Third commissary district of Solomon (1 K 4:10).

Arumah (ȧ-rōō'mȧ, height). Place near Shechem where Abimelech dwelt (Ju 9: 41). H: Tormah; KJ privily; RV: craftily in Ju 9:31.

Arvad (är'văd. Aradus in 1 Mac 15:23). Island (Ruwad) off coast of Phoenicia (Eze 27:8, 11).

Arvadite (är'vȧ-dīt). Native of Arvad (Gn 10:18; 1 Ch 1:16).

Arza (är'zȧ). Steward of Elah in whose house Zimri killed Elah (1 K 16:8-10).

Asa (ā'sȧ, physician). 1. Son of Abijam; 3d king of Judah; reign began with ten years of peace (2 Ch 14:1); conducted religious reformation (2 Ch 14:3-5; 15: 1-17); defeated Ethiopian Zerah (2 Ch 14:9-15); invited Ben-hadad of Damascus against Baasha of Israel (1 K 15: 16-22; 2 Ch 16:1-10); reigned 41 years. 2. Levite (1 Ch 9:16).

Asadias (ăs-ȧ-dī'ăs. RSV: Hasadiah). Ancestor of Baruch (Bar 1:1).

Asael (ăs'ȧ-ĕl). See *Asiel 3*.

Asahel (ăs'ȧ-hĕl, God has made). 1. Nephew of David, killed by Abner (2 Sm 2:18 to 23). 2. Levite; legal instructor (2 Ch 17:8). 3. Temple overseer (2 Ch 31:13). 4. Priest (Ez 10:15; 1 Esd 9:14 [RV, KJ: Azael]).

Asahiah (ăs-ȧ-hī'ȧ). See *Asaiah 4*.

Asaiah (ȧ-sā'yȧ, LORD has made). 1. Simeonite prince (1 Ch 4:36). 2. Levite; head of Merari family (1 Ch 6:30; 15:6, 11). 3. Shilonite (1 Ch 9:5). Maasiah in Neh 11:5. 4. Officer sent by Josiah to inquire of prophetess Huldah about Law (2 K 22:12, 14 [KJ: Asahiah]; 2 Ch 34:20).

Asaias (ȧ-sā'yăs). See *Isshijah*.

Asana (ăs'ȧ-nȧ). See *Asnah*.

Asaph (ā'săf, collector). 1. Levite; son of Berechiah; sounded cymbals for religious functions (1 Ch 6:39; 15:16-19; 16:4, 5, 7). Ps 50 and 73 to 83 attributed to him. Celebrated as poet (1 Ch 9:15; Neh 11:17). 2. Father of Joah, Hezekiah's recorder (2 K 18:18; Is 36:3, 22). 3. Keeper of royal forest in Palestine under Artaxerxes Longimanus (Neh 2:8).

Asara (ăs'ȧ-rȧ). See *Azara*.

Asaramel (ȧ-săr'ȧ-mĕl. KJ: Saramel). Variously interpreted as title for Simon Maccabaeus, forecourt of temple, or sentence indicating Israel had no temporal ruler (1 Mac 14:28).

Asareel, Asarel (á-să'rê-ĕl, ăs'á-rĕl, God has bound). Descendant of Judah (1 Ch 4:16).

Asarelah (ăs-á-rē'lá). See *Asharelah*.

Asbasareth (ăs-băs'á-rĕth). See *Azbazareth*.

Ascalon (ăs'ká-lŏn). See *Ashkelon*.

ascension. Name applied to that event in which risen Christ removed His visible presence from men and passed into the heavens (Mk 16:19; Lk 24:50, 51; Jn 6:62; 20:17; Acts 1:1-12; Eph 4:8-10; 1 Ti 3:16; 1 Ptr 3:22; Hb 4:14).

ascents, song of. See *degrees, song of*.

Aseas (á-sē'ăs). See *Isshijah*.

Asebebia, Asebebias (á-sĕb-ĕ-bī'á, -bī'ăs). See *Sherebiah*.

Asebia, Asebias (ăs-ê-bī'á, -bī'ăs). See *Hashabiah 6*.

Asenath (ăs'ê-năth, devotee of Neith, Egyptian goddess). Egyptian wife of Joseph; daughter of Potiphera, priest of On (Gn 41:45, 50; 46:20).

Aser (ā'sĕr). See *Asher; Hazor 1*.

Aserer (ăs'ê-rĕr). See *Sisera 2*.

ash. Probably Syrian fir (Is 44:14. RV: fir tree. RSV: cedar).

Ashan (ā'shăn, smoke. Ain in Jos 21:16). Levitical city (1 Ch 6:59); assigned to Judah (Jos 15:42) and Simeon (Jos 19:7; 1 Ch 4:32).

Asharelah (ăsh-á-rē'lá. KJ: Asarelah. Jesharelah in 1 Ch 25:14). Son of Asaph; in charge of temple music (1 Ch 25:2).

Ashbea (ăsh'bĕ-á). Meaning doubtful. KJ, RV: house of Ashbea. RSV: linen workers at Beth-ashbea (1 Ch 4:21).

Ashbel (ăsh'bĕl, man of lord). 2d son of Benjamin (Gn 46:21; Nm 26:38; 1 Ch 8:1). See also *Jediael 1*.

Ashchenaz (ăsh'kê-năz). See *Ashkenaz*.

Ashdod (ăsh'dŏd. G: Azotus). One of five chief cities of Philistia, between Gaza and Joppa. Worshiped Dagon (Jos 13:3 [RSV]; 1 Sm 5); assigned to Judah but not taken (Jos 15:46, 47); ark carried to it but returned (1 Sm 5; 6); Uzziah broke its walls (2 Ch 26:6); Sargon captured it (Is 20:1); destroyed by Psammetichus of Egypt (c 630 BC). Azotus in 1 Mac 5:68; 10:83, 84; 16:10; Acts 8:40.

Ashdodites, Ashdothites (ăsh'dŏd-īts, ăsh'-dŏth-īts). Inhabitants of Ashdod (Jos 13:3; Neh 4:7).

Ashdoth-pisgah (ăsh'dŏth-pĭz'gá. RV, RSV: slopes of Pisgah. KJ: springs of Pisgah in Dt 4:49). Slopes of Pisgah, E of Dead Sea (Dt 3:17; 4:49; Jos 12:3; 13:20).

Asher (ăsh'ĕr, happiness. KJ in NT: Aser). 1. 8th son of Jacob (Gn 30:12, 13; 35:26). 2. Territory on sea N of Carmel (Jos 19:24-31). 3. Perhaps a town (Jos 17:7). 4. See *Hazor 1*.

Asherah (á-shē'rá. KJ: grove). Canaanite goddess of sex and war; wife or sister of El. Word denotes goddess or wooden image (Dt 16:21; Ju 6:25-30; 1 K 15:13; 16:33; 2 K 13:6; 23:4-15). See also *Ashtoreth*.

Asherim (á-shē'rĭm). Plural of Asherah.

Asherites (ăsh'ĕr-īts). Of the tribe of Asher (Ju 1:32).

Asheroth (á-shē'rŏth). Plural (f.) of Asherah.

ashes. To sprinkle with, or sit in, ashes showed humiliation, grief, or penitence (Gn 18:27; 2 Sm 13:19; Est 4:3; Jb 2:8; Jer 6:26; Lm 3:16; Mt 11:21). To reduce to ashes implied complete destruction (Eze 28:18; 2 Ptr 2:6). Eating ashes is symbolic of dejection (Ps 102:9). Ashes

of red heifer were used for cleansing (Nm 19:17-22).

Ashhur (ăsh'ĕr, blackness. KJ: Ashur). Son of Hezron; founder of Tekoa (1 Ch 2:24; 4:5).

Ashima (á-shī'má, offense). Divinity of Hamath (2 K 17:30).

Ashkelon (ăsh'ke-lŏn, migration. KJ at times: Askelon). City of Philistia, 12 mi N of Gaza; captured (Ju 1:18), but lost by Judah (Ju 14:19; 1 Sm 6:17). Taken by Jonathan Maccabaeus (1 Mac 10:86; 11:60. KJ, RV: Ascalon; RSV: Askalon). Destroyed AD 1270 by Bibars.

Ashkenaz (ăsh'kê-năz. KJ: Ashchenaz in 1 Ch 1:6; Jer 51:27). Grandson of Japhet (Gn 10:3). Descendants lived near Ararat.

Ashnah (ăsh'ná). Two towns of Judah (Jos 15:33, 43).

Ashpenaz (ăsh'pê-năz). Master of Babylonian eunuchs (Dn 1:3).

Ashriel (ăsh'rĭ-ĕl). See *Asriel*.

Ashtaroth, Astaroth (ăsh'tá-rŏth, ăs'tá-rŏth). 1. Plural of Ashtoreth. 2. City of Bashan, E of Jordan (Dt 1:4; Jos 9:10; 12:4; 13:12, 31); capital of Og (Dt 1:4) and seat of worship of Astarte (Tell Ashtarah).

Ashterathite (ăsh'tê-răth-īt). Native of Ashtaroth (1 Ch 11:44).

Ashteroth-karnaim (ăsh'tê-rŏth-kär-nā'ĭm, Ashteroth near Karnaim, or two-horned Ashteroth. KJ: Asteroth Karnaim). Place of victory of Chedorlaomer (Gn 14:5); probably different from Ashtaroth and (though near) Karnaim.

Ashtoreth (ăsh'tŏ-rĕth). Canaanite goddess (identified with planet Venus); Ishtar of Babylonians; Astarte of Greeks and Romans. Worship entrenched at Sidon (1 K 11:5, 33; 2 K 23:13) and occasionally practiced in Israel (Ju 2:13; 10:6). Solomon introduced her worship (1 K 11:5; 2 K 23:13).

Ashur (ăsh'ĕr). See *Ashhur*.

Ashurites (ăsh'ĕr-īts). People belonging to Ishbosheth (2 Sm 2:9).

Ashvath (ăsh'văth). Asherite; son of Japhlet (1 Ch 7:33).

Asia (ā'zhá). Used in NT for Asia Minor (Acts 19:26), Proconsular Asia (Acts 20:4; 1 Cor 16:19), or more restricted areas (Acts 2:9).

Asiarch (ā'shĭ-ärk. KJ: chief of Asia). One of ten deputies elected by cities of Asia to conduct games and festivals in honor of gods or emperor (Acts 19:31).

Asibias (ăs-ĭ-bī'ăs). See *Malchijah 4*.

Asideans (ăs-ĭ-dē'ăns). See *Hasideans*.

Asiel (ā'sĭ-ĕl, made by God). 1. Simeonite (1 Ch 4:35). 2. Scribe under Esdras (2 Esd 14:24). 3. Ancestor of Tobit (Tob 1:1. KJ: Asael).

Asipha (ăs'ĭ-fá). See *Hasipha*.

Askalon, Askelon (ăs'ká-lŏn, ăs'ke-lŏn). See *Ashkelon*.

Asmodeus (ăz-mō-dē'us). Evil spirit, classed with Abaddon and Apollyon (Tob 3:8-17).

Asmonaean (ăz-mō-nē'ăn, H *hashman*). Descendant of Hashman of the family of Jehoiarib, ancestor of the Maccabees (Ant XII, vi, 1; 1 Mac 2:1; 1 Ch 24:7).

Asnah (ăs'ná, bramble. KJ, RV: Asana in 1 Esd 5:31). Head of family which returned from captivity (Ez 2:50).

Asnapper (ăs-năp'ĕr). See *Osnappar*.

Asom (ā'som). See *Hashum 1*.

asp. Poisonous serpent (H *pethen;* G *aspis*. Dt 32:33; Jb 20:14, 16; Is 11:8; Ro 3:13). See *serpent*.

aspalathus (ăs-păl'á-thŭs). RSV: camel's thorn. Perfume or ointment (Sir 24:15).

Aspatha (ăs-pā'thá). Haman's son (Est 9:7).

Asphar (ăs'fär). Pool of Tekoa (1 Mac 9:33).

Aspharasus (ăs'fär'á-sŭs). See *Mispar*.

Asriel (ăs'rĭ-ĕl, vow of God. KJ: Ashriel in 1 Ch 7:14). Descendant of Manasseh and founder of family (Nm 26:31; Jos 17:2).

ass. Beast of burden and riding animal (Gn 12:16; 22:3; Ex 4:20; Mt 21:7).

Assalimoth (ă-săl'ĭ-mŏth). See *Shelomith 6*.

Assamias, Assanias (ăs-á-mī'ăs, ăs-á-nī'ăs). See *Hashabiah 7*.

Assaphioth (á-sā'fĭ-ŏth). See *Sophereth*.

assassins (á-săs'ĭns. RSV, RV marg. KJ, RV: murderers). Ruffians who terrorized Judea, AD 50—70 (Acts 21:38).

assembly. 1. Congregation (RSV: Ex 12: 6, 16). 2. Festal gathering (Nm 29:35; Dt 16:8; Heb 12:23). 3. Called meeting (Is 1:13). 4. Deliberative assembly (Acts 19:39).

Asshur (ăs'shoōr). 2d son of Shem (Gn 10:22; 1 Ch 1:17). Descendants peopled Assyria. See *Assyria*.

Asshurim (á-shoō'rĭm). Tribe descended from Abraham (Gn 25:3).

Assideans (ăs-ĭ-dē'ănz). See *Hasideans*.

Assir (ăs'ēr, prisoner). 1. Levite (Ex 6:24; 1 Ch 6:22). 2. Forefather of Samuel (1 Ch 6:23, 37). 3. Son of Jeconiah (1 Ch 3:17).

Assos (ăs'ŏs). Seaport of Mysia (Asso. Acts 20:13, 14).

Assur (ăs'ēr). 1. See *Ashhur*. 2. See *Harhur*.

Assyria (á-sĭr'ĭ-á, KJ at times: Asshur, Assur). Empire (capital: Nineveh) which dominated Biblical world from 9th to 7th c BC and which, at its height, embraced land between Black Sea, Caspian Sea, Persian Gulf, and Mediterranean Sea (included Egypt). People Semitic; wrote with ideograms and syllabic signs. Originated with Babylonian colonists (Gn 10:11). Chief gods: Asshur, Anu, Bel, Ea. Kings frequently invaded Israel (2 K 15:19, 29; 16:7-9; 2 Ch 28:20), finally carried people into captivity (721 BC. 2 K 17:6; 18:11). Nineveh fell 612 BC.

Astad (ăs'tăd). See *Azgad*.

Astaroth (ăs'tá-rŏth). See *Ashtaroth*.

Astarte (ăs-tär'tē). See *Ashtoreth*.

Astath (ăs'tăth). See *Azgad*.

astrologers (ăs-trŏl'ō-jērz). Those who attempt to foretell future by course of stars (Dn 2:27; 4:7; 5:7, 11. See Dn 1:20; Is 47:12, 13).

Astyages (ăs-tĭ'á-jēz). Last king of Medes (Bel 1).

Asuppim (á-sŭp'ĭm, collections). Building used for storing temple goods (1 Ch 26: 15, 17. RV, RSV: storehouse).

Asur (ä'soōr). See *Harhur*.

Asyncritus (á-sĭng'krĭ-tŭs, incomparable). Friend of Paul at Rome (Ro 16:14).

Atad (ā'tăd, thorn). Name of person or place (Gn 50: 10, 11).

Atar (ā'tär). See *Ater 2*.

Atarah (ăt'á-rä, crown). Mother of Onam (1 Ch 2:26).

Atargatis (á-tär'gá-tĭs). Syrian goddess of fertility (2 Mac 12:26).

Ataroth (ăt'á-rŏth, crowns). 1. City near Gilead (Nm 32:3, 34). 2. City on boundary of Ephraim and Benjamin (Jos 16:2). Ataroth-addar in Jos 16:5; 18:13 (AV: -adar). 3. See *Atroth-beth-joab*. 4. Place on E frontier of Ephraim (Jos 16:7).

Ataroth-addar, or **-adar** (ăt'á-rŏth-ăd'är, -ä'där). See *Ataroth 2*.

Ater (ā'tēr, shut). 1. Descendants returned from captivity (Ez 2:16; Neh 7:21). See also *Hezekiah 6*. 2. Porter (Ez 2:42; Neh 7:45; 1 Esd 5:28 [KJ: Jatal; RV: Atar]).

Aterezias (á-tēr-ē-zī'-ăs). See *Hezekiah 6*.

Ateta (á-tē'tá). See *Hatita*.

Athach (ā'thăk, lodging place). Town in S Judah (1 Sm 30:30). Modern Kirbet 'Attir.

Athaiah (á-thā'yá). Son of Uzziah (Neh 11:4).

Athaliah (ăth-á-lī'á, afflicted of LORD). 1. Wicked wife of Jehoram who introduced worship of Baal, usurped throne, was slain by her guard (2 K 11; 2 Ch 22—24). 2. Benjaminite (1 Ch 8:26). 3. Head of family which returned from captivity (Ez 8:7). Gotholias (RSV: Gotholiah) in 1 Esd 8:33.

Atharias (ăth-á-rī'ăs). See *Tirshatha*.

Atharim (ăth'á-rim. RSV, RV. KJ, RV margin: way of the spies). Route of Israelites approaching Canaan (Nm 21:1).

Athenians (á-thē'nĭ-ănz). Inhabitants of Athens (Acts 17:21).

Athenobius (ăth-ē-nō'bĭ-ŭs). Envoy of Antiochus VII (1 Mac 15:28-36).

Athens (ăth'ĕnz, city of Athena). Capital of Attica, near Gulf of Aegina; chief seat of Grecian learning and civilization. Grew up around Acropolis (512 ft high); connected with harbor Piraeus by 5-mi walls. Paul preached on its Areopagus (Acts 17:19-22).

Athlai (ăth'lä-ī, afflicted or exalted). Divorced foreign wife after captivity (Ez 10:28). KJ: Amatheis; RV: Ematheis; RSV: Emathis in 1 Esd 9:29.

Atipha (ăt'ĭ-fá). See *Hatipha*.

atonement (á-tōn'ment, H *kaphar*: cover, cancel; G *katallage*: exchange, reconcile). Reconciliation between persons or beings (Ro 5:11) and that which produces reconciliation (Ex 30:16). Atonement is reconciliation between world and God by life and death of Jesus Christ.

Atonement, Day of. H festival on 10th day of 7th month, observed with fasting, humiliation, and looking to cleansing from sin (Ex 30:16; Lv 16; 23:27-32).

Atroth (ăt'rŏth). See *Atroth-shophan*.

Atroth-beth-joab (ăt'rŏth-bĕth-jō'ăb, crowns of house of Joab. KJ: Ataroth, the house of Joab). Village of Judah (1 Ch 2:54).

Atroth-shophan (ăt'rŏth-shō'făn, crowns of Shophan). KJ: Atroth, Shophan). Town rebuilt by Gadites (Nm 32:35).

Attai (ăt'á-ī, ready). 1. Grandson of Sheshan (1 Ch 2:35, 36). 2. Gadite (1 Ch 12:11). 3. Son of Rehoboam (2 Ch 11:20).

Attalia (ăt-á-lī'á). Coast town of Pamphylia (Acts 14:25).

Attalus (ăt'á-lŭs, increased). King of Pergamos (1 Mac 15:22).

Attharates, Attharias (á-thăr'á-tēs, ăth-á-rī'ăs). See *Tirshatha*.

attire. See *dress*.

Attus (ăt'ŭs). See *Hattush 2*.

augia (ô'jĭ-á). See *Agia 2*.

augury. Divination. Forbidden (Lv 19:26; 2 K 21:6; 2 Ch 33:6. KJ: enchantments). See also *enchantment*; *magic*.

Augustus (ô-gŭs'tŭs, venerable). Imperial title of Gaius Julius Caesar Octavianus, 1st Roman emperor (27 BC—AD 14). Christ born during his reign (Lk 2:1).

Augustus' band. Cohort of Roman soldiers (Acts 27:1. RV: Augustan band. RSV: Augustan Cohort).

Auranus (ô-rā′nŭs. RV: Hauran). Rioter (2 Mac 4:40).

Ava (a′vá). See *Avva*.

Avaran (ăv′á-răn). Surname of Eleazar (1 Mac 2:5; 6:43 [KJ: Savaran]).

Aven (a′ven, nothingness). 1. Heliopolis in Egypt (Eze 30:17). 2. "High places of Aven," places of idolatry in Bethel (Hos 10:8). 3. Perhaps Baalbek (Am 1:5).

avenge. To exact just satisfaction (Lk 18:8; 1 Th 4:6). "Avenger of blood," pursuer of slayer to avenge death of relative (Dt 19:6).

Avim, Avims, Avites (ā′vĭm, ā′vīmz, ā′vīts). See *Avvim*.

Avith (ā′vĭth). Capital city of Hadad in Edom (Gn 36:35; 1 Ch 1:46).

Avva (ăv′á. KJ: Ava). City of Assyrian Empire from which people were brought to colonize Samaria (2 K 17:24, 31). Ivvah (KJ: Ivah) in 2 K 18:34; 19:13.

Avvim, Avites (ăv′ĭm, ā′vīts). 1. Aborigines in country of Gaza (Dt 2:23). 2. Town, probably named after Avites (Jos 18:23). LXX and Jerome identify Avvim with Hivites (see Jos 9:7, 17; 18:22-27).

awl. See *Trade* 5; *9*; *10*.

axe. H *garzen* (Is 10:34), instrument like adze; *herebh* (Eze 26:9), instrument for destroying walls; *kashil* (KJ: Ps 74:6), probably hatchet (RV, RSV); *magzerah* 2 Sm 12:31; *ma'atsad* (Jer 10:3), used for felling trees; *qardom* (Ju 9:48; 1 Sm 13:20), used for cutting brushwood; G *axine* (Mt 3:10).

Ayyah (ī′yá. AV: Gaza; RV: Assah). Town of Ephraim (1 Ch 7:28).

Azael, Azaelus (ăz′á-ĕl, äz-á-ē′lus). 1. See *Asahel* 4. 2. Listed in 1 Esd 9:34.

Azal (ā′zăl). See *Azel*.

Azaliah (ăz-á-lī′á, LORD has spared). Father of Shaphan, scribe (2 K 22:3).

Azaniah (ăz-á-nī′á, whom LORD hears). Father of Jeshua (Neh 10:9).

Azaphion (á-zā′fī-ŏn). See *Sophereth*.

Azara (ăz′á-rá. RV: Asara; RSV: Hasrah). Listed in 1 Esd 5:31.

Azarael (á-zā′rá-ĕl). See *Azarel*.

Azaraias (á-zä-rá-ī′ás). 1. See *Seraiah* 4. 2. See *Azariah* 8.

Azareel (á-zā′rē-ĕl). See *Azarel*.

Azarel (ăz′á-rĕl. KJ: Azareel; once, Neh 12:36, Azarael). 1. Koharite; joined David at Ziklag (1 Ch 12:6). 2. Temple musician (1 Ch 25:18). Uzziel in 1 Ch 25:4. 3. Prince of Dan (1 Ch 27:22). 4. Divorced foreign wife (Ez 10:41; 1 Esd 9:34 [KJ: Esril; RV: Ezril]). 5. Priest (Neh 11:13). 6. Priest's son (Neh 12:36).

Azariah (ăz-á-rī′á, helped by LORD). 1. Descendant of Zadok (1 K 4:2). 2. Son of Nathan; officer of Solomon (1 K 4:5). 3. Son of Amaziah; 10th king of Judah (2 K 14:21; 15:1-7; 1 Ch 3:12). Usually called Uzziah. 4. Ethan's son (1 Ch 2:8). 5. Jehu's son (1 Ch 2:38, 39). 6. High priest; son of Ahimaaz (1 Ch 6:9). Possibly same as 1. 7. High priest, perhaps in reigns of Abijah and Asa (1 Ch 6: 10, 11); ancestor of Ezra (Ez 7:3; 2 Esd 1:2 [KJ, RV: Aziei]). KJ: Ezias; RV: Ozias; RSV omits in 1 Esd 8:2. 8. High priest (1 Ch 6:13, 14; 9:11; Ez 7:1; 1 Esd 8:1 [KJ: Ezerias; RV: Zechrias]; 2 Esd 1:1 [KJ: Azarias; RV: Azaraias]). Seraiah in Neh 11:11. 9. Levite; ancestor of Samuel (1 Ch 6:36). Uzziah in 1 Ch 6:24. 10. Prophet; caused reformation under Asa (2 Ch 15:1-8). 11. 12. Two sons of Jehoshaphat (2 Ch 21:2). 13. See *Ahaziah* 2. 14. Son of Jeroham; captain of Joash (2 Ch 23:1). 15. Son of Obed;

captain of Joash (2 Ch 23:1). 16. High priest in reign of Uzziah (2 Ch 26:16-20). 17. Captain of Ephraim (2 Ch 28:12). 18. High priest in reign of Hezekiah (2 Ch 31:10, 13). 19. 20. Two Levites (Kohathite and Merarite); participated in cleansing of temple under Hezekiah (2 Ch 29:12). 21. Levite; assisted Ezra and Nehemiah (Neh 3:23, 24). 22. See *Seraiah 8*. 23. H name of Abednego (Dn 1:7; 2:17). 24. Opponent of Jeremiah (Jer 42:1 [KJ, RV: Jezaniah]; 43:2). Jaazaniah in 2 K 25:23. Jezaniah in Jer 40:8. 25. Levite; assisted at reading of law (Neh 8:7; 1 Esd 9:48 [KJ, RV: Azarias]). Possibly same as 21. 26. Sealed covenant with Nehemiah (Neh 10:2). Possibly same as 21. 27. Prince of Judah (Neh 12:33). Possibly same as 21. 28. Divorced foreign wife (1 Esd 9:21. KJ, RV: Azarias). Uzziah in Ez 10:21. 29. Captain of Judas Maccabaeus (1 Mac 5:18, 55-62. KJ, RV: Azarias). 30. Listed in 1 Esd 9:43 (KJ, RV: Azarias).

Azarias (ăz-á-rī′ás). 1. Name assumed by angel Raphael (To 5:12; 6:6, 13; 7:8; 9:2). 2. 3. 4. 5. 6. See *Azariah 8; 25; 28; 29; 30*.

Azaru (ăz′á-rōō. KJ: Azuran). Listed in 1 Esd 5:15.

Azaz (ā′zăz, strong). Reubenite (1 Ch 5:8).

Azazel (á-zā′zĕl. KJ: scapegoat). Meaning of word doubtful (Lev 16). Has been interpreted as meaning: 1. solitary place; 2. scapegoat led away; 3. epithet of devil; 4. abstraction: "utter removal."

Azaziah (ăz-á-zī′á, LORD is strong). 1. Levite musician (1 Ch 15:21). 2. Chief of Ephraim (1 Ch 27:20). 3. Custodian of temple offerings under Hezekiah (2 Ch 31:13).

Azbazareth (ăz-băz′á-rĕth. RV: Asbasareth. RSV: Esarhaddon). Probably Esarhaddon (1 Esd 5:69).

Azbuk (ăz′bŭk, devastation). Father of a Nehemiah (Neh 3:16).

Azekah (á-zē′ká, dug over). Town of Judah (Jos 10:10, 11; 15:35; 1 Sm 17:1; 2 Ch 11:9; Neh 11:30; Jer 34:7).

Azel (ā′zĕl). 1. Descendant of Jonathan (1 Ch 8:37, 38; 9:43). 2. Perhaps a town (Zch 14:5. KJ: reach unto Azal [RV: Azel]; RSV: touch the side of it).

Azem (ā′zĕm). See *Ezem*.

Azephurith (ăz-ē-fū′rĭth). See *Hariph 1*.

Azetas (á-zē′tás). Listed in 1 Esd 5:15.

Azgad (ăz′găd, strong of fortune). Large number of his descendants returned with Zerubbabel (Ez 2:12; 8:12; Neh 7:17; 1 Esd 5:13 [KJ: Sadas; RV: Astad]; 1 Esd 8:38 [KJ, RV: Astath]). Probably same man in Neh 10:15.

Azia (á-zī′á). See *Uzza 1*.

Aziei (á-zī′ē-ī). See *Azariah 7*.

Aziel (ā′zī-ĕl). See *Jaaziel*.

Aziza (á-zī′zá, strong. KJ: Sardeus; RV: Zardeus; RSV: Zerdaiah in 1 Esd 9:28). Divorced foreign wife after captivity (Ez 10:27).

Azmaveth (ăz-mā′vĕth, death is strong). 1. One of David's heroes (2 Sm 23:31); sons came to David at Ziklag (1 Ch 12:3). 2. Descendant of Mephibosheth (1 Ch 8: 36; 9:42). 3. David's treasurer (1 Ch 27:25); perh same as 1. 4. Village between Geba and Anathoth (Ez 2:24; Neh 12:29). Beth-azmaveth in Neh 7:28. Bethasmoth (KJ: Bethsamos) in 1 Esd 5:18.

Azmon (ăz′mŏn, strong). Place in S Palestine (Nm 34:4, 5; Jos 15:4).

Aznoth-tabor (ăz′nŏth-tā′bôr, tops of Tabor). Place on boundary of Naphtali near Tabor (Jos 19:34).

Azor (ā'zôr). Ancestor of Christ (Mt 1:13, 14).

Azotus (a-zō'tus). See *Ashdod*.

Azriel (ăz'rĭ-ĕl, help of God). 1. Mighty man of Manasseh (1 Ch 5:24). 2. Father of Jerimoth (1 Ch 27:19). 3. Father of Seraiah (Jer 36:26).

Azrikam (ăz'rĭ-kăm, avenging help). 1. Descendant of Zerubbabel (1 Ch 3:23). 2. Descendant of Saul (1 Ch 8:38; 9:44). 3. Levite (1 Ch 9:14; Neh 11:15). 4. Governor of Ahaz' palace (2 Ch 28:7).

Azubah (a-zū'bá, forsaken). 1. Jehoshaphat's mother (1 K 22:42; 2 Ch 20:31). 2. Caleb's wife (1 Ch 2:18, 19).

Azur (ā'zēr). See *Azzur 1, 2*.

Azuran (ăz'ū-răn). See *Azaru*.

Azzah (ăz'á, strong). See *Ayyah*; *Gaza*.

Azzan (ăz'ăn, very strong). Father of Paltiel of Issachar (Nm 34:26).

Azzur (ăz'ēr, helpful). 1. Father of the Hananiah who urged Zedekiah against Babylonians (Jer 28:1. KJ: Azur). 2. Father of false prophet Jaazaniah (Eze 11:1. KJ: Azur). 3. Signed covenant with Nehemiah (Neh 10:17).

B

Baal (bā'ăl, lord, possessor). 1. Name for iord among Phoenicians. Used of master of house (Ex 22:7), land (Jb 31:39), or cattle (Ex 21:28). 2. Storm-god of Phoenicians and Canaanites; adored on high places with self-torture and human offerings (Jer 19:5); worship early infected Hebrews (Nm 22:41; Dt 4:16; Ju 2:13; 6:28-32); Jezebel championed Baal worship in Israel (1 K 16:31, 32; 18:17-40) and Athaliah in Judah (2 Ch 17:3; 21:6; 22:2; 2 K 11:18). Worship of Baal persisted in Israel and Judah (Hos 2:8; 2 Ch 28:2; 2 K 21:3; 23:4, 5; Jer 19:4, 5). Often associated with Ashtoreth (Ju 2:13; 6:30; 1 K 16:32, 33). 3. Reubenite; father of Beerah (1 Ch 5:5). 4. Son of Jeiel of Gibeon (1 Ch 8:30; 9:36). 5. See *Baalath-beer*.

Baalah (bā'á-lá, mistress). 1. See *Kiriath-jearim*. 2. Hill in Judah between Shikkeron and Jabneel (Jos 15:11). 3. Town in Judah (Jos 15:29) assigned to Simeon. Balah in Jos 19:3. Bilhah in 1 Ch 4:29.

Baalath (bā'ăl-ăth, mistress). Town in Dan (Jos 19:44; 1 K 9:18; 2 Ch 8:6).

Baalath-beer (bā'ăl-ăth-bē'ēr, mistress of well). City of Simeon (Jos 19:8). Baal in 1 Ch 4:33. Identified with Ramoth-negeb.

Baalbek (bā'ăl-bĕk). See *Baal-gad*.

Baal-berith (bā'ăl-bē'rĭth, Baal of the covenant. El-berith [KJ: god of Berith] in Ju 9:46). God worshiped at Shechem (Ju 8:33; 9:4).

Baale, Baale-judah (bā'á-lĕ-jōō'dá, Baal of Judah. KJ: Baale of Judah. RV: Baale Judah). Same as Kiriath-jearim.

Baal-gad (bā'ăl-găd, Baal of fortune). City near Mt Hermon (Jos 11:17; 12:7); often identified with Baal-hermon and/or Baalbek (Heliopolis).

Baal-hamon (bā'ăl-hā'mon, Baal of a multitude). Place where Solomon had vineyard (SS 8:11).

Baal-hanan (bā'ăl-hā'năn, Baal is gracious). 1. Son of Achbor; king of Edom (Gn 36:38, 39; 1 Ch 1:49, 50). 2. David's overseer of olive and sycamore trees (1 Ch 27:28).

Baal-hazor (bā'ăl-hā'zôr, Baal of a village). Place near Ephraim which Gesenius identified with Hazor (2 Sm 13:23. See Neh 11:33).

Baal-hermon (bā'ăl-hûr'mon, Baal of Hermon). 1. City near Hermon (1 Ch 5:23). See *Baal-gad*. 2. Mountain forming NW limit of Manasseh (Ju 3:3).

Baali (bā'ăl-ī, my master. RSV: My Baal). Name given God by Israel (Hos 2:16).

Baalim (bā'ăl-ĭm. RSV: Baals). Plural of Baal (Ju 2:11).

Baalis (bā'á-lĭs). King of Ammonites (Jer 40:14).

Baal-meon (bā'ăl-mē'ŏn, Baal of house. Beth-baal-meon in Jos 13:17. Beon in Nm 32:3. Beth-meon in Jer 48:23). Amorite city rebuilt by Reubenites (Nm 32:38; Eze 25:9). Moabite Stone speaks of it; ruins excavated at Ma'în, 4 mi SW of Medeba.

Baal-peor (bā'ăl-pē'ôr, Baal of Peor). 1. Baal worshiped at Peor (Nm 25:1-9; Ps 106:28 [RSV: Baal of Peor]). 2. RSV makes Baal-peor place name in Dt 4:3; Hos 9:10.

Baal-perazim (bā'ăl-pē-rā'zĭm, Baal of openings. Perazim in Is 28:21). Place where David conquered Philistines (2 Sm 5:20; 1 Ch 14:11).

Baalsamus (bā-ăl'sá-mus). See *Maaseiah 11*.

Baal-shalishah (bā'ăl-shăl'ĭ-shá, Baal of Shalishah. KJ: Baal-shalisha). Place in Ephraim near Gilgal (2 K 4:42).

Baal-tamar (bā'ăl-tā'mär, Baal of palm). Place near Gibeah (Ju 20:33).

Baal-zebub (bā'ăl-zē'bŭb. Originally possibly Baalzebul: Baal is lofty one, Baal exalts, *or* Baal of manure; Baalzebub: Baal of flies). Name of god of Ekron (2 K 1:2-6). See also *Beelzebub, Beelzebul*.

Baal-zephon (bā'ăl-zē'fŏn). Place on Red Sea (Ex 14:2, 9; Nm 33:7).

Baana (bā'á-ná, son of affliction). 1. Solomon's purveyor; son of Ahilud (1 K 4:12). 2. Solomon's purveyor; son of Hushai (1 K 4:16. KJ: Baanah). 3. Zadok's father (Neh 3:4).

Baanah (bā'á-ná, son of affliction). 1. Son of Rimmon; with brother slew Ishbosheth (2 Sm 4:2-12). 2. Netophathite; father of Heleb (or Heled, 2 Sm 23:39; 1 Ch 11:30). 3. Returned from captivity (Ez 2:2; Neh 7:7; 10:27; 1 Esd 5:8 [KJ, RV: Baana]). 4. See *Baana 2*.

Baani (bā'á-nī). See *Bani 4*.

Baanias (bā-á-nī'ăs). See *Benaiah 8*.

Baara (bā'á-rá). Wife of Shaharaim (1 Ch 8:8). Hodesh in 1 Ch 8:9.

Baaseiah (bā-á-sē'yá). Levite ancestor of Asaph (1 Ch 6:40).

Baasha (bā'á-shá). 3d king of Israel; son of Ahijah; tribe of Issachar; foe of Asa of Judah; built Ramah; reigned 24 years (1 K 15:27-34; 16:7).

babbler (băb'lēr). In Ec 10:11 (RSV: charmer) means either charmer or slanderer. In Acts 17:18 (G: "seed picker") it has connotation of talkative parasite.

Babel (bā'bel, gate of God). 1. City in plain of Shinar; beginning of Nimrod's kingdom (Gn 10:10; 11:9). 2. Tower of Babel, brick structure, built on plain of Shinar to prevent very confusion and dispersion it brought about (Gn 11:4-9). Some regard this tower as prototype of ziggurat.

Babi (bā'bī). See *Bebai*.
Babylon (băb'ĭ-lon, Greek form of Babel). Beginnings of Babylon mentioned in Gn 10. City-state began conquests in 19th c BC; in 18th c Hammurabi became ruler; reached zenith under Nebuchadnezzar II (605—562 BC); conquered by Cyrus of Persia, 539 BC; noted for temple of Bel (Marduk), ziggurats, hanging gardens, bridges, palace, Ishtar Gate, strength, and splendor. Prophets frequently prophesied concerning it (Is 13; 14; 21; 46; 47; Jer 50; 51). In NT often used figuratively for that which opposes God within and without church (1 Ptr 5:13; Rv 14:8; 16:19; 17:5; 18:2, 10, 21).
Babylonia (băb-ĭ-lō'nĭ-à). Region of W Asia with Babylon as capital; also called Shinar (Gn 10:10; 11:2; Is 11:11) and land of Chaldeans (Jer 24:5; Eze 12:13). Lower alluvial plain in ancient times had Accad in N (cities: Agade, Babylon, Borsippa, Kish, Kuthah, Sippar) and Sumer in S (cities: Erech, Eridu, Lagash, Larsa, Nippur, Umma, Ur); inhabited by Sumerians before arrival of Semites. Sumerians developed cuneiform. Earliest culture called Obeid. In 3d millennium BC Sumerian kings appeared in leading cities. About 2400 BC Akkadian period began. This was followed, c 2100, by Neo-Sumerian period. About 1900 BC Elamites and Amorites invaded territory. Next period is the Babylonian (see Babylon).
Babylonish garment (RV: Babylonish mantle. RSV: mantle from Shinar). Full robe, decorated with figures, which originated in Babylon (Jos 7:21).
Baca (bā'kà, weeping, or balsam tree). Usually interpreted figuratively as denoting any vale of tears (Ps 84:6. RV: Weeping). Some identify Baca with Rephaim because of balsam (KJ, RV: mulberry) trees there (2 Sm 5:22-24).
Bacchides (băk'ĭ-dēz). Syrian general (1 Mac 7:8).
Bacchurus (bă-kū'rus. RSV: Zaccur). Listed in 1 Esd 9:24.
Bacchus (băk'us). See *Dionysus*.
Bacenor (bà-sē'nôr). Jewish captain (2 Mac 12:35).
backbite. To tattle or speak evil about someone (Pr 25:23; Ps 15:3 [RV, RSV: slander]; Ro 1:30 [RSV: slanderers]; 2 Co 12:20 [RSV: slander]).
Bachrites (băk'rīts). See *Becher*.
backslide. See *apostasy*.
badger. KJ for H *tahash* (Ex 26:14; 35:7; Nm 4:25; Eze 16:10). RV: seal: porpoise in margin. RSV: goatskin (Ex 26:14; 35:7), sheepskin (Nm 4:25), leather (Eze 16:10). Badger skin not suited for purposes mentioned. See *rock badger*.
Baean (bē'ăn. KJ: Bean). Probably Bedouin tribe (1 Mac 5:4).
bag. Used for carrying weights (Dt 25:13), money (2 K 5:23; 12:10), stones (1 Sm 17:40), etc. Judas' "bag" (KJ, RV) was probably chest (RSV: money box. Jn 12:6; 13:29).
Bago (bā'gō). See *Bigvai 2*.
Bagoas (bà-gō'ăs). Servant of Holofernes (Jdth 12:11).
Bagoi (băg'ō-ĭ). See *Bigvai 1*.
bagpipe. Wind instrument (Dn 3:5, 10, 15. KJ, RV: dulcimer).
Baharumite (bà-hā'rum-īt). Native of Bahurim (1 Ch 11:33. RSV: of Baharum). Barhumite (RSV: of Bahurim) in 2 Sm 23:31.
Bahurim (bà-hū'rĭm). Village between Jerusalem and Jordan (2 Sm 3:16; 16:5; 17:18). Modern Râs et-Tmîm.

Baiterus (bī-tē'rus. KJ: Meterus). Listed in 1 Esd 5:17.
Bajith (bā'jĭth, house. RV: Bayith. RSV text variant: daughter of). Perhaps a temple or place (Is 15:2).
Bakbakkar (băk-băk'ēr). Levite (1 Ch 9: 15).
Bakbuk (băk'bŭk, bottle). Head of family of Nethinim (Ez 2:51; Neh 7:53; 1 Esd 5:31 [KJ, RV: Acub]).
Bakbukiah (băk-bū-kī'à, effusion of LORD). Levite; high official (Neh 11:17); gatekeeper (Neh 12:9, 25).
bakemeats. Baked foods (as RSV. Gn 40: 17).
baker. Potentates had bakers (Gn 40; 1 Sm 8:13). There were professional bakers in Israel (1 Sm 8:13; Jer 37:21).
Balaam (bā'lăm). Son of Beor (Dt 23:4); from land of Amaw (Nm 22:5); when Balak employed him to curse Israel, God inspired him to bless (Nm 22—24); put stumbling block in way of Israel (Rv 2: 14; Nm 31:15, 16); slain by Hebrews (Nm 31). Balaam's error (Jude 11) is surrender to natural morality. "Balaam's way" (2 Ptr 2:15) is commercializing of prophecy.
Balac (bā'lăk). See *Balak*.
Baladan (băl'à-dăn, Marduk gave a son). Father of Merodach-baladan (2 K 20:12; Is 39:1).
Balah (bā'là). See *Baalah 3*.
Balak (bā'lăk, destroyer). King of Moab; hired Balaam to curse Israel (Nm 22—24; Jos 24:9; Ju 11:25; Rv 2:14 [KJ: Balac]).
Balamo, Balamon (băl'à-mō, -mon). Place near which Judith's husband, Manasses, was buried (Jdth 8:3).
balance. Instrument for weighing (Lv 19: 36; Eze 45:10; Hos 12:7; Am 8:5). Used figuratively for measuring worth (Ps 62:9; Dn 5:27) or calamity (Jb 6:2) of man; emblem of fair dealing (Jb 31:6; Pr 11:1).
Balasamus (bà-lăs'à-mus). See *Maaseiah 11*.
baldness. Priests forbidden to make selves bald (Lv 21:5; Eze 44:20). "Baldhead," cry of contempt (2 K 2:23). Sign of leprosy (Lv 13:40-43), misery (Is 3:24), mourning (Jer 16:6; Eze 7:18). Artificial baldness forbidden to Israelites (Dt 14: 1, 2) and punishment for captives (Dt 21:12). Baldness by shaving marked end of Nazarite vow (Nm 6:9, 18).
ballad singers. Singers of narrative poems (Nm 21:27. KJ, RV: they that speak in proverbs).
balm of Gilead. Aromatic vegetable product obtained especially in Gilead (Gn 37:25; Jer 8:22; 46:11) and exported from Palestine (Gn 37:25; Eze 27:17). Used for healing (Jer 51:8). Identified as coming from tree *Balsamodendron Gileadense* or *B. opobalsamum*, no longer found in Palestine. Mentioned as growing in Palestine by Pliny (XIV, 25) and Josephus (*Ant*, XIV, iv, 1; XV, iv, 2; *War* I, vi, 6).
Balnuus (băl-nū'us). See *Binnui 2*.
balsam tree. Plant in Palestine; identity unknown (2 Sm 5:22-24; 1 Ch 14:14, 15. KJ, RV: mulberry). See also *Baca*.
Baltasar, Balthasar (băl-tā'zēr, băl-thā'zēr). See *Belshazzar*.
Bamah (bä'mä, high place). Place of idolatrous worship (Eze 20:29).
Bamoth (bā'mŏth, heights). Camp of Israel in land of Moabites (Nm 21:19, 20). Probably same as Bamoth-baal.
Bamoth-baal (bā'mŏth-bā'ăl, high places of Baal). Place E of Jordan on Arnon river (Jos 13:17) near Nebo.
Ban (băn). See *Tobiah 1*.

Banaias (băn-â-ĭ'ăs). See *Benaiah 11*.
band. 10th part of Roman legion; cohort. (Mt 27:27 [RSV: battalion]; Acts 21:31 [RSV: cohort]). Italian and Augustan bands (RSV: cohort) are named (Acts 10:1; 27:1). See also *army*.
Bani (bā'nĭ). 1. One of David's heroes (2 Sm 23:36). 2. Forefather of Ethan (1 Ch 6:46). 3. Judahite (1 Ch 9:4). 4. Head of family which returned with Zerubbabel (Ez 2:10), some of whom divorced foreign wives (Ez 10:29; 1 Esd 9:30 [KJ, RV: Mani]), Binnui in Neh 7:15. 5. Another whose sons divorced foreign wives (Ez 10:34; 1 Esd 9:34 [KJ: Maani; RV: Baani]). 6. Son of 5; divorced foreign wife (Ez 10:38). 7. Prominent Levite after exile (Neh 8:7 [KJ: Anus; RV: Annus; RSV; Anniuth in 1 Esd 9:48]; 9:4, 5). Binnui in Neh 3:24; 10:9; 12:8. 8. Levite; father of Rehum (Neh 3:17). Possibly same as 7. 9. Prominent Levite after exile (Neh 9:4; 10:13). 10. Levite of sons of Asaph; father of Uzzi (Neh 11:22). Possibly same as 7 or 9. 11. A "chief of people" who signed covenant (Neh 10:14). Possibly same as 6.
Banias, Banid (bá-nī'ăs, bā'nĭd. RSV: Bani). Listed in 1 Esd 8:36. RSV (and LXX: Baani) inserts in Ez 8:10. Possibly same as Bani 5.
bank, bankers. Mentioned in Mt 25:27 (KJ: exchangers) and Lk 19:23.
Bannaia (bă-nā'yá). See *Zabad 6*.
Banneas (băn'ê-ăs). See *Benaiah 8*.
banner. See *ensign*.
Bannus (băn'us). See *Binnui 3*.
baptism (băp'tiz'm). LXX uses G *bapto* for dip or bathe (2 K 5:14; Ps 68:23). Jews baptized proselytes; ceremonial washings *(baptismoi)* were common (Mk 7:3, 4; Heb 9:10; cf. Lv 14:7; 15; Nm 8:7). John's baptism was connected with repentance and worked forgiveness of sins (Mt 3; Mk 1:4-8; Lk 3:3-18; Jn 1:25 to 28) but differentiated from baptism of Jesus (Lk 3:16; Jn 1:26; Acts 1:5; 11:16; 19:4-6). Jesus' baptism was into work of salvation (Mt 3:13-15; Mk 10:38; Lk 12:50). Baptism brings all benefits (justification, sanctification) which flow from that work (1 Ptr 3:21; Acts 2:38; 22:16; Gl 5:16), since individual thereby participates in death and resurrection of Christ (Ro 6:3-11; Col 2:12) and is made member of Christ (1 Co 1:13; Gl 3:27; Eph 4:5). Baptism is connected with Word and places individual into body of Christ, the church (1 Co 12:13; Gl 3:27, 28; Eph 5:26). Faith receives blessings of baptism (Ro 6:11). Mode of baptism undoubtedly varied (Jn 3:23; Acts 2:38; 8:12, 36; 10:47, 48; 16:15, 33). NT makes no distinction between adult and infant baptism.
Baptism with fire refers to inner purification of Spirit (Mt 3:9-12; Lk 3:16, 17; Acts 2:3; See Is 6:6, 7; Zch 13:9; Ml 3:2, 3; 1 Ptr 1:7).
Barabbas (bá-răb'ăs, son of Abba). Prisoner freed by Pilate at Jesus' trial (Mt 27:16 to 26; Mk 15:7-15; Lk 23:18-25; Jn 18:40). Some G mss: Jesus Barabbas in Mt 27:16, 17.
Barachel (băr'á-kĕl, blessed of God). Buzite: father of Elihu (Jb 32:2, 6).
Barachiah, Barachias (băr-á-kī'á, -ăs, LORD has blessed). Father of Zechariah, priest slain between temple and altar (Mt 23:35).

Barak (bâr'ăk, lightning). Israelite; defeated Sisera at command of Deborah (Ju 4; 5:1, 12; Heb 11:32).
barbarian (rude). Originally, any person who did not speak Greek. Term connoted vulgarity. Later designated all not of Greco-Roman culture. No vulgar connotation in NT (Acts 28:4 [RSV: native]; Ro 1:14; Col 3:11; 1 Co 14:11 [RSV: foreigner]).
barber. Mentioned once (Eze 5:1).
Barchus (bâr'kus). See *Barkos*.
barefoot. To go barefoot was sign of distress (2 Sm 15:30; Is 20:2-4; Jer 2:25 [unshod]) and reverence for holy places (Ex 3:5).
Barhumite (bär-hū'mīt). See *Baharumite*.
Bariah (bá-rī'á, fugitive). Descendant of Shecaniah (1 Ch 3:22).
Bar-Jesus (bär-jē'zus). See *Elymas*.
Bar-jona (bär-jō'ná, son of Jonah. RV: Bar-Jonah. RSV: Bar-Jona). Surname of Peter (Mt 16:17). RV, RSV: Son of John in Jn 1:42; 21:15-17.
Barkos (bär'kŏs). One of Nethinim; founder of returned family (Ez 2:53; Neh 7:55; 1 Esd 5:32 [KJ: Charcus. RV: Barchus]).
barley (H *se'orah*, bristling). Grain with long awns cultivated in Palestine (Lv 27:16; Ru 1:22), Egypt (Ex 9:31), neighboring region. Provender for horses, mules, asses, etc. (1 K 4:28). Made into cakes or loaves (Ju 7:13; Jn 6:9); eaten especially by poor (2 K 4:42); sometimes mixed with other grain (Eze 4:9). Jealousy offering (Nm 5:15). See *food 1*.
Barnabas (bär'ná-bás, son of exhortation). Levite from Cyprus; surname Joses (Acts 4:36, 37); early friend of Paul (Acts 9:27); worked with Paul at Antioch and on first missionary journey (Acts 11—14); with Paul at Jerusalem council (Acts 15); separated before 2d missionary journey of Paul because latter refused to take John Mark (Acts 15:36-41). Paul in epistles speaks approvingly of Barnabas (1 Co 9:6; Gl 2:1, 9, 13; Col 4:10) and Mark (2 Ti 4:11).
Barodis (bá-rō'dĭs). Listed in 1 Esd 5:34.
barracks. See *castle*.
barren. Barrenness considered disgrace and punishment (Gn 11:30; Ex 23:26; 1 Sm 1:6, 7; Is 49:21).
Barsabas, Barsabbas (bär'sá-bás, bär-săb'ás, son of Sabas). Surname of Joseph (Acts 1:23) and of Judas (Acts 15:22). Possibly brothers.
Bartacus (bär'tá-kus). Soldier of Darius (1 Esd 4:29).
Bartholomew (bär-thŏl'ô-mū, son of Tolmai). One of 12 apostles (Mt 10:3; Mk 3:18; Lk 6:14; Acts 1:13). Perhaps Nathanael (Jn 1:45).
Bartimaeus (bär-tĭ-mē'us, son of Timaeus). Blind beggar of Jericho (Mk 10:46-52).
Baruch (bâr'uk, blessed). 1. Jeremiah's friend, scribe, and fellow prisoner (Jer 32:12; 36:4-32; 43:3-6). 2. Nehemiah's co-worker (Neh 3:20; 10:6). 3. Judahite (Neh 11:5). 4. Apocryphal book.
Barzillai (bär-zĭl'lá-ī, strong). 1. Gileadite; friend of David (2 Sm 17:27; 19:32-39; 1 Esd 5:38 [KJ: Berzelus; RV: Zorzelleus]). 2. Father-in-law of Saul's daughter Michal (2 Sm 21:8). 3. Priest who married Barzillai's daughter and assumed his name (Ez 2:61; Neh 7:63). See *Addus 2*.
Basaloth (băs'á-lŏth). See *Bazlith*.
Bascama (băs'ká-má. RSV: Baskama). Place in Gilead (1 Mac 13:23).

Basemath (băs'ê-măth, fragrance. KJ: Bashemath and once Basmath [1 K 4:15]). **1.** Hittite wife of Esau (Gn 26:34). Adah in Gn 36:2. **2.** Esau's wife; daughter of Ishmael (Gn 36:3, 4, 13, 17). Mahaloth in Gn 28:9. **3.** Daughter of Solomon (1 K 4:15).

Bashan (bā'shăn). Region from Gilead to Hermon, Jordan to Salcah; productive (Ps 22:12; Jer 50:19); parts noted for fine cattle (Dt 32:14; Eze 39:18); its Argob had 60 fenced cities (Dt 3:4, 5; 1 K 4:13); given to half tribe of Manasseh (Jos 13:29, 30).

Bashan-havoth-jair (bā'shăn-hā'vŏth-jā'ĭr). KJ reading in Dt 3:14 (RV: he called them, even Bashan, after his own name, Havvoth-jair. RSV: and called the villages after his own name, Havvoth-jair). See *Havoth-jair*.

Bashemath (băsh'ê-măth). See *Basemath*.

basilisk. See *serpent*.

Baskama (băs'ka-ma). See *Bascama*.

basket. See *cage 1; trade 2*.

Basmath (băs'măth). See *Basemath*.

Bassa, Bassai (băs'ā, -â-ī). See *Bezai*.

Bastai (băs'tā-ī). See *Besai*.

bastard. One born within prohibited degrees (Dt 23:2).

Basthai (băs'thâ-ī). See *Besai*

bat. Classed with fowls, considered unclean (Lv 11:19; Dt 14:18); lived in caverns of rocks and cliffs (Is 2:19-21).

bath. See *measures 3c*.

bathe. Bathing and cleanliness practiced by Israelites from earliest times (Ru 3:3; 2 Sm 12:20; SS 5:3, 12). Concept of cleanliness before God is prominent in rituals (Ex 19:10; Lv 13—16; 17:15, 16. See Jn 13:5-11).

Bath-rabbim (băth'răb-ĭm, daughter of many). Gate of Heshbon (SS 7:4).

Bath-sheba (băth-shē'bà, daughter of oak. Bath-shua in 1 Ch 3:5). Became wife of David (after David had her husband Uriah killed in battle); mother of Solomon (2 Sm 11:3, 4; 12:24; 1 K 1:11-53; 2:13-25).

Bath-shua (băth'shū'à). **1.** RV has this proper noun in 1 Ch 2:3 (see Gn 38:2, 12). KJ, RSV: daughter of Shua. **2.** See *Bath-sheba*.

Bathzacharias (băth-zăk-à-rī'ăs). See *Bethzacharias*.

battalion (bă-tăl'yun). See *band*.

battlement. See *parapet*.

Bavai, Bavvai (băv-â-ī). Helped build walls of Jerusalem (Neh 3:18).

Bayith (bā'yĭth). See *Bajith*.

bay tree. KJ translation in Ps 37:35 (RV: a green tree in its native soil. RSV: cedar of Lebanon).

Bazlith, Bazluth (băz'lĭth, -lŭth). Head of family of Nethinim (Neh 7:54; Ez 2:52; 1 Esd 5:31 [KJ, RV: Basaloth]).

bdellium (dĕl'ĭ-um). Fragrant gum resin listed with precious stones (so regarded in LXX. Gn 2:12; Nm 11:7).

beacon. Translation of KJ, RV (Is 30:17. RSV: flagstaff).

beads. Used as ornaments (Nm 31:50. KJ: tablets. RV: armlets).

Bealiah (bē'à-lī-à, LORD is lord). Benjaminite; came to David at Ziklag (1 Ch 12:5).

Bealoth (bē'à-lŏth, mistresses). **1.** Village in S Judah (Jos 15:24). Perhaps Baalath-beer. **2.** Locality in Asher (1 K 4:16. KJ: in Aloth).

Bean (bē'ăn). See *Baean*.

bean. See *food 3*.

Bear, The. See *Arcturus*.

bear. Syrian bear, once abundant in Palestine (2 K 2:24); cunning (Lm 3:10);

ferocious (1 Sm 17:34-36); 2 Sm 17:8; Pr 17:12; Hos 13:8; Am 5:19); used symbolically in Is 11:7.

beard. Badge of manly dignity. Tearing, cutting, or neglecting it was sign of mental aberration (1 Sm 21:13), affliction (2 Sm 19:24), mourning (Ez 9:3; Is 15:2; Jer 41:5). To mutilate it was outrage (2 Sm 10:4); taken hold of in salutation (2 Sm 20:9); removed in leprosy (Lv 4:9); shaved in Egypt (Gn 41:14); shaving corners of beard was probably heathen religious act (Lv 19:27; Jer 9:26; 25:36).

beast. **1.** Mammal, not man, as distinguished from fowl and creeping things (Gn 1: 29, 30). **2.** Wild beasts (Ez 26:22; Is 13:21, 22; Jer 50:39; Mk 1:13). **3.** Animals, including birds and reptiles (Ps 147:9; Ec 3:18; Acts 28:5). **4.** Destructive power hostile to God's kingdom and people (Dn 7; Rv 12:3; 13:1-10; 17: 3-18). See *Leviathan*. **5.** In Rv 13:2-18 beast fights Christians and "beast with horns like a lamb" persuades men to worship first beast. Has been identified with Antichrist. **6.** Beast (KJ) in Rv 4: 6-9 is living creature (RSV, RV).

beatitudes (bē-ăt'ĭ-tūds). Declarations of blessedness, especially Mt 5:3-11; Lk 6: 20-22. Isolated: Mt 11:6; 13:16; 16:17; Lk 7:23; 10:23; 11:28; 12:37, 43; Jn 13:17; 20:29; Ja 1:12, 25; 1 Ptr 3:14; 4:14; Rv 1:3; 14:13; 16:15; 19:9; 20:6; 22:7, 14. See also *blessing*.

Bebai (bē'bā-ī). Founder of family which returned from captivity and members of family (Ez 2:11; 8:11; 10:28; Neh 7:16; 10:15; 1 Esd 8:37 [KJ, RV: Babi]).

Becher (bē'kēr, young camel). **1.** 2d son of Benjamin (Gn 46:21; 1 Ch 7:6, 8). Family not in registry (Nm 26:38; 1 Ch 8: 1-6), but sons of Becher are listed (1 Ch 7:8, 9). **2.** In Nm 26:35 a Becher, father of Bachrites (RSV: Becherites), is mentioned as Ephraimite. Bered in 1 Ch 7:20.

Bechorath, Becorath (bē-kō'răth). Ancestor of Saul (1 Sm 9:1).

bed. Poor and travelers often slept on ground (Gn 28:11; Ex 22:26, 27) or mat (Mt 9:6; Mk 2:4-12 [RSV: pallet]). Bedsteads used early; wood, iron (Dt 3:11), even ivory (Dt 3:11; 2 K 1:4, 6; Am 6:4); had mattress, covering, pillow (Ex 22:27; 1 Sm 19:13; Is 28:20); at times ornamental and canopied (Am 6:4; Est 1:6; 2 K 4:10). See also *homes; litter*.

Bedad (bē'dăd). Father of Hadad, king of Edom (Gn 36:35; 1 Ch 1:46).

Bedan (bē'dăn). **1.** Judge in Israel according to KJ, RV (1 Sm 12:11). RSV (and LXX, Syriac): scribal error for Barak. **2.** Great-grandson of Manasseh (1 Ch 7:17).

Bedeiah (bē-dē'yà, servant of LORD). Divorced foreign wife (Ez 10:35; 1 Esd 9:34 [KJ: Pelias; RV: Pedias]).

bee. Plentiful in Palestine (Ex 3:8; Dt 1:44; 1 K 14:3; Eze 27:17). Nested in rocks (Ps 81:16), woods (1 Sm 14:25), even carcasses (Ju 14:8).

Beeliada (bē'ê-lī'à-dà, Baal has known). See *Eliada 1*.

Beelsarus (bē-ĕl'sà-rus). See *Bilshan*.

Beeltethmus (bē-ĕl-tĕth'mus. RSV: Beltethmus). Officer of Artaxerxes (1 Esd 2:16).

Beelzebub, Beelzebul (bē-ĕl'zē-bŭb, -bŭl). Prince of demons (Mt 10:25; 12:24; Mk 3:22; Lk 11:15, 18, 19; Satan (Lk 11:18). See also *Baalzebub*.

Beer (bē'ēr, well). **1.** Encampment of Israel (Nm 21:16-18). **2.** Place to which Jotham fled (Ju 9:21).

Beera (bē-ē'rȧ, well). Zophah's son (1 Ch 7:37).

Beerah (bē-ē'rȧ, well). Reubenite prince (1 Ch 5:6).

Beer-elim (bē'ẽr-ē'lĭm, well of heroes). Place on border of Moab (Is 15:8); probably same as *Beer 1*.

Beeri (bē-ē'rī, of a well). 1. Hittite; father of one of Esau's wives (Gn 26:34). 2. Father of Hosea (Hos 1:1).

Beer-lahai-roi (bē'ẽr-lȧ-hī-roi, well of living one who sees me). Hagar's well (Gn 16:6-14; 24:62; 25:11).

Beeroth (bē-ē'rŏth, wells). 1. Hivite city (Jos 9:17; 1 Esd 5:19 [KJ, RV: Beroth]). 2. See *Bene-jaakan*.

Beerothite (bē-ē'rō-thīt. Berothite in 1 Ch 11:39. RSV: of Beeroth). Native of Beeroth (2 Sm 4:2; 23:37).

Beer-sheba (bē'ẽr-shē'bȧ, well of oath, or of seven). Place in S Palestine where Abraham made compact with Abimelech and dug well (Gn 21:31; 26:33; 1 Ch 4:28; 1 Sm 8:2; Am 5:5; 8:14; Neh 11:27, 30).

Beeshterah (bē-ēsh'tē-rȧ, house of Ashterah). Levitical city given to Gershonites in Manasseh beyond Jordan (Jos 21:27). Ashtaroth in 1 Ch 6:71. See *Ashteroth-karnaim*.

beetle. RV, RSV (correctly): cricket (Lv 11:22).

beeves. Cattle of bovine species (Lv 22:19. RSV: bulls).

beggar. See *alms; poverty*.

beginning. 1. Temporal beginning (Gn 1:1; Heb 1:10). 2. Eternity (Jn 1:1; 1 Jn 1:1; 2:13). 3. Source (Rv 21:6; 22:13).

Behemoth (bē-hē'moth). H for hippopotamus (Jb 40:15-24).

beka, bekah (bē'kȧ). Half shekel (Ex 38:26).

Bel (bāl, lord). Marduk, patron god of Babylon, whom Hebrews called Merodach (Is 46:1; Jer 50:2; 51:44; Bel 3-22; Herodotus I, 181).

Bela (bē'lȧ, devouring). 1. King of Edom (Gn 36:32). 2. Reubenite chief (1 Ch 5:8). 3. Son of Benjamin (Gn 46:21 [KJ: Belah]; Nm 26:38). 4. See *Zoar*.

Belah (bē'lȧ). See *Bela 3*.

Belaite (bē'lȧ-īt). Descendant of Bela 3 (Nm 26:38).

Belemus (bĕl'ē-mus). See *Bishlam*.

Belial (bē'lĭ-ȧl, worthlessness, wickedness, restlessness). Should not be regarded proper noun in OT (Dt 13:13; Ju 19:22; 1 Sm 2:12. RV, RSV: base fellows, worthless men). Personified once in NT (2 Co 6:15).

belief, believe, believer. See *body 6; church; faith*.

bell. Bells of gold appended to priestly robes (Ex 28:33-35; 39:25). Ornaments for ankles (Is 3:16-18), horses (Zch 14:20).

bellows. Pair of skins used for blowing fire (Jer 6:29).

Belmaim, Belmen (bĕl'mȧ-ĭm, bĕl'men). Town of Samaria (Jdth 4:4).

Belnuus (bĕl'nū'us). See *Binnui 2*.

Belshazzar (bĕl-shăz'ẽr, Bel protect king). Last ruler of Neo-Babylonian Empire; Son of Nabonidus (Dn 5; Bar 1:11, 12 [KJ: Balthasar; RV: Baltasar]).

belt. See *girdle*.

Belteshazzar (bĕl-tē-shăz'ẽr, protected by Bel). Name given Daniel by Nebuchadnezzar (Dn 1:7).

Beltethmus (bĕl-tĕth'mus). See *Beelteth-mus*.

Ben (bĕn, son). Levite (1 Ch 15:18. RSV omits as copyist's error).

Ben-abinadab (bĕn-ȧ-bĭn'ȧ-dăb. KJ: son of Abinadab). Son-in-law of Solomon (1 K 4:11).

Benaiah (bē-nā'yȧ, son of the LORD). 1. Son of Jehoiada; priest (1 Ch 27:5); known for deeds of valor (2 Sm 23:20, 21; 1 Ch 11:22, 23); captain of David's bodyguard (2 Sm 8:18); commander-in-chief of Solomon's army (1 K 1:36; 2:34-46). 2. One of David's mighty men (2 Sm 23:30; 1 Ch 11:31). 3. Levite harpist (1 Ch 15:18, 20; 16:5). 4. Priest, trumpeter (1 Ch 15:24; 16:6). 5. 6. Two Levites (2 Ch 20:14; 31:13). 7. Simeonite prince (1 Ch 4:36). 8. 9. 10. 11. Four who divorced foreign wives (Ez 10:25 [KJ: Baanias; RV: Banneas in 1 Esd 9:26], 30 [Naidus in 1 Esd 9:31], 35 [KJ: Mabdai: RV, RSV: Mamdai in 1 Esd 9:34], 43 [KJ, RV: Banaias in 1 Esd 9:35]). 12. Pelatiah's father (Eze 11:1, 13).

Ben-ammi (bĕn-ăm'ī, son of my kindred). Lot's son; ancestor of Ammonites (Gn 19:38).

Ben-deker (bĕn-dē'kẽr. KJ: son of Dekar). Purveyor of Solomon (1 K 4:9).

Bene-berak (bĕn'ē-bē'răk, sons of lightning). Town of Dan (Jos 19:45). Modern Ibn Ibrak.

Bene-jaakan (bē'nē-jā'ȧ-kăn, sons of Jaakan). Israelite encampment in wilderness (Nm 33:31, 32). Beeroth Bene-jaakan (KJ: Beeroth of the children of Jaakan) in Dt 10:6. See also *Jaakan*.

benevolence, due (bē-nĕv'ō-lens). Conjugal rights (as RSV: 1 Co 7:3. RV: her due).

Ben-geber (bĕn-gē'bẽr. KJ: son of Geber). Purveyor of Solomon (1 K 4:13).

Ben-hadad (bĕn-hā'dăd, son of Hadad). 1. King of Damascus, called Ben-hadad I; helped Asa against Baasha (1 K 15:18-21; 2 Ch 16:1-6). 2. Another king (identified with 1 by some) defeated by Ahab (1 K 20:1-34). In days of Jehoram again attacked Israel (2 K 6:24—7:20; 8:28); killed and succeeded by Hazael (2 K 8:7-15). 3. Ben-hadad II, son of Hazael. In days of Jehoahaz, Hazael and then Ben-hadad attacked ten tribes (2 K 13:3-13); but Ben-hadad defeated by Joash (2 K 13:22-25).

Ben-hail (bĕn-hā'īl, son of strength). Prince in Judah (2 Ch 17:7).

Ben-hanan (bĕn-hā'năn, son of grace). Son of Shimon (1 Ch 4:20).

Ben-hesed (bĕn-hē'sĕd. KJ: son of Hesed). Purveyor of Solomon (1 K 4:10).

Ben-hur (bĕn-hûr'. KJ: son of Hur). Purveyor of Solomon (1 K 4:8).

Beninu (bē-nī'nū, our son). Levite; sealed covenant with Nehemiah (Neh 10:13).

Benjamin (bĕn'jȧ-mĭn, son of right hand). 1. Youngest son of Jacob; called Benoni by dying Rachel (Gn 35:16-20); beloved by Jacob (Gn 42); visited Egypt (Gn 43). 2. Tribe was distinguished as Jacob prophesied (Gn 49:27; Ju 20:16); received territory between Judah and Ephraim (Jos 18:11-28); severely punished for ravishing old man's concubine (Ju 20; 21). Saul (1 Sm 9:1, 2) and Paul (Ph 3:5) were Benjaminites. 3. Head of Benjaminite family (1 Ch 7:10). 4. One of returned (Ez 10:32; Neh 3:23; 12:34).

Benjamin, Gate of. Gate in Jerusalem (Jer 20:2; 38:7; Zch 14:10).

Beno (bē'nō, his son). Levite (1 Ch 24:26, 27).

Ben-oni (bĕn-ō'nī, son of my sorrow). See *Benjamin 1*.

Ben-zoheth (bĕn-zō'hĕth, son of Zoheth). Judahite (1 Ch 4:20).

Beon (bē'ŏn). See Baal-meon.

Beor (bē'ôr, torch). 1. Father of Bela, king of Edom (Gn 36:32; 1 Ch 1:43). 2. Balaam's father (Nm 22:5; 2 Ptr 2:15 [KJ: Bosor]).

Bera (bē'rȧ). King of Sodom (Gn 14:2).

Beracah, Berachah (bĕr'ȧ-kä, blessing). 1. Benjaminite; joined David at Ziklag (1 Ch 12:3). 2. Valley in Judah near Tekoa where Jehoshaphat celebrated his victory (2 Ch 20:26).

Berachiah (bĕr-ȧ-kī'ȧ). See Berechiah 1.

Beraiah (bĕr-ā-ī'ȧ, created of LORD). Son of Shimei, Benjaminite (1 Ch 8:21).

Berea (bē-rē'ȧ). 1. City in Judea (1 Mac 9:4). 2. Syrian city (Aleppo, 2 Mac 13:4). KJ, RV: Beroea. 3. See Beroea.

Berechiah (bĕr-ê-kī'ȧ, LORD has blessed). 1. Levite; father of Asaph (1 Ch 6:39 [KJ: Berachiah]; 15:17). 2. Levite; doorkeeper of ark (1 Ch 15:23). 3. Ephraimite; took part of captives from Judah (2 Ch 28:12). 4. Son of Zerubbabel (1 Ch 3:20). 5. Levite (1 Ch 9:16). 6. Father of Meshullam (Neh 3:4, 30). 7. Father of prophet Zechariah (Zch 1:1, 7).

Bered (bē'rĕd, hail). 1. Place in S Palestine near Kadesh and Beer-lahai-roi (Gn 16:7-14). 2. Ephraimite (1 Ch 7:20). See Becher 2.

Beri (bē'rī, well). Asherite (1 Ch 7:36).

Beriah (bē-rī'ȧ). 1. Son of Asher. Descendants called Beriites (Gn 46:17; Nm 26:44, 45; 1 Ch 7:30, 31). 2. Son of Ephraim (1 Ch 7:23). 3. Benjaminite (1 Ch 8:13). 4. Levite (1 Ch 23:10).

Beriites (bē-rī'īts). See Beriah 1.

Berites (bē'rīts. RSV: Bichrites). People in N Palestine (2 Sm 20:14).

Berith (bē'rīth). See Baal-berith.

Bernice (bēr'nī'sē, bringing victory). Oldest daughter of Herod Agrippa. Married Herod of Chalcis. Close association with brother Agrippa (Acts 25:23; 26:30) caused scandal. Mistress of Vespasian and Titus.

Berodach-baladan (bē-rō'dăk-băl'ȧ-dăn). See Merodach-baladan.

Beroea (bē-rē'ȧ. KJ: Berea). City of Macedonia (Acts 17:10-14; 20:4).

Beroth (bē'rŏth). See Beeroth 1.

Berothah, Berothai (bē-rō'thȧ, bē-rō'thī). City (modern Bereitan) between Hamath and Damascus (Eze 47:16; 2 Sm 8:8). Cun in 1 Ch 18:8 (KJ: Chun).

Berothite (bē'rŏth-īt). See Beerothite.

beryl (bĕr'īl). Precious stone in high priest's breastplate (Ex 28:20; 39:13. See Eze 28:13; Dn 10:6; Rv 21:20). See Chrysolite.

Berzelus (bĕr-zē'lus). See Barzillai 1.

Besai (bē'sī). One of Nethinim (Ez 2:49; Neh 7:52; 1 Esd 5:31 [KJ: Bastai; RV: Basthai]).

Bescaspasmys (bĕs-kăs'păs-mis). See Mattaniah 8.

Besodeiah (bĕs-ô-dē'yȧ, familiar with LORD). Father of Meshullam (Neh 3:6).

besom (bē'zum. RSV: broom). Broom (Is 14:23).

Besor (bē'sôr, cool). Brook of Ziklag; probably Nahr Ghazzeh (1 Sm 30:9, 10, 21).

Betah (bē'tȧ, confidence). Tibhath in 1 Ch 18:8). City of Syria-Zobah (2 Sm 8:8).

Betane (bĕt'ȧ-nē. RSV: Bethany). Place near oak of Abraham (Jdth 1:9).

Beten (bē'tĕn, hollow). Border city of Asher (Jos 19:25).

Bethabara (bĕth-ăb'ȧ-rȧ, house of ford. RV, RSV: Bethany). Place near Jordan where John baptized Jesus (Jn 1:28).

Beth-anath (bĕth-ā'năth, house of Anath). Fortified city of Naphtali (Jos 19:38; Ju 1:33).

Beth-anoth (bĕth-ā'nŏth, house of Anoth). Town in Judah (Jos 15:59).

Bethany (bĕth'ȧ-nĭ, house of affliction). 1. Village on Mt of Olives close to Bethphage (Mt 21:17; Mk 11:1; Lk 19:29) about 2 mi from Jerusalem (Jn 11:18). Modern el'Azariyeh. 2. See Bethabara. 3. See Betane.

Beth-arabah (bĕth-ăr'ȧ-bȧ, house of the desert. Arabah in Jos 18:18). Town on N end of Dead Sea assigned to Judah (Jos 15:6, 61; 18:22).

Beth-aram (bĕth-ā'răm). See Beth-haran.

Beth-arbel (bĕth-är'bĕl, house of ambush). Town destroyed by Shalman with horrible cruelty (Hos 10:14). Perhaps Arbela, 4 mi NW of Tiberias.

Beth-ashbea (bĕth-ăsh'bē-ȧ, house of witness). See Ashbea.

Bethasmoth (bĕth-ăz'mŏth). See Azmaveth 4.

Beth-aven (bĕth-ā'vĕn, house of nothingness). 1. Town near Ai E of Bethel (Jos 7:2; 18:12; 1 Sm 13:5; 14:23). 2. Bethel (Hos 4:15; 5:8; 10:5).

Beth-azmaveth (Bĕth-ăz-mā'vĕth). See Azmaveth 4.

Beth-baal-meon (bĕth-bā'ăl-mē'ŏn). See Baal-meon.

Beth-barah (bĕth-bâr'ȧ, house of ford). Ford of Jordan (Ju 7:24).

Bethbasi (bĕth-bā'sī). Place near Jordan (1 Mac 9:62, 64).

Beth-birei, Beth-biri (bĕth-bĭr'ê-ī, -bĭr'ī. Beth-lebaoth in Jos 19:6. Lebaoth in Jos 15:32). Simeonite town (1 Ch 4:31).

Beth-car (bĕth'kär, house of the lamb). Place to which Israelites pursued Philistines (1 Sm 7:11).

Beth-dagon (bĕth-dā'gŏn, house of Dagon). 1. City near Lydda (Jos 15:41). Modern Khirbet Dajun. 2. Town of Asher (Jos 19:27).

Beth-diblathaim (bĕth-dĭb-lȧ-thā'ĭm, house of figcakes). Town of Moab (Jer 48:22); perhaps Almon-diblathaim.

Beth-eden (bĕth-ē'd'n). See Eden 2.

Beth-eked (bĕth-ē'kĕd. KJ, RV: shearing house). Place in Samaria (2 K 10:12, 14).

Bethel (bĕth'el, house of God). 1. Town about 12 mi N of Jerusalem (Gn 28:19), where Abraham encamped (Gn 12:8; 13:3). Called Luz by Canaanites, but Bethel by Jacob after his vision (Gn 28:11-19; Jos 16:2; Gn 35:1-15; Hos 12:4). Assigned to Benjamin (Jos 16:2; 18:13, 22); captured by Ephraim (Ju 1:22-26). Ark brought to Bethel from Shiloh (Ju 20:1, 27). Jeroboam made it center of idolatry (1 K 13:1-32). Its children mocked Elisha (2 K 2:23, 24; 1 Esd 5:21 [KJ: Betolius; RV: Betolion]). Ruins called Beitin. 2. See Bethuel 2.

Beth-emek (bĕth-ē'mĕk, house of the valley). Town of Asher (Jos 19:27).

Bether (bē'thĕr, house of cutting). Figurative mountains (SS 2:17. See 8:14).

Bethesda (bē-thĕz'dȧ, probably from Aramaic beth- 'esdatain, house of twin outpourings. RSV: Beth-zatha. Some mss: Bethsaida). Spring-fed pool with 5 porches in Jerusalem (Jn 5:2), probably one found (1888) near St. Anne's Church.

Beth-ezel (bĕth-ē'zel, neighboring house?). Place in Judah (Mi 1:11).

Beth-gader (bĕth-gā'dĕr, house of wall). Place in Judah (1 Ch 2:51). Perhaps same as Geder or Gedor.

Beth-gamul (bĕth-gā'mul, house of reward). Town of Moab (Jer 48:23. Jemeil, E of Dibon).

Beth-gilgal (bĕth-gĭl'găl). KJ: house of Gilgal (Neh 12:29). Possibly same as *Gilgal 2.*

Beth-haccerem, Beth-haccherem (bĕth-hăk'sē-rĕm, -hă-kē'rĕm, house of the vineyard). Town of Judah (Neh 3:14; Jer 6:1) from whose heights signals were given. Modern Ain Karim.

Beth-haggan (bĕth-hăg'ăn. KJ, RV: garden house). Place to which Ahaziah fled from Jehu (2 K 9:27).

Beth-haram, Beth-haran (bĕth-hā'răm, -hā'răn. KJ: Beth-aram in Jos 13:27). City E of Jordan (Nm 32:36).

Beth-hoglah (bĕth-hŏg'lá, house of partridge). Village of Benjamin near Judah (Jos 15:6 [KJ: Beth-hogla]; 18: 19, 21).

Beth-horon (bĕth-hō'rŏn, house of the hollow). Twin towns 1¾ mi apart, about 11 m NW of Jerusalem (Jos 16:3, 5; 18:13; 1 Ch 7:24); assigned to Kohathites (Jos 21:22; 1 Ch 6:68; Jdth 4:4 [KJ: Bethoron]). Modern Beit 'Uret Tahta and el-Foka.

Beth-jeshimoth (bĕth-jĕsh'ĭ-mŏth, house of desert). Town E of Jordan about 9 mi. SE of Jericho (Jos 12:3; 13:20; Nm 33:49 [KJ: Bethjesimoth]; Eze 25:9).

Beth-le-aphrah (bĕth-lĕ-ăf'rá. KJ: house of Aphrah). Name of place, possibly in Philistine plain (Mi 1:10).

Beth-lebaoth (bĕth-lĕb-ā'ŏth, house of lionesses?). See *Beth-birei.*

Bethlehem (bĕth'lĕ-em, house of bread). 1. Town 6 mi S of Jerusalem; originally called Ephrath or Ephrathah. Bethlehemjudah (RSV: in Judah) in Ju 17:7. Bethlehem Ephrathah in Mi 5:2. KJ, RV: Bethlomon in 1 Esd 5:17. Rachel buried there (Gn 35:19); home of Ruth (Ru 1:19); birthplace of David (1 Sm 17:12) and Christ (Mt 2:1, 2; Lk 2:15-18). 2. Town in Zebulun (Jos 19:15).

Bethlomon (bĕth-lō'mŏn). See *Bethlehem 1.*

Beth-maacah, Beth-maachah (bĕth-mā'á-ká). See *Abel-beth-maacah.*

Beth-marcaboth (bĕth-mär'ká-bŏth, house of chariots). Town of Simeon (Jos 19:5; 1 Ch 4:31).

Beth-meon (bĕth-mē'ŏn). See *Baal-meon.*

Beth-millo (bĕth-mĭl'lō). See *Millo 2.*

Beth-nimrah (bĕth-nĭm'rá, house of lepers. Nimrah in Nm 32:3). Town in Jordan valley fortified by Gad (Nm 32:36; Jos 13:27).

Bethoron (bĕth-ō'rŏn). See *Beth-horon.*

Beth-palet (bĕth-pā'lĕt). See *Beth-pelet.*

Beth-pazzez (bĕth-păz'ĕz, house of dispersion). City of Issachar (Jos 19:21).

Beth-pelet (bĕth-pē'lĕt, house of escape). Town in S Judah (Jos 15:27 [KJ: Beth-palet]; Neh 11:26 [KJ: Beth-phelet]).

Beth-peor (bĕth-pē'ôr, house of Peor). Place in Moab where Israel encamped while fighting Sihon and Og (Dt 3:29; 4:46; Jos 13:20). Moses buried in valley opposite it (Dt 34:6).

Beth-phage (bĕth'fá-jē, house of figs). Village near Bethany (Mk 11:1; Lk 19:29) not far from descent of Mt of Olives (Mt 21:1).

Beth-phelet (bĕth-fĕ'lĕt). See *Beth-pelet.*

Beth-rapha (bĕth-rā'fá, house of Rapha). Son of Eshton (1 Ch 4:12).

Beth-rehob (bĕth-rē'hŏb, house of Rehob). See *Rehob 3.*

Bethsaida (bĕth-sā'ĭ-dá, house of fishing). 1. City on Sea of Galilee (Jn 1:44; 12:21); home of Peter, Andrew, Philip; rebuked

by Jesus for not receiving His teachings (Mt 11:21; Lk 10:13); probably close to Capernaum (see Mk 6:45 and Jn 6:17). 2. Bethsaida of Gaulonitis (Julias). On E side of Sea of Galilee (Lk 9:10-17; Mk 8:22-26). Rebuilt by Philip the tetrarch and called Julias in honor of Augustus' daughter (Ant XVIII, ii, 1).

Bethsamos (bĕth-sā'mŏs). See *Azmaveth 4.*

Beth-shan, Beth-shean, Beth-san (bĕth-shăn', -shē'ăn, -săn', house of security, or house of Shahan). Fortress city (modern Beisan) strategically located in valley of Jezreel; dates to early part of 3d millennium BC; under Egyptian rule for 3 c; had chariots of iron; could not be taken (Jos 17:11-16); Saul's body was hanged on its wall (1 Sm 31:10-13; 2 Sm 21: 12-14), his armor put in temple of Ashtoreth (1 Sm 31:10), his head in temple of Dagon (1 Ch 10:10).

Beth-shemesh (bĕth-shē'mĕsh, house of sun). 1. City of N Judah (Jos 15:10) set aside for sons of Aaron (Jos 21:16); Jehoash there defeated Amaziah (2 K 14: 11, 13); occupied by Philistines during Ahaz' reign (2 Ch 28:18); kine brought ark to it (1 Sm 6:1-21. *Ant* VI, i, 4). Ir-shemesh in Jos 19:41. 2. Town of Issachar between Tabor and Jordan (Jos 19:22). 3. City of Naphtali (Jos 19:38; Ju 1:33). 4. Egyptian city (Jer 43:13. RSV: Heliopolis); probably On.

Beth-shittah (bĕth-shĭt'á, house of acacia). City between valley of Jezreel and Zererah (Ju 7:22).

Bethsura, Bethsuron (bĕth-sū'rá, -sū'ron). See *Beth-zur.*

Beth-tappuah (bĕth-tăp'ū-á, house of apples). Town in Judah near Hebron (Jos 15:53). Tephon (KJ: Taphon) in 1 Mac 9:50.

Beth-togarmah (bĕth-tō-gär'má. KJ, RV: house of Togarmah). City in N, possibly in Armenia; exported war horses and mules (Eze 27:14; 38:6). See also *Togarmah.*

Bethuel (bē-thū'el, house of God?). 1. Nephew of Abraham; father of Laban and Rebecca (Gn 22:20-24; 24:15, 29; 25:20; 28:2, 5). 2. Simeonite town in Judah (1 Ch 4:30). Bethul in Jos 19:4. Bethel in 1 Sm 30:27. Chesil in Jos 15:30.

Bethul (bĕth'ul). See *Bethuel 2.*

Bethulia (bĕth-û-lī'á). Home of Judith (Jdth 4:6; 6:11-14).

Bethzacharias (bĕth-zăk-á-rī'ăs. KJ: Bathzacharias. RSV: Bethzechariah). Town 8 mi from Beth-zur (1 Mac 6:32, 33).

Beth-zaith (bĕth-zā'ĭth). See *Bezeth.*

Beth-zatha (bĕth-zā'thá). See *Bethesda.*

Bethzechariah (bĕth-zĕk-á-rī'á). See *Bethzacharias.*

Beth-zur (bĕth-zûr', house of rock. KJ, RV: Bethsura *or* Bethsuron in Mac). Town in Judah, 4 mi N of Hebron (Jos 15:58; 2 Ch 11:7; Neh 3:16). Judas Maccabee there defeated Lysias (1 Mac 4:29; 2 Mac 11:5; 13:19, 22).

Betolion, Betolius (bē-tō'lĭ-ŏn, -us). See *Bethel 1.*

Betomasthaim, -masthem, -mesthaim, mestham (bĕt-ō-măs'thā-ĭm, -măs'them, -mĕs'thā-ĭm, -mĕs'thăm). Town near Esdraelon (Jdth 4:6; 15:4).

Betonim (bĕt'ō-nĭm). Town in Gad (Jos 13:26) on Mt Gilead.

betrothal (bē-trŏth'al). See *marriage.*

Beulah (bū'lá, married). Name for Palestine when in right relationship with God (Is 62:4, 5. RSV: Married).

Bezai (bĕ'zâ-ī). Head of returned family (Ez 2:17; Neh 7:23; 1 Esd 5:16 [KJ: Bassa; RV: Bassai]); joined Nehemiah in making covenant (Neh 10:18).
Bezaleel, Bezalel (bĕ-zăl'ē-ĕl, bĕz'-á-lĕl, in shadow of God). 1. Grandson of Hur (1 Ch 2:20); tabernacle artificer (Ex 31:1-11; 35:30-35). 2. Returned Jew; divorced foreign wife (Ez 10:30). Sesthel in 1 Esd 9:31.
Bezek (bĕ'zĕk). 1. Town near Jabesh-gilead identified as Ibzik (1 Sm 11:8, 11). 2. Place in territory of Judah where Adoni-bezek was defeated (Ju 1:1-5).
Bezer (bĕ'zēr, fortress). 1. Asherite (1 Ch 7:37). 2. Levitical city of refuge in territory of Judah (Dt 4:43; Jos 20:8).
Bezeth (bĕ'zĕth. RSV: Beth-zaith). Place near Jerusalem where Bacchides encamped (1 Mac 7:19).
Biatas (bī'á-tăs). See *Pelaiah 2.*
Bible (book). Name given to collection of 39 OT and 27 NT books. See *canon; versions.*
Bichri (bĭk'rī). Benjaminite (2 Sm 20:1).
Bichrites (bĭk'rīts). See *Berites.*
Bidkar (bĭd'kär). Captain of Jehu (2 K 9:25).
bier. Stretcher used to carry dead to grave (2 Sm 3:31; 2 Ch 16:14; Lk 7:14).
Bigtha (bĭg'thá). Chamberlain of Ahasuerus (Est 1:10).
Bigthan, Bigthana (bĭg'thăn, bĭg-thä'ná). Chamberlain of Ahasuerus (Est 2:21; 6:2). Gabatha in Ap Est 12:1.
Bigvai (bĭg'vá-ī, happy). 1. Descendants returned with Zerubbabel (Ez 2:14; Neh 7:19; 1 Esd 5:14 [KJ, RV: Bagoi]). 2. Chief of Zerubbabel (Ez 2:2; Neh 7:7). KJ: Reelius; RV: Reelias; RSV: Reeliah in 1 Esd 5:8. Bago in 1 Esd 8:40. 3. Descendants returned with Ezra (Ez 8:14). Possibly same as 1. 4. Family which sealed covenant (Neh 10:16). Possibly same as 1, 3. 5. See *Nahamani.*
Bildad (bĭl'dăd, Bel has loved). Shuhite; friend of Job (Jb 2:11); made three speeches (Jb 8; 18; 25).
Bileam (bĭl'ē-ăm). See *Ibleam.*
Bilgah (bĭl'gá, cheerful). 1. Aaronite; family made 15th course of priests (1 Ch 24:14). 2. Priest; returned with Zerubbabel (Neh 12:5, 18); probably same as Bilgai.
Bilgai (bĭl'gâ-ī, cheerful). Joined Nehemiah in making covenant (Neh 10:8). Probably same as Bilgah 2.
Bilhah (bĭl'há). 1. Rachel's handmaid; Jacob's concubine; mother of Dan and Naphtali (Gn 29:29; 30:3-8; 35:22, 25; 46:25; 1 Ch 7:13). 2. See *Baalah 3.*
Bilhan (bĭl'hăn). 1. Horite; son of Ezer (Gn 36:27). 2. Benjaminite (1 Ch 7:10).
bill. Written document (Dt 24:1, 3; Is 50:1; Lk 16:6. See Mt 5:31).
Bilshan (bĭl'shăn). One of 12 chiefs who returned with Zerubbabel (Ez 2:2; Neh 7:7; 1 Esd 5:8 [KJ, RV: Beelsarus]).
Bimhal (bĭm'hăl). Asherite; son of Japhlet (1 Ch 7:33).
binding and loosing. See *key.*
Binea (bĭn'ē-á). Descendant of Jonathan (1 Ch 8:37).
Binnui (bĭn'ū-ī, building). 1. Levite; father of Noadiah (Ez 8:33; 1 Esd 8:63 [KJ: Sabban; RV: Sabannus]). 2. One who divorced foreign wife (Ez 10:30). Balnuus (RSV: Belnuus) in 1 Esd 9:31. 3. Another who divorced foreign wife (Ez 10:38; 1 Esd 9:34 [KJ, RV: Bannus]). 4. See *Bani 7.* 5. See *Bani 4.*
bird. Clean and unclean birds mentioned (Lv 11:13-19; Dt 14:11-19). Charac-

teristics of eagle, ostrich, hawk, birds generally, mentioned (Jb 39:13-30; Mt 6:26). Birds trapped (Jb 18:8-10); eggs eaten (Dt 22:6; Is 10:14; Lk 11:12).
Birsha (bĭr'shá). King of Gomorrah (Gn 14:2).
birthright. See *first-born 1.*
Birzaith, Birzavith (bĭr-zā'ĭth, -vĭth). Town in Asher (1 Ch 7:31).
Bishlam (bĭsh'lăm). Persian official who complained to Artaxerxes about rebuilding of Jerusalem (Ez 4:7; 1 Esd 2:16 [KJ, RV: Belemus]).
bishop (G *episkopos*). 1. Classical: gods and men as overseers and governors. 2. LXX: superintendent, overseer (Nm 4:16) in religion, state, army (Ju 9:28; 2 K 12:11; 2 Ch 34:12, 17). 3. NT: alternative for presbyter (Tts 1:5, 7; 1 Ti 3:1; 4:14; 5:17, 19); applied to those who rule (Ro 12:8), supervise (Acts 20:17, 28; 1 Ptr 5:2), care for (Acts 20:28) church.
Bithiah (bĭ-thī'á, daughter of Lord). Daughter of Pharaoh; wife of Mered (1 Ch 4:18).
Bithron (bĭth'rŏn, gorge). KJ, RV: proper noun; ravine of Arabah. RSV: marching the whole forenoon (2 Sm 2:29).
Bithynia (bĭ-thĭn'ĭ-á). Country in NW Asia Minor; capital: Nicaea (Acts 16:7; 1 Ptr 1:1).
bitter, bitterness. 1. Opposite of sweet (Ex 15:23). 2. Sorrow; affliction (Ex 1:14; Jb 7:11). 3. Inward displeasure (Eph 4:31). 4. Pernicious; evil (2 Sm 2:26). 5. Hostile wickedness (Acts 8:23). 6. Wickedness which corrupts (Heb 12:15).
bitter herbs. Used in Passover feast to recall servitude in Egypt (Ex 12:8; Nm 9:11).
bittern (bĭt'ẽrn). H *qippod.* RV: porcupine. RSV: hedgehog (Is 14:23; 34:11 [RSV: porcupine]; Zph 2:14).
bitumen (bĭ-tū'men, KJ, RV: slime). Mineral pitch, or asphalt (Gn 11:3; 14:10; Ex 2:3. See Gn 6:14); used for sealing wood, bricks, etc., together. Bitumen pits found along Euphrates, Dead Sea, other places.
Biziothiah, Bizjothjah (bĭz-ĭ-ō-thī'á, -jŏth'já). Town of Judah (Jos 15:28). Perh same as Baalath-beer.
Biztha (bĭz'thá). Chamberlain of Ahasuerus (Est 1:10).
black. See *color.*
blain. Blister full of serum arising on skin (Ex 9:8-11. RSV: sore).
blasphemy (blăs'fē-mĭ). Speaking evil of God (Ps 74:10, 18; Is 52:5; Rv 16:9, 11, 21). Punished by stoning (Lv 24:16). False charges of blasphemy brought against Naboth (1 K 21:10-13), Stephen (Acts 6:11), Jesus (Mt 9:3; 26:65, 66).
blasphemy against the Holy Spirit. See *sin, unpardonable.*
Blastus (blăs'tus, sprout). Chamberlain of Herod Agrippa (Acts 12:20).
blemish. Any deformity; spot (Lv 21:18-20; 22:20-24).
blessing. 1. Blessing by God (2 Sm 6:11) or utterance by Him regarding future favor (Gn 1:22; 12:1-3). 2. Blessing by man; appeal to God to confer blessing on object and regarded as directly beneficial (Gn 12:2; 27:28, 29; Nm 23; 24). 3. Direct application of grace through Word (Gn 48:17-19; Lv 9:22; Nm 6:22-27; Mt 19:13; Lk 24:51). 4. Well-known benedictions: 1. Mizpah (Gn 31:49). 2. Aaronic (Nm 6:22-27). 3. Apostolic (2 Co 13:14).
blindness. Prevalent in Bible lands, hence blind beggars frequent (Mt 9:27; 12:22).

Some ancient tribes blinded their captives (Ju 16:21; 1 Sm 11:2). Kindness toward blind enjoined (Lv 19:14; Dt 27:18).

blood. Often made synonymous with life (Gn 9:4; Lv 17:11, 14; Dt 12:23). Eating of blood forbidden (Gn 9:4; Acts 15:20, 29). Without shedding blood there is no remission of sins (Heb 9:22; Lv 17:11). Blood used for life (Gn 9:6; Mt 27:25), race (Acts 17:26). "Blood of Christ" delivers from sin and death (1 Co 10:16; Eph 2:13; 1 Ptr 1:2, 19).

blood, issue of. Flowing of blood (as RSV: Lv 12:7), hemorrhage (as RSV: Mt 9:20).

bloodguilt. Guilt of murder (Ex 22:2, 3; Lv 17:4; 1 Sm 25:26, 33; Hos 12:14).

bloody flux. See *dysentery*.

bloody sweat. Christ in severe mental distress of Gethsemane perspired sweat as clots of blood (Lk 22:44).

blot. To obliterate or abolish. Used of removing sin (Is 44:22); removing men from God's people (Ps 69:28) or fellowship (Ex 32:32).

blue. See *color*.

Boanerges (bō-à-nûr'jĕz, sons of thunder). Surname given by Christ to James and John (Mk 3:17).

boar. Found wild in thickets of Jordan and on Lebanon range (Ps 80:13)

boats. In Palestine limited to small fishing (Mt 4:21; Mk 1:19), passenger (Mt 9:1; 14:13; Jn 6:17) vessels on Sea of Galilee and (possibly) ferryboats or small boats on swift Jordan. Solomon built fleet of ships at Ezion-geber on Red Sea (1 K 9:26) and fleet which sailed Mediterranean with that of Hiram (1 K 10:22; 2 Ch 9:21). Jehoshaphat and Ahaziah later built ships at Ezion-geber (2 Ch 20:35-37). Frequent references to ships of other nations. Luke's description of ships is source material on shipping (Acts 27; 28. See Rv 18:17).

Boaz (bō'ăz. KJ in NT: Booz). 1. Bethlehemite kinsman and husband of Ruth (Ru; Mt 1:5). 2. Left pillar in porch of Solomon's temple (1 K 7:21; 2 Ch 3:17; Jer 52:21).

Boccas (bŏk'ăs). See *Bukki* 2.

Bocheru (bō'ke-rōō). Son of Azel (1 Ch 8:38; 9:44).

Bochim (bō'kĭm, weepers). Place near Gilgal where Israelites repented and wept (Ju 2:1-5).

body. 1. OT, various words (bones, bowels, belly), esp flesh. 2. NT (*soma*), corpse (Mt 14:12; Mk 15:43; Lk 23:52). 3. Living body (Mt 26:12; Mk 5:29; Ro 12:4; 1 Co 5:3); external appearance (2 Co 10:10); contrasted with inner man (1 Co 5:3). Medium for reception and possession of life (Ro 4:19; 2 Co 4:7. See Lv 17:11, 14; Dn 7:15) through which psyche operates (2 Co 5:10; 1 Co 9:27; Heb 13:3). 4. Sinfulness of human nature brought about and manifested by body (Ro 6:6, 12, 13; 1 Co 6:18; Col 1:22; 2:11; Heb 10:22). 5. Joined to Spirit (*pneuma*) in believers (Ro 8:10, 13; 1 Co 6:19, 20) for new life and its manifestation (2 Co 4:7, 10; Gl 6:17). 6. By participation in Him (1 Co 1:9) believers are one body with Christ (Ro 12:5; 1 Co 10:17; 12:27; Eph 5:30), into whom they are baptized (1 Co 12:13). His Spirit manifests Himself through this body (Eph 4:3, 4). 7. See *Lord's Supper*.

Bohan (bō'hăn, covering?). Descendant of Reuben; stone on Judah-Benjamin boundary named after him (Jos 15:6; 18:17).

boil. Inflamed ulcer (Ex 9:8-11; Dt 28:27, 35 [KJ: botch]); symptom in leprosy (Lv 13:18-20); disease of Hezekiah (2 K 20:7) and Job (Jb 2:7). See also *disease*.

bone. Used to show close association (Gn 2:23; Ju 9:2; 2 Sm 19:12).

bonnet. Headdress for men (Eze 44:18. RV: tire. RSV: turban) and women (Is 3:20. RV: headtire. RSV: headdress).

Book. See *writing*.

Book of the Chronicles of the Kings of Israel (Judah). Source frequently quoted in 1, 2 K.

booth. Temporary hut, usually of boughs (Gn 33:17; Lv 23:34; Jb 27:18; Is 1:8). See also *homes*.

booty. Spoils of war (Gn 14:11, 12, 16; Nm 31:9, 26-52). At conquest of Canaan all living things to be destroyed (Nm 33:52). Portion of spoils given to Levites (Nm 31:26-47); shared with baggage guards (1 Sm 30:21-25).

Booz. (bō'ŏz). See *Boaz*.

Borashan (bôr-ăsh'ăn). See *Chor-ashan*.

Borith (bō'rĭth). See *Bukki* 2.

Boscath (bŏs'kăth). See *Bozkath*.

bosom. See *lap*.

Bosor (bō'sôr). See *Beor*.

Bosora (bŏs'ô-rà). Town of Gilead (1 Mac 5:26, 27); either Bozrah or, more likely, the Roman Bostra.

boss. Knob on shield or buckler (Jb 15:26).

botch. See *boil*.

bottle. Vessel of skin (Jb 32:19; Mt 9:17) or earthenware (Jer 19:1, 10, 11). Lachrymatory (Ps 56:8). See *vineyard* 3.

bottomless pit. See *abyss*.

bow. See *archery*.

bow. Mode of salutation by bending one knee, bending head forward (Gn 23:7; 33:3; 43:28; 1 K 1:53; 2:19).

bowels. KJ translates several H words and G *splanchna* to designate emotions (Gn 43:30; Is 16:11; Ph 1:8; Cl 3:12. RV, RSV: heart, soul, affection, compassion).

bowl. See *homes; pommel; trade* 6.

box. Flask for holding oil or perfume (2 K 9:1, 3 [RV: vial. RSV: flask]; Mk 14:3 [RV: cruse. RSV: jar]; Is 3:20 [KJ: tablet]). See *bag*.

box tree. KJ, RV for H *te'asshur* (Is 41:19; 60:13) from which boat seats (Eze 27:6. KJ: ivory. RSV: pine) and tablets were made (2 Esd 14:24). RSV: pine. RV margin once: cypress.

Bozez (bō'zĕz, shining). One of two crags near Gibeah; the other called Seneh (1 Sm 14:4, 5).

Bozkath (bŏz'kăth, craggy). Town in S Judea near Lachish (Jos 15:39; 2 K 22:1 [KJ: Boscath]).

Bozrah (bŏz'rà). 1. City of Edom (Gn 36:33; 1 Ch 1:44; Is 34:6; 63:1). Amos (1:12) and Jeremiah (49:13, 22) predicted its destruction. Modern Buseirah. 2. City of Moab (Jer 48:24).

bracelet. Wrist and arm ornament worn by both sexes (Gn 24:22, 30; Eze 16:11). Badge of royalty (2 Sm 1:10. RSV: armlet). KJ: bracelet in Gn 38:18, 25 (RV, RSV: cord) and Ex 35:22 (RV, RSV: brooches). See *armlet*.

bramble. Ju 9:14, 15. See *thorns and thistles*.

branch. Title for the Messiah as offspring of David (Jer 23:5; 33:15; Zch 3:8; 6:12). Branch is symbol of prosperity (Is 49:22. See Eze 17:3) and productivity (Ps 80:11).

brand. Firebrand (as RSV, Is 7:4) or torch (as RSV, Ju 15:5).

brass, brazen. See *copper*.

brazen serpent. Copper, or bronze, serpent erected by Moses in wilderness. When people were bitten by fiery serpents, they looked at it and were saved from death (Nm 21:1-9). Type of Christ (Jn 3:14).

brazier (brā'zhĕr). See *hearth; homes* 5.

bread. See *food 1; 2.*

Breaking of Bread. See *Lord's Supper.*

breastplate (RSV: breastpiece). 1. Sacred article of dress worn by high priest (Ex 28; 29:5; 35:9, 27; 39). 2. Armor to protect body in battle (1 K 22:34; Is 59:17; Rv 9:9). 3. Figuratively, righteousness (Is 59:17; Eph 6:14), faith and love (1 Th 5:8).

breath. See *soul; spirit.*

breeches. See *dress.*

brickkiln. Kiln for enclosing bricks while they are burned (2 Sm 12:31; Nah 3:14 [RV margin, RSV: brickmould (mold)]; Jer 43:9 [RV: brickwork. RSV: pavement]).

bride, bridegroom. See *marriage.*

brier. See *thorns and thistles.*

brigandine (brig'an-dēn). KJ in Jer 46:4 (RV, RSV: coat of mail).

brimstone. Sulphur (Gn 19:24). Often figuratively for destruction, punishment (Jb 18:15; Ps 11:6; Is 34:9; Rv 21:8).

bronze. See *copper.*

brooches. Ornaments of women (Ex 35:22. KJ: bracelets).

brook. Small stream like Kishon (1 K 18: 40) and Kidron (2 Sm 15:23). Usually stream which flows only in rainy season (Dt 2:13).

broom. Bush with many, almost leafless, branches and pinkish white flowers (1 K 19: 4, 5; Jb 30:4; Ps 120:4. KJ: juniper. RV: juniper, except in Jb 30:4).

brother. 1. Kinsman of same parents (Gn 27:6) or of same father (Gn 38:1) or mother (Ju 8:19). 2. Relative, such as nephew (Gn 14:16), cousin (Mt 12:46). 3. Ally (Am 1:9); coreligionist (Acts 9:17: 1 Co 6:6), often in plural of Christians (Mt 23:8; Ro 1:13). 4. Of same tribe (Nm 8:26; Neh 3:1). 5. Fellow countryman (Ju 14:3; Mt 5:47). 6. Friend or companion (Jb 6:15; Neh 5:10). 7. Peer (Mt 23:8). 8. Someone greatly beloved (2 Sm 1:26). 9. All men (Gn 9:5; Mt 5:22; 18:35).

brotherly affection, kindness, love (G *philadelphia*). Affection for all mankind (Ro 12:10; Heb 13:1; 2 Ptr 1:7).

brothers of the Lord. James, Joses, Simon, and Judas called Lord's brothers (Mt 13: 55); sisters referred to (Mt 13:56). Many regard these as Jesus' full brothers, others as cousins, children of levirate marriage, or children of Joseph by former wife.

brother's wife. See *levirate marriage.*

bruise. Used figuratively for hurting, or inflicting fatal injury (Gn 3:15). Also indicates inability or weakness (2 K 18:21; Is 42:3; Lk 4:18).

buck. See *roebuck.*

buckler. See *armor; arms.*

buffet. To maltreat harshly (Mt 26:67; 1 Co 4:11; 2 Co 12:7; 1 Ptr 2:20).

Bukki (bŭk'ī). 1. Prince of Dan (Num 34: 22). 2. Descendant of Aaron (1 Ch 6:5, 51; Ez 7:4). Borith in 2 Esd 1:2. KJ, RV: Boccas in 1 Esd 8:2.

Bukkiah (bu-kī'á). Levite; leader of 6th division of musicians (1 Ch 25:4, 13).

Bul. See *time* 4.

bull, bullock. H *shor,* generic for ox, cattle (Ps 22:12); bullock in Is 65:25; cow in Eze 4:15; oxen in Gn 12:16. "Wild bull" and "wild ox" (KJ) correctly "antelope" in RV, RSV (Dt 14:5; Is 51:20). Ox used for plowing (Dt 22:10), threshing (Dt 25:4), draught (Nm 7:3), burden bearing (1 Ch 12:40), beef (Dt 14:4), sacrifices (1 K 1:9).

bulrush. 1. H *gome'* (Ex 2:3; Is 18:2 [RV, RSV: papyrus]) includes papyrus and related marsh plants. 2. H *'agmon.* Swamp plant translated reed, rush (Is 19:15).

bulwark. Figuratively for God's salvation (Is. 26:1) and church in its relationship to truth (1 Tí 3:15. KJ, RV: ground).

Bunah (bū'ná, prudence). Descendant of Judah (1 Ch 2:25).

Bunni (bŭn'ī, built). 1. Levite who made confession (Neh 9:4); afterwards co-covenanter (Neh 10:15). 2. Levite; father of Shemaiah (Neh 11:15).

burden. 1. Heavy load (literal or figurative. Ex 23:5; Nm 11:11; Mt 11:30). 2. See *oracle.*

burial. Body washed (Acts 9:37), wrapped in cloth or closely bound in bands (Mt 27:59; Jn 11:44), anointed (if wealthy) with spices and perfumes (Jn 12:7; 19:39; Jer 34:5), carried on bier to grave (2 Sm 3:31; Lk 7:14), cavity in ground but usually cave or cavity cut in rocks (Gn 25:9, 10; Mt 27:60). Friends joined in lamentation (Mk 5:38); mourners even hired (Jer 9:17).

burnt offering. See *sacrifice.*

bushel. See *measures 2h.*

butler. Officer of royal household in charge of wines and drinking vessels (Gn 40; 41:9). Also called cupbearer (1 K 10:5; 2 Ch 9:4; Neh 1:11).

butter. See *food 8.*

Buz (bŭz, contempt). 1. Son of Nahor (Gn 22:21); also tribe of Arabia descended from him (Jer. 25:23). 2. Gadite (1 Ch 5:14).

Buzi (bū'zī). Father of Ezekiel (Eze 1:3).

Buzite (bū'zīt). Of the tribe of Buz (Jb 32:2, 6).

bypath, byway. Byways were traveled to escape danger (Ju 5:6). Bypaths (Jer 18:15. KJ: paths), figuratively, departure from way of God.

byword (bī'wûrd). Object of taunt; often for H *sh:ninah,* as Dt 28:37; or *mashal,* as Jb 17:6.

C

cab. See *measures 2b.*

Cabbon (kăb'on). Village in plain of Judah (Jos 15:40) perhaps same as Machbenah (1 Ch 2:49).

Cabul (kā'bul, fettered land). 1. Town of Asher 9 mi SE of Acre (Jos 19:27). Modern Kabûl. 2. District in N Naphtali given to Hiram by Solomon (1 K 9:13).

Caddis (kăd'is). See *Gaddi.*

Cades (kā'dēz). See *Kedesh 3.*

Cades-Barne (-bär'nē). See *Kadesh 1.*

Cadmiel (kăd'mī-ĕl). See *Kadmiel 1; 2.*

Caesar (sē'zēr). Title of Roman emperors after Julius Caesar (Mt 22:17; Lk 23:2; Jn 19:15; Acts 17:7; 25:11, 12, 21). Emperors directly or indirectly mentioned in NT: Augustus (Lk 2:1), Tiberius (Lk 3:1; 20:22), Claudius (Acts 11:28), Nero (Acts 25:8).

Caesarea (sĕs-á-rē'á, for Caesar). City c 23 mi S of Mt Carmel; built (25-13 BC) by Herod the Great; Roman capital of Palestine; evangelized by Philip (Acts 8:40; 21:8); home of Cornelius (Acts 10:1, 24; 11:11); prominent city in life of Paul (Acts 9:30; 18:22; 21:8, 16; 23:23, 33; 25). Modern Kaisariyeh.

Caesarea Philippi (fĭ-lĭp'ĭ). City at foot of Mt Hermon, enlarged by Philip the Tetrarch and called Caesarea. Here Peter's confession was made (Mt 16:13-20; Mk 8:27-30).

cage. 1. Basket for birds (Jer 5:27. RSV: basket). 2. Prisoner cage (Eze 19:9. KJ: ward). 3. Haunt (Rv 18:2. RV: hold. RSV: haunt).

Caiaphas (kā'yȧ-fȧs). Appointed high priest by Valerius Gratus (*Ant* XVIII, ii, 2); high priest during public ministry of Jesus (Lk 3:2); conceived (Jn 11:49-53; 18:14), plotted (Mt 26:3-5), and participated in condemnation of Jesus (Mt 26: 57; Jn 18:28). Took part in trial of Peter and John (Acts 4:6-22). Deposed by Vitellius, 36 AD (*Ant* XVIII, iv, 3).

Cain (kān, acquisition, spear). 1. Oldest son of Adam; murdered Abel (Gn 4). 2. See *Kain 2.*

Cainan (kȧ-ī'nȧn. RV, RSV: Kenan in OT). 1. Son of Enos (Gn 5:9-14; 1 Ch 1:2 [KJ: Kenan]; Lk 3:37, 38). 2. Son of Arphaxad (Lk 3:36).

cake. Loaf or wafer. See *food 1; 2.*

Calah (kā'lä). City of Assyria; built by Nimrod (Gn 10:11).

Calamolalus (kăl-ȧ-mŏl'ȧ-lŭs). Probably conflation of Lod and Hadid (1 Esd 5:22. RSV: other Elam. See Ez 2:31, 33; Neh 7:34, 37).

calamus (kăl'ȧ-mŭs, reed, cane). Sweet-smelling plant used in anointing oil and sacrifices (Ex 30:23 [RSV: aromatic cane]; SS 4:14; Eze 27:19). Sweet cane in Is 43:24; Jer 6:20.

Calcol (kăl'kŏl, sustenance). Wise man; son of Mahol (1 K 4:31 [KJ: Chalcol]); but son of Zerah in 1 Ch 2:6.

caldron (kôl'drŭn). Vessel for boiling meat (1 Sm 2:14; 2 Ch 35:13; Jb 41:20 [RV, RSV: burning bushes]; Mi 3:3). Figuratively, Eze 11:3, 7, 11.

Caleb (kā'lĕb, dog). 1. Son of Jephunneh (Nm 32:12; Jos 15:17; 1 Ch 4:15); one of 12 spies sent into Canaan; gave faithful report with Joshua; entered Holy Land (Jos 14; 15; Nm 13:14). 2. Son of Hezron (1 Ch 2:18, 42); ancestor of Hur and Bezalel (1 Ch 2:19). Chelubai in 1 Ch 2:9. Carmi in 1 Ch 4:1. 3. Caleb's district (1 Sm 30:14).

Caleb-ephratah, -ephrathah (ĕf'rȧ-tȧ, -thä. RSV: Caleb went in to Ephrathah). KJ, RV consider it a place name; RSV, name of Hezron's wife (1 Ch 2:19, 24).

calendar. See *time.*

calf. Young bull or cow. Fatted calf a luxury (Gn 18:7; 1 Sm 28:24; Am 6:4; Lk 15:23). Aaron made golden calf as idol (Ex 32:4). Jeroboam instituted calf worship at Bethel, and Dan (1 K 12:28, 29). Calf worship denounced (Hos 8; 10; 13).

Calitas (kăl'ĭ-tȧs). See *Kelita.*

call, calling. See *vocation.*

Callisthenes (kȧ-lĭs'thē-nēz). Friend of Nicanor (2 Mac 8:33).

Calneh (kăl'nĕ). 1. KJ, RV: city of Nimrod (Gn 10:10. RSV: all of them). 2. City mentioned in Amos (6:2). Canneh in Eze 27:23.

Calno (kăl'nō). City which vainly resisted Assyria (Is 10:9).

Calphi (kăl'fī). See *Chalphi.*

Calvary (kăl'vȧ-rĭ. KJ: Lk 23:33. RV: The skull. RSV: The Skull). Latin (*calvaria*) corresponding to H Golgotha (Mt 27:33;

Mk 15:22; Jn 19:17), where Christ was crucified; near His grave (Jn 19:41); outside city gate (Mt 28:11; Heb 13:11-13). Name may be due to shape of elevation or because of executions there.

camel. One-humped camel, either draught animal (2 K 8:9) or dromedary (Is 66:20 RSV). Used for carriage and source of wealth (Gn 12:16; Ju 7:12; 2 Ch 14:15; Jb 1:3; 42:12; Is 30:6). Unclean (Lv 11:4). Hair used for clothing (2 K 1:8; Zch 13:4; Mt 3:4). Used figuratively (Mt 19:24; 23:24).

camel's thorn. See *aspalathus.*

Camon (kā'mon). See *Kamon.*

camp, encampment (H *mahaneh*, place of pitching a tent). Station of party (Gn 32:21), body of people (Ex 14:9), or army (1 Sm 4:1, 5; 2 K 7:7). Camp of Israelites kept clean (Dt 23:9-14) and orderly (Nm 1:47—2:34; 3:14-39).

camphire (kăm'fīr). See *henna.*

Cana (kā'nȧ). Town in Galilee near Nazareth (Jn 2:1-11; 4:46; 21:2).

Canaan (kā'nan). 1. Son of Ham (Gn 10: 6, 15; 1 Ch 1:8, 13). 2. Country between Jordan and Mediterranean (Ex 6:4; Lv 25:38; Nm 34:3-12). Originally applied to Phoenician coast. Called Holy Land after captivity (Zch 2:12). KJ: Chanaan in Acts 7:11; 13:19; Jdth 5:3. Kinahhi in Tell el Amarna Letters.

Canaanite (kā'nȧn-īt). 1. Inhabitant of Canaan (Gn 10:18-20; 13:7; 15:21; Nm 13:29; Jos 11:3; 24:11). Canaanites had developed arts and sciences. Language Phoenician and Ugaritic; deities immoral (El, Baal, Anath, Astarte, Asherah). 2. See *Zealot.*

canal. Irrigation canals of Egypt referred to in Ex 7:19; 8:5 (KJ: rivers. RV: streams); Is 19:6 (KJ, RV: rivers).

Cananaean (kā'nȧ-nē'ȧn). See *Zealots.*

Candace (kăn'dȧ-sē). Ethiopian queen (Acts 8:27).

candle, candlestick. See *lamp.*

cane. See *calamus.*

cankerworm. Probably undeveloped locust (Jl 1:4; 2:25; Nah 3:15, 16; also RV in Ps 105:34; Jer 51:27. RSV: hopping locust, hopper, locust).

Canneh (kăn'ĕ). See *Calneh.*

canon. Collection of books of Bible. Collection of OT books completed by NT times (Ro 3:2; 1 Mac 4:46; 9:27; 12:9; 2 Mac 2:13-15). Books of NT canonized gradually. Distinction between homologoumena (universally recognized) and antilegomena (genuineness doubted by some) was preserved. 39 OT and 27 NT books.

Canticles (kăn'tĭ-k'lz). See *Song of Songs.*

Capernaum (kȧ-pûr'nȧ-um, town of Nahum). City on NW coast of Sea of Galilee (Mt 4:13; Jn 6:24) which had customs station (Mt 9:9) and synagog (Lk 7:5). Headquarters of Jesus (Mt 9:1; Mk 2:1).

Capharsalama (căf-är-săl'ȧ-mä). Battlefield (1 Mac 7:31).

Caphenatha (kȧ-fĕn'ȧ-thä). See *Chaphenatha.*

Caphthorim (kăf'thō-rĭm). See *Caphtorim.*

Caphtor (kăf'tôr). Place from which Philistines came (probably Crete. Dt 2:23; Jer 47:4; Am 9:7).

Caphtorim (kăf'tō-rĭm). Inhabitants of Caphtor (Gn 10:14; Dt 2:23; 1 Ch 1:12 [KJ: Caphthorim]).

capital. 1. Ruling city (Est 1:2. KJ, RV: palace). 2. Decorative crown of candlesticks, pillars, etc. (KJ: knop or chapiter. Ex 25:33; 1 K 7:16-22).

Cappadocia (kăp-à-dō'shĭ-à). Province in E part of Asia Minor (Acts 2:9; 1 Ptr 1:1).

captain. Military title applied to officers ranging from commander-in-chief (Gn 21:22. RSV: commander) to commander of body guard (Gn 37:36). "Captain of the temple" (Acts 4:1) was in charge of temple guard. Christ is Captain of our salvation (Heb 2:10; see Jos 5:14).

captive. Prisoners of war treated with cruelty (Ju 1:7; 8:7; 2 Sm 12:31; 2 Ch 28:8-15) and indignity (1 K 20:32; Jos 10:24).

captivity. Bondage to enemies, especially in foreign land. Assyrians and Babylonians practiced wholesale deportation. Captivity of Ten Tribes was long process by Tiglath-pileser (2 K 15:29; 1 Ch 5:26), Shalmaneser (2 K 17:3, 5), Sargon II, and Esarhaddon. Deportation of Judah also was by stages (2 K 18:13; 24:14; 25:11; 2 Ch 36:20). Ezra and Nehemiah describe return of captives. Figuratively, Christ is described as leading His enemies captive (Eph 4:8).

Carabasion (kăr-à-bā'zĭ-ŏn). See *Meremoth 1.*

caravan (kăr'à-văn). Company of traveling merchants, pilgrims, etc. Animals used: camels, asses, horses (Gn 37:25 [KJ: company. RV: traveling company]; Ju 5:6; Is 21:13 [KJ, RV: traveling companies]). Regular routes were followed (Ju 8:11 [KJ, RV: way of them that dwelt in tents]; Jb 6:18, 19 [KJ: paths]), famous one leading from Damascus across Esdraelon to Mediterranean.

carbuncle (kär'bŭng-k'l). Precious gem; 3d stone in 1st row of high priest's breastpiece (Ex 28:17; 39:10; Eze 28:13; Is 54:12).

Carcas (kär'kăs. RSV: Carkas). Chamberlain of Ahasuerus (Est 1:10).

carcass. The Jews were unclean after touching carcass of unclean animal, or clean animal which had died (Lv 11; Dt 14:8). Contact with corpse also rendered unclean (Nm 6; 9:10; 19:11-19).

Carchamis, Carchemish (kär'kà-mĭs, kär'ke-mĭsh). Hittite city on bank of Euphrates (2 Ch 35:20 [KJ: Charchemish]; Is 10:9; Jer 46:2; 1 Esd 1:25 [KJ: Carchamis]), where Babylon defeated Egypt (605 BC).

care (RSV: anxiety, fearfulness, etc.). 1. OT, anxious foreboding (Eze 4:16; 12:18). 2. NT, concern with (Mk 4:38); anxious concern for (Lk 10:41; 1 Co 7:32). 3. NT warnings against care (Mt 6:25-34; Ph 4:6; 1 Ptr 5:7) are against false orientation (Mk 4:19; Lk 21:34; 1 Co 7:32-35) and anxiety from which trust in God frees us (1 Co 7:29-31; Ph 4:6; 1 Ptr 5:7).

Careah (kà-rē'à). See *Kareah.*

Caria (kā'rĭ-à). SW province of Asia Minor (1 Mac 15:23). Cities: Cnidus and Miletus.

Carites (kăr'ĭ-tēz). See *Cherethites.*

Carkas (kär'kăs). See *Carcas.*

carme (kär'mē). See *Harim 1.*

Carmel (kär'mĕl, garden). 1. Translated as productive field (Is 10:18; Jer 48:33. KJ erroneously makes H word proper noun in 2 K 19:23; 2 Ch 26:10). 2. Mountain (c 1,700 ft) in Asher; SW boundary of Esdraelon; juts into Mediterranean (Jos 19:26; 1 K 18:17-40; 2 K 2:25; Is 33:9; 35:2; Jer 50:19). 3. Town in Judah (Jos 15:55); home of Nabal (1 Sm 25:2-44); 7 mi SE of Hebron.

Carmi (kär'mī, vinedress). 1. Son of Reuben; progenitor of Carmites (Gn 46:9;

Ex 6:14; Nm 26:6). 2. Descendant of Judah; father of Achan (Jos 7:1; 1 Ch 2:7). 3. See *Caleb 2.*

Carmites (kär'mĭts). Descendants of Carmi 1 (Nm 26:6).

Carnaim (kär'nā-ĭm). See Karnaim.

carnal. See *flesh 6.*

carnelian (kär-nĕl'yăn, H *odem;* G *sardios*). Red or brownish-red gem (Eze 28:13; Rv 4:3; 21:20. KJ, RV: sardius).

Carnion (kär'nĭ-on). See *Karnaim.*

carpenter. Artificer in wood; general term for builder (2 Sm 5:11; 2 K 12:11; 22:6; 1 Ch 14:1; 22:15; 2 Ch 24:12; 34:11; Ez 3:7; Is 44:13). Joseph, husband of Mary, was carpenter (Mt 13:55; Mk 6:3). See *trade 5.*

carpet (RV, RSV in Ju 5:10; RSV in Eze 27:24). See *homes; trade 2.*

Carpus (kär'pus). Paul's friend (2 Ti 4:13).

carriage. KJ for things carried (Ju 18:21; 1 Sm 17:22; Is 10:28; 46:1; Acts 21:15).

Carshena (kär'shē-nà). Persian prince (Est 1:14).

cart. Two-wheeled vehicle for transporting people or freight, usually drawn by oxen (1 Sm 6:7-16; Am 2:13).

carve, carving. Art of engraving, sculpturing, or carving in materials as wood, stone, ivory (Ex 31:5; 35:33; 1 K 6; 2 Ch 2:7-14; Ps 74:6; Zch 3:9).

casement. See *homes; lattice.*

Casiphia (kà-sĭf'ĭ-à). Place where Levites settled during captivity (Ez 8:17).

Casluhim (kăs'lŭ-hĭm). Mizraite people (Gn 10:14; 1 Ch 1:12).

Casphon, Casphor (kăs'fŏn, kăs'fôr). See *Chaspho.*

Caspin, Caspis (kăs'pĭn, kăs'pĭs). City taken by Judas Maccabee (2 Mac 12:13, 14). Perhaps Chaspho.

cassia (kăsh'ĭ-à, H *qiddah*). Aromatic wood; used in anointing oil; probably flavor of cinnamon (Ex 30:24; Ps 45:8; Eze 27:19).

castanets (kăs'tà-nĕtz, KJ: cornets). Pair of small, spoon-shaped cymbals (2 Sm 6:5).

castle. 1. Fortified building or stronghold (Neh 7:2 [KJ: palace]; Pr 18:19). 2. Tower of Antonia in Jerusalem (Acts 21:34, 37; 22:24; 23:10, 16, 32. RSV: barracks).

Castor and Pollux (kăs'tĕr, pŏl'ŭks). See *Twin Brothers.*

cat. Mentioned in Bar 6:22.

caterpillar. Species of locust, or undeveloped locust (1 K 8:37; 2 Ch 6:28; Ps 78:46; Is 33:4).

Cathua (kà-thū'à). See *Giddel 1.*

cattle. Domestic bovine animals such as horned cattle, horses, asses, camels, sheep, and goats (Gn 1:24; 25; 13:2; Ex 12:29; 34:19; Nm 20:19; 32:16; Ps 50:10; Jb 1:3).

Cauda (kô'dà. KJ: Clauda). Small island near SW shore of Crete (Acts 27:16). Modern Gozzo.

caul (kôl). 1. Net for woman's hair (Is 3:18. RSV: headband. KJ, RV margin: networks). 2. Membrane, or inner lining of belly, which covers stomach and part of liver (Ex 29:13, 22; Lv 3:4, 10, 15. RSV: appendage). 3. Covering of heart, or breast (Hos 13:8. RSV: breast).

cave. Hollow place or cavern frequently found in limestone of Palestine. Used as dwellings (Gn 19:30; 1 K 19:9), as places of refuge (Gn 6:2; 1 Sm 14:11), for burial (Gn 23:1-20; 49:29; Mt 27:60; Jn 11:38). See *homes 1.*

cedar. Usually cedar of Lebanon; its timber extensively used for palaces, temples (2 Sm 5:11; 1 K 5:5, 6; 7:1-12; Ez 3:7),

idols (Is 44:14, 15), ship masts (Eze 27:5). Probably different variety of cedar in Lv 14:4; Nm 19:6; 24:6; Eze 31:8.
Cedron (sē'dron). See *Kidron; Kidron, Brook.*
Ceilan (sē'lăn). See *Kilan.*
ceiling. Hebrew temple ceiling was of cedar (1 K 6:9-15).
cellar. Underground storage place (1 Ch 27:27, 28).
Celosyria (sē-lŏ-sĭr'ĭ-á). See *Coelesyria.*
Cenchrea, Cenchreae (sĕn-krē'á, sĕn'krē-ē). Port of Corinth (Acts 18:18); had Christian church (Ro 16:1).
Cendebaeus, Cendebeus (sĕn-dē-bē'us). Syrian general (1 Mac 15:38).
censer. Vessel for burning incense. Censers for tabernacle were of copper (Lv 16:12; Nm 16:39), those for temple of gold (1 K 7:50; 2 Ch 4:22. Cf Rv 8:3, 5). "Censer" (KJ) of Heb 9:4 is better rendered "altar of incense" (RSV).
census (RSV. KJ: sum of, number). In OT several censuses recorded (Ex 38:26; Nm 1:2, 3; 26:51; 1 Ch 21:1-6; 27:24; 1 K 5:15; 2 Ch 2:17, 18; Ez 2:64). NT mentions Roman census in Lk 2:1 (KJ: taxed; RSV: enrolled) and Acts 5:37 (KJ: taxing).
centurion (sĕn-tū'rĭ-un, hundred). Roman officer in command of 100 soldiers (Mt 8:5; Mk 15:39; Lk 7:1-10; Acts 10:1).
Cephas (sē'făs, rock). Aramaic for Peter (Jn 1:42; 1 Co 1:12).
Ceras (sē'răs). See *Keros.*
cereal offering (RV: meal offering; KJ: meat offering). Offering of fine flour, salt, and (except in sin offerings) olive oil (Lv 2:1, 4, 13, 14; 7:13-37; 1 Ch 21:23); contained no meat.
Cetab (sē'tăb). See *Ketab.*
Chabris (kā'brĭs). Ruler of Bethulia (Jdth 6:15).
Chadias, Chadiasai, Chadiasans (kā'dĭ-ăs, kăd-ĭ-ā'sī, -ā'săns). Listed in 1 Esd 5:20.
Chaereas (kē'rē-ăs. KJ: Chereas). Commander at Gazara (Gezer); defeated by Judas Maccabeus (2 Mac 10:32-38).
chaff (chăf). 1. H *mois,* refuse of winnowed grain (Jb 21:18; Ps 1:4; Is 17:13; Hos 13:3; Zph 2:2). 2. H *hashash,* dry grass (as in RV, RSV. Is 5:24). 3. H *teben,* straw (as RV, RSV. Jer 23:28). 4. Figuratively, that which is worthless or evil (Jer 13:24 [KJ, RV: stubble]; Ps 1:4; Mt 3:12).
chains. Used as badges of office (Gn 41:42; Eze 16:11; Dn 5:7), ornaments (Pr 1:9; Is 3:20), fetters (Is 45:14; Jer 40:1; Nah 3:10; Mk 5:4; Acts 12:6). Figuratively: oppression, punishment (Lm 3:7; Ps 73:6; 149:8).
chalcedony (kăl-sĕd'ō-nĭ). Perhaps agate (as RSV. Rv 21:19).
Chalcol (kăl'kŏl). See *Calcol.*
Chaldea (kăl-dē'á). Originally Babylonia on Persian Gulf; later, practically all of Babylonia (Gn 10:10; 11:31; Jb 1:17; Is 48:20; Jer 50:10). See also *Leb-kamai.*
Chaldeans, Chaldees (kăl-dē'ánz, -dēz'). Chaldeans existed 1000 BC. In 8th c BC Chaldean kings conquered and ruled Babylon and began to extend their rule (2 K 24:2; 25; Is 13:19-22; Jer 21:4-14; Dn 1:4). Chaldeans noted as astronomers (Dn 2:2; 4:7).
chalkstone. Limestone rock (Is 27:9) used to make mortar. See *lime.*
Chalphi (kăl'fī. KJ: Calphi). Father of Judas, captain of Jonathan Maccabaeus (1 Mac 11:70).
chamber. Room of house (Gn 43:30; Ps 19:5; Mk 14:14). Figuratively, heaven

(Ps 104:3), place of earnest prayer (Is 26:20). "Chamber of imagery" (Eze 8:12) is "room of pictures" in RSV.
chambering. Debauchery (as RSV, Ro 13:13).
chamberlain (chăm'bēr-lĭn). Confidential and influential officer of a ruler (2 K 23:11; Est 1:10; Acts 12:20).
chameleon (ká-mē'lē-un). 1. Meaning of H *qoah* (Lv 11:30) is uncertain. RV, RSV: land crocodile. 2. H *tinshemeth* (Lv 11:30. KJ: mole).
chamois (shăm'ĭ). See *mountain sheep.*
Chanaan (kā'năn). See *Canaan.*
chancellor (chán'se-lēr). Title applied to Rehum (Ez 4:8. RSV: commander).
Channuneus, Chanuneus (kăn-û-nē'us. RSV: Hananiah). In 1 Esd 8:48, where Ez 8:19 has Merari.
chaos. Disorder in the beyond of death (Jb 10:22. KJ, RV: without any order); confusion (Is 24:10; 34:11; 45:18. KJ, RV: waste, confusion, etc.).
Chaphenatha (ká-fĕn'á-thá. KJ: Caphenatha). Probably portion of E wall of Jerusalem (1 Mac 12:37).
chapiter. See *capital* 2.
chapman. Merchant, peddler (1 K 10:15; 2 Ch 9:14. RSV: trader).
Charaathalan, Charaathalar (kăr-á-ăth'á-lăn, -lär). Perhaps Cherub, Addan (as RSV and RV margin. 1 Esd 5:36).
Characa (kăr'á-ká). See *Charax.*
Charashim (kăr'á-shĭm). See *Ge-harashim.*
Charax (kăr'ăx). Place mentioned in 2 Mac 12:17 (KJ: Characa).
Charchemish (kär'kē-mĭsh). See *Carchemish.*
charcoal. See *coal.*
Charcus (kär'kus). See *Barkos.*
Charea (kā'rē-á). See *Harsha.*
charger. 1. Deep dish or receptacle (Nm 7:13-85; Ez 1:9. RSV: plate, basin. 2. Platter (Mt 14:8, 11; Mk 6:25, 28. RSV: platter). 3. Horse (Nah 2:3. KJ: fir tree. RV: spear).
chariot. Two-wheeled vehicle for travel and war (Gn 41:43; 46:29; 1 K 18:44; 2 K 5:9; Acts 8:28). Used by enemies of Israel (Ex 14:7; Jos 11:4; Ju 4:3; 1 Sm 13:5) and by Israel from David on (2 Sm 8:4; 1 K 9:19; 10:26; 22:34; 2 K 9:16; Is 31:1).
charity. See *love.*
Charme (kär'mē). See *Harim* 1.
charmer. See *magic.*
Charmis (kär'mĭs). Ruler of Bethulia (Jdth 6:15).
Charran (kăr'ăn). See *Haran.*
Chaseba (kăs'ē-bá. RSV: Chezib). Listed in 1 Esd 5:31.
Chaspho (kăs'fō. RV: Casphor). City in Gilead (1 Mac 5:26 [KJ: Casphor], 36 [KJ: Casphon]). Perh Caspis.
chastisement (chăs'tĭz-ment. RSV: discipline; chastening). Action for instruction *(paideia)* and correction (Dt 8:5; Pr 13:24; 19:18; 1 Co 11:32; Eph 6:4); not punishment for sin.
Chebar (kē'bär). River of Chaldea on whose banks Ezekiel had visions (Eze 1:1, 3).
Chedorlaomer (kĕd-or-lā-ō'mēr, servant of god Lagamar). King of Elam against whom Abraham fought (Gn 14).
cheek. To strike on cheek regarded as insult (1 K 22:24; Jb 16:10; Ps 3:7; Mt 5:39; Lk 6:29).
cheese. See *food* 8
Chelal (kē'lăl, completion). Divorced foreign wife (Ez 10:30)
Chelcias (kĕl'shĭ-ăs. RV: Helkias. RSV: Hilkiah). 1. Ancestor of Baruch (Bar

1:1). **2. Father of high priest Jehoiakim** (Bar 1:7). **3. Father of Susannah** (Sus 2, 29, 63); perh same as Hilkiah 6.

Chelluh (kĕl'ū). See Cheluhi.

Chelius, Chelous (kĕl'us, kē'lŏoz). Place W of Jordan (Jdth 1:9).

Chelub (kē'lŭb, basket). **1. Brother of Shuah** (1 Ch 4:11). **2. Father of David's chief gardener** (1 Ch 27:26).

Chelubai (kĕ-lōo'bī). See Caleb 2.

Cheluhi (kĕ-lōo'hī. KJ: Chelluh). Divorced foreign wife (Ez 10:35).

Chemarim (kĕm'á-rĭm). Word (RV) in Zph 1:4 (KJ: Chemarims) and in margins of 2 K 23:5; Hos 10:5. RSV: idolatrous priests.

Chemosh (kē'mŏsh, subduer). God of Moabites (Nm 21:29; Jer 48:46); worshiped with child sacrifices (2 K 3:27). Solomon built a high place to him (1 K 11:7); destroyed by Josiah (2 K 23:13).

Chenaanah (kĕ-nā'á-nä). **1. Benjaminite** (1 Ch 7:10). **2. Father of false prophet Zedekiah** (1 K 22:11, 24).

Chenani (kĕ-nā'nī, firm). Levite; assisted returned exiles in worship (Neh 9:4).

Chenaniah (kĕn-á-nī'á, LORD is firm). Leader of Levites in music (1 Ch 15:22, 27); judge (1 Ch 26:29).

Chephar-ammoni, Chephar-haammonai (kē'-fär-ăm'mō-nī, -hä-ăm'ō-nī, village of Ammonites). Town of Benjamin (Jos 18:24).

Chephirah (kĕ-fī'rá, village). Gibeonite town (Jos 9:17; 18:26; Ez 2:25; Neh 7:29) 8 mi from Jerusalem. Modern Kefireh.

Cheran (kē'răn). Horite (Gn 36:26; 1 Ch 1:41).

Chereas (kē'rē-ăs). See Chaereas.

Cherethims, Cherethites (kĕr'ĕ-thĭmz, -thīts, Cretans?). Philistines who lived in SW Canaan (1 Sm 30:14; Eze 25:16 [KJ: Cherethims]; Zph 2:5). Some were members of David's bodyguard (2 Sm 8:18; 15:18). Carites in 2 K 11:4, 19 (KJ: captains).

Cherith (kē'rĭth, gorge). Brook of Transjordan where Elijah sojourned (1 K 17:3, 5).

cherub (chĕr'ub, pl cherubim [KJ: cherubims]). Guards of Paradise (Gn 3:24). Two golden cherubim placed on ark of covenant (Ex 25:18-22; 37:7-9; Heb 9:5). Cherubim embroidered on curtain and veil of tabernacle (Ex 26:1, 31). Solomon placed two cherubim in temple Holy of Holies (1 K 6:23-28; 8:7; 2 Ch 3:10-13; 5:7, 8). The LORD is described as dwelling between cherubim (Nm 7:89; 1 Sm 4:4; Ps 80:1; 99:1) and riding on them (2 Sm 22:11; Ps 18:10). Described as fourwinged and four-faced (Eze 1:5-12; 10:1-22. See Rv 4:6, 9).

Cherub (kē'rŭb). Exile who returned with Zerubbabel (Ez 2:59; Neh 7:61).

Chesalon (kĕs'á-lŏn). Landmark of Judah (Kesla) 10 mi W of Jerusalem (Jos 15:10).

Chesed (kē'sĕd). Son of Nahor by Milcah (Gn 22:22).

Chesil (kē'sĭl). See Bethuel 2.

chest. 1. Treasure chest (2 K 12:9, 10; 2 Ch 24:8). **2. Trunk** (Eze 27:24. RSV: carpet).

Chestnut tree. See plane.

Chesulloth (kĕ-sŭl'ŏth). Town of Issachar (Jos 19:18), probably same as Chisloth-tabor.

Cheth (kāth). See Heth 2.

Chettiim (kĕ-tī'ĭm). See Kittim 2.

Chezib (kē'zĭb). See Achzib 2; Chaseba.

Chidon (kī'don). See Nacon.

Chief. Title frequent, especially in KJ, with official terms: chief butler, chief baker, chief of herdsmen, chief of three, chief officer, chief of princes, chief priest, chief commander, chief captain.

chief of Asia. (á'zhá). See Asiarch.

chief priest. See priest.

child, children. See family.

Chileab (kīl'ĕ-ăb). David's son by Abigail (2 Sm 3:3). Daniel in 1 Ch 3:1.

Chilion (kīl'ĭ-ŏn, pining). Son of Elimelech and Naomi (Ru 1:2, 5; 4:9).

Chilmad (kīl'măd). Place mentioned with Sheba and Asshur. Site unknown (Eze 27:23).

Chimham (kĭm'hăm, pining). **1. David's friend** (2 Sm 19:37, 38, 40). **2. Inn at Bethlehem later named after him** (Jer 41:17). See Geruth Chimham.

Chinnereth, Chinneroth (kĭn'ĕ-rĕth, -rŏth, harp). **1. Fortified city of Naphtali** (Jos 19:35. Thutmose III's list at Thebes). **2. Region where city was located** (1 K 15:20. KJ: Cinneroth). **3. Ancient name for Sea of Galilee** (Nm 34:11; Dt 3:17; Jos 11:2; 12:3; 13:27; 34:11). See also Galilee, Sea of.

Chios (kī'ŏs). Island of Grecian Archipelago between Lesbos and Samos (Acts 20:15).

Chisleu, Chislev (kĭs'lū, kĭs'lĕv). KJ: Casleu in Mac 1:54. See time 4.

Chislon (kĭs'lŏn, strength). Chief of Benjamin (Nm 34:21).

Chisloth-tabor (kĭs'lŏth-tā'bĕr). Place near Tabor probably identical with Chesulloth (Jos 19:12).

Chitlish (kĭt'lĭsh, KJ: Kithlish). Village in lowlands of Judah (Jos 15:40).

Chittim (kĭt'ĭm). See Kittim.

Chiun (kī'un). Probably Kaiwan (as RSV), Syrian star god Saturn (Am 5:26). Probably same as Rephan.

Chloe (klō'ĕ, green grass). Christian woman of Corinth (1 Co 1:11).

Choba, Chobai (kō'bá, kō'bâ-ī). Place in Bethulia (Jdth 4:4; 15:4).

Chola (kō'lá). See Kola.

choose. See elect.

Chor-ashan (kôr-ăsh'ăn. RV: Cor-ashan; RSV: Borashan). Hunting place of David (1 Sm 30:30). Probably same as Ashan.

Chorazin (kō-rā'zĭn). City on Sea of Galilee. Identified with Kerazeh, 2½ mi N of Capernaum (Mt 11:21; Lk 10:13).

Chorbe (kôr'bē). See Zaccai.

Chosamaeus, Chosameus (kŏs-á-mē'us). Surname of Simon (1 Esd 9:32). See Shimeon.

Chozeba (kō-zē'bá). See Achzib 2.

Christ (krīst). See Jesus Christ; Messiah.

Christian. Follower of Christ. First so called at Antioch, Syria (Acts 11:26; 26:28; 1 Ptr 4:16).

Chronicles (krŏn'ĭ k'lz). Two historical books of OT. H name is "Acts of the Days"; in LXX erroneously called Paraleipomena ("that passed over"). Present name traced to Jerome. Two books originally one. Emphasize priestly history from death of Saul to end of captivity. Outline: 1. Genealogies from Adam to end of captivity (1 Ch 1:1—9:44). 2. David's history (1 Ch 10:1—29:30). 3. Solomon's history (2 Ch 1:1—9:31). 4. History of Judahite kings (2 Ch 10:1—36:23). Tradition assigned authorship to Ezra. Sources mentioned (1 Ch 29:29; 2 Ch 9:29; 12:15; 13:22; 25:26; 26:22).

Chronicles. Sources referred to in OT. Following names associated with them: David (1 Ch 27:24); Samuel, Nathan, Gad (1 Ch 29:29); Shemaiah, Iddo (2 Ch 12:15); Jehu (2 Ch 20:34). Other Chronicles: of Seers (2 Ch 33:19); of Medes and Persians (Est 2:23; 6:1; 10:2).

Chronicles of the Kings. See *Book of the Chronicles of the Kings of Israel (Judah).*

chronology (krō-nŏl'ō-jĭ). Dating of Biblical events. Statements in Bible (Lk 3:1, 2) and extrabiblical history used. Chronology of Ussher has been used as convenient orientation, though few scholars agreed completely or accepted older dates. Some prominent dates often given are: Patriarchs: c 2100—1800 BC. Exodus: 1441 (or late date 1290) BC. Kings: 1000—587 BC. Captivity of Israel: c 740 to 600 BC. Captivity of Judah: 587—400 BC. Birth of Christ: 6—5 BC. See *time.*

chrysolite, chrysolyte (krĭs'ō-līt, gold stone). Yellow topaz and other precious stones with golden tint (Rv 21:20). KJ, RV: beryl in Eze 1:16; 10:9; 28:13.

chrysoprase, chrysoprasus (krĭs'ō-prāz, krĭsŏp'rá-sŭs, golden-green stone). Gem, often considered variety of chalcedony but not satisfactorily identified (Rv 21: 20).

Chub (kŭb). See *Cub.*

Chun (kŭn). See *Berothah.*

church (G *ekklesia*). 1. In the classics, assembled citizens. 2. LXX: *ekklesia* translates *qahal* (convoke, assemble); nature of assembly varied (Dt 23:2; 1 Sm 19:20; 2 Ch 20:5; Ps 149:1; Ez 10:8); synonym for synagog (Gn 28:3; Nm 20:4). 3. NT: believers considered collectively (whether in meeting or not) in city (Acts 5:11; 7: 38; 8:1; Ro 16:1; 1 Co 1:2; 1 Th 1:1), territory (Acts 9:31; Gl 1:13), world (Mt 16:18; 1 Co 10:32). Church belongs to God in Christ (Acts 20:28; 1 Co 1:2; Gl 1:22; 1 Th 2:14), gathered by, and active in, Word (Mt 28:19, 20; Acts 20:28; 1 Co 4:17; 2 Co 8:18; Ph 4:15). See *body; fellowship; kingdom of God.*

churning. RSV: pressing (Pr 30:33). See *food 8.*

Chushan-rishathaim (kū'shăn-rĭsh-á-thā'ĭm). See *Cushan-rishathaim.*

Chuzi (kū'sī). Place held by Assyrians (Jdth 7:18).

Chusa (kū'zá, jug). Steward of Herod (Lk 8:3).

Cilicia (sĭ-lĭsh'ĭ-á). Province of Asia Minor with Tarsus as capital (Acts 15:41).

cinnamon. Inner bark of cinnamon tree (Ex 30:23; Pr 7:17; SS 4:14; Rv 18:13).

Cinneroth (sĭn'e-rŏth). See *Chinnereth.*

Cirama (sĭr'á-má. See *Ramah 5.*

circumcision (sûr-kum-sĭzh'un, cutting around). Removing foreskin of male organ, rite enjoined upon Abraham and his descendants as token of covenant (Gn 17). Made legal institution by Moses (Lv 12:3; Jn 7:22, 23). Neglected in wilderness (Jos 5:2-7). Jews despised uncircumcised (Ju 14:3; 15:18; 1 Sm 14:6). Other nations (e. g., Egyptians) practiced circumcision. "The circumcision" in NT means Jews (Gl 2:8; Col 4:11). Christianity refused to force Gentiles to be circumcised (Acts 15:5; Gl 5:2). Circumcision signified putting away carnal lust (Col 2:11); symbol for purity of heart (Dt 10:16; 30:6), ears (Acts 7:51).

Cis (sĭs). See *Kish 1.*

Cisai (sĭ'sá-ī). See *Kish 5.*

cistern. Reservoir dug in earth or rock to retain water from rain or spring (Pr 5:15; Ec 12:6; Is 36:16; Jer 2:13). Empty cisterns sometimes used as prisons (Gn 37:22-24).

Citims (sĭt'ĭmz). See *Kittim 2.*

citizen, citizenship. 1. Inhabitant of city (Ju 9:2-20 [KJ, RV: men]; Acts 21:39)

or country (Lk 15:15; 19:14). 2. Roman citizenship carried special privileges (including right of appeal to emperor); acquired by birth, purchase, or through special service and favor (Acts 16:37-39; 22:25-29; 23:27). Christians are citizens of heaven (their commonwealth) with saints (Eph 2:19; Ph 3:20).

City of God. See *Jerusalem.*

city of refuge. See *refuge, cities of.*

clasps. Used to fasten veil and curtains of tabernacle (Ex 26:6, 11, 33; 36:13, 18. KJ: taches).

Clauda (klô'dá). See *Cauda.*

Claudia (klô'dĭ-á). Female friend of Paul (2 Ti 4:21).

Claudius (klô'dĭ-us). Roman emperor (41—54 AD) succeeded Caligula. Banished Jews from Rome (Acts 18:2).

Claudius Lysias (klô'dĭ-us lĭs'ĭ-ăs). See *Lysias.*

clean. 1. Free from filth (Nm 19:9). 2. Pure (Ps 51:10; Jn 13:10). 3. Ceremonially clean (Lv 13:6). 4. Edible (Gn 7:2). See *purification; unclean.*

cleanliness. See *bathe; clean.*

Clement (klĕm'ent, mild). Co-worker of Paul (Ph 4:3).

Cleopas (klē'ō-păs, of renowned father). One of two disciples to whom Christ appeared on way to Emmaus (Lk 24:18).

Cleopatra (klē-ō-păt'rá, name of many Egyptian princesses). Wife of Alexander Balas (1 Mac 10:57, 58), Demetrius Nicator (11:12), Antiochus VII (*Ant* XIII, vii); mother of Antiochus VIII.

Cleophas, Clopas (klē'ō-făs, klō'păs). Name for Alphaeus (Jn 19:25).

cloak. See *dress; wimple.*

closet. 1. Bridal couch with curtains (RSV: chamber, Jl 2:16. See Ps 19:5). 2. Private room (Mt 6:6 [RV: inner chamber; RSV: room]; Lk 12:3 [RV: inner chamber; RSV: private room]).

cloud. Shows God's power and wisdom (Ps 135:7; Pr 8:28; Nah 1:3). Figuratively, multitude (Is 60:8; Heb 12:1), calamity (Eze 30:3), danger (Is 44:22), vanity (Jb 30:15; 2 Ptr 2:17). See *pillar 3.*

Cnidus (nī'dus). City of Caria on SW coast of Asia Minor (Acts 27:7; 1 Mac 15:23).

coal. Usually live coals (Lv 16:12; Ps 18:8; Is 6:6; Ro 12:20). Coal of smiths probably charcoal (as RSV, Pr 26:21. See Is 44:12), though coal may have been known (see Jn 18:18; 21:9. RSV: charcoal).

coast. KJ for edge of water, border, boundary (as Ju 11:20; Mt 8:34).

coastland. See *isle; island 3; 4.*

coat. See *dress.*

cock. RSV mentions cock once in OT (Pr 30:31). Crowing of cock referred to (Mt 26:34; Mk 13:35; Lk 22:34).

cockatrice (kŏk'á-trĭs). Fabulous monster of Europeans. KJ for H *tsiph'oni* (Is 11:8; 59:5; Jer 8:17) and *tsepha'* (Is 14:29). RV: basilisk; RV margin, RSV: adder. Adder in Pr 23:32.

cockle. Foul weed (as RSV. Jb 31:40).

Coelesyria (sē-lē-sĭr'ĭ-á. KJ: Celosyria). Valley between Lebanon and Anti-Lebanon (1 Mac 10:69).

coffer. KJ, RV for box (RSV) fastened to cart on which ark was returned by Philistines (1 Sm 6:8, 11, 15).

coffin. Probably chest in which mummy was placed (Gn 50:26).

cohort. See *army; band.*

Cola (kō'lá). See *Kola.*

Col-hozeh (kŏl-hō'zĕ, all-seeing). 1. Shallum's father (Neh 3:15). 2. Baruch's father (Neh 11:5). Probably same as 1.

Colitus, Colius (kŏ'lĭ-tus, -us). See *Kelita*.
collar. 1. Opening (Jb 30:18) like modern collar. 2. Pendant for ears (Ju 8:26. RV, RSV: pendant).
college (RV, RSV: second quarter). Suburb of Jerusalem (2 K 22:14; 2 Ch 34:22. KJ correctly in Zph 1:10).
collop (kŏl'up). Slice, or layer, of meat or fat (Jb 15:27).
colony. Settlement of Roman citizens which served as garrison in conquered territory (Acts 16:12).
color. Bible refers to following natural colors: black, brown (Gn 30:32; Lv 13:31; Mi 3:6); white (Gn 49:12; Is 1:18); green (SS 1:16. Often of grass and living plants; red (2 K 3:22; Nm 19:2); yellow (Lv 13:30). Artificial colors: purple, made from shellfish (Ju 8:26; Lk 16:19); blue, also from shellfish (Nm 15:38; Eze 27:7); crimson, from insect (Is 1:18); vermillion, pigment for decorating walls, beams (Jer 22:14; Eze 23:14). White, emblem of purity (Mk 16:5), joy (Ec 9:8), victory (Rv 6:2). Black, typical of death, sorrow, calamity (Jer 14:2; Rv 6:5). Red, symbolic of life in its egotism (Gn 9:4-6). Green signifies life, vigor. Blue, color of sky; revealed God (Ex 24:10). Purple, rich and regal color (Ju 8:26; Lk 16:19).
Colossae, Colosse (kŏ-lŏs'ē). City of Phrygia (Cl 1:2).
Colossians, Epistle to (kŏ-lŏsh'anz). Written by Paul while in captivity (at Caesarea, Ephesus, or Rome). Purpose is to combat Judaic-Gnostic heresy. Outline: 1. Introduction (1:1-8). 2. Doctrinal Section (1:9—3:4). 3. Practical Exhortations (3:5—4:6). 4. Personal Matters (4:7-18).
colt. Young of camel (Gn 32:15) or ass (Gn 49:11; Mt 21:2).
Comforter. See *Paraclete*.
commander. See *army; Philarches*.
commandments. See *Decalog*.
commerce. Bible refers to traders of Phoenicia (Is 23:8; Eze 27) and Egypt (Gn 39:1). Early Israelites were pastoral and agricultural people. Solomon built up extensive foreign trade (1 K 5:10-12; 9:26-28; 10:22, 28, 29). Thereafter Israelites were prominent merchants and traders (Acts 12:20; Ja 4:13).
commonwealth. See *citizen, citizenship*.
communion. See *body; fellowship; Lord's Supper*.
community of goods. Early church practiced voluntary community of goods in Jerusalem (Acts 2:44, 45; 4:32-37; 5:3, 4).
compass. KJ: "fetch a compass" for "make a circuit" (2 Sm 5:23; Acts 28:13).
compassion. See *mercy*.
Conaniah (kŏn-à-nī'à, Lord has established). 1. Levite in charge of offerings and tithes under Hezekiah (2 Ch 31: 12, 13. KJ: Cononiah). 2. Levite at time of Josiah (2 Ch 35:9). Jeconias (RSV: Jeconiah) in 1 Esd 1:9.
concision (kon-sĭzh'un). Sarcastic word for circumcision (Ph 3:2. RSV: those who mutilate the flesh).
concubine (kŏng'kû-bīn). Secondary wife of inferior status (Gn 16:1; 22:24; Ju 8:31; 2 Sm 3:7; 5:13). Laws protected her rights (Ex 21:7-9; Dt 21:10-14).
concupiscence (kŏn-kû'pĭ-sens). Love of, and seeking after, carnal things (Ro 7: 7:23; Cl 3:5; 1 Th 4:5. RV, RSV: covetousness; desire; lust). See *lust*.
conduit. Aqueduct, cut in rock or constructed underground (2 K 18:17; 20:20; Is 7:3; 36:2).

coney (kō'nĭ). See *rock badger*.
confection (RSV: incense). Incense made by temple apothecary (Ex 30:35). Confectionary is perfumer (1 Sm 8:13 [RSV: perfumer]).
confess. 1. Publicly own and acknowledge as one's own (Mt 10:32; Lk 12:8). 2. Profess Christ and His Gospel and obey Him (Mt 10:32; Lk 12:8; 1 Jn 2:23; 4:15). 3. Acknowledge and reveal sins publicly or privately to God or neighbor (Lv 5:5; Ps 32:5; Mt 3:6; Ja 5:16; 1 Jn 1:9). 4. Acknowledge, praise, and thank God (Is 48:1; Dn 9:4). 5. Profess faith (Heb 3:1; 4:14; 10:23).
confusion of tongues. See *Babel*.
congregation. Israel viewed as collective, holy religious group (Nm 16:3) whether in assembly (Ex 12:6; 35:1) or not (Ex 12:3; Lv 4:13). Congregation often represented by leaders (Jos 23:12; Ju 20:1, 2; 21:10-20). See *church*.
Coniah (kō-nī'à). See *Jeconiah; Jehoiachin*.
Cononiah (kŏ-nō-nī'à). See *Conaniah 1*.
conscience. G *syneidesis*. Consciousness that one's conduct is in harmony with, or contrary to, an acknowledged standard. (Acts 23:1; 1 Ti 1:5; Heb 13:18; 1 Ptr 3:16, 21). In Ro 13:5 and 1 Ptr 2:19 conscience is related to God. "Weak" conscience has faulty norm (1 Co 8: 10-13). "Seared" is injured conscience (1 Ti 4:2).
consecrate. To set aside for God, e. g., Levites for priesthood (Ex 13:2; Nm 3:12), precious metals, vessels (Jos 6:19), persons (Nm 6:2-13), nations (Ex 19:6), fields (Lv 27:28), cattle (2 Ch 29:33). etc. All Christians are consecrated (1 Ptr 2:9); there are also special consecrations (Acts 13:2). See *ordination*.
contrition (kon-trĭsh'un). Conviction of sin and dread of God's wrath which is indispensable before conversion (Ps 51:17; Is 57:15; 66:2; Jl 2:12; Mk 1:15; Lk 15: 18; 18:13; 24:47; Acts 2:37; 16:29).
conversion (kon-vûr'shun). Act of divine grace by which sinner is turned from power of darkness, translated into kingdom of Christ (Cl 1:13). In its entirety this is process by which man is transferred from his carnal state into spiritual state of faith and enters upon and continues in spiritual life. In specific sense conversion is bestowal of faith by Spirit through Word (Ps 51:13; Is 55; 60 5; Jn 1:45-50; 3:16; 6:63; Acts 3:19; 8:34-38; 9:35; 11: 21; 14:15; 16:13-34; 26:18; Ro 1:16; 10: 17; 2 Co 3:16; 1 Ptr 2:25).
conviction. 1. Being found guilty. Law convicts all of sin. Individual convicted (convinced) of sin by conscience (Jn 16:8; 1 Co 14:24; Ja 2:9; Jude 15). 2. Firm belief, or that which engenders it (1 Th 1:5 [KJ, RV: assurance]; Heb 11:1 [KJ: evidence RV: proving]).
convocation. Meeting called for worship (Lv 23:2-8; Nm 28:18-25; 29:1-16).
cooking. See *food*.
Coos (kō'ŏs). See *Cos*.
copper. H *nehosheth*, G *chalcos*, usually: bronze; abundantly used in ancient Asia and Europe (Ex 38; Lv 6:28; 2 Sm 21:16). KJ usually: brass (copper and zinc) when should be: copper, bronze (copper and tin). RSV: copper (7 times), bronze (151 times), brass (3 times: Lv 26:19; Dt 28:23; Is 48:4).
cor. See *measures 2j*.
coral. Highly prized by Hebrews; ranked with precious stones (Jb 28:18; Lm 4:7 [KJ, RV: ruby]; Eze 27:16).
Cor-ashan (kôr-ăsh'ăn). See *Chor-ashan*.

corban (kôr'băn, offering). H *qorban* is offering or oblation for God (Lv 1:2, 3; 2:1; 3:1; Nm 7:12-17); hence money or service dedicated to God (Mk 7:11).

Corbe (kôr'bē). See *Zaccai*.

Cord. Made of flax, hide, date tree fibers, camel hide reeds, etc. Used for fastening tents (Ex 35:18), binding prisoners (Ju 15:13; 16:7), scourges (Jn 2:15), ship ropes (Acts 27:32), etc. Frequently used figuratively (Jb 30:11; 36:8; Ec 4:12).

Core (kō'rē). See *Korah* 3.

Coriander (kō-rĭ-ăn'dēr). Plant (Coriandrum sativum) producing aromatic seeds. Manna was size of coriander seeds (Ex 16:31; Nm 11:7). See *food* 4.

Corinth (kôr'ĭnth). Greek, wealthy, but immoral city on isthmus connecting Peloponnesus and mainland. Destroyed by Romans 146 BC and rebuilt by Caesar 46 BC. Paul founded church there (Acts 18:1; 20:2, 3).

Corinthians, 1st Epistle to (kō-rĭn'thĭ-ánz). Written by Paul at Ephesus to correct abuses and strengthen faith of church at Corinth. Outline: 1. Paul's Ministry; Factions (1—4). 2. Immorality (5). 3. Courts (6). 4. Marriage (7). 5. Meat Offered to Idols (8—10). 6. Veils; Lord's Supper (11). 7. Spiritual Gifts (12—14). 8. Resurrection (15). 9. Collection; Closing Remarks (16).

Corinthians, 2d Epistle to. Written by Paul in Macedonia to praise repentance of Corinthians and exalt ministry. Outline: 1. Joy over Repentance (1—2). 2. Exaltation of Ministry (3—6). 3. Joy over Corinthians (7). 4. Collection for Saints (8, 9). 5. Paul's Defense (10—13).

cormorant (kôr'mō-rant). A large swimming bird (Phalacrocorax carbo); regarded unclean (Lv 11:17; Dt 14:17). Probably different bird in Is. 34:11 (RV: pelican; RSV: hawk); Zph 2:14 (RV: pelican; RSV: vulture).

corn. See *grain*.

Cornelius (kôr-nēl'yus, of a horn). Roman centurion and 1st Gentile convert (Acts 10).

corner gate. NW gate of Jerusalem (2 K 14:13; 2 Ch 25:23).

cornerstone. Foundation stone laid at corner as starting point for building (Jb 38:6; Is 28:16). Head stone (Ps 118:22; Mk 12:10; Lk 20:17; Acts 4:11). Christ is Cornerstone (or Head Stone) of church (Mt 21:42; Eph 2:20; 1 Ptr 2:5-7).

cornet. 1. H *shophar* (RSV: horn. 1 Ch 15:28; 2 Ch 15:14; Ps 98:6; Hos 5:8), usually: trumpet. 2. H *m:na'an:im* (2 Sm 6:5. RV, RSV: castanets). 3. H *qeren* (RSV: horn. Dn 3:5, 7, 10, 15). "Cornet" does not occur in RSV. See also *trumpet*.

corpse. See *carcass*.

correction. 1. Reforming, making right (2 Ti 3:16; Jer 2:30). 2. See *chastisement*.

corrupt, corruption. 1. Putrefaction (Acts 2:27, 31; 13:35, 36). 2. Infectious and poisonous nature of sin, which is vicious and totally biased by carnal interest and evil inclinations (Gn 6:11, 12; Ps 14:1; Gl 6:8; Eph 4:22; 2 Ti 3:8; 2 Ptr 2:19). 3. Other meanings (KJV): consume (Mt 6:19), break (Ml 2:8), entice (2 Co 11:3), spoil (1 Co 15:33), pollute (Ex 32:7).

Cos (kŏs). Island in Aegean Sea (Acts 21:1 [KJ: Coos]; 1 Mac 15:23).

Cosam (kō'săm). Ancestor of Christ (Lk 3:28).

cote. Sheepfold (2 Ch 32:28).

cottage. See *homes* 2.

cotton. Mentioned twice (Est 1:6 [KJ, RV: green]; Is 19:9. (KJ: networks; RV: white cloth]).

couch. See *homes* 5.

coulter (kōl'tēr). See *agriculture* 2; *plowshare*.

council. 1. Two or more people gathered for deliberation (Gn 49:6 [KJ: secret]; 2 K 9:5 [KJ, RV: sitting]; Acts 25:12). 2. Sanhedrin (Mt 26:59; Acts 5:34) and lesser courts (Mt 10:17; Mk 13:9). See also *appeal; Sanhedrin*.

countenance. 1. Face, especially as it expresses feelings (Gn 4:5, 6; 1 Sm 1:18; Jb 9:27; Mk 10:22). 2. Light of God's countenance is His love and favor (Nm 6:26; Ps 4:6).

court. See *appeal; Sanhedrin*.

court, courtyard. Enclosed yard of house (2 Sm 17:18), palace (2 K 20:4), prison (Jer 32:2). Outer area of tabernacle (Ex 27:9; Lv 6:16), temple (1 K 6:36; 2 K 21:5; 23:12; 2 Ch 23:6). See also *homes* 6.

cousin. 1. Uncle's son (Lv 25:49; Jer 32:8, 9, 12). 2. Kinsfolk (Lk 1:36, 58. RV, RSV: kinswoman, kinsfolk). 3. Cousin (Cl 4:10. KJ: sister's son).

Coutha (kou'thá). See *Cutha*.

covenant. 1. Pact between tribes, nations, individuals (Gn 21:27; Jos 9:6, 15; 1 Sm 11:1; 20:8) in which, after Near E custom, God was witness (Gn 31:50; 1 Sm 20:8). 2. Covenants with Noah (Gn 9:9-16), Abraham (Gn 15:7-21) are pledges of grace. Third covenant was made with Israel in which people participated, blood was sprinkled and obligations imposed (Ex 24). It is like suzerainty covenants in form. 3. Prophets spoke of new covenant (Jer 31:31-34) which would center in a person (Is 42:6; 49:8). 4. NT covenant (testament) harks back to the Abrahamic (Acts 3:25, 26; Gl 3:17, 18), places man in relationship to his Maker through work of Christ (Heb 7:22; 8:6-13; 2 Co 3:6-18), which stresses forgiveness (Ro 11:26, 27) in blood of Christ (Mt 26:28), and leads to holy life (Gl 5:22-26; Heb 8—10). See also *baptism; circumcision; Lord's Supper; passover*.

covet, covetousness. 1. Rightful desire (1 Co 12:31). 2. Inordinate, lawless, wrongful desire (Ex 20:17; Dt 5:21; Acts 20:33; Ro 7:7; 13:9). See also *lust*.

cow. Cows (oxen, kine) mentioned early (Gn 12:16; 41; 1 Sm 6:7-14). Milk used as food (1 Sm 6:7). Cows used for concluding covenants (Gn 15:9); for peace (Lv 3:1), sin (Nm 19:2; Heb 9:13), and burnt (1 Sm 6:14) offerings.

Coz (kŏz, thorn). See *Hakkoz* 1.

Cozbi (kŏz'bī, liar). Daughter of Zur, prince of Midian (Nm 25:6-18).

Cozeba (kō-zē'bá). See *Achzib* 2.

Cracknels. Hard cakes (RSV: cakes. 1 K 14:3).

craft. See *trade*.

crane. Meaning of H *'agur* uncertain (Is 38:14; Jer 8:7. KJ: swallow). H *sus* (twitterer) probably martin, swallow, swift (Is 38:14; Jer 8:7. KJ: crane. RV, RSV: swallow).

Crates (krā'tēz). Deputy of Sostratus (2 Mac 4:29).

creation. Act of God by which He calls into being (Gn 1; 2). God is subject, object is new thing. Creation was by Word (Jn 1:3; Eph 3:9; Col 1:16; Heb 1:2).

creeping thing. Land or water animal which creeps on belly or feet (Gn 1:24, 25; 6:7; Lv 11:41, 42; Ps 104:25).

Crescens (krĕs'ĕnz, increasing). Paul's helper (2 Ti 4:10).

Cretans (krē'tăns). Inhabitants of Crete, known for being good sailors; skillful in archery; also for untruthfulness (Tts 1:12. KJ: Cretians). Some present on first Pentecost (Acts 2:11. KJ: Cretes).

Crete (krēt). Island in Mediterranean (Candia), 165 mi long, 6—35 wide. Paul founded church there (Acts 27:7-13; Tts 1:5-14). Also called Caphtor.

Cretes, Cretians (krēts, krē'shăns). See *Cretans.*

crib. Rack of stone (trough) for fodder (Jb 39:9; Prov 14:4; Is 1:3). See also *manger.*

cricket. Leaping, winged insect of grasshopper class (Lv 11:22. KJ: beetle).

crimson. See *color.*

crisping pins. KJ in Is 3:22 (RV: satchels; RSV: handbags).

Crispus (cris'pus, curled). Ruler of synagog at Corinth; converted by Paul (Acts 18:8; 1 Co 1:14).

crocodile. See *chameleon.*

crocus. See *rose.*

cross. Four common forms: 1. Simple, | ; 2. St. Andrew's *(decussata),* ×; 3. St. Anthony's *(commissa),* T; 4. The Latin *(immissa),* †. The Greek (+) and the double and triple cross are additional forms. Cross as emblem predates Christianity. Instrument used for Christ's execution (Mt 27:32-35). Used figuratively for Gospel (Gl 6:14), all Christ's sufferings (Eph 2:16), and that which is suffered as, and as a result of being, a disciple (Mt 16:24).

crown. Headdress of priests, kings, queens (Ex 28:36-38; 2 Ch 23:11; Est 2:17). symbol of victory (1 Co 9:25; 2 Ti 2:5), power, honor (Pr 12:4; Lm 5:16), and eternal life (Ja 1:12; 1 Ptr 5:4; Rv 2:10). Crown of thorns placed on Jesus to insult Him (Mt 27:29). See also *diadem.*

crucible. See *furnace 4.*

crucifixion. Method of inflicting death practiced by Egyptians (Gn 40:19), Persians (Ez 6:11), Greeks, Romans, and other ancient civilizations. Jesus crucified by Romans (Mt 27; Mk 15; Lk 23; Jn 19). See also *cross.*

cruse. Translation for three H words: 1. *tsappahath:* flask for holding oil (1 K 17:12) or water (1 Sm 26:11. RSV: jar). 2. *baqbuq* (1 K 14:3. RSV: jar. See Jer 19:1, 10). 3. *ts:lohith:* shallow saucer (2 K 2:20. RSV: bowl. See 2 K 21:13).

crystal (ice). Clear and brilliant substance (Jb 28:17 [RV, RSV: glass]; Jb 28:18 [KJ: pearl]; Eze 1:22; Rv 4:6; 22:1). See also *glass.*

Cub (kŭb). Ally of Egypt (Eze 30:5. KJ: Chub. RSV, LXX: Libya).

cubit. See *measures 1, d.*

cuckoo. KJ mistranslation for unclean bird of sea gull family (Lv 11:16; Dt 14:15. RV: sea mew. RSV: sea gull).

cucumber. See *food 4.*

cumi (kū'mī). Aramaic: arise (Mk 5:41).

cummin (kŭm'ĭn). See *food 4.*

cun (kŭn). See *Berothah.*

cup. Drinking vessel of horn, clay, or metal (Gn 44:2; 1 Sm 16:13; 1 K 7:26; Mt 26:27). Figuratively, contents of cup (1 Co 10:16). One's lot in life (Ps. 11:6; 16:5; 23:5; Mt 26:39; Mk 10:38). See *homes 5.*

cupbearer. See *butler.*

curds. See *food 8.*

curious arts. See *magic.*

curse. To call down evil, suffering, or calamity on someone (Gn 9:25; 49:7). God cursed serpent and earth after fall (Gn 3:14, 17). Curse of God pronounced on various sins in Dt 27:15-26. Death penalty for cursing father or mother (Lv 20:9). Christians to return blessing for cursing (Mt 5:11; Lk 6:28; Ro 12:14).

Cush (kŭsh). 1. Son of Ham; father of Nimrod (Gn 10:8; 1 Ch 1:10). 2. Territory in region of Tigris and Euphrates (Gn 2:13). 3. See *Ethiopia.* 4. Benjaminite (Ps 7 title).

Cushan (kū'shăn). Form of Cush or country in Arabia (Hab. 3:7).

Cushan-rishathaim (kū'shăn-rĭsh-á-thā'ĭm. KJ: Chushan-rishathaim). Hittite king; annexed Mesopotamia; held Israel in subjection 8 yrs (Ju 3:8-11).

Cushi (kū'shī, Ethiopian). 1. Father of Zephaniah (Zph 1:1). 2. Ancestor of Jehudi (Jer 36:14). 3. KJ where RV, RSV: the Cushite in 2 Sm 18:21-32.

Cushite (kŭsh-īt). Ethiopian (Nm 12:1).

Cuth, Cuthah (kŭth, kū'thá). City of Babylonia which worshiped Nergal and sent colonists to Samaria (2 K 17:24, 30).

Cutha (kū'thá). KJ: Coutha. Listed in 1 Esd 5:32.

cuttings. See *tattoo.*

Cyamon (sī'á-mŏn). Place near Carmel (Jth 7:3). Perhaps Jokneam.

cymbal H *tsilts:lim, m:tsilthayim,* G *kymbalon.* Musical percussion instrument (2 Sm 6:5; 1 Ch 13:8; 16:5; Ps 150:5; 1 Co 13:1).

cypress. 1. H *b:rosh;* tall evergreen, probably the *cupressus sempervirens* (1 K 5:8, 10; 6:15, 34; Is 14 8; 37:24. KJ, RV: fir. RV margin usually: cypress. RSV: cypress, but fir in Ps 104:17; Eze 27:5; 31:8). 2. KJ for H *thirzah* (Is 44:14. RV, RSV: holm).

Cyprian (sĭp'rĭ-ăn). Dweller in Cyprus (2 Mac 4:29).

Cyprus (sī'prus). Island in Mediterranean off coast of Syria, 148 mi long, 50 mi wide. Known for copper. Many Jews lived there (1 Mac 15:23). Home of Barnabas (Acts 4:36). Stephen preached there (Acts 11:19, 20). Visited by Paul, Barnabas, and Mark (Acts 13:4; 15:39). See also *Kittim.*

Cyrene (sī'rē'nē). Greek colonial city, capital of Cyrenaica (Tripoli) in Africa (Mt 27:32; Mk 15:21; Acts 2:10; 6:9).

Cyrenius (sī-rē'nī-us). See *Quirinius.*

Cyrus (sī'rus). Founder of Persian Empire; King of Anshan; defeated Median Astyages (c 559 BC), Lydian Croesus (c 546 BC), and captured Babylon (539 BC). Humane king who returned captives to native land. Issued decree giving Jews permission to return from captivity (2 Ch 36:22, 23; Ez 1:1-14; Is 44:28; 45:1-7). Died 530 BC. See *Daniel; Ezra.*

D

Dabareh (dăb'á-rĕ). See *Daberath.*

Dabbasheth, Dabbesheth (dăb'á-shĕth, dăb'-ĕ-shĕth, hump). Town on W border of Zebulun (Jos 19:11).

Daberath (dăb'ĕ-răth, pasture). Levitical city of Issachar (Daburiyeh on W slope of Tabor. Jos 19:12; 21:28 [KJ: Dabareh]; 1 Ch 6:72).

Dabria (dă'brĭ-á). Scribe (2 Esd 14:24).
Dacobi, Dacubi (dá-kō'bī, dá-kū'bī). See *Akkab* 2.
Daddeus (dă-dē'us). See *Iddo* 8.
dagger. KJ for H *herebh* (Ju 3:16, 21, 22. RV, RSV: sword).
Dagon (dā'gŏn, *daghan*, grain?; *dagh*, fish?). Deity with body of fish, head and hands of man. God of natural powers, especially of grain. Worshiped in Mesopotamia and by Canaanites. National god of Philistines; temples at Ashdod (1 Sm 5:1-7), Gaza (Ju 16:21-30), and in Israel (1 Ch 10:10).
Daisan (dā'săn). See *Rezin* 2.
Dalaiah (dăl-á-ĭ'á). See *Delaiah* 4.
Dalan (dā'lăn). See *Delaiah* 5.
Dale, King's. Valley near Jerusalem (Gn 14:17 [RV: King's Vale]; 2 Sm 18:18). RSV: King's Valley.
Dalmanutha (dăl-má-nū'thá). Place on W coast of Sea of Galilee near Magdala (Mk 8:10. See Mt 15:39).
Dalmatia (dăl-mā'shĭ-á). See *Illyrium*.
Dalphon (dăl'fŏn). Haman's son (Est 9:7).
Damaris (dám'á-rĭs, gentle). Athenian woman converted by Paul (Acts 17:34).
Damascus (dá-măs'kus). City of Syria, on plateau (2,300 ft above sea level) watered by Abana (Barada) and Pharpar (2 K 5:12) at E foot of Anti-Lebanon. Old city (Gn 14:15; 15:2); captured by David (2 Sm 8:6) and Jeroboam II (2 K 14:28). Rulers of Damascus played prominent role in history of Israel and Judah: Rezon (1 K 11:23-25); Ben-hadad (1 K 15:19, 20; 22:15-37; 2 K 8:15; 2 Ch 16:3); Hazael (2 K 8:15; 13:22-25); Rezin (2 K 16:5, 7, 8). Paul converted nearby (Acts 9).
damnation. Unbelievers will be damned (Mk 16:16) and punished with everlasting destruction (Mt 23:33; 2 Th 1:9). Punishment described as fire (Mk 9:44), outer darkness (Mt 8:12), and imprisonment (Mt 5:26).
Dan (dăn, judge). 1. 5th son of Jacob by Bilhah (Gn 30:5, 6). 2. Tribe descended from Dan and territory allotted to it (Nm 1:12, 38, 39; Jos 19:40-48; 21:5, 23; Ju 1:34, 35). 3. City (formerly Laish) in extreme N captured and renamed by Danites when crowded from lowlands of their possessions by Amorites (Jos 19:47; Ju 18). For KJ translation in Eze 27:19 see *Vedan*.
Dan to Beer-sheba. The length of Palestine (Ju 20:1; 1 Ch 21:2).
dance. Dance used to express joy (Jb 21:11; Jer 31:4, 13; Mt 11:17; Lk 15:25); to celebrate victory (Ex 15:20, 21; Ju 11:34; 1 Sm 18:6) and vintage (Ju 21:21); especially for religious expression (2 Sm 6:14; Ps 149:3). Also evil purposes (Ex 32:19; Mk 6:22).
Daniel (dăn'yel, God is my judge). 1. See *Chileab*. 2. Judahite prophet and minister at Babylonian court (there called Belteshazzar); held influential positions under Nebuchadnezzar, Belshazzar, Darius, and Cyrus; showed concern for his people. 3. Priest; sealed covenant (Ez 8:2; Neh 10:6). Gamael in 1 Esd 8:29.
Daniel, Book of. Prophetic book which Hebrew Canon places in 3d division because Daniel had gift of prophecy but not prophetic vocation. Apocalyptic character and figurative language occasioned varying interpretations. Date also debated. Title "Son of Man" often used by Christ is in Daniel (7:13, 14). References to Daniel: Mt 24:15; Lk 1:19, 26; Heb 11:33, 34. Outline: 1. Introduction

(1). 2. Historic section in Aramaic (2—6). 3. Apocalyptic visions (7—12).
Dan-jaan (dăn-jā'án. RSV: from Dan). Name of place, apparently extreme N city. Reading in original offers difficulties (2 Sm 24:6).
Dannah (dăn'á, murmuring). City in hill country of Judah near Hebron (Jos 15:49).
Daphne (dăf'nê). Shrine of Apollo near Antioch (2 Mac 4:33).
Dara (dä'rá). See *Darda*.
Darda (där'dá, pearl of wisdom). Son of Mahol; famed for wisdom (1 K 4:31). Dara, son of Zerah, in 1 Ch 2:6.
Daric (dăr'ĭk. KJ: dram). Persian gold coin with picture of king with bow and javelin on one side, square figure on other. Worth c $5. (1 Ch 29:7; Ez 2:69; 8:27; Neh 7:70-72).
Darius (dá-rī'us). 1. Darius the Mede, probably Gobryas, son of Ahasuerus (Dn 5:31; 9:1); governor of Babylon under Cyrus; prominent in Daniel (6:1, 6, 9, 25, 28; 11:1). 2. Darius Hystaspes, 4th king of Persian (521—486 BC) empire; organized satrapies; fought Greeks at Marathon; renewed edict of Cyrus and assisted in rebuilding temple (Ez 4:5, 24; 5:5-7; 6:1-12; Hg 1:1; 2:1, 10, 18; Zch 1:1, 7; 7:1). 3. Darius the Persian, last king (Codomannus, 336—330 BC) of Persia; defeated by Alexander (1 Mac 1:1; Ant XI, viii, 3; Neh 12:22).
darkness. See *light and darkness*.
Darkon (där'kŏn. Lozon in 1 Esd 5:33). Progenitor of family of Solomon's servants who returned from Babylon (Ez 2:56; Neh 7:58).
dart. Arrow or light spear (2 Sm 18:14; Jb 41:26; Eph 6:16). See *armor; arms*.
Dathan (dā'thăn, of a spring). Reubenite; leader in rebellion of Korah (Nm 16; 26:7-11; Dt 11:6; Ps 106:17).
Dathema (dăth'ê-má). Fortress in Gilead (1 Mac 5:9).
daughter. 1. Daughter (Gn 11:29) or female descendant (Gn 24:48). 2. Female inhabitant (Gn 24:3; Nm 25:1; Ju 21:21; Lk 23:28). 3. Female worshiper (Is 43:6; Ml 2:11). 4. City (Is 37:22). 5. Citizens (Zch 2:10).
David (dā'vĭd, beloved?). 2d king of Israel. Son of Jesse; Bethlehemite of tribe of Judah (1 Sm 16:1-13; 1 Ch 2:13-15); anointed king by Samuel (1 Sm 16:13) and men of Judah (2 Sm 2:4); played harp (RSV: lyre) for Saul (1 Sm 16:14-23); killed Goliath (1 Sm 17); loved by Jonathan but feared and envied by Saul (1 Sm 18); persecuted by Saul (1 Sm 19; 20); fled to Nob; feigned madness at Gath (1 Sm 21; Ps 34 title); dwelt in cave (1 Sm 22); gathered small band, protected Israelites and expected provisions in return (1 Sm 23—25); pursued by Saul (1 Sm 26); dwelt in Ziklag (1 Sm 27—30). King of Judah (2 Sm 2—4) and Israel (2 Sm 5). Took Jerusalem; made it his capital and thoroughly defeated Philistines (2 Sm 5:17-25; 1 Ch 14:8-17; 2 Sm 21:15-22); brought ark to Jerusalem (2 Sm 6; 1 Ch 13; 15:1-3); organized worship (1 Ch 15; 16); planned temple (2 Sm 7; 1 Ch 17; 22:7-10); subdued Moabites, Aramaeans, Ammonites, Edomites, Amalekites (2 Sm 8; 10; 12:26-31); made Solomon his successor (1 K 1; 2); reigned forty years (2 Sm 2:11; 5:4, 5; 1 Ch 29:27); sinned grievously (2 Sm 11:1—12:23; Ps 51; 2 Sm 24; 1 Ch 21); had family problems (2 Sm 12—19; 1 K 1). Called sweet

psalmist of Israel (2 Sm 23:1. See 1 Sm 16:18-23; 2 Sm 1:17-27; 3:33, 34; 6:5; 22; 23:1-7; Am 6:5; Ez 3:10; Neh 12:24, 36, 45, 46); 73 psalms ascribed to him. Man after God's own heart (1 Sm 13:14; Acts 13:36). Prominent in ancestry of Jesus (Mt 22:41-45).

David, City of. 1. Portion of Jerusalem occupied by David; S of temple area (2 Sm 5:6-9). 2. Bethlehem (Lk 2:4).

day. See *time* 5, 6.

Day of Atonement. See *Atonement, Day of.*

Day of the LORD. 1. OT: day of victory for kingdom of God and defeat of evil (Is 2:12; 13:6, 9; Eze 13:5; Zph 1:14). 2. NT: day when Christ comes in glory of Father (parousia). To unbeliever, day of terror (Mt 10:15; Ro 2:5, 6; 2 Ptr 3: 7, 12); to believer, day of joy (Mt 16:27; 24:30; Jn 6:39; 2 Co 1:14; Ph 1:6, 10). See also *parousia.*

day's journey. See *measures* 1 h.

daysman. Arbitrator, moderator (Jb 9:33. RSV: umpire).

dayspring. Dawn (as RSV. Jb 38:12; Lk 1:78).

day star. (G *phosphoros*, light bringer). 1. Christ is Light who brings illumination to His people (RSV: morning star. 2 Ptr 1:19; see Rv 2:28; 22:16). 2. King of Babylon compared to planet Venus (Is 14:12. RSV: Day Star; RV: day star; KJ: Lucifer).

deacon (minister). 1. G *diakonein* (and derivatives) used for "to serve" (Lk 22: 25-27; Mk 10:45; Acts 6:1, 2). 2. Hence any service in early church usually in behalf of group and often connected with preaching and evangelism (Acts 6:4; 20:24; Ro 11:13; 15:25; 2 Co 6:3, 4; 8:19, 20). 3. In Ph 1:1; 1 Ti 3 *diakonos* is an office associated with that of bishop.

deaconess. Female helper in church (Ro 16:1 [KJ, RV: servant]; perh 1 Ti 5:9-12).

dead. 1. Body deprived of life (Gn 23). 2. Collectively, the deceased (Rv 20:12). 3. Figuratively, spiritual condition of unbelievers (Eph 2:1). 4. Believers are dead to Law (Col 2:20). 5. Of faith not active in works (Ja 2:17). See also *burial; carcass; death; shades.*

Dead Sea. See *Salt Sea.*

deaf. Protected by law (Lv 19:14).

death. Universal (Heb 9:27); results from sin (Gn 2:17; Ro 5:12-14); for believer prelude to eternal bliss (2 Co 5:1; Ph 1:23; 2 Ti 4:6-8; Ja 1:12). Described as separation from body (Ec 12:7; 2 Co 5: 1-5; 2 Ptr 1:14), departure (2 Ti 4:6).

Debir (dē'bẽr). 1. King of Eglon; defeated by Joshua (Jos 10:3-23). 2. Levitical city in hill country of Judah, 12 mi SW of Hebron (Jos 10:38, 39; 21:15). Canaanites called it Kirjath-sannah (KJ: Kirjath-sanna, Jos 15:49) or Kiriath-sepher (book town. KJ: Kirjath-sepher. Jos 15:15, 16; Ju 1:11, 12). 3. Town near Achor (Jos 15:7). 4. Town E of Jordan (Jos 13:26).

Deborah (dĕb'ō-rá, bee). 1. Nurse of Rebekah (Gn 24:59; 35:8). 2. Prophetess and judge; urged Barak to fight Sisera (Ju 4:4-14); composed song of triumph (Ju 5).

debt. 1. That which is owed. In later Judaism notes were used. Within certain limitations (Dt 15:1-15; 24:6-13) creditor might seize debtor's property, family, or person as payment (Lv 25: 25-41). 2. Failure to meet obligations to God and fellow men (Mt 6:12). 3. Moral obligation (Ro 8:12).

Decalog (dĕk'á-lŏg). OT, H: ten words (Ex 34:28; Dt 4:13), words (Ex 20:1; Dt 5:22). NT: commandments (Mt 19:17; Eph 6:2). Precepts spoken by God from Sinai (Ex 20) and written on tables of stone (Ex 31:18; 32:15-19; 34:1-4, 27-29; Dt 10: 1-5). Ten Commandments form basis of divine Law. Christ's interpretation in Mt 5:17-48; Mt 19:16-22; Mk 2:24-27; Lk 6: 1-10; 13:10-16. Love is fulfillment (Mt 22:35-40).

Decapolis (dē-kăp'ō-lĭs, ten cities). District containing 10 cities beginning where Esdraelon opens into Jordan and eastward (Mt 4:25; Mk 5:20; 7:31).

Decision, Valley of. See *Jehoshaphat, Valley of.*

Dedan (dē'dăn). 1. Cush's grandson (Gn 10:7). 2. Son of Jokshan; grandson of Abraham and Keturah (Gn 25:3; 1 Ch 1:32 [RSV: Deban?]). 3. Cushite people or territory (Jer 25:23; 49:8; Eze 25:13; 38:13). See also *Rhodes.*

Dedanim, Dedanites (dĕd'dăn-ĭm, - īts). Descendants of Dedan (Is 21:13).

dedication. Act of devoting something to holy use (tabernacle — Ex 40; Nm 7; altar — Nm 7:84, 88; temple — Ez 6: 16, 17; other things — Dt 20:5; 2 Ch 24:7; Lv 27:17). Feast of Dedication commemorated cleansing of temple (1 Mac 4:52-59; Jn 10:22).

deep. 1. Sea or its deepest part (Gn 7:11; Jb 38:30; Is 51:10; Jon 2:5 [KJ: depth]; Lk 5:4). 2. See *abyss.*

deer. See *hart, roebuck.*

defile. To pollute, or render unclean. Could be external or ceremonial defilement (Gn 34; Lv 13:46; 18; Nm 5; Eze 18:11) or inner, moral and spiritual (Mt 15:20; Mk 7:15; 1 Co 8:7; 2 Co 7:1; 2 Ptr 2:20). Inner and external usually associated. See also *clean; unclean.*

degree. Rank or station (1 Ch 15:18 [RSV: order]; 1 Ch 17:17 [RSV: future generations]; Ps 62:9 [RSV: estate]; Lk 1:52).

degrees, song of (RSV: Song of Ascents). Title given to each of psalms from 120 to 134. Jewish tradition holds that they were sung on 15 steps from court of women to court of men. It is also held that "degrees" refer to progressive (step) poetry or to the melody.

degrees of glory. See *glory* 4.

Dehaites, Dehavites (dē-hā'īts, dē-hā'vīts). Interpreted as referring to Dai or Dahi, nomadic Persian tribes. Not proper noun in RSV (Ez 4:9).

deity. See *God.*

Dekar, Deker (dē'kär, dē'kẽr). See *Bendeker.*

Delaiah (dē-lā'yá, LORD has delivered). 1. Ancestor of 23d course of priests (1 Ch 24:18). 2. Father of Shemaiah (Neh 6:10). 3. Son of Shemaiah; interceded for preservation of Jeremiah's scroll (Jer 36:12, 25). 4. Descendant of Zerubbabel (1 Ch 3:24. KJ: Dalaiah). 5. Ancestor of returned family (Ez 2:60; Neh 7:62; 1 Esd 5:37 [KJ: Ladan; RV: Dalan]).

Delilah (dē-lī'lá, coquette). Woman of Sorek; loved by Samson; bribed by Philistines to discover secret of Samson's strength (Ju 16:4-20).

Delos, Delus (dē'lŏs, -lŭs). One of Cyclades islands (1 Mac 15:23).

Demas (dē'măs). Fellow laborer who deserted Paul (Phmn 24; Cl 4:14; 2 Ti 4:10).

Demetrius (dē-mē'trĭ-*us*, belonging to Demeter). 1. Silversmith at Ephesus (Acts 19:23-30). 2. Disciple (3 Jn 12). 3.

Demetrius I (Soter), king of Syria 162 to 150 BC (1 Mac 7:1-4; 9:1; 10:48-50). 4. Demetrius II (Nicator), king of Syria, 148—138; 128 BC (1 Mac 11:12-40; 13:36-40).

demons (KJ: devil; evil spirit). Evil spirit, opposed to God, bent on evil. Unclean spirits in Mk 5:9. Constituted hierarchy of Satan (Mt 12:22-29). Took possession of persons in peculiar ways (Mt 8:16; Mk 1:32; Lk 8:36).

Demophon (dĕm'ō-fŏn). Opponent of Judas Maccabaeus (2 Mac 12:2).

denarius (dē-nâr'ĭ-ŭs, KJ, RV: penny). Silver coin, weighing 52 (Nero) to 60 (Augustus) grams; worth about 15 cents (Mt 18:28; 20:2, 9, 10, 13; Mk 6:37; 14:5; Lk 7:41; 10:35; Jn 6:7; 12:5; Rv 6:6).

deputy. One empowered to act for another; a regent (1 K 22:47; Jer 51:28 [KJ: ruler]. See also proconsul.

Derbe (dûr'bē). City of Lycaonia in Asia Minor (Acts 14:6, 20; 16:1; 20:4).

desert. Desolate, uncultivated, often arid plain (Dt 32:10; Jb 24:5). See also wilderness.

Desire of all nations. Often understood of Messiah or His kingdom (Hg 2:7. RV: the desirable things of all nations; RSV: the treasures of all nations).

Dessau (dĕs'ō. RV: Lessau). Village (2 Mac 14:16).

Destiny. See Meni.

destroyer, destruction. See Abaddon.

Deuel (dū'ĕl, knowledge of God. Reuel in Nm 2:14). Father of Eliasaph (Nm 1:14; 7:42, 47; 10:20).

Deuteronomy (dū-tẽr-ŏn'ō-mĭ). Called "Words" by Jews. Last book of Pentateuch. Claims Mosaic authorship (31:9, 24, 26). Contains 3 addresses of Moses; ratified as covenant. Outline: 1. 1st discourse (1—4). 2. 2d discourse (5—26). 3. 3d discourse (27—30). 4. Historical notes (31—34).

devil (G diabolos. KJ also for G daimon). See demon; Satan.

devoted. See accursed; anathema.

dew. Heavy dew refreshed earth and regarded as source of fertility (Gn 27:28; Ju 6:37-40). Absence of dew considered an evil (2 Sm 1:21; 1 K 17:1). Figuratively, silent blessings (Dt 32:2; Ps 110:3; Pr 19:12).

diadem. 1. Headdress of men (Jb 29:14. RV margin, RSV: turban), women (Is 3:23. KJ: hood; RV, RSV: turban), high priests (RV margin in Zch 3:5 [KJ: miter; RSV: turban]; Eze 21:26 [RV: miter. RSV: turban]), and kings (Is 28:5; 62:3). Beast (Rv 12:3; 13:1) and rider of white horse (Rv 19:12) wore diadems (KJ: crowns). Ancient diadems were cloth (silk), often covered with gems.

dial. See time 6.

diamond. 1. Precious stone (H yahalom) not definitely identified as diamond (Ex 28:18; 39:11). 2. Hard stone (H shamir, corundum?) used to point engraving tools (Jer 17:1). Adamant in Eze 3:9; Zch 7:12.

Diana (dī-ăn'à). See Artemis.

Diblah (dĭb'là). See Diblath.

Diblaim (dĭb-lā'ĭm, cakes). Father-in-law of Hosea (Hos 1:3).

Diblath (dĭb'lăth. RV: Diblah). Probably Riblah 1 (as RSV. Eze 6:14).

Dibon (dī'bŏn, wasting). 1. Town of Gad E of Jordan (Nm 21:30; 32:3, 34); allotted to Reuben (Jos 13:9, 17); later held by Moabites (Is 15:2; Jer 48:18, 22). Dibon-

gad in Nm 33:45. Modern Dhiban, where Moabite Stone was found. 2. Town in S Judah (Neh 11:25). 3. See Dimon.

Dibon-gad (dī'bŏn-găd). See Dibon 1.

Dibri (dĭb'rī, orator). Danite (Lv 24:11-14).

Didymus (dĭd'ĭ-mus, twin. RSV: the Twin). Surname of Thomas (Jn 11:16; 20:24; 21:2).

dignities. Persons of honor, probably angels (2 Ptr 2:10; Jude 8. RSV: glorious ones).

Diklah (dĭk'là, palm). Joktan's son (Gn 10:27; 1 Ch 1:21)

Dilan, Dilean (dī'lăn, dĭl'ē-ăn, cucumber field). Lowland city of Judah (Jos 15:38).

dill. H qetsah (Is 28:25, 27. KJ, RV: fitch) and G anethon (Mt 23:23. KJ, RV: anise). Anethum graveolens, umbelliferous plant used in cooking and medicine. See food 3; 4.

Dimnah (dĭm'nä). See Rimmon 3.

Dimon (dī'mŏn. RSV: Dibon). Stream in Moab (Is 15:9).

Dimonah (di-mō'nà). City of S Judah (Jos 15:22); probably same as Dibon 2.

Dinah (dī'nà, judged). Daughter of Jacob and Leah; seduced by Shechem (Gn 30:21; 34).

Dinaites (dī'na-īts. RSV: judges). Colonists of Samaria (Ez 4:9).

Dinhabah (dĭn'hà-bä). City of Bela, king of Edom (Gn 36:32; 1 Ch 1:43).

Dionysius (dī-ō-nĭsh'ĭ-ŭs, devotee of Dionysus). Member of Areopagite court at Athens; converted by Paul (Acts 17:34). Patristic writings incorrectly ascribed to him.

Dionysus (dī-ō-nī'sus. KJ, RV: Bacchus). Greek god (2 Mac 6:7; 14:33).

Dioscorinthius (dī-ŏs-kŏ-rĭn'thĭ-ŭs). Month in Cretan calendar (2 Mac 11:21).

Diotrephes (dī-ŏt'rē-fēz, nourished by Zeus). Vainglorious and arbitrary person condemned by John (3 Jn 9, 10).

Diphath (dī'făth). See Riphath.

discerning of spirits. Ability to decide source of proclamation, whether of God or evil (1 Co 12:10. RSV: ability to distinguish between spirits. See 1 Jn 4:1).

disciple (learner). 1. Follower of school of prophet (Is 8:16), Jesus (Mt 5:1; 8:21), John the Baptist (Mt 9:14), Pharisees (Mt 22:16). 2. The Twelve (Mt 10:1; 11:1; 20:17). See apostle.

discipline. See chastisement; education.

discover. KJ for uncover (Ps 29:9; Is 22:8; Mi 1:6).

disease. Physical diseases mentioned in the Bible are: fever (Lv 26:16 [KJ: ague]; Mt 8:14); boils (blains, botch. Ex 9:9, 10; Jb 2:7; 2 K 20:7); gangrene (KJ: canker [cancer]. 2 Ti 2:17); dropsy (Lk 14:2); emerods (Dt 28:27 [RSV: ulcers]; 1 Sm 5:6, 9, 12 [RV, RSV: tumors]); flux (Acts 28:8. RV, RSV: dysentery); itch (Dt 28:27); scab (Dt 28:27. RV, RSV: scurvy); scurvy (Lv 21:20; 22:22); leprosy (Ex 4:6); insanity (Dt 28:28; 1 Sm 21:15); murrain (Ex 9:3. RSV: plague); palsy (RSV: paralytic. Mt 9:2); wen (RSV: discharge, Lv 22:22); worms (Acts 12:23); fractures (Lv 21:19); bruises (Is 1:6); lameness (Lk 14:21); impotence (Jn 5:3); infirmity (Lk 13:11; Jn 5:5 [RSV: ill]); inflammation (Lv 13:28); issue (Lv 15:2. RSV: discharge); sores (Is 1:6); wounds (Lk 10:34). Physicians are rarely mentioned in OT (Gn 50:2; Jb 13:4; 2 Ch 16:12). Tribute to physicians in apocrypha (Sir 38:1-15). In NT medicine was regular profession (Mt 9:12; Lk 4:23; Cl 4:14). Figuratively, sin is described as a terrible disease (Is 1).

Dishan (dī'shăn, antelope). Seir's youngest son (Gn 36:21, 28, 30; 1 Ch 1:38, 42).
Dishon (dī'shon, antelope). 1. Seir's 5th son (Gn 36:21, 30; 1 Ch 1:38). 2. Seir's grandson (Gn 36:25; 1 Ch 1:41).
dispensation. RSV in 2 Co 3:7, 8, 9 (KJ, RV: ministrations); KJ in 1 Co 9:17 (RV: stewardship. RSV: commission); KJ, RV in Eph 1:10 (RSV: plan); 3:2 (RSV: stewardship); Cl 1:25 (RSV: divine office).
dispersion. Scattering of Jews by deportation (as by Assyria and Babylon) or by migration. In NT times Jewish groups were found in practically all civilized countries (Jer 25:34; Jn 7:35; Ja 1:1; 1 Ptr 1:1).
distaff. See *trade 3.*
divination (dĭv-ĭ-nā'shun). Heathen counterpart of prophecy (1 Sm 6:2; Eze 21:21; Dn 2:2); forbidden (Lv 19:26; Dt 18:10; Is 19:3; Acts 16:16). Means used included rods (Hos 4:12), arrows (Eze 21:21), cups (Gn 44:5), liver (Eze 21:21), dreams (Dt 13:3), oracles (Is 41:21-24).
Diviners' Oak. See *Meonenim.*
divorce. See *marriage.*
Di-zahab (dĭ'zá-hăb, having gold). Place in Sinai wilderness near Dead Sea (Dt 1:1).
doctor (RSV: teacher). Teacher (Lk 2:46; 5:17. See 1 Co 12:28). See also *disease.*
doctrine. OT: that which is taught (Dt 32:2; Pr 4:2. RSV: teaching, precept). NT: act of teaching (1 Ti 4:13, 16; 5:17; 2 Ti 3:10. RV, RSV: teaching). That which is taught (Mt 15:9; 2 Ti 4:3 [RSV: teaching]).
Docus (dō'kus). See *Dok.*
Dodai (dō'dī). See *Dodo 2.*
Dodanim (dō'da-nĭm). Race descended from Javan (Gn 10:4 [LXX, Samaritan text: Rodanim]; 1 Ch 1:7 [H, RV, RSV: Rodanim]). See *Javan; Rhodes.*
Dodavah, Dodavahu (dō'da-va, dō-dăv'a-hū, loved of LORD). Eliezer's father (2 Ch 20:37).
Dodo (dō'dō, loving). 1. Ancestor of Tola (Ju 10:1). 2. Ahohite, Eleazar's father (2 Sm 23:9 [RV: Dodai]; 1 Ch 11:12). Dodai in 1 Ch 27:4. 3. Father of Elhanan (2 Sm 23:24; 1 Ch 11:26).
Doeg (dō'ĕg, timid). Edomite; chief of Saul's herdsmen. Reported to Saul that Ahimelech had given David sword and food. Slew Ahimelech and massacred inhabitants of Nob (1 Sm 21:7; 22:7-23; Ps 52 title).
dog. An unclean animal (Ex 11:7; Dt 23:18); regarded with contempt (Ex 22:31; 1 Sm 17:43; 24:14; 2 Sm 3:8; 9:8; 1 K 22:38; 2 K 8:13; Mt 7:6). Sometimes spoken of in kinder terms (Lk 16:21). Applied figuratively to cruel enemies (Ps 22:16, 20); lustful people (Dt 23:18); those who do not appreciate the holy (Mt 7:6), teach false doctrine (Ph 3:2), return to sin (2 Ptr 2:22); Gentiles (Mt 15:26); wicked people (Rv 22:15).
Dok (dŏk. KJ: Docus). Stronghold near Jericho built by Ptolemy, son of Abubus (1 Mac 16:15).
door. 1. Christ is access to salvation (Jn 10:9). 2. Access to sinner's heart (Rv 3:20). 3. Access to God's grace (Lk 13:25). 4. Opportunity to preach Gospel (Acts 14:27; 1 Co 16:9; Col 4:3). 5. Access to heaven (Rv 4:1). 6. "To be at door" indicates nearness (Gn 4:7; Mt 24:33; Ja 5:9). See *homes 4.*
doorkeeper. See *gatekeeper.*

doorpost. Important matters often inscribed on doorposts, following Egyptian custom (Dt 6:9).
Dophkah (dŏf'ka). Camp of Israel between Red Sea and Rephidim (Nm 33:12, 13).
Dor, Dora (dôr, dō'ra, dwelling). Town of Canaanites on Mediterranean Sea (Jos 11:2; 12:23; 17:11; Ju 1:27; 1 K 4:11; 1 Mac 15:11 [KJ: Dora]). See also *Naphath-dor; Naphoth-dor.*
Dorcas (dôr'kăs, gazelle). G for Tabitha.
Dorymenes (dō-rĭm'ĕ-nēz). Father of Ptolemy Macron (1 Mac 3:38; 2 Mac 4:45).
Dositheus (dō-sĭth'ē-us, gift of God). 1. Captain of Judas Maccabaeus (2 Mac 12:19, 24). 2. Soldier of Judas Maccabaeus (2 Mac 12:35). 3. Priest (Ap Est 11:1).
Dothaim, Dothan (dō'thá-im, -thăn, two wells). Place near Shechem and Samaria where Joseph was sold (Gn 37:17-28) and Elisha had vision (2 K 6:13-23; Jdth 4:6 [KJ, RV: Dothaim]).
dough. See *food 2.*
dove. Gentle (SS 1:15), timid (Hos 11:11) bird which housed in clefts (Jer 48:28; Eze 7:16). Spirit of God appeared as dove (Mt 3:16). Turtledove was sacrifice of poor (Lv 12:6-8; Lk 2:24). See also *pigeon.*
dove's dung. Eaten in time of famine (2 K 6:25).
dowry. Stipend paid by groom to bride's father (Gn 29:15-20; 34:12; 1 Sm 18:25). Wedding present for daughter (1 K 9:16).
doxology (dŏks-ŏl'ō-jĭ). Words or songs of praise to God (Ps 96:6; 112:1; 113:1; Lk 2:14; Ro 11:36; Eph 3:21; 2 Ti 1:17). Church has especially used four doxologies: Greater (Gloria in Excelsis), Lesser (Gloria Patri), Trisagion, and the long-meter doxology ("Praise God, from Whom All Blessings Flow").
dragon. 1. Sea monster (Ps 74:13; Is 27:1). Egypt is called dragon (Eze 29:3). 2. Mythical monster typifying Satan (Rv 12:3).
dragon well. See *Jackal's Well.*
dram. See *daric.*
draught house. Latrine (as RSV. 2 K 10:27).
dream. Bible speaks of: 1. Ephemeral and empty dreams (Jb 20:8; Ps 73:20; Is 29:8). 2. Dreams intended to affect inner life or emotions (Ju 7:13; Mt 27:19). 3. Prophetic or directive dreams (Gn 20:3; 28:12; 37:5-11; 40:5; Dn 2; 4; Mt 1:20). Interpretation of dreams was exceptional gift (Gn 40:5-23; Dn 4:19-27).
dregs. Sediment of wine. Figuratively portion of wicked (Ps 75:8; Is 51: 17, 22).
dress. Earliest dress made of leaves (Gn 3:7). Other materials: skin (Gn 3:21; Mt 7:15), hair (Mt 3:4. See Ex 26:7), wool (Gn 38:12; Lv 13:47), linen (Gn 41:42; Pr 31:13), cotton (Is 19:9. RV: white cloth. KJ: networks). Dress of men consisted of tunic (Ex 28:4; Mt 5: 40; Mk 6:9), outer tunic (1 Sm 24:4; Lk 3:11), mantle (almost square cloth, Ex 12:34), used also as bed (Ex 22:26; Dt 24:13), breeches (worn by priests, Ex 28: 42), girdle (2 K 4:29; Jn 21:7; Acts 12:8. RSV: belt in Jb 12:21; Ps 109:19; Eze 23:15; Mt 10:9; Mk 6:8), cap, or turban (Ex 28:40; Jb 29:14), sandals (Ex 3:5; Mt 3:11). Dress of women similar but longer and of finer material; women wore veil (Gn 38:14), ornaments (Is 3:18-23). See *color.*
drink. Hebrews drank water (Gn 24:11-18), milk (Ju 4:19), vinegar and oil (Ru 2:14), wine (Gn 14:18; Jn 2:3), and strong drink (Lv 10:9).

drink offering. See *libation*.
drink, strong. Intoxicating beverage. Jews probably had barley beer, cider, honey wine, date wine, raisin wine, etc. Strong drink frequently mentioned (Gn 9:21; Ps 107:27; Is 24:20; Jn 2:1-11) and warned against (Pr 20:1; Is 5:11).
dromedary. See *camel*.
dropsy. See *disease*.
drought. Dryness due to lack of rain. Little rain fell in Palestine from May to October (Ps 32:4).
drowning. Capital punishment practiced by Greeks, Phoenicians, Romans, Syrians (Mt 18:6).
drunk. 1. Many references to drunkenness (Gn 9:20, 21; 1 Sm 25:36; 1 K 16:9; Lk 12:45; 1 Th 5:7). Drunkenness forbidden (Lv 10:9; Dt 21:20; Pr 23:21; 1 Co 5:11; 6:10; Gl 5:21). 2. Figuratively, of strong emotional feelings which inhibit reason (Is 29:9; 63:6; Jer 51:7).
Drusilla (droo-sil'a). Daughter of Herod Agrippa I; wife of Azizus of Edessa; later of Felix (Acts 24:24).
duke. 1. Chief (as RSV) of Edom (Gn 36: 15; Ex 15:15; 1 Ch 1:51-54). 2. Prince (as RSV, RV. Jos 13:21).
dulcimer (dŭl'si-mĕr). See *bagpipe*.
Dumah (dū'ma). 1. Son of Ishmael; descendants in NW Arabian peninsula (Gn 25:14; 1 Ch 1:30; Is 21:11, 12). 2. Town

in Judah, 10 mi SW of Hebron (Jos 15: 52).
dung. Rules were laid down regarding excrement of human beings (Dt 23:12-14) and sacrifices (Ex 29:14). Used for fertilizer (Is 25:10; Lk 13:8) and fuel (Eze 4:12). Beggars often lay on dunghills (1 Sm 2:8; Ps 113: 7; Lm 4:5). As punishment man's house was made dunghill (Dn 2:5. See 2 K 10:27).
dungeon. See *prison*.
Dura (dū'ra, circle). Plain of Babylon (Dn 3:1).
dust. Sign of mourning (Jos 7:6), degradation (Is 47:1), submission ("mouth in the dust" Lm 3:29), feebleness (Gn 18:27; Jb 30:19), grave (Jb 7:21), death (Gn 3:19; Ps 22:15), multitudes (Gn 13:16), low condition (1 Sm 2:8), anger (2 Sm 16:13; Acts 22:23), renunciation (Mt 10:14; Mk 6:11). Dust rain as punishment (Dt 28:24).
duty. That which one owes, or that which ought to be done; includes duties in home, church, school, and state (1 Sm 10:25; Neh 13:30; Lk 17:10; Ro 13:7; 1 Ti 4:15; 6:2).
dwarf. Could not serve in sanctuary (Lv 21:20).
dysentery. Hemorrhage caused by inflammation of large intestine (Acts 28:8. KJ: bloody flux). See *disease*.

E

eagle. Eagles and vultures (see also *vulture*). Bird of prey (Jb 9:26; 39:30), scavenger (Mt 24:28), large (Eze 17:3, 7), unclean (Lv 11:13; Dt 14:12), builds lofty nests (Jb 39:27-30; Jer 49:16), swift and lofty in flight (Dt 28:49; 2 Sm 1:23; Jb 9:26; Pr 23:5; Jer 4:13), tireless (Is 40:31), youth renewed (Ps 103:5), sights prey from afar (Jb 39:29), tender toward its young (Ex 19:4; Dt 32:11, 12).
Eanes (ē'a-nēz). See *Maaseiah 7*.
ear. Blood was put on ear of priests at consecration (Ex 29:20), and lepers at cleansing (Lv 14:14). Uncircumcised (Jer 6:10; Acts 7:51) or heavy ear is disobedient; open ear, obedient (Is 50:5) or attentive (Ps 34:15; 116:2).
earing. Plowing (as RV, RSV. Gn 45:6; Ex 34:21; Dt 21:4; 1 Sm 8:12).
earnest. Advance deposit or guarantee (2 Co 1:22; 5:5; Eph 1:14. RSV: guarantee). See also *loan*.
earring. Egyptians and Assyrians wore earrings. Ring worn by both sexes (Ex 32:2) as earring (Gn 35:4) or nose-ring (Gn 24:47). "Earring" (KJ, RV) in Is 3:20 is better rendered "amulet" (RSV).
earth. 1. World (Gn 1:1). 2. Dry land (Gn 1:10). 3. Inhabitants of world (Gn 6:11). 4. Carnal things (Jn 3:31; Cl 3:2). 5. Soil (Ex 20:24).
earthquake. Vibratory movement of earth (Nm 16:32; 1 K 19:11; Am 1:1; Zch 14: 4, 5; Mt 27:51-54; 28:2; Acts 16:26; Rv 16:18, 19). Figuratively, God's judgment (Ju 5:4; 2 Sm 22:8; Ps 77:18; 97:4; Is 24:20; 29:6; Jer 4:24; Hg 2:6; Rv 6:12).
East. 1. Hebrews faced E when determining direction; hence H *qedem* (front. Gn 2:8). 2. Toward rising sun (Gn 3:24; Jos 12: 3). 3. Territory toward E (Gn 10:30; Mt 2:1).
East, children (RSV: people) of. Easterners (Gn 29:1; Ju 6:3; Jb 1:3) from point of subject.

east country. Region E of Palestine, especially Syria and Arabia (Gn 25:1-7).
east gate. Potter's Gate in Jerusalem (Jer 19:2. RSV: Potsherd Gate. RV: gate Harsith).
east sea. See *Salt Sea*.
east wind. Hot, dry wind from E (Gn 41: 23, 27; Eze 17:7-10; 19:12).
Easter. (Teutonic goddess of light and spring). Name applied to Christ's resurrection by 8th c. Occurs incorrectly in KJ (Acts 12:4. RV, RSV: Passover).
eating. Eating together a sign of community life (2 Sm 9:7; Jer 52:33) or covenant (Ps 41:9; Jer 41:1; Jn 13:18). Unsatisfactory if not associated with righteous life (Mi 6:14; Eze 12:18). Christ is spiritual food (Jn 6) and drink (Jn 4:14). See also *feast; food*.
Ebal (ē'băl). 1. See *Obal*. 2. Mountain, 2,700 ft above sea, separated by valley of Shechem from Gerizim (2,600 ft above sea). Gerizim was mount of blessing, Ebal of cursing (Dt 11:29; 27:12-26; 28; Jos 8:30-35). 3. Descendant of Seir (Gn 36:23; 1 Ch 1:40).
Ebed (ē'bĕd, servant). 1. Father of Gaal (Ju 9:26-35). 2. Returned from captivity (Ez 8:6). KJ, RV: Obeth; RSV: Obed in 1 Esd 8:32.
Ebed-melech (ē'bĕd-mē'lĕk, king's servant). Ethiopian eunuch who drew Jeremiah from pit (Jer 38:7-13; 39:15-18).
Ebenezer (ĕb-en-ē'zĕr, stone of help). 1. Place where Philistines defeated Israel (1 Sm 4:1, 2; 5:1). 2. Memorial stone set up by Samuel between Mizpeh and Shen after defeat of Philistines (1 Sm 7:12).
Eber (ē'bĕr, beyond. KJ: Heber in 1 Ch 5: 13; 8:22; Lk 3:35). 1. Descendant of Shem; progenitor of Hebrews, Joktanide Arabs, and Aramaeans (Gn 10:21-30; 11: 14-17; Lk 3:35). 2. Priest (Neh 12:20). 3. Gadite (1 Ch 5:13). 4. Benjaminite; son of Elpaal (1 Ch 8:12). 5. Benjaminite; son of Shashak (1 Ch 8:22).

Ebez (ē'bĕz). See *Abez.*

Ebiasaph (ĕ-bī'ȧ-săf). See *Abiasaph.*

ebony. Hard, heavy, dark wood (*Diospyros ebenum*) used for ornamental work (Eze 27:15).

Ebron (ē'bron. KJ: Hebron). Town on boundary of Asher (Jos 19:28). Probably same as Abdon 5.

Ebronah (ĕ-brō'nȧ). See *Abronah.*

Ecanus (ĕ-kā'nus). See *Ethanus.*

Ecbatana (ĕk-bȧt'ȧ-nȧ, RSV). See *Achmetha.*

Ecclesiastes (ĕ-klē-zǐ-ăs'tēz, preacher). H title: *Qoheleth*, G: *Ecclesiastes:* one who addresses assembly. Book is philosophical, answers questions regarding value. Theoretically, there can be no gain in life since same fate comes to all (9). Man's source of satisfaction lies in himself, in use of his mind and body (2:24) for toil (3:13; 5:18) and enjoyment at proper time (3:1-9). Enjoyment of good things in life is gift of God (2:24, 25; 3:13; 5:19). Good things are simple pleasures (9:7-10; 11). In all activity man is to remember his Creator; chief duty, to fear God and keep His commandments (12:13). Traditionally ascribed to Solomon. Luther regarded it as one of latest books of OT.

Ed (ĕd, witness. RSV: Witness). Name of altar built by Reuben, Gad, Manasseh near Jordan (Jos 22:10, 34).

Edar (ē'dȧr). See *Eder.*

Eddias (ĕ-dī'ȧs). See *Izziah.*

Eddinus (ĕd'ǐ-nus). See *Jeduthun.*

Eden (ē'd'n, delight). 1. Garden in which God placed Adam and Eve (Gn 2:15). 2. Region in Mesopotamia called Bit-Adini in Assyrian documents (2 K 19:12; Is 37:12; Eze 27:23; Am 1:5 [RSV: Beth-eden]). 3. Levite (2 Ch 29:12; 31:15).

Eder (ē'dẽr, flock). 1. Tower (Gn 35:21. KJ: Edar). 2. Town in S Judah (Jos 15:21). 3. Levite of family of Merari (1 Ch 23:23; 24:30). 4. Benjaminite (1 Ch 8:15. KJ: Ader).

Edes (ē'dēz). See *Iddo 4.*

edification (ĕd-i-fi-kā'shun, building). Growth in knowledge and grace of life (1 Co 14:3-5; Eph 4:11, 12).

Edna (ĕd'nȧ, rejuvenation). Wife of Raguel (Tob 7:2-16).

Edom (ē'dum, red). 1. Name given to Esau because he sold his birthright for red pottage (Gn 25:30). 2. Descendants of Esau (Ps 83:6) and their country (Idumaea), located at SE border of Palestine (Ju 11:17; Nm 34:3). Seir in Gn 36:8; Jos 24:4. Capital: Sela (Petra).

Edomites (ē'dum-īts). Descendants of Esau (Dt 23:7) who expelled Horites (Dt 2:12); refused passage to Israel through their country (Nm 20:18-21); defeated by Saul (1 Sm 14:47); subdued by David (1 K 11:15, 16; 2 Sm 8:13, 14); continual enemies of Israel (1 K 11:14-22; 2 Ch 21; 25; Is 34:5-8; 63:1-4; Jer 49:17). Under Maccabees Idumea incorporated with Israel.

Edos (ē'dŏs). See *Iddo 4.*

Edrei (ĕd'rē-ī, strong). 1. Town of Bashan (Nm 21:33; Dt 3:10; Jos 12:4) where Og was defeated (Nm 21:33-35; Dt 1:4; 3:1). 2. Town of N Palestine (Jos 19:37).

education. In earliest Hebrew times the children were taught religious ideas and national traditions by parents. Later Deuteronomy was used as textbook (Dt 4:9; 6:6, 7). Moses and the prophets were educational leaders. Ezra increased teachers (Ez 8:16) and promoted knowledge of reading, which before was ability of few (2 K 5:7; 22:8-10; 23:2). In pre-exilic period "the wise" became teachers. Proverbs gives educational ideas of period. After Exile professional teachers taught in synagog schools; c 75 BC compulsory education was introduced, schools divided into Beth Sepher (elementary), Beth Talmud (secondary), and Beth Hammidrash (advanced). Learning was mostly by exact memorization of the master's teaching.

Eglah (ĕg'lȧ, heifer). Wife of David (2 Sm 3:5; 1 Ch 3:3).

Eglaim (ĕg'lȧ-ĭm, ponds). Moabite town (Is 15:8).

Eglath-shelishiyah (ĕg'lȧth-shĕl-ĭsh'ī-yȧ. KJ: an heifer of three years old). Place in Moab (Is 15:5; Jer 48:34).

Eglon (ĕg'lŏn, calflike). 1. Moabite king who captured Jericho and exacted tribute from Israel for 18 yrs; slain by Ehud (Ju 3:12-30). 2. City in S Palestine, whose king, Debir, slain by Joshua (Jos 10; 12: 12; 15:39).

Egypt (ē'jĭpt). NE country of Africa (Gn 10:6. KJ, RV: Mizraim); country of Ham (Ps 105:23, 27); watered by Nile; divided into narrow valley and delta bounded by desert. Ruler called Pharaoh. Wrote with hieroglyphics, later (800 BC) demotic Religion: spiritualized nature worship (gods: Ptah, Ra, Thum, Amon). Powerful kingdom in OT times, cultural center in NT times. Bondage place of Israel (Ex 1—14); often in contact with Hebrews (1 K 3:1; 14:25, 26). "City of sin" called Sodom and Egypt (Rv 11:8).

Egyptian Sea. See *Red Sea.*

Ehi (ē'hī). See *Aharah.*

Ehud (ē'hŭd, union). 1. Benjaminite (1 Ch 7:10). 2. Judge of Israel who assassinated Eglon (Ju 3:15-30).

Eker (ē'kẽr, transplanted). Descendant of Hezron (1 Ch 2:27).

Ekrebel (ĕk'rẽ-bel. RSV: Acraba). Place in Esdraelon (Jdth 7:18).

Ekron (ĕk'rŏn. KJ: Accaron in 1 Mac 10: 89). One of five leading Philistine cities. Ark was carried to Ekron (Jos 13:3; 15: 11, 45, 46; Ju 1:18; 1 Sm 5:10; 6:16, 17; 7:14; 17:52; 2 K 1:2-16; Jer 25:20; Am 1:8; Zph 2:4; Zch 9:5, 7). Modern Akir, 11 mi from Gath.

El (ĕl, God; Divine Being). Name for God which is traced to Canaanites. Frequent in compounds. Elohim (plural) usual word for God in OT.

Ela (ē'lȧ, terebinth). 1. Father of Shimei, purveyor of Solomon (1 K 4:18. KJ: Elah). 2. See *Elam 4.*

Eladah (ĕl'ȧ-dȧ, God has adorned. RV, RSV: Eleadah). Descendant of Ephraim (1 Ch 7:20).

Elah (ē'lȧ, terebinth). 1. See *Ela 1.* 2. Chief of Edom (Gn 36:41; 1 Ch 1:52). 3. 4th king of Israel; son and successor of Baasha, king of Israel; killed by Zimri (1 K 16:8-10). 4. Father of Hoshea, king of Israel (2 K 15:30; 17:1; 18:1). 5. Son of Caleb (1 Ch 4:15). 6. Benjaminite chief (1 Ch 9:8). 7. Valley, SW of Jerusalem, where David killed Goliath (1 Sm 17:2, 19; 21:9).

Elam (ē'lăm). 1. Son of Shem (Gn 10:22; 1 Ch 1:17); descendants dwelt E of Babylonia; in days of Abraham ruled Babylonia (Gn 14:1-11). Capital: Shushan (See Is 21:2; 22:6; Jer 49:34-39; Eze 32: 24; Dn 8:2; Ez 4:9; Acts 2:9). 2. Korahite Levite (1 Ch 26:3). 3. Benjaminite; son of Shashak (1 Ch 8:24). 4. Progenitor of family which returned with Zerubbabel (Ez 2:7; Neh 7:12) and Ezra (Ez 8:7; 10:2, 26; 1 Esd 9:27 [KJ, RV: Ela]).

5. "Other Elam" whose descendants, or inhabitants, returned (Ez 2:31; Neh 7:34). 6. Priest (Neh 12:42). 7. Sealed covenant with Nehemiah (Neh 10:14).

Elasa (ĕl'á-sá. KJ: Eleasa). Place where Judas Maccabaeus camped (1 Mac 9:5).

Elasah (ĕl'á-sá, God has made). 1. Priest who divorced his foreign wife (Ez 10:22; 1 Esd 9:22 [KJ: Talsas; RV: Saloas]). 2. Son of Shaphan; brought letter from Jeremiah to exiles (Jer 29:3).

Elath (ē'lăth, palm grove). Town on Gulf of Aqaba (Dt 2:8) near modern Tell el Kheleifeh. Eloth in 1 K 9:26. See also *Paran.*

El-berith (ĕl-bē'rĭth). See *Baal-berith.*

El-bethel (ĕl-bĕth'ĕl, God of Bethel). Name given by Jacob to altar he built at Bethel (Gn 35:7).

Elcia (ĕl'shĭ-á). See *Elkiah.*

Eldaah (ĕl-dā'á, God of knowledge). Last son of Midian (Gn 25:4; 1 Ch 1:33).

Eldad (ĕl'dăd, God has loved). One of 70 elders appointed to assist Moses (Nm 11: 16, 26-29).

elder. Great respect was paid to aged among Hebrews because of their wisdom and experience (Lv 19:32; Dt 32:7; Jb 32:6). Elders, by primogeniture, became heads of families and clans (Dt 22:15; Ex 3:16; 19:7; Gn 50:7), and leaders in various activities (Gn 24:2; 2 Sm 12:17; Eze 27:9). Elders of city replaced elders of tribe (Dt 21:3; 22:18). Elders also became "rulers of synagog." Elders (presbyters) of Christian churches were men chosen under leadership of apostles. Name presbyter was interchangeable with bishop. Exercised spiritual oversight (Acts 20:17, 28; 1 Ti 5:17; Tts 1:5-9; 1 Th 5:12; 1 Ptr 5:1-3).

Elead (ĕ'lē-ăd, God has testified). Ephraimite (1 Ch 7:21)

Eleadah (ĕl-ē-ā'dá). See *Eladah.*

Elealeh (ē'lē-ā'lĕ). Amorite town assigned to Judah (Nm 32:3, 37; Is 15:4; 16:9; Jer 48:34). Modern El-Al.

Eleasa (ĕl-ē-ā'sá). See *Elasa.*

Eleasah (ĕl-ē-ā'sá, God has made. In H same as Elasah). 1. Judahite (1 Ch 2:39). 2. Descendant of Saul and Jonathan (1 Ch 8:37; 9:43).

Eleazar (ĕl-ē-ā'zẽr, God has helped). 1. 3d son of Aaron and successor in priestly office (Ex 6:23; Nm 20:25-28); overseer of temple custodians (Nm 3:32); assisted in division of land (Jos 14:1). 2. Son of Abinadab; consecrated to keep ark (1 Sm 7:1, 2). 3. Levite of family of Merari (1 Ch 23:21, 22; 24:28). 4. One of David's mighty men (2 Sm 23:9; 1 Ch 11: 12). 5. Priest, son of Phinehas (Ez 8:33). 6. Son of Parosh (Ez 10:25). 7. Priest and musician (Neh 12:42), probably same as 5. 8. Brother of Judas Maccabaeus (1 Mac 2:5; 6:43). 9. Scribe (2 Mac 6: 18). 10. Father of Jason (1 Mac 8:17). 11. Son of Eliud (Mt 1:15). 12. See *Eliezer 8.* — See also *Eliezer.*

Eleazurus (ĕl-ē-á-zū'rus). See *Eliashib 4.*

elect, election. Man's salvation, its conception, method, outcome, is God's work. In OT God is described as choosing (H *baḥar*) Israel, not because of their qualifications (Dt 7:7; 9:4-6) but because of divine love (Dt 4:37; 7:8; 10:15; 23:5). Election to be followed by fidelity (Dt 7:6-11. See Gn 18:19). Remnant is to inherit blessings of election (Is 4:3; 37: 31, 32). OT speaks of God choosing individuals (Neh 9:7; Ps 78:70; 105:26). Gospels speak of Christ choosing (*ekle-*

gesthai) disciples (Lk 6:13). The elect (*eklektoi*) are Messianic community (Mt 24:22, 24; Mk 13:20-27). In epistles previous thoughts are systematized: Election (*ekloge*) roots in eternity, is in Christ, places individuals in company of elect, results from divine love, is understood in entire process of salvation (Ro 9—11; 1 Co 1:27-31; Eph 1:4-14; 1 Ptr 1:2). Election cannot lead to carnal security (2 Ptr 1:10). Elect are members of church (Ro 8:33; 16:13; Col 3:12; Tts 1:1; 1 Ptr 1:1; 2 Jn 13). Reprobation, opposite of election, is absent in NT.

El-elohe-israel (ĕl-ē-lō'hĕ-ĭz'rá-ĕl, God, the God of Israel). Name of Jacob's altar near Shechem (Gn 33:20).

elemental spirits. See *elements 3.*

elements (G *stoicheia*). 1. Basic elements (2 Ptr 3:10, 12). 2. Basic principles (Heb 5:12). 3. Basic principles of orientation in fallen, demonic world (Gl 4:3, 9 [RV: rudiments; RSV: elemental spirits]; Cl 2:8, 20 [KJ, RV: rudiments; RSV: elemental spirits]).

Eleph (ē'lĕf, ox. RSV: Ha-eleph). Town of Benjamin (Jos 18:28). Modern Neby Samvil.

elephant. Used in warfare (1 Mac 3:34; 6: 28-46; 8:6); ivory mentioned (1 K 10: 18, 22; 2 Ch 9:17, 21).

Eleutherus (ē-lū'thẽr-us). Syrian river (1 Mac 11:7).

Eleven, The. Name given to original twelve disciples after defection of Judas (Mt 28: 16; Mk 16:14; Lk 24:9, 33; Acts 1:26; 2:14).

Elhanan (ĕl-hā'năn, grace of God). 1. Son of Dodo; one of David's heroes (2 Sm 23:24). 2. Son of Jair, slew a Goliath (2 Sm 21:19. KJ interpolates "brother of") who is called Lahmi, brother of Goliath, in 1 Ch 20:5.

Eli (ē'lī, high). 1. Descendant of Aaron (Lv 10:12); judge (1 Sm 4:18); devoted high priest (1 Sm 1:17; 2:20-30; 3:11-18) but failed to discipline sons (1 Sm 2:12 to 3:13). As result evil befell him (1 Sm 4:18); priesthood was given to line of Zadok (1 K 2:27). 2. Ancestor of Ezra (2 Esd 1:2. RV: Heli).

Eli, Eli, lama sabachthani (ā'lē, ā'lē, lä'mä sä-bäk-tä'nē). See *Eloi,* etc.

Eliab (ē-lī'ăb, God is Father). 1. Chief of Zebulun (Nm 1:9; 2:7; 7:24, 29; 10:16). 2. Reubenite; father of Dathan and Abiram (Nm 16:1; 26:8). 3. Levite musician (1 Ch 15:18-20). 4. David's oldest brother (1 Sm 16:6; 17:13, 28; 1 Ch 2:13; 2 Ch 11:18). Elihu in 1 Ch 27:18. 5. Gadite; came to David at Ziklag (1 Ch 12:8, 9). 6. See *Elihu 1.* 7. Son of Nathanael (Jdth 8:1).

Eliada (ē-lī'á-dá, whom God notices). 1. Son of David (2 Sm 5:16; 1 Ch 3:8). Beeliada in 1 Ch 14:7. 2. Benjaminite general (2 Ch 17:17). 3. Father of Rezon (1 K 11:23. KJ: Eliadah).

Eliadah (ē-lī'á-dá). See *Eliada 3.*

Eliadas (ē-lī'á-dăs). See *Elioenai 6.*

Eliadun (ē-lī'á-dŭn). See *Iliadun.*

Eliah (ē-lī'á). See *Elijah 2, 4.*

Eliahba (ē-lī'á-bá, God hides). One of David's heroes (2 Sm 23:32; 1 Ch 11:33).

Eliakim (ē-lī'á-kĭm, whom God establishes). 1. Ruler over Hezekiah's house (2 K 18:18; 19:2; Is 22:20). Sent by Hezekiah to receive message from invading Assyrians and report to Isaiah (2 K 18:18, 26, 27; 19:2; Is 36; 37:1-7). Isaiah highly praised him (Is 22:20-25). 2. Original name of King Jehoiakim (2 K

23:34; 2 Ch 36:4). **3.** Priest (Neh 12:41). **4.** Descendant of Zerubbabel and ancestor of Christ (Mt 1:13). **5.** Ancestor of Christ (Lk 3:30).

Eliali, Elialis (ē-lī'á-lī, -lĭs). Listed in 1 Esd 9:34.

Eliam (ē-lī'ăm, God is kinsman). **1.** Father of Bathsheba (2 Sm 11:3. Ammiel in 1 Ch 3:5). **2.** Son of Ahithophel; mighty man of David (2 Sm 23:34). Ahijah in 1 Ch 11:36.

Eliaonias (ē-lī-á-ō-nī'ăs). See *Eliehoenai 2.*

Elias (ē-lī'ăs). See *Elijah 1.*

Eliasaph (ē-lī'á-săf, God has added). **1.** Head of Gad in wilderness (Nm 1:14; 2:14; 7:42). **2.** Levite; chief of Gershonites (Nm 3:24).

Eliashib (ē-lī'á-shĭb, God restores). **1.** Head of 11th course of priests (1 Ch 24:12). **2.** Judahite (1 Ch 3:24). **3.** High priest; father of Joiada (Neh 12:10); helped rebuild walls of Jerusalem (Neh 3:1, 20, 21); related to Tobiah, the Ammonite (Neh 13:4, 7); probably father of Jehohanan (Ez 10:6). **4.** Levite singer; divorced foreign wife (Ez 10:24; 1 Esd 9:24 [KJ: Eleazurus. RV: Eliasibus]). **5.** Israelite; divorced foreign wife (Ez 10:27; 1 Esd 9:28 [KJ: Elisimus; RV: Eliasimus]). **6.** Israelite; divorced foreign wife (Ez 10:36; 1 Esd 9:34 [KJ, RV: Enasibus]).

Eliasibus (ĕl-ĭ-ăs'ĭ-bus). See *Eliashib 4.*

Eliasimus (ĕl-ĭ-ăs'ĭ-mus). See *Eliashib 5.*

Eliasis (ē-lī'á-sĭs). See *Jaasu.*

Eliathah (ē-lī'á-thá, God has come). Leader of 20th division of temple musicians (1 Ch 25:4, 27).

Elidad (ē-lī'dăd, God has loved). Chief of Benjamin; assisted in division of Canaan (Nm 34:21).

Eliehoenai (ē-lī-ē-hō'ē-nī, to God are my eyes). **1.** Korahite porter (1 Ch 26:3. KJ: Elioenai). **2.** Leader who returned with Ezra (Ez 8:4 [KJ: Elihoenai]; 1 Esd 8:31 [KJ, RV: Eliaonias]).

Eliel (ē'lī-ĕl, my God is God). **1.** See *Elihu 1.* **2. 3.** Two of David's heroes (1 Ch 11:46, 47). **4.** Gadite; came to David at Ziklag (1 Ch 12:11). **5.** Levite; son of Hebron (1 Ch 15:9, 11). **6. 7.** Two chiefs of Benjamin (1 Ch 8:20, 22). **8.** Chief of Manasseh (1 Ch 5:24). **9.** Overseer of tithes and offerings (2 Ch 31:13).

Elienai (ĕl-ĭ-ē'nī, to God my eyes). Chief of tribe of Benjamin (1 Ch 8:20).

Eliezar (ĕl-ĭ-ē'zēr). See *Eliezer 8.*

Eliezer (ĕl-ĭ-ē'zēr, God is help). **1.** Steward of Abraham (Gn 15:2, 3; see 24:2). **2.** Younger son of Moses (Ex 18:2-4; 1 Ch 23:15-17; 26:25). **3.** Chief of Benjamin (1 Ch 7:8). **4.** Priest; trumpeter before ark (1 Ch 15:24). **5.** Prophet; predicted shipwreck of Jehoshaphat's vessels (2 Ch 20:37). **6.** Chief sent by Ezra to induce Levites and Nethinim to return (Ez 8:16). **7.** Reubenite chief (1 Ch 27:16). **8.** Priest; divorced foreign wife (Ez 10:18). Eleazar (RSV: Eliezar) in 1 Esd 9:19. **9.** Levite; divorced foreign wife (Ez 10:23). Jonas (RSV: Jonah) in 1 Esd 9:23. **10.** Israelite; divorced foreign wife (Ez 10:31). Elionas in 1 Esd 9:32. **11.** Ancestor of Christ (Lk 3:29). See also *Eleazar.*

Elihoenai (ĕl-ĭ-hō-ē'nī). See *Eliehoenai 2.*

Elihoreph (ĕl-ĭ-hō'rĕf). Scribe of Solomon (1 K 4:3).

Elihu (ē-lī'hū, my God is he). **1.** Greatgrandfather of Samuel (1 Sm 1:1). Eliab in 1 Ch 6:27. Eliel in 1 Ch 6:34. **2.** See

Eliab 4. 3. Captain of Manasseh; joined David (1 Ch 12:20). **4.** Temple porter (1 Ch 26:7). **5.** Friend of Job (Jb 32 to 37). **6.** Ancestor of Judith (Jdth 8:1. KJ: Eliu. RSV: Elijah).

Elijah (ē-lī'já, my God is LORD). **1.** Tishbite. When Ahab, influenced by Jezebel, threatened to suppress worship of Jehovah, made Baal worship court religion, Elijah prophesied drought. During 3 yrs of drought, Elijah was fed by ravens at brook Cherith, later lived in house of widow at Zarephath. Challenged prophets of Baal to test; fire from heaven consumed his sacrifice. People slew 400 priests of Baal. Jezebel plotted against his life; he went to Horeb, met God in vision, learned that God's rule is established in "still, small voice." Anointed Hazael king over Syria, Jehu over Israel, Elisha as his successor. Prophesied God's judgment on Ahab for murder of Naboth. Taken to heaven in chariot (1 K 17—19; 21; 2 K 1; 2; 2 Ch 21:12-15). Later Jews esteemed his memory (Sir 48:1-12; 2 Esd 7:39 [KJ: Helias]). John Baptist is called Elijah (Mt 11:14; 17:10-13; Lk 1:17. See Ml 4:5, 6). Referred to 29 times in NT (KJ: Elias). **2.** Benjaminite chief (1 Ch 8:27. KJ: Eliah). **3.** Priest; divorced foreign wife (Ez 10:21). **4.** Israelite; divorced foreign wife (Ez 10:26 [KJ: Eliah]; 1 Esd 9:27 [KJ, RV: Aedias]). **5.** See *Elihu 6.*

Elika (ē-lī'ká). One of David's heroes (2 Sm 23:25).

Elim (ē'lĭm, large trees). 2d camp of Israel. There were 12 wells and 70 palms (Ex 15:27; 16:1; Nm 33:9). Modern Wadi Gharandel.

Elimelech (ē-lĭm'e-lĕk, my God is king). Husband of Naomi (Ru 1:1-3).

Elioenai (ē-lī-ō-ē'nī, to God are my eyes). **1.** Descendant of Zerubbabel (1 Ch 3:23, 24). **2.** Prince of Simeon (1 Ch 4:36). **3.** See *Eliehoenai 1.* **4.** Grandson of Benjamin (1 Ch 7:8). **5.** Priest; divorced foreign wife (Ez 10:22; see Neh 12:41; 1 Esd 9:22 [KJ, RV: Elionas]). **6.** Singer; divorced foreign wife (Ez 10:27; 1 Esd 9:28 [KJ, RV: Eliadas]).

Elionas (ĕl-ĭ-ō'năs). **1.** See *Elioenai 5.* **2.** See *Eliezer 10.*

Eliphal (ē-lī'făl. God judged. Eliphelet in 2 Sm 23:34). Son of Ur; one of David's mighty men (1 Ch 11:35).

Eliphalat (ē-lĭf'á-lăt). See *Eliphelet 5; 6.*

Eliphalet (ē-lĭf'á-lĕt). See *Eliphelet 2; 4; 5.*

Eliphaz (ĕl'ĭ-făz, God is gold). **1.** Son of Esau by Adah (Gn 36:4; 1 Ch 1:35, 36). **2.** Friend of Job; argued perfection of retribution and majesty of God (Jb 3—8; 15; 22—24).

Elipheleh, Eliphelehu (ē-lĭf'e-lĕ, ē-lĭf'ē-lē-hū). Levite porter; played on harp when ark was brought to Jerusalem (1 Ch 15:18, 21).

Eliphelet (ē-lĭf'e-lĕt, God is deliverance). **1.** Son of David born at Jerusalem (1 Ch 3:6). Elpelet (KJ: Elpalet) in 1 Ch 14:5. **2.** Another son of David born at Jerusalem (1 Ch 3:8). KJ: Eliphalet in 1 Ch 14:7; 2 Sm 5:16. **3.** See *Eliphal.* **4.** Descendant of Jonathan (1 Ch 8:39). **5.** One who returned with Ezra (Ez 8:13; 1 Esd 8:39 [KJ: Eliphalet; RV: Eliphalat]). **6.** Israelite; divorced foreign wife (Ez 10:33; 1 Esd 9:33 [KJ, RV: Eliphalat]).

Elisabeth (ē-lĭz'á-bĕth, God is oath. RSV: Elizabeth). Wife of Zacharias; mother of John the Baptist (Lk 1).

Eliseus (ĕl-ĭ-sē'us). See *Elisha.*

Elisha (ê-lī'shà, God is salvation). Son of Shaphat of tribe of Issachar; successor of Elijah; prophetic work belonged to reigns of Jehoram, Jehu, Jehoahaz, and Joash; many miracles by him (2 K 2—9; 13). KJ: Eliseus in Lk 4:27.

Elishah (ê-lī'shà). Son of Javan; name given to ancient people (Gn 10:4; Eze 27:7).

Elishama (ê-lĭsh'à-mä, God has heard). 1. Captain of tribe of Ephraim at Exodus; ancestor of Joshua (Nm 1:10; 2:18; 7:48, 53; 10:22; 1 Ch 7:26). 2. Son of David born at Jerusalem (1 Ch 3:6). Elishua in 2 Sm 5:15; 1 Ch 14:5. 3. Another son of David born at Jerusalem (1 Ch 3:8; 14:7; 2 Sm 5:16). 4. Prince; grandfather of Ishmael, who murdered Gedaliah (2 K 25:25; Jer 41:1). 5. Judahite (1 Ch 2:41). 6. Priest (2 Ch 17:8). 7. Scribe of Jehoiakim (Jer 36:12, 20, 21).

Elishaphat (ê-lĭsh'à-făt, God has judged). Captain of 100 under Jehoiada (2 Ch 23:1).

Elisheba (ê-lĭsh'ê-bà, God of oath). Wife of Aaron (Ex 6:23).

Elishua (ĕl-ĭ-shū'à). See Elishama 2.

Elisimus(ê-lĭs'ĭ-mŭs). See Eliashib 5.

Eliu (ê-lī'ū). See Elihu 6.

Eliud (ê-lī'ŭd). Ancestor of Jesus (Mt 1: 14, 15).

Elizabeth (ê-lĭz'à-bĕth). See Elisabeth.

Elizaphan (ĕl-ĭ-zā'făn, God has protected). 1. Chief of Kohathites in wilderness (Ex 6:22; Nm 3:30); with brother Mishael carried away corpses of Nadab and Abihu (Lv 10:4). Elzaphan in Ex and Lv. 2. Prince of Zebulun (Nm 34:25).

Elizur (ê-lī'zēr, God is rock). Reubenite prince (Nm 1:5; 2:10; 7:30, 35; 10:18).

Elkanah, Elkonah (ĕl-kā'nà, ĕl-kō'nà, God has acquired). 1. Kohathite; brother of Abiasaph (Ex 6:24; 1 Ch 6:23). 2. 3. 4. Kohathites; descendants of Abiasaph (1 Ch 6:36, son of Joel; 6:26, 35, son of Mahath; 6:27, 34, son of Jeroham and father of Samuel. See 1 Sm 1:1; 2:11, 20). 5. Korahite; joined David at Ziklag (1 Ch 12:6). 6. Gatekeeper for ark (1 Ch 15:23). Possibly same as 5. 7. High official of Ahaz (2 Ch 28:7). 8. Head of Levitical family (1 Ch 9:16).

Elkiah (ĕl-kī'à. KJ: Elcia). Ancestor of Judith (Jdth 8:1).

Elkosh (ĕl'kŏsh). Birthplace of Nahum (Nah 1:1).

Ellasar (ĕl-lā'sär). City of Arioch identified with Larsa (G Larissa. Gn 14:1-9).

elm. See oak.

Elmadam, Elmodam (ĕl-mā'dăm, -mō'dăm). Ancestor of Christ (Lk 3:28).

Elnaam (ĕl-nā'ăm, God is delight). Father of two of David's warriors (1 Ch 11:46).

Elnathan (ĕl-nā'thăn, gift of God). 1. Grandfather of Jehoiachin (2 K 24:8; Jer 26:22). 2. Names of three men sent to obtain priests from Iddo (Ez 8:16). 1 Esd 8:44 lists only two (KJ: Alnathan, Eunatan. RV: Ennatan as the 2d).

Elohim (ê-lō'hĭm). See El.

Eloi, eloi, lama sabachthani (ê-lō'ī, ê-lō'ī, lä'mà sà-băk'thà-nī, My God, My God, why hast Thou forsaken Me?). Jesus' 4th utterance on cross (Ps 22:1; Mt 27:46; Mk 15:34, KJ: Eli, Eli . .).

Elon (ê'lŏn, oak). 1. Father of Basemath (Gn 26:34; 36:2). 2. Son of Zebulun (Gn 46:14; Nm 26:26). 3. Zebulonite; judge of Israel (Ju 12:11, 12). 4. Town of Dan (Jos 19:43). Elon-beth-hanan in 1 K 4:9

Elon-beth-hanan (ê'lŏn-bĕth-hā'năn). See Elon 4.

Eloth (ê'lŏth). See Elath.

Elpaal (ĕl-pā'ăl, God of doing). Benjaminite (1 Ch 8:11, 12).

Elpalet (ĕl-pā'lĕt). See Eliphelet 1.

El-paran (ĕl-pā'răn). See Paran.

Elpelet (ĕl-pē'lĕt). See Eliphelet 1.

Elteke, Eltekeh (ĕl'tê-kē, -kĕ). City of Dan (Jos 19:44; 21:23).

Eltekon (ĕl'tê-kŏn). Town in mts of Judah (Jos 15:59).

Eltolad (ĕl-tō'lăd). Town in S Judah assigned to Simeon (Jos 15:30; 19:4). Tolad in 1 Ch 4:29.

Elul (ê'lōol). See time 4.

Eluzai (ê-lū'zā-ī, God my strength). Benjaminite; joined David at Ziklag (1 Ch 12:5).

Elymaeans (ĕl-ĭ-mê'ans). Elamites (Jdth 1:6).

Elymas (ĕl'ĭ-măs, wise). Jew named Bar-Jesus; sought to hinder conversion of Sergius Paulus; smitten with blindness (Acts 13:6-12).

Elzabad (ĕl-zā'băd, God has given). 1. Gadite; joined David at Ziklag (1 Ch 12:12). 2. Levite porter (1 Ch 26:7).

Elzaphan (ĕl-zā'făn). See Elizaphan.

Emadabun (ê-mà-dà'bŭn. KJ: Madiabun). Levite listed in 1 Esd 5:58.

Ematheis, Emathis (ĕm-à-thē'ĭs, ĕm'à-thĭs). See Athlai.

embalm. Jacob was embalmed by Egyptians at command of Joseph; likewise Joseph (Gn 50:2, 26).

embroidery. Weaving, sewing, artistic needlework done by Hebrews and their neighbors (Ex 38:23; Ju 5:30; Ps 45: 13, 14). Embroidery decorated hangings of temple (Ex 26:36) and attire of priests (Ex 28:33, 39; 39:29).

Emek-keziz (ê'mĕk-kē'zĭz, vale cut off. KJ: valley of Keziz). Town of Benjamin near Jericho (Jos 18:21).

emerald. Jews probably became acquainted with emeralds in Egypt (Ex 28:18; 39:11; Eze 28:13; Rv 4:3; 21:19).

emerod (ĕm'ēr-ŏd). External or internal tumor in anal region; hemorrhoid (Dt 28:27 [RSV: ulcers]). RV, RSV: tumors in 1 Sm 5:6-12; 6:4-11. See disease.

Emim (ê'mĭm). See giants 4.

Emmanuel (ê-măn'ū-ĕl). See Immanuel.

Emmaus (ê-mā'us, hot springs). Village near Jerusalem. Site uncertain (Lk 24: 13-33).

Emmer, Emmeruth (ĕm'ēr, ĕm-ê-rōōth'). See Immer 1.

Emmor (ĕm'or). See Hamor.

Enaim (ê-nā'ĭm, two springs. KJ: open, openly). Town between Adullam and Timnath (Gn 38:14, 21).

Enam (ê'năm, having fountains). City in lowlands of Judah (Jos 15:34). Perhaps Enaim.

Enan (ê'năn, having eyes). Father of Ahira, prince of Naphtali (Nm 1:15; 2:29; 7:78, 83; 10:27).

Enasibus (ê-năs'ĭ-bus). See Eliashib.

encampment. See camp.

enchantment. Use of magic arts, spells, or charms, as Egyptian arts (Ex 7:11-22; 8:7); Balaam's omens (Nm 24:1); sorceries (2 K 9:22; Mi 5:12; Nah 3:4); serpent charming (Ec 10:11); magical spells (Is 47:9-12). See augury; magic.

En-dor (ĕn'dôr, fountain of Dor). Village near Mt Tabor (Jos 17:11; Ps 83:10; 1 Sm 28:7).

En-eglaim (ĕn-ĕg'lâ-ĭm, fountain of two calves). Place on Dead Sea (Eze 47:10).

Enemessar (ĕn-ê-mĕs'ēr). See Shalmaneser 2.

Eneneus, Enenius (ĕ-nē'nē-*us*, -nĭ-*us*). See *Nahamani*.

En-gaddi (ĕn-găd'ī). See *En-gedi*.

En-gannim (ĕn-găn'ĭm, fountain of gardens). 1. Levitical city of Issachar (Jos 19:21; 21:29). Anem in 1 Ch 6:73. Modern Jenin, 7 mi SW of Mt Gilboa. 2. City of Judah (Jos 15:34).

En-gedi (ĕn-gē'dī, fountain of wild goat). Town on oasis on W shore of Dead Sea fed by warm spring water, 15 mi SE of Hebron (Jos 15:62; Eze 47:10; 1 Sm 24: 1-7; SS 1:14; Sir 24:14 [KJ: En-gaddi; RV: on the sea shore]). Hazazon-tamar (Gn 14:7 [KJ: Hazezon-tamar]; 2 Ch 20·2).

engine. Military equipment; ballista (2 Ch 26:15); battering ram (as RSV: Eze 26:9. See Eze 4:2; 21:22).

engraving. Well known in Palestine and neighboring regions (2 Ch 2:14). Examples: commandments (Ex 32:16); stones and signets (Ex 28:11, 36); idols (Ex 20:4; 32:4).

En-haddah (ĕn-hăd'ă, vehement fountain). Border village of Issachar (Jos 19:21).

En-hakkore (ĕn-hăk'ō-rē, fountain of the crier). Samson's fountain (Ju 15:19).

En-hazor (ĕn-hā'zôr, fountain of the village). Fenced city of Naphtali (Jos 19:37).

En-mishpat (ĕn-mĭsh'păt, fountain of judgment). Early name of Kadesh 1 (Gn 14:7).

enmity. Antagonism between serpent and man (Gn 3:15), carnality, worldliness and God (Ro 8:7, 8; Ja 4:4). Carnality leads to enmity among men (Gl 5:20).

Ennatan (ĕ-nā'tăn). See *Elnathan 2*.

Enoch (ē'nŭk, dedicated). 1. 1st son of Cain (Gn 4:17). 2. Father of Methuselah; transported to heaven (Gn 5:18-24; 1 Ch 1:3 [KJ: Henoch]; Heb 11:5; Jude 14). 3. City built by Cain (Gn 4:17). 4. Behemoth (as RV, RSV: 2 Esd 6:49-51).

Enos, Enosh (ē'nos, ē'nŏsh). Son of Seth (Gn 4:26; 5:6-11; 1 Ch 1:1; Lk 3:38).

En-rimmon (ĕn-rĭm'on, fountain of pomegranate). Place occupied by Judahites after exile (Neh 11:29; Jos 19:7 [KJ: Ain, Remmon. RV: Ain, Rimmon]). Probably villages Ain and Rimmon (Jos 15:32). See also *Ain 2; Rimmon 1*.

En-rogel (ĕn-rō'gel, spy's fountain). Spring outside Jerusalem's walls (Jos 15:7; 18:16; 2 Sm 17:17; 1 K 1:9).

enrolled. See *census; genealogy*.

En-shemesh (ĕn-shē'mĕsh, fountain of sun). Spring on Judah-Benjamin boundary, probably near Bethany (Jos 15:7; 18:17).

ensign (ĕn'sīn). 1. Signal exhibited on pole (Is 13:2. KJ: banner; RSV: signal). 2. Standard, perhaps emblem, given to four divisions of army (Nm 2:2). 3. Sign given tribes (Nm 2:2). Used figuratively (Is 11:10).

En-tappuah (ĕn-tăp'û-ȧ, fountain of Tappuah). Spring near Tappuah (Jos 17:7).

envoy. See *ambassador*.

envy. Spite and hostile grudge which result from hostility to God and corrupt human nature (Mk 7:22 [KJ, RV: an evil eye]; Ro 1:29; Gl 5:21).

Epaenetus (ĕ-pē'nē-*tus*, praised). Christian; first fruit of Asia; greeted by Paul (Ro 16:5).

Epaphras (ĕp'ȧ-frăs, lovely). Colossian Christian; visited imprisoned Paul (Cl 1:7, 8; 4:12; Phmn 23).

Epaphroditus (ē'păf-rō-dī'*tus*, lovely). Christian sent by church at Philippi to imprisoned Paul (Ph 2:25-30; 4:18).

ephah (ē'fȧ). See *measures 2 d*.

Ephah (ē'fȧ, gloom). 1. Son of Midian (Gn 25:4; 1 Ch 1:33; Is 60:6). 2. Caleb's concubine (1 Ch 2:46). 3. Judahite (1 Ch 2:47).

Ephai (ē'fī). Netophathite; sons, left in Judah, informed Gedaliah of plots against him (Jer 40:7-16).

Epher (ē'fēr). 1. Son of Midian (Gn 25:4; 1 Ch 1:33). 2. Judahite (1 Ch 4:17). 3. Manassite (1 Ch 5:24).

Ephes-dammim (ē'fēs-dăm'ĭm, end of Dammim). Place between Soco and Azekah, where David fought Goliath (1 Sm 17:1). Pas-dammim in 1 Ch 11:13.

Ephesians, Epistle to (ē-fē'zhănz). Traditionally regarded as circular letter written to congregations in province of which Ephesus was pro-city; ascribed to Paul (1:1; 3:1; 4:1). Contains sublime thoughts concerning the Lord of the church and the relation of the church to its Lord. Concludes with admonitions. Outline: 1. Doctrine (election, adoption, Christ, conversion, church. 1—3). 2. Life (unity, sin, duties. 4—6).

Ephesus (ĕf'e-*sus*). Capital of Roman province of Asia, 3 mi from Aegean Sea on Cayster River. Commercial city; racial melting pot; dedicated to worship of Phoenician Astarte (G Artemis; L Diana). Paul established church there (Acts 19; 20; 1 Co 16:8).

Ephlal (ĕf'lăl). Judahite (1 Ch 2:37).

ephod (ĕf'ŏd, covering). Apronlike garment with shoulder straps and girdle worn by high priests. Its adornments described in Ex 29. Later worn by other than priests (1 Sm 2:18; 2 Sm 6:14; 1 Ch 15:27).

Ephod (ē'fŏd). Manassite; father of Hanniel (Nm 34:23).

ephphatha (ĕf'ȧ-thȧ, be opened). Spoken by Christ (Mk 7:34).

Ephraim (ē'frȧ-ĭm). 1. 2d son of Joseph by Asenath, daughter of Potipherah (Gn 46:20). Jacob preferred Ephraim to Manasseh, conferred on him birthright blessing (Gn 48:8-20). Descendants were numerous (Nm 1:33; 26:37). Tribe was assigned land between Manasseh (W), and Dan and Benjamin (Jos 16). Ephraim became heart of N Kingdom (1 K 12; Is 7:2; 11:13; Eze 37:15-22). 2. City near Absalom's sheep farm (2 Sm 13:23). 3. City NE of Jerusalem (Jn 11:54). 4. Gate of Jerusalem (2 K 14:13; 2 Ch 25:23).

Ephraim, Mount. Central range of mts in Samaria (Jos 19:50; 1 Sm 1:1. RV, RSV: hill country of Ephraim). Hill country (KJ: mountains) of Israel in Jos 11:21; mountains of Samaria in Jer 31:5; Am 3:9.

Ephrain (ē'frȧ-ĭn). See *Ephron 2*.

Ephratah (ĕf'rȧ-tȧ). See *Ephrath; Ephrathah*.

Ephrath (ĕf'răth, fruitful). 1. Ancient name of Bethlehem-Judah (Gn 35:16, 19; 48:7). Ephrathah (KJ: Ephratah) in Ru 4:11; Ps 132:6; Mi 5:2. 2. See *Ephrathah 2*.

Ephrathah (ĕf'rȧ-thȧ, KJ: Ephratah). 1. See *Ephrath 1*. 2. Wife of Caleb; mother of Hur (1 Ch 2:24, 50; 4:4). Ephrath in 1 Ch 2:19.

Ephrathite (ĕf'rȧ-thīt). 1. Inhabitant of Bethlehem (Ephrath. Ru 1:2). 2. Ephraimite (as RV, RSV: 1 Sm 1:1; 1 K 11:26).

Ephron (ē'frŏn, fawnlike). 1. Hittite who sold Machpelah to Abraham (Gn 23:8-20; 49:29; 50:13). 2. City taken from Jeroboam by Abijah (2 Ch 13:19. KJ: Ephrain). 3. Mt ridge on Judah-Benjamin boundary (Jos 15:9). 4. City E of Jordan captured by Judas Maccabaeus (1 Mac 5: 46-52; 2 Mac 12:27).

Epicureans (ĕp-ĭ-kû-rē'ănz). Followers of Epicurus (d 270 BC). Philosophy aimed at happiness, which consisted in mental peace and freedom from fear. Denied life after death (Acts 17:16-32).

epileptic. See *disease*.

Epiphanes (ē-pĭf'á-nēz). See *Antiochus 3*.

epistle (ē-pĭs''l. RSV: letter). Formal letter or treatise containing Christian doctrine and admonition (Acts 15:30; Ro 16:22). Name given to 21 NT books, divided into Pauline and Catholic (or General) epistles. Christians are epistles written by Holy Spirit (2 Co 3:2, 3).

Er (ûr, on watch). 1. Oldest son of Judah (Gn 38:2-7; Nm 26:19). 2. Son of Shelah (1 Ch 4:21). 3. Ancestor of Christ (Lk 3:28).

Eran (ē'răn, watchful). Grandson of Ephraim; head of Era.ites (Nm 26:36).

Erastus (ē-răs'tŭs, beloved). Convert of Paul; lived in Corinth (Ro 16:23; 2 Ti 4:20); with Paul at Ephesus (Acts 19:22).

Erech (ē'rĕk, Uruk). City 50 mi NW of Ur (Gn 10:10); excavated.

Eri (ē'rī, watcher). Son of Gad (Gn 46:16; Nm 26:16).

error. Mistake, or departure from truth in life (Ro 1:27; Ja 5:20; 2 Ptr 2:18) and conviction or doctrine (Is 32:6; 1 Jn 4:6). There are errors of ignorance (Nm 15:22-26; Eze 45:20) and malicious error (2 Ptr 3:17). Spirit of error is worldly orientation (1 Jn 4:5, 6).

Esaias (ē-zā'yás). See *Isaiah*.

Esarhaddon (ĕz-ẽr-hăd''n, Asshur has given brother). Son and successor of Sennacherib. Ruled 681—669 BC (2 K 19:37; Is 37:38). Rebuilt Babylon; defeated Egypt; laid tribute on, and took Manasseh captive (2 Ch 33:11); colonized Samaria (Ez 4:2; Tob 1:21, 22 [KJ, RV: Sarchedonus]). See also *Azbazareth*.

Esau (ē'sô, hairy). 1. 1st of twin sons of Isaac and Rebecca (Gn 25:25); sold birthright (Gn 27:28, 29, 36) to brother Jacob for red pottage (Gn 25:29-34; Heb 12:16, 17), hence called Edom (red); married two Canaanites (Gn 26:34; 36:2) and an Ishmaelite (Gn 28:9); sought to kill Jacob (Gn 27:41-45) but reconciled (Gn 33). Edom is country of his descendants (Gn 36). 2. See *Ziha 1*.

Esay (ē'zā). See *Isaiah*.

eschatology (ĕs-ká-tŏl'ŏ-jĭ, doctrine of last things). Presentation of ultimate existence and state; events leading to end; all that follows life. OT emphasis was on destiny of chosen people (Is 43:6; Am 9:11-15) and Day of Jehovah, when world would be judged in righteousness (Is 13:6, 9; Jl 3:14; Zph 1:7). Individual exists in Sheol after death (see *Sheol*). Resurrection taught in Is 26:19-21; Dn 12:2 (see Jb 19:25, 26; Is 53:10). NT emphasizes return of Christ (see parousia) to judge world (Mt 24:25); resurrection (Ro 8:11; 1 Co 15); consummation (1 Co 15:24), when wicked are cast into Gehenna (Mt 5:29, 30; 25; Mk 9:43) and righteous enter into joy of Father (Mt 25:31-46).

Esdraelon (ĕs-drá-ē'lŏn). See *Jezreel, Valley of*.

Esdras (ĕz'drăs). See *Ezra; Apocrypha*.

Esebon (ĕs'ē-bŏn). See *Heshbon*.

Esebrias (ĕs-ē-brī'ás). See *Sherebiah*.

Esek (ē'sĕk, strife). Well dug by Isaac's herdsmen in valley of Gerar (Gn 26:20).

Eserebias (ĕs-ē-rē'bĭ-ăs). See *Sherebiah*.

Eshan (ē'shăn, support. KJ: Eshean). Village in Judah (Jos 15:52).

Eshbaal (ĕsh'bā-ăl). See *Ishbosheth*.

Eshban (ĕsh'băn). Descendant of Seir (Gn 36:26; 1 Ch 1:41).

Eshcol (ĕsh'kŏl). 1. One of 3 Amorite brothers in alliance with Abraham (Gn 14:13, 24). 2. Valley near Hebron celebrated for large grapes (Nm 13:22, 23; Dt 1:24).

Eshean (ĕsh'ē-ăn). See *Eshan*.

Eshek (ē'shĕk). Descendant of Saul (1 Ch 8:39).

Eshkalonites (ĕsh'ká-lŏn-īts). Inhabitants of Ashkelon (Jos 13:3. RV: Ashkelonites).

Eshtaol (ĕsh'tâ-ŏl). Town 13 mi NW of Jerusalem (Jos 15:33), given to Dan (Jos 19:41). Samson active in this area (Ju 13:24, 25; 16:31).

Eshtaolites, Eshtaulites (ĕsh'tâ-ŏl-īts, ĕshtâ-ū'lits). Inhabitants of Eshtaol (1 Ch 2:53).

Eshtemoa (ĕsh-tē-mō'á). 1. Village 9 mi S of Hebron, given to priests (Jos 21:14; 1 Ch 6:57; 1 Sm 30:28). Eshtemoh in Jos 15:50. Modern Semua. 2. A Maacathite (1 Ch 4:19).

Eshtemoh (ĕsh'tē-mō). See *Eshtemoa 1*.

Eshton (ĕsh'tŏn, restful). Judahite (1 Ch 4:11, 12).

Esli (ĕs'lī). Ancestor of Jesus (Lk 3:25).

Esora (ē-sō'rá. RV, RSV: Aesora). Perhaps Hazor or Zorah (Jdth 4:4).

espouse. See *marriage*.

Esril (ĕs'rĭl). See *Azarel 4*.

Esrom (ĕs'rŏm). See *Hezron 2*.

Essene (ē-sēn'). Jewish sect (2d c BC—2d c AD); chief colonies around Dead Sea. While there were variations in related groups, societies generally taught celibacy, community of property, sanctity of Law, cleanliness, immortality; opposed slavery, animal sacrifice. Not named in Bible but described in Josephus, Philo, Dead Sea scrolls.

estate (ĕs-tāt'). 1. Rank or condition in life (Eze 16:55; Lk 1:48). See also *degree*. 2. Property, especially in land (1 K 2:26 [KJ, RV: fields]; Gl 4:1 [KJ: omits]).

Esther (ĕs'tẽr, Ishtar, Babylonian goddess; star). Jewess, cousin of Mordecai; became wife of Ahasuerus (Xerxes I, 486 to 465 BC); saved lives of her countrymen. Hebrew name was Hadassah (myrtle. Est 2:7). See *Esther, Book of*.

Esther, Book of. Called Megilloth Esther and belonged to Writings. Relates how Esther became queen and saved her people. Author familiar with Persian government and palace of Shushan. Explains origin of Feast of Purim, referred to in 2 Mac 15 as "the day of Mordecai" (Est 9:21-32). Outline. 1. Esther Becomes Queen (1—2:17). 2. Jewish Plight (2: 18—3:15). 3. Jews Delivered (4—10).

Esyelus (ĕs-ĭ-ē'lŭs). See *Jehiel 6*.

Etam (ē'tăm, hawkground). 1. Border town of Judah (1 Ch 4:32). 2. "Rock Etam," place where Samson dwelt (Ju 15:8, 11). 3. Town 2 mi SW of Bethlehem (2 Ch 11:6).

eternal life. Participation in life of Jesus, Son of God (Jn 1:4: 10:10; 17:3; Ro 6:23); reaches full fruition in resurrection and subsequent glory (Mt 25:46; Jn 6:54; Ro 2:7; Tts 3:7).

eternity. Described as "forever," or "from everlasting to everlasting" (Ps 90:2). God is before (Jer 1:5; Ps 90) and after all things (Rv 1:8; 21:6). His reign, power, glory is eternal (Ps 29:10; Is 44:6; 57:15).

God's eternity envelopes time and creatures, while He is unaffected by change (Ps 90; 2 Ptr 3:8; Rv 1:4; 4:8).

Etham (ē'thăm) 2d encampment of Israel (Ex 13:20; Nm 33:6).

Ethan (ē'thăn, permanent). 1. Wise man (1 K 4:31; 1 Ch 2:6; Ps 89 title). 2. See *Joah 2*. 3. Levite singer (1 Ch 6:44; 15: 17-19). See also *Jeduthun*.

Ethanim (ĕth'á-nĭm, rains). Name of Tishri, 7th month (October, 1 K 8:2).

Ethanus (ē-thā'nus. KJ: Ecanus). Scribe (2 Esd 14:24).

Ethbaal (ĕth-bā'ăl, with Baal). King of Sidon; father of Jezebel (1 K 16:31).

Ether (ē'thĕr, plenty). City in lowlands of Judah (Jos 15:42); allotted to Simeon (Jos 19:7); 1 mi N of Beit Jibrin.

Ethiopia (ē-thǐ-ō'pǐ-á, *possibly* sunburnt, *or foreign word*). G and L for H: Cush. Versions vary between "Cush" and "Ethiopia." (Gn 10:6-8; 1 Ch 1:8; 2 Ch 12:3; 14:9; Eze 30:9; Acts 8:27). Ethiopians described as merchants (Is 45:14); strong military power (2 Ch 14:9-12). See also *Cush*.

Eth-kazin (ĕth-kā'zĭn. KJ: Ittah-kazin). Place on boundary of Judah (Jos 19:13).

Ethma (ĕth'má). See *Nebo 3*.

Ethnan (ĕth'năn, gift). Judahite (1 Ch 4:7).

Ethni (ĕth'nī, liberal). See *Jeaterai*.

Eubulus (û-bū'lus, prudent). Roman Christian (2 Ti 4:21).

Eucharist (ū'ká-rĭst). See *Lord's Supper*.

Eunatan (ū-nā'tăn). See *Elnathan 2*.

Eunice (û-nī'sē, û'nĭs, victorious). Mother of Timothy (Acts 16:1; 2 Ti 1:5).

eunuch (ū'nuk, G "bedkeeper." H *saris*). Castrated male. Eunuchs were court officials (Dn 1:3; Acts 8:27); guardians of women and children (2 K 20:18; Jer 41: 16; Est 1:10-15; 2:21). According to Josephus, castration was not practiced by Jews (Ant LV, viii, 40). Eunuchs not permitted to enter congregation (Dt 23:1).

Euodia, Euodias (û-ō'dĭ-á, -ăs, fragrant). Christian woman at Philippi (Ph 4:2).

Euphrates (û-frā'tēz). River about 1,780 mi long from Armenia to Persian Gulf. River of Eden (Gn 2:14). Called "great river" (Gn 15:18), "the River" (Dt 11:24). Regarded as ideal boundary of Palestine (Dt 11:24; Jos 1:4) and of David's conquests (2 Sm 8:3; 1 Ch 18:3).

Eupolemus (û-pŏl'ē-mus). Envoy (1 Mac 8:17).

Euraquilo (û-răk'wĭ-lō, NE wind. KJ: Euroclydon, SE wind, a reading found in some ancient mss. RSV: the northeaster). Wind typical on Mediterranean; shipwrecked Paul (Acts 27:14).

Euroclydon (û-rŏk'lĭ-dŏn). See *Euraquilo*.

Eutychus (ū'tĭ-kus, fortunate). Youth, who falling asleep while Paul preached, fell from 3d story; restored to life by Paul (Acts 20:9, 10).

evangelist (ē-văn'je-lĭst, publisher of good tidings). 1. Preacher inferior to apostles yet superior to pastors and teachers (Acts 8:4-40; 21:8; Eph 4:11; 2 Ti 4:5). 2. Writer of Gospel.

Eve (ēv, life). 1st woman; mother of all living (Gn 2:18-25; 3; 4).

Evi (ē'vī, desire). King of Midian (Nm 31:8; Jos 13:21).

evil. 1. Material conditions which create disorder in the universe (Gn 3; Jb 2:10; Ps 23:4; Pr 15:15; Lk 16:25). 2. See *sin*.

Evil-merodach (ē'vĭl-mē-rō'dăk, man of Marduk). King of Babylon (562—560 BC), successor of Nebuchadnezzar (2 K 25:27; Jer 52:31).

exchanger. See *bank, banker*.

excommunication (ĕks-ko-mū-ni-kā'shun). Jews practiced temporary and permanent excommunication. NT: separation from church for good of individual and welfare of church (1 Co 5:5). Restored after repentance (2 Co 2:5-11. See Mt 16:19; 18:17; Tts 3:10).

excrement (ĕks'krē-ment). See *dung*.

exile. See *captivity; dispersion*.

exodus (ĕk'sō-dus, departure). Departure of Israel from Egypt (Ex; Heb 11:22. KJ: departing; RV: departure).

Exodus, Book of. H *w:'elleh shemoth* (and these are the names); Exodus from LXX. 2d book of Pentateuch; describes Israel's redemption from Egypt and establishment of nation under covenant with law, priesthood, sacrificial system. Outline: 1. Deliverance in Egypt (1—12:36). 2. Israel in wilderness (12:37—18:37). 3. Organization of Israel at Sinai (19—40). See also *Moses*.

exorcism (ĕk'sôr-sĭz'm). Driving out demons and evil spirits by using magical formulas and ceremonies (Mt 12:27; Mk 9:38; Acts 19:13).

expiation (ĕks-pĭ-ā'-shun). See *atonement; propitiation*.

eye. Frequently used figuratively in Bible: light of the body (Mt 6:22), jealousy (Mt 20:15), lust (Eze 6:9; 2 Ptr 2:14), pity (Dt 7:16), and others.

Ezar (ē'zēr). See *Ezer*.

Ezbai (ĕz'bā-ī, shining). Father of Naarai (1 Ch 11:37).

Ezbon (ĕz'bŏn, bright). 1. Son of Gad (Gn 46:16). Ozni in Nm 26:16. 2. Benjaminite (1 Ch 7:7).

Ezechias (ĕz-ê-kī'ăs). See *Hezekiah 1; Jahzeiah*.

Ezecias (ĕz-ê-sī'ăs). See *Hilkiah 8*.

Ezekias (ĕz-ê-kī'ăs). See *Hezekiah 1; Jahzeiah*.

Ezekiel (ê-zēk'yel, God strᴇ.ıgthens). Prophet-priest; son of Buzi (Eze 1:3); carried into captivity (597 BC) with Jehoiachin (Eze 33:21; 40:1; 2 K 24: 11-16); lived on Chebar Canal in Babylonia (Eze 1:1, 3; 3:15), where he began his prophecies (Eze 1:1, 2).

Ezekiel, Book of. Written by prophet in captivity to comfort Israel and to show God's people they were not forsaken. Last part emphasizes New Covenant. Book abounds in imagery (valley of bones; Good Shepherd; showers of blessing). Outline: 1. Prophecies Against Judah and Jerusalem Before Destruction of Temple (1—24). 2. Prophecies Against Nations (Ammon, Moab, Edom, Philistia, Tyre, Sidon, Egypt. 25—32). 3. Prophecies Concerning Israel and Other Nations After Restoration (33—39). 4. Vision of Worship in Kingdom (40—48).

Ezel (ē'zĕl, separation). Place of separation of David and Jonathan (1 Sm 20:19).

Ezem (ē'zĕm, bone. KJ: Azem in Jos). Village in Judah near Edom later given to Simeon (Jos 15:29; 19:3; 1 Ch 4:29).

Ezer (ē'zēr, help). 1. Horite tribe and chieftain (Gn 36:21, 27, 30; 1 Ch 1:38 [KJ: Ezar]). 2. Ephraimite killed by Philistines (1 Ch 7:21). 3. Descendant of Hur (1 Ch 4:4). 4. Gadite who joined David at Ziklag (1 Ch 12:9). 5. Levite; son of Jeshua (Neh 3:19). 6. Priest (Neh 12:42).

Ezerias (ĕz-ê-rī'ăs). See *Azariah 8*.

Ezias (ê-zī'ăs). See *Azariah 7*.

Ezion-gaber, -geber (ē'zĭ-ŏn-gā'bĕr, -gē'-bĕr, backbone of giant. KJ: Ezion-gaber in Nm and Dt). Place where Israelites camped on N end of Gulf of Aqabah (Nm 33:35, 36; Dt 2:8). Naval port and copper refining center of Solomon (1 K 9:26; 22:48; 2 Ch 8:17). Its site (Tell el-Kheleifeh) has been excavated.

Eznite (ĕz'nĭt). See *Josheb-basshebeth*.

Ezora (ĕ-zō'rà. KJ: Ozora). Listed in 1 Esd 9:34.

Ezra (ĕz'rà, help). **1.** Jewish priest, scribe, and prophet (Ez 7:6-12; 1 Esd 8:1; 9:49; 2 Esd 1:1; 14:44); with assistance of Artaxerxes, led group of exiles back to Jerusalem (c 459 BC); reformed Jewish life, worship, government; practiced public reading of Law; rebuilt Temple (Ezra-Nehemiah). **2.** Chief priest (Neh 12:1).

Possibly same as Azariah 26. 3. See *Ezrah.*

Ezra, Book of. 15th book of OT describes activities of Ezra, the scribe. Records return and re-establishment of Israelitish people in home country, their separation from foreign customs and idolatry. Outline: 1. Return of Exiles (1—6). 2. Reforms of Ezra (7—10).

Ezrah (ĕz'rà. KJ: Ezra). Judahite (1 Ch 4:17).

Ezrahite (ĕz'rà-hīt), Patronymic of Heman and Ethan (1 K 4:31; titles of Ps 88:89).

Ezri (ĕz'rī, my help). Overseer of David's farm laborers (1 Ch 27:26).

Ezril (ĕz'rĭl). See *Azarel 4.*

F

fable. 1. Fictitious story in which acts of higher beings are ascribed to lower (Ju 9:8-15; 2 K 14:9). **2.** Invention (RSV: myth. 1 Ti 1:4; 4:7; 2 Ti 4:4; Tts 1:14; 2 Ptr 1:16).

face (or countenance). **1.** Essential for beauty; to fall on face is act of reverence (Gn 17:3), petition (Nm 14:5), or sorrow (Jos 7:6). Shame, grief, other emotions shown in face (Gn 4:6, 7; 1 Sm 1:18; 2 Sm 19:5; Ps 44:15). **2.** No one can see God's face and live (Ex 33:20). God's face is hidden or turned away on account of evil (Dt 33:18) or against evil (Ps 34: 16). Moses spoke with God face to face (Dt 34:10). Face of God is God in His active presence (Nm 6:25, 26). To "seek God's face" is to worship Him (Ps 27:8).

Fair Havens. Small bay on S side of Crete (Acts 27:8-13).

faith. 1. Acceptance of God's promises in Christ worked by Holy Spirit, through which individual is justified, brought into right relation to God, saved (Ro 5:1; 1 Co 2:10-13; Eph 2:8). Described in OT by *'aman* (believe, Gn 15:6; Ex 14:31), *batah* (trust in, Ps. 28:7), *hasah* (take refuge in, 2 Sm 22:3). Frequent in prophets and psalms. In NT (*pistis*) occurs on almost every page, and is described as apprehension of Christ in Gospel as Lord, who has brought redemption with His blood and with His innocent suffering and death (Lk 24:46-48; Jn 3:16; 20:31; Acts 2:36; 16: 31; Ro 10:6-15; Gl 2:20; 1 Jn 1:7). This faith is worked by the Gospel in all its forms (Ro 1:16; 10:17) and thereby individual dies (Cl 3:3), is buried (Ro 6:4), raised (Cl 2:12), and lives (Ro 6:8) with Christ. Faith works through love (Gl 5:6) and determines conduct (Ro 6:14-23; Gl 2:20). **2.** Doctrine of Gospel (Acts 24:24; Gl 1:23). **3.** Historical faith (Lk 4:34; Ja 2:19).

falcon (fôl'kŭn). See *vulture.*

fall. Act whereby man apostatized from God, lost his integrity, virtue, and innocence (Gn 3), and involved himself and posterity in sin, misery, and death (Ro 5:12-21). As one man's fall involves all, so atonement of Christ brings grace to all (Ro 5:18).

fallow deer. See *roebuck.*

false Christs. Persons who falsely claimed to be Messiah (Mt 24:24; Mk 13:22).

false prophet. Prophet not sent by, or responsible to, God (Jer 29:9; Eze 13). See also *prophet.*

familiar spirit. Spirit of dead person or divining demon which entered into conjurer (RSV: medium. Lv 19:31; 20:6, 27; Dt 18:11; 1 Sm 28:3, 7-25; 2 K 21:6; 23:24).

family (H *mishpahah*). Fundamental social unit established by God (Gn 2:24; Mt 19:5). Father head of household, religious, social institution (Gn 18:19; Ex 12: 26; Eph 5:23). Wives to be loved (Eph 5:25); to care for home and children (1 Ti 5:10, 14). Children considered blessings from God (Ps 127:3-5). See also *homes; marriage.*

famine 1. Deficiency of food and drink caused by lack of rain (Gn 12:10; 26:1; 1 K 17:1) or war (2 K 6:25). **2.** Lack of God's Word (Am 8:11, 12. See Mt 4:4; Jn 4:14; 6:35).

fan (RSV: fork). Fork to throw threshed grain into air to clean it of chaff (Is 30: 24; Mt 3:12). See also *agriculture 6.*

farthing. Two Roman bronze coins; one (G *kodrantes*) worth 3.8 mills (Mt 5:26; Mk 12:42); the other (G *'assarion*) 1½ cents (Mt 10:29; Lk 12:6). RSV: penny.

fasting. Partial or total abstinence from food. Moses fasted on Sinai 40 days and nights (Ex 34:28). Fasting may be found in phrase "afflict the soul" (Lv 16:29, 31. RSV: afflict yourselves). Expressed religious humiliation; originally prescribed only for Day of Atonement (Lv 16:29; 23: 27-32); days of national calamity and others added. In NT disciples of John fasted, but not those of Jesus (Mt 9:14-17; Lk 5:33-39). Jesus fasted 40 days and nights in desert (Mt 4:2); approved fasting but opposed ostentation (Mt 6:16-18). RV, RSV on basis of textual criticism omit in Mt 17:21; Mk 9:29; Acts 10:30; 1 Co 7:5. Special fasts: 1 Sm 7:6; Jer 36:6-10; Est 4:16.

fat. 1. All fat of sacrificial animals belonged to God (Lv 3:16; 7:23, 25; Ex 29: 13, 22). **2.** Used of pasture (1 Ch 4:40), land (Neh 9:25), people (Ju 3:17). **3.** Wine vat (as in RSV. Jl 2:24; 3:13; Hg 2:16).

father. 1. Progenitor (Gn 19:31). **2.** Ancestor (1 K 15:11; Nm 18:2; Mt 3:9). **3.** Ancestor head or founder of community (1 Ch 2:51; 4:14), tribe, or nation (Gn 10:21; 17:4, 5). **4.** Founder of trade, art (Gn 4:20, 21). **5.** Author of group animated by same spirit (Ro 4:11). **6.** God as Creator (Ml 2:10; Is 63:16) or Savior (Ro 8:15; Gl 4:6). **7.** God as Father of Jesus (Mt 11:26; Mk 14:36; Lk 22:42). **8.** Benefactor (Jb 29:16; Is 22: 21), teacher (2 K 2:12). **9.** Spiritual father (1 Co 4:15).

fear. Used in versions to denote reverence (Acts 10:2, 22), terror (Gn 9:2; Dt 2:25; Mt 14:26), dread (Dt 28:67), trembling (Pr 29:25; Dt 20:3), fright (Jb 41:33). Fear of God is primarily reverential awe for His holiness (Ps 34:11; Ec 12:13).

feast. 1. Sumptuous meal attended by joyfulness (Dn 5:1; Lk 5:29; Jn 2:1). 2. Time appointed for sacred joy. Major feasts of Jews were: a. Passover (Feast of Unleavened Bread, Lv 23:5-8; Nm 28: 17-25). b. Feast of Weeks (Pentecost, Harvest, First Fruits, Ex 23:16; Nm 28: 26-31). c. Feast of Tabernacles (Booths, Ingathering, Lv 23:34-36; Dt 16:13-17). Lesser festivals: a. Feast of Dedication, or Lights (*Hanukkah*, 1 Mac 4:52-59; Jn 10:22); b. Purim (Est 9:21-28); c. Feast of Wood Offering (Neh 10:34); d. Sheep-Shearing (1 Sm 25:4-11).

feet. Used in euphemism, e. g.: to cover the feet (1 Sm 24:3. RSV: to relieve himself). Respect was shown by falling at feet (1 Sm 25:24; Lk 8:41). To wash feet was sign of hospitality (Gn 18:4; Jn 13:5, 6). To remove shoes was sign of reverence (Ex 3:5); also kissing feet (Lk 7:38). "To be at feet of" meant to be disciple (Acts 22:3). There are numerous figurative expressions (Jos 10:24; Is 18:7).

Felix (fē'lĭks, happy). Roman procurator of Judea (Acts 23:26).

fellowship (G *koinonia*). Christian fellowship is common sharing (communion) in Gospel (Ph 1:5-7), faith (Phmn), and other spiritual gifts. It is creation of God, who calls us into participation in Christ (Ro 6:1-8; 14:8; Ph 3:10) so that we share in His work, blessing, glory (1 Co 1:9; 1 Jn 1:3, 6, 7). Believers have oneness in Christ through Spirit (Jn 17:11, 21, 22; 2 Co 13: 14; Gl 3:28; 1 Jn 1:7). Mark of fellowship is love (1 Co 13; 1 Ptr 1:22; 1 Jn). See also *body* 5; 6.

fenced city. See *fort.*

ferret. See *gecko.*

festival. See *feast.*

Festus, Porcius (fĕs'tŭs, pôr'shĭ-ŭs). Successor of Felix as procurator of Judea (Acts 24:27).

fetters. Shackles or chains for binding feet of prisoners (Ju 16:21; 2 Ch 33:11; Ps 105:18; Mk 5:4).

fever. See *disease.*

field. Open area beyond enclosed gardens and vineyards (Gn 4:8; 27:5). Boundaries indicated by stones (Dt 19:14). See also *agriculture.*

fig. Common in Palestine (Dt 8:8; Is 34:4). Blossoms appear before leaves (Mt 21:19). See *orchard* 2.

figure. See *antitype.*

finger. Used figuratively to denote agency (Ex 8:19; Lk 11:20).

fir. See *cypress.*

fire. Used for cooking (Is 44:16), warmth (Jer 36:22; Mk 14:54); not kindled on Sabbath (Ex 35:3). Used to consume sacrifices (Lv 21:6; 22:22; 23:8); was to burn continuously on altar (Lv 6:9-13). Symbol of God's presence (Ex 3:2; 19: 18). His wrath burns like fire (Ps 79:5; 89:46). Christ will appear in fire (2 Th 1:8). World to be destroyed by fire (2 Ptr 3:7).

fire pan. Metal pan used to carry fire to altars (Ex 27:3; Nm 4:14 [KJ: censers]). H *mahtah* often; censer, snuff dish, tray (Ex 25:38; 37:23; Nm 16:46).

firkin (fûr'kĭn). See *measures* 3d.

firmament. Visible vault of sky separating primeval waters (Gn 1:6, 7; Ps 19:1; Eze 1:22-26. See Ps 148:4).

first-born, firstling. 1st of mother's offspring (Ex 12:12). 1. Birthright. Oldest son received double portion of inheritance (Dt 21:17); became head of family (Gn 43: 33; 35:23; 2 Ch 21:1-3); birthright at times transferred to younger son (Gn 25:

23; 27; 49:4) but later prohibited (Dt 21: 15-17). 2. Firstborn (man) and firstling (animal) belonged to God (Ex 13:2, 15). Firstborn priest of family, but redeemed after Aaronic priesthood was established (Nm 3:12-15; 18:15, 16). Firstlings were given to sanctuary; clean to be sacrificed, unclean redeemed or killed (Ex 13:2, 11-15; 22:30; 34:19, 20; Lv 27:26-29).

first fruits. 1. Whether raw (grain, fruit) or prepared (wine, oil, flour), were offerings and priest's perquisites (Ex 22:29; 23:19; 34:26; Lv 2:12; 23:10-12; Nm 18: 12; Dt 18:3, 4). 2. Day of First Fruits. See *Pentecost.*

fish. The Sea of Galilee, principal fishing ground of Jews, abounded in large variety of fish (Lk 5:5). Sold in Jerusalem (2 Ch 33:14; Neh 13:16). Caught by spearing (Jb 41:7), angling (Is 19:8; Am 4:2; Mt 17:27), dragnet (Lk 5:4-9), casting net (Hab 1:15). Without scales were unclean (Lv 11:9-12). Figuratively: Egyptians (Eze 29:4, 5), church (Mt 13:48), captives (Hab 1:14). Letters of G word for fish (IXTHYS) became symbol for: "Jesus Christ, God's Son, Savior" (*Iesous Christos Theou Uios Soter*). See *food* 6.

fish gate. Jerusalem gate near fish market (2 Ch 33:14).

fisher. Disciples were fishers of men (Mt 4:19; Mk 1:17).

fishhook. See *fish.*

fitches. 1. Spelt, inferior wheat (as RV, RSV. Eze 4:9). 2. Cummin, aromatic seed (as RSV. Is 28:25-27). See also *dill; food* 3; *spelt.*

flag. Grasslike plant in swamps and along rivers (Ex 2:3-5 [RSV: reeds]; Jb 8:11 [RSV: reed]; Is 19:6 [RSV: rushes]).

flagon (skin). 1. Bottle or pitcher of skin or earthenware (Is 22:24). 2. KJ for cake of raisins (as RV, RSV. 2 Sm 6:19; 1 Ch 16:3; SS 2:5; Hos 3:1).

flagstaff. See *beacon.*

flax. *Linum sativum;* fibers of bark used to make linen (Ex 9:31; Jos 2:6; Ju 15:14; Is 19:9), lamp wicks (Is 42:3; Mt 12:20. RSV: wick).

flea. Common insect in E (1 Sm 24:14; 26:20).

flesh. 1. Flesh as distinguished from other parts of body (Gn 41:2, 19; Jb 33:21; Lk 24:39). 2. All beings possessed of flesh (Gn 6:13, 19; Acts 2:17; Ro 3:20). 3. Meat (Ex 16:12; Lv 7:19). 4. Flesh as contrasted with spirit (Jb 14:22; Jn 6:52; 1 Co 5:5). 5. Human nature as functional organism (Gn 2:23; Mt 19:5, 6; 1 Co 6: 16); shared by Christ (Jn 1:14; Ro 1:3; Cl 1:22; Heb 5:7); relatives participate in common flesh (Gn 29:14; Ju 9:2; Ro 9:8), as do countrymen (Ro 9:3; Acts 2: 30) and all men (Is 58:7). 6. Human nature corrupted by sin; carnality (Ro 7:5; 8:5-8; 2 Co 7:1; Gl 5:16-20; 2 Ptr 2:10).

fleshhook (RSV: fork). Instrument for taking meat in sacrificial services (Ex 27:3; 1 Sm 2:13, 14; 1 Ch 28:17).

flint. Any hard compact rock (but strictly quartz. Dt 8:15; 32:13; Ps 114:8). Figuratively, uncompromising firmness (Is 50:7; Eze 3:9).

float. Raft (as RSV) of floating timber (1 K 5:9; 2 Ch 2:16).

flock. 1. Sheep (Lk 2:8). 2. Israel as covenant nation (Is 40:11). 3. NT church (Mt 26:31; Acts 20:28, 29; 1 Ptr 5:2, 3; see Jn 10:1-18).

flood. 1. Water, as river (Jos 24:2; Ps 66:6); inundation (Is 44:3); destructive flood (Dn 9:26; Mt 7:25); sea (Ex 15:8; Ps

24:2). 2. Deluge by which God destroyed living things of earth, except creatures in Noah's ark (Gn 6—9).

flour. See *food 1.*

flowers. Palestine noted for flowers; beauty appreciated (SS 2:12; Mt 6:28); embroidered and used in temple ornaments (Ex 25:31-40; 37:17; 1 K 7:26, 49). Symbolic of vanishing beauty and glory (Is 28:1, 4; 40:6, 7; 1 Ptr 1:24). Flower of age (1 Co 7:36. RSV: if his passions be strong).

flute. Wind instrument consisting of reed with holes or reeds of various lengths (Dn 3:5-10 [RSV: pipe]). KJ, RV: pipe in 1 Sm 10:5; Is 5:12; 30:29; Jer 48:36; 1 Co 14:7. See also *music; pipe.*

flux. See *disease; dysentery.*

fly. Immense number and great variety of species found in E (Ex 8:21-31; Ps 78:45; Ec 10:1; Is 7:18).

food. 1. Bread and water are "stay and staff" of life (Is 3:1). Wheat most commonly used for flour. Barley, spelt, millet, and lentils also ground in emergencies, or eaten by poor (Eze 4:9, 10). Primitive method of grinding flour was to crush it between two stones. Canaanites used rotary type mill in which cone of upper millstone fit into depression in lower millstone. Common Hebrew mill consisted of two stones: lower stone, 20 to 24 in in diameter and 4 in thick; upper stone slightly smaller. In center of lower stone peg was inserted which was passed through center of wooden crosspiece wedged in 4-in hole in upper stone. Projecting peg near edge of upper stone served as handle. Grain fed into center hole of revolving upper stone was crushed as it moved outward between stones (Mt 24:41; Ex 11:5). Flour carefully sifted. 2. Flour, yeast, salt, olive oil, and water or milk used in making bread. Simplest oven (used in camp or vineyard) was slightly convex, circular plaque of sheet iron, about 30 in in diameter. After plaque had been heated, crackerlike thickness of dough was spread over it and quickly baked. Another type of oven consisted of dome of clay, about 3 ft in diameter and 1½ ft high. Small loaves were placed under this dome and the dome was covered with fire. Another common oven was cylindrical clay structure 3 ft high and 2 ft in diameter, covered by lid. Fire was built in cylinder; after it had burned to live coals, loaves were stuck on inside surface to bake. Community ovens were probably also used. Besides bread Jewish women baked confections of many kinds (Ex 16:31). 3. Vegetables, grown in private plots by family or by truck gardeners, were important part of Hebrew diet. Legumes were extensively grown in all periods of Israel's history. Beans of varieties similar to modern ones were grown in large quantities, dried, and threshed. Lentils, which look like small split peas, are reddish tan in color (Gn 25:34; 2 Sm 17:28). Fitches (RSV: dill) used chiefly as flavoring material (Is 28:25, 27). 4. Melons (Nm 11:5) and cucumbers (Nm 11:5; Is 1:8) grew in both Palestine and Egypt. Onions, garlic, and leeks (Nm 11:5) were always favorites of Israelites. Dill (RSV: Is 28:25, 27; Mt 23:23), mustard (Mt 13:31), coriander seed (Ex 16:31; Nm 11:7) provided strong flavoring. Cinnamon bark (Ex 30:23), mint, cummin (Mt 23:23), saffron (SS 4:14) flavored both food and wine. Parsley, celery, let-

tuce, cabbage grown. Favorite dish was vegetable stew. 5. Best meat scarce in Palestine and used for special occasions (Lk 15:23; Ex 12:3-10). Meats were stewed or used to flavor vegetable stew. Calf or kid might be stewed in milk but not in that of its mother (Ex 23:19). On special occasions whole animals might be roasted (barbecued) and served (Gn 18:7; Lk 15:23). 6. Fish were taken chiefly from Sea of Galilee, Jordan, and Mediterranean (Mt 4:18-31). Roasted over live charcoal or salted and dried for later use (Jn 21:9-13; Mk 8:7). 7. Fowl, both wild (Lv 11:13-19; Lk 2:13, 24) and domestic (Mt 23:37; Jn 18:27), and eggs (Is 10:14; Lk 11:12) good source of protein. 8. Milk and its products were chief supply of protein, calcium, and fat. Milk of cows (1 Sm 6:7), sheep, and goats (Dt 32:14; Is 7:21, 22) used as beverage at meals (Gn 18:8), especially by children (Heb 5:12, 13). Curds of milk eaten (Gn 18:8; Dt 32:14; Pr 30:33. KJ, RV: butter). Cheese prepared from soured milk (1 Sm 17:18). Butter (Ps 55:21) churned in suspended goatskin from cream skimmed from top of soured milk. (Klinck)

fool. Person who has no wisdom or judgment (Pr 12:15; Lk 12:20) or is morally or religiously defective (Ps 14:1; 92:6; Jer 17:11).

footmen. 1. Infantry (2 K 13:7). 2. Guard (as RV, RSV. 1 Sm 22:17). 3. Men on foot (Jer 12:5). Possibly same as 1.

footstool. Used by kings (2 Ch 9:18). Earth is God's footstool (Ps 110:1; Is 66:1; Mt 5:35).

forehead (fôr'ĕd). Priests wore inscribed golden plates on forehead (Ex 28:38). Special marks placed on forehead (Eze 9:4; Jer 3:3; Rv 17:5). Mark of beast on forehead (Rv 13:16; 20:4). God's name is on forehead of saints (Rv 14:1; 22:4).

foreigner (KJ usually: stranger). One not of Hebrew stock (Ex 12:45; Eph 2:12). Those who are not citizens of God's kingdom (Eph 2:19; 1 Ptr 2:11).

foreknowledge. God's knowledge of all future events. See also *elect.*

forerunner. Preparer of way (Heb 6:19, 20).

forest. Woods, forests, trees, shrubs frequently mentioned; probably more extensive then in Palestine than now. See *ash; cedar; cypress; oak; pine; plane.*

fork. See *fan; fleshhook; homes 5.*

forgiveness. Act of God which ends alienation caused by man's sin and puts man in proper relationship to God. Forgiveness unmerited (Mt 18:23-25); given for Christ's sake (Mk 2:5, 7, 10; Lk 24:47; Jn 20:23; Eph 1:7; Cl 1:14; 1 Jn 2:12). Forgiveness of brethren is consequence of Christ's forgiveness (Mt 6:12-14; Eph 4:32). Contrition precedes forgiveness (Ps 51; Is 57:15; Jer 14:20).

fornication. Illicit sex relation especially with unmarried person (Mt 5:32; 1 Co 5:9; 6:9; 2 Co 12:21; Eph 5:3; Cl 3:5). Figuratively, infidelity to God (Eze 16:2; Jer 2:20).

fort, fortification, fortress. Cities of Canaan were strongly fortified with walls when Hebrews entered. Famous fortified towns: Gibeah, Jerusalem, Samaria, Damascus. KJ often: fenced. God's protection is figuratively called a fortress (2 Sm 22:2; Ps 31:3; Jer 6:27).

Fortunatus (fôr-tû-nā'tus, fortunate). Corinthian Christian (1 Co 16:17).

Fortune. See *Gad 4.*

Forum of Appius (fō'rum ŏv ăp'ĭ-us). See *Appii Forum.*

fountain. Springs highly prized in Palestine (Gn 16:7; Dt 8:7; 33:28; 1 Sm 29:1). With God is fountain of life (Ps 36:9; Jer 17:13; Pr 10:11). Drink Jesus gives becomes spring of living water (Jn 4:14).

fowl. See *food 7.*

fowler. One who catches birds, usually with noose of hair or cords (Ps 91:3; 124:7; Pr 6:5).

fox. H *shu'al* is jackal as well as fox (should be jackal in Ju 15:4; Ps 63:10; Neh 4:3). Two varieties of foxes (*Vulpes nilotica; V. flavescens*) found in Palestine (Mt 8:20; Lm 5:18; Lk 13:32; Eze 13:4).

frankincense (frăngk'ĭn-sĕns). Fragrant gum resin of tree used in anointing oil for priests (Ex 30:34), meal offering (Lv 2:1), burned (Lv 6:15), on showbread (Lv 24:7).

freedmen. See *libertines.*

fringes. Tassels made of twisted blue thread fastened on each corner of garment. Jews commanded to wear them as reminder of Law (Nm 15:37-40; Dt 22:12. RSV: tassel).

frog. Amphibian common in Egypt and Palestine (Ex 8:2-14; Ps 78:45; 105:30; Rv 16:13).

frontlet. Jewel or amulet between eyes. Later Jews, interpreting Ex 13:16; Dt 6:8; 11:18 literally, inscribed Ex 13:2-10, 11-16; Dt 6:4-9; 11:13-21 on frontlets or wore them on left arm. G: phylacteries (Mt 23:5).

frying pan. See *pan.*

fuller. One who bleaches, cleanses, thickens, or dyes cloth (Ml 3:2; Mk 9:3). Had place outside E wall of Jerusalem (2 K 18:17; Is 7:3; 36:2).

furlong. See *measures 1i.*

furnace. 1. Bake oven (as RSV. Neh 3:11). 2. Furnace for smelting iron (Dt 4:20; 1 K 8:51). 3. Kiln for burning bricks (as RSV. Ex 9:8, 10; 19:18). 4. Crucible for melting silver and gold (Pr 17:3; 27:21 [RSV: crucible]; Eze 22:20). 5. Furnace for various purposes (Gn 19:28; Dn 3:6, 11; Mt 13:42, 50; Rv 1:15; 9:2). 6. Figuratively, trial (Is 48:10). 7. Everlasting punishment (see Mt 13:42; 25:41). See *food; trade 7.*

furniture. 1. Camel's canopied saddle (Gn 31:34. RSV: camel's saddle). 2. Furnishings (vessels) of tabernacle (Ex 25:9; 40:9; 1 Ch 9:29). 3. Furnishings of palaces. 4. Furnishings of private dwellings (Neh 13:8. KJ: household stuff). See *homes.*

furrow. 1. Trench made by plow (Ps 65:10; Hos 10:4). 2. Iniquity (as RSV: Hos 10:10).

future life. See *eschatology; eternal life; eternity.*

G

Gaal (gā'ăl). Son of Ebed; conspired against Abimelech (Ju 9:26-45).

Gaash (Gā'ăsh, quaking). Hill in Ephraim where Joshua was buried (Jos 24:30; Ju 2:9; 2 Sm 23:30; 1 Ch 11:32).

Gaba (gā'bà). See *Geba 1.*

Gabael (găb'ā-ĕl). 1. Ancestor of Tobit (Tob 1:1). 2. Poor Jew to whom Tobit lent money (Tob 1:14).

Gabatha (găb'à-thà). See *Bigthan.*

Gabbai (găb'ā-ī, taxgatherer). Benjaminite (Neh 11:8).

Gabbatha (găb'à-thà). Place where tribunal of Pilate stood (G *lithostroton,* pavement. Jn 19:13).

Gabbe, Gabdes (găb'ē, -dēz). See *Geba 1.*

Gabrias (gā'brĭ-ăs). Brother (or father) of Gabael (Tob 1:14; 4:20).

Gabriel (gā'brĭ-el, man of God). Angel who interpreted visions to Daniel (Dn 8:16-27; 9:20-27); announced birth of John the Baptist (Lk 1:11-22) and Jesus (Lk 1:26-38).

Gad (găd, good fortune). 1. Jacob's 7th son (Gn 30:9-11; 49:19). 2. Tribe of Gad (Nm 1:14, 24, 25; 26:15-18; Dt 27:13; Eze 48:27); settled between Reuben and half tribe of Manasseh E of Jordan (Nm 32); carried into captivity by Tiglath-pileser (1 Ch 5:26). 3. David's seer (1 Sm 22:5; 2 Sm 24:11-14; 2 Ch 29:25) and chronicler (1 Ch 29:29). 4. Idol (RV, RSV: Fortune. KJ: troop. Is 65:11).

Gadarenes (găd-à-rēnz'). Inhabitants of Gadara, decapolis city (perhaps modern Um-Keis, about 6 mi SE of Sea of Galilee, or of Gerasa (Gergesa, modern Kersa) on E coast (Mt 8:28 [KJ: Gergesenes]). RV, RSV: Gerasenes in Mk 5:1; Lk 8:26, 37.

Gaddi (găd'ī, fortunate). 1. One of twelve spies (Nm 13:11). 2. John; son of Mattathias (1 Mac 2:2. KJ: Caddis. RV: Gaddis).

Gaddiel (găd'ĭ-ĕl, fortune of God). One of twelve spies (Nm 13:10).

Gaddis (găd'ĭs). See *Gaddi 2.*

gadfly. Figuratively of punishment for Egypt (Jer 46:20. KJ, RV: destruction).

Gadi (gā'dī, Gadite). Father of Menahem (2 K 15:14, 17).

Gaham (gā'hăm, to burn). Son of Nahor (Gn 22:24).

Gahar (gā'här, hiding place). Progenitor of Nethinim who returned from captivity (Ez 2:47; Neh 7:49; 1 Esd 5:30 [KJ, RV: Geddur]).

Gai (gā'ī, valley. KJ: valley. RSV: Gath). Place mentioned in pursuit of Philistines (1 Sm 17:52).

Gaius (gā'yus, L, Caius). 1. Macedonian companion of Paul at Ephesus (Acts 19:29). 2. Co-worker of Paul from Derbe (Acts 20:4). 3. Christian at Corinth baptized by Paul (Ro 16:23; 1 Co 1:14). 4. Addressee of 3 Jn. (Scholars regard some of these as identical).

Galaad (găl'à-ăd). See *Gilead.*

Galal (gā'lăl). Two Merarite Levites (1 Ch 9:15, 16; Neh 11:17).

Galatia (gà-lā'shĭ-à). Region of inner Asia Minor around the Halys, S of Black Sea; named for Gauls who settled there in 3d c BC. After Pompey's conquest (64 BC) Roman province was formed which included region visited by Paul on 1st journey (Acts 16:6; 18:23; 1 Co 16:1; Gl 1:2; 2 Ti 4:10; 1 Ptr 1:1).

Galatians, Epistle to. Written by Paul, probably to churches established on 1st missionary journey and soon after that journey. Purpose: to stress justification by faith over against tenets of Judaizers. Outline: 1. Apostolic Vindication (1; 2). 2. Justification by Faith (3; 4). 3. Practical Applications (5; 6).

galbanum (găl'bà-num). Gum resin with pungent odor used in sacred incense (Ex 30:34).

Galeed (găl'ē-ĕd, heap of witness). Heap of stones commemorating covenant between Jacob and Laban (Gn 31:47, 48).

Galgala (găl'gȧ-lȧ). See *Gilgal 4.*

Galilean (găl-i-lē'ȧn). See *Galilee.*

Galilee (găl'i-lē, circle). The N of 3 provinces of Palestine (Jos 20:7; 1 K 9:11; 2 K 15:29; 1 Ch 6:76). Originally given to Zebulun (Jos 19:10-16), Asher (Jos 19:24-31), and Naphtali (19:32-39). In time of Christ extended from Hermon to Carmel, from Jordan to Mediterranean. Land fertile; "way of the sea" (trade route, Is 9:1) crossed lower Galilee. Ruled by Herod Antipas. Galileans were simple, impulsive, pious, generous. Jesus performed major part of ministry there (Capernaum). Twelve, with exception of Judas Iscariot, were Galileans. Leaders of Judea despised Galileans, who were recognized by dialect (Mk 14:70).

Galilee, Sea of (Mt 4:18; 15:29). Also called Sea of Chinnereth, or Chinneroth (Nm 34:11; Jos 12:3; 13:27); Lake of Gennesaret(h) (Lk 5:1; 1 Mac 11:67 [KJ: Gennesar]); Sea of Tiberias (Jn 6:1; 21:1). Lake formed by Jordan 680 ft below sea level, 13 mi long, 7 wide, 160 ft deep. Blue, sweet water abounds with fish.

gall. 1. Bitter secretion of liver (Jb 16:13; 20:25). 2. Poison of serpents believed to be gall (Jb 20:14). 3. Poisonous bitter herb (H *rosh.* Dt 29:18 [RSV: poisonous fruit]; Hos 10:4 [RSV: poisonous weeds; KJ, RV: hemlock]). 4. Ingredient of drink offered Christ (Mt 27:34). 5. Figuratively, bitter experience (Jer 8:14; Acts 8:23).

gallery. In architecture, projection of story or veranda (Eze 42:3, 5). RV, RSV: tresses in SS 7:5. RSV: walls in Eze 41:15.

galley. Low, flat-built vessel with banks of oars (Is 33:21).

Gallim (găl'ĭm, heaps). Town of Benjamin N of Jerusalem (1 Sm 25:44; Is 10:30).

Gallio (găl'ĭ-ō). Roman proconsul (KJ: deputy) of Achaia (AD 51—52); brother of Seneca, the philosopher (Acts 18: 12-17).

gallows. Mentioned in Esther (2:23; 5:14; 6:4; 7:9, 10; 8:7; 9:13, 25) as means for execution.

Gamad, men of (găm'ăd). RV, KJ: Gammadim(s). Defenders of tower of Tyre (Eze 27:11).

Gamael (găm'ȧ-el). See *Daniel 3.*

Gamaliel (Gȧ-mā'lǐ-el, reward of God). 1. Prince of Manasseh (Nm 1:10; 2:20; 7:54; 10:23). 2. Grandson of Hillel; Pharisee; member of Sanhedrin (Acts 5: 34); teacher of Paul (Acts 22:3); gave wise counsel at trial of Peter and apostles (Acts 5:38-40). Called "rabban" and highly regarded in rabbinic circles.

games. Children's games mentioned: playing "wedding" and "funeral" (Mt 11:17), keeping birds (Jb 41:5). Children played in streets (Zch 8:5). Recreation of adults included merrymaking (Jer 15:17), riddles (Ju 14:12-19), music and dancing (Lk 15:25), racing (Ps 19:5; Ec 9:11), bow and sling (Ju 20:20; Ju 20:16; 1 Ch 12:2). Paul acquainted with Greek games (1 Co 9:24-27; 15:32; Ph 3:14; Cl 3:15; 2 Ti 2:5; 4:7, 8). Gaming board found in Saul's castle at Gibeah. See also *music; dance.*

Gammadim (găm'ȧ-dĭm). See *Gamad, men of.*

Gamul (gā'mul, recompensed). Chief of 22d course of priests (1 Ch 24:17).

gangrene (găng'grēn). See *disease.*

Gar (gär). See *Gas.*

garden. Enclosed plot of ground for flowers (SS 6:2), vegetables (Dt 11:10), fruit (SS 4:16; 6:11), spices (SS 6:2), and parks (Est 1:5). Gardens were well watered (Gn 13:10; Nm 24:6) and protected (Is 1:8).

Gareb (gā'rĕb, scab). 1. One of David's heroes (2 Sm 23:38; 1 Ch 11:40). 2. Hill near Jerusalem (Jer 31:39).

Garizim (găr'ĭ-zĭm). See *Gerizim.*

garlic. See *food 4.*

garment. See *dress.*

Garmite (gär'mīt). Appelation of Keilah (1 Ch 4:19).

garrison. Military post or fortified and manned place (1 Sm 13:23; 14:1-15; 1 Ch 11:16).

Gas (găs. KJ: Gar). Listed in 1 Esd 5:34.

Gashmu (găsh'mū). See *Geshem.*

Gatam (gā'tăm). Son of Eliphaz; chief of Edom (Gn 36:11, 16; 1 Ch 1:36).

gate. Placed as entrances to cities (Gn 19:1), tabernacle (Ex 27:16), camp (Ex 32:26), temple (2 Ch 8:14), mansions (Lk 16:20), houses (Acts 10:17), rivers (Nah 2:6), prisons (Acts 12:10). Market and judgment places were near gates of cities (2 Sm 15:2; 2 K 7:1; Dt 17:5; Ru 4:1-12). Symbols of power (Gn 22:17; Is 24:12; Mt 16:18). Figuratively: gate of heaven (Gn 28:17); gates of New Jerusalem (Rv 21:12, 21); gate of righteousness (Ps 118:19, 20); gate of death (Jb 38:17).

gatekeeper (Usually KJ: porter; RV: doorkeeper; RSV: gatekeeper). Keeper of city, temple, palace, or private doors and gates (2 K 7:10; 1 Ch 23:5; Ps 84:10; Ez 7:24; Mk 13:34).

Gath (găth, wine press). One of 5 great Philistine cities (Jos 13:3; 1 Sm 6:17), site uncertain (Am 6:2); home of Goliath (1 Sm 17); refuge of David (1 Sm 21: 10), who later captured it (1 Ch 18:1). See 2 Ch 11:8).

Gath-hepher (găth-hē'fêr, wine press of Hepher. KJ: Gittah-hepher in Jos 19: 13). Town in Zebulun 3 mi from Nazareth; Jonah's town (2 K 14:25). Modern el Meshad.

Gath-rimmon (găth-rĭm'un, pomegranate press). 1. Levitical city of Dan near Joppa (Jos 19:45; 21:24; 1 Ch 6:69). 2. Probably scribal error for Bileam (Jos 21:25. See 1 Ch 6:70).

Gaza (gā'zȧ). Capital of Philistia (Gn 10: 19); assigned to Judah (Jos 10:41; 15:47; Ju 1:18); scene of Samson's exploits (Ju 16) and of Philip's Christian activity (Acts 8:26). KJ: Azzah in Dt 2:23; 1 K 4:24; Jer 25:20. Modern Ghazzeh. See also *Ayyah.*

Gazara (Gȧ-zā'rȧ). See *Gezer.*

Gazathites (gā'zăth-īts). See *Gazites.*

gazelle (gȧ-zĕl'). H *ts:bi, Gazella dorcas.* Clean animal; smallest of Palestinian antelopes (Dt 12:15, 22; 15:22; Pr 6:5; SS 2:9, 17. KJ: roebuck).

Gazer (gā'zêr). See *Gezer.*

Gazera (gȧ-zē'rȧ). 1. See *Gezer.* 2. See *Gazzam.*

Gazez (gā'zĕz, shearer). Son of Caleb (1 Ch 2:46).

Gazites (gā'zīts). Inhabitants of Gaza (Jos 13:3 [KJ: Gazathites]; Ju 16:2).

Gazzam (găz'ăm, devourer). Gazera in 1 Esd 5:31 [RSV: Gazzan]). Ancestor of Nethinim who returned with Zerubbabel (Ez 2:48; Neh 7:51).

Geba (gē'bà, hill). 1. Levitical city of Benjamin (modern Jeba), 6 mi N of Jerusalem (KJ: Gaba in Jos 18:24; Ez 2:26; Neh 7:30; Gibeah [with which text at times confuses Geba] in Ju 20:33; 1 Sm 13:16; 14:5; all versions: Geba in Jos 21:17; 1 Sm 13:3; 1 K 15:22; 2 K 23:8; 1 Ch 6:60; 8:6; Neh 11:31; 12:29; Is 10: 29; Zch 14:10). KJ: Gabdes; RV: Gabbe in 1 Esd 5:20. 2. Town in Jezreel (Jdth 3:10). 3. See Gibeon.

Gebal (Gē'băl, mountain). Phoenician city on Mediterranean (Ps 83:7; Eze 27:9). G Byblos. Modern Jebeil.

Gebalites (gē'băl-īts, KJ: Giblites). Inhabitants of Gebal (Jos 13:5; 1 K 5:18 [KJ: stonesquarers; RSV: men of Gebal]).

Geber (gē'bĕr, man). Purveyor of Solomon (1 K 4:19). Ben-geber (1 K 4:13) probably his son.

Gebim (gē'bĭm, cisterns). City of Benjamin (Is 10:31).

gecko (gĕk'ō, ferret). Lizard which emits plaintive sound (Lv 11:30. KJ: ferret; LXX: shrew).

Gedaliah (gĕd-à-lī'à, LORD makes great). 1. Levite harpist (1 Ch 25:3, 9). 2. Ancestor of Zephaniah (Zph 1:1). 3. Son of Pashhur; conspired against Jeremiah (Jer 38:1). 4. Made governor of Judea by Nebuchadnezzar (2 K 25:22); protector of Jeremiah (Jer 39:14; 40:5-16). 5. Priest; divorced foreign wife (Ez 10:18). Joadanus (RSV: Jodan) in 1 Esd 9:19. 6. See Jozabad 7.

Geddur (gĕd'ẽr). See Gahar.

Gedeon (gĕd'ē-un). See Gideon.

Geder (gē'dẽr, wall). Town in S Judah (Jos 12:13). Perhaps Gedor 2.

Gederah (gĕ-dē'rà, wall). Town in lowlands of Judah (Jos 15:36; 1 Ch 4:23 [KJ: hedges]). Modern Jedireh.

Gederoth (gĕ-dē'rŏth, enclosures). Town in Judah (Jos 15:41); captured by Philistines (2 Ch 28:18). Perhaps modern Katrah, 4 mi SW of Ekron. See also Kidron.

Gederothaim (gĕd-ē-rŏ-thā'ĭm, two walls). Town of Judah (Jos 15:36).

Gedor (gē'dôr, wall). 1. Benjaminite (1 Ch 8:31). 2. Town in Judah, 7½ mi NW of Hebron (Jos 15:58; 1 Ch 4:4, 18). Modern Jedur. 3. Town, perhaps in Simeon (1 Ch 4:39). 4. Town of Benjamin (1 Ch 12:7).

Ge-harashim (gē-hăr'à-shĭm, valley of craftsmen. KJ: Charashim). Place near Jerusalem (as KJ, RV). Or name of person (as RSV. 1 Ch 4:14. See Neh 11:35).

Gehazi (Gē-hā'zī, valley of vision). Servant of Elisha (2 K 4:12-36; 5:20-27).

Gehenna (gē-hĕn'à, "valley of [son, children of] Hinnom" in OT, "hell" in NT). Deep valley S of Jerusalem (Jos 15:8) where Jews had offered their children to Moloch (2 K 23:10; Jer 7:31; 19:2-6). Later became dump for unclean matter; fires burned in it continually NT uses word as place of destiny for damned (Mt 5:22, 29, 30; 10:28; 18:9; 23:15, 33; Mk 9:43, 45, 47; Lk 12:5). Identical with "lake of fire" (Rv 19:20; 20:10). See also hell.

Geliloth (gĕ-lī'lŏth). See Gilgal 1.

Gemalli (gĕ-măl'ĭ, camel owner). Danite; father of spy Ammiel (Nm 13:12).

Gemariah (gĕm-à-rī'à, LORD has perfected). 1. Son of Hilkiah; messenger of Zedekiah (Jer 29:3). 2. Prince; son of Shaphan; urged king not to burn Jeremiah's scroll (Jer 36:10-26).

genealogy (jĕn-ē-ăl'ō-jĭ, birth record. KJ at times: generations). Tracing forward or backward of ancestral relationship of tribes and families (Gn 35:22-26; Nm 1: 2, 18; 1 Ch 9:2; Neh 7:5; Mt 1:1-16; Lk 3:23-38). Genealogies contained gaps (e. g., in Ex 6:16-24).

generation. 1. Begetting or producing (Gn 2:4). 2. Offspring or successions of offspring (Gn 5:1). 3. Age as period of time (Gn 15:16; Dt 32:7; Ps 45:17). 4. Men of specific time (Lv 3:17; Mt 11:16; 17:17; 24:34).

Genesis (jĕn'ē-sĭs, beginning). First book of Bible and of Pentateuch, attributed to Moses in Scripture. Book of beginnings; describes origins of physical universe, plants, animals, human life, and institutions. Outline: 1. History of Creation, Adam, Deluge, Noah, First Inhabitants, Babel (1—11). 2. History of Patriarchs Abraham, Isaac, Jacob, and Joseph (12 to 50). See Pentateuch; creation; flood; Abraham; Isaac; Jacob.

Gennesar, Gennesaret, Gennesareth (gĕ-nē'-sär, gĕ-nĕs'à-rĕt, -rĕth). 1. Plain NW of Sea of Galilee (Mt 14:34; Mk 6:53). 2. See Galilee, Sea of.

Genneus (gĕ-nē'us). Father of Apollonius (2 Mac 12:2).

Gentiles. H goyim; RSV 3 times: Goiim. 1. Non-Hebrew nations of world (Gn 10:5; 14:1; Ju 4:2, 13, 16; Neh 5:8). 2. In NT ethnos means nation (Acts 2:5; Lk 7:5) and in the plural, Gentiles (Mt 4:15). 3. Hellen (Greek) is sometimes rendered "Gentile" in KJ (Ro 2:9, 10; 1 Co 10:32. RV, RSV: Greek). 4. People outside Jewish and Christian faith (1 Co 5:1; 10:20. RSV: pagan).

Genubath (gĕ-nū'băth, theft). Edomite; son of Hadad (1 K 11:20).

Geon (gē'ŏn). See Gihon.

Gera (gē'rà). 1. Descendants of Benjamin (Gn 46:21; 1 Ch 8:3, 5, 7). 2. Benjaminite; father of Ehud (Ju 3:15). 3. Benjaminite; father of Shimei (2 Sm 16:5).

gerah (gē'rà). Smallest Jewish coin; worth c 3 cents (Ex 30:13; Lv 27:5; Nm 3:47; 18:16; Eze 45:12).

Gerar (gē'rär). Philistine city near Gaza (Gn 10:19; 20:1; 26:26; 2 Ch 14:13, 14).

Gerasenes, Gergesenes (gĕr'à-sēnz, gŭr'gĕ-sēnz). See Gadarenes.

Gerizim (gĕr'ĭ-zĭm. KJ: Garizim in 1 Mac 5:23). Mt c 2,850 ft high; opposite Mt Ebal. Blessings were read from it (Dt 11:29; 27:12); site of Samaritan temple (see 2 K 17:33; Jn 4:20).

Gerr(h)enians (gĕ-rē'nĭ-ăns). People of Gerar (2 Mac 13:24).

Gershom (gŭr'shom, sojourner). 1. Son of Moses and Zipporah (Ex 2:22; 18:3; 1 Ch 23:15, 16; 26:24). 2. Son of Manasseh and father of Jonathan, the priest (Ju 18:30). 3. One who returned with Ezra (Ez 8:2; 1 Esd 8:29 [KJ, RV: Gerson]). 4. See Gershon.

Gershon (gŭr'shon, sojourner). Son of Levi (Gn 46:11; Ex 6:16). Gershom in 1 Ch 6:16, 17, 20, 43, 62, 71; 15:7. Founder of Gershonites (1 Ch 6:62; 26:21; 29:8), who were given 13 cities (Jos 21:6).

Gerson (gŭr'sun). See Gershom 3.

Geruth Chimham (gē'rŭth kĭm'hăm, lodging place of Chimham). Probably khan (Jer 41:17. KJ: habitation of Chimham).

Gesem (gē'sém). See Goshen.

Gesham, Geshan (gē'shăm, -shăn). Descendant of Caleb (1 Ch 2:47).

Geshem (gē'shĕm. KJ: Gashmu in Neh 6:6). Arabian opponent of Jews after their return from captivity (Neh 2:19; 6:1, 2).

Geshur (gē'shẽr, bridge). Region between Mt Hermon and Bashan (Dt 3:14; Jos 12:5); given to Manasseh, but original inhabitants not expelled (Jos 13:13); Aramaean kingdom (2 Sm 13:37; 15:8. See 2 Sm 3:3).

Geshuri, Geshurites (gē-shōō'rī, -rīts). Inhabitants of Geshur (Dt 3:14; Jos 13:2, 11, 13; 1 Sm 27:8).

Gether (gē'thẽr). 3d son of Aram (Gn 10:23; 1 Ch 1:17).

Gethsemane (gēth-sĕm'á-nē, oil press). Olive yard E of Jerusalem; scene of Christ's agony and betrayal (Mt 26:36-56; Mk 14:26-52; Lk 22:39-54; Jn 18:1-13).

Geuel (gē-ū'ĕl, majesty of God). Gadite; son of Machi; spy (Nm 13:15).

Gezer (gē'zẽr. KJ: Gazer in 2 Sm 5:25; 1 Ch 14:16. Gazara in 1 Mac 4:15 [KJ: Gazera]; 9:52; 2 Mac 10:32). Ancient city 18 mi NW of Jerusalem; Tell Jezer; modern Khirbet Yerdeh. Joshua defeated king of Gezer (Jos 12:12) but could not take city (Ju 1:29). Assigned to Levites (Jos 21:21; 1 Ch 6:67). Egyptian Pharaoh destroyed city, gave it to Solomon (1 K 9:16). See also Gob.

Gezrite (gēz'rīt). See Girzite.

ghost. Used three times (Is 29:4; Mt 14:26; Mk 6:49) in KJV, RSV. Frequently in KJ, RV for life, spirit, breath (Gn 25:17; Jb 11:20; Jer 15:9; Mt 27:50). See also Holy Spirit; soul, spirit.

Giah (gī'á, bursting forth). Place opposite Ammah (2 Sm 2:24).

giants. Men abnormally tall and powerful. 1. Nephilim (fallen ones). Sons of Anak; unnatural offspring before flood (Gn 6:4; Nm 13:33). 2. Rephaim (shades). Aborigines of Canaan, Edom, Moab, and Ammon (Gn 14:5; 15:20; Dt 3:11; Jos 12:4; 13:12). 3. Anakim. Gigantic race connected with Rephaim (Nm 13:33; Dt 2:10, 11, 12); found at Hebron (Nm 13:22) and hill country (Jos 11:21). 4. Emim (KJ: Emims). Ancient inhabitants of Moabite country (Gn 14:5; Dt 2:10, 11). 5. Zamzummim (KJ: Zamzummims). Ancient inhabitants of country of Ammonites (Dt 2:20). Probably same as Zuzim (Gn 14:5).

Gibbar (gīb'är, mighty man). See Gibeon.

Gibbethon (gīb'ĕ-thŏn, height). Town of Dan assigned to Kohathites (Jos 19:44; 21:23; 1 K 15:27; 16:17).

Gibea (gīb'ĕ-á, hill). Village; probably Gibeah (1 Ch 2:49).

Gibeah (gīb'ĕ-á, hill). 1. Gibeah of Judah, 10 mi SW of Jerusalem (Jos 15:57). 2. Gibeah of Benjamin (Ju 19:13, 14; 1 Sm 13:2; 2 Sm 23:29). "Gibeah of Saul" (1 Sm 11:4), birthplace of Saul; residence after he became king (1 Sm 10:26; 15:34). Site (Tell el-Fûl) including castle excavated. 3. Gibeah at Kiriath-jearim; place where ark was kept after returned by Philistines (2 Sm 6:3, 4. RV, RSV: the hill). 4. Gibeah (KJ: hill) of Phinehas; place in Mt Ephraim (Jos 24:33). 5. Gibeah often translated "hill" (Ju 7:1; 1 Sm 23:19; 26:1; 2 Sm 2:24; Jer 31:39).

Gibeath (gīb'ĕ-ãth). Probaby Gibeah 2 (Jos 18:28. RSV: Gibeah).

Gibeath-elohim (gīb'ĕ-ãth-ĕ-lō'hĭm, KJ, RV: hill of God). Place in Benjamin where Saul met and joined prophets (1 Sm 10:5). Sometimes identified with Gibeah 2.

Gibeath-haaraloth (gīb'ĕ-ãth-há-är'á-lŏth, hill of the foreskins). Place where Joshua circumcised Israelites after crossing Jordan (Jos 5:3. KJ, RV: hill of the foreskins).

Gibeon (gīb'ĕ-un, hill city). City in Benjamin given to Levites (Jos 18:25; 21:17). Originally Hivite city (Jos 11:19), whose people made treaty with Joshua under false pretenses, thereby saving city but bringing slavery on themselves (Jos 9; 10; 2 Sm 21:1-9). Geba in 2 Sm 5:25. Gibbar in Ez 2:20.

Giblites (gīb'līts). See Gebalites.

Giddalti (gĭ-dăl'tī, I magnify). Son of Heman; leader of the 22d musical course (1 Ch 25:4, 29).

Giddel (gĭd'el). 1. Ancestor of Nethinim who returned (Ez 2:47; Neh 7:49). Cathua in 1 Esd 5:30. 2. Ancestor of Solomon's servants who returned (Ez 2:56; Neh 7:58; 1 Esd 5:35 [KJ, RV: Isdael]).

Gideon (gĭd'ĕ-un, cutting down. KJ in NT: Gedeon). Son of Joash of tribe of Manasseh (Ju 6:11); called to deliver Israel; cut down Baal's altar (hence called Jerubbaal: let Baal plead. Ju 6:32); defeated Midianites; destroyed Succoth; refused king's crown (Ju 6—8; Heb 11:32). Called Jerubbesheth (contender with Shame. 2 Sm 11:21).

Gideoni (gĭd-ĕ-ō'nī, cutting off). Benjaminite (Nm 1:11).

Gidom (gī'dŏm, cutting). Place E of Gibeah (Ju 20:45).

gier eagle (jẽr ē'g'l). See vulture.

gift (gĭft). Given more often in E than in W. Given to show esteem (Est 9:22), good will (Gn 45:22), or secure favor (Gn 32:13-21; Ex 23:8; Pr 18:16). Bridegroom paid parents, gave gifts to bride (Gn 34:12). Subjects brought gifts as tribute (2 Sm 8:2, 6). God's gifts: eternal life (Jn 4:10; Ro 6:23); Holy Spirit (Acts 2:38); others (Eph 4:8).

Gihon (gī'hŏn, gushing forth). 1. River of Paradise (Gn 2:13). 2. Spring in Kidron valley; its water confined within city of Jerusalem (1 K 1:33-38; 2 Ch 32:30; 33:14; Sir 24:27 [KJ: Geon]).

Gilalai (gil'á-lī). Levite musician (Neh 12:36).

Gilboa (gĭl-bō'á). Mt range overlooking Jezreel; Saul slain there (1 Sm 31; 2 Sm 1:21).

Gilead (gĭl'ĕ-ăd, to be rough). 1. Land E of Jordan extending from Sea of Galilee to Dead Sea (Gn 31:21-25; Dt 3:12-17). KJ: Galaad in Jdth 1:8; 1 Mac 5:9, 55. Modern Jelûd. 2. City of Gilead (Hos 6:8). 3. Grandson of Manasseh (Nm 26:29, 30; Jos 17:1); founder of Gileadites (Ju 12:4, 5). 4. Father of Jephthah (Ju 11:12). 5. Gadite (1 Ch 5:14).

Gilgal (gĭl'găl, circle). 1. Place in Jordan valley near Jericho where Israel encamped (Jos 4:19-24); became city and headquarters (Jos 9:6; 15:7. Geliloth in Jos 18:17); Saul there crowned (1 Sm 10:8; 11:15), forfeited kingdom (1 Sm 13:4-15). 2. City of Elijah and Elisha near Bethel (2 K 2:1, 2; 4:38). 3. Name in difficult phrase in Jos 12:23. RSV: Galilee. 4. Place mentioned in 1 Mac 9:2 (KJ: Galgala).

Giloh (gī'lŏh). Town in mts of Judah (Khirbet Jala? Jos 15: 51; 2 Sm 15:12).

Gimzo (gĭm'zō, place of sycamores). Place 3 mi from Lydda in Judah (2 Ch 28:18). Modern Jimzu.

gin. Snare for birds (Is 8:14; Am 3:5. RSV: trap).

Ginath (gī'năth). Father of Tibni (1 K 16:21, 22).

Ginnetho, Ginnethoi, Ginnethon (gĭn'ĕ-thō, -thō-ī, -thŏn). Priest (Neh 10:6; 12:4, 16).

girdle (gûr'd'l). See *dress*.

Girgashite, Girgasite, (gûr'ga-shīt, -sīt). Aborigines of Canaan (Gn 10:16; 15:21; Dt 7:1; Jos 3:10; 24:11; 1 Ch 1:14; Neh 9:8).

Girzite (gûr'zīt. KJ: Gezrite). People living S of Philistia otherwise unknown (1 Sm 27:8).

Gishpa, Gispa (gĭsh'pa, gĭs'pa). Overseer of Nethinim (Neh 11:21).

Gittah-hepher (gĭt'ä-hē'fēr). See *Gath-hepher*.

Gittaim (gĭt'ä-ĭm, two wine presses). Village of Benjamin (2 Sm 4:3; Neh 11:33).

Gittite (gĭt'it). Native of Gath (2 Sm 6: 10, 11).

gittith (gĭt'ĭth). Feminine of "Gittite"; musical term; possibly instrument of Gath or a melody ("Of Gath" or "Of Winepress." Ps 8; 81; 84 titles).

Gizonite (gĭ'zō-nīt). Appellation of Hashem (1 Ch 11:34); perhaps variant for Gunite (Nm 26:48).

gladness. See *joy*.

glass. Opaque glass early used by Phoenicians and Egyptians (c 1500 BC. Jb 28: 17. KJ: crystal). Transparent glass produced in Roman period (Rv 4:6; 15:2; 21:18, 21). See also *crystal; mirror*.

gleaning. Gathering grain left by reapers, or grapes after vintage. Owners were to leave gleanings of grain, grapes, and fallen fruit for poor (Lv 19:9, 10; Dt 24: 19-21; Ru 2).

glede. Bird of vulture family (Dt 14:13. RSV: buzzard).

glorious ones. See *dignities*.

glory. 1. Manifestation of that which shows character or excellence of subject. God's glory is expression of His holiness (Ex 33:19-23; Mt 17:2; Lk 2:9; Jn 1:14; 2:11; 17:4, 5, 22). Man's glory are those things which display his highest character (soul: Ps 16:9; reputation: Pr 3:35; Christian experience: Ph 2:16; service: 1 Th 2:20). 2. The glory itself (Is 42:8; 3:8). Thus God is glory of His people (Jer 2:11. See Lk 2:29-32). 3. Believers participate in spiritual (Jn 17:22; 1 Co 2:7; 2 Co 3:18; 1 Ptr 1:8) and eternal (Mk 10:37; Ro 8:18; 1 Co 15:43) glory, will have glorified bodies (Ph 3:21). 4. Teaching of degrees of glory in heaven based on Dn 12:3; Lk 19:12-26; 1 Co 15:41, 42.

gnat. H *ken;* G *konops*. Small bloodsucking insect (Mt 23:24). KJ, RV: lice; RV margin: sandflies or fleas in Ex 8:16-19; Ps 105:31; KJ, RV: in like manner in Is 51:6. Translation uncertain. Marsh gnats and lice were common in Egypt.

Gnosticism (nŏs'ti-siz'm, G *gnosis*, knowledge). Movement which reached its peak in 2d, 3d c AD. Taught redemption from material world and entrance into freedom through union of soul with fullness (*pleroma*) of God. Gnostic tendencies opposed in NT (Jn; Cl; 2 Ptr; 1, 2, 3 Jn; Jude; Ti; Rv).

goad. Rod sharpened at one end for guiding oxen (1 Sm 13:21; Ju 3:31). Used figuratively (Ec 12:11).

Goah (gō'a, lowing. KJ: Goath). Place near Jerusalem (Jer 31:39).

goat. Often mentioned (Gn 27:9; 30:32); hair woven for cloth (Ex 25:4; 35:26); flesh and milk used for food (Lv 7:23; Dt 14:4); used for burnt and sin offerings (Gn 15:9; Lv 3:12; 4:24; 9:15). See *Azazel*. Figuratively, the damned (Mt 25: 32, 33). Wild goat found among hills and rocks (Dt 14:5; 1 Sm 24:2; Jb 39:1; Ps 104:18).

Goath (gō'ăth). See *Goah*.

Gob (gŏb, pit). Place where war was waged between Israel and Philistia (2 Sm 21:18, 19). Gezer in 1 Ch 20:4.

goblet. Drinking vessel (Est 1:7 [KJ, RV: vessel]; SS 7:2 [RSV: rounded bowl]).

God. Being unlimited in power, knowledge, wisdom, not confined to time and space; made world and man; to Him man is responsible. God manifests Himself through created things, but this truth (basic to every human system of religion) is changed into a lie by fallen man (Ro 1; 2; Ps 19; Acts 17). God reveals Himself to man in incarnation of Jesus Christ (Jn 1:18; 2 Co 5.18-20). Chief OT names for God: Elohim (connoting power) and Yahveh (see *Jehovah*). Anthropomorphic (Gn 3:8; Ex 16:12; Ps 2:4; Is 7:18) and anthropopathic (Ex 20:5; Lv 20:23; Zph 3:17) expressions used of God who, however, is not man (Is 31:3; 55:8, 9; Hos 11:9). God is One (Dt 6:4; 1 Co 8:4; Gl 3:20). "God" is properly used of Trinity or of each Person (Eph 1:3; Jn 1:1; Acts 5:3, 4). See *Trinity; gods, false; Jesus Christ; Holy Spirit*.

God fearers. See *proselytes*.

God Most High. See *High, Most*.

gods, false. See *Adrammelech; Anammelech; Artemis; Asherah; Ashima; Ashtoreth; Astarte; Baal; Baal-berith; Baal-peor; Baal-zebub; Bel; Castor and Pollux; Chemosh; Chiun; Gad 4; Hermes; Malcham; Meni, Merodach; Milcom; Molech; Nehushtan; Nergal; Nibhaz; Nisroch; Rephan; Rimmon; Sakkuth; satyr; Succoth-Benoth; Tammuz; Tartak; Zeus*.

Gog (gŏg). 1. Reubenite (1 Ch 5:4). 2. Prince of Rosh, Meshech, and Tubal; prophetically described as invading Israel in Last Times (Eze 38:39. See Rv 20:8-15).

Goiim (goi'ĭm). See *Gentiles*.

Golan (gō'lăn, exile). Refuge city in Bashan (Dt 4:43; Jos 20:8; 21:27).

gold. Precious metal obtained from Havilah (Gn 2:11, 12), Sheba (1 K 10:2), Ophir (1 K 22:48). Used for ornaments (Gn 24:22), money, temple furnishings (Ex 36:34-38). Symbol of purity (Jb 23:10; Lm 4:1).

goldsmith. See *trade 7*.

Golgotha (gŏl'gō-tha). See *Calvary*.

Goliath (gō-lī'ăth). 1. Philistine giant slain by David (1 Sm 17). 2. The Goliath slain by Elhanan (2 Sm 21:19) identified as Lahmi, brother of Goliath. Probably of Anakim.

Gomer (gō'mēr). 1. Son of Japheth (Gn 10:2; 1 Ch 1:5); ancestor of tribe (Eze 38:6). 2. Wife of Hosea (Hos 1:3).

Gomorrah, Gomorrha (gō-môr'a, submersion). City of plain destroyed by fire (Gn 14; 18:20; 19:24, 28). See also *Sodom*.

good. Not autonomous reality but essence of God (Ps 118:1; Mk 10:18; Lk 18:19). God's acts are good (Ex 18:9; Jer 32:40; Ro 7:12). Salvation is good which God gives man and which centers in Christ (Eph 1:3; Heb 10:1). To do good is to live in Christ (Rom 6; Gal 5:24-26).

gopherwood. Unknown wood of Noah's ark (Gn 6:14).

Gorgias (gôr'ji-ăs). Syrian general (1 Mac 3:38).

Gortyna (gôr-tī'na). Capital of Crete (1 Mac 15:23).

Goshen (gō'shen). 1. NE province of Egypt; c 40 mi long (Gn 46:28; 47:6; Jdth 1:9 [KJ: Gesem]). 2. District of S Palestine (Jos 10:41; 11:16). 3. Town in mts of Judah (Jos 15:51).

gospel (good news. G *euaggelion* [evangel]). Message of salvation of world in Jesus Christ (Ro 1:16, 17), that He died and rose again (1 Co 15:1-5).

gospels. 1st four books of NT; attributed from earliest times to Matthew, Mark, Luke, and John. 1st three called synoptic Gospels since they may be set side by side for comparison. Writers are called evangelists.

Gotholiah, Gotholias (gŏth-ō-lī'á, -lī'ás). See *Athaliah 3.*

Gothoniel (gō-thō'nĭ-el). Father of Chabris (Jdth 6:15).

gourd. 1. Perhaps castor oil plant (Jon 4:6-10). **2.** Wild gourd is perhaps colocynth (2 K 4:39). **3.** Ornamental figures in Solomon's temple. KJ, RV: knops in 1 K 6:18 (margins: gourd); 7:24; oxen in 2 Ch 4:3.

governor. Although also applied to other dignitaries, usually one who governs city, province, etc., under supreme ruler (Gn 42:6; Ez 5:14; Neh 5:14). G *hegemon* (L procurator): provincial governor appointed by emperor (Mt 27:2; Acts 23:24; 26:30). See also *Tirshatha.*

Gozan (gō'zăn). Place on Habor R NW of Nineveh (2 K 17:6; 18:11; 19:12; 1 Ch 5:26; Is 37:12).

Graba (grä'bá). See *Hagaba.*

grace. OT *ḥesed* (KJ: loving-kindness; RSV: steadfast love), persistent love, especially as related to covenant, comes nearest to NT *charis* (LXX translates *ḥen* with *charis*). Grace is relationship which God establishes between Himself and men (2 Sm 7:15; Ps 31:21). Grace for man is forgiveness of sins (Ex 34:6, 7; Ps 103:8; Is 43:25). NT *charis* applied to Christ (Jn 1:14; Tts 2:11-13) and His work (Ro 5:15, 21; 1 Co 1:4), whereby forgiveness, life, and salvation are accomplished (1 Co 15:10; Gl 2:15-21; Eph 2:8). See *steadfast love.*

grain. (KJ: corn). Grain of various kinds, but not maize or Indian corn. Chief grains were wheat, barley, millet, vetch, beans, lentils, and fitches. See also *food.*

grape. See *vineyard.*

grass. Green herbage generally (Gn 1:11, 12; Mt 6:30). Figuratively (Ps 90:5, 6; Is 40:6, 8; Ja 1:10, 11; 1 Ptr 1:24) describes life's brevity.

grasshopper. See *locust.*

grave, grave clothes. See *burial.*

graving tool. See *trade 7.*

Great Sea. See *Mediterranean Sea.*

greaves. See *armor.*

Grecia, Greece (grē'shá, grēs). Country in SE Europe including Macedonia (Acts 20:2), Epirus, Achaia, and Peloponnesus. H *Javan* (Ionia) in Gn 10:2-5; Dn 8:21; Jl 3:6, representative for isles afar off (Is 66:19; Eze 27:13).

Grecian, Greek (grē'shăn, grēk). **1.** Language of Greece of which *koine* is form in NT times. **2.** Inhabitants of Greece; NT versions distinguish "Greeks" (Hellenes), that is, Greeks by birth (Acts 17:12), or all non-Jews (Ro 1:16; Gl 3:28), and Hellenists (G *hellenistai*). KJ: Grecians; RV: Grecian Jews [margin: Hellenists]), that is, Greek-speaking Jews (Acts 6:1; 9:29).

greyhound. KJ, RV in obscure passage (Pr 30:31. RSV: strutting cock).

griddle. See *pan.*

grove. See *Asherah.*

Gudgodah (gŭd-gō'dá, cutting). Encampment of Israel between Mt Hor and Jotbath (Dt 10:7). Hor-haggidgad (KJ: Hor-hagidgad) in Nm 33:32.

guest. See *hospitality.*

guest chamber. Room for guests (Mk 14:14; Lk 22:11).

guilt. See *conscience; sin.*

Guni (gū'nī, painted). **1.** Son of Naphtali (Gn 46:24; Nm 26:48; 1 Ch 7:13); ancestor of Gunites (Nm 26:48). **2.** Gadite (1 Ch 5:15).

Gur (gŭr, whelp). Place near Ibleam where Ahaziah was slain (2 K 9:27).

Gurbaal (gŭr-bā'ăl, sojourn of Baal). Place in Arabia (2 Ch 26:7).

H

Haahashtari (hä-á-hăsh'tá-rī). Son of Ashhur (1 Ch 4:6).

Habaiah (há-bā'yá, LORD has hidden). Priest whose descendants returned with Zerubbabel (Ez 2:61) but were excluded from priesthood (Neh 7:63 [RV, RSV: Hobaiah]; 1 Esd 5:38 [KJ, RV: Obdia]).

Habakkuk (há-băk'uk, embrace). Prophet; wrote during Chaldean period (1:6; c 600 BC); temple still standing (2:20; 3:19; 2 Esd 1:40 [KJ, RV: Abacuc]; Bel 33-39 [KJ: Habbacuc]). Outline: 1. Twofold Complaint (Judah's sin, 1:1-4; Chaldean cruelty, 1:12—2:1) and Twofold Answer (1:5-11; 2:2-20). 2. Prayer (3).

Habaziniah, Habazziniah (hăb-á-zĭ-nī'á, Lord's light). Rechabite; father of Jaazaniah (Jer 35:3).

Habbacuc (há-băk'uk). See *Habakkuk.*

habergeon (hăb'ēr-jŭn). Obsolete KJ word for coat of mail (Ex 28:32; 39:23; 2 Ch 26:14; Neh 4:16; Jb 41:26).

Habor (hā'bôr, joining?). Tributary (modern Khabur) of Euphrates (2 K 17:6; 18:11; 1 Ch 5:26).

Hacaliah, Hachaliah (hăk-á-lī'á). Father of Nehemiah (Neh 1:1).

Hachilah (há-kī'lá, dark). Hill in Ziph (1 Sm 23:19; 26:1, 3).

Hachmoni, Hachmonite (hăk'mō-nī, -nīt). Ancestor (patronymic) of Jashobeam and Jehiel (1 Ch 11:11; 27:32). Tahchemonite (KJ: Tachmonite) in 2 Sm 23:8.

Hadad (hā'dăd, thunderer?). **1.** Aramaean deity of storm and thunder (Baal of Canaanites; Addu of Phoenicians; Adad of Mesopotamians). Perhaps also title. **2.** Son of Ishmael (Gn 25:15 [KJ: Hadar]; 1 Ch 1:30). **3.** King of Edom; son of Bedad (Gn 36:35; 1 Ch 1:46). **4.** Another king of Edom (1 Ch 1:50). Hadar in Gn 36:39. **5.** Prince of Edom who escaped massacre of Joab (1 K 11:14-25).

Hadadezer (hăd-ăd-ē'zēr, Hadad is help. KJ, RV often: Hadarezer). Son of Rehob; king of Zobah; twice defeated by David (2 Sm 8:3-5; 10:15-18; 1 K 11:23; 1 Ch 18:3-10; 19:16-19).

Hadadrimmon (hä-dăd-rĭm'on, Hadad, Rimmon, names for Syrian god). Place in valley of Megiddo (Zch 12:11. See 2 Ch 35:22-25; Eze 8:14).

Hadar (hā'där). See *Hadad 2; 4.*

Hadarezer (hăd-á-rē'zēr). See *Hadadezer.*

Hadashah (há-dăsh'á). Town in lowland of Judah (Jos 15:37).

Hadassah (há-dăs'á). See *Esther.*

Hadattah (há-dăt'á). See *Hazor-hadattah.*

Hades (hā'dēz). Classical Greek: person, then place for all dead in depth of earth. In LXX translated "Sheol." NT: beyond of death, place of departed; negative connotation (Mt 11:23; Lk 10:15; 16:23; Acts 2:27, 31; Rv 1:18; 6:8; 20:13, 14. KJ: hell). See also *Gehenna; hell; sheol.*

Hadid (hā'dĭd, pointed). Place in Benjamin (Ez 2:33; Neh 7:37; 11:34). Probably same as Adida (1 Mac 12:38; 13:13). Modern Haditheh near Lydda.

Hadlai (hăd'lī, resting). Ephraimite, father of Amasa (2 Ch 28:12).

Hadoram (ha-dō'răm). 1. Son of Joktan; progenitor of tribe (Gn 10:27; 1 Ch 1:21). 2. Son of Tou of Hamath; ambassador to David (1 Ch 18:10). Joram in 2 Sm 8:10. 3. See *Adoniram.*

Hadrach (hā'drăk). Syrian country (Zch 9:1). Ancient Hatarrika on Orontes.

Ha-eleph (ha-ē'lĕf). See *Eleph.*

Hagab (hā'găb, locust). One of Nethinim who returned from Babylon (Ez 2:46; 1 Esd 5:30 [KJ: Agaba. RV: Accaba]).

Hagaba, Hagabah (hăg'a-bä). One of Nethinim who returned from Babylon (Neh 7:48). Hagabah in Ez 2:45; 1 Esd 5:29 (KJ: Graba. RV: Aggaba).

Hagar (hā'gär, flight). Egyptian handmaid of Sarah; bore Ishmael to Abraham as proxy for Sarah; expelled by Sarah and Abraham (Gn 16; 21; 25:12). Type of legal bondage (Gl 4:24, 25. KJ: Agar).

Hagarenes, Hagarites, Hagerites (hăg'a-rēnz, hā'gär-īts, hā'gēr-īts). See *Hagrites.*

Haggai (hăg'ā-ī, festive). Prophet in days of Darius Hystaspes (520 BC. Hg 1:1) and leader in rebuilding temple (Ez 5:1; 6:14). KJ: Aggeus; RV: Aggaeus in 1 Esd 6:1; 7:3; 2 Esd 1:40. Outline: 1. Reproof and Encouragement to Rebuild Temple (1). 2. Future Glory of House of God and Doom of Heathen (2).

Haggedolim (hăg'ē-dō-lĭm, great men). Father of Zabdiel (Neh 11:14. KJ: great men).

Haggeri (hăg'e-rī). See *Hagri.*

Haggi (hăg'ī, festive). Son of Gad (Gn 46:16; Nm 26:15).

Haggiah (hă-gī'a, festival of Lord). Levite (1 Ch 6:30).

Haggith (hăg'ĭth, festive). Wife of David; mother of Adonijah (2 Sm 3:4; 1 K 1:5, 11; 2:13; 1 Ch 3:2).

Hagia (hā'gī-a). See *Hattil.*

Hagiographa (hăg-ĭ-ŏg'ra-fa, sacred writings). 3d division of OT (H *Kethubhim;* writings): Ruth, Chronicles, Ezra, Nehemiah, Esther, Job, Psalms, Proverbs, Ecclesiastes, Song of Solomon, Lamentations, Daniel.

Hagri (hăg'rī. KJ: Haggeri). Father of Mibhar (1 Ch 11:38).

Hagrites (hăg'rīts). Descendants of Hagar, Ishmaelites (1 Ch 5:10, 18-22; 27:31. KJ: Hagarite, Hagerite. KJ, RV, RS 83:6: Hagarenes).

Hai (hā'ī). See *Ai.*

hail. 1. Greeting (Mt 2:49). 2. Plague of Egypt (Ex 9:18-29); feared because of destructiveness (Ps 78:47, 48; 148:8). 3. Figuratively, divine retribution (Is 28:2).

hair. Considered ornament by Jews; bald head despised (2 K 2:23; Is 3:24; Jer 47:5). Long hair worn by youths (2 Sm 14:26), Nazarites (Nm 6:5), and women (SS 4:1; Lk 7:38). Certain customs forbidden or censured (Lv 19:27; 21:5; Dt 14:1; 1 Ti 2:9; 1 Ptr 3:3). Barbers mentioned (Eze 5:1); also shaving and polling (44:20).

Hakkatan (hăk'a-tăn, smallest). Father of Johanan (Ez 8:12; 1 Esd 8:38 [KJ: Acatan; RV: Akatan]).

Hakkoz (hăk'ŏz). 1. Judahite (1 Ch 4:8 [RSV: Koz; KJ: Coz]). 2. Head of 7th division of priests (1 Ch 24:10). KJ: Koz in Ez 2:61; Neh 3:4, 21; 7:63. KJ: Accoz; RV: Akkos in 1 Esd 5:38.

Hakupha (hă-kū'fä). Ancestor of family of Nethinim (Ez 2:51; Neh 7:53; 1 Esd 5:31 [KJ: Acipha. RV: Achipha]).

Halah (hā'lá). Region of N Mesopotamia (2 K 17:6; 18:11; 1 Ch 5:26; Ob 20 [KJ, RV: this host]).

Halak (hā'lăk, smooth). Mountain in S Palestine (Jos 11:17; 12:7), perhaps same as Akrabbim.

Halhul (hăl'hŭl). Village in Judah (Jos 15:58).

Hali (hā'lī). Town of Asher (Jos 19:25).

Halicarnassus (hăl-ĭ-kär-năs'ŭs). City in Caria, Asia Minor (1 Mac 15:23).

Hallel (hă-lāl'). Ps 113—118, chanted in liturgy of certain festivals.

Hallelujah (hăl'ē-loo'ya, praise Lord). Liturgical ejaculation urging all to praise Jehovah. Occurs at beginning of Ps 106, 111—113, 117, 135, 146—150 and at end of Ps 104—106, 113, 115—117; 135; 46—150 (translated: praise. See KJ, RV margins, sometimes: Hallelujah). In NT: Rv 19:1, 3, 4, 6 (KJ: Alleluia).

Hallohesh (hă-lō'hĕsh, speaker of charms). Sealed covenant with Nehemiah (Neh 3:12 [KJ: Halohesh]; 10:24).

hallow (H *qadash;* separate). Set apart from ordinary to sacred use (Ex 20:11; 29:36; Is 65:5; Jn 17:19; Acts 20:32).

Halohesh (hă-lō'hĕsh). See *Hallohesh.*

Ham (hăm, black. Egyptian name for Egypt). 1. 3d son of Noah (Gn 5:32); provoked father by act of indecency (Gn 9:21-27); sons: Cush, Mizraim, Put, Canaan (1 Ch 1:8); descendants lived in S Arabia, Ethiopia, Egypt, Canaan (Gn 10:6-14). 2. Poetic name for Egypt (Ps 78:51; 105:23, 27; 106:22). 3. Place where Chedorlaomer defeated Zuzim (Gn 14:5).

Haman (hā'măn). Prime minister of Ahasuerus (Est 3:1; Ap Est 10:7 [KJ, RV: Aman]).

Hamath (hā'măth, fortress). 1. City (modern Hama) on Orontes in Syria (Gn 10:18; Nm 13:21; 1 K 8:65). 2. Province centering in Hamath (1 Mac 12:25 [KJ: Amathis]; 2 K 17:24, 30; 23:33). KJ: Hemath in 1 Ch 13:5; Am 6:14.

Hamath-zobah (hā'măth-zō'bà). Probably same as Hamath (2 Ch 8:3).

Hammath (hăm'ăth, hot springs). 1. Fortified city of Naphtali (Jos 19:35); near Tiberias; identified by Josephus (Ant XVIII, ii, 3) with Emmaus. Hammothdor in Jos 21:32; Hammon in 1 Ch 6:76. 2. Ancestor of Rechabites (1 Ch 2:55).

Hammeah (hăm'ē-à). See *Meah.*

Hammedatha (hăm-ē-dā'thà). Father of Haman (Est 3:1; Ap Est 12:6 [KJ, RV: Amadathus]; 16:10 [KJ: Amadatha; RV: Amadathus]).

Hammelek (hăm'e-lĕk, the king). Proper name in KJ, RV. RSV: king (Jer 36:26; 38:6).

hammer. 1. Tool used for driving tent pins (Ju 4:21), tearing down structures (Ps 74:6), beating gold (Is 41:7), quarrying (Jer 23:29), or as workman's tool (1 K 6:7). 2. Figuratively, any crushing power (Jer 23:29; 50:23). See also *trade 5; 7; 11.*

Hammiphkad (hă-mĭf'kăd). See *Miphkad.*

Hammolecheth, Hammoleketh (hă-mŏl'ĕ-kĕth, the queen). Sister of Gilead (1 Ch 7:18).

Hammon (hăm'on, hot springs). **1.** City in Asher (Jos 19:28). **2.** See *Hammath.*

Hammoth-dor (hăm'oth-dôr). See *Hammath 1.*

Hammuel (hăm'û-ĕl, warmth of God. KJ: Hamuel). Simeonite (1 Ch 4:26).

Hammurabi (hăm-*u*-rä'bĕ). 6th king of 1st dynasty of Babylon (1726—1686 BC; not Amraphel of Gn 14:1); military genius; builder; lawgiver (Code of Hammurabi).

Hamonah (hå-mō'nå, multitude). Figurative city near which Gog is defeated (Eze 39:16).

Hamon-gog (hā'mŏn-gŏg, multitude of Gog). Symbolical name for valley in which forces of Gog are buried (Eze 39:11).

Hamor (hā'môr, ass). Father of Shechem (Gn 33:19; 34:26; Acts 7:16 [KJ: Emmor]).

Hamran (hăm'răn). See *Hemdan.*

hamstring. See *hough.*

Hamuel (hăm-û'ĕl). See *Hammuel.*

Hamul (hā'mŭl, pitied). Son of Perez; progenitor of Hamulites (Gn 46:12; Nm 26:21).

Hamutal (hå-mū'tăl, akin to dew). Wife of Josiah; mother of Jehoahaz, Zedekiah (2 K 23:31; 24:18; Jer 52:1).

Hana (hā'nå). See *Hanan 4.*

Hanameel, Hanamel (hăn'å-mēl, -mĕl, God has pitied). Cousin of Jeremiah (Jer 32:6-12).

Hanan (hā'năn, gracious). **1.** Benjaminite (1 Ch 8:23). **2.** One of David's mighty men (1 Ch 11:43). **3.** Descendant of Jonathan (1 Ch 8:38; 9:44). **4.** Founder of family of Nethinim (Ez 2:46; Neh 7:49). Anan (RSV: Hana) in 1 Esd 5:30. **5.** Teacher of Law (Neh 8:7 [KJ, RV: Ananias in 1 Esd 9:48]; 10:10). **6, 7.** Covenanters with Nehemiah (Neh 10:22, 26). **8.** Assistant treasurer of Nehemiah (Neh 13:13). **9.** Man of God (Jer 35:4).

Hananeel, Hananel (hå-năn'ĕ-ĕl, hăn'å-nĕl, God has been gracious). Gave name to tower in Jerusalem wall (Neh 3:1; 12:39; Jer 31:38).

Hanani (hå-nā'nī, gracious). **1.** Head of 18th division of temple musicians (1 Ch 25:4, 25). **2.** Seer; father of prophet Jehu (1 K 16:1; 2 Ch 16:7). **3.** Brother of Nehemiah (Neh 1:2; 7:2). **4.** Priest (Ez 10:20; 1 Esd 9:21 [KJ, RV: Ananias]). **5.** Levite musician (Neh 12:36).

Hananiah (hăn-å-nī'å, LORD has favored). **1.** Benjaminite (1 Ch 8:24). **2.** Leader of 16th division of temple musicians (1 Ch 25:4, 23). **3.** Captain of Uzziah (2 Ch 26:11). **4.** Father of Zedekiah (Jer 36:12). **5.** False prophet (Jer 28:1-17). **6.** Hebrew name of Shadrach (Dn 1:3-19). **8.** Son of Zerubbabel (1 Ch 3:19). Grandson Joanan (KJ: Joanna) in Lk 3:27. **9.** Divorced foreign wife (Ez 10:28; 1 Esd 9:29 [KJ, RV: Ananias]). **10.** Perfumer (Neh 3:8. KJ: son of perfumer). **11.** Repaired wall (Neh 3:30). **12.** Sealed covenant with Nehemiah (Neh 10:23). **13.** Governor of castle (Neh 7:2). **14.** Priest (Neh 12:12). Probably same in Neh 12:41. **15.** See *Channuneus.*

hand. 1. Figuratively: **a.** Power, strength (H Jos 8:20; Ps 76:5). **b.** Hand of God refers to His activity (Ex 13:3, 14, 16; Nm 11:23; 1 Sm 5:6). **c.** Many phrases which are often translated literally (Gn 41:35; Ps 16:8; 73:23). **d.** Open hand: liberality (Dt 15:8). **2.** Right hand: South; left hand: North (Jb 23:9; 1 Sm 23:19). **3.** Right hand: place of honor (1 K 2:19; Mt 25:33). **4.** Imposed to bestow blessing (Mk 10:16; 2 Ti 1:6).

handbag. See *crisping pin.*

handbreadth. See *measures 1b.*

handful. See *measures 2a.*

handkerchief (hăng'kẽr-chĭf, G *soudarion,* sweat cloth). Used to wrap money (napkin; Lk 19:20); wrap head of corpse (napkin, cloth; Jn 11:44); and, chiefly, as article of dress (Acts 19:12).

Hanes (hā'nēz). Place in Egypt (Is 30:4).

hanging. See *punishment.*

Haniel (hăn'ĭ-ĕl). See *Hanniel.*

Hannah (hăn'å, grace). Mother of Samuel (1 Sm 1; 2).

Hannathon (hăn'å-thŏn, favored). Place in N Zebulun (Jos 19:14).

Hanniel (hăn'ĭ-ĕl, grace of God). **1.** Prince of Manasseh (Nm 34:23). **2.** Asherite (1 Ch 7:39. KJ: Haniel).

Hanoch (hā'nŏk, dedicated). **1.** Son of Midian and descendant of Abraham by Keturah (Gn 25:4; 1 Ch 1:33 [KJ: Henoch]). **2.** Son of Reuben (Gn 46:9; Ex 6:14; Nm 26:5; 1 Ch 5:3).

Hanun (hā'nun, favored). **1.** King of Ammon (2 Sm 10:1-4; 1 Ch 19:1-6). **2. 3.** Jews who repaired portions of wall of Jerusalem (Neh 3:13, 30).

Hapharaim, Haphraim (hăf-å-, hăf-rā'ĭm, two pits). Place in Issachar between Shunem and Shihon (Jos 19:19).

Happizzez (hăp'ĭ-zĕz, dispersion). Head of 18th course of priests. (1 Ch 24:15. KJ: Aphses).

Hara (hā'rå, mountainous). Province in Assyria (1 Ch 5:26).

Haradah (hå-rā'då). Encampment of Israel in desert (Nm 33:24).

Haran (hā'răn, road). **1.** Brother of Abraham (Gn 11:26-31). **2.** Son of Caleb (1 Ch 2:46). **3.** Levite (1 Ch 23:9). **4.** City in Mesopotamia, on Belikh River, 60 mi above confluence with Euphrates. Abraham located there after leaving Ur (Gn 11:31, 32; 24:10; 27:43; Acts 7:2, 4 [KJ: Charran]).

Hararite (hā'rå-rīt, mountain dweller). Designation of 3 of David's heroes (2 Sm 23:11, 33 [RV: Ararite]; 1 Ch 11:34, 35).

Harbona, Harbonah (här-bō'nå). Chamberlain of Ahasuerus (Est 1:10; 7:9).

hardness of heart. Stubbornness; disposition unresponsive to discipline or appeal (Ex 7—10; Mk 8:17; Acts 19:9).

hare. Species of rabbit, probably *Lepus Syriacus* (Lv 11:6; Dt 14:7).

Hareph (hā'rĕf, plucking). Son of Caleb (1 Ch 2:51).

Hareth (hā'rĕth). See *Hereth.*

Harhaiah (här-hā'yå). Father of Uzziel (Neh 3:8).

Harhas (här'hăs, poor). Ancestor of Shallum (2 K 22:14). Hasrah in 2 Ch 34:22.

Har-heres (här-hē'rĕz, Mount Heres). See *Heres.*

Harhur (här'hûr, inflammation). Progenitor of family of Nethinim (Ez 2:51; Neh 7:53). Asur (KJ: Assur) in 1 Esd 5:31.

Harim (hā'rĭm, consecrated). **1.** Head of 3d priestly course (1 Ch 24:8; Neh 12:15). Rehum in Neh 12:3. Probably same in Ez 2:39; Neh 7:42; 1 Esd 5:25 (KJ: Carmе; RV: Charme). Descendants divorced foreign wives (Ez 10:21). **2.** Priest; sealed covenant (Neh 10:5); possibly priest course collectively. **3.** Place whose natives returned (Ez 2:32; Neh 7:35); divorced foreign wives (Ez 10:31); repaired wall (Neh 11:3). Annas

(RSV: Annan) in 1 Esd 9:32. 4. Sealed covenant (Neh 10:27); possibly collectively for 3.

Hariph (hā'rif, autumnal). 1. Founder of family which returned with Zerubbabel (Neh 7:24). Jorah in Ez 2:18 and RSV in 1 Esd 5:16 (KJ: Azephurith; RV: Arsiphurith). 2. Sealed covenant with Nehemiah (Neh 10:19).

harlot, harlotry (KJ often: whore, whoredom). Religious and common prostitution widespread in Semitic world; both common (Lv 19:29) and religious (Lv 21:7, 9, 14; Dt 23:18) forbidden.

Har-Magedon (här-má-gĕd'un). See *Armageddon.*

Harnepher (här'ne-fẽr). Asherite (1 Ch 7: 36).

Harod (hā'rŏd, fear). Spring (KJ: well) where Gideon encamped (Ju 7:1); identified with modern Jalûd; village probably located there (2 Sm 23:25).

Haroeh (há-rō'ĕ). See *Reaiah 1.*

Harosheth (há-rō'shĕth). City in N Palestine; home of Sisera (Ju 4:2, 13, 16). Identified as Tell 'Amar, 16 mi NW of Megiddo.

harp. See *music.*

harrow. KJ, RV in 2 Sm 12:31; 1 Ch 20:3 (RSV: pick). Some regard instrument as threshing machine. See *agriculture 2.*

Harsha (här'shá. Charea in 1 Esd 5:32). Head of family of Nethinim which returned with Zerubbabel (Ez 2:52; Neh 7:54).

Harsith (här'sĭth). See *east gate.*

hart. Male fallow deer (*Cervus dama; H 'ayyal*) once found in Palestine (Dt 12: 15, 22; 14:5; 15:22; 1 K 4:23; Ps 42:1; Is 35:6; Lm 1:6).

Harum (hā'rum, high). Judahite (1 Ch 4:8).

Harumaph (há-rōo'măf, snub-nosed). Father of Jedaiah (Neh 3:10).

Haruphite (há-rōo'fĭt). Designation of Shephatiah (1 Ch 12:5).

Haruz (hā'rŭz). Grandfather of Amon (2 K 21:19).

harvest. See *agriculture 4; orchard; vineyard.*

harvest, feast of. See *Pentecost.*

Hasadiah (hăs'á-dī'á, loved by LORD). 1. Son of Zerubbabel (1 Ch 3:20). 2. See *Asadias.*

Hasenuah (hăs-ē-nū'á). See *Hassenuah.*

Hashabiah (hăsh-á-bī'á, LORD imputes). 1. Two Merarite Levites: descendant of Amaziah (1 Ch 6:45) and of Bunni (1 Ch 9:14; Neh 11:15). 2. Son of Jeduthun (1 Ch 25:3, 19). 3. David's official W of Jordan (1 Ch 26:30). 4. Ruler of Levites (possibly same as 3) in David's time (1 Ch 27:17). 5. Chief Levite (2 Ch 35: 9; 1 Esd 1:9 [KJ: Assabias; RV: Sabias]). 6. Levite under Ezra (Ez 8:19; 1 Esd 8:48 [KJ: Asebia; RV: Asebias]). 7. Chief priest in charge of bullion and temple equipment (Ez 8:24; 1 Esd 8:54 [KJ: Assanias; RV: Assamias]). 8. Bani's father (Neh 11:22). 9. Levite (Neh 3:17; 10:11; 12:24). 10. Priest (Neh 12:21). 11. See *Malchijah 4.*

Hashabnah (há-shăb'ná). Chief who sealed Nehemiah's covenant (Neh 10:25).

Hashabneiah, Hashabniah (hăsh-ăb-nĕ-ī'á, -nī'á, LORD regarded). 1. Father of Hattush (Neh 3:10). 2. Levite; exhorted Israelites to worship God (Neh 9:5).

Hashbadana, Hashbadanah, Hashbaddana hăsh-băd'á-ná). Stood by Ezra as latter read Law (Neh 8:4). Nabarias (RSV: Nabariah) in 1 Esd 9:44.

Hashem (hā'shĕm. Jashen in 2 Sm 23:32). Father of members of David's guard (1 Ch 11:34).

Hashmonah (hăsh-mō'ná). Station of Israel in Arabah near Mt Hor (Nm 33:29).

Hashub (hā'shŭb). See *Hasshub.*

Hashubah (há-shōo'bá, esteemed). Descendant of Solomon (1 Ch 3:20).

Hashum (hā'shŭm). 1. His descendants returned with Zerubbabel (Ez 2:19; 10:33; Neh 7:22; 1 Esd 9:33 [KJ, RV: Asom]). Arom in 1 Esd 5:16. 2. Stood by Ezra as latter read law (Neh 8:4); sealed covenant (10:18). Lothasubus in 1 Esd 9:44.

Hashupha (há-shōo'fá). See *Hasupha.*

Hasideans (hăs-ĭ-dē'ănz, pious. KJ: Asideans; Assideans). Party among Jews which held to old faith (1 Mac 2:42; 7:13; 2 Mac 14:6).

Hasmonaeans (hăz-mŏ-nē'ănz). See *Asmonaean; Maccabees.*

Hasrah (hăz'rá). 1. See *Harhas.* 2. See *Azara.*

Hassenaah (hăs-ĕ-nā'á). Descendants rebuilt Fishgate (Neh 3:3). Senaah in Ez 2:35; Neh 7:38; 1 Esd 5:23 (KJ: Annaas; RV: Sanaas).

Hassenuah (hăs-ĕ-nū'á). Benjaminite; descendants lived in Jerusalem after captivity (1 Ch 9:7 [KJ: Hasenuah]; Neh 11:9 [KJ: Senuah]).

Hasshub (hăsh'ŭb, thoughtful. KJ: Hashub in Neh). 1. Repaired part of Jerusalem wall (Neh 3:11). 2. Also repaired wall (Neh 3:23). He or 1 sealed covenant (Neh 10:23). 3. Father of Shemaiah (1 Ch 9:14; Neh 11:15).

Hassophereth (hăs-ō-fē'rĕth). See *Sophereth.*

hasty fruit (Neh 3:1). See *orchard 2.*

Hasupha (há-sū'fá, made bare). Ancestor of Nethinim who returned (Ez 2:43; Neh 7:46 [KJ: Hashupha]; 1 Esd 5:29 [KJ, RV: Asipha]).

hat. Probably kind of cap. (Dn 3:21. RV: mantle).

Hatach, Hathach (hā'tăk, hā'thăk). See *Hathath 2.*

hate. 1. Abhor; loathe; regard as ugly; cherish dislike for. Regard with feelings contrary to love (2 Ch 18:7; Ps 45:7; Mt 24:10). 2. Withdrawal from and denial of every relationship orientated from the fallen state so that the Christian's relationships have their right and meaning in the Lord (Lk 14:26. See "deny," Lk 9:23; "in the Lord," 1 Co 7:39; "as to the Lord," Eph 5:21-33).

Hathath (hā'thăth, fear). 1. Son of Othniel (1 Ch 4:13). 2. Eunuch of Ahasuerus (Est 4:5. KJ: Hatach. RV: Hathach).

Hatipha (há-tī'fá, captive). Progenitor of family of Nethinim (Ez 2:54; Neh 7:56: 1 Esd 5:32 [KJ, RV: Atipha]).

Hatita (há-tī'tá, dug up). Temple porter whose descendants returned (Ez 2:42; Neh 7:45; 1 Esd 5:28 [KJ: Teta; RV: Ateta]).

Hattil (hăt'ĭl, vacillating). Servant of Solomon whose descendants returned (Ez 2:57; Neh 7:59; 1 Esd 5:34 [KJ: Hagia; RV: Agia]).

Hattush (hăt'ŭsh). 1. Judahite; son of Shemaiah (1 Ch 3:22). 2. Descendant of David who returned with Ezra (Ez 8:2; 1 Esd 8:29 [KJ: Lettus; RV: Attus]). 3. Rebuilt part of Jerusalem wall (Neh 3:10). Perhaps same as 2. 4. Sealed covenant of Nehemiah (Neh 10:4). 5. Chief priest who returned with Zerubbabel (Neh 12:2).

Hauran (hô-rän', hollow land?). 1. Plateau of E Syria S of Damascus. In Greco-Roman period called Auranitis. Covered

with extinct volcanic mounds (Eze 47:
16, 18. See Josephus *Ant* XVII, xi, 4;
XVIII, iv, 6; *Wars* I, xx, 4; II, vi, 3; III,
iii, 5). 2. See *Auranus*.
Havilah (hăv'ĭ-lä, sandy). **1.** Region surrounded by Pison R (Gn 2:11). Name
later applied to region of Cushites (Gn
10:7; 1 Ch 1:9), Joktanites (Gn 10:29;
1 Ch 1:23), and Ishmaelites (Gn 25:18).
2. Son of Cush (Gn 10:7; 1 Ch 1:9). **3.**
Son of Joktan (Gn 10:29; 1 Ch 1:23).
Havoth-jair, Havvoth-jair (hä'vŏth-, hăv'-
ŏth-jā'ĭr, villages of Jair). Unwalled
towns in NW Bashan captured by Jair
(Nm 32:41; Dt 3:14; Ju 10:4; 1 Ch 2:23).
hawk (H *nets*). Unclean predatory bird
ranging from sparrow hawk to buzzard
(Lv 11:16; Dt 14:15; Jb 39:26).
hay. **1.** KJ for grass (Pr 27:25; Is 15:6).
2. Cut herbage or grass (1 Co 3:12. See
Ps 72:6). Hay not made in Palestine.
Hazael (hăz'ā-ĕl, God sees). King of Assyria (844—804 BC); successor of Ben-
hadad II (1 K 19:15-18; 2 K 8:7-15);
seized Israel's land E of Jordan (2 K
10:32, 33; Am 1:3, 4); overcame Jehoahaz (2 K 13:3-7, 22-25) and besieged
Jerusalem (2 K 12:17, 18).
Hazaiah (hȧ-zā'yȧ, Lord has seen). Judahite (Neh 11:5).
Hazar (hā'zär, enclosure, village). Often
prefixed to descriptive place names. Also
used for encampments of nomads.
Hazar-addar (hā'zär-ăd'är). See *Addar 1*.
Hazar-enan, -enon (hā'zär-ē'năn, -ē'non,
village of fountains). Village near Damascus (Nm 34:9, 10; Eze 47:17, 18;
48:1).
Hazar-gaddah (hā'zär-găd'ȧ, village of good
fortune). Village in S Judah (Khirbet
Ghazza? Jos 15:27).
Hazar-hatticon (hā'zär-hăt'ĭ-kŏn, middle
village. RV, RSV: Hazer-hatticon). Vil-
lage on boundary of Hauran (Eze 47:16).
Hazar-maveth (hā'zär-mā'vĕth, village of
death). Son of Joktan; descendants in
Arabia (Gn 10:26; 1 Ch 1:20).
Hazar-shual (hā'zär-shōō'ăl, fox village).
Town in S Judah (Jos 15:28; 19:3; 1 Ch
4:28; Neh 11:27).
Hazar-susah, -susim (hā'zär-sū'sȧ, -sū-sĭm,
village of mare, horses). City of Simeon
(Jos 19:5; 1 Ch 4:31). Probably modern
Sbalat Abu Susein.
Hazazon-tamar (hăz'ȧ-zŏn-tā'mēr, pruning
of palm). See *En-gedi*.
hazel (hā'z'l). Almond (as RV, RSV. Gn
30:37).
Hazelelponi (hăz-e-lĕl-pō'nĭ). See *Hazzelel-
poni*.
Hazer-hatticon (hā'zēr-hăt'ĭ-kŏn). See *Ha-
zar-hatticon*.
Hazerim (hȧ-zē'rĭm). Proper noun in KJ.
RV, RSV (correctly): villages (Dt 2:23).
Hazeroth (hȧ-zē'rŏth, villages). Israelite en-
campment before Paran (Nm 11:35; 12:16;
33:17, 18; Dt 1:1). There sedition of
Aaron and Miriam occurred (Nm 12).
Hazezon-tamar (hăz'e-zŏn-tā'mēr). See *En-
gedi*.
Haziel (hā'zĭ-ĕl, vision of God). Levite;
son of Shimei (1 Ch 23:9).
Hazo (hā'zō, vision). Son of Nahor and
Milcah (Gn 22:22).
Hazor (hā'zôr, enclosure). **1.** City of N Gal-
ilee near headwaters of Jordan; ruled by
Jabin; taken by Joshua (Jos 11:1-14; 12:
19); given to Naphtali (Jos 19:36). A
later Jabin of Hazor defeated by Deborah
and Barak (Ju 4; 1 Sm 12:9). Thence
Tiglath-pileser III carried captives to Assyria (2 K 15:29). There Jonathan Maccabaeus defeated Demetrius (1 Mac 11:

67. KJ: Nasor). Asher (KJ: Aser) in
Tob 1:2. **2.** Town in S Judah (Jos 15:23).
3. See *Hazor-hadattah*. **4.** See *Kerioth-
hezron*. **5.** Benjaminite town near Jerusalem (Neh 11:33). **6.** Capital of Syrian
Bedouins (Jer 49:28-33).
Hazor-hadattah (hā'zôr-hȧ-dăt'ȧ, New Hazor.
KJ: Hazor, Hadattah). Town in extreme
S Judah (Jos 15:25).
Hazzelelponi (hăz-ĕl-ĕl-pō'nĭ. KJ: Hazelelponi). Judahitess; daughter of Etam (1
Ch 4:3).
head. **1.** Part of body. **2.** Whole person
(Pr 10:6; Eze 9:10). **3.** Capital (Is 7:8).
4. Chief in society (Is 9:14, 15). **5.** One
who has pre-eminence over another (Eph
5:23). **6.** "Upon the head": responsibility
(Jos 2:19). **7.** "Lift up head": exalt (Gn
40:20; Ps 83:2).
Head of the church. Christ, who gives life,
strength, goal to every believer and rules
the church (Eph 1:22; 4:13-16).
headband. 1. See *caul 1*. **2.** Probably sash
(as RV, RSV. Is 3:20).
headdress. See *bonnet; dress*.
head stone. See *cornerstone*.
heal. See *apothecary; disease*.
hear. 1. Receive sound by ear (2 Sm 15:10).
2. Listen to God's Word (Mt 13:19). **3.**
Comprehend and assent to God's Word
(Jn 8:47; 10:27). **4.** Approve (1 Jn 4:5).
5. Answer prayer (Ps 116:1).
heart. 1. Center of bodily life (Ju 19:5;
1 Sm 25:37; Ps 40:12). **2.** Center of
thought (Dt 29:4 [RSV: mind]; Pr 14:10),
understanding (Is 44:18. RSV: mind),
deliberation (Neh 7:5. RSV: mind), will
(1 Co 7:37), emotion (Pr 25:20; Is 65:14),
morality (Ps 73:26; 7:21; Ro 1:21 [RSV:
mind]; 2:15; 1 Ptr 3:4). **3.** Dwelling
place of Christ and Spirit (Eph 3:17; 2
Co 1:22).
hearth (härth). **1.** Brazier (as RV, RSV.
Jer 36:22, 23). **2.** Fire pan (Zch 12:6.
RV: pan; RSV: pot). **3.** Hearth on altar
(Lv 6:9 [KJ: burning]; Eze 43:15, 16
[KJ: altar]). **4.** Burning mass (Is 30:14).
5. Brand or fagot (Ps 102:3. RSV: furnace. RV: firebrand).
heath (hēth). Heath grew in Lebanon (Jer
17:6 [RSV: shrub]; 48:6 [RSV: wild
ass]).
heathen. See *barbarian; gentile*.
heave offering (hēv ŏf'ēr-ĭng, H *t:rumah*,
something lifted). **1.** Contributions or offerings set aside; specifically, offering set
aside for priests and Levites (Ex 29:27,
28 [RSV: priests' portion]; Lv 7:34 [RSV:
that is offered]; 10:14 [RSV: that is of-
fered]; Nm 15:19-21 [RSV: offering]).
heaven (hĕv'en). **1.** Atmosphere (Dn 4:12;
7:13; Mt 6:26; Mk 14:62). **2.** Firmament
(Gn 1:6; Jb 38:37; Ps 148:4; Is 40:22).
3. Invisible world, abode and throne of
God (1 K 8:30; 2 Ch 30:27; Ez 1:2) and
angels (1 K 22:19; Mk 12:25; Lk 2:13).
Christ is in heaven (Acts 7:55; Heb 8:1)
and receives believers there (Mt 5:12; Jn
14:1-3; Col 1:5; 1 Ptr 1:4). See also
Paradise.
Heber (hē'bēr, unite). **1.** Chief of Benjamin
(1 Ch 8:17). **2.** Grandson of Asher;
founder of Heberites (Nm 26:45). **3.** Kenite husband of Jael, who slew Sisera (Ju
4:11-24; 5:24). **4.** Judahite; patriarch of
Soco (1 Ch 4:18). See also *Eber*.
Hebrew (hē'brōō). Semitic language in
which most of OT was written (see Aramaic). Called Canaanite language (Is 19:
18) and Jewish language (2 K 18:26, 28).
Closely related to old Phoenician; probably Canaanite dialect adapted by patri-

archs. Hebrew script (consonants) came from Phoenician; existed in 15th c B C. Vowel points added by Massoretes (A D 600—800).

Hebrew of the Hebrews. Self-description of Paul, indicating pure H descent and adherence to H customs (Ph 3:5).

Hebrews. Abram is 1st in OT to be called "Hebrew" (Gn 14:13); thereafter name given to his descendants in O and NT. H word means "pass over" and may refer to Abram's crossing of Euphrates. May also be patronymic from Eber, ancestor of Israelites (Gn 10:21). Habiru of Amarna and Nuzian-Hittite documents are usually identified with Hebrews.

Hebrews, Epistle to. 19th book of NT; written to Christians who were in danger of lapsing from faith. Early 3d-c Eastern Church ascribed authorship to Paul; but West denied Pauline authorship. Tertullian ascribed it to Barnabas. Outline: 1. The Pre-eminence of Jesus, Author of Salvation, over Angels, Moses, Joshua, Levitical High Priest (1:1—5:10). 2. Warning Against Apostasy (5:11—6:12). 3. Finality of Christ's Sacrifice (6:13—10:39). 4. Roll call of Heroes and Heroines of Faith (11). 5. Exhortation to Faith and Godliness (12). 6. Exhortation to Social and Religious Duties; Salutations (13).

Hebron (hē'bron, union). 1. Levite; son of Kohath (Ex 6:18; Nm 3:19). 2. Descendant of Caleb (1 Ch 2:42, 43). 3. City 19 mi SW of Jerusalem (Jos 15:48, 54) originally called Kiriath-arba (Gn 20:2; Neh 11:25). Abraham is closely associated with Hebron (Gn 13:18; 18:23). Spies found Anakim there (Nm 13:22). Conquered by Joshua (Jos 10:39; 11:21-23). David was anointed king there (2 Sm 2:11). 4. See Ebron.

hedge. Enclosure, often of thorns (Is 5:5; Hos 2:6; Mt 21:33). See bittern.

hedgehog. See bittern.

Hegai, Hege (hĕg'à-ī, hē'gē). Eunuch in charge of harem of Ahasuerus (Est 2:3, 8, 15).

heifer. Young cow which has not produced calf (Ju 14:18). Frequent in metaphors (Ju 14:18; Is 15:5; Jer 46:20; 48:34; 50: 11; Hos 4:16; 10:11). Red heifer used for purification (Nm 19) and sin offering (Nm 19:9, 7).

heir. Inheritance divided among sons of legitimate wives (Gn 21:10; 24:36; 25:5), oldest usually receiving double portion and becoming head of family (Dt 21:15-17). Succession of heirs: sons, daughters, brothers, paternal uncles, kinsmen (Nm 27:8-11). Sons of concubines received presents (Gn 25:6).

Helah (hē'là). Wife of Ashhur (1 Ch 4:5, 7).

Helam (hē'lăm). Place between Jordan and Euphrates where David defeated army of Hadadezer (2 Sm 10:16-20).

Helbah (hĕl'bà, fatness). Town of Asher (Ju 1:31).

Helbon (hĕl'bŏn, fat). City in Syria 3½ mi N of Damascus (Eze 27:18).

Helchiah, Helchias (hĕl-kī'à, hĕl-kī'ăs). See Hilkiah 6.

Heldai (hĕl'dà-ī). 1. Descendant of Othniel, David's commander for 12th month (1 Ch 27:15). Heled in 1 Ch 11:30; Heleb in 2 Sm 23:29. 2. Exile who returned from Babylon (Zch 6:10, 11. KJ, RV Helem in v 14).

Heleb (hē'lĕb). See Heldai 1.

Helech (hē'lĕk. KJ, RV: with thine army). Name of place (Eze 27:11).

Heled (hē'lĕd). See Heldai 1.

Helek (hē'lĕk, portion). Son of Gilead; ancestor of Helekites (Nm 26:30; Jos 17:2).

Helem (hē'lĕm). 1. See Heldai 2. 2. Greatgrandson of Asher (1 Ch 7:35). Probably Hotham (1 Ch 7:32).

Heleph, (hē'lĕf). City at NW boundary of Naphtali (Jos 19:33).

Helez (hē'lĕz, strength). 1. Paltite; David's commander for 7th month (2 Sm 23:26; 1 Ch 11:27; 27:10). 2. Judahite; descendant of Hezron (1 Ch 2:39).

Heli (hē'lī). 1. Grandfather of Christ (Lk 3:23). 2. See Eli 2.

Helias (hē-lī'ăs). See Elijah 1.

Heliodorus (hē-lī-ō-dôr'us). Syrian treasurer (2 Mac 3).

Heliopolis (hē-lī-ŏp'ô-lĭs). See second On.

Helkai (hĕl'kà-ī, smooth). Priest (Neh 12:15).

Helkath (hĕl'kăth, portion. Hukok in 1 Ch 6:75). Levitical city on E border of Asher (Jos 19:25; 21:31).

Helkath-hazzurim (hĕl'kăth-hăz'û-rĭm, field of sharp knives, or of liers in wait). Plain near pool of Gibeon where men of David and Ishbosheth fought (2 Sm 2:16).

Helkias (hĕl-kī'ăs). See Chelcias; Hilkiah 6.

hell. Eternal punishment of damned called Gehenna; eternal (Mt 18:8, 9), unquenchable (Mt 3:12; Mk 9:44) fire; eternal punishment (Mt 25:46); fire and worm (Mk 9:48); lake of fire (Rv 20:14) and brimstone (Rv 14:10; 19:20); furnace of fire (Mt 13:42); torment (Rv 14:10, 11); outer darkness (Mt 8:12; 22:13; 25:30). Unbelievers are damned and under the wrath of God (Jn 3:36. See Dn 12:2). See Gehenna; Hades.

Hellenist (hĕl'ĕn-ĭst). See Greek.

helmet. See armor.

Helon (hē'lŏn, strong). Father of Eliab 1 (Nm 1:9; 2:7; 7:24, 29; 10:16).

hem. RV, RSV: skirt (Ex 28:33, 34; 39:24-26); RSV: fringe, RV: border (Mt 9:20; 14:36). Pharisees made long fringes (Mt 23:5) on basis of Nm 15:38, 39.

Hemam (hē'măm). See Homam.

Heman (hē'măn). 1. See Homam. 2. Wise man (1 K 4:31; 1 Ch 2:6; Ps 88 title). 3. Grandson of Samuel; musician of David (1 Ch 6:33; 15:17-19; 16:41, 42; 25:1; 2 Ch 5:12; 29:14; 35:15). Zacharias (RSV: Zechariah) in 1 Esd 1:15.

Hemath (hē'măth). See Hamath 2; Hammath 2.

Hemdan (hĕm'dăn, pleasant). Oldest son of Dishon (Gn 36:26). Hamran (KJ: Amram) in 1 Ch 1:41.

hemlock. See gall 2; wormwood.

hen. Domestic fowl common in Palestine (Mt 23:37; Lk 13:34).

Hen (hĕn, grace). See Josiah 2.

Hena (hē'nà). City of Mesopotamia (Ana? 2 K 18:34; 19:13; Is 37:13).

Henadad (hĕn'à-dăd, favor of Hadad). Levite; sons repaired Jerusalem wall, sealed covenant (Ez 3:9; Neh 3:18, 24; 10:9).

henna (hĕn'à. KJ: camphire). Plant with clusters of fragrant white and yellow flowers (SS 1:14; 4:13).

Henoch (hē'nŏk). See Enoch 2; Hanoch 1.

Hepher (hē'fēr, pit). 1. Son of Gilead; founder of Hepherites (Nm 26:32, 33; 27:1; Jos 17:2, 3). 2. Son of Ashhur (1 Ch 4:6). 3. One of David's guard (1 Ch 11:36). 4. City near Soco (Jos 12:17; 1 K 4:10).

Hephzibah (hĕf'zĭ-bà, my delight is in her). 1. Wife of Hezekiah (2 K 21:1). 2. Symbolic name for Zion (Is 62:4).

herald. 1. Crier (Dn 3:4. RSV in Is 40:9; 41:27). 2. Preacher (2 Ptr 2:5).

Hercules (hûr'kû-lēz). A god identified with Melkart (2 Mac 4:19).

herd. See *cattle.*

herdsman. Person in charge of cattle (Gn 13:7) or swine (Mt 8:33). Herdsmen honorable in Israel (Gn 47:6; 1 Sm 11:5; 21:7; 1 Ch 27:29) but despised in Egypt (Gn 46:34).

hereafter. See *eschatology; eternal life; Gehenna; heaven; hell.*

Heres (hē'rēz, sun). 1. City of Dan; probably same as Beth-shemesh 1 (Ju 1:35. RSV: Har-heres). 2. Ascent of Heres, pass E of Jordan (Ju 8:13. KJ: before the sun was up).

Heresh (hē'rĕsh). Levite (1 Ch 9:15).

heresy (hĕr'e-sĭ, G *hairesis,* choice). 1. Sect or party; applied to Pharisees (Acts 15:5), Sadducees (Acts 5:17), Christians (Acts 24:5, 14). 2. Divisions in church occasioned by difference of motive, goal, and doctrine (Acts 20:29; 1 Co 11:19; Gl 5: 20; Tts 3:10; 2 Ptr 2:1).

Hereth (hē'rĕth, thicket. KJ: Hareth). Forest in Judah (1 Sm 22:5).

Hermas (hûr'măs). 1. Friend of Paul at Rome (Ro 16:14). 2. See *Ramiah.*

Her'mes (hûr'mēz). 1. Greek messenger god, called Mercury in Latin (Acts 14:12. KJ: Mercurius; RV: Mercury). 2. Friend of Paul at Rome (Ro 16:14).

Hermogenes (hûr-mŏj'ĕ-nēz, born of Mercury). Resident of Asia who turned from Paul (2 Ti 1:15).

Her'mon (hûr'mon, sacred mountain). Mt 30 mi SW of Damascus; 9,101 ft above sea level; water from its snow feeds Jordan; N limit of Israel's conquests (Dt 3: 8); regarded high mt of Mt 17:1; Mk 9:2; Lk 9:28; mentioned in poetry (Ps 42:6; 133:3); Sidonians call it Sirion (Dt 3:9; Ps 29:6; Jer 18:14); Amorites, Senir (Dt 3:9; 1 Ch 5:23; SS 4:8; Eze 27:5). KJ: Shenir in Dt and SS. In SS Hermon and Senir are distinct peaks. Also called Sion (Dt 4:48. RSV: Sirion). Hermon was seat of Baal worship (Ju 3:3). Modern Jebel esh Sheikh.

Herod (hĕr'ud, heroic). Idumaean rulers of Palestine (55 B C—A D 93). Line started by Antipater, whom Hyrcanus II forced to be circumcized. 1. Herod the Great, procurator of Judea (47 B C) and king of the Jews (37—4 B C); to remain on side of victorious parties in Rome, rebuilt Caesarea, temples at Jerusalem and Samaria; domestic and political life marked by intrigue and bloodshed; slaughtered innocents at Bethlehem (Mt 2:1-18). 2. Herod Archelaus. Son of Herod the Great by Malthace, Samaritan. Ruled Idumea, Judea, and Samaria (4 B C— A D 6. Mt 2:22). 3. Herod Antipas. (4 B C— A D 39). Sly, ambitious; lived sumptuously. Jesus called him "fox" (Lk 13:32). 4. Herod Philip. Married Herodias (Mt 14:3; Mk 6:17; Lk 3:19). 5. Herod Philip II, tetrarch of Batanaea, Trachonitis, Gaulanitis, and parts of Jamnia. Best of Herods (Lk 3:1). 6. Herod Agrippa I. Grandson of Herod the Great; tetrarch of Galilee; king of Palestine (A D 37—44). Persuaded Caligula not to put his statue in temple. Persecuted Christians (Acts 12:1-23). 7. Herod Agrippa II. King of territory E of Galilee (c A D 53 —70). Paul was brought before him (Acts 25:13—26:32).

Herodians (hē-rō'dĭ-ănz). Partisans of Herods and Roman rule (Mt 22:16; Mk 3:6; 8:15).

Herodias (hē-rō'dĭ-ăs). Granddaughter of Herod the Great. Caused death of John Baptist (Mt 14:3-6; Mk 6:17; Lk 3:19).

Herodion (hē-rō'dĭ-ŏn). Kinsman of Paul (Ro 16:11).

heron (hĕr'un). Large unclean, aquatic bird (Lv 11:19; Dt 14:18).

Hesed (hē'sĕd). See *Ben-hesed.*

Heshbon (hĕsh'bŏn, device. KJ: Esebon in Jdth 5:15). Moabite city NE of Dead Sea (Hesban); ruled by Sihon of Amorites (Nm 21:25); given by Moses to Reuben (Nm 32:37; Jos 13:17); later assigned as town of Gad to Levites (Jos 21:39; 1 Ch 6:81).

Heshmon (hĕsh'mŏn). Town in S Judah (Jos 15:27).

Heth (hĕth). Forefather of Hittites (Gn 10: 15; 1 Ch 1:13. See Gn 23; 25:10; 49:32).

Hethlon (hĕth'lŏn). Name of place in N Palestine (Eze 47:15; 48:1).

Hezeki (hĕz'ĕ-kī). See *Hizki.*

Hezekiah (hĕz-ĕ-kī'á, strength is LORD). 1. Son of Ahaz; father of Manasseh; 13th king of Judah; inaugurated religious reforms; reign marked by material prosperity; involved in struggle for power between Egypt and Mesopotamia; built Siloam tunnel. In his reign occurred destruction of Sennacherib's army; Isaiah prophesied (2 K 18—20; 2 Ch 29—32; Is 1:1; 36—39. KJ: Ezekias in Mt 1:9, 10; Ezechias in 2 Esd 7:40). 2. Ancestor of Zephaniah (Zph 1:1. KJ: Hizkiah). 3. Son of Neariah (1 Ch 3:23. RV, RSV: Hizkiah). 4. Sealed covenant with Nehemiah (Neh 10:17. KJ: Hizkijah). 5. See *Hilkiah 8.* 6. Named with Ater in Ez 2:16; Neh 7:21; 1 Esd 5:15 (KJ conflates the two: Aterezias; RV: Ezekias).

Hezion (hē'zĭ-on, vision). Grandfather of Ben-hadad I of Syria (1 K 15:18). Perh same as Rezon (1 K 11:23).

Hezir (hē'zĕr, swine, or apple). 1. Head of 17th course of priests (1 Ch 24:15). 2. Sealed covenant with Nehemiah (Neh 10: 20).

Hezrai, Hezro (hĕz'rá-ī, hĕz'rō). One of David's mighty men (2 Sm 23:35; 1 Ch 11:37).

Hezron (hĕz'rŏn, surrounded). 1. Son of Reuben (Gn 46:9; Ex 6:14; 1 Ch 4:1; 5:3). 2. Son of Perez (Gn 46:12; Nm 26: 21; Ru 4:18; 1 Ch 2:5. KJ: Esrom in Mt 1:3; Lk 3:33). 3. Place on S boundary of Judah (Jos 15:3).

Hezronites (hĕz'rŏn-īts). Descendants of Hezron 1 and 2 (Nm 26:6, 21).

Hiddai (hĭd'â-ī). One of David's mighty men (2 Sm 23:30). Hurai in 1 Ch 11:32.

Hiddekel (hĭd'ĕ-kĕl). Ancient name of Tigris river (Gn 2:14; Dn 10:4).

Hiel (hī'ĕl, brother of God). Rebuilt Jericho in days of Ahab (1 K 16:34) and brought curse on himself (Jos 6:26).

Hierapolis (hī-ĕr-ăp'ŏ-līs, holy city). City in Phrygia near Colossae (Cl 4:13).

Hiereel (hī-ĕr'ĕ-ĕl). See *Jehiel 8.*

Hieremoth (hī-ĕr'ĕ-moth). See *Jeremoth 6; 8.*

Hierielus (hī-ĕr-ĭ-ē'lus). See *Jehiel 9.*

Hiermas (hī-ûr'măs). See *Ramiah.*

hieroglyphic (hī-ĕr-ŏ-glĭf'ĭk, sacred carving). Picture writing of ancient Egypt and other nations.

Hieronymus (hī-ĕr-ŏn'ĭ-mus). A governor (2 Mac 12:2).

Higgaion (hĭ-gā'yŏn). Musical term (Ps 9: 16). Elsewhere: melody (Ps 92:3. KJ, RV: solemn sound), meditation (Ps 19: 14).

High, Most. Name applied to God (Ps 9:2; 21:7; 87:5; Mk 5:7; Lk 8:28). Melchizedek served El Elyom (God Most High. Gn 14:18-20).

high places. Places of worship originally on high ground (Gn 12:8; Nm 22:41; 1 K 11:7). Israelites enjoined to destroy high places of Canaanites (Nm 33:52; Dt 33: 29), often connected with licentiousness (Hos 4:11-14; Jer 3:2). On high places stood altar (1 K 12:32), Asherah (Dt 16: 21; Ju 6:25), and often house (1 K 12: 31). Jews at times worshiped Jehovah on high places (1 K 3:2, 4).

high priest. See *priest 2.*

Hilen (hī'lĕn). See *Holon.*

Hilkiah (hĭl-kī'á, portion is LORD). 1. Merarite Levite; son of Amzi (1 Ch 6:45, 46). 2. Merarite Levite; son of Hosah (1 Ch 26:11). 3. Father of Eliakim (2 K 18:18, 26; Is 22:20; 36:3). 4. Father of Jeremiah (Jer 1:1). 5. Father of Gemariah (Jer 29:3). 6. High priest in days of Josiah; ancestor of Ezra; found Book of Law (2 K 22:4-14; 23:4; 1 Ch 6:13; 9: 11; 2 Ch 34:9-22; Ez 7:1; Neh 11:11; 1 Esd 8:1 [KJ: Helchiah; RV: Helkias]; 2 Esd 1:1 [KJ: Helchias; RV: Helkias]). 7. Chief priest who returned with Zerubbabel (Neh 12:7, 21). 8. Stood by Ezra as he read Law (Neh 8:4). KJ: Ezecias; RV: Ezekias; RSV: Hezekiah in 1 Esd 9: 43. 9. 10. See *Chelcias 1; 2.*

hill. 1. Isolated elevation (Mt 5:14; Lk 3:5). H *gibh'ah* in Jos 24:33 (KJ, RV: hill); 1 Sm 11:4. 2. Ascent (as RV. 1 Sm 9:11). 3. Horn or top (Is 5:1). 4. H *har:* mountain (Ex 24:4; Nm 14:44; 1 K 11:7. RV, RSV: mountain).

Hillel (hĭl'ĕl, he has praised). Father of Abdon (Ju 12:13, 15).

hin (hĭn). See *measures 3b.*

hind (hīnd). Female deer (Gn 49:21; Jb 39:1).

Hinnom (hĭn'om). See *Gehenna.*

Hirah (hī'rá). Adullamite (Gn 38:1, 12).

Hiram (hī'răm, brother of exalted one). 1. King of Tyre; sent cedar and workmen to David for his house (2 Sm 5:11; 1 Ch 14:1) and timber (1 K 5:1) and gold (1 K 9:11-14) to Solomon for temple. Huram in Ch. 2. Artificer for Solomon's temple (1 K 7:13-46). Huram in 2 Ch 4:11. Huram-abi in 2 Ch 2:13 (KJ, RV: Huram my father); 4:16 (KJ, RV: Huram his father).

Hircanus (hûr-kā'nus). Son of Tobias (2 Mac 3:11). RV, RSV: Hyrcanus.

hiss. 1. Way of showing astonishment (1 K 9:8) and contempt (Jb 27:23; Jer 19:8). 2. To call (Is 7:18 [RSV: whistle]; Zch 10:8 [RSV: signal]).

Hittites (hĭt'īts). Descendants of Heth (Gn 10:15); frequently mentioned in OT (Gn 23:1-20; 26:34; Jos 9:1). Archaeology has uncovered their civilization; language deciphered; Indo-European.

Hivites (hī'vīts). Nation of Canaan (Dt 7: 1); seemed to be centered in N country (Jos 11:3; Ju 3:3; 2 Sm 24:7), though found in other localities (Gn 34:2); unwarlike, after deceiving Joshua, became hewers of wood and drawers of water (Jos 9).

Hizki (hĭz'kī, LORD strengthened). Son of Elpael (1 Ch 8:17, 18. KJ: Hezeki).

Hizkiah (hĭz-kī'á). See *Hezekiah 2; 3.*

Hizkijah (hĭz-kī'já). See *Hezekiah 4.*

Hobab (hō'băb, beloved). Brother-in-law of Moses (Nm 10:29; Ju 4:11 [KJ, RSV: father-in-law]). See also *Jethro.*

Hobah (hō'bá). Place N of Damascus (Gn 14:15).

Hobaiah (hō-bā'yá). See *Habaiah.*

Hod (hŏd, majesty). Asherite; son of Zophah (1 Ch 7:37).

Hodaiah (hō-dá'yá). See *Hodaviah 1.*

Hodaviah (hō-dá-vī'á, LORD is praise). 1. Descendant of David (1 Ch 3:24. KJ: Hodaiah). 2. Chief in Manasseh (1 Ch 5:24). 3. Benjaminite (1 Ch 9:7). 4. Levite, whose descendants returned with Zerubbabel (Ez 2:40). Hodevah in Neh 7:43. Judah in Ez 3:9. Sudias in 1 Esd 5:26. Joda in 1 Esd 5:58.

Hodesh (hō'dĕsh, new moon). See *Baara.*

Hodevah (hō'dē-vä). See *Hodaviah 4.*

Hodiah (hō-dī'á, majesty of LORD). 1. Man reckoned as belonging to Judah (1 Ch 4:19. KJ incorrect). 2. Levite; explained law to people (Neh 8:7; 10:10). 3. Levite; sealed covenant (Neh 10:13). 4. Sealed covenant (Neh 10:18). KJ: Hodijah in Neh.

Hodijah (hō-dī'já). See *Hodiah 3; 4; 5.*

Hoglah (hŏg'lá, partridge). Daughter of Zelophehad (Nm 26:33; 27:1-8; 36:1-12).

Hoham (hō'hăm). King of Hebron; joined league against Joshua (Jos 10:1-27).

holm (hōm). See *cypress.*

Holofernes (hŏl-ō-fûr'nēz). General slain by Judith (Jdth 2:4).

Holon (hō'lŏn). 1. Levitical town in hill country of Judah (Jos 15:51; 21:15). Hilen in 1 Ch 6:58. 2. Moabite town (Jer 48:21).

holy. That which is separated from common and consecrated to sacred. Jehovah is holy because He is above created world (Is 6; 57:15). He demands that His people be holy, i. e., separated for God (Nm 15:40, 41; Dt 7:6). Jesus is Holy One of God (Mk 1:24; Lk 4:34; Jn 6:69). Holiness of God imparts itself to men through election and mighty acts (Dt 26:18, 19) culminating in work of Jesus (Jn 17:19; 1 Co 1:2; Eph 4; 1 Ptr 2:1-10).

Holy Land (hō'lĭ lănd). See *Canaan.*

Holy Spirit. 3d person of Godhead; proceeds from Father (Jn 1:2; Jn 15:26) and Son (Jn 14:26; 15:26; Acts 1:8). Works in creation and preservation (Gn 1:2; Jb 33:4), and in leader (Ju 3:10) of God's people. He gave divine understanding to prophets (Is 61:1; Mi 3:8; 1 Ptr 1:10, 11; 2 Ptr 1:21). Spirit was given without measure to Jesus (Mk 1:8; Jn 1:32, 33; 3:34; Acts 10:38). Spirit is Spirit of Christ (Ro 8:9; 2 Co 3:18; Gl 4:6). Holy Spirit creates church (Eze 37: 1-14; Jl 2:28; Acts 2; 9:31). Lives in those added to Church (Acts 2:38. See Eph 3:20, 21). Believer is new creation (Jn 3:3-8. See 2 Co 5:17) of Spirit and brought by Him into communion with Father and Son (Ro 8:14-17; Gl 4:1-7), hence with all believers (Ph 2:1,2) in one unity of Spirit (1 Co 12). Holy Spirit converts and edifies through Word (Jn 6:63; 1 Co 12:2, 3; 1 Jn 5:6-12).

Holy Spirit, sin against. See *sin, unpardonable.*

Homam (hō'măm). Grandson of Seir (1 Ch 1:39). Hemam (RSV: Heman) in Gn 36: 22.

homer (hō'mēr). See *measures 2e.*

homes. 1. Limestone ridge of Palestine honeycombed with caves; these served as homes for shepherds, exiles (1 Sm 24:3; 1 K 18:4; 19:9), outcasts, lepers. 2. Temporary shelters were booths made of 4 upright poles covered with network of twigs and leaves (Jb 27:18; Is 1:8 [KJ: cottage]; Jon 4:5. See Lv 23:34-43). In Jordan valley seasonal homes may have been constructed of woven river reeds, sometimes plastered with mud. 3. Nomadic people dwelt in tents (Gn 4:20), often woven of dark-colored goat or camel hair. Desert tent large, with 2 or more center poles (Ex 26:32) from which tent cloth sloped to within 3 or 4 ft of ground, was held in place by cords (Jer 10:20) tied to tent pins (Is 54:2. See Ju 4:21). 4. In rocky sections of Palestine houses constructed of limestone held together by mortar of slaked lime and sand. Along Mediterranean, as in ancient Shinar (Gn 11:3), houses made of clay. Homes preferably placed on solid footing (Mt 7:24-27), built by placing layer on layer of stone. Door openings made by building squared masonry sides or inserting framework. Doors of heavy planks or slabs of stone. Window openings narrow, high up in walls, usually fitted with latticework of wooden slats (Ju 5:28; 2 K 1:2; Pr 7:6; SS 2:9). At sufficient height roof beams were laid from wall to wall; smaller branches were laid crosswise, covered with rushes or straw; this then covered with alternating layers of clay and straw, finished with pure clay. Wall continued about 3 ft above roof line (Dt 22:8; Jos 2:6; Acts 10:9). Stairway led from street level to roof line. Upper rooms might be built at one side of building (Mk 14:15; Acts 1:13; 1 K 17:19; 2 K 4:10). House might also have one large room with mezzanine floor running along one side, with living quarters above, room for sheep and goats below. 5. On floor were mats and rugs woven of wool, grass, straw, or other fiber; these served as mattresses at night (wealthier homes had couches and beds), took place of chairs during day. In middle of house stood brazier or stove (of iron or bronze) consisting of three legs riveted to one or two circular hoops; or simply circular hole in earthen floor. Fuel was straw, brushwood, charcoal, dried animal dung. Pots and pans were beaten out of copper or bronze. Ladles, spoons, and forks (flesh hooks) were also copper. Knives were of bronze or iron, of various sizes, fitted with wooden handles. Many household utensils (jugs, pitchers, cups, saucers, bowls) were of pottery. Very large pottery jars stored wheat. Every home had its flour mill (Dt 24:6). Wineskins, rings of onions and garlic, dried raisins, etc., were suspended from crossbeams of ceiling. 6. Wealthier homes had walled courtyards or were series of rooms built around open court. As the nation prospered, the wealthy and influential built luxurious mansions and palaces (Am 5: 11; 6:4-11; Jn 18:13-27). (Klinck)

homosexuals. See *abuse, abuser.*

honey. Honey was plentiful in Palestine. Wild honey deposited in rocks (Dt 32: 13), carcasses (Ju 14:8), trees (1 Sm 14:25), etc. Eaten in comb or in various preparations (Ex 16:31; 1 Sm 14:27; SS 5:1).

hooks. Hooks were used for fishing (Jb 41: 1; Hab 1:15); hanging curtains (Ex 26: 32, 37; 27:10-14; 36:36-38; 38:11-17); for leading animals and captives (2 K 19: 28; 2 Ch 33:11 [KJ: among the thorns]; Eze 19:4 [KJ: chains]); pruning (Jl 3: 10; Mi 4:3); hanging meat (Eze 40:43), lifting boiled meat (1 Sm 2:14. RSV: fork).

hoopoe (hōō'pōō). Unclean, migratory bird (Lv 11:19; Dt 14:18. KJ: lapwing).

hope. Christian hope is fruit of justification (Ro 5:4, 5), is joined with faith and love (1 Co 13:13), centers in Christ (Cl 1:27; 1 Ti 1:1; Heb 6:18). Hope comforts in trials (Ps 43:5; Ro 12:12), stimulates Christian life (1 Jn 3:3), takes Christ's resurrection as pledge of our resurrection (1 Ptr 1:3, 4).

Hophni (hŏf'nī). Impious son of Eli (1 Sm 2:12—4:22).

Hophra (hŏf'rà). See *Pharaoh 11.*

hopper. See *cankerworm.*

Hor (hôr, mountain). 1. Mt at edge of Edom (Nm 20:23; 33:37) where Aaron died (Nm 20:22-29; 33:37). Identified with Nebi-Harun, or, better, Madurah. 2. Mt on N boundary of Palestine. Probably Lebanon range or peak (Nm 34:7, 8).

Horam (hō'răm, elevation). King of Gezer killed by Joshua (Jos 10:33).

Horeb (hō'rĕb, dryness). Lower peak of Sinai (Gesenius); range of which Sinai is peak (Hengstenberg); later name for Sinai (Ewald) (Ex 3:1; 33:6; Dt 1:2; 2 Esd 2:33 [KJ: Oreb]). Horeb and Sinai used interchangeably (e. g., Ex 17:6; 19:11). See also *Sinai.*

Horem (hō'rĕm, consecrated). Fenced city of Naphtali (Jos 19:38).

Horesh (hō'rĕsh, thicket). Place where David hid (1 Sm 23:15-19. KJ, RV: wood).

Hor-haggidgad (hôr-hà-gĭd'găd). See *Gudgodah.*

Hori (hō'rī). 1. Grandson of Seir (Gn 36:22; 1 Ch 1:39). 2. Simeonite; father of spy Shaphat (Nm 13:5).

Horim, Horite (hō'rĭm, -rīt). People defeated by Chedorlaomer (Gn 14:6) and Esau's descendants (Gn 36:29, 30; Dt 2:12, 22 [KJ Horims]). Identified by archaeology (especially excavations at Nuzi) with Hurrians, non-Semitic people.

Hormah (hôr'mä, asylum). Canaanite city in S Palestine (Nm 14:45; 21:1-3; Dt 1: 44; Jos 12:14; 15:30; 19:4). Early name Zephath (Ju 1:17).

horn. First made of animal horns, later of metal (Nm 10:2). Used for giving signals (Jos 6:5; Ps 98:6), as container (1 Sm 16:1). Projections of corners of altar were called horns (Ex 27:2; 1 K 1:50). Symbolically horn denoted honor and strength (e. g., Ps 18:2; Dn 7:7; Lk 1:69; Ps 132:17; 75:10).

horned owl. See *water hen.*

hornet. Several species found in Holy Land (Ex 23:28; Dt 7:20; Jos 24:12).

Horonaim (hŏr'ō-nā'ĭm, two hollows). City of Moab (perh el-Arak. 2 Sm 13:34 [KJ, RV: behind him]; Is 15:5; Jer 48:3, 5, 34).

Horonite (hŏr'ō-nīt). Appellation of Sanballat (Neh 2:10, 19; 13:28) as inhabitant of Beth-horon.

horse. Mentioned in time of Jacob (Gn 49: 17); used in Egypt (Ex 14:9; 15:19). Israelites commanded not to keep horses taken in war (Dt 17:16; Jos 11:4-9); kings later kept horses (1 Sm 8:11; 2 Sm 8:4; 1 K 1:5; 4:26). Used chiefly for war (Ex 14:9).

horseleech (hôrs'lēch). See *leech.*

Hosah (hō'sà, refuge). 1. Doorkeeper of ark in Jerusalem (1 Ch 16:38) and of temple (1 Ch 26:10-16). 2. City on boundary of Asher (Jos 19:29).

Hosanna (hō-zăn'à, save now). Ps 118:25, 26 chanted at feast of tabernacles. Chanted when Jesus entered Jerusalem (Mt 21:9-15; Mk 11:9, 10).

Hosea (hō-zē'á, salvation. KJ in NT: Osee). Prophet in days of Uzziah, Jotham, Ahaz, and Hezekiah of Judah and Jeroboam II of Israel (Hos 1:1). Contemporary of Isaiah, Amos, Micah (2 Esd 1:39 [KJ, RV: Oseas]). Book is extract of many discourses. Outline: 1. Israel's Unfaithfulness and Restoration Under Symbol of Harlots (1—3), 2. Gross Iniquity of People, Priests, Rulers and Need for Repentance (4:1—6:3). 3. Punishment Which Must Come for Sin (6:4—10:15). 4. Hopeful Remonstrance and Expostulation (11 to 13). 5. Entreaty and Promise of Acceptance for Penitent (14).

hosen (hō'z'n). Breeches or other tight-fitting covering of legs (Dn 3:21. RV, RSV: tunics).

Hoshaiah (hō-shā'yá, LORD has saved). 1. Assisted at dedication of Jerusalem's walls (Neh 12:32). 2. Father of Jezaniah (Jer 42:1; 43:2).

Hoshama (hōsh'á-má, LORD has heard). Son of Jehoiachin (1 Ch 3:18).

Hoshea (hō'shē'á, salvation). H same as Hosea). 1. See *Joshua 1*. 2. Prince of Ephraim (1 Ch 27:20). 3. 19th and last king of Israel; conspired with Tiglath-pileser against Pekah and slew him (2 K 15:30); paid tribute to Assyria (2 K 17:3). Shalmaneser invaded his territory and his successor, Sargon, took Samaria and carried ten tribes into captivity (2 K 17:1-23; Hos 13:16; 2 Esd 13:40 [KJ, RV: Osea]). 4. Sealed covenant with Nehemiah (Neh 10:23).

hospitality (hŏs-pi-tăl'i-ti). Enjoined by Mosaic law (Lv 19:34); encouraged in OT (Gn 18:1-8; Jb 31:32) and NT (Lk 14:12-14; Ro 12:13; 1 Ptr 4:9).

host. 1. Of heaven. Sun, moon, stars described as army (Ju 5:20); worshiped (Dt 4:19; 2 K 17:16). 2. Lord of hosts (H Sabaoth). God is Lord of angels (Gn 28: 12); stars (Is 40:26; 45:12); forces of nature (Neh 9:6; Ps 103:21); sun, moon, stars, sea (Jer 31:35). 3. Host of heaven. Company of holy people and beings (1 K 22:19-23; Dn 8:10, 11). 4. One who shows hospitality (Ro 16:23; Lk 10:35); army (Ex 14:4), etc.

Hotham (hō'thăm). 1. See *Helem 2*. 2. Aroerite; 2 sons were heroes of David (1 Ch 11:44. KJ: Hothan).

Hothan (hō'thăn). See *Hotham 2*.

Hothir (hō'thêr). Son of Heman (1 Ch 25: 4, 28).

hough (hŏk). Hamstring (as RSV: Jos 11:6, 9; 2 Sm 8:4).

hours. See *time*.

house. 1. Family line (Ex 2:1; Nm 12:7). 2. House of God: place where God makes His presence known, e. g., Bethel (Gn 28: 17), tabernacle (Ex 34:26; 40:19-35; Dt 23:18), temple (1 K 6:1). 3. See *homes*.

Hozai (hō'zá-ī, LORD sees. KJ, RSV: seers). Writer of history of Manasseh (2 Ch 33:19).

Hukkok (hŭk'ŏk). Town on border of Naphtali (Jos 19:34).

Hukok (hū'kŏk). See *Helkath*.

Hul (hŭl). Grandson of Shem (Gn 10:23; 1 Ch 1:17).

Huldah (hŭl'dá, weasel). Wife of Shallum; prophetess (2 K 22:14-20; 2 Ch 34:22-28).

humiliation of Christ (hū-mĭl-ĭ-ā'shun). See *Jesus Christ*.

humility. Lowliness of mind. Whereas pride overestimates self, humility sees self in proper perspective, avoids overestimation (Ro 12:3. See Pr 15:33; Mt 18:4; Eph 4:2; Cl 3:12).

Humtah (hŭm'tá, place of lizards). Town in Judah (Jos 15:54).

hunting. Israelites hunted deer (Gn 25:28), gazelle, hart (Dt 12:15, 22), roebuck, wild goat, ibex, antelope, mountain sheep (Dt 14:5), partridge (1 Sm 26:20) and other birds. Bows and arrows (Gn 27:3), slingstones, darts (Jb 41:28, 29), nets (Jb 19: 6), pits (Ps 9:15), snares (Ps 9:15; 64:5) used.

Hupham (hū'fŭm). Benjaminite; founder of Huphamites (Nm 26:39). Probably same as Huppim (Gn 46:21; 1 Ch 7:12) and perhaps Huram (1 Ch 8:5).

Huppah (hŭp'á, covering). Priest in charge of 13th division (1 Ch 24:13).

Huppim (hŭp'ĭm). See *Hupham*.

Hur (hûr). 1. With Aaron, held up hands of Moses at Rephidim (Ex 17:10-13; 24:14). 2. Grandfather of Bezalel (Ex 31:2; 35:30; 38:22; 1 Ch 2:19, 20). 3. King of Midian (Nm 31:8; Jos 13:21). 4. See *Ben-hur*. 5. Father of Rephaiah (Neh 3:9).

Hurai (hū'rá-ī). See *Hiddai*.

Huram (hū'răm). 1. 2. See *Hiram 1; 2*. 3. See *Hupham*.

Huram-abi (hū'răm-á'bī). See *Hiram 2*.

Huri (hū'rī). Gadite (1 Ch 5:14).

Hushah (hū'shá). Person or place (1 Ch 4:4).

Hushai (hū'shā-ī). Archite; wise man who overthrew advice of Ahithophel to Absalom (2 Sm 15:32-37; 17:5-16).

Husham (hū'shăm). King of Edom (Gn 36: 34, 35).

Hushathite (hū'shăth-īt). See *Sibbecai*.

Hushim (hū'shĭm). 1. Son of Dan (Gn 46:23). Shuham in Nm 26:42. 2. Sons of Aharah (1 Ch 7:12). 3. Wife of Shaharaim and mother of Abitub and Elpaal (1 Ch 8:8, 11).

husks. Pods of carob tree, an evergreen (Lk 15:16. RSV: pods).

Huz (hŭz). See *Uz 4*.

Huzzab (hŭz'áb). Probably erroneously rendered as proper noun by KJ, RV (Nah 2:7. RSV: mistress. KJ, RV margins: established, decreed).

hyacinth (hī'á-sĭnth). See *jacinth*.

Hydaspes (hī-dăs'pēz). River in India (Jdth 1:6).

hyena (hī-ē'ná). Common in Palestine (Is 13:22; 34:14. KJ: wild beasts. RV: wolves).

Hymenaeus (hī-me-nē'us, G god of marriage). Convert who made shipwreck of his faith (1 Ti 1:20; 2 Ti 2:17, 18).

hymn. Spiritual song (Psalms; Ex 15:1-19; Dt 32:1-43; Ju 5; 1 Sm 2:1-10; Lk 1: 46-55, 68-79). Christians are exhorted to use psalms, hymns, spiritual songs (Eph 5:19; Cl 3:16).

hypocrisy (hī-pŏk-ri-sĭ). H *haneph* (profane, godless) rendered hypocrite by KJ. G *hupokrisis* (play a part) is making outward show of being religious, but at heart not so (Mt 7:5; 23:28; Mk 12:15; Lk 12:1; 1 Ti 4:2; 1 Ptr 2:1).

Hyrcanus (hûr-kā'nus). See *Hircanus; Maccabees*.

hyssop (hĭs'up). Plant mentioned several times but apparently not always same species. Ex 12:22 probably refers to bushy type; Jn 19:29, to plant with long stem (see Mt 27:48; Mk 15:36). Used in purification for lepers (Lv 14:4, 6); plague (Lv 14:49); in red heifer ceremony (Nm 19:6); to sprinkle blood on doorposts (Ex 12:22); figuratively (Ps 51:7).

I

I Am. See *Jehovah*.
Iadinus (ĭ-ăd'ĭ-nŭs). See *Jamin 3*.
Ibhar (ĭb'här, choice). Son of David (2 Sm 5:15; 1 Ch 3:6; 14:5).
ibex (ī'běks, H *dishon*, leaper). Clean animal, probably large, light colored antelope (Dt 14:5; KJ, RV: pygarg).
ibis (ī'bĭs). Bird related to herons (Dt 11:17. KJ: great owl).
Ibleam (ĭb'lē-ăm, people fail. Bileam in 1 Ch 6:70). City assigned to Manasseh, probably modern Tell Bel'ameh, 1¼ mi S of Jenin (Jos 17:11; Ju 1:27; 2 K 9:27; 15:10 [KJ, RV: before the people]).
Ibneiah (ĭb-nē'yȧ, Lord builds). Benjaminite (1 Ch 9:8).
Ibnijah (ĭb-nī'jȧ, Lord builds). Benjaminite (1 Ch 9:8).
Ibri (ĭb'rī, Hebrew). Son of Jaaziah (1 Ch 24:27).
Ibsam (ĭb'săm, fragrant). Issacharite (1 Ch 7:2. KJ: Jibsam).
Ibzan (ĭb'zăn). 10th judge of Israel (Ju 12:8-10).
ice. Snow and ice occasionally found on central range of Palestine (Jb 6:16; 37:10; 38:29; Ps 147:17).
Ichabod (ĭk'ȧ-bŏd, glory is not). Son of Phinehas (1 Sm 4:19-22).
Iconium (ī-kō'nĭ-ŭm). City on SW edge of central plain of Asia Minor. Visited by Paul (Acts 13:51; 14:1-22; 16:2; 2 Ti 3:11).
Idalah (ĭd'ȧ-lȧ. Border town of Zebulun (Jos 19:15).
Idbash (ĭd'băsh). Judahite (1 Ch 4:3).
Iddo (ĭd'ō). 1. Father of Ahinadab (1 K 4:14). 2. See *Adaiah 2*. 3. Chief of David over half tribe of Manasseh (1 Ch 27:21). 4. Divorced foreign wife (Ez 10:43 [KJ: Jadau; RSV: Jaddai]; 1 Esd 9:35 [KJ: Edes; RV: Edos]). 5. Seer and chronicler in reign of Rehoboam, Jeroboam, and Abijah (2 Ch 9:29; 12:15). 6. Grandfather of Zechariah (Zch 1:1, 7; 1 Esd 6:1 [KJ, RV: Addo]). 7. Head of family which returned (Neh 12:4, 16). 8. Head of Nethinim (Ez 8:17; 1 Esd 8:45, 46 [KJ: Saddeus, Daddeus; RV: Loddeus]).
idol, idolatry (ī'dul, ī-dŏl'ȧ-trĭ). Image fashioned in symbolic form as object of worship (Ex 20:4, 5, 23; Ju 17:3; 2 Ch 33:7; 1 Co 8:7); of silver, gold, wood, stone, other material (Is 40:19, 20; 44: 9-20; Jer 10:9); some small (Gn 31:34), others large (1 Sm 19:16; Dn 3:1). Idol is called nonentity (1 Co 8:4), horrible thing (1 K 15:13), abomination (Eze 37:23), dumb (Hab 2:18).
Iduel (ĭd'ū-ĕl). See *Ariel 1*.
Idumea, Idumaea (ĭd-ū-mē'ȧ). Greek name for Edom (Mk 3:8; Is 34:5 [RV, RSV: Edom]).
Ieddias (ī-ĕ-dī'ăs. See *Izziah*.
Iezer (ī-ē'zēr). See *Abiezer 1*.
Iezerite (ī-ēz'ēr-īt). See *Abiezrite*.
Igal (ī'găl, he redeemed). 1. Spy of Issachar (Nm 13:7). 2. Son of Nathan of Zobah; one of David's heroes (2 Sm 23:36). Joel, brother of Nathan, in 1 Ch 11:38. 3. Descendant of King Jeconiah (1 Ch 3:22. KJ: Igeal).
Igdaliah (ĭg-dȧ-lī'ȧ, great is Lord). Father of Hanan (Jer 35:4).
Igeal (ī'gē-ăl). See *Igal 3*.
ignorance. Want of true knowledge of God and spiritual things. Sometimes excusable (Eze 45:20; Acts 17:30), at other times inexcusable (Eph 4:18; 1 Ptr 1:14; 2:15).

Iim (ī'ĭm, ruins). 1. Town in S Judah (Jos 15:29). 2. See *Iye-abarim*.
Ije-abarim (ī'jē-ăb'ȧ-rĭm). See *Iye-abarim*.
Ijon (ī'jŏn, springs). Fortified city of Naphtali (1 K 15:20; 2 K 15:29).
Ikkesh (ĭk'ĕsh). Father of Ira (2 Sm 23:26; 1 Ch 11:28; 27:9).
Ilai (ī'lā-ī, exalted). One of David's heroes (1 Ch 11:29). Zalmon in 2 Sm 23:28.
Iliadun (i-lī'ȧ-dŭn. KJ: Eliadun). Levite (1 Esd 5:58). Possibly same as Henadad.
Illyricum (ĭ-lĭr'ĭ-kum). Roman province on E coast of Adriatic; later Dalmatia (2 Ti 4:10); now part of Yugoslavia. Reached by Paul (Ro 15:19).
image. See *idol; teraphim*.
image of God. Man is created in image of God (Gn 1:26, 27). Vestiges of this image remain after fall (Gn 9:6; Ja 3:9), though original sin continually destroys image (Ro 3:23; Eph 4:24; Cl 3:10). Likeness is spiritual rather than corporeal. Christ is image of God (Col 1:15; Heb 1:3. See Jn 1:1; 17:25, 26) through whom man receives likeness (Ro 8:29; Cl 3:10, 11).
Imalcue, Imalkue (ī-măl-kū'ē). Arabian chief; brought up Antiochus, son of Alexander (1 Mac 11:39. RV: Imalcue. KJ: Simalcue).
Imla, Imlah (ĭm'lȧ, God fills). Father of Micaiah (1 K 22:8, 9; 2 Ch 18:7, 8).
Immanuel (ĭ-măn'ū-el, God with us. KJ, RSV in Mt 1:23: Emmanuel). Name of child which maiden (KJ, RV, RSV margin: virgin. RSV: young woman) would bear (Is 7:14), who was to be worthy Son of David at whose birth salvation would be near. Immanuel is Promised One around whom prophecy clusters (Is 8:9, 10; 9:6, 7; 11:1; Mi 5:2, 3; Mt 1:22, 23).
Immer (ĭm'ēr). 1. Head of 16th division of priests (1 Ch 24:14; Jer 20:1; Ez 2:37; 10:20; Neh 3:29; 11:13; 1 Esd 5:24 [KJ: Meruth; RV: Emmeruth]; 9:21 [KJ, RV: Emmer]). 2. Place in Babylonia (Ez 2:59; Neh 7:61).
immortality (ĭm-ôr-tăl'ĭ-tĭ). See *eschatology; eternal life*.
Imna (ĭm'nȧ). Asherite (1 Ch 7:35).
Imnah (ĭm'nȧ). 1. Son of Asher (Gn 46:17 [KJ: Jimnah]; Nm 26:44 [KJ: Jimna]; 1 Ch 7:30). 2. Levite; father of Kore (2 Ch 31:14).
imputation (ĭm-pū-tā'shun). Word used to describe ascription of Adam's sin to all men (Ro 5:12-21); human guilt to Christ, Christ's righteousness to man (2 Co 5: 19-21).
Imrah (ĭm'rȧ, resist). Asherite (1 Ch 7:36).
Imri (ĭm'rī, eloquent). 1. Judahite (1 Ch 9:4). 2. Father of Zaccur (Neh 3:2).
incarnation (ĭn-kär-nā'shun). See *Jesus Christ*.
incense. Aromatic compound for burning. Ingredients of incense used in worship given in Ex 30:34, 35. Burned morning and evening on altar of incense (Ex 30: 1-10). Carried into Holy of Holies on Day of Atonement (Lv 16:12, 13). Symbol of prayer (Ps 141:2; Rv 5:8; 8:3, 4). Also used in idolatrous worship (1 K 13:2; 2 Ch 28:25; Jer 44:18).
incest. Forbidden (Lv 20:11-17; Dt 27: 20-23; 1 Co 5:1).
incorruption (ĭn-ko-rŭp'shun). See *eternal life*.
India (ĭn'dĭ-ȧ). Country which bounded empire of Ahasuerus on E (Est 1:1; 8:9).

indignation of God (ĭn-dĭg-nā'shŭn). See *wrath.*

inheritance. See *heir.*

iniquity (ĭ-nĭk'wĭ-tĭ). See *sin.*

ink. Compound made of charcoal or lamp-black mixed with water and gum (Jer 36:18; 2 Co 3:3; 2 Jn 12; 3 Jn 13).

inkhorn. Pen case with inkwell (Eze 9:2, 3, 11. RSV: writing case).

inn. Lodging places mentioned (Gn 42:27; 43:21; Ex 4:24), but Israelite hospitality made inns and hotels in our sense practically unnecessary. In Lk 2:7 (G *kataluma*) probably similar to khan or hostelry. In Lk 10:34 (G *pandocheion*) lodging place kept by innkeeper. See also *hospitality.*

insanity. See *disease.*

insect. Abundant in Palestine. See *ant; bee; cankerworm* (locust); *caterpillar; cricket* (beetle); *color* (crimson, or scarlet, from cochineal insect); *flea; fly; gnat* (lice); *hornet; locust* (grasshopper); *moth; palmerworm; scorpion; spider; wasp; worm* (larvae).

inspiration. Special influence of Holy Spirit by which He guided His chosen instruments to speak and write that which He desired (1 Co 2:13; 1 Ptr 1:10, 11; 2 Ptr 1:19-21; 2 Ti 3:16; 1 Th 2:13) without suspension of their personality or individual activity (Lk 1:1-4; 1 Ptr 1:10, 11).

instant. KJ for constant, earnest, steadfast, urgent (Lk 7:4; 23:23; Acts 26:7; Ro 12:12).

intercession. See *prayer.*

interest. See *loans.*

intermediate state. Interval of time, according to this-world reckoning, which elapses between death and resurrection of believers (1 Th 4:14; Lk 23:43; Ph 1:23; Rv 14:4).

Iob (yŏb). See *Jashub 1.*

Ionia (ī-ō'nĭ-á). India in 1 Mac 8:8.

iota (ī-ō'tá). See *jot.*

Iphdeiah, Iphedeiah (ĭf-dē'yá, ĭf-ĕ-dē'yá, LORD delivers). Benjaminite (1 Ch 8:25).

Iphtah (ĭf'tá, he opens. KJ: Jiphtah). Town of Judah (Jos 15:43).

Iphtahel (ĭf'tá-ĕl, God opens. KJ: Jiphthahel). Valley on boundary between Zebulun and Asher (Jos 19:14, 27). Probably Tell Jephât 9 mi N of Nazareth.

Ir (ûr, city). Benjaminite (1 Ch 7:12). Iri in 1 Ch 7:7.

Ira (ī'rá, watchful). 1. Jairite; chief minister of David (2 Sm 20:26). 2. One of David's heroes (2 Sm 23:26; 1 Ch 11:28). 3. Ithrite; one of David's heroes (2 Sm 23:38; 1 Ch 11:40).

Irad (ī'răd). Son of Enoch (Gn 4:18).

Iram (ī'răm, of a city). Chief of Edom (Gn 36:43; 1 Ch 1:54).

Iri (ī'rĭ). 1. See *Ir.* 2. See *Uriah 3.*

Irijah (ĭ-rī'já, LORD sees). Captain who arrested Jeremiah (Jer 37:13, 14).

Ir-nahash (ûr-nā'hăsh, city of serpent). City of Judah (1 Ch 4:12).

Iron (ī'rŏn, pious). City of Naphtali (Jos 19:38).

iron. Iron of Gn 4:22 was probably meteoric. Hebrew iron age dates from 1200 to 300 BC. Philistines learned to work with iron from Hittites; David's conquest of Philistines brought extensive iron industries to Israelites. Hebrews had iron mines in Jordan-Arabah. Iron used for instruments and weapons (Dt 19:5; Nm 35:16; 1 Sm 17:7); vessels (Jos 6:19, 24); chariots (Jos 17:16); chains (Ps 105:18); graving instruments (Jb 19:24); bars

(Acts 12:10); etc. Figuratively, iron is symbol of strength.

ironsmith. See *trade 7.*

Irpeel (ûr'pĕ-ĕl, God heals). City of Benjamin (Jos 18:27).

irrigation. Known to Israelites in Egypt (Dt 11:10).

Ir-shemesh (ûr-shē'mĕsh). See *Beth-shemesh 1.*

Iru (ī'rōō, of a city). Son of Caleb (1 Ch 4:15).

Isaac (ī'sák, laughter). Only son of Abraham by Sarah (Gn 17:19); circumcised on 8th day (Gn 21:4); showed himself dutiful son when Abraham was commanded to sacrifice him (Gn 22:1-18); married Rebekah of Mesopotamia (Gn 24); had 2 sons, Esau and Jacob (Gn 25); denied wife (Gn 26); gave Jacob 1st blessing (Gn 27); died at Mamre (Gn 35:27-29).

Isaias (ī-zā'yá, LORD is salvation. KJ: Esaias in NT; Esay in 2 Esd 2:18; Sir 48:20, 22). Prophet of Judah during reign of Uzziah, Jotham, Ahaz, Hezekiah (Is 1:1); son of Amoz; lived in Jerusalem; saw vision year Uzziah died (Is 6); married (Is 8:3); had 2 sons (Is 7:3; 8:3); dress coarse; respected by Hezekiah (2 K 19:1-11).

Isaiah, Book of. 1st of greater prophets. Emphasized spiritual and social problems. Reproved sins of Judah, predicted destruction, but promised salvation of world through remnant; prophesied coming of Christ. Outline: 1. Introduction (1). 2. Prophecy Against Jerusalem (2—5). 3. Vision (6). 4. Prophecies Concerning Nations (13—23). 5. Judgment on World and Jewish Blessing (24—27). 6. Prophecies Concerning Judah and Samaria and Conclusions (28—35). 7. History (36—39). 8. Consolation Based on Relation of Israel to Jehovah, to Nations, and Its Future Glory (40—60).

Iscah (ĭs'ká). Sister of Lot (Gn 11:27, 29).

Iscariot (ĭs-kăr'ĭ-ot). See *Judas 3.*

Isdael (ĭs'dá-ĕl). See *Giddel 2.*

Ishbah (ĭsh'bá). Judahite (1 Ch 4:17).

Ishbak (ĭsh'băk). Son of Abraham and Keturah; progenitor of people in N Arabia (Gn 25:2; 1 Ch 1:32).

Ishbi-benob (ĭsh'bī-bē'nŏb, dweller on height). One of the Rephaim (2 Sm 21:16).

Ish-bosheth (ĭsh-bō'shĕth, man of shame). Originally called Eshbaal (1 Ch 8:33; 9:39). Son of Saul who ruled two years at Mahanaim but was defeated by David's men and assassinated (2 Sm 2:8-32; 3; 4:5-12).

Ishhod (ĭsh'hŏd, man of splendor). Manassite (1 Ch 7:18. KJ: Ishod).

Ishi (ĭsh'ī, salutary). 1. Judahite; son of Appaim (1 Ch 2:31). 2. Judahite; father of Zoheth (1 Ch 4:20). 3. Simeonite; sons defeated Amalekites (1 Ch 4:42). 4. Manassite (1 Ch 5:24).

Ishiah (ī-shī'á). See *Isshiah 1.*

Ishijah (ī-shī'já). See *Isshijah.*

Ishma (ĭsh'má). Judahite (1 Ch 4:3).

Ishmael (ĭsh'má-el, God hears). 1. Son of Abraham and Hagar (Gn 16:3, 15); circumcised (Gn 17:25); Sarah insisted he be cast out after he played with (KJ: mocked) Isaac (Gn 21:9, 10. See Gl 4:29); progenitor of Ishmaelites (Gn 17:20; 25:12-16). 2. Descendant of Jonathan (1 Ch 8:38; 9:44). 3. Judahite; father of Zebadiah (2 Ch 19:11). 4. Judahite; conspired against Athaliah

(2 Ch 23:1). **5.** Son of Nethaniah; assassinated Gedaliah (2 K 25:25; Jer 40:7 —41:18). **6.** Son of Passhur; divorced foreign wife (Ez 10:22; 1 Esd 9:22 [KJ, RV: Ismael]).

Ishmaelites (ĭsh'mā-el-īts. KJ at times: Ishmeelites). Desert dwellers and traders (Gn 37:25-28; 39:1; 1 Ch 27:30) descended from Ishmael.

Ishmaiah (ĭsh-mā'yá, LORD hears). **1.** Gibeonite; joined David at Ziklag (1 Ch 12:4. KJ: Ismaiah). **2.** Son of Obadiah; head of Zebulunites (1 Ch 27:19).

Ishmeelites (ĭsh'mĕ-el-īts). See **Ishmaelites**.

Ishmerai (ĭsh'mĕ-rī, LORD keeps). Benjaminite (1 Ch 8:18).

Ishod (ī'shŏd). See **Ishhod**.

Ishpah (ĭsh'pá). Benjaminite (1 Ch 8:16. KJ: Ispah).

Ishpan (ĭsh'păn). Son of Shashak (1 Ch 8:22).

Ish-tob (ĭsh'tŏb). See **Tob**.

Ishuah (ĭsh'û-á). See **Ishvah**.

Ishuai, Ishui (ĭsh'û-ī). See **Ishvi 1; 2.**

Ishvah (ĭsh'vá, like). Son of Asher; did not perpetuate family (Gn 46:17 [KJ: Ishuah]; 1 Ch 7:30 [KJ: Isuah]).

Ishvi (ĭsh'vī, like). **1.** 3d son of Asher; founder of family (Gn 46:17 [KJ: Isui]; Nm 26:44 [KJ: Jesui]; 1 Ch 7:30 [KJ: Ishuai]). **2.** Son of Saul (1 Sm 14:49. KJ: Ishui).

isle, island (īl, ī'lănd). **1.** Habitable land as opposed to water (Is 42:15). **2.** Island (Jer 47:4; Acts 13:6; Rv 1:9). **3.** Maritime land (Gn 10:5; Is 20:6 23:2 Eze 27:7. RV, RSV: coastland or coast). **4.** Remote regions of earth (Is 41:5; 49:1; 66:19; Jer 31:10. RSV: coastland); often mentioned to indicate broad scope of Messianic prophecy (Zph 2:11); majesty of God (Ps 97:1).

Ismachiah (ĭs-má-kī'á), LORD supports). Overseer of temple sacrifices (2 Ch 31:13).

Ismael (ĭs'má-el). See **Ishmael 6.**

Ismaerus (ĭs-mā-ē'rus). See **Amram 2.**

Ismaiah (ĭs'mā'yá). See **Ishmaiah 1.**

Ispah (ĭs'pá). See **Ishpah.**

Israel (ĭz'rā-ĕl, he strives with God, or God strives). **1.** Name given to Jacob (Gn 32:28; 35:10). **2.** Jacob, through 12 sons, is progenitor of 12 tribes of Israel (Ex 3:16), collectively called Israel (more than 2,000 times). **3.** After revolt of 10 tribes, N kingdom called Israel to distinguish it from Judah, the S kingdom (1 Sm 11:8; 1 K 14:19, 29). Capital at Shechem (1 K 12:25), later at Samaria (1 K 16:24). Remnant collectively still referred to as Israel after exile (Ez 10:10). **4.** True Israelites: those (whether Jew or Gentile) who follow in faith of Abraham, Isaac, Jacob (Ps 73:1; Is 45:17; Jn 1:47; Ro 11:13-36; Gl 6:15, 16).

Israelites (ĭz'rā-el-īts). See **Israel.**

Israel, mountains of. See **Ephraim, Mount.**

Issachar (ĭs'á-kär, hired laborer). **1.** 9th son of Jacob, 5th by Leah (Gn 30:14-18). Jacob compared Issachar to ass that loved ease and became burden bearer of others (Gn 49:14, 15). **2.** Territory W of Jordan, S of Zebulun and Naphtali and N of Manasseh (Jos 19:17-23); included plain of Esdraelon.

Isshiah (ĭs-shī'á, LORD lends or forgets). **1.** Issacharite; family of Tola (1 Ch 7:3. KJ: Ishiah). **2.** Came to David at Ziklag (1 Ch 12:6. KJ: Jesiah). **3.** Levite (1 Ch 24:21). **4.** Kohathite Levite (1 Ch 23:20 [KJ: Jesiah]; 24:25).

Isshijah (ĭs-shī'já, LORD lends or forgets). Divorced foreign wife (Ez 10:31. KJ: Ishijah). Aseas (RSV: Asaias) in 1 Esd 9:32.

issue. See **disease.**

Istalcurus (ĭs-tăl-kū'rus). See **Zabbud.**

Isuah (ĭs'û-á). See **Ishvah.**

Isui (ĭs'û-ī). See **Ishvi 1.**

Italian Cohort (ĭ-tăl'yăn kō'hôrt). See **band.**

Italy (ĭt'ál-ī). Whole peninsula between Alps and Messina (Acts 18:2; 27:1, 6; Heb 13:24).

itch. See **disease.**

Ithai (ĭth'á-ī). See **Ittai 2.**

Ithamar (ĭth'á-mär, palm coast). Youngest son of Aaron (Ex 6:23; 1 Ch 6:3; 24:1); consecrated to priesthood (Ex 29); family continued after exile (Ez 8:2).

Ithiel (ĭth'ĭ-ĕl, God with me). **1.** Friend of Agur (Pr 30:1). **2.** Benjaminite (Neh 11:7).

Ithlah (ĭth'lá). Town in Dan (Jos 19:42; KJ: Jethlah).

Ithmah (ĭth'mä). Moabite; one of David's guard (1 Ch 11:46).

Ithnan (ĭth'năn). City in S Judah (Jos 15:23).

Ithra (ĭth'rá, abundance). Ishmaelite; married Abigail, David's sister; father of Amasa (2 Sm 17:25. KJ, RV: an Israelite). Jether in 1 K 2:5, 32; 1 Ch 2:17.

Ithran (ĭth'răn, abundance). **1.** Horite (Gn 36:26; 1 Ch 1:41). **2.** Asherite (1 Ch 7:37). Jether in v 38.

Ithream (ĭth'rē-ăm, residue of people). Son of David by Eglah (2 Sm 3:5; 1 Ch 3:3).

Ithrite (ĭth'rīt). Family of Kiriath-jearim (1 Ch 2:53). Patronymic of two of David's heroes (2 Sm 23:38; 1 Ch 11:40).

Ittah-kazin (ĭt'á-kā'zĭn). See **Eth-kazin.**

Ittai (ĭt'á-ī). **1.** Inhabitant of Gath; loyal to David; led 3d of his army against Absalom (2 Sm 15:18-22; 18:2, 5). **2.** One of David's heroes (2 Sm 23:29). Ithai in 1 Ch 11:31.

Ituraea (ĭ-tû-rē'á). Small province NW of Palestine, including part of Anti-Lebanon. Inhabited by Jetur, son of Ishmael (Gn 25:15; 1 Ch 1:31; Lk 3:1).

Ivah (ī'vá). See **Avva.**

ivory. Imported into Palestine (1 K 10:22; Eze 27:15); used to decorate houses (1 K 22:39; Ps 45:8; Am 3:15), furniture (1 K 10:18), etc.

Ivvah (ĭv'á). See **Avva.**

Iye-abarim (ī'yē-ăb'á-rĭm, ruins of Abarim). Station of Israel on border of Moab (Nm 21:11; 33:44. KJ: Ije-abarim). Contracted to Iyim in Nm 33:45 (KJ: Iim).

Iyim (ī'yĭm). See **Iye-abarim.**

Izehar (ĭz'ē-här). See **Izhar 1.**

Izhar (ĭz'här, bright; oil). **1.** Levite; son of Kohath (Ex 6:18, 21; Nm 3:19 [KJ: Izehar]; 1 Ch 6:18, 38). Amminadabin 1 Ch 6:22. **2.** Judahite; son of Asshur (1 Ch 4:5-7. KJ: Jezoar).

Izharite (ĭz'här-īt). Descendants of Izhar 1 (Nm 3:27; 1 Ch 24:22; 26:23, 29).

Izliah (ĭz-lī'á, LORD delivers). Son of Elpaal (1 Ch 8:18. KJ: Jezliah).

Izrahiah (ĭz-rá-hī'á, LORD arises). Issacharite of family of Tola (1 Ch 7:3).

Izrahite (ĭz'rá-hīt). Patronymic of Shamkuth (1 Ch 27:8).

Izri (ĭz'rī). Levite; leader of 4th division of singers (1 Ch 25:11). Zeri in v 3.

Izziah (ĭz-ī'á, LORD sprinkles?). Son of Parosh; divorced foreign wife (Ez 10:25 [KJ: Jeziah]; 1 Esd 9:26 [KJ: Eddias. RV: Ieddias]).

J

Jaakan (jā'á-kăn. Akan in Gn 36:27). Horite; grandson of Seir (1 Ch 1:42. KJ: Jakan). See also Bene-jaakan.
Jaakobah (jā-á-kō'bá). Simeonite prince (1 Ch 4:36).
Jaala, Jaalah (jā'á-lá, wild goat. Jaalah in Ez 2:56). Ancestor of family of Solomon's servants who returned (Neh 7:58; 1 Esd 5:33 [KJ, RV: Jeeli]).
Jaalam (jā'á-lăm). See Jalam.
Jaanai (jā'á-nī). See Janai.
Jaar (jā'âr, forest. KJ, RV: wood). Place, perhaps Kiriath-jearim (Ps 132:6).
Jaareoregim (jā-á-rĕ-ôr'ĕ-jĭm). See Jair 4.
Jaareshiah (jā-á-rĕ-shī'á, LORD nourishes. KJ: Jaresiah). Benjaminite; son of Jeroham (1 Ch 8:27).
Jaasau (jā'á-sô). See Jaasu.
Jaasiel (jā-á'sĭ-ĕl). 1. One of David's heroes (1 Ch 11:47. KJ: Jasiel). 2. Son of Abner (1 Ch 27:21). Perhaps same as 1.
Jaasu (jā'á-sū). Divorced foreign wife (Ez 10:37. KJ: Jaasau). Eliasis in 1 Esd 9:34.
Jaazaniah (jā-ăz-á-nī'á, LORD hears). 1. See Azariah 24. 2. Son of Jeremiah (not prophet. Jer 35:3). 3. Idolater; son of Shaphan (Eze 8:11). 4. Prince denounced by Ezekiel (Eze 11:1).
Jaazer (jā'á-zēr). See Jazer.
Jaaziah (jā-á-zī'á). Levite (1 Ch 24:26, 27).
Jaaziel (jā-á'zĭ-ĕl, God comforts). Levite; musician (1 Ch 15:18). Aziel in 1 Ch 15:20. Jeiel in 1 Ch 16:5.
Jabal (jā'băl). Son of Lamech; ancestor of nomadic herdsmen (Gn 4:20).
Jabbok (jăb'ok, effusion). River of Gilead; rises near Amman; flows through deep canyon; enters Jordan 23 mi N of Dead Sea (Gn 32:22; Nm 21:24; Jos 12:2).
Jabesh (jā'bĕsh, dry). 1. Father of King Shallum (2 K 15:10-14). 2. See Jabesh-gilead.
Jabesh-gilead (jā'bĕsh-gĭl'ĕ-ăd, Jabesh of Gilead. Or simply: Jabesh). City E of Jordan; 10 mi SE of Beth-shan in territory of Manasseh; males destroyed for not cooperating at Mizpah; inhabitants friends of Saul (Nm 32:39, 40; Ju 21:8-14; 1 Sm 11:1-11; 31:11-13; 2 Sm 2:4, 5; 21:12; 1 Ch 10:11, 12).
Jabez (jā'bĕz, he makes sorrowful). 1. Judahite; noble, God-fearing (1 Ch 4:9, 10). 2. Place inhabited by scribes (1 Ch 2:55).
Jabin (jā'bĭn, he discerns). 1. King of Hazor; defeated by Joshua (Jos 11:1-14). 2. Another king of Hazor whose general, Sisera, was defeated by Barak (Ju 4; 1 Sm 12:9; Ps 83:9).
Jabneel (jā'bnĕ-ĕl, God builds). 1. Town on N border of Judah (Jos 15:11). Jabneh in 2 Ch 26:6. Later Jamnia in Jdth 2:28 (KJ, RV: Jemnaan); 1 Mac 4:15. Modern Jebuah. 2. Town on border of Naphtali (Jos 19:33).
Jabneh (jăb'nĕ). See Jabneel 1.
Jacan, Jachan (jā'kăn). Gadite (1 Ch 5:13).
Jachin (jā'kĭn). 1. Son of Simeon (Gn 46:10; Ex 6:15). Jarib in 1 Ch 4:24. 2. Head of 21st course of priests (1 Ch 24:17). 3. Priest (1 Ch 9:10; Neh 11:10). 4. Jachin and Boaz were names of two temple pillars (1 K 7:15-22; 2 Ch 3:15-17).
jacinth (jā'sĭnth). Classical hyacinth was probably blue sapphire, though at times described as yellow or golden (Rv 9:17 [RSV: sapphire]; 21:20; Ex 28:19 [KJ: ligure]; 39:12 [KJ: ligure]).
jackal. 1. RV, RSV for H tannim (monster.

Jb 30:29; Is 34:13; Jer 9:11; 10:22; Mi 1:8. KJ: dragon); RSV, at times, for shu'al (fox, jackal. Ps 63:10. KJ, RV: foxes). RSV for 'iyyim (Is 13:22; 34:14. KJ: wild beasts. RV: wolves.)
Jackal's Well. Well at Jerusalem (Neh 2:13. KJ: dragon well).
Jacob (jā'kub, supplanter). 1. Son of Isaac and Rebekah; younger twin of Esau (Gn 25:21-26); bought birthright from Esau for pottage of lentils (Gn 25:29-34); through fraud obtained blessing (Gn 27:1-41); fled to Haran and on way had vision of ladder (Gn 27:42—28:22); served Laban for at least 20 yrs and married his daughters: Leah, Rachel (Gn 29:1-30); 12 sons, 1 daughter born to him by Leah (Reuben, Simeon, Levi, Judah, Issachar, Zebulun, Dinah), Rachel (Joseph, Benjamin), Leah's maid, Zilpah (Gad, Asher), and Rachel's maid, Bilhah (Dan, Naphtali) (29-31—30:24; 35:16-26); fled from Laban, wrestled with God (Gn 30:25—32:32); reconciled with Esau, settled in Canaan (Gn 33); blessed (Gn 35); went to Egypt (Gn 42—46); blessed sons and died (Gn 49). 2. Patronymic of Israelites (Nm 23:10; Ps 59:13). 3. Father of Joseph, husband of Mary (Mt 1:15, 16).
Jacubus (já-kū'bus). See Akkub 4.
Jada (jā'dá, wise). Judahite; son of Onam (1 Ch 2:28, 32).
Jadau, Jaddai (jā'dô, jăd'ī). See Iddo 4.
Jaddua (jā-dū'á, known). 1. Sealed covenant with Nehemiah (Neh 10:21). 2. Son of Jonathan; last high priest named in OT (Neh 12:11, 22).
Jaddus (jăd'us). See Addus 2.
Jadon (jā'don, judge). Repaired part of Jerusalem's wall (Neh. 3:7).
Jael (jā'el, wild goat). Wife of Heber; killed Sisera with tent pin (Ju 4:17-27).
Jagur (jā'gēr). Town in S Judah (Jos 15:21). Probably modern Tell Ghurr.
Jah (jä). Form of JHVH (Jahveh, Jehovah) occurring in poetry (Ps 68:4; RV: 89:8. RSV: LORD). Also in compounds of many proper names.
Jahath (jā'hăth). 1. Descendant of Hezron (1 Ch 4:2). 2. Levite; son of Libni (1 Ch 6:20, 43). 3. Levite; son of Shimei (1 Ch 23:10). 4. Levite; descendant of Izhar (1 Ch 24:22). 5. Merarite Levite (2 Ch 34:12).
Jahaz, Jahaza, Jahazah (jā'hăz, já-hā'zá). Place (apparently fortified) in Moab where Israelites defeated Sihon, the Amorite (Nm 21:23; Dt 2:32; Ju 11:20). Assigned to Reuben (Jos 13:18 [KJ: Jahaza]; 21:36 [KJ: Jahazah]). Jahzah in 1 Ch 6:78; Jer 48:21 (KJ: Jahazah).
Jahaziah (jā-há-zī'á). See Jahzeiah.
Jahaziel (já-hā'zĭ-ĕl, God sees). 1. Kohathite Levite (1 Ch 23:19). 2. Benjaminite; joined David at Ziklag (1 Ch 12:4). 3. Priest; blew trumpet before ark (1 Ch 16:6). 4. Levite prophet in days of Jehoshaphat (2 Ch 20:14). 5. Ancestor of family which returned (Ez 8:5; 1 Esd 8:32 [KJ, RV: Jezelus]).
Jahdai (jā'dă-ī). Descendant of Caleb (1 Ch 2:47).
Jahdiel (jä'dĭ-ĕl, God makes glad). Manassite (1 Ch 5:24).
Jahdo (jä'dō). Gadite (1 Ch 5:14).
Jahleel (jā'lē-ĕl, wait for God). Son of Zebulun; founder of family (Gn 46:14; Nm 26:26).

Jahmai (jä'må-ī, may LORD protect). Issacharite, descendant of Tola (1 Ch 7:2).

Jahve, Jahwe, Jahweh (yä'vĕ, yä'wĕ). See Jehovah.

Jahzah (jä'zå). See Jahaz.

Jahzeel (jä'zē-ĕl, God allots). Son of Naphtali; founder of family (Gn 46:24; Nm 26:48). Jahziel in 1 Ch 7:13).

Jahzeiah (jä-zē'yå, LORD sees). Son of Tikvah; prominent in matter of divorcing foreign wives (Ez 10:15 [KJ: Jahaziah]; 1 Esd 9:14 [KJ: Ezechias; RV: Ezekias]).

Jahzerah (jä'ze-rá). See Ahzai.

Jahziel (jä'zĭ-ĕl). See Jahzeel.

Jair (jä'ẽr, enlighten). 1. Descendant of Manasseh; grandson of Hezron (1 Ch 2: 21-23; Nm 32:41; Dt 3:14); conquered Amorites on border of Gilead and Bashan; called villages Havoth-jair (Nm 32:41). 2. Judge (Ju 10:3-5). 3. Ancestor of Mordecai (Est 2:5; Ap Est 11:2 [KJ, RV: Jairus]).

Jair (jä'ẽr, forest). Father of Elhanan (1 Ch 20:5). Jaareoregim in 2 Sm 21:19 through scribal error.

Jairus (jä'ĭ-rus, jå-ī'rus, G of Jair). 1. Ruler of synagog, probably at Capernaum (Mk 5:22; Lk 8:41). 2. See Reaiah 3. See Jair 3.

Jakan (jä'kăn). See Jaakan.

Jakeh (jä'kĕ). Father of Agur (Pr 30:1).

Jakim (jä'kĭm, he sets up). 1. Head of 12th course of priests (1 Ch 24:12). 2. Benjaminite (1 Ch 8:19).

Jalam (jä'lăm). Son of Esau; Edomite chieftain (Gn 36:5, 18; 1 Ch 1:35. KJ: Jaalam).

Jalon (jä'lŏn). Judahite; son of Ezrah (1 Ch 4:17).

Jambres (jăm'brēz). Egyptian magician who opposed Moses (2 Ti 3:8, 9. See Ex 7: 9-13).

Jambri (jăm'brī). Perhaps Amorites (1 Mac 9:36-41).

James (jāmz, H Jacob). 1. Son of Zebedee and Salome (Mt 27:56; Mk 1:19; 15:40); brother of John (Mk 5:37); fisherman (Lk 5:10); called to discipleship (Mt 4:21; Mk 1:19); Peter, James, John intimately associated with Jesus; present at transfiguration (Mt 17:1; Mk 9:2; Lk 9:28), raising of Jairus' daughter (Mk 5:37), agony in Gethsemane (Mt 26:37; Mk 14:33); martyred by Herod (Acts 12:2). With John called Boanerges (sons of thunder) by Jesus (Mk 3:17. See Lk 9: 52-54). 2. James the Less; apostle; son of Alphaeus (Mt 10:3; Mk 3:18; Lk 6:15; Acts 1:13), and probably Mary (Mt 27:56; Mk 15:40;Lk 24:10). 3. The brother of the Lord (Mt 13:55; Mk 6:3); at first did not believe (Jn 7:5); converted, possibly by postresurrection appearance (Acts 1: 13, 14; 1 Co 15:5, 7); leader in early church (Gl 1:19; 2:12); presided at Jerusalem council (Acts 15:13; 21:18).

James, Epistle of. Written by James (1:1. Often regarded as son of Alphaeus or brother of Lord) to Jews outside Palestine to comfort them in trials, warn against indifference and dead orthodoxy. Outline: 1. Comfort (1). 2. Warning Against Indifference, Faith Without Works, Pride (2—4). 2. Encouragement to Patience and Prayer (5).

Jamin (jä'mĭn, right hand). 1. Son of Simeon and founder of family (Gn 46:10; Ex 6:15; Nm 26:12). 2. Judahite (1 Ch 2:27). 3. Levite; read Law to returned Jews (Neh 8:7, 8; 1 Esd 9:48 [KJ: Adinus]).

Jamlech (jăm'lĕk, made king). Simeonite prince (1 Ch 4:34).

Jamnia (jăm'nĭ-á). See Jabneel 1.

Janai (jä'ná-ī. KJ: Jaanai). Gadite chief (1 Ch 5:12).

Janim (jăn'ĭm. KJ: Janum). Village in Judah SW of Hebron (Jos 15:53).

Janna, Jannai (jăn'á, jăn'á-ī). Ancestor of Christ (Lk 3:24).

Jannes (jăn'ēz). Egyptian magician; opposed Moses (2 Ti 3:8, 9. See Ex 7:9-13).

Janoah (jå-nō'á, rest). 1. Town of Naphtali; captured by Tiglath-pileser (2 K 15:29). 2. Town on border of Ephraim, 7 mi SE of Shechem (Jos 16:6, 7. KJ: Janohah). Modern Yânûn.

Janohah (jå-nō'há). See Janoah 2.

Janum (jä'num). See Janim.

Japheth (jä'fĕth, beauty, or enlarged). 1. Son of Noah (Gn 5:32; 6:10; 7:13; 10:21); father of Gomer, Magog, Madai, Javan, Tubal, Meshech, and Tiras (Gn 10:2); descendants occupied isles of Gentiles (Gn 10:5), i. e., Indo-Europeans; dutiful behavior brought him blessing (Gn 9:20-27). 2. Unidentified region (Jdth 2:25).

Japhia (jå-fī'á, shining). 1. Lachish king executed by Joshua (Jos 10:3-26). 2. Son of David (2 Sm 5:15; 1 Ch 3:7; 14:6). 3. Town on S edge of Zebulun (Jos 19:12). Modern Yâfa, 2 mi SW of Nazareth.

Japhlet (jăf'lĕt). Asherite (1 Ch 7:32, 33).

Japhleti, Japhletites (jăf'le-tī, -tīts). People on border of Ephraim (Jos 16:3).

Japho (jä'fō). See Joppa.

jar. See cruse.

Jarah (jä'rá, honey). Descendant of Saul (1 Ch 9:42). Jehoaddah (KJ: Jehoadah) in 1 Ch 8:36.

Jareb (jär'ĕb, contentious). KJ, RV: name of Assyrian king. RSV: the great king (Hos 5:13; 10:6).

Jared (jä'rĕd, descent). Father of Enoch (Gn 5:15-20; 1 Ch 1:2 [KJ: Jered]; Lk 3:37).

Jaresiah (jär-ē-sī'á). See Jaareshiah.

Jarha (jär'há). Egyptian slave (1 Ch 2: 34, 35).

Jarib (jä'rĭb, adversary). 1. Chief with Ezra (Ez 8:16; 1 Esd 8:44 [KJ, RV: Joribus]). 2. Priest; divorced foreign wife (Ez 10:18; 1 Esd 9:19 [KJ, RV: Joribus]). 3. See Jachin 1. 4. See Jehoiarib 1.

Jarimoth (jär'ĭ-mŏth). See Jeremoth 7.

Jarmuth (jär'mŭth, height). 1. Town in Judah identified with Yarmûk (Jos 10: 3:27; 12:11; 15:35; Neh 11:29). 2. Levitical town of Issachar (Jos 21:28, 29). Ramoth in 1 Ch 6:73. Remeth in Jos 19:21.

Jaroah (jå-rō'á). Gadite (1 Ch 5:14).

Jasael, Jasaelus (jå'sá-ĕl, jăs-á-ē'lus). See Sheal.

Jashar (jä'shẽr, upright. KJ: Jasher). Author of lost poetic book (Jos 10:13; 2 Sm 1:18. LXX: 1 K 8:53).

Jashen (jä'shen). See Hashem.

Jasher (jä'shẽr). See Jashar.

Jashobeam (jä-shō'bĕ-ăm, let the people return). 1. Hachmonite; chief of David's heroes (1 Ch 11:11). Perhaps same as son of Zabdiel (1 Ch 27:2, 3). Joshebbasshebeth in 2 Sm 23:8. 2. Benjaminite; joined David at Ziklag (1 Ch 12:6).

Jashub (jä'shŭb, he returns). 1. Son of Issachar; founder of family (Nm 26:24; 1 Ch 7:1). Iob in Gn 46:13 (KJ: Job). 2. Divorced foreign wife (Ez 10:29; 1 Esd 9:30 [KJ, RV: Jasubus]).

Jashubi-lehem (jå-shoō'bī-lĕ'hĕm). KJ, RV as person or place. RSV: returned to Lehem (1 Ch 4:22).

Jasiel (jä'sĭ-ĕl). See Jaasiel 1.

Jason (jā'sun, healing). **1.** Christian; showed Paul hospitality at Thessalonica (Acts 17: 5-9). **2.** Probably same in Ro 16:21. **3.** Envoy of Judas Maccabaeus (1 Mac 8:17). **4.** High priest (2 Mac 4:7-26). **5.** Of Cyrene; historian (2 Mac 2:23).

jasper. Opaque quartz stained red, brown, green, yellow, etc. In ancient times included chalcedonies (Ex 28:20; 39:13; Eze 28:13; Rv 4:3; 21:11, 18, 19).

Jasubus (ja-sū'bus). See *Jashub 2.*

Jatal (jā'tăl). See *Ater 2.*

Jathan (jā'thăn. KJ: Jonathas). Son of Shemaiah (Tob 5:13).

Jathniel (jăth'nĭ-ĕl, God gives). Levite gatekeeper of temple (1 Ch 26:2).

Jattir (jăt'ẽr). Town in mountains of Judah given to priests (Jos 15:48; 21:14; 1 Sm 30:27; 1 Ch 6:57). Probably 'Attir, 13 mi SW of Hebron.

Javan (jā'văn). **1.** 4th son of Japheth; father of Elishah, Tarshish, Kittim, and Dodanim (Gn 10:2, 4; 1 Ch 1:5, 7); identical with G *Ion*, ancestor of Ionian Greeks. See *Grecia, Greece.* **2.** KJ, RV, H: place name in Arabia (Eze 27:19. RSV, LXX: and wine from Uzal).

javelin (jăv'lĭn). Short, light spear. See *armor, arms.*

Jazar, Jazer (jā'zẽr, helpful). Ammonite city E of Jordan, probably about 14 mi N of Heshbon; captured by Israel from Amorites; assigned to Gad; given to Merarite Levites but fell into Moabite hands (Nm 21:24 [KJ: strong]; 21:32 [KJ: Jaazer]; 32:1, 3; 32:35 [KJ: Jaazer]; Jos 13:25; 21:39; 2 Sm 24:5; 1 Ch 6:81; 26:31; Is 16:8, 9; Jer 48:32). Judas Maccabaeus took it from Ammon (1 Mac 5:8. KJ: Jazar).

Jaziz (jā'zĭz). Overseer of David's flocks (1 Ch 27:30).

jealousy offering. Wife suspected of infidelity brought to priest with offering of barley meal. Priest put holy water and dust into earthen bowl, required woman under oath to state her innocence. Thereafter she drank water, which brought curse if guilty (Nm 5:11-31).

Jearim (jē'a-rĭm, forests). Mt on N boundary of Judah (Jos 15:10).

Jeaterai, Jeatherai (jē-ăt'ē-rī, jē-ăth'ē-rī). Levite (1 Ch 6:21); probably same as Ethni (1 Ch 6:41).

Jeberechiah (jē-bĕr-ē-kī'a, Lord blesses). Father of a Zechariah whom Isaiah used as witness (Is 8:2).

Jebus (jē'bus). Name of Jerusalem under Jebusites (Jos 15:63; 18:28 [KJ: Jebusi; RV: the Jebusite]; Ju 19:10, 11; 1 Ch 11:4, 5); city taken by Judah (Ju 1:8), but stronghold (Ju 1:21) not taken until David's times (2 Sm 5:7, 8); S of Moriah. See *Zion.*

Jebusi (jĕb'ū-sī). See *Jebus; Jebusites.*

Jebusites (jĕb'ū-zīts). Mountain tribe of Canaan (Gn 10:16; 15:21; Nm 13:29; Jos 11:3). Lived at Jebus. Joshua slew their king (Jos 10:23-27), assigned their territory to Benjamin (Jos 18:16, 28).

Jecamiah (jĕk-a-mī'a). See *Jekamiah 2.*

Jechiliah, Jecholiah (jĕk-ĭ-lī'a, jĕk-ō-lī'a). See *Jecoliah.*

Jechoniah, Jechonias (jĕk-ō-nī'a, jĕk-ō-nī'as). See *Jeconiah 1; Shecaniah 5.*

Jecoliah (jĕk-ō-lī'a, Lord has prevailed). Mother of Azariah (2 K 15:2 [KJ: Jecholiah]; 2 Ch 26:3 [RV: Jechiliah]).

Jeconiah (jĕk-ō-nī'a, Lord establishes). **1.** Variant of Jehoiachin (1 Ch 3:16, 17; Est 2:6; Jer 24:1; 27:20; 28:4; 29:2). Jechoniah (KJ: Jechonias) in Mt 1:11, 12.

Coniah in Jer 22:24, 28; 37:1. **2.** See *Conaniah 2.* **3.** See *Jehoahaz 2.*

Jeconias (jĕk-ō-nī'as). See *Conaniah 2.*

Jedaiah (jē-dā'ya, Lord knows). **1.** Head of 2d course of priests (1 Ch 9:10; 24:7), whose descendants returned from Babylon (Ez 2:36; Neh 7:39; 1 Esd 5:24 [KJ, RV: Jeddu]). **2. 3.** Two chief priests who returned with Zerubbabel (Neh 12: 6, 7, 19, 21). **4.** Priest; officiated in Jerusalem after captivity (Neh 11:10). **5.** Brought gifts for temple after captivity (Zch 6:10-14). Some of 2—5 may be identical.

Jedaiah (jē-dā'ya, praising Lord). **1.** Simeonite (1 Ch 4:37). **2.** Repaired part of wall of Jerusalem (Neh 3:10).

Jeddu (jĕd'ōō). See first *Jedaiah 1.*

Jedeus (jē-dē'us). See *Adaiah 5.*

Jediael (jē-dī'a-ĕl, known of God). **1.** Benjaminite (1 Ch 7:6-11). Identified, perhaps erroneously, with Ashbel (Nm 26:38). **2.** One of David's heroes (1 Ch 11:45). **3.** Perhaps same as 2; joined David at Ziklag (1 Ch 12:20). **4.** Horahite Levite of sons of Asaph; gatekeeper of tabernacle (1 Ch 26:2).

Jedidah (jē-dī'da, beloved). Mother of Josiah (2 K 22:1).

Jedidiah (jĕd-ĭ-dī'a, beloved by Lord). Name given to Solomon by Nathan (2 Sm 12:25).

Jeduthun (jē-dū'thun). Merarite Levite; appointed head of sanctuary musicians by David (1 Ch 1:41-43; 25:1); identified with Ethan (see 1 Ch 15:17, 19); ancestor of gatekeepers (1 Ch 16:42), who later became musicians (2 Ch 5:12; 29:14; 35:15; Neh 11:17); supplied musical tonality for Ps 39; 62; 77; seer (2 Ch 35:15; 1 Esd 1:15 [RV, RSV: Eddinus]).

Jeeli (jē-ē'lī). See *Jaala.*

Jeelus (jē-ē'lus). See *Jehiel 9.*

Jeezer (jē-ē'zẽr). See *Abiezer 1.*

Jeezerite (jē-ē'zẽr-īt). See *Abiezrite.*

Jegar-sahadutha (jē'gär-sā-ha-dū'tha, heap of witness). Aramaic name given by Laban to heap of stones piled up as memorial of covenant between him and Jacob. Jacob called it Galeed (Gn 31: 47, 48).

Jehaleleel, Jehalelel (jē-ha-lē'lē-ĕl, jē-hăl'-ē-lĕl). See *Jehallelel.*

Jehallelel (jē-hăl'ē-lĕl, he praises God). **1.** Judahite (1 Ch 4:16. KJ: Jehaleleel). **2.** Merarite Levite (2 Ch 29:12. KJ: Jehalelel).

Jehdeiah (jē-dē'ya, Lord makes joyful). **1.** Kohathite Levite (1 Ch 24:20). **2.** Meronothite in charge of David's asses (1 Ch 27:30).

Jehezekel, Jehezkel (jē-hĕz'ē-kĕl, jē-hĕz'-kĕl, God strengthens). Head of 20th course of priests (1 Ch 24:16).

Jehiah (jē-hī'a, Lord lives). See *Jeiel 4.*

Jehiel (jē-hī'ĕl, God lives). **1.** Levite musician (1 Ch 15:18, 20; 16:5). **2.** Gershonite Levite (1 Ch 23:8); ancestor of family Jehieli (1 Ch 26:21, 22). **3.** Son of Hachmoni (1 Ch 27:32). **4.** Son of Jehoshaphat; in charge of fenced cities (2 Ch 21:2-4). **5.** Kohathite Levite who aided Hezekiah in his reformation (2 Ch 29:14 [RV, RSV: Jehuel]; 2 Ch 31:13). **6.** Temple ruler in days of Josiah (2 Ch 35:8; 1 Esd 1:8 [KJ: Syelus; RV: Esyelus]). **7.** Father of Obadiah who returned with Ezra (Ez 8:9; 1 Esd 8:35 [KJ, RV: Jezelus]). **8.** Priest; divorced foreign wife (Ez 10:21; 1 Esd 9:21 [KJ, RV: Hiereel]). **9.** Father of Shecaniah; divorced foreign wife (Ez 10:2, 26; 1 Esd 9:92 [KJ, RV:

Jeelus]; 9:27 [KJ: Hierielus; RV: Jezrielus]). 10. 11. See *Jeiel 1; 2.*
Jehieli (jĕ-hī'e-lī). See *Jehiel 2.*
Jehizkiah (jĕ-hiz-kī'á, LORD strengthens). Ephraimite chief in days of Pekah (2 Ch 28:12).
Jehoadah, Jehoaddah (jĕ-hō'á-dá, jē-hō-ăd'á). See *Jarah.*
Jehoaddan, Jehoaddin (jĕ-hō-ăd'ăn, -ăd'ĭn, LORD makes pleasant?). Mother of Amaziah (2 Ch 25:1; 2 K 14:2 [RV, RSV: Jehoaddin]).
Jehoahaz (jĕ-hō'á-hăz, LORD has laid hold of). 1. 11th king of Israel; successor of Jehu (2 K 10:35; 13:1); continued idolatry of Jeroboam; Hazael and Benhadad of Syria successfully campaigned against him (2 K 13:1-9). RV, RSV: Joahaz in 2 K 14:1. 2. 17th king of Judah; son and successor of Josiah; evil; after three-month reign carried to Egypt by Pharaoh Neco (2 K 23:30-34; 2 Ch 36:1-4). Shallum in 1 Ch 3:15; Jer 22: 10-12. Joachaz (RSV: Jeconiah) in 1 Esd 1:34. Called lion's whelp (Eze 19:1-4). 3. See *Ahaziah 2.*
Jehoash (jĕ-hō'ăsh). See first *Joash 1; 2.*
Jehohanan (jĕ-hō'há'năn, LORD is gracious). 1. David's tabernacle gatekeeper (1 Ch 26:3). 2. Captain of Jehoshaphat (2 Ch 17:15). Probably same in 2 Ch 23:1. 3. Divorced foreign wife (Ez 10:28; 1 Esd 9:29 [KJ: Johannes; RV: Joannes]). 4. Priest at time of Joiakim (Neh 12:13). 5. Priest and musician (Neh 12:42). 6. Son of Eliashib (Ez 10:6 [KJ: Johanan]; 1 Esd 9:1 [KJ: Joanan; RV: Jonas]). 7. Son of Tobiah (Neh 6:18. KJ: Johanan).
Jehoiachin (jĕ-hoi'á-kĭn, LORD establishes). 19th king of Judah; son and successor of Jehoiakim; evil; carried into captivity by Nebuchadnezzar and imprisoned; released by Evil-Merodach (2 K 24:8-16; 25: 27-30; 2 Ch 36:9, 10; Jer 39:2; 52:28-34; Eze 17:12; 1 Esd 1:43 [KJ: Joacim; RV: Joakim]). See also *Jeconiah.*
Jehoiada (jĕ-hoi'á-dá, LORD has known). 1. Father of Benaiah (2 Sm 23:22; 1 K 4:4; probably priest (1 Ch 27:5) who acknowledged David king at Hebron (1 Ch 12:27). 2. Son of Benaiah; counselor of David; successor of Ahithophel (1 Ch 27:34). 3. High priest; wife concealed Joash; planned overthrow of Athaliah. While he lived, Joash was true to Jehovah (2 K 11:1—12:16; 2 Ch 22:10—24:22). 4. Priest (Jer 29:26). 5. Repaired gate of Jerusalem (Neh 3:6. RV, RSV: Joiada). 6. See *Joiada 1.*
Jehoiakim (jĕ-hoi'á-kĭm, LORD establishes). 1. 18th king of Judah; son of Josiah; name changed from Eliakim to Jehoiakim by Pharaoh Neco; evil; paid tribute to Pharaoh Neco; after battle of Carchemish, to Nebuchadnezzar; rebelled 3 years later; died ignoble death (2 K 23:34-37; 24:1-6; 2 Ch 36:4-8; Jer 1:3; 22; 24—28; 35—37; 45; 46; 52; Dn 1:1, 2; 1 Esd 1: 37-39 [KJ: Joacim; RV: Joachim]; Bar 1:3 [KJ: Joacim. RV: Joakim]). 2. High priest (Bar 1:7. KJ: Joachim; RV: Joakim).
Jehoiarib (jĕ-hoi'á-rĭb, LORD pleads). 1. Head of 1st course of temple priests (1 Ch 9:10; 24:7). Joiarib in Neh 11:10. Joarib in 1 Mac 2:1. 2. See *Joiarib.*
Jehonadab (jĕ-hŏn'á-dăb). See *Jonadab 2.*
Jehonathan (jĕ-hŏn'á-thăn, LORD has given). 1. Uzziah's son; overseer of treasuries under David (1 Ch 27:25. RV, RSV: Jonathan). 2. Levite; taught Law to people (2 Ch 17:8) 3. Priest (Neh 12:18).

Jehoram (jĕ-hō'răm). See *Joram.*
Jehoshabeath (jĕ-hō-shăb'ĕ-ăth). See *Jehosheba.*
Jehoshaphat (jĕ-hŏsh'á-făt. LORD has judged). 1. Recorder of David and Solomon (2 Sm 8:16; 1 K 4:3). 2. Solomon's purveyor (1 K 4:17). 3. Father of Jehu (2 K 9:2, 14). 4. 4th king of Judah; son of Asa; good; sent princes and Levites to teach people Law; made peace with Israel; rebuked for joint enterprises with Ahab and Ahaziah; successful in his wars (1 K 15:24; 2 K 8:18, 26; 2 Ch 17—21:1; Mt 1:8 [KJ: Josaphat]). 5. See *Josaphat 1.*
Jehoshaphat, Valley of. Valley where all nations shall be gathered by Jehovah for judgment (Jl 3:2, 12. V 14: Valley of Decision). Some, since Eusebius, have identified with Kidron. Others interpret symbolically.
Jehosheba (jĕ-hŏsh'ĕ-bá, LORD is an oath. Jehoshabeath in 2 Ch 22:11). Daughter of Jehoram; wife of Jehoiada; hid Joash from Athaliah (2 K 11:2).
Jehoshua (jĕ-hŏsh'ū-á). See *Joshua 1.*
Jehovah (jĕ-hō'vá). Name of God of Israel; translated: LORD (RV: Jehovah; KJ occasionally: Jehovah). Jews, out of reverence for name, read "Adonai" where Tetragrammaton YHWH (often JHVH) pronounced Yahwe(h) (also written Yahve[h], Jahwe[h], Jahve[h], occurred. Vowel points for Adonai were placed under the four consonants, thus giving Jehovah. Jehovah abbreviated to jah or iah in many compound words. YHWH is connected with qal of verb *hayah*, "to be" (see Ex 3:13-15), thereby showing God's self-existence (some, on basis of hiphil: giver of existence).
Jehovah-jireh (jĕ-hō'vá-jī'rĕ. RSV: The LORD will provide). Abraham's name for place where Isaac was placed on the altar (Gn 22:14).
Jehovah-nissi (jĕ-hō'vá-nĭs'ī. RSV: The LORD is my banner). Altar built by Moses at Rephidim to commemorate victory over Amalek (Ex 17:15, 16).
Jehovah-shalom (jĕ-hō'vá-shā'lŏm. RSV: The LORD is peace). Name given to altar in Ophrah by Gibeon (Ju 6:23, 24).
Jehovah-shammah (jĕ-hō'vá-shăm'á. KJ, RV, RSV: The LORD is there). Name given to prophetic Jerusalem (Eze 48:35; see Is 60:14-22; Rv 21:3).
Jehovah-tsidkenu (jĕ-hō'vá-tsĭd'kĕ-nū. KJ: The LORD Our Righteousness. RV, RSV: The LORD is our righteousness). Name given by Jeremiah to prophetic Righteous King (Jer 23:6) and to His city (Jer 33: 16).
Jehozabad (jĕ-hŏz'á-băd, LORD has given). 1. Korahite porter (1 Ch 26:4). 2. One of assassins of Joash (2 K 12:21; 2 Ch 24:26; 25:3). 3. Captain of Jehoshaphat (2 Ch 17:18).
Jehozadak (jĕ-hŏz'á-dăk, LORD is righteous. Jozadak in Ez and Neh. KJ: Josedech in Hg and Zch. RV: Josedec; RSV: Josedek; RSV: Jozadak in 1 Esd and Sir). Son of Seraiah; high priest at time of captivity (1 Ch 6:14, 15. See 2 K 25:18-21); son Joshua (Jeshua) was high priest after return (Ez 3:2, 8; 5:2; 10:18; Neh 12:26; Hg 1:1, 12, 14; 2:2, 4; Zch 6:11).
Jehu (jĕ'hū, LORD he). 1. Benjaminite; came to David at Ziklag (1 Ch 12:3). 2. Prophet; rebuked Baasha (1 K 16:1, 7, 12) and Jehoshaphat (2 Ch 19: 1-3), whose chronicler he was (2 Ch 20:34). 3. 10th king of Israel; slew Jehoram of

Israel, Ahaziah of Judah, Jezebel, heirs of Ahab, prophets of Baal; submitted to Shalmaneser III; Aramaeans devastated his land (2 K 9; 10; 2 Ch 22:7-9). 4. Judahite (1 Ch 2:38). 5. Simeonite who moved into valley of Gedor (1 Ch 4:35-41).

Jehubbah (jĕ-hŭb'ȧ). Asherite (1 Ch 7:34).

Jehucal (jĕ-hū'kǎl, LORD is able). Sent by Zedekiah to ask for prayers of Jeremiah (Jer 37:3). Jucal in Jer 38:1.

Jehud (jē'hŭd, praise). Town of Dan (Jos 19.45). Modern Yazur, 5 mi SE, or el-Yehûdiyeh, 10½ mi ESE of Joppa.

Jehudi (jĕ-hū'dī, Jew). Sent by court of Jehoiakim to ask Baruch to read Jeremiah's roll (Jer 36:14-23).

Jehudijah (jĕ-hū-dī'jȧ). Not proper noun, as KJ, but adjective: Jewish (1 Ch 4:18).

Jehuel (jĕ-hū'ĕl). See *Jehiel 5.*

Jehush (jē'hŭsh). See *Jeush 3.*

Jeiel (jĕ-ī'ĕl). 1. Gibeon's father; ancestor of Saul (1 Ch 8:29 [KJ, H omit]; 9:35 [KJ: Jehiel]). 2. Aroerite in time of David (1 Ch 11:44. KJ: Jehiel). Perhaps same in 1 Ch 5:7, 8. 3. See *Jaaziel.* 4. Levite musician (1 Ch 15:18, 21); minister for ark (1 Ch 16:5). Jehiah in 1 Ch 15:24. 5. Descendant of Asaph (2 Ch 20: 14). 6. Scribe of Uzziah (2 Ch 26:11). 7. Levite in days of Josiah (2 Ch 35:9). Ochiel (RV: Ochielus) in 1 Esd 1:9. 8. Divorced foreign wife (Ez 10:43). 9. 10. See *Jeuel 2; 3.*

Jekabzeel (jĕ-kǎb'zĕ-ĕl). See *Kabzeel.*

Jekameam (jĕk-ȧ-mē'ǎm, he gathers people). Levite (1 Ch 23:19; 24:23).

Jekamiah (jĕk-ȧ-mī'ȧ, LORD strengthens). 1. Judahite (1 Ch 2:41). 2. Descendant of Jeconiah (1 Ch 3:18). KJ: Jecamiah).

Jekuthiel (jĕ-kū'thĭ-ĕl, preservation of God). Judahite (1 Ch 4:18).

Jemima, Jemimah (jĕ-mī'mȧ, dove). Job's daughter (Jb 42:14).

Jemnaan (jĕm'nȧ-ăn). See *Jabneel 1.*

Jemuel (jē-mū'ĕl, desire of God). Son of Simeon (Gn 46:10; Ex 6:15). Nemuel in Nm 26:12; 1 Ch 4:24.

Jephthae, Jephthah (jĕf'thē, jĕf'thȧ, he opens). Judge of Israel; illegitimate son; driven from home by father's heirs; lived in land of Tob; called back by elders of tribes to fight Amorites, whom he defeated; sacrificed daughter, only child, because of rash promise (Ju 11:1—12:7; Heb 11:32 [KJ: Jephthae]).

Jephunneh (jĕ-fŭn'ĕ). 1. Judahite; father of spy Caleb (Nm 13:6). 2. Asherite (1 Ch 7:38).

Jerah (jē'rȧ, moon). Son of Joktan (Gn 10: 26; 1 Ch 1:20).

Jerahmeel (jĕ-rä'mĕ-ĕl, God has mercy). 1. Son of Hezron (1 Ch 2:9, 42). 2. Merarite Levite (1 Ch 24:29). 3. Sent by Jehoiakim to take Jeremiah and Baruch captive (Jer 36:26).

Jerahmeelites (jĕ-rä'mĕ-ĕl-īts). Descendants of Jerahmeel 1.

Jerechu, Jerechus (jĕr'ĕ-kū, -kus). See *Jericho.*

Jered (jē'rĕd). See *Jared.*

Jeremai (jĕr'ĕ-mī, exalted). Divorced foreign wife (Ez 10:33; 1 Esd 9:34 [KJ, RV: Jeremias]).

Jeremiah (jĕr-ĕ-mī'ȧ, LORD exalts or appoints). 1. Prophet (c 640—587 BC); son of Hilkiah in territory of Benjamin (Jer 1:1); prophesied in days of last Judean kings (Josiah, Jehoahaz II, Jehoiakim, Jehoiachin, Zedekiah); called to prophetic activity by vision instructing "to destroy and to overthrow, to build and to plant"

(Jer 1:4-10); probably assisted Josiah in reforms (2 K 23); warned Jehoiakim against Egyptian alliance and favored Chaldeans; roll dictated to Baruch destroyed by king (Jer 36); princes persecuted him in days of Zedekiah (Jer 37; 38); after Jerusalem was captured, Nebuchadnezzar showed him great kindness (Jer 39:11, 12); finally moved to Egypt, where he probably died (Jer 43:6, 7). KJ: Jeremy in Mt 2:17; 27:9; Jeremias in Mt 16:14. 2. Josiah's father-in-law (2 K 23:31; 24:18). 3. Manassite (1 Ch 5:24). 4. Benjaminite; came to David at Ziklag (1 Ch 12:4). 5. 6. Gadites (1 Ch 12:10, 13). 7. Priest (Neh 10:2; 12:34). 8. Priest; returned with Zerubbabel (Neh 12:1). 9. Rechabite (Jer 35:3).

Jeremiah, Book of. See *Jeremiah 1.* Outline: 1. Call of Prophet (1). 2. Warnings to Jews (2—29). 3. Promise of Restoration of Israel (30—33). 4. Prophecies Occasioned by Jehoiakim and Zedekiah (34—39). 5. Ministry of Jeremiah to Remnant in Egypt (40—44). 6. Prophecy for Baruch (45). 7. Prophecies Against Egypt, Philistia, Moab, Ammon, Edom, Damascus, Elam, Arabia, Babylon (46—51). 8. Jerusalem's Fall (52). Prophecies spoken (2:2; 34:2); later written (Jer 36; 45). Core of book deals with Righteous Branch (23:5, 6; 30; 31; 33).

Jeremias (jĕr-ĕ-mī'ȧs). See *Jeremai; Jeremiah 1.*

Jeremiel (jĕr-ĕ-mī'ĕl). See *Uriel 4.*

Jeremy (jĕr'ĕ-mī). See *Jeremiah 1.*

Jeremoth (jĕr'ĕ-mŏth, high or thick). 1. Benjaminite; descendant of Becher (1 Ch 7:8. KJ: Jerimoth). 2. Benjaminite; son of Beriah (1 Ch 8:14). 3. Merarite Levite (1 Ch 23:23). Jerimoth in 1 Ch 24:30. 4. See *Jerimoth 5.* 5. Chief of Naphtali (1 Ch 27:19. KJ: Jerimoth). 6. Divorced foreign wife (Ez 10:26; 1 Esd 9: 27 [KJ, RV; Hieremoth]). 7. Divorced foreign wife (Ez 10:27; 1 Esd 9:28 [KJ, RV: Jarimoth]). 8. Divorced foreign wife (Ez 10:29 [KJ: and Ramoth]; 1 Esd 9:30 [KJ, RV: Hieremoth]).

Jeriah (jĕ-rī'ȧ). Kohathite Levite; chief at Hebron (1 Ch 23:19; 24:23). Jerijah in 1 Ch 26:31.

Jeribai (jĕr'ĭ-bī, LORD defends). One of David's heroes (1 Ch 11:46).

Jericho (jĕr'ĭ-kō, place of fragrance or moon-city). City, 825 ft below sea level, 6 mi W of Jordan, near Dead Sea. Jericho's mounds have series of sites. OT Jericho examined by archaeologists (1908 to 1910; 1930—1936; 1952—). Oldest known city has been regarded as located at Jericho. Conquered by Joshua (Jos 2 to 6); given to Benjamin (Jos 18:21); rebuilt by Hiel (1 K 16:34). Thereafter frequently mentioned (2 K 2:1-22; 25:5; Ez 2:34; Mt 20:29; Mk 10:46; Lk 10:30; 1 Esd 5:22 [KJ: Jerechus; RV: Jerechu]).

Jeriel (jĕr'ĭ-ĕl, founded by God). Issacharite (1 Ch 7:2).

Jerijah (jĕ-rī'jȧ). See *Jeriah.*

Jerimoth (jĕr'ĭ-mŏth, high or thick). 1. Benjaminite; son of Bela (1 Ch 7:7). 2. See *Jeremoth 3.* 3. Benjaminite; joined David at Ziklag (1 Ch 12:5). 4. See *Jeremoth 3.* 5. Levite; head of 13th course of musicians (1 Ch 25:4. Jeremoth in 1 Ch 25:22). 6. See *Jeremoth 5.* 7. Son of David; father of Mahalath (2 Ch 11:18). Possibly same as Ithream. 8. Levite overseer (2 Ch 31:13).

Jerioth (jĕr'ĭ-ŏth). Caleb's wife (1 Ch 2· 18).

Jeroboam (jĕr'ô-bō'ăm, he pleads people's cause). **1.** Jeroboam I; 1st king of Israel after division, superintendent under Solomon (1 K 11:28); Ahijah designated him king of 10 tribes (1 K 11:29-40); fled to Egypt (1 K 11:40); became king with Shechem as capital and Tirzah as residence (1 K 12:1-25); built shrines in Bethel and Dan with golden calves (1 K 12:25-33); downfall foretold (1 K 13; 14. See 2 Ch 10—13). **2.** Jeroboam II; 13th king of Israel; successful in war with Syria and others; extended territory of Israel; idolatry and immorality continued in his reign (Amos and Hosea). Excavations at Samaria show splendor of period (2 K 14:23-29).

Jeroham (jĕ-rō'hăm). **1.** Grandfather of Samuel (1 Sm 1:1; 1 Ch 6:27, 34). **2.** Benjaminite (1 Ch 8:27). Perhaps same in 1 Ch 9:8. **3.** Priest (1 Ch 9:12; Neh 11:12). **4.** Benjaminite; father of two who came to David at Ziklag (1 Ch 12:7). **5.** Father of Azarel (1 Ch 27:22). **6.** Father of Azariah (2 Ch 23:1).

Jerubbaal, Jerubbesheth (jĕr-ub-bā'ăl, -bē'-shĕth). See *Gideon.*

Jeruel (jĕ-rōō'ĕl, God founded). Place near En-gedi (2 Ch 20:16).

Jerusalem (jĕ-rōō'sá-lĕm). Name probably connected with H *shalom* (peace); Tell el Amarna tablets call it Urusalim (city of peace); 33 mi E of Mediterranean, 14 mi W of Dead Sea, on rocky plateau, 2,550 ft high; mean temperature: 63 degrees; water supplied by Gihon Spring (Virgin's Fountain) in Kidron Valley and En-rogel (Job's Well) at juncture of Kidron and Hinnom valleys; reservoirs built in city. Hezekiah cut tunnel in rock to conduct water from Gihon to Upper Pool of Siloam (2 Ch 32:30). Kidron Valley on E side of Jerusalem, Valley of Hinnom (Gehenna) on W and S; Tyropoeon (Valley of Cheesemongers) passed through city.

Jebusite city of David's day was on hill S of Ophel (SE corner of Jerusalem) and was 1,250 × 400 ft (1 Ch 11:4-8). Solomon extended walls to protect his palaces and temple (1 K 3:1; 9:15). Manasseh extended wall (2 Ch 33:14), and Nehemiah rebuilt it, extending it on N. Herod built or extended walls as found in time of Christ. Hadrian built walls in AD 135. Modern walls are by Suleiman the Magnificent AD 1542. Temple stood on Rock Moriah (Mt Zion), considered site of Gn 22:2-4, 14. Jerusalem has been considered the Salem of Melchizedek (Gn 14:18). Also called Salem (Ps 76:2), Jebus (Ju 19:10, 11), "City of David," Zion (1 K 8:1; 2 K 14:20), City of Judah (2 Ch 25:28), City of God (Ps 46:4), City of the great King (Ps 48:2), Holy City (Neh 11:1).

Jerusalem, the New. City of God; described in Rv 21:2, 10 as coming down from heaven. In Gl 4:26 described as mother of believers (see Heb 11:8-10; 12:22-24).

Jerusha, Jerushah (jĕ-rōō'shá, possessed). Daughter of Zadok; wife of Uzziah (2 K 15:33). Jerushah in 2 Ch 27:1.

Jesaiah (jĕ-sā'yá). See *Jeshaiah 3; 6.*

Jeshaiah (jĕ-shā'yá, LORD saves). **1.** Musician; son of Jeduthun (1 Ch 25:3). **2.** Levite (1 Ch 26:25). **3.** Descendant of Zerubbabel (1 Ch 3:21. KJ: Jesaiah). **4.** Son of Athaliah; returned with Zerubbabel (Ez 8:7; 1 Esd 8:33 [KJ: Josias; RV: Jesias]) **5** Merarite Levite re-

turned with Zerubbabel (Ez 8:19; 1 Esd 8:48 [KJ, RV: Osaias]). **6.** Benjaminite (Neh 11:7. KJ: Jesaiah).

Jeshanah (jĕsh'á-ná). City; probably 3¼ mi N of Bethel (2 Ch 13:19; 1 Sm 7:12 [KJ, RV: Shen]).

Jesharelah (jĕsh-á-rē'lá). See *Asharelah.*

Jeshebeab (jĕ-shĕb'ē-ăb, father's dwelling). Head of 14th course of priests (1 Ch 24:13).

Jesher (jē'shēr, uprightness). Caleb's son (1 Ch 2:18).

Jeshimon (jĕ-shī'mŏn, waste, desert. RV: desert. RSV: desert in Nm). Desert area N of Dead Sea (Nm 21:20; 23:28; 1 Sm 23:19,24; 26:1, 3).

Jeshishai (jĕ-shĭsh'á-ī, old). Gadite (1 Ch 5:14).

Jeshohaiah (jĕsh-ō-hā'yá, LORD humbles). Simeonite (1 Ch 4:36).

Jeshua, Jeshuah (jĕsh'ū-á, LORD is salvation. Late form of Joshua). **1.** See *Joshua 1.* **2.** Head of 9th course of priests (1 Ch 24:11 [KJ: Jeshuah]; Ez 2:36; Neh 7:39). KJ, RV: Jesus in 1 Esd 5:24; Sir 49:12. **3.** Levite (2 Ch 31:15). **4.** High priest; returned with Zerubbabel (Ez 2:2; 3:2-9; Neh 7:7). Joshua in Zch 3; 6:11-13; Hg 1:1, 14. KJ, RV: Jesus in 1 Esd 5:8, 48, 56. **5.** Descendants returned with Zerubbabel (Ez 2:6; Neh 7:11; 1 Esd 5:11 [RV: Jesus]). **6.** Levite; returned with Zerubbabel (Ez 2:40; 8:33; Neh 7:43; 12:8; 1 Esd 5:26 [KJ: Jessue; RV: Jesus]; 8:63 [KJ, Jesu; RV: Jesus]); assisted high priest Jeshua (Ez 3:9); sealed covenant (Neh 10:9). **7.** Father of Ezer (Neh 3:19). **8.** Levite; explained law (Neh 8:7). Perh same as 6. **9.** Village of Judah (Neh 11:26).

Jeshurun (jĕsh'ū-rŭn, upright). Surname given to Israel in poetry and representing Israel as righteous people (Dt 32:15; 33:5, 26; Is 44:2 [KJ: Jesurun]).

Jesiah (jĕ-sī'á). See *Isshiah 2; 4.*

Jesias (jĕ-sī'ás). See *Jeshaiah 4.*

Jesimiel (jĕ-sĭm'ĭ-ĕl, God will set up). Simeonite (1 Ch 4:36).

Jesse (jĕs'ē). Son of Obed; grandson of Ruth (Ruth 4:17, 22; Mt 1:5). David was youngest of his 8 sons (1 Sm 17:12. See 1 Sm 16:11; 20:31; 22:3, 7; 25:10).

Jessue, Jesu (jĕs'ū-ē, jĕsōō). See *Jeshua 6.*

Jesui (jĕs'ū-ī). See *Ishvi 1.*

Jesurun (jĕs'ū-rŭn). See *Jeshurun.*

Jesus (jē'zus, Savior). **1.** G form of Jeshua and Joshua. See *Jeshua 1; 4; 5; 6; Jose; Joshua 1.* **2.** Compiler of Sirach (Ecclesiasticus). **3.** Paul's friend, also called Justus (Cl 4:11).

Jesus Christ (jē'zus krīst. Jesus is G for H *y:hoshu'a:* savior. Christ is G for H *Mashiah:* the anointed). Jesus signifies Savior (Mt 1:21, 25; Lk 1:31). Christ signifies Anointed One (Acts 10:38), the promised Messiah (Mt 16:13-23; Lk 2:25, 26; Jn 1:35-41). See also *Messiah.*

Logos. Jesus is called Logos (Word; Jn 1:1-14; 1 Jn 1:1; Rv 19:13); shows Messiah as pre-existing Person before incarnation. Logos is Himself living and gives life; creative (Jn 1:3; Ps 147:15-18; Mt 8:24-27; 9:1-8; Cl 1:15-20); preservative (Cl 1:17). Spirit of Word inspired prophets (1 Ptr 1:10, 11).

Son of God. Applied to Jesus in unique sense (Mt 11:27; 16:16; 21:33-41; Mk 12:6, 7; 13:32; Jn 1:14, 18; 3:16-18) which makes Father and Son equal (Jn 10:30; 12:45; 14:8-11; 17). Jesus is distinct Person, eternal Son, begotten by eternal Father (Jn 3:16; Ro 8:3), yet of one substance with Father (Cl 1:19; 1 Jn 5:20); hence He has same attributes (Jn 5:21; 21:17), works (Mt 9:1-8; Jn 5:17, 21, 25; Cl 1:15-20), honor (Jn 5:23).

Son of Man. Jesus used this expression to emphasize His humanity especially in connection with His ministry (Lk 9:56; 19:10), power (Mt 9:6; 12:8), death (Mk 14:21; Lk 22:48; Jn 3:14), resurrection (Mt 17:9; Mk 9:9), ascension (Jn 6:62), 2d coming and judgment (Mt 25:31). He is prophesied man (Gn 3:15; Is 7:14; Gl 4:1-7), New Man, New Adam (Ro 5:12-21; 1 Co 15:22; Ph 2:5-11), who brought in new humanity. Shared in flesh and blood as children do (Ro 9:5; Heb 2:14). Thus Christ is God and man in one person (Jn 1:14; 1 Ti 2:5; Cl 2:9).

Earthly Life. Conceived by Holy Ghost; born of virgin Mary at Bethlehem; circumcised; presented at temple; taken to Egypt; lived at Nazareth (Lk 2:39); visited temple when 12 yrs old (Lk 2:40-52); when about 30 yrs old, baptized by John (Mt 3:13-17; Mk 1:9-11; Lk 3:21-23); tempted by Satan (Mt 4:1-11); began public ministry. Major portion of ministry in Galilee with Capernaum as headquarters; also included Judea, Samaria, even distant regions as that of Tyre and Sidon. Announced and taught kingdom of God, did good, performed miracles, was opposed by Jewish leaders (lawyers, scribes, Pharisees). Taken captive by Jewish leaders in Gethsemane; condemned by judges gathered by high priest; crucified by Pilate on Golgotha; buried in nearby garden; rose from dead on 3d day; appeared to disciples; ascended to heaven. Gospels present facts of Christ's life that fit their objectives (see Jn 20:30, 31).

Servant of God. Jesus is Servant of God (Mt 12:18; Acts 3:13, 26) because He did that which God willed (Mk 14:32-42; Jn 1:29; 4:34; 5:30); served God by saving men (Acts 3:26) in spite of human opposition (Acts 4:27). Thus ultimate fulfillment of Is 53 is seen in Christ (Mk 8:31; 10:33; Ro 4:25).

Savior. Jesus is promised Savior (Lk 2:11, 22-32), who by His life, death, resurrection, and proclamation saves (Mt 1:21; Lk 19:10; Jn 4:42; Acts 4:12; 11:14; 16:31; Ro 5:10; 10:9, 10) those who believe (Acts 16:31) from sin, wrath, and death (Mt 1:21; 1 Ti 1:1; 2; Eph 5:23).

Mediator. Jesus is Mediator between God and man (Gl 3:19, 1 Ti 2:5; Heb 8:6; 9:15; 12:24) by bringing men to God as Prophet, Priest, King. See *Offices* (below).

Lamb of God. Jesus is Lamb of God in sense that He is sacrificed for sins of world (Jn 1:29, 36; Acts 8:32; 1 Co 5:7; 1 Ptr 1:19; Heb 7:27. See Ex 12; Is 53:7).

Offices. Christ as Prophet announces kingdom of God; reveals to man God in His holiness, mercy, love; performed signs of Kingdom; forgives sins; and through apostles and church proclaims Gospel (Gospels). Christ as Priest fulfilled all righteousness and atoned for all sin in place of mankind by His vicarious life, death, and resurrection (Ro 4:25; 2 Co 5:19; Heb 7). Christ is King in sense that He rules men with truth of God (Jn 18:33-38), namely, New Covenant (Jer 31:31-34; 32:40, 41). He is Son of David, through whom God had

covenanted with Israel (2 Sm 7; 23:1-7). Jesus is King of kings and Lord of lords (Mt 28:18). See *Lord* (below).

States. To perform work of redemption, Christ according to human nature did not use prerogatives He might rightfully claim (humiliation. Ph 2:6-8). Resumption of full and constant use is exaltation (Eph 4:8; Ph 2:9-11).

Lord. God made Jesus Lord (in sense that *kurios* translates JHVH [Lord, Jehovah], Mk 1:3—Is 40:3) by resurrection from dead (Acts 2:31-36; Ro 1:4; Eph 4:5; Ph 2:5-11; 1 Ti 6:15; Rv 11:15). Authority of Jesus-Lord is authority of God (Mt 28:18; 1 Co 8:4-6). Jesus' lordship is won (Eph 1:21; Ph 2:5-11; Cl 2:6-15) and will be fully revealed at Parousia (Mt 25:31; 1 Co 15:26-28). He is Lord of individual by faith (Lk 23:42; Acts 5:14; 11:17; 1 Co 12:3; 2 Co 3:17; Eph 1:3), and believers for Him (Ro 14:6-8; 1 Co 15:58; 16:10; Eph 2:21; 5:8-10; 6:4; Cl 1:10). As Lord, Jesus is Head of church, both as supreme authority and as goal (Eph 1:22, 23; 4:15, 16; 5:23, 24; Cl 1:18; 2:10, 19).

Jether (jē'thēr, eminence, abundance). **1.** Judahite; son of Jerahmeel (1 Ch 2:32). **2.** Judahite; son of Ezra (1 Ch 4:17). **3.** See *Ithra.* **4.** See *Ithran* **2.** **5.** Gideon's son (Ju 8:20; 9:18).

Jetheth (jē'thĕth). Chief of Edom (Gn 36: 40; 1 Ch 1:51).

Jethlah (jĕth'la). See *Ithlah.*

Jethro (jĕth'rō, excellence). Priest and prince of Midian; father of Zipporah (Ex 3:1; 4:18); advised Moses (Ex 18). Jethro is probably surname or title of Reuel (Ex 2:18) or Raguel (Nm 10:29). Hobab was probably brother-in-law (Ju 4:11 makes him father-in-law. RV: brother-in-law).

Jetur (jē'tĕr). Son of Ishmael (Gn 25:15; 1 Ch 1:31); descendants (1 Ch 5:19) were Itureans (Lk 3:1).

Jeuel (jē-ū'ĕl, treasure of God?). **1.** Judahite; family of Zerah (1 Ch 9:6). **2.** Levite; participated in reforms of Hezekiah (2 Ch 29:13. KJ: Jeiel). **3.** Returned with Ezra (Ez 8:13 [KJ: Jeiel]; 1 Esd 8:39).

Jeush (jē'ūsh). **1.** Son of Esau (Gn 36:5, 18). **2.** Benjaminite (1 Ch 7:10). **3.** Descendant of Jonathan (1 Ch 8:39. KJ: Jehush). **4.** Levite; son of Shimei (1 Ch 23:10, 11). **5.** Son of Rehoboam (2 Ch 11:19).

Jeuz (jē'ūz). Benjaminite (1 Ch 8:10).

Jew (jōō, H *y:hudi,* G *Judaios.* See Judah). Tribe or country of Judah, son of Jacob. At first used to distinguish Kingdom of Judah from N Kingdom (Israel) (2 K 15:36. See 14:28; 16:6; 25:25; Est 3:6). After Babylonian Captivity, since men of Judah were majority of remnant, all Hebrews called Jews (frequent in Ez, Neh, Est). Broader use in Maccabees (2 Mac 9:17) and NT (Mt 27:11; Mk 7:3; Acts 2:5; Ro 3:9). "Hebrew" denotes descent from Abraham, "Israel" from Jacob, "Jew" from Judah. "Jew" not applied to Gentile converts as "Israel" is. See also *Hebrew; Israel.*

jewel, jewelry. See *ornaments.*

Jezaniah (jĕz'a-ni'á). See *Azariah* **24.**

Jezebel (jĕz'e-bel, unmarried or unexalted). Wife of Ahab (1 K 16:31); daughter of Ethbaal, priest of Astarte, king of Tyre and Sidon; introduced worship of Baal and Astarte (1 K 16:31, 32; 18:19); slew prophets of the Lord (1 K 18:13); opposed Elijah (1 K 19:1); planned death of Naboth (1 K 21); killed by Jehu (2 K 9:30-37). Symbol of licentious evil and idolatry (2 K 9:22; Rv 2:20).

Jezelus (jĕ-zē'lŭs). See *Jehaziel 5; Jehiel 7*.

Jezer (jē'zēr, formation). Naphtalite (Gn 46:24; 1 Ch 7:13); founder of tribe (Nm 26:49).

Jeziah (jē-zī'á). See *Izziah*.

Jeziel (jē'zī-ĕl, assembly of God). Benjaminite; came to David at Ziklag (1 Ch 12:3).

Jezliah (jĕz-lī'á). See *Izliah*.

Jezoar (jē-zō'ēr). See *Izhar 2*.

Jezrahiah (jĕz-rá-hī'á, LORD shines). Levite; in charge of singers at dedication of Jerusalem's walls (Neh 12:42).

Jezreel (jĕz'rē-ĕl, God sows). 1. Judahite (1 Ch 4:3). 2. Oldest son of Hosea (Hos 1:4, 5). 3. City of Issachar (modern Zerin), 5 mi N of Jerusalem (Jos 19:18; 1 Sm 29:1). Kings of Israel had palace there (2 Sm 2:9; 1 K 18:45, 46; 21:1). Nearby was Naboth's vineyard. 4. Town in hill country of Judah (Jos 15:56).

Jezreel, Valley of. Plain; 20 mi long and 14 wide between ridges of Gilboa and Moreh (Jos 17:16; Ju 6:33; Hos 1:5). Esdraelon in Jdth 3:9; 4:6.

Jezrielus (jĕz-rī-ē'lŭs). See *Jehiel 9*.

Jibsam (jĭb'săm). See *Ibsam*.

Jidlaph (jĭd'lăf, he weeps). Son of Nahor and Milcah (Gn 22:22).

Jimna, Jimnah (jĭm'ná). See *Imnah 1*.

Jiphtah (jĭf'tá). See *Iphtah*.

Jiphthahel (jĭf'thá-ĕl). See *Iphtahel*.

Joab (jō'ăb, LORD is father). 1. Son of Zeruiah, half sister of David (2 Sm 2:18); brother of Asahel and Abishai; defeated forces of Ish-bosheth (2 Sm 2:8-32); killed Abner (2 Sm 3:22-39); became commander-in-chief at Jebus (1 Ch 11:4-9); defeated Syria, Edom, Ammon (2 Sm 10—12); arranged murder of Uriah (2 Sm 11); killed Absalom (2 Sm 18:9-15) and Amasa (2 Sm 20:4-13); sided with Adonijah (1 K 1); killed at order of Solomon (1 K 2:28-34). 2. Son of Seraiah; father (or founder) or Ge-harashim (1 Ch 4:13, 14). 3. Founder of family which returned (Ez 2:6; 8:9; Neh 7:11). 4. See *Atroth-beth-joab*.

Joachaz (jō'á-kăz). See *Jehoahaz 2*.

Joachim (jō'á-kĭm). See *Jehoiakim 1; 2*.

Joacim (jō'á-sĭm). See *Jehoiakim 1; 2; Jehoiachin; Joiakim; Joakim 4; 5*.

Joadanus (jō-á-dā'nŭs). See *Gedaliah 5*.

Joah (jō'a, LORD is brother). 1. Son of Obed-edom (1 Ch 26:4). 2. Levite; descendant of Gershom (1 Ch 6:21); probably one who helped Hezekiah in reformation (2 Ch 29:12). Ethan in 1 Ch 6:42. 3. Son of Asaph; recorder of Hezekiah (2 K 18:18, 26; Is 36:3, 11, 22). 4. Recorder of Josiah (2 Ch 34:8).

Joahaz (jō'á-hăz). 1. Father of Joah 4 (2 Ch 34:8). 2. See *Jehoahaz 1*.

Joakim (jō'á-kĭm). 1. See *Jehoiachin*. 2. See *Jehoiakim 1; 2*. 3. See *Joiakim*. 4. High priest (Jdth 4:6, 8, 14. KJ: Joacim). 5. Husband of Susannah (Sus 1, 4, 28, 29, 63. KJ: Joacim).

Joanan (jō-á'năn). See *Hananiah 8; Jehohanan 6*.

Joanna (jō-ăn'á, LORD has been gracious). 1. See *Hananiah 8*. 2. Wife of Chuza (Lk 8:3; 24:10).

Joannan (jō-ăn'ăn). See *John 2*.

Joannes (jō-ăn'ēz). See *Jehohanan 3; Johanan 8*.

Joarib (jō'á-rĭb). See *Jehoiarib 1*.

Joash (jō'ăsh, LORD has given. Long form Jehoash interchangeable in 2 K). 1. 8th

king of Judah; son of Ahaziah (2 K 11:2); saved from Athaliah by aunt Jehosheba, wife of high priest Jehoiada; crowned through efforts of Jehoiada; restored religion of Jehovah under guidance of Jehoiada; apostatized after Jehoiada's death; ordered murder of Zechariah, Jehoiada's son; slain by servants (2 K 11; 12; 2 Ch 24). 2. 12th king of Israel; followed sins of Jeroboam (perhaps in early years); visited Elisha on his deathbed; defeated Syrians, Moabites, Amaziah of Judah; died in peace (2 K 13; 14; 2 Ch 25). 3. Judahite (1 Ch 4:22). 4. Father of Gideon (Ju 6:11-32). 5. Benjaminite; came to David at Ziklag (1 Ch 12:3). 6. Son of Ahab (1 K 22:26; 2 Ch 18:25).

Joash (jō'ăsh, LORD has come to help). 1. Son of Beecher (1 Ch 7:8). 2. Keeper of David's oil cellars (1 Ch 27:28).

Joatham (jō'á-thăm). See *Jotham 2*.

Job (jŏb). See *Jashub 1*.

Job, Book of. Regarded as literary masterpiece; in it are dramatic, lyric, and epic poetry; didactic and reflective; name from chief character. Estimated dates range from 200 to 1000 B C. Asks how suffering of righteous is compatible with concept of just God. Is human conduct justly rewarded or punished on earth? Job concludes that as he knows God, so God knows him; that his Redeemer lives and he shall see God. Though God's rule is mysterious, He rules for best. True piety needs no external indication but lives on through all conditions (13:15). Outline: 1. Prolog (1, 2). 2. Job Bewails His Birth, Yearns for Death (3). 3. Three Series of Debates Between Job and His Friends (4—31). 4. Speech of Elihu (32—37). 5. Speech of LORD from Storm Cloud (38 to 41). 6. Job's Submission and Restoration (42).

Jobab (jō'băb). 1. Son of Joktan (Gn 10:29; 1 Ch 1:23). 2. Edomite king (Gn 36:33, 34; 1 Ch 1:44, 45). 3. King; with Jabin and Hazor fought Joshua (Jos 11:1). 4. 5. Benjaminites (1 Ch 8:9, 18).

Jochebed (jŏk'ē-bĕd, LORD is glory). Mother of Moses and Aaron (Ex 6:20; Nm 26:29).

Joda (jō'dá). 1. See *Hodaviah 4*. 2. Ancestor of Jesus (Lk 3:26, KJ: Juda).

Jodan (jō'dăn). See *Gedaliah 5*.

Joed (jō'ĕd). Benjaminite (Neh 11:7).

Joel (jō'ĕl, LORD is God). 1. See *Joel, Book of*. 2. Samuel's son (1 Sm 8:2; 1 Ch 6:28 [KJ: Vashni]). 3. Simeonite (1 Ch 4:35). 4. Reubenite (1 Ch 5:4, 8). 5. Gadite (1 Ch 5:12). 6. Son of Azariah; father of Elkanah (1 Ch 6:36). 7. Issacharite (1 Ch 7:3). 8. See *Igal 2*. 9. Levite; assisted in removing ark (1 Ch 15:7, 11); probably same in 1 Ch 23:8; 26:22. 10. Manassite chief (1 Ch 27:20). 11. Kohathite Levite in Hezekiah's time (2 Ch 29:12). 12. Divorced foreign wife (Ez 10:43; 1 Esd 9: 35 [KJ, RV: Juel]). 13. Benjaminite; overseer of Jerusalem (Neh 11:9). 14. See *Uel*.

Joel, Book of. Dates assigned have ranged from 932 to 400 B C. Plague of locusts viewed by prophet as punishment for sin, causes his prophetic vision to see Judgment Day. Time of recuperation led to prophecy of time when God would pour out Spirit on all flesh (Acts 2:16-21). Outline: 1. Plague of Locusts (1:1—2:17). 2. Lord Pities and Gives Spiritual Blessings (2:18-27). 3. Ultimate Blessing of God and Visitation of Judgment (2:28—3: 21).

Joelah (jō-ē'lá). Benjaminite; joined David at Ziklag (1 Ch 12:7).

Joezer (jō-ē'zēr, LORD is help). Korahite; joined David at Ziklag (1 Ch 12:6).

Jogbehah (jŏg'bē-hä, lofty). Town of Gad, 6 mi NW of Rabbah 1 (Nm 32:35; Ju 8: 11). Modern Jubeîhât or Ajbehât.

Jogli (jŏg'lī). Father of Bukki (Nm 34:22).

Joha (jō'há). 1. Benjaminite (1 Ch 8:16). 2. One of David's heroes (1 Ch 11:45).

Johanan (jō-hā'năn, LORD is merciful). 1. Jewish chief; supported Gedaliah (2 K 25:23; Jer 40:8—41:16); led Jeremiah and other Jews into Egypt (Jer 40—43). 2. Benjaminite; joined David at Ziklag (1 Ch 12:4). 3. Son of Josiah (1 Ch 3: 15). 4. Descendant of Zerubbabel (1 Ch 3:24); possibly Nahum (KJ: Naum) in Lk 3:25. 5. Son of Azariah; father of Azariah 16, the high priest (1 Ch 6:9, 10). 6. Gadite; joined David at Ziklag (1 Ch 12:12). 7. Ephraimite (2 Ch 28:12). 8. Returned with Ezra from Babylon (Ez 8:12; 1 Esd 8:38 [KJ: Johannes; RV: Joannes]). 9. 10. See *Jehohanan 6; 7.* 11. High priest (Neh 12:22, 23). Jonathan in Neh 12:11.

Johannes (jō-hăn'ēz). See *Jehohanan 3; Johanan 8.*

John (jŏn, LORD has been gracious, H *yohanan*). 1. Father of Mattathias (1 Mac 2 1). 2. Son of Mattathias (1 Mac 2:2. KJ: Joannan). 3. Obtained special privileges for the Jews (2 Mac 4:11). 4. John Hyrcanus, son of Simon Maccabaeus (1 Mac 13:53; 16). 5. Envoy sent to Lysias (2 Mac 11:17). 6. Father of apostle Peter (Jn 1:42 [KJ: Jona]; 21:15-17 [KJ: Jonas]). 7. John Mark. See *Mark.* 8. Jewish dignitary who called Peter and John to account (Acts 4:6). 9. See *John the Apostle.* 10. See *John the Baptist.*

John the Apostle. Son of Zebedee; brother of James (Mt 4:21; Acts 12:1, 2); mother was Salome (Mk 15:40; Mt 27:56); fisherman (Mk 1:19, 20) of Bethsaida (Lk 5:10; Jn 1:44); introduced to Jesus by John the Baptist (Jn 1:35, 39); followed Jesus (Jn 1:43; 2:2, 12, 23; 4:5); called as apostle (Mk 1:19, 20; Lk 5:10); one of inner circle; at raising of Jairus' daughter (Mk 5:37; Lk 8:51), transfiguration (Mt 17:1; Mk 9:2; Lk 9:28), Gethsemane (Mt 26:37; Mk 14:33); called *Boanerges* (sons of thunder) with James (Mk 3:17); asked Jesus to call fire from heaven (Lk 9:54); his mother asked for highest places for him and James (Mt 20: 20; Mk 10:35-45); prepared Passover with Peter (Lk 22:8). Identified as beloved disciple; leaned on Jesus' breast at Last Supper (Jn 13:23); gained admittance to Caiaphas' palace (Jn 18:15, 16); was only disciple at cross (Jn 19:26, 27); first to believe resurrection (Jn 20:1-10); recognized Jesus at Sea of Galilee (Jn 21:1-7). Waited in Jerusalem after Ascension (Acts 1:13); active with Peter (Acts 3:1—4:22; 8:14-17; Gl 2:9). Connected by tradition with Ephesus. Lived to old age. Gospel and Epistles of John and Revelation ascribed to him.

John the Baptist (jŏn băp'tĭst). Forerunner of Jesus; son of priest Zacharias and Elizabeth (Lk 1:5-25, 56-80); in austere life followed pattern of Elijah (Lk 1:17; Mt 11:12-14; 17:11, 12); began ministry in 15th year of Tiberias Caesar in regions of Jordan (Lk 3:1-3); preached baptism of repentance (Lk 3:4-14) and approach of kingdom of heaven (Mt 3:1-12); met and baptized Jesus (Mt 3:13-17; Mk 1:9,

10; Lk 3:21; Jn 1:32); bore witness to Jesus, called Him Messiah (Jn 1:24-42); imprisoned (Mk 6:17-20); beheaded (Mt 14:6-12; Mk 6:21-28). Jesus highly praised John (Mt 11:7-14; Lk 7:24-28). John's baptism continued for some time Acts 18:25). See also Josephus, *Ant* XVIII, v.

John, Gospel of. Written by "the disciple whom Jesus loved" (Jn 21. See *John the Apostle);* eyewitness of events described; purpose is to show that "Jesus is the Christ, the Son of God; and that believing you may have life in His name" (Jn 20: 30, 31). Acts and words of Jesus are presented to reveal unique Person of Christ and His significance to world. Reaction of individual to True Light is delineated (Jn 1:9-13). It describes Jesus as eternal Logos (1:1-18), Messiah (1:41-51; 4:25, 26; 6:14; 7; 10:22-25; 17:3), Son of Man (3:12-15; 5:22-27; 6:62; 12: 27-36), Son of God (3:16; 5:17-31; 8:58; 10:29-39; 14:1). Outline: 1. Incarnate Word (1:1-9). 2. Initial Testimony (1: 19—2:11). 3. Self-Revelation Through Words and Deeds (2:12—12:50). 4. Self-Revelation in Connection with Passion and Resurrection (13—21). See *Jesus Christ.*

John, 1st Epistle of. Written to warn against Gnosticism and strengthen readers in Christian loyalty. Keynote: faith and love. Ascribed by early church to apostle John. Dated near end of 1st c. Outline: 1. Basis and Character of Fellowship (1:1—2:6). 2. Love of Brethren (2:7-27). 3. Abiding in God by Obedience and Love (2:28—3:24). 4. True Confession (4). 5. Adherence to Apostolic Teaching (5).

John, 2d Epistle of. Written to encourage readers to walk in light and warn against error. "Elect lady" (1) regarded as church or individual.

John, 3d Epistle of. Letter addressed to Gaius to commend him for truth of his life, service to brethren, to censure Diotrephes, and to praise Demetrius.

Joiada (joi'á-dá, LORD knows). 1. High priest (Neh 12:10, 11, 22; 13:28 [RSV: Jehoiada]). 2. See *Jehoiada 5.*

Joiakim (joi'á-kĭm, LORD establishes). High priest; son of Jeshua (Neh 12:10, 12, 26). Joakim (KJ: Joacim) in 1 Esd 5:5.

Joiarib (joi'á-rĭb, LORD defends. Used interchangeably with Jehoiarib). 1. See *Jehoiarib 1.* 2. Chief priest who returned with Zerubbabel (Neh 12:6, 19). 3. Secured Nethinim and Levites for temple service (Ez 8:16, 17). 4. Judahite (Neh 11:5).

Jokdeam (jŏk'dē-ăm). City of Judah (Jos 15:56).

Jokim (jō'kĭm). Judahite (1 Ch 4:22).

Jokmeam (jŏk'mē-ăm, people's existence). Levitical town of Ephraim (1 K 4:12 [KJ: Jokneam]; 1 Ch 6:68). Kibzaim in Jos 21:22.

Jokneam (jŏk'nē-ăm, people permitted to possess). 1. Levitical city (Tell Kaimon) 12 mi SW of Nazareth on Zebulun's boundary (Jos 12:22; 19:11; 21:34). 2. See *Jokmeam.*

Jokshan (jŏk'shăn, fowler). Son of Abraham (Gn 25:2, 3; 1 Ch 1:32).

Joktan (jŏk'tăn, small). Son of Eber; ancestor of 13 Arabian tribes (Gn 10:25-30; 1 Ch 1:19-23).

Joktheel (jŏk'thē-ĕl, subject to God?). 1. City of Judah (Jos 15:38). 2. Name given by Amaziah to Sela, city of Edom (2 K 14:7).

Jona (jō'ná). See *John 6.*

Jonadab (jŏn'á-dăb, LORD is bounteous). **1.** Son of David's brother Shimeah (2 Sm 13:3-35). **2.** Son (or descendant) of Rechab (Jer 35). Jehonadab, friend of Jehu, in 2 K 10:15, 23.

Jonah (jō'ná, dove. KJ in NT: Jonas). **1.** Son of Amittai of Gath-hepher; predicted victories over Syrians to Jeroboam II; preached to Nineveh (2 K 14:23-25; Jon 1:1). **2.** See *Eliezer 9.*

Jonah, Book of. Written to rebuke exclusive spirit and show that God's mercy extends to all (4:11). Not prophecy in strict sense but typical in character (Mt 12:39-41; 16:4). Outline: 1. Jonah's Commission, Disobedience, Punishment (1:1-16). 2. Jonah's Deliverance (1:17—2:10). 3. Jonah Preaches, Nineveh Repents (3). 4. God's Mercy Defended (4).

Jonam, Jonan (jō'năm, jō'năn). Ancestor of Christ (Lk 3:30).

Jonas (jō'nás). See *Eliezer 9; Jehohanan 6; John 6; Jonah 1.*

Jonathan (jŏn'á-thăn, LORD has given). **1.** Levite; officiated before image for Micah and later for Danites (Ju 17; 18). **2.** Son of Saul (1 Sm 13:16; 14:49; 1 Ch 8:33); successfully fought Philistines (1 Sm 13; 14); devoted to David and (ignoring fact that he himself was successor) stripped himself of royal robe, girdle, and sword, and pledged loyalty to David (1 Sm 18:4; 20:42); defended David from Saul's anger (1 Sm 19:1-7; 20); killed with Saul at Mt Gilboa (1 Sm 31:2-10; 2 Sm 1:17-27). **3.** Son of Abiathar; friend of David (2 Sm 15:27, 36; 17:17-21; 1 K 1:42, 43). **4.** Uncle of David (1 Ch 27:32). **5.** Nephew of David; slew giant (2 Sm 21:21). **6.** One of David's heroes (1 Ch 11:34; 2 Sm 23:32). **7.** See *Jehonathan.* **8.** Son of Kareah (Jer 40:8). **9.** Scribe in whose house Jeremiah was imprisoned (Jer 37: 15, 20). **10.** Son of Jada (1 Ch 2:32). **11.** Father of Ebed (Ez 8:6). **12.** Son of Asahel; prominent in matter of divorcing foreign wives (Ez 10:15). **13.** See *Johanan 11.* **14.** Levite (Neh 12:35). **15.** Priest (Neh 12:14). **16.** See *Maccabees.*

Jonathas (jŏn'á-thăs). See *Jathan.*

Jonath-elem-rechokim (jō'năth-ē'lĕm-rĕ-kō'kĭm). Probably melody (Ps 56 title. RSV: according to The Dove on Far-off Terebinths. RV: Jonath-elem-rehokim).

Joppa, Joppe (jŏp'á, jŏp'ĕ, beauty). Ancient walled seaport (modern Jaffa) 34 mi NW of Jerusalem; named in the lists of Thutmose III and Amarna Letters; assigned to Dan (Jos 19:46 [KJ: Japho]; 2 Ch 2:16; Ez 3:7; Jon 1:3). Conquered by Jonathan Maccabeus (1 Mac 10:74-76. KJ: Joppe). Simon Peter active there (Acts 9—11).

Jorah (jō'rá, autumn rain). See *Hariph 1.*

Jorai (jō'rā-ī). Gadite (1 Ch 5:13).

Joram (jō'răm, LORD is high. Interchangeable with longer form Jehoram). **1.** See *Hadoram 2.* **2.** Levite; descendant of Eliezer (1 Ch 26:25). **3.** 9th king of Israel; son of Ahab; with kings of Judah and Edom defeated Moabites (2 K 3: 1-27); undoubtedly king to whom Naaman came (2 K 5) and who sent Syrians home unmolested (2 K 6:8-23); killed by Jehu, who threw his body in Naboth's vineyard (2 K 9:14-26). **4.** Priest (2 Ch 17:8). **5.** Son of Jehoshaphat; 5th king of Judah; his father killed his brothers and princes of Judah; his wife, daughter of Ahab, led him into idolatry; harassed by Edomites, Philistines, Arabs (2 K 8: 16-24; 2 Ch 21). **6.** See *Jozabad 5.*

Jordan (jôr'd'n, downrusher). Chief river of Palestine; flows in fissure which extends from between Lebanon and Anti-Lebanon through Sea of Galilee to Dead Sea (and beyond). Valley is 160 mi long, 2 to 15 mi wide, and as much as 1,292 ft below sea level. River is 3 to 10 ft deep and about 100 ft wide (Gn 13:10; Jos 2:7; Ju 3:28; Mt 3:13).

Joribus (jôr'ĭ-bus). See *Jarib 1; 2.*

Jorim (jō'rĭm). Ancestor of Christ (Lk 3: 29).

Jorkeam, Jorkoam (jôr'kĕ-ăm, jôr'kō-ăm). Descendant of Caleb (1 Ch 2:44) or place in Judah (Jokdeam).

Josabad (jŏs'á-băd). See *Jozabad 1; 6; Zabbai 1.*

Josabdus (jō-săb'dŭs). See *Jozabad 6.*

Josaphat (jŏs'á-făt). See *Jehoshaphat 4.*

Josaphias (jŏs-á-fī'ás). See *Josiphiah.*

Jose (jō'sĕ. RV, RSV: Jesus). Ancestor of Christ (Lk 3:29).

Josech (jō'sĕk. KJ: Joseph). Ancestor of Christ (Lk 3:26).

Josedec, Josedech, Josedek (jŏs'ĕ-dĕk). See *Jehozadak.*

Joseph (jō'zef, he adds). **1.** Son of Jacob and Rachel (Gn 30:22-24); Jacob's favorite child (Gn 37:3, 4); sold into Egypt (Gn 37); resisted temptation of Potiphar's wife and imprisoned (Gn 39); promoted to high officer by Pharaoh (Gn 40; 41); saved his family from famine (42—45); settled them in Goshen (Gn 47); d at 110; bones brought to Shechem (Jos 24: 32). **2.** Issacharite; father of spy Igal (Nm 13:7). **3.** Son of Asaph; leader of 1st division of musicians (1 Ch 25:2, 9). **4.** Divorced foreign wife (Ez 10:42; 1 Esd 9:34 [KJ, RV: Josephus]). **5.** Priest (Neh 12:14). **6. 7. 8.** Ancestors of Christ (Lk 3:24, 26 [see *Josech*], 30). **9.** General under Judas Maccabaeus (1 Mac 5:18, 56). **10.** Husband of Mary, mother of Jesus (Mt 1:16; Lk 3:23); carpenter (Mt 13:55); took home his wife (Mt 1:18-23); went to Bethlehem for census; Jesus born there (Lk 2:4-6); presented Jesus in temple (Lk 2:22-40); took Jesus and His mother to Egypt (Mt 2:13-18); returned to Nazareth (Mt 2:19-23); took 12-yr-old Jesus to Jerusalem (Lk 2:41-52). **11.** Joseph of Arimathea; member of Sanhedrin; acknowledged Christ (Mt 27: 57-60; Mk 15:42-46; Lk 23:50-53). **12.** Barsabbas, surnamed Justus (Acts 1:23). **13.** "Brother of the Lord" (Mt 13:55 [KJ: Joses]; 27:56 [KJ, RV: Joses]). Joses in Mk 6:3; 15:40, 47. **14.** Personal name of Barnabas (Acts 4:36. KJ: Joses). **15.** Brother of Judas Maccabeus (2 Mac 8:2). **16.** Ancestor of Judith (Jdth 8:1).

Josephus (jō-sē'fus). See *Joseph 4.*

Joses (jō'sēz, G for Joseph). **1.** See *Joseph 13. 2.* See *Jose. 3.* See *Joseph 14.*

Joshah (jō'shá). Simeonite prince (1 Ch 4: 34).

Joshaphat (jŏsh'á-făt, LORD has judged). **1.** Priest; blew trumpet before ark (1 Ch 15:24. KJ: Jehoshaphat). **2.** One of David's heroes (1 Ch 11:43).

Joshaviah (jŏsh-á-vī'á). One of David's warriors (1 Ch 11:46).

Joshbekashah (jŏsh-bĕ-kā'shá, he returns a hard fate?). Son of Heman; leader of 17th course of musicians (1 Ch 25:4, 24).

Josheb-basshebeth (jō'shĕb-băs-shē'bĕth. KJ: Adino the Eznite. KJ margin: Josheb-bassebet the Tachmonite. H shebeth). One of David's heroes (2 Sm 23:8). Probably Jashobeam (1 Ch 11:11).

Joshibiah (jŏsh-ĭ-bī'á, LORD gives dwelling. KJ: Josibiah). Simeonite (1 Ch 4:35).

Joshua (jŏsh'ū-á, LORD is salvation. Later Jeshua, Jesus). 1. Assistant and successor of Moses; Ephraimite; son of Nun (Ex 33:11; Nm 13:8, 16; 1 Ch 7:27); commander against Amalekites (Ex 17:8-16); went part of way up Sinai (Ex 32:17); in charge of tabernacle (Ex 33:11); spy of Canaan (Nm 13 [here Moses changed his name Hoshea — KJ: Oshea — to Joshua — KJ: Jehoshua]; 14); succeeded Moses (Dt 31; Jos 1); entered Canaan, conquered land, apportioned it (Jos); died and buried at Timnath-serah (Jos 24:29). Jeshua in Neh 8:17. KJ: Jesus in Acts 7:45; Heb 4:8. 2. Native of Bethshemesh (1 Sm 6:14). 3. Governor of Jerusalem (2 K 23:8). 4. See *Jeshua 4.*

Joshua, Book of. In Bible, first of "former prophets." In later times made last book of Hexateuch. Purpose: teach God's will for Israel and show how God gave His people land promised them while still strangers (Heb 11:13). Outline: 1. Conquest of Canaan (1—12). 2. Partition of Territory (13—22). 3. Joshua's Farewell Address (22—24). See *Joshua 1.*

Josiah (jŏ-sī'á, LORD supports). 1. 16th king of Judah; son of Amon and Jedidah (2 K 22:1); in 8th year of reign began to seek after God of David (2 Ch 34:3); suppressed idolatry in Judah and Israel; repaired temple and found book of Law which was publicly read; defeated and killed by Pharaoh-Necho at Megiddo (2 K 22; 23; 2 Ch 34; 35). KJ, RV: Josias in Mt 1:10, 11; 1 Esd 1:1; Bar 1:8. 2. Son of Zephaniah (Zch 6:10). KJ, RV: Hen in v. 14.

Josias (jŏ-sī'as). 1. G form of Josiah. See *Josiah 1.* 2. See *Jeshaiah 4.*

Josibiah (jŏs-ĭ-bī'á). See *Joshibiah.*

Josiphiah (jŏs-ĭ-fī'-á, LORD will add). Progenitor of family which returned with Ezra (Ez 8:10; 1 Esd 8:36 [KJ, RV: Josaphias]).

jot. Smallest letter in H (*yodh*, y) and G (*iota*, i) alphabet (Mt 5:18. RSV: iota).

Jotbah (jŏt'bá, pleasantness). City of Haruz, grandfather of Amon (2 K 21:19).

Jotbath, Jotbathah (jŏt'băth, jŏt'bá-thá, pleasantness). Encampment of Israel; perh near Ezion-geber (Nm 33:33, 34; Dt 10:7 [KJ: Jotbath]).

Jotham (jō'thăm, LORD is upright). 1. Son of Gideon. When Shechem made Abimelech king, Jotham told parable of trees and bramble (Ju 9). 2. 11th king of Judah; regent of father Uzziah and later sole king; good; fortified Jerusalem, built fortresses in Judah; fought successfully against Ammonites (2 K 15; 2 Ch 27); contemporary with Isaiah (Is 1:1), Hosea (Hos 1:1) and Micah (Mi 1:1); ancestor of Jesus (Mt 1:9. KJ: Joatham). 3. Judahite (1 Ch 2:47).

journey. See *measure 1.*

joy. OT: delight of mind; gladness in its mild form, tumultous, excited exaltation (H *gil*, leap, spin) in its stronger phases. It is expressed over Law (Ps 119), judgments (Ps 48:11), pardon (Ps 51), salvation (Ps 9:14; 13:5), presence of God (Dt 12:7-18; 14:26). NT: expressed over God's salvation (Lk 1:47), presence of bridegroom (Jn 3:29), outpouring of Spirit (Acts 13:52), Lord's Supper (Acts 2:46). Joy is gift of Spirit (Gl 5:22) through nearness of Lord (Ph 4:4. See 2 Co 13:11; 1 Th 5:16), exultation over grace (Ro 5:2, 11), element of fellowship (2 Co 1:24; Ph 1:25, 26; 1 Th 2:20), even expressed in affliction (2 Co 13:9; Cl 1:11; Ja 1:2; 1 Ptr 1:8).

Jozabad (jŏz'á-băd, LORD has bestowed). 1. Gederathite; joined David at Ziklag (1 Ch 12:4. KJ: Josabad). 2. 3. Manassites; joined David at Ziklag (1 Ch 12:20). 4. Levite, supervisor of tithes (2 Ch 31:13). 5. Levite (2 Ch 35:9). Joram in 1 Esd 1:9. 6. Levite; son of Jeshua (Ez 8:33; 1 Esd 8:63 [KJ: Josabad; RV: Josabdus]). Probably same in Ez 10:23; Neh 8:7; 11:16; 1 Esd 9:23 (RV: Jozabdus). 7. Priest; divorced foreign wife (Ez 10:22). Ocidelus (RSV: Gedaliah) in 1 Esd 9:22.

Jozabdus (jŏ-zăb'dŭs). See *Jozabad 6; Zabbai 1.*

Jozacar, Jozachar (jŏz'á-kär, LORD has remembered). One of assassins of Joash (2 K 12:21). Zabad in 2 Ch 24:26.

Jozadak (jŏz'á-dăk). See *Jehozadak.*

Jubal (jōō'băl, perh related to H *jobel*: ram's horn). Son of Lamech; inventor of instruments of music (Gn 4:19-21).

jubilee (jōō'bĭ-lē, blast of trumpets). Celebrated every 50th year, or after 7 sabbaths of years (7×7). Announced by blast of trumpet; land rested that year; landed property returned to original owner; Israelite slaves freed (Lv 25:8-55; 27:16-25; Eze 46:17).

Jucal (jōō'kăl). See *Jehucal.*

Juda (jōō'dá). See *Joda 2; Judah 1; 2; Judas 2; 4.*

Judaea (jōō-dē'á). See *Judea.*

Judah (jōō'dá, praise). 1. 4th son of Jacob and Leah (Gn 29:35); suggested that Joseph be sold to Ishmaelites instead of slain (Gn 37:26, 27); married Canaanite woman (Gn 38:1-11); had twin sons by Tamar, his daughter-in-law (Gn 38: 12-30); became leader of family (Gn 43: 3-10; 44:16-34); received blessing of Scepter (Gn 49:8-12). KJ: Juda, Judas in NT.
2. Tribe of Judah marched with Issachar and Zebulun in van (Nm 2:3-9); acquired most of S Palestine (Jos 15. 20-63); David and Solomon were kings of Israel from Judah; Jesus came from tribe of Judah through Boaz, Jesse, and David (Lk 3:23-32). KJ: Juda in NT.
3. Kingdom of Judah began when 10 N tribes withdrew from Rehoboam (c 912) and lasted until 587 BC, when Jerusalem fell. In 538 Cyrus permitted Jews to return (1 K 12—22; 2 K; 2 Ch 11—36; Ez; Neh).
4. Levite (Neh 12:8). 5. Benjaminite (Neh 11:9). 6. See *Hodaviah 4.* 7. Levite; divorced foreign wife (Ez 10:23; 1 Esd 9:23 [KJ, RV: Judas]). 8. Prince of Judah; took part in dedication of Jerusalem wall (Neh 12:34). 9. Levite musician; took part in dedication of Jerusalem wall (Neh 12:36). Perhaps same as 4 and/or 7.

Judas (jōō'dás, H Judah). 1. See *Judah 1.* 2. Ancestor of Jesus (Lk 3:30. KJ: Juda). 3. Iscariot (man of Kerioth); called apostle (Mt 10:4; Mk 3:19; Lk 6:16); steward for Jesus and apostles (Jn 12: 4-6; 13:29); became greedy (Mt 26:6-13; Mk 14:3-9; Jn 12:3-9); betrayed Jesus (Mt 26:47-49); regretted deed; hanged himself (Mt 27:3-5; Acts 1:17, 18). 4. Brother of Jesus (Mt 13:55; Mk 6:3. KJ: Juda). See *Jude, Epistle of.* 5. Judas, surnamed Thaddeus (Mt 10:3; Mk 3:18) and Lebbaeus (heart; KJ: Mt 10:3) as appears from placement of names in lists; apostle; son or brother of a James (Lk 6:16. See Jn 14:22). 6. Man in Damascus to whom Paul went after his conversion (Acts 9:11). 7. Barsabbas (Acts 15:22, 27, 32). 8. Judas of Galilee; rebel (Acts 5:37). 9. See *Judah 7.* 10. See *Maccabees.*

Jude (jōōd). See *Judas 4; 5.*
Jude, Epistle of. Catholic epistle written by "Jude . . . brother of James"; identified with Judas 4. Outline: 1. Salutation and Preface (1-4). 2. Condemnation of False Teachers (5-16). 3. Admonitions (17-23). 4. Doxology (24, 25).
Judea (jōō-dē'à, RV once, KJ: Judaea). Term used in Ez 5:8 (KJ) and 9:9 (RSV) for province to which tribes of Judah and Benjamin returned (usually called Judah, Neh 2:7). Province mentioned in 1 Esd 1:35, 39; 1 Mac 5:45; 7:10 (KJ). At time of Christ (Mt 2:1; often), S division of three (Galilee, Samaria, Judea) regions into which Roman Province of Palestine was divided. About 55 mi long and wide, located E of Jordan and Dead Sea from Beersheba in S to line from Joppa to 10 mi N of Dead Sea in N.
judges. Governors, leaders, and deliverers of Israelites between times of Joshua and Saul (Othniel, Ehud, Shamgar, Deborah, Barak, Gideon, Abimelech, Tola, Jair, Jephthah, Ibzan, Elon, Abdon, Samson). Eli (high priest), Samuel (prophet) functioned as judges. Their activity described in Book of Judges.
Judges, Book of. History of Israel from death of Joshua to time of Samuel. Chronology of book has presented difficulty since more than one judge may have ruled in different sectors at same time. Book covers period of about 300 years. Outline: 1. Introduction (1:1 to 3:6). 2. Deeds of the Judges (3:7—16). 3. Founding of the Sanctuary at Dan (17, 18). 4. Outrage of the Benjaminites at Gibeah (19—21).
judgment. OT: Occasionally administration of justice (2 Sm 15:4; 1 K 3); usually keeping people in right relation to covenant (Is 11; 61). God's judgments are salvation, victory, deliverance of covenant God (Dt 32:36; Ju 5:11; Is 30:18; Jer 30:11). Judgment, however, is not on purely national line but based on relationship to Jehovah (Is 2:12; Am 5: 18). Judgment preserves remnant (Is 6: 13). Judgments point to final judgment, Day of Jehovah, which centers in God's self-expression (Is 25; Zch 14). NT: Sometimes administration of law (Jn 18: 31; Acts 23:3); usually judgment of God and includes salvation of believers (Lk 18:1-8; 2 Th 1:5-10; Ro 1:18-32; 1 Co 11:29-32), culminates in Final Judgment

(Mt 11:20-24; 25:31-46; Jn 16:11; 1 Th 4:13-18). Final judgment belongs to God (Mt 18:35; Ro 14:10) and administered by Christ (Mt 25:31-46). Angels (Mk 8: 38), believers collaborate (1 Co 6:2, 3). Judgment is salvation to believers, condemnation to unbelievers (Mt 25:31-46). Criterion of judgment is Law (Mt 25); since Law has been fulfilled by Christ, relationship to Him is decisive factor (Mt 10:32, 33; Ro 8:1-17; Gl 5:13-25).
Judgment Hall. See *Praetorium.*
Judith (jōō'dith, praised; Jewess). 1. Wife of Esau (Gn 26:34). Oholibamah (KJ: Aholibamah, my tent is a high place) in Gn 36:2. 2. Heroine of Jdth.
Juel (jōō'el). See *Joel 12; Uel.*
Julia (jōōl'yà, soft-haired). Christian woman at Rome (Ro 16:15).
Julius (jōōl'yus, soft-haired). Centurion of Augustan band who conducted Paul and other prisoners to Rome (Acts 27).
Junia, Junias (jōō'nǐ-à, -ǎs). Friend of Paul at Rome (Ro 16:7).
juniper (jōō'nǐ-pẽr). See *broom.*
Jupiter (jōō'pǐ-tẽr). See *Zeus.*
Jushab-hesed. (jōō'shǎb-hē'sĕd, stedfast love is returned). Son of Zerubbabel (1 Ch 3:20).
justice. Based solely on God as source of righteousness. Justice in Israel derives from God's dealings in harmony with His covenant (Ex 19:4-6; 20; Dt 29; 30), which is basis of Law. This justice embraces every Israelite; includes service to fellows (Ex 20; Is 1:10-31; Mi 6:6-11) and same for all (Ex 22:21-27; Dt 24: 14-22).
justification. Act of God whereby He applies Christ's universal reconciliation to believers (2 Co 5:18-21), though they are unworthy because of transgression of God's Law (Ro 1—3; 5:12-20). By faith (Gn 15:6; Lk 15; Ro 4:16; Gl 3:22) they receive Christ's righteousness offered in Gospel (Ro 1:16; Jn 15:3; Gl 3:27). See *reconciliation.*
Justus (jŭs'tus, just). 1. Surname of Barsabbas (Acts 1:23). 2. Christian at Corinth (Acts 18:7). 3. See *Jesus 3.*
Jutah, Juttah (jōō'tà, jŭt'à, extend). Town in Judah, 5½ mi SW of Hebron, assigned to priests (Jos 15:55 [RV: Jutah]; 21:16). Modern Yuttah. Perhaps same as "city of Judah" (Lk 1:39), birthplace of John the Baptist.

K

kab (kǎb). See *measures 2b.*
Kabzeel (kǎb'zē-ĕl, God brings together). City in S Judah (Jos 15:21); home of Benaiah (2 Sm 23:20; 1 Ch 11:22). Jekabzeel in Neh 11:25.
Kades (kā'dēz). See *Kadesh 1.*
Kadesh (kā'dĕsh, consecrated). 1. Camp site of Israel in desert c 70 mi S of Hebron; earlier called En-mishpat (Gn 14:7); Hagar fled to its regions (Gn 16:7, 14); Miriam died there (Nm 20:1); Moses struck rock there instead of speaking to it; hence called Meribah (strife. Nm 20: 2-13); thence Moses sent messengers to Edom (Nm 20:14-21) and spies to Palestine (Nm 13:21-26; Dt 1:19-25); Israel spent 37 yrs in vicinity. KJ: Kades in Jdth 1:9. Often Kadesh-barnea (as Nm 32:8; Dt 2:14; Jdth 5:14 [KJ: Cades-Barne]). 2. Place (according to G) men-

tioned in 2 Sm 24:6 (RSV. KJ, RV, H: Tahtim-hodshi). See *Kedesh 3.*
Kadesh-barnea (-bär'nē-à). See *Kadesh 1.*
Kadmiel (kǎd'mǐ-ĕl, God is ancient one). 1. Progenitor of Levitical family which returned with Ezra (Ez 2:40; Neh 7:43; 12:8, 24; 1 Esd 5:26 [KJ: Cadmiel]). 2. One or more Levites who helped rebuild temple (Ez 3:9; 1 Esd 5:58 [KJ: Cadmiel]); took part in penance (Neh 9:4, 5); sealed covenant (Neh 10:9).
Kadmonites (kǎd'mon-īts, people of E). Ancient Arab tribe (Gn 15: 19-21).
Kain (kān). 1. Term for Kenite (Nm 24: 22. KJ: Kenite). 2. Town in Judah 3 mi SE of Hebron (Jos 15:57. KJ: Cain). Modern Yaqin.
Kaiwan (kī'wän). See *Chiun.*
Kallai (kǎl'à-ī, swift). Chief priest (Neh 12:20).

Kamon (kā'mŏn). Place of Jair's burial (Ju 10:5. KJ: Camon).

Kanah (kā'nà, place of reeds). 1. Stream between Ephraim and Manasseh; empties into Mediterranean (Jos 16:8; 17:9). 2. Town SE of Tyre assigned to Asher (Jos 19:28).

Kareah (kà-rē'à, bald). Father of Johanan and Jonathan, contemporaries of Jeremiah (2 K 25:23 [KJ: Careah]; Jer 40:8).

Kariathiarius (kā-rĭ-ăth-ĭ-â'rĭ-us). See Kiriath-jearim.

Karka, Karkaa (kär'kà, kär'kâ-à, floor). Place on Judah's S boundary (Jos 15:3).

Karkor (kär'kôr, soft level ground). Place E of Jordan where Gideon attacked Zebah and Zalmunna (Ju 8:10).

Karnaim (kär-nā'ĭm, two horns). City in Gilead where Syrian nature goddess Atargatis was worshiped (Am 6:13. KJ, RV: horns). Carnaim in 1 Mac 5:26, 43, 44; 2 Mac 12:21, 26 (KJ, RV: Carnion).

Kartah (kär'tà, city). Levitical town of Zebulun (Jos 21:34).

Kartan (kär'tăn, twin cities?). See Kiriathaim 2.

Kattath (kăt'ăth). Town of Zebulun (Jos 19:15). Sometimes identified with Kitron or Kartah.

Kedar (kē'dēr, dark). 1. Son of Ishmael (Gn 25:13; 1 Ch 1:29); progenitor of tribe. 2. Arabians who lived in black tents, had flocks and camels (SS 1:5; Is 21:13-17; 42:11; 60:7; Jer 49:28, 29; Eze 27:21).

Kedemah (kĕd'ê-mà, eastward). Son of Ishmael; progenitor of tribe (Gn 25:15; 1 Ch 1:31).

Kedemoth (kĕd'ê-mŏth, east). 1. Wilderness E of Dead Sea (Dt 2:26). 2. Levitical town of this region assigned to Reuben (Jos 13:18; 21:37; 1 Ch 6:79).

Kedesh (kē'dĕsh, sacred place). 1. Town in S Judah (Jos 15:23). Probably Kadesh 1. 2. Levitical town of Issachar (1 Ch 6:72). Kishion in Jos 19:20; 21:28 (KJ: Kishon). 3. City of refuge in Naphtali, NW of Lake Huleh (Jos 19:37; 1 Mac 11:63-73 [KJ: Cades. RSV: Kadesh]); king slain by Joshua (Jos 12:22); captured by Tiglath-pileser (2 K 15:29). Kedesh-naphtali (RSV: Kedesh in Naphtali), home of Barak, in Ju 4:6. Kedesh Naphtali (KJ: that city which is rightfully called Nephtali) in Tob 1:2. Kedesh in Galilee in Jos 20:7; 21:32; 1 Ch 6:76.

Kedesh-naphtali, Kedesh Naphtali. See Kedesh 3.

Kedron (kĕd'rŏn). See Kidron.

Kehelathah (kē-hê-lā'thà, assembly). Encampment of Israel in desert (Nm 33:22, 23).

Keilah (kē-ī'là). 1. City in lowlands of Judah (Jos 15:44); David delivered it from Philistines (1 Sm 23:7-13); prominent after Exile (Neh 3:17, 18). 2. Grandson of Hodiah (1 Ch 4:19).

Kelaiah (kē-lā'yà). See Kelita.

Kelita (kĕl'ĭ-tà, dwarf). Levite; read Law to people (Neh 8:7; 1 Esd 9:48 [KJ, RV: Calitas]); sealed covenant (Neh 10:10). Kelaiah (divorced foreign wife) in Ez 10:23 (KJ, RV: Colius in 1 Esd 9:23), with surname Kelita (KJ: Colitus; RV: Calitas in 1 Esd 9:23).

Kemuel (kĕm'ū-ĕl, congregation of God). 1. Son of Nahor; father of Aram (Gn 22:21). 2. Ephraimite; helped apportion land (Nm 34:24). 3. Levite; father of Hashabiah (1 Ch 27:17).

Kenan (kē'năn). See Cainan.

Kenath (kē'năth, possession). City W of Hauran Mts; easternmost of Decapolis cities (1 Ch 2:23). For a while called Nobah after one of its conquerors (Nm 32:42). Modern Kanawat.

Kenaz (kē'năz). 1. Descendant of Esau; ancestor of Kenizzites (Gn 36:11, 15, 42). 2. Descendant of Caleb (1 Ch 4:15). 3. Father of Othniel (Jos 15:17; Ju 1:13; 3:9).

Kenezite (kē'nĕz-īt). See Kenizzites.

Kenites (kē'nīts). Bedouin smiths, Midianites related to Kenizzites (Gn 15:19). Moses' father-in-law was Kenite (Ju 1:16); Hobab, son of Raguel, Kenite, guided Israel in desert (Nm 10:29-32; Ju 1:16; 4:11). Rechabites were Kenites (1 Ch 2:55); on friendly terms with Israelites and settled in Wadi Arabah (Nm 24:20-22), near Hebron (Ju 1:16), in Naphtali (Ju 4:11), and S Judah (1 Sm 15:6; 27:10; 30:29).

Kenizzites (kē'nĭz-īts). Descendants of Kenaz (Gn 36:11); inhabitants of S Canaan before Israel. Apparently conquered by and merged with Edomites (Gn 15:19; Dt 2:12). Caleb (Nm 32:12; Jos 14:6, 14), Othniel (Jos 15:17) were Kenizzites. Tribe or part of it may have merged with Judah.

kenosis (kē-nō'sĭs, G emptying). Term applied to Jesus' humiliation (Ph 2:7).

Keras (kē'răs). See Keros.

Keren-happuch (kĕr'en-hăp'uk, horn of antimony). Job's 3d daughter born after his trial (Jb 42:14).

Kerioth (kē'rĭ-ŏth, cities). 1. See Kerioth-hezron. 2. Town of Moab (Jer 48:24, 41); described as having palaces (Am 2:2. KJ: Kirioth); often identified with Ar.

Kerioth-hezron (kē'rĭ-ŏth-hĕz'rŏn. KJ: Kerioth and Hezron). City in S Judah (Jos 15:25), probably home of Judas Iscariot. Also called Hazor.

Keros (kē'rŏs, reed of weaver's loom). Ancestor of Nethinim (Ez 2:44; Neh 7:47; 1 Esd 5:29 [KJ: Ceras; RV: Keras]).

Ketab (kē'tăb. KJ: Cetab). Listed in 1 Esd 5:30.

Keturah (ke-tū'rà, incense). Wife of Abraham (Gn 25:1-6; 1 Ch 1:32, 33) by whom he became progenitor of E nations.

key. Piece of wood with pegs to fit holes in wooden bolt (Ju 3:25; Is 22:22). Figuratively: power; authority (Is 22:22; Lk 11:52; Rv 3:7). Keys of Kingdom are power given by Christ through apostles (Mt 16:19; 18:18) to church to admit to, or exclude from (loose or bind), kingdom of heaven, i. e., to forgive or retain sins.

Kezia, Keziah (ke-zī'à, cassia). Job's 2d daughter born after his trial (Jb 42:14).

Keziz (kē'zĭz). See Emek-keziz.

Kibroth-hattaavah (kĭb'rŏth-hă-tā'à-và, graves of lust). Encampment of Israel c 30 mi NE of Sinai. There Israel buried those who died in plague because they lusted for fleshpots of Egypt (Nm 11:34, 35; 33:16, 17; Dt 9:22).

Kibzaim (kĭb-zā'ĭm, double heap). See Jokmeam.

kid. Young goat; favorite food (Gn 38:17; 1 Sm 16:20; Lk 15:29); used for sacrifice (Ju 13:15-19).

kidnapers. See menstealers.

kidney. Used with surrounding fat for burnt offering (Ex 29:13, 22; Lv 3:4-15). Figuratively: seat of emotion and desire (Ps 73:21; Jb 16:13; 19:27; Pr 23:16. KJ: reins. RV, RSV: heart, except Jb 16:13 [RV: reins. RSV: kidneys]).

Kidron (kǐd'rŏn. KJ: Cedron. RSV: Kedron). Town named with Jamnia and Azotus; fortified by Cendebeus; burned by Maccabees (1 Mac 15:39-41; 16:9, 10). Some identify with Gederoth.

Kidron, Brook. Ravine and winter brook which begins NW of Jerusalem, joins with Valley of Hinnom to extend 20 mi to Dead Sea; early became burial ground (2 K 23:6), dumping place for destroyed idols and their altars (1 K 15:13; 2 Ch 29:16; 30:14 [RSV: Kidron valley]). David fled across it from Absalom (2 Sm 15:23); Jesus crossed it on way to Gethsemane (Jn 18:1 [KJ: Cedron. RSV: Kidron valley]).

Kilan (kī'lăn. KJ: Ceilan). Listed in 1 Esd 5:15.

kiln (kĭl). See *furnace 3; trade 6.*

Kinah (kī'na, dirge). City in S Judah (Jos 15:22).

kindness, loving-kindness. See *steadfast love.*

kine. KJ, RV at times for cattle, cows.

king. LORD (Jehovah) King of Israel (Dt 33:1-5; 1 Sm 8:7; 10:19; 12:12). Kings under God, subject to democratic processes (1 K 12:16), moral law, and denunciation of prophets (2 Sm 12; 1 K 12:16; 21:20-24); Israel had kings from Saul to Zedekiah (c 1020—587 BC). Kings had scepters (Ps 45:6), crown (2 K 11:12), throne (1 K 2:19), palace (1 K 7:1-12), etc. Officers of king included army officers (1 Sm 14:50), captain of bodyguard (2 Sm 20:23), recorder (2 Sm 8:16; 20:24), secretary (2 Sm 8:17), overseers (1 K 4:6; 2 Sm 20:24), counselors (2 Sm 15:12), and others.

kingdom of God. In OT God is described as King, that is, majestic and sovereign (Nm 23:21; Dt 33:5). He is King over whole earth (Ps 47:7), Israel (1 Sm 12:12; Is 44:6. Kings were God's representatives), remnant faithful to LORD (Mi 4:7), future spiritual kingdom (Is 9; 11; 61; Jer 23:5, 6; 33:15, 16) which includes all nations (Is 2:4; Jl 3:9-11; Zch 9:10). Gospel of Kingdom is proclamation of coming of God's reign. Kingdom comes through Word (Lk 4:43; 8:1; 9:11), actions (Mt 11:4, 5), casting out demons (Mt 12:25-28). Christ is Bearer and Fulfiller of Kingdom (Mt 12:28; Lk 17:20, 21). People enter Kingdom through repentance and faith (Mt 18:3, 4; Jn 3: 3—5). Membership in Kingdom produces self-denial and conformity to virtues of Kingdom (Mt 5—7; 19:12; Lk 9:60-62), culminates in cross and resurrection (Mt 26:29; Mk 14:25; Lk 22:15-30). Christ entered Kingdom by resurrection and ascension (Mt 28:18; Lk 24:26. See *Jesus Christ*). Its disclosure awaits *Parousia* (Acts 1:11). Church proclaims Kingdom by proclaiming Christ.

Kings, Books of. Originally one book; religious history; emphasize reward of good and punishment of evil; frequent mention of sources. Cover period from c 1000—560 BC. Archaeology has augmented or corroborated historical data. Outline: 1. Solomon's Reign (1 K 1—11). 2. Kings of Israel and Judah (1 K 12— 2 K 18). 3. Kings of Judah to Exile (2 K 18—25). See *kings of Judah and Israel.*

kings of Judah and Israel. Dates are only approximations which seek roughly to adhere to H text. There are textual and other difficulties (e. g., regencies; co-rule). 1. United kingdom: Saul (1030—1010 BC); David (1010—970); Solomon (970—931).

2. Judah: Rehoboam (931—915); Abijah (915—913); Asa (913—873); Jehoshaphat (873—849); Joram (849—843); Ahaziah (842); Athaliah (842—837); Joash (837 —800); Amaziah (800—?); Uzziah (?— 742); Jotham (750—735); Ahaz (735— 719); Hezekiah (719—690); Manasseh (690—639); Amon (639—638); Josiah (638—608); Jehoahaz (608); Jehoiakim (608—598); Jehoiachin (598); Zedekiah (598—587). 3. Kings of Israel: Jeroboam I (931—910); Nadab (910—909); Baasha (909—887); Elah (887—886); Zimri (886); Omri (886-875); Ahab (875— 853); Ahaziah (853—852); Joram (852 —842); Jehu (842—815); Jehoahaz (815 —799); Joash (799—784); Jeroboam II (784—745); Zechariah (745); Shallum (745); Menahem (745—736); Pekahiah (736—735); Pekah (?—730); Hoshea (730—722).

Kir (kûr, wall). 1. Place to which Tiglath-pileser led captive people of Damascus (2 K 16:9; Am 1:5); original home of Aramaeans (Am 9:7). 2. Fortified city of Moab built on 3,370-ft mt, c 11 mi E of Dead Sea (Is 15:1). Kir-hareseth in 2 K 3:25 (KJ: Kir-haraseth); Is 16:7. Kir-heres in Is 16:11 (KJ: Kir-haresh); Jer 48:31, 36. Modern Kerak.

Kirama (kǐr'à-mà). See *Ramah 5.*

Kir-haraseth, Kir-hareseth, Kir-haresh, Kir-heres (kûr-hăr'à-sĕth, -hăr'ĕ-sĕth, -hā'rĕsh, -hē'rĕs, wall of bricks or pottery). See *Kir 2.*

Kiriath (kǐr'ĭ-ăth, city. KJ: Kirjath). City of Benjamin (Jos 18:28).

Kiriathaim (kǐr-ĭ-à-thā'ĭm, twin city). 1. Town in Moab N of Arnon R, E of Dead Sea. Assigned to Reuben (Nm 32:37; Jos 13:19. KJ: Kirjathaim); later occupied by Moabites (Jer 48:1, 23; Eze 25:9). Site called Khirbet el Qereiyat. Shaveh-kiriathaim (plain of Kiriathaim) is probably surrounding region (Gn 14:5). 2. Levitical city (Khirbet el Qureiyeh) near Sea of Galilee (1 Ch 6:76. KJ: Kirja-thaim). Kartan in Jos 21:32.

Kiriath-arba (kǐr'ĭ-ăth-är'bà, city of Arba. KJ: Kirjath-arba except in Gn 35:27; Jos 15:13; 21:11: city of Arbah). Ancient name for Hebron (Gn 23:2; Jos 14:15; 15:54; 20:7; Ju 1:10; Neh 11:25).

Kiriath-arim (kǐr'ĭ-ăth-ā'rĭm). See *Kiriath-jearim.*

Kiriath-baal (kǐr'ĭ-ăth-bā'ăl, city of Baal). See *Kiriath-jearim.*

Kiriath-huzoth (kǐr'ĭ-ăth-hū'zŏth, city of streets. KJ: Kirjath-huzoth). City near Bamoth-baal (Nm 22:39).

Kiriathiarius (kǐr-ĭ-ăth-ĭ-à'r-ĭus). See *Kiriath-jearim.*

Kiriath-jearim (kǐr'ĭ-ăth-jē'à-rĭm, city of thickets. KJ: Kirjath-jearim. Kiriath-baal in Jos 15:60 [KJ: Kirjath-baal]. Kiriath-arim in Ex 2:25 [KJ: Kirjath-arim]; 1 Esd 5:19 [KJ: Kiriathiarius; RV: Hariathiarius]. Baalah in Jos 15: 9, 10. Baale-judah [KJ: Baale of Judah; RV: Baale Judah] in 2 Sam 6:2). Gibeonite town (Jos 9:17); assigned to Judah (Jos 15:60); later to Benjamin (Jos 18:28); located around Mt Jearim; ark remained there 20 yrs (1 Sm 6:19—7:2).

Kiriath-sannah, Kirith-sepher (kǐr'ĭ-ăth-săn'à, -sē'fĕr, city of scribes). See *Debir 2.*

Kirioth (kǐr'ĭ-ŏth). See *Kerioth.*

Kirjath (kûr'jăth). See *Kiriath* and its compounds.

Kiseus (kĭs'ē-us). See *Kish 5.*

Kish (kĭsh). 1. Benjaminite; father of Saul (1 Sm 9:3; 10:11; 1 Ch 9:39; Acts 13:21 [KJ: Cis]); son of Abiel (1 Sm 9:1). Called son of Ner in 1 Ch 8:33; 9:39. 2. Uncle of Kish, father of Saul (1 Ch 8:30; 9:36). 3. Merarite Levite (1 Ch 23:21, 22; 24:29). 4. Later Merarite Levite (2 Ch 29:12). 5. Ancestor of Mordecai (Est 2:5; Ap Est 11:2 [KJ: Cisai; RV: Kiseus]).

Kishi (kĭsh'ĭ). See Kushaiah.

Kishion (kĭsh'ĭ-ŏn). See Kedesh 2.

Kishon (kī'shŏn, winding). 1. See Kedesh 2. 2. Small river; sources are springs near Tabor, stream starting near Gilboa, meeting in plain of Esdraelon (Ju 4:7, 13; 5:21; 1 K 18:40; Ps 83:9 [KJ: Kison]).

Kison (kī'sŏn). See Kishon 2.

kiss. Affectionate salutation (Gn 29:11-13; Ru 1:14; Lk 15:20). Early church practiced kiss of charity as symbolic of fraternity (Ro 16:16; 1 Co 16:20; 1 Ptr 5:14). Judas used kiss to betray Jesus (Lk 22:47-53). Feet kissed as sign of reverence or submission (Ps 2:12; Lk 7:45).

kite. See vulture.

Kithlish (kĭth'lĭsh). See Chithlish.

Kitron (kĭt'rŏn, burning). Town of Zebulun, probably Kattath (Ju 1:30).

Kittim (kĭt'tĭm, KJ usually: Chittim). 1. Descendants of Javan; place where they dwelt (Gn 10:4; Nm 24:24; 1 Ch 1:7; Dn 11:30). Name probably extended from Citium to all Cyprus, then loosely to Mediterranean coasts and islands. Is 23:12; Jer 2:10; Eze 27:6 have H Kittiyim (KJ: Chittim. RV: Kittim. RSV: Cyprus). 2. Macedonia or Macedonians (1 Mac 1:1 [KJ: Chettim. RV: Chittim]; 8:5 [KJ: Citims. RV: Chittim. RSV: Macedonians]). See also Macedonia.

kneading-trough. Shallow pottery or wooden vessel for kneading dough with hands (Ex 8:3 [RSV: kneading bowls]; Dt 28:5, 17 [KJ: store]).

knee, kneel. To bow the knee, or kneel, is attitude of reverence (Gn 41:43; 2 K 1:13), worship (Ps 95:6), prayer (2 Ch 6:13; Mt 17:14; Lk 22:41), subjection (Is 45:23; Ph 2:10).

knife. In primitive times of flint (Jos 5: 2, 3); Philistines already had knives of metal, which did not become common in Israel until later monarchy; used for killing and cutting (Lv 7:33, 34; 8:20; 1 K 18:28), sharpening pens (Jer 36:23), pruning (Is 18:5), as razors (Eze 5:1).

knop (nŏp). Archaic word for knob or bud of flower (Ex 25:31-36. RSV: capital); gourd (as RSV, 1 K 6:18; 7:24). See capital.

knowledge. 1. Intellectual grasp; knowing as fact (1 K 2:32; Est 2:22; Mt 24:32; Lk 12:47; 18:20; Acts 21:37). 2. Understanding of relationship and ultimate significance (Jb 38:2; Pr 1:7; Mt 22:29; Mk 12:24; Jn 13:7). 3. Omniscience of God (1 Sm 2:3; Jb 21:22; Jn 21:17). 4. Understanding which takes hold of subject, or causes subject to enter experience (loss, suffering: Is 47:8; 53:3; intimacy with man, woman: Nm 31:17; Ju 19:25; power, love of God, Christ: Ex 6:7; Jer 16:21; Eze 25:14; Jn 14:4; Eph 3:19; 1 Jn 4:8). 5. God intervening, binding Himself by covenant, helping (Hos 13:5; Am 3:2). 6. Acceptance of God's covenant (Hos 2:20) and remembrance of His acts (Dt 11:2; Is 41:20). 7. To know God, who has first known man; to accept Christ by faith (Jn 6:69; 8:31, 32; 1 Co 8:2, 6, 7). See also wisdom.

Koa (kō'a). People E of Euphrates (Eze 23:23).

Kohath (kō'hăth). Son of Levi (Gn 46:11; Ex 6:16-18; Nm 3:17); descendants (Kohathites), one of 3 Levite branches, included priestly family of Aaron (Ex 6:18-20).

Kola (kō'la). City in Bethulia (Jdth 15:4. KJ: Cola. RV: Chola).

Kolaiah (kō-lā'yȧ, voice of LORD). 1. Benjaminite (Neh 11:7). 2. Father of false prophet Ahab (Jer 29:21).

Kona, Konae (kō'nȧ, kō'nē). A place (Jdth 4:4. KJ: the villages).

Korah (kō'rȧ, ice, or baldness). 1. Son of Esau by Oholibamah (Gn 36:5, 14; 1 Ch 1:35). 2. Probably inserted by copyist (Gn 36:16. See Gn 36:11, 12; 1 Ch 1:36). 3. Levite; conspired with Dathan and Abiram against Moses; earth opened and swallowed them (Nm 16; 17). KJ: Core in Jude 11. 4. Son of Hebron (1 Ch 2:43).

Korahite, Korathite (kō'rȧ-īt, kō'rȧth-īt. KJ: Korathite once, Korahite twice, otherwise Korhite). Descendant of Levite Korah 3; Heman and Samuel were Korahites (1 Ch 6:33-38). Became famous temple singers (1 Ch 15:17; 16:41, 42; 25:4, 5; Ps 42; 44—49, 84, 85, 87, 88 titles).

Kore (kō'rĕ, caller, partridge). 1. Korahite Levite; father of Shallum (1 Ch 9:19; 26:1). 2. KJ for Korahites (as RV, RSV: 1 Ch 26:19). 3. Levite in charge of thank offerings (2 Ch 31:14).

Korhite (kôr'hīt). See Korahite.

Koz (kŏz). See Hakkoz.

Kushaiah (kû-shā'yȧ. Kĭshi in 1 Ch 6:44). Merarite Levite (1 Ch 15:17).

L

Laadah (lā'ȧ-dȧ). Judahite (1 Ch 4:21).

Laadan (lā'ȧ-dăn). See Ladan.

Laban (lā'băn, white). 1. Descendant of Nahor; brother of Rebekah (Gn 24:29; 25:20); lived at Haran in Paddan-aram (Gn 11:31, 32; 24:4, 10); gave Rebekah to Abraham (Gn 24); Jacob served him 14 yrs for Leah and Rachel, 6 yrs for cattle (Gn 29—31). 2. Place in desert (Dt 1:1); perhaps Libnah 1.

Labana (lăb'ȧ-nȧ). See Lebana.

labor. Dignified by fact that God's work of creation was designated as labor (Gn 2:2. See Ex 20:9-11). God's continued work in world was cited by Jesus in defense of work on Sabbath (Jn 5:17). Work is honorable (Ps 128:2; Pr 21:25; 1 Th 4: 11). Laborer was protected by laws (Dt 24:14).

Laccunus (lă-kū'nus. KJ: Lacunus). Listed in 1 Esd 9:31.

lace. Cord which tied high priest's breastplate to ephod (Ex 28:28).

Lacedemonians (lăs-ê-dê-mō'nĭ-ăns). Spartans (as RV, RSV. 1 Mac 12:2-21).

Lachish (lā'kĭsh). Canaanite royal city on mound of Tell ed-Duweir, 30 mi SW of Jerusalem and 15 mi W of Hebron; king defeated by Joshua (Jos 10:3-35); Rehoboam strengthened its defenses (2 Ch 11:9); Amaziah slain there (2 K 14:19); captured by Sennacherib (2 K 18:14, 17);

twice destroyed by Nebuchadnezzar together with Jerusalem: 598 BC (2 K 24) and 587 BC (2 K 25; Jer 34:7); occupied after exile (Neh 11:30). Archaeologists found many important evidences at Lachish including Lachish Letters (ostraca) from time of Jeremiah.

Lacunus (lä-kū'nŭs). See *Laccunus*.

Ladan (lä'dăn, appoint? KJ: Laadan). 1. Ephraimite (1 Ch 7:26). 2. Gershonite Levite (1 Ch 23:7-9; 26:21). Perhaps same as Libni 1. 3. See *Delaiah* 5.

ladder. Perhaps staircase in dream of Jacob (Gn 28:12).

Lael (lä'el, devoted to God). Father of Eliasaph (Nm 3:24).

Lahad (lä'hăd, swarthy?). Judahite (1 Ch 4:2).

Lahai-roi (lä-hī'roi). See *Beer-iahai-roi*.

Lahmam (lä'măm). Village in lowlands of Judah (Jos 15:40).

Lahmi (lä'mī). Brother of Goliath (1 Ch 20:5).

Laish (lä'ĭsh, lion). 1. Father of Palti (1 Sm 25:44). 2. City in N Palestine at head of Jordan (Ju 18:7-29). Leshem in Jos 19:47. Renamed Dan. See *Dan 3*. 3. See *Laishah*.

Laishah (lä'ĭ-shä, lion. KJ: Laish). Village of Benjamin (Is 10:30).

Lakkum, Lakum (lăk'ŭm, lä'kŭm, obstruction). Place in NE Naphtali (Jos 19:33).

lamb. Used for food (Lv 3:7; 7:15; 2 Sm 12:4) and sacrifices (Gn 22:7; Ex 29:38-41; Nm 28:9-29), especially Passover (Ex 12:3-5). Sacrificial lambs typical of Christ (Jn 1:29; Rv 5:6, 8). Christians, especially young, compared to lambs (Jn 21:15); likewise inoffensive teachers (Jer 11:19). Beast had two horns like lamb (Rv 13:11).

Lamech (lä'měk). 1. Father of Jabal, Jubal, Tubal-cain, Naamah (Gn 4:18-24). 2. Father of Noah (Gn 5:25, 28-31).

Lamentations, Book of. LXX placed this book after Jeremiah, H among Hagiographa between Ruth and Ecclesiastes. Contains elegies or laments on destruction of Jerusalem. Righteous God (1:18; 2:17; 3:33) allows suffering to result from sin (1:22; 4:13, 22). Five poems make up five chapters; first 4 acrostics. G versions assigned authorship to Jeremiah.

lamp (KJ often: candle). Vessel for holding inflammable liquid and wick which burned to give illumination (Ex 27:20; 2 K 4:10 [KJ, RV: candlestick]). Lamps of golden candlestick (RSV: lampstand) of tabernacle and temple were of gold (Ex 25:31-40; 37:17-24; 1 K 7:49) and burned olive oil (Ex 27:20). Used in marriage processions (Mt 25:1). Figuratively, Word of God (Ps 119:105), guidance of God (Ps 18:28), wise leaders (Jn 5:35).

lance, lancet. Javelin or light spear (1 K 18:28; Jer 50:42 [RV, RSV: spear]).

landmarks. Marks (stones, stakes, double furrows) used to designate boundary of land; not to be removed (Dt 19:14; 27: 17; Pr 22:28; Hos 5:10 [KJ: bound]).

language. Gift of God. Language diversity consequence of sin (Gn 11). OT world polyglot (Sumerian, Akkadian, Egyptian, Phrygian, Phoenician, Canaanite, Hittite, others). Chief languages in NT Palestine: Aramaic (Hebrew), Greek, Latin (Jn 19: 20), though other languages frequently heard (Acts 2:8-11).

lantern. Lamp with some kind of covering (Jn 18:3).

Laodicea (lä-ŏd-ĭ-sē'á). City in Lycus valley of Asia Minor, originally Diospolis; later named for wife of Antiochus II (Cl 2:1; 4:15; Rv 1:11; 3:14-22).

Laodiceans, Epistle to. Letter referred to in Cl 4:16. May refer to copy of Ephesians, or letter sent by Laodiceans.

lap. Folds of garment in which articles were carried (2 K 4:39; Neh 5:13; Lk 6: 38 [KJ, RV: bosom]).

Lapidoth, Lappidoth (lăp'ĭ-dŏth, torches). Husband of Deborah (Ju 4:4).

lapwing. See *hoopoe*.

lasciviousness (lä-sĭv'ĭ-us-nĕs), RSV: licentiousness (Mk 7:22; 2 Co 12:21; Gl 5:19; Eph 4:19; 1 Ptr 4:3; Jude 4).

Lasea (lä-sē'á). Seaport of Crete near Fair Havens (Acts 27:8).

Lasha (lä'shá, fissure). Place mentioned with cities of plain (Gn 10:19). Ancient authorities identified it with Callirrhoë, E of Dead Sea.

Lasharon, Lassharon (lä-shä'ron, lä-shä'ron, of Sharon). Canaanite town (Jos 12:18).

Last Day. See *judgment*.

Last Times. See *eschatology*.

Lasthenes (lăs'thê-nēz). Cretan (1 Mac 11: 31, 32).

latchet. See *sandal-thong*.

Latin (lăt'ĭn). Language of the Romans (Jn 19:20. KJ also Lk 23:38).

lattice. Window lattice (SS 2:9), lathed opening (Ju 5:28; Pr 7:6 [KJ: casement]), or screen (2 K 1:2).

laughter. Expression of joy (Gn 21:6; Lk 6:21), disbelief (Gn 18:13), security over danger (Jb 5:22), derision (Ps 2:4).

laver (lä'vĕr). Vessel for priestly washings. Tabernacle laver of bronze (Ex 30:18. KJ: brass) with basin and pedestal. Temple had "molten sea" (10 cubits in diameter) and 10 lavers (1 K 7:23-39).

law. 1. Will of God revealed to man in judgments, words, precepts, acts, etc (Ex 20:1-17; 21:1; Dt 7:6-16; Ps 19; 119; Is 1:10). 2. Torah, first 5 books of OT (Mt 5:17; Lk 16:16). 3. OT (Jn 10:34; 12: 34). 4. Basic law (Ten Commandments) given to Moses (Ex 20:2-17; Dt 5:6-21; Jn 7:19) which was core of system governing man's relation to God, to man, and to animals (Lv; Dt). Jesus showed respect and love for the Law and showed its deeper significance (Mt 5:17-48). Paul emphasized that Law showed man's sinfulness but could not provide victory over sin (Ro 3—7; Gl). Law prepares for Gospel (Gl 3:24). See *appeal; council 2; judgment; justice; righteousness*.

lawyer. Professional interpreter, often scribe, of OT (Mt 22:35; Lk 10:25).

laying on of hands. Act signifying impartation; associated with blessing; used to dedicate priests (Nm 8:5-20), animals (Lv 1:4), bestow blessings of various kinds (Gn 48:5-20; Mk 10:16; Lk 4:40; 13:13), and set people apart for special service (Acts 6:6; 13:3; 1 Ti 4:14; 2 Ti 1:6; Heb 6:2).

Lazarus (lăz'á-rus, H Eleazer. God has helped). 1. Brother of Mary and Martha (Jn 11; 12). 2. Type of poverty and distress in parable (Lk 16:19-31).

lead. Listed among metals early known; imported and used by Hebrews (Ex 15: 10; Nm 31:22; Jer 6:29; Eze 22:18).

leaf. Leaves of trees, of doors (Eze 41:24), of gold (Ex 39:3), of books or scrolls (Jer 36:23. RSV: column). Green leaves symbolic of prosperity (Ps 1:3; Pr 11:28 [KJ: branch]; Jer 17:8), dry leaves of ruin and decay (Jb 13:25; Is 1:30; 64:6; Jer 8:13).

Leah (lē'á, languid). Wife of Jacob by trickery of Laban, her father (Gn 29; 30; 49:31).

leasing (lēz'ĭng). Obsolete KJ word for falsehood (Ps 4:2; 5:6).

leather. Used for clothing (Lv 13:48), tents (Ex 26:14), bottles (Jdth 10:5; Mt 9:17), shoes (Eze 16:10), girdles (2 K 1:8; Mk 1:6), parchment for writing (2 Ti 4:13). See trade 8, 9.

leaven (lĕv'en). Substance, usually old fermented dough (Mt 13:33), used to make dough rise (Ex 12:15, 20); removed from houses during Passover (Ex 12); not used in meal offerings (Lv 2:11). Symbol of corruption (Mt 16:12; 1 Co 5:6-8) and of moral influence, whether good or bad (Mt 13:33; Mt 16:6).

Lebana, Lebanah (lē-bā'ná, white). Progenitor of family which returned from captivity (Ez 2:45; Neh 7:48; 1 Esd 5:29 [KJ, RV: Labana]).

Lebanon (lĕb'á-nun, white). 110-mi-long mt ranges of Lebanon and Anti-Lebanon running NE to SW from Taurus Mts to lower mt ranges of Palestine and beyond. Between two ranges is Coelesyria (hollow Syria; El-Beka). Mt Hermon (9,383 ft) is spur of Anti-Lebanons. Highest points are Jebel Makmal and Kurnat es-Sauda, both over 10,000 ft. Lebanons proper formed boundary of Palestine (Dt 1:7) and frequently referred to. Known especially for cedars (Ju 9:15; 1 K 5; 1 Esd 4:48 [KJ, RV: Libanus]).

Lebaoth (lē-bā'ŏth, lionesses?). See Bethbirei.

Lebbaeus (le-bē'us). See Judas 5.

Leb-kamai (lĕb-kā'mī). Cryptic spelling for Chaldea (Jer 51:1). KJ: midst of them that rise up against me. RSV: Chaldea).

Lebonah (lē-bō'ná, frankincense). Town N of Shiloh (Ju 21:19). Modern Lubban.

Lecah (lē'ká). Son of Er (1 Ch 4:21).

leech. Translation (uncertain) in Pr 30:15 (KJ, RV: horseleach. RV margin: vampire).

leek. Onionlike herb (Nm 11:5). See food 4.

lees. Sediment of wine (Is 25:6). "To settle on the lees" is indolent, luxurious, unhampered, stupid life (Jer 48:11; Zph 1:12).

left. Usual meanings; north (Gn 14:15); ill omen among Greeks and Romans and less favored than right in Scripture (Mt 25:33).

legion. 1. See army. 2. Multitude (Mt 26:53; Mk 5:9).

Lehabim (lē-hā'bĭm). Midianite people (Gn 10:13; 1 Ch 1:11). Undoubtedly same as Libyans.

Lehi (lē'hī, jawbone). Place where Samson slew Philistines with jawbone of ass (Ju 15:9-19). Ramath-lehi in Ju 15:17.

Lemuel (lĕm'û-el, belonging to God). Unidentified king (Pr 31:1-9).

lentil. Seed of Ervum lens, leguminous plant which grows wild in Moab, cultivated in Palestine (Gn 25:34; 2 Sm 23:11; Eze 4:9). See also food 1, 3.

leopard (lĕp'ĕrd). Spotted, wily, fierce animal; symbol of wild destruction (Jer 5:6; Hos 13:7).

leprosy (lĕp'rŏ-sī). Disease characterized by whiteness (Ex 4:6) and disfiguring skin eruptions. Levitical leprosy perhaps included diseases beyond commonly known leprosy of today (Lv 13; 14). Type of mildew or mold (Lv 13:47-59; 14:33-37). Jesus cleansed lepers (Mt 8:2-4; Lk 17:11-19).

Leshem (lē'shĕm). See Laish 2.

Lessau (lĕs'ô). See Dessau.

lethech (lē'thĕk. KJ, RV: half homer). Dry measure, c 4 bushels.

letters. Correspondence common in Biblical times (2 Sm 11:14; 2 K 19:14; 2 Co 3:1; Acts 18:27). Forms of Persian (Ez 4), Roman (Acts 23:26-30) letters given. Excavations have brought many letters to light. Private individuals arranged own deliveries. 21 letters, or epistles, in NT. See alphabet.

Lettus (lĕt'us). See Hattush 2.

Letushim (lē-tū'shĭm). Tribe descended from Dedan (Gn 25:3).

Leummim (lē-ŭm'ĭm, nations). Tribe descended from Dedan (Gn 25:3).

Levi (lē'vī, joined). 1. Third son of Jacob by Leah (Gn 29:34); avenged with Simeon seduction of Dinah (Gn 34); joined in plot against Joseph (Gn 37); three sons: Gershon, Kohath, Merari (Gn 46: 11; 1 Ch 6:16-48). 2. 3. Two ancestors of Christ (Lk 3:24, 29). 4. See Matthew. 5. See Levis.

leviathan (lē-vī'á-thăn). Poetical passages describe it as in some ways similar to crocodiles (Jb 41), serpents (Is 27:1), or sea monster (Ps 104:26). Similar to mythical Canaanite monster Lotan. Figuratively: unrestrained power (Jb 3:8; 41), evil (Ps 74:14; 104:26; Is 27:1). See beast 4.

levirate marriage (lĕv'ī-rát măr'ĭj). When an Israelite died without male children nearest relative should marry widow; firstborn son to be heir of first husband (Dt 25:5-10).

Levis (lē'vĭs. RSV: Levi). For Levite in 1 Esd 9:14. See Ez 10:15.

Levites (lē'vīts). Descendants of Levi 1 through Gershon, Kohath, Merari (Ex 6: 16-25; Lv 25:32; Nm 35:2-8; Jos 21:3); substituted for first-born in duties pertaining to God (Nm 3:11-13; 8:16); duty was to preserve Law of Jehovah and His worship (Lv 10:11; Dt 17:18; 31:9-13). Different duties assigned to families of 3 sons (Nm 3:5-39). Priests descended from Kohath through Aaron, sons Eleazar and Ithamar (Ex 28:1; Nm 18:7). Received no tribal territory (Nm 18:20; Dt 10:9) but were assigned 48 cities (Nm 35) and tithes (Lv 27:30-33; Nm 18:21-24).

Leviticus (lē-vĭt'ĭ-kus). 3d book of OT; manual of priesthood. Stresses holiness of God, approach to Him through priesthood, and holiness (spiritual, moral, physical) required of man. Outline: 1. Sacrifices and Offerings (1—7). 2. Priests (8—10). 3. Cleanliness and Holiness (11 to 22). 4. Feasts (23). 5. General Rules (25—27). See law.

levy. Israelites forced to labor under Hiram (1 K 5:13-18); also levy of slaves (1 K 9:20, 21).

lewdness. Licentiousness (Jer 13:27; Eze 16:43, 58; 22:9; 23:21-49; 24:13; Hos 2:10; Acts 18:14 [RSV: vicious crime. RV: wicked villainy]).

Libanus (lĭb'á-nus). See Lebanon.

libation (lī-bā'shun). Pouring wine or other liquids (especially on morning and evening sacrificial lamb) as act of worship (Ex 29:40, 41; Jer 44:17-25. KJ, RV: drink offering).

libertines (lĭb'ĕr-tēnz KJ, RV). Freedmen (RSV, Acts 6:9).

liberty. Prized in OT (Is 61:1; Jer 34), though Israelites were frequently tributary or in bondage. Israelites who had become slaves (Lv 25:39) were to be freed in year of jubilee (Lv 25:8-17). Spiritual depth of OT prophecy regarding liberty reaches fulfillment in Christ (Is 61:1; Lk 4:18; Jn 8:31-36), who frees from Satan (Acts 26:18), sin (Jn 1:29; Ro 6; 7), death, judgment, fear (Ro 8), law (Gl 3). Christian has liberty in matters morally indifferent (adiaphora, Ro 14; 1 Co 8).

Libnah (lib′nạ, whiteness). 1. Camp site of Israel (Nm 33:20, 21). See also *Laban 2.* 2. Canaanite city N of Lachish captured by Joshua (Jos 10:29-31); given to Judah; Levitical city (Jos 21:13; 1 Ch 6:57); home of Hamutal (2 K 23:31), Zedekiah (2 K 24:18).

Libni (lib′nị, whiteness). 1. Son of Gershon (Ex 6:17; Nm 3:18, 21; 1 Ch 6:17, 20). Perhaps same as Ladan 2. 2. Merarite Levite (1 Ch 6:29).

Libya (lib′ị-a). Country W of Egypt in N Africa (Eze 30:5 [RV: Put]; Acts 2:10). See also *Put 2.*

Libyans (lib′ị-ăns). Inhabitants of Libya (Jer 46:9 [RV, RSV: Put]; Nah 3:9 [KJ, RV: Lubim]). KJ: Lubims; RV: Lubim in 2 Ch 12:3; 16:8. See also *Lehabim; Lud 2; Put 2.*

lice. See *gnats.*

licentiousness (lī-sĕn′shus-nĕs). See *lasciviousness.*

lie. 1. Falsehood (Ju 16:10; Ps 144:8; Pr 6:19; Is 16:6; 2 Co 11:31; Gl 1:20). 2. God is truth; hence that which comes from Him cannot be lie (Nm 23:19; 1 Sm 15:29). Devil, God's opposition, is liar and source of lies (Jn 8:44, 45). Idols, distortions of truth, are lies (Ro 1:25; Hab 2:18). Distortions of divinely revealed truth are lies (Jer 8:8; 27:9, 10). Failure to live by truth is lie (1 Jn 1:6).

lieutenant (lū-tĕn′ănt). See *satrap.*

life. 1. Animation of animal existence (Gn 6:17; Ex 1:14; Jb 3:20, 21; Ec 2:17). 2. Spiritual life, whereby we live to God (Ro 8:6; Cl 3:3); eternal life given by faith in Christ (Eph 2:8-10; Jn 17:3; 1 Jn 5:12); believer never dies (Jn 11:25, 26). 3. Christ is source of all life (Jn 1:4; 11: 25; Cl 3:4. See Cl 1:15, 16).

light, darkness. Light figurative of God (Ps 104:2; 1 Jn 1:5), from whom every good gift comes (Ja 1:17); Jesus, Light of world (Jn 1:4-9); Word (Ps 119:105; 2 Ptr 1:19); believers (Mt 5:14-16); godliness (Ro 13:11-14; 1 Jn 1:7). Darkness figurative of evil (Lk 22:53; Cl 1:13; Eph 6:12) and all results of powers of evil: spiritual blindness (1 Jn 1:6), evil deeds (Jn 3:19, 20), death (Jb 10:21, 22), hell (Mt 22:13), suffering (Jl 2:2).

lignaloes (lin-ăl′ŏz). See *Aloes.*

ligure (lig′ūr). See *jacinth.*

likeness. See *idol; image of God.*

Likhi (lĭk′hī, learned). Manassite (1 Ch 7:19).

lily. Several varieties abundant in Palestine; referred to figuratively (1 K 7:26; 2 Ch 4:5; SS 2:1, 2, 16; 4:5; 5:13; 6:2, 3; 7:2; Hos 14:5; Mt 6:28; Lk 12:27).

lime. Mts of Palestine largely limestone; Israelites knew how to burn limestone to make lime for plaster, etc. (Is 27:9 [chalkstones]; 33:12; Am 2:1). See *homes.*

lineage (lĭn′ē-ĭj). See *genealogy.*

linen. See *flax.* Used for garments (Gn 41: 42; Eze 9:2; Mk 14:51, 52; Rv 18:12), priests' apparel (Ex 28:5-42; Lv 6:10), temple veil (2 Ch 3:14), choral robes (2 Ch 5:12), shrouds (Mk 15:46; Jn 19: 40; 20:5), etc. Symbol of wealth (Lk 16:19), purity (Rv 19:8, 14).

lintel. Transverse piece over door or casement (Ex 12:7 [KJ: upper door post], 22, 23; 1 K 6:31).

linus (lī′nus). Roman friend of Paul (2 Ti 4:21).

lion. Jordan valley favorite haunt of lions (Jer 49:19); also found in rest of Palestine (1 Sm 17:34; 2 K 17:25; 2 Ch 9:18). Usually figuratively in NT (1 Ptr 5:8; Rv 4:7; 9:8).

lip. 1. Part of mouth (Lv 13:45; 1 Sm 1: 13). 2. Language and speech (Jb 2:10; Ps 12:2; 21:2; Pr 5:3; 10:18; Mk 7:6). 3. Emotions expressed by lip movements (Ps 22:7 [RSV: make mouths]; 59:7; Pr 16:30; Hab 3:16). 4. At times deceitful (Is 29:13; Mt 15:8; Ro 3:13).

litter. Couch or chair for conveying passengers (SS 3:7 [KJ: bed]; Is 66:20).

little way. See *measures 1g.*

liver. Used in sacrifice (Ex 29:13; Lv 3:4-15), for divination (Eze 21:21); considered center of life and feeling (Pr 7:23 [RSV: entrails]; Lm 2:11).

lizard. Reptile of family which includes gecko, lizard, crocodile, and chameleon; unclean (Lv 11:30).

lizard, great. Land monitor; reaches length of 6 ft; or, another, 2 ft (Lv 11:29. KJ: tortoise).

Lo-ammi (lō-ăm′ī, not my people). Symbolic name of Hosea's son (Hos 1:9. RSV: Not my people).

loans. OT permits and enjoins loans, allows enslavement because of poverty, but Israelite servants to be released in 7th year and debts of Israelites to be canceled in year of jubilee (Lv 25:39-41; Dt 15:1-11). Interest (KJ, RV: usury) not charged to Israelites, permitted in case of strangers (Lv 25:36, 37; Dt 23:19, 20). Usury denounced (Neh 5:7, 10; Ps 15:5; Pr 28:8; Eze 22:12).

lock. Bar of wood or iron fixed by sliding pins (Neh 3:3, 6, 13-15; SS 5:5. RV, RSV: bolt). See also *key.*

locks. See *hair.*

locust. 8 H words apparently refer to species of locusts or grasshoppers; clean animals (Lv 11:22; Mt 3:4); noted for destructiveness (Ju 6:5; 7:12; Jer 46:23. KJ: grasshopper). See also *cankerworm.*

Lod (lŏd). City of Benjamin (1 Ch 8:12; Ez 2:33; Neh 7:37; 11:35) identified with Lydda.

Loddeus (lŏd′ē-us). See *Iddo 8.*

Lo-debar (lō-dē′bär, thing of nought?). Place E of Jordan in Gilead, perhaps Debir (2 Sm 9:4, 5; 17:27; Am 6:13 [KJ, RV: thing of nought]).

log (hollow). See *measures 3a.*

Logos (lŏg′ŏs). See *Jesus Christ.*

loin. Part of back and sides between hips and false ribs. Loose garments of Orientals tied at loins before walking, working. Figuratively (Jb 31:20; 38:3; Ps 38:7; Eph 6:14).

Lois (lō′ĭs, pleasing). Timothy's grandmother (2 Ti 1:5).

Longimanus (lŏn-jĭm′a-nus). See *Artaxerxes 2.*

long-suffering), KJ (and RV less frequently), for slow to anger (as 2 Ptr 3:9).

looking glass. See *mirror.*

loom. See *measure 4.*

Lord. 1. Jehovah (YHWH. Written with capital and small capitals: LORD. Gen 2:4). 2. H ′adon. Denotes ownership by human beings (Gn 24:14) or God (Ps 114:7). 3. H ′adonai. Used when submission is expressed (Ex 4:10, 13). Spoken by Jews instead of Jahveh. See *Jehovah.*

4. H *ba'al.* Denotes master, owner; applied to human beings and idols (Ex 22:8; Ju 2:11, 13). **5. G** *kurios.* Human master (Mt 20:8); God as ruler (Mt 8:25; 21:9); Christ, who by His death and resurrection is Lord (Ro 14:9). See also *Jehovah; Jesus Christ.*

Lord of Hosts. See *host* 2.

Lord's day. 1st day of week, commemorating resurrection of Jesus (Jn 20:1-25), pouring out of Spirit (Acts 2:1-41); set aside for worship (Acts 20:7), although some (Acts 2:46) still observed Sabbath (Rv 1:10. See Ro 14:5; 1 Co 16:2; Cl 2:16; Gl 4:10). See also *Sunday.*

Lord's Prayer. Prayer spoken by Jesus as model (Mt 6:9-13 [RV, RSV omit doxology]; Lk 11:2-4).

Lord's Supper. Instituted by Christ on night of His betrayal to take place of paschal feast, convey to celebrants His sacrifice for their sins, and be memorial of His death. In supernatural, sacramental manner Christ gives His body and blood with bread and wine (Mt 26:26-28; Mk 14:22-24; Lk 22:19, 20; 1 Co 10:16, 17; 11:20-26). Also called Breaking of Bread (Acts 2:42; 20:7; 1 Co 10:16), Communion (participation, 1 Co 10:16), Eucharist (blessing, 1 Co 10:16), Lord's Table (1 Co 10:21). Self-examination precedes celebration of Lord's Supper (1 Co 11:27-32).

Lo-ruhamah (lō-rōō-hā'má). Symbolic name of Hosea's daughter (Hos 1:6, 8. RSV: Not pitied).

lot. Casting lots usually had religious associations (Pr 16:33; Jon 1:7; Acts 1:26); used to divide land, inheritance, or settle other difficult matters (Jos 18:6-28; 1 Ch 25:8; Mt 27:35).

Lot (lŏt, covering?). Son of Haran; nephew of Abraham (Gn 11:27-31); accompanied Abraham to Egypt and Canaan (Gn 13:1-7); settled in Jordan valley (Gn 13:8-13); escaped destruction of Sodom and Gomorrah (Gn 19); ancestor of Moab and Ammon (Gn 19:36-38).

Lotan (lō'tăn). Horite prince (Gn 36:20-29; 1 Ch 1:38, 39).

Lothasubus (lŏth-á-sū'bus). See *Hashum* 2.

lotus tree (lō'tus. KJ: shady tree). *Zizyphus lotus,* low thorny shrub (Jb 40:21, 22).

love. (OT: H *'ahabah*) **1.** Sensuous love (Gn 29:18). **2.** Love within family (Gn 25:28). **3.** Attachment (1 Sm 20:17. See 1 Sm 18:1). **4.** Israel's love for God (Ex 20:6). **5.** Expression of covenant love (see *steadfast love*) wherein God's unmotivated love seeks good of its object (Dt 7:7-9, 12); wrath of injured love is converse (Dt 7:10, 11).

G: 1. *Eros:* motivated love; seeks value in its object (LXX, Pr 7:18; 30:16). **2.** *Storge:* family or group affection (not in Bible). **3.** *Philia:* noble, unselfish love and friendship (Mt 10:37; Jn 5:20; 12:25; 15:19; 16:27; 21:15-17; Tts 3:15; Rv 3:19). **4.** *Agape:* divine, unmotivated, spontaneous love; bestows value on its object (Jn 3:16; 1 Jn 4:8); love of Christians (Mt 5:44, 45; 1 Co 13; 1 Jn 4). KJ frequently: charity. See also *grace; mercy; steadfast love.*

love feasts. Feasts expressing mutual love held in connection with Lord's Supper (Jude 12 [KJ: feasts of charity]; 2 Ptr 2:13 [KJ: deceivings; RSV: dissipation]).

loving-kindness. See *steadfast love.*

low country, lowland. See *Shephelah.*

Lozon (lō'zŏn). See *Darkon.*

Lubim (lū'bĭm). See *Lehabim; Libya; Libyans.*

Lucas (lū'kăs). See *Luke.*

Lucifer (lū'sĭ-fẽr, light bringer). See *day star.*

Lucius (lū'shĭ-us). **1.** Roman official (1 Mac 15:16). **2.** Cyrenian; Christian teacher at Antioch (Acts 13:1; Ro 16:21).

Lud (lŭd). **1.** People and place in Asia Minor which included Lydians (Gn 10:22; 1 Ch 1:17). See also *Lydia* 1. **2.** People and place related to Egyptians (Gn 10:13; 1 Ch 1:11; Is 66:19; Jer 46:9 [KJ: Libyans]; Eze 27:10; 30:5). Lubim in Gn and Ch.

Luhith (lū'hĭth). Moabite town (Is 15:5; Jer 48:5).

Luke (lūk). Physician and companion of Paul; well educated, probably Greek; named 3 times in NT (Cl 4:14; Phlm 24 [KJ, RV: Lucas]; 2 Ti 4:11); author of Luke, Acts, which give additional information: joined Paul at Troas (Acts 16:10, where first person plural is used for 1st time in Acts); joined Paul on third journey at Philippi (Acts 20:5).

Luke, Gospel of. 3d book of NT, whose Lucan authorship is generally acknowledged. Vocabulary, style, and dedication to Theophilus (Lk 1:3) show that author of Luke and Acts (1:1) are same. Outline: 1. Prolog (1:1-4). 2. Birth and Incidents Before Jesus' Baptism (1:5—4:13). 3. Ministry in Galilee (4:14—9:50). 4. Journey Toward Jerusalem (9:51—19:28). 5. Last Days and Crucifixion (19:29—23:55). 6. Resurrection and Ascension (24). Gives account of Christian beginnings (1:1-4), shows universality of Christian message. See *Jesus Christ.*

lunatic. Probably epileptic (as RV, RSV. Mt 4:24; 17:15).

lust. Sin of heart and will of man (often: covet, desire: Ex 20:17; Dt 5:21) resulting from fact that man does not love God with all his heart (Dt 6:5) but seeks all things for self-gratification (Ja 3:14—4:2. RV: pleasures — lust; RSV: passions — desire). Sexual lust plays major role (Ro 1:24), but other objects of lust are included (Ex 20:17; Mi 2:2; Acts 20:33); whole personality involved (Ro 1:24; 1 Jn 2:16). Law shows man his real condition by showing him nature of his lust (Ro 7:7).

lute (lūt). Stringed instrument (Ps 92:3 [KJ, RV: instrument of ten strings]; Ps 150:3 [KJ, RV: psaltery]).

Luz (lūz, almond). **1.** Canaanite town, including territory of later Bethel (Gn 28:19; 35:6; 48:3; Jos 16:2; 18:13; Ju 1:23). **2.** Hittite town (Ju 1:22-26).

Lycaonia (lĭk-ā-ō'nĭ-á, wolf land). High tableland of Asia Minor, bounded by Isauria, Cilicia, Pisidia, Phrygia, and Cappadocia. Annexed to Galatia 35 BC (Acts 14:6, 11).

Lycia (lĭsh'ĭ-á). Province of SW Asia Minor Acts 21:2; 27:5).

Lydda (lĭd'á. H Lud, Lod). Town in plain of Sharon, 11 m SE of Joppa (Acts 9:32-38). See also *Lod.*

Lydia (lĭd'ĭ-á). **1.** Region on W Coast of Asia Minor; capital: Sardis (Jer 46:9 [RV: Ludim. RSV: Lud]; Eze 30:5 [RV, RSV: Lud]). See also *Lud* 1. **2.** Woman in Philippi; dealer in purple dyes, whom Paul converted and at whose house he stayed (Acts 16:14, 15, 40).

lye. See *nitre.*

lyre. H *kinnor;* LXX *kithara.* Probably small, portable, musical instrument made of frame with 2 arms joined by crossbar from which sheep-gut strings were stretched to frame (Gn 4:21; 1 Sm 10:5; 1 Ch 25:3; Jb 21:12; Ps 33:2; Is 5:12. KJ, RV: harp).

Lysanias (lī-sā'nī-ăs). Tetrarch of Abilene, region with Abila (18 mi NW of Damascus) as capital (Lk 3:1).

Lysias (lĭs'ĭ-ăs). General of Antiochus Epiphanes and Antiochus Eupator (1 Mac 3; 4).

Lysias, Claudius (lĭs'ĭ-ăs, klô'dĭ-us). Chief captain of Roman soldiers in Jerusalem; rescued Paul and sent him to Caesarea (Acts 21—24).

Lysimachus (lī-sĭm'a-kus). 1. Son of Ptolemy (Ap Est 11:1. RSV omits). 2. Brother of Menelaus (2 Mac 4:29-42).

Lystra (lĭs'trá). City (Roman colony) in Lycaonia (Acts 14:6-21; 16:1, 2; 2 Ti 3: 11).

M

Maacah (mā'á-ká, oppression. KJ: Maachah exc 2 Sm 3:3; 10:6, 8). 1. Child of Nahor by Reumah (Gn 22:24). 2. Wife of David; mother of Absalom (2 Sm 3:3; 1 Ch 3:2). 3. Syrian city and kingdom at foot of Mt Hermon (Jos 13:13 [RV, RSV: Maacath]; 2 Sm 10:6-8. See Gn 22:24). Aram-maacah (KJ: Syria-maachah) in 1 Ch 19:6. 4. Father of Achish of Gath (1 K 2:39). Maoch in 1 Sm 27:2. 5. Wife of Rehoboam; mother of Abijah (1 K 15:2, 10, 13); granddaughter of Absalom (2 Ch 11:20-22). Micaiah (KJ: Michaiah) in 2 Ch 13:2. 6. Concubine of Caleb (1 Ch 2:48). 7. Wife of Machir (1 Ch 7:15, 16). 8. Ancestress of Saul (1 Ch 8:29; 9:35). 9. Father of Hanan (1 Ch 11:34). 10. Father of Shephatiah (1 Ch 27:16).

Maacath (mā'á-kăth). See Maacah 3.

Maacathites, Maachathites (má-ăk'á-thīts). People of Maacah (Dt 3:14 [KJ: Maachathi]; Jos 12:5; 13:11, 13).

Maachah (mā'á-ká). See Maacah.

Maachathi (má-ăk'á-thī). See Maacathites.

Maadai (mā-á-dā'ī). Divorced foreign wife (Ez 10:34; 1 Esd 9:34 [KJ, RV: Momdis]).

Maadiah (mā-á-dī'á, ornament of Lord). Chief priest who returned from captivity (Neh 12:5). Probably same as Moadiah (Neh 12:17).

Maai (mā-ā'ī). Priest and musician (Neh 12:36).

Maaleh-acrabbim (mā'á-lē-á-krăb'ĭm). See Akrabbim.

Maani (mā'á-nī. See Bani 5; Meunim.

Maarath (mā'á-răth, desolate). Place in Judah near Hebron (Jos 15:59).

Maareh-geba (mā'á-rĕ-gē'bá). See meadow 3.

Maasai (mā'á-sī). Priest in Jerusalem after exile (1 Ch 9:12. KJ: Maasiai).

Maaseas (mā'á-sē'ás). See Mahseiah.

Maaseiah (mā'á-sē'yá, work of Lord). 1. Levite musician (1 Ch 15:18, 20). 2. Captain; assisted Jehoiada in overthrowing Athaliah (2 Ch 23:1). 3. Steward under Uzziah (2 Ch 26:11). 4. Prince slain during Pekah's invasion (2 Ch 28:7). 5. Governor of Jerusalem under Josiah (2 Ch 34:8). 6. Priest of house of Jeshua; divorced foreign wife (Ez 10:18; 1 Esd 9:19 [KJ: Matthelas; RV: Mathelas]). 7. Priest of house of Harim; divorced foreign wife (Ez 10:21; 1 Esd 9:21 [KJ: Eanes; RV: Manes]). 8. Priest of house of Pashhur; divorced foreign wife (Ez 10:22; 1 Esd 9:22 [KJ, RV: Massias]). 9. Israelite; divorced foreign wife (Ez 10:30). Moossias (KJ: Moosias) in 1 Esd 9:31. 10. Father of Azariah (Neh 3:23). 11. Priest; co-worker of Ezra (Neh 8:4; 12:41). Baalsamus (KJ: Belasamus) in 1 Esd 9:43. 12. Stood by Ezra at reading of law (Neh 8:7; 1 Esd 9:48 [KJ: Maianeas; RV: Mainnas]). Perhaps same in Neh 12:42. 13. Chief; sealed covenant with Nehemiah (Neh 10:25). 14. See

Asaiah 3. 15. Benjaminite (Neh 11:7). 16. Priest; father of a Zephaniah (Jer 21:1; 29:25; 37:3). 17. Father of false prophet Zedekiah (Jer 29:21). 18. Son of Shallum; gatekeeper of temple (Jer 35:4). 19. See Mahseiah.

Maasiai (mā-ăs'ĭ-ī). See Maasai.

Maasias (mā-á-sī'ás). See Mahseiah.

Maasmas (mā-ăs'măs). See Shemaiah 18.

Maath (mā'áth). Ancestor of Jesus (Lk 3:26).

Maaz (mā'ăz, anger). Descendant of Jerahmeel (1 Ch 2:27).

Maaziah (mā-á-zī'á, decision of Lord?). 1. Head of 24th course of priests (1 Ch 24: 18). 2. Priest; sealed covenant with Nehemiah (Neh 10:8).

Mabdai (măb'dá-ī). See Benaiah 10.

Macalon (măk'á-lŏn). See Michmash.

Maccabees (măk'á-bēz, hammer?). Asmonaean family called Maccabaeus after surname of Judas; won freedom for Jews and ruled 166—63 BC; rebellion against Antiochus IV began with Mattathias, priest, was continued by his sons (Johanan, Simon, Judas, Eleazar, Jonathan). Prominent leaders: Judas (166—160 BC), Jonathan (160—142 BC), Simon (142 to 134 BC), John Hyrcanus (134—104 BC), Aristobulus (104—103 BC), Alexander Jannaeus (103—76 BC), Alexandra (76 to 67 BC), Aristobulus II (66—63 BC), Hyrcanus II (high priest, 63—40 BC), Antigonus II (high priest, 40—31 BC). History in Books of Maccabees.

Macedonia (măs-ĕ-dō'nĭ-á). State N of Greece (Balkan Peninsula) ruled by Philip (359—336 BC), extended by Alexander (336—323 BC), conquered by Rome (168 BC); often visited by Paul (Acts 16:9-12; 17:1-15; 20:1-6; Ro 15: 26; 1 Co 16:5; 2 Co 1:16; 2:13; 7:5; 8:1; 9:2; 11:9; Ph 4:15; 1 Th 1:7; 4:10; 1 Ti 1:3). See also Kittim 2.

Machaerus (má-kē'rus, black fortress). Place, overlooking Dead Sea, fortified by Alexander Jannaeus. Prison of John the Baptist (Josephus, Wars VII, vi, 2; Ant XVIII, v, 2).

Machbanai, Machbannai (măk'bá-nī). Gadite; came to David at Ziklag (1 Ch 12: 13).

Machbena, Machbenah (măk-bē'ná). See Cabbon.

Machi (mā'kī). Gadite; father of spy Geuel (Nm 13:15).

Machir (mā'kĭr, sold). 1. Son of Manasseh (Gn 50:23; Nm 27:1; 32:39, 40; Jos 17: 1-6; 1 Ch 2:21; 7:14). Machirites descended from him (Nm 26:29). 2. Son of Ammiel; brought provisions to David (2 Sm 9:4, 5; 17:27).

Machirites (mā'kĭr-īts). See Machir.

Machmas (măk'măs). See Michmash.

Machnadebai (măk-năd'ĕ-bī, liberal). Divorced foreign wife (Ez 10:40). RSV in 1 Esd 9:34 instead of Mamnitanemus.

Machpelah (măk-pē'lă, double). Cave purchased by Abraham in W portion of Hebron where Abraham, Sarah, Isaac, Rebeccah, Jacob, Leah were buried (Gn 23; 25:9, 10; 49:30, 31; 50:13). Mohammedan mosque now stands on site.

Macron (mā'krŏn). See *Ptolemy Macron.*

mad. Deprived of reason (1 Sm 21:14; Acts 26:24; 1 Co 14:23); infatuated, impetuous, or furious with zeal for cause or object (Jer 50:38; Acts 26:11 [RSV: raging fury]); foolish and deceitful (Hos 9:7); perplexed or confused in mind (Dt 28:34; Jer 25:16; Acts 26:24).

Madai (măd'ā-ī, Mede). Descendants of Japheth (Gn 10:2; 1 Ch 1:5). See also *Mede.*

Madiabun (mȧ-dī'ȧ-bŭn). See *Emadabun.*

Madian (mā'dī-ăn). See *Midian 2.*

Madmannah (măd-măn'ȧ, dunghill). Town S of Gaza (Jos 15:31; 1 Ch 2:49).

Madmen (măd'mĕn, dunghill). Town in Moab (Jer 48:2).

Madmenah (măd-mē'nȧ, dunghill). Town N of Jerusalem (Is 10:31).

Madon (mā'dŏn, strife). Canaanite city (perh Madin) ruled by Jobab (Jos 11:1; 12:19).

Maelus (mā-ē'lŭs). See *Mijamin 2.*

Magadan (măg'ȧ-dăn). Place on W shore of Sea of Galilee (Mt 15:39. KJ: Magdala). Dalmanutha in Mk 8:10.

Magbish (măg'bĭsh, rendezvous). Unknown person or place (Ez 2:30; 1 Esd 5:21 [KJ: Nephis; RV: Niphis]).

Magdala (măg'dȧ-lȧ). See *Magadan.*

Magdalene (măg'dȧ-lēn). See *Mary 3.*

Magdiel (măg'dĭ-ĕl, praise of God). Chief of Edom (Gn 36:43; 1 Ch 1:54).

Maged (mā'gĕd). See *Maked.*

maggot. See *worm.*

Magi (mā'jī). Title for priests and learned men among Babylonians, Medes, Persians (see Dn 1; 2; 5); astronomy, astrology probably major part of study; influential advisers of rulers (see Herodotus I). Magi (Wise Men) came from E to worship infant Jesus (Mt 2:1-11). Word used with negative connotation in Acts 8:9 (see Acts 13:8).

magic. Supposed supernatural powers gained through occult science or mysterious arts (Gn 41:8; Ex 7:11, 22; 8:7, 18; Acts 13: 6-12). Includes necromancy (1 Sm 28:8), exorcism (Acts 19:13), dreams (Dt 13: 1-4), shaking arrows (Eze 21:21), inspecting entrails of animals (Eze 21:21), divination (Dt 18:10, 14), sorcery (Is 47:9; Ml 3:5), astrology (Dn 2:27; 4:7; 5:7, 8), enchantment, soothsaying (Dt 18: 10, 14; Jos 13:22; 2 K 21:6; Acts 16:16), divining by rods (Hos 4:12), witchcraft (Lv 19:26. KJ: enchantment).

magistrate. G *strategos*; L *praetor.* Chief civil magistrate in Roman colony (Acts 16:12-40).

Magog (mā'gŏg, Gog's land). 1. 2d son of Japheth (Gn 10:2; 1 Ch 1:5). 2. Gog's land, often identified with Scythia (Josephus) or Lydia (Eze 38; 39:1, 11). Used symbolically for forces of evil (Rv 20:7-9).

Magor-missabib (mā'gor-mĭs'ȧ-bĭb. RSV: Terror on every side). Name given by God to Pashhur through Jeremiah (Jer 20:3).

Magpiash (măg'pĭ-ăsh, moth killer?). Sealed covenant with Nehemiah (Neh 10:20). Perh same as Magbish.

Mahalab (mȧ-hā'lăb. KJ: from the coast. RV: by the region). City of Asher (Jos 19:29).

Mahalah (mȧ-hā'lä). See *Mahlah 2.*

Mahalaleel, Mahalalel (mȧ-hā'lȧ-lē-ĕl, -lĕl, praise of God). 1. Descendant of Seth (Gn 5:12-17; 1 Ch 1:2; Lk 3:37 [KJ: Maleleel]). 2. Judahite (Neh 11:4).

Mahalath (mā'hȧ-lăth). 1. Daughter of Ishmael; wife of Esau (Gn 28:9). Basemath in Gn 36:3. 2. Wife of Rehoboam (2 Ch 11:18). 3. Title of Ps 53; (with Leannoth) 88; probably refers to melody.

Mahali (mā'hȧ-lī). See *Mahli 1.*

Mahanaim (mā-hȧ-nā'īm, two camps). Place E of Jordan, N of Jabbok; on boundary between Gad and Manasseh (Jos 13:26, 30); Levitical city (Jos 21:38). Angels met Jacob there (Gn 32:2); Ish-bosheth ruled there (2 Sm 2:8); thither David fled from Absalom (2 Sm 17:24; 19:32; 1 K 2:8); commissary depot of Solomon (1 K 4:14).

Mahaneh-dan (mā'hȧ-nĕ-dăn', camp of Dan). Place W of Kiriath-jearim (Ju 13: 25 [KJ: camp of Dan]; 18:12).

Maharai (mȧ-hăr'ā-ī, swift). One of David's heroes (2 Sm 23:28; 1 Ch 11:30); commander for 11th month (1 Ch 27:13).

Mahath (mā'hăth, seizing?). 1. See *Ahimoth.* 2. Kohathite Levite; participated in restoring temple under Hezekiah (2 Ch 29:12; 31:13).

Mahavite (mā'hȧ-vīt). Designation of Eliel (1 Ch 11:46).

Mahazioth (mȧ-hā'zĭ-ŏth, visions). Son of Heman (1 Ch 25:4, 30).

Maher-shalal-hashbaz (mā'hĕr-shăl'ăl-hăsh' băz, spoil speeds, prey hastens). Symbolic name given by Isaiah to son (Is 8:1-4).

Mahlah (mä'lȧ, sick). 1. Daughter of Zelophehad (Nm 26:33; 27:1-8; 36:1-12; Jos 17:3, 4). 2. Child of Hammolecheth (1 Ch 7:18. KJ: Mahalah).

Mahli (mä'lī, sickly). 1. Levite; son of Merari (Ex 6:19 [KJ: Mahali]; Nm 3:20; 1 Ch 6:19; 23:21; 24:26; 1 Esd 8:47 [KJ: Moli; RV: Mooli]). 2. Grandson of Merari (1 Ch 6:47; 23:23; 24:30).

Mahlites (mä'līts). Descendants of Mahli (Nm 3:33; 26:58).

Mahlon (mä'lŏn, sickly). Son of Elimelech and Naomi; husband of Ruth (Ru 1:2; 4:10).

Mahol (mā'hŏl, dancing). Father of Heman, Calcol, Darda (1 K 4:31).

Mahseiah (mä-sē'yȧ, LORD is refuge). Ancestor of Baruch and Seraiah (Jer 32:12; 51:59. KJ: Maaseiah). KJ: Maasias; RV: Maaseas in Bar 1:1.

Maianeas, Maianness (mī-ăn'ē-ăs, -ăn'ăs). See *Maaseiah 12.*

maid, maiden. 1. Female servant (Gn 16:1). 2. Virgin (Dt 22:17) or young woman (2 Ch 36:17; Jer 2:32). 3. Harlot (Am 2:7).

majesty. 1. Dignity and splendor of God (Ex 15:7 [KJ: excellence]; 1 Ch 16:27 [KJ: honor]; Ps 104:1). 2. Splendor of rulers (Est 1:4).

Makaz (mā'kăz, end). Place in district of son of Dekar (1 K 4:9).

Maked (mā'kĕd). City of Gilead (1 Mac 5:26). KJ: Maged in 5:36.

maker. 1. Human fabricator (Eze 20:49 [KJ: speaker; RV: speaker]; Is 45:16; Hab 2:18). 2. God as creator (Gn 14:19 [KJ, RV: possessor]; Jb 4:17; Ps 95:6; Pr 14: 31; Heb 11:10).

Makheloth (măk-hē'lŏth, assemblies). Encampment of Israel in wilderness (Nm 32:25, 26).

Makkedah (mă-kē'dȧ, place of sheep marking?). Canaanite city N of Lachish (Jos 10:10-29; 12:16; 15:41).

Maktesh (măk'tĕsh, mortar. RSV: Mortar). Mortar-shaped valley in Jerusalem (Zph 1:11).

Malachi (măl'à-kī, my messenger. KJ, RV: Malachy in 2 Esd 1:40). Nothing (beyond statements in book) known of this prophet; regarded contemporary of Nehemiah (Mal 2:11-17 — see Neh 13:23 to 31; Mal 3:8-11 — see Neh 13:10-13). Outline of book: 1. Preamble (1:1-5). 2. Sins of the Priests (1:6—2:9). 3. Sins of the People (2:10—4:1). 4. The Rising of the Sun of Righteousness (4:2-6).

Malcam, Malcham (măl'kăm, their king). 1. Benjaminite (1 Ch 8:9). 2. See *Milcom.*

Malchiah (măl-kī'à). See *Malchijah.*

Malchiel (măl'kī-ĕl, God is king). Grandson of Asher; progenitor of Malchielites (Gn 46:17; Nm 26:45; 1 Ch 7:31).

Malchijah (măl-kī'jà, LORD is king. KJ usually: Malchiah). 1. Levite, ancestor of Asaph (1 Ch 6:40). 2. Head of 5th course of priests (1 Ch 24:1, 9); house of Pashhur, prominent in exilic days, descended from him. See *Pashhur* 4. 3. Divorced foreign wife (Ez 10:25; 1 Esd 9:26 [KJ, RV: Melchias]). 4. Sons of Parosh; divorced foreign wives (Ez 10:25 [RSV: Hashabiah]). Asibias in 1 Esd 9:26. 5. Divorced foreign wife (Ez 10:31); helped rebuild Jerusalem's walls (Neh 3:11). Melchias in 1 Esd 9:32. 6. Son of Rechab; repaired dung gate (Neh 3:14). 7. Goldsmith; repaired wall (Neh 3:31). 8. Priest; participated in reading of Law (Neh 8:4; 1 Esd 9:44 [KJ, RV: Melchias]), dedication of Jerusalem's walls (Neh 12:42); probably same who sealed covenant with Nehemiah (Neh 10:3). 9. Prince into whose dungeon Jeremiah was cast (Jer 21:1 [KJ: Melchiah]; 38:1, 6. RSV: Malchiah).

Malchiram (măl-kī'răm, king is exalted). Son of Jehoiachin (1 Ch 3:18).

Malchi-shua (măl-kī-shoō'à, king is help. KJ: Melchi-shua in 1 Sm 14:49; 31:2). Son of Saul (1 Ch 8:33; 9:39; 10:2).

Malchus (măl'kus, king). High priest's servant whose ear Peter cut off (Jn 18:10. See Mt 26:51; Lk 22:50).

malefactor (măl'ĕ-făk-tēr). KJ (Jn 18:30), KJ, RV (Lk 23:32-43) for evildoer, criminal.

Maleleel (mà-lē'lĕ-ĕl). See *Mahalaleel.*

malice, maliciousness. Vicious disposition and expression thereof (Ro 1:29; Tts 3:3).

mallet. See *trade* 5.

Mallos (măl'os). See *Mallus.*

Mallothi (măl'ō-thī). Son of Heman; temple musician (1 Ch 25:4, 26).

mallow (H *malluah*, salt plant. RV: saltwort). Plant used as food (Jb 30:4).

Malluch (măl'uk, ruling). 1. Levite; ancestor of Ethan (1 Ch 6:44). 2. Son of Bani; divorced foreign wife (Ez 10:29; 1 Esd 9:30 [KJ, RV: Mamuchus]). 3. Native of Harim; divorced foreign wife (Ez 10:32). 4, 5. Two who sealed covenant (Neh 10:4, 27). 6. Priest; head of father's house (Neh 12:2). Malluchi in Neh 12:14 (KJ, RV marg: Melicu). Possibly same as 4.

Malluchi (măl'lû-kī). See *Malluch* 3.

Mallus (măl'us. KJ: Mallos). City of Cilicia (2 Mac 4:30).

Malta (môl'tà). See *Melita.*

Maltanneus (măl-tă-nē'us). See *Mattenai* 2; 3.

Mamaias (mà-mā'yăs). See *Shemaiah 18.*

Mamdai (măm'dà-ī). See *Benaiah 10.*

mammon (măm'un, Aramaic *mamona,* wealth). Riches and its personification (Mt 6:24; Lk 16:9, 11, 13).

Mamnitanaimus, Mamnitanemus (măm-nǐ-tà-nā'mus, -nē'mus). Listed in 1 Esd 9:34 (RSV: Machnadebai); probably conflation of Mattaniah and Mattenai (Ez 10:37).

Mamre (măm'rĕ, strength?). 1. Amorite; confederate of Abraham (Gn 14:13, 24). 2. Residence of Abraham near or in Hebron (Gn 13:18; 14:13; 18:1; 23:17, 19; 25:9; 35:27; 49:30; 50:13).

Mamuchus (mà-mū'kus). See *Malluch 2.*

man. Creature of God (Gn 1:26, 27), transitory (Jb 14; Ps 103:15, 16), dependent on God (Mt 6:26-30; Acts 17:24-28), endowed with body (Mt 6:25; Ro 12:4; 1 Co 12:12), flesh (Ps 145:21; Is 40:6; Ro 1:3; 1 Co 1:26), soul, spirit (Gn 2:7; 41:8; Ps 76:12; Mt 10:28; Lk 9:56; Ph 1:27), intelligence (Pr; Ec; Lk 2:19; Jn 12:40; Ro 2:15; 12:2). He is self-conscious and free as being responsible to God; created in image and likeness of God (Gn 1:26, 27; 9:6; 1 Co 11:7; Cl 3:10). Man fell into sin (Gn 3; Ro 5:15-21); refuses to honor and thank God, reverences and worships created things (Ro 1:19-25); subject to death (Ro 5:17). God confronts man in Law, shows his alienation (Ro 7:14-24), saves him through faith in Jesus Christ (Ro 5:15 to 21), and conforms believer to His Son's image (Ro 8:29; 1 Co 15:48, 49; Cl 1:15; 3:10). Names: H: 1. *'adham* (earthy creature, mankind. Gn 1:27). 2. *'ish* (man as individual; distinguished from woman. Gn 3:16). 3. *'enosh* (mortal. 2 Ch 14:11). 4. *ba'al* (master. Gn 20:3). 5. *gebher, gibhor* (strong man, hero. Ex 10:11). 6. *zakhar* (male. Lv 15:33). G: 1. *anthropos* (generic. Ro 5:12). 2. *aner* (man as individual. Mt 7:24). 3. *arsen* (male. Ro 1:27). See *body; flesh; Jesus Christ; sin; soul; spirit.*

Man of Sin. Man of lawlessness; exalts self over God; sits in God's temple; proclaims self God; brings rebellion, deception, delusion; revealed at Parousia (2 Th 2:3-12. See Dn 7; 1 Jn 2:18; Rv 13; 19).

Man, Son of. See *Jesus Christ.*

Manaen (măn'à-ĕn, comforter). Christian prophet or teacher at Antioch (Acts 13:1).

Manahath (măn'à-hăth, rest). 1. Horite; son of Shobal (Gn 36:23; 1 Ch 1:40). 2. Place to which Benjaminites were carried captive (1 Ch 8:6).

Manahathites, Manahethites (mà-nā'hăth-īts, -hĕth-īts). Descendants of Manahath (1 Ch 2:54). See also *Menuhoth.*

Manasseas (măn-ă-sē'ăs). See *Manasseh 5.*

Manasseh (mà-năs'ĕ, cause to forget). 1. 1st son of Joseph and Asenath (Gn 41:50, 51); blessed by Jacob (Gn 48:8-22). 2. Tribe descended from Manasseh (Gn 50:23; Nm 26:28-34; Jos 17:1; Rv 7:6 [KJ: Manasses]); half of tribe possessed Gilead and Bashan E of Jordan (Nm 32:33-42; Jos 12:4-6; Dt 3:13-17); other half settled W of Jordan, S of Asher and Issachar, N of Ephraim (Jos 17:5-10). 3. H in Ju 18:30 for Moses (RV, RSV). 4. 14th king of Judah; son and successor of Hezekiah; wicked; restored many forms of heathen worship; carried into captivity by Assyrians (2 K 21; 2 Ch 33; Jer 47—49; Zph 2:4-9; Mt 1:10 [KJ: Manasses]). Mentioned in inscription of Esarhaddon. 5. Divorced foreign wife (Ez 10:30). Manasseas in 1 Esd 9:31. 6. Divorced foreign wife (Ez 10:33; 1 Esd

9:33 [KJ, RV: Manasses]). 7. Husband of Judith (Jdth 8:2. KJ, RV: Manasses).

Manasses (ma-năs'ēz). 1. Mentioned in Tob 14:10 (RSV: Ahikar). 2. See *Manasseh*.

Manassites (ma-năs'īts). Descendants of Manasseh (Dt 4:43; 2 K 10:33).

mandrake (măn'drăk). Narcotic, slightly poisonous plant with whitish or violet-purple flowers and forked roots; regarded as love potion (Gn 30:14-16; SS 7:13).

maneh (măn'ĕ). See *mina*.

Manes (mā'nēz). See *Maaseiah 7*.

manger (măn'jẽr, G *phatne*). Trough for cattle (Lk 2:7-16; 13:15). See also *crib*.

Mani (mā'nī). See *Bani 4*.

Manius, Manlius (mā'nī-us, măn'lī-us). See *Titus 2*.

manna (măn'a, what?) Food; like hoarfrost in appearance; miraculously provided Israel in desert (Ex 16:14-36; Nm 11:7-9; Dt 8:3; Jos 5:12. See Heb 9:4). Jesus is true manna from heaven (Jn 6:31-40).

Manoah (ma-nō'a, rest). Father of Samson (Ju 13).

mansion. See *homes 5*.

manslayer. One who accidentally kills; could find asylum in cities of refuge (Nm 35; Dt 4:42; 19:3-10; Jos 20:3).

mantle. See *dress*.

mantle of Shinar (shī'när). See *Babylonish garment*.

manuscripts (măn'û-skrĭpts). Original manuscripts of Bible lost. Before Christian era OT written with consonants only; Massoretes added vowels and notes. Until recently (see *scrolls, Dead Sea*) oldest OT manuscript was dated AD 916. Important NT uncials: Sinaiticus (4th c), Vaticanus (4th c), Alexandrinus (5th c), Ephraemi (5th c), Bezae (6th c). Important for NT are older papyri (e. g., Chester Beatty). See *writing*.

Maoch (mā'ŏk, oppression). See *Maacah 4*.

Maon (mā'ŏn, dwelling). 1. Town 8½ mi S of Hebron (Jos 15:55; 1 Sm 23:24, 25; 25:2). Modern Tell Main. 2. Son of Shammai (1 Ch 2:45).

Maonites (mā'on-īts). See *Meunim*.

Mara (mā'ra, bitter). Name given to herself by Naomi (Ru 1:20).

Marah (mā'ra, bitter). Spring of bitter water in wilderness of Shur (Ex 15: 22-25; Nm 33:8, 9).

Maralah (măr'a-lä, trembling. RSV: Mareal). Place 4 mi from Nazareth on boundary of Zebulun (Jos 19:11).

maranatha (măr-a-năth'a). See *anathema Maranatha*.

marble. Limestone which can be highly polished (1 Ch 29:2; Est 1:6; Rv 18:12).

Marcus (mär'kus). See *Mark*.

Mardocheus (mär-dô-kē'us). See *Mordecai*.

Mareal (măr'ē-ăl). See *Maralah*.

Mareshah (ma-rē'sha, summit). 1. City between Hebron and Gaza; fortified by Rehoboam (Jos 15:44; 2 Ch 11:8; 14:9, 10; 20:37; Mi 1:15). Marisa in 2 Mac 12:35. Excavated in 20th c. 2. Judahite (1 Ch 2:42). 3. Son of Laadah (1 Ch 4:21). 4. See *Mesha 3*.

Marimoth (măr'ī-mŏth). See *Meraioth 1*.

Marisa (măr'ī-sa) See *Mareshah 1*.

Mark (märk, KJ: Marcus in Cl 4:10; Phlm 24; 1 Ptr 5:13). John Mark (Acts 12:12, 25; 15:37. Sometimes John: Acts 13:5, 13); native of Jerusalem (Acts 12:12-17); relative of Barnabas (Cl 4:10); spiritual son of Peter (1 Ptr 5:13); accompanied Paul and Barnabas to Antioch (Acts 12: 25; 13:1); deserted on 1st missionary journey (Acts 13:13); cause of strife between Paul and Barnabas (Acts 15:36-

41); went with Barnabas to Cyprus (Acts 15:39); later, helper of Paul (2 Ti 4:11; Cl 4:10; Phlm 24); perhaps young man of Mk 14:51, 52. Tradition makes Mark interpreter of Peter (see 1 Ptr 5:13) and founder of church of Alexandria.

Mark, Gospel of. 2d and shortest of 4 Gospels. According to Papias, Mark wrote Peter's Gospel. Author well acquainted with Jewish thought and life. Primarily addressed to Gentile Christians. Outline: 1. Baptism and Temptation of Jesus (1: 1-13). 2. Early Galilean Ministry (1:14 to 7:23). 3. Tour to Tyre and Sidon (7: 24-30). 4. Later Galilean Ministry (7: 31—9). 5. Ministry in Perea (10). 6. Passion Week and Resurrection Morning (11—16). See *Jesus Christ*.

market. Place in cities for public transactions, community fellowship, and sale of goods (Ps 55:11 [KJ, RV: streets]; Pr 7:12 [KJ: streets; RV: broad places]; Mt 11:16; Lk 11:43; Acts 16:19; 17:17).

Market of Appius (ăp'ī-us). See *Apii Forum*.

Marmoth (mär'mŏth). See *Meremoth 2*.

Maroth (mā'rŏth, bitterness). Town of Judah (Mi 1:12).

marriage. Permanent union between man and woman (Gn 1:26-31; 2:18-25; Mt 19:5). While monogamy is Biblical ideal (Mt 19:5; 1 Ti 3:2), bigamy (Gn 4:19) and polygamy (Gn 30; 1 K 11:3) were practiced in OT, probably also in NT (1 Ti 3:2). Israelites forbidden to marry Canaanites (Dt 7:3, 4); there were legal restrictions on Ammonites, Moabites, Edomites, Egyptians (Dt 23:3-8. See *Ru* 1:4). Foreign wives divorced after exile (Ez 9; 10). Marriage between flesh of flesh (Lv 18; 20) forbidden. Some additional instances (Lv 21; Nm 36:5-9).

Marriage highly regarded as creation of God (Pr 25:24; 31:10-31). Procreation (Gn 1:28; 29:32; 30:1), assistance, companionship (Gn 2:18-24) are objects of marriage. Sexual life in marriage is honorable (Pr 5:15-19; 1 Th 4:1-5; Heb 13: 4) but regulated (1 Sm 21:3-6; 2 Sm 11: 11-13; Lv 12; 15:18-33).

Divorce not part of God's plan (Mt 19: 3-7); allowed (Dt 24:1-4; Mt 19:7-9) with restrictions (Dt 22:13-29); enjoined under certain circumstances (Ez 10:11-44); conscience of divorced believer pacified (1 Co 7:12-16). Divorce, except for fornication, is commission of adultery (Mt 5:31, 32; 19:3-10; Mk 10:2-12; Lk 16: 18).

Fathers often secured wives for sons. Marriage customs differed. Betrothal was formal, legal proceeding confirmed by oath and dowry (H *mohar*). Thereafter two regarded as man and wife (Mt 1:18-20. See Tob 7:14). Marriage celebration occurred when bridegroom removed bride from her father's house to his home (Is 61:10; SS 3:11; 1 Mac 9:39; Mt 25:1-13). Covenant union between God and Israel spoken of as marriage (Is 62:1-5; Jer 2:2). Church is bride of Christ the Bridegroom (Lk 5:34; 2 Co 11:2; Rv 21:2).

marriage, levirate. See *levirate marriage*.

Marsena (mär-sē'na). Persian prince (Est 1:14).

Mars' Hill (märz). See *Areopagus*.

Martha (mär'tha, lady). Sister of Lazarus and Mary (Lk 10:38-41; Jn 11; 12:2).

martyr (mär'tẽr, witness). G *martus* usually: witness. KJ: martyr in Acts 22:20;

Rv 2:13; 17:6; RV, RSV in Rv 17:6; developed meaning of witnessing by giving life in early church.

Mary (mâr'ĭ, rebellion). Miriam in OT. 1. See *Mary, mother of Jesus.* 2. Mary, wife of Clopas (Jn 19:25); mother of James and Joses (Mt 27:56; Mk 15:40; Lk 24:10); witnessed crucifixion (Mt 27: 56; Mk 15:40; Lk 24:10) and burial (Mt 27:61; Mk 15:47); visited grave on resurrection morning (Mt 28:1; Mk 16:1; Lk 24:10). 3. Mary Magdalene, often regarded as woman of Lk 7:37-50 (See Mk 16:9; Lk 8:1, 2); witnessed crucifixion and burial (Mt 27:56, 61; Mk 15:40, 47; Jn 19:25); came to tomb on resurrection morning (Mt 28:1; Mk 16:1; Lk 24:1; Jn 20:1); saw risen Lord (Mt 28:9; Jn 20: 11-29). 4. Mary of Bethany, sister of Lazarus and Martha (Jn 11:1); sat at Jesus' feet while Martha served (Lk 10: 38-41); anointed Jesus' feet (Jn 12:1-8; see Jn 11). 5. Mary, mother of Mark; sister of Barnabas (Cl 4:10); opened her Jerusalem home to Peter (Acts 12:12). 6. Christian at Rome (Ro 16:6).

Mary, mother of Jesus. Wife of Joseph (Mt 1:18-25); lineage of David (Lk 1:27; Ro 1:3); gave birth to Jesus at Bethlehem (Mt 1:18, 20; Lk 2:1-20); went to temple for purification (Lk 2:22-38); fled with Joseph, Jesus to Egypt (Mt 2:13-15); lived at Nazareth (Mt 2:19-23; Lk 2:39, 40); with 12-yr-old Jesus at temple (Lk 2:41-50); at wedding of Cana (Jn 2:1-12); entrusted by Jesus to care of John (Jn 19:25-27); with early believers (Acts 1:14). Mary called blessed among women (Lk 1:42, 48. See Lk 1:28; 11: 27, 28); pondered mission of Jesus (Lk 2:51); believed in His powers (Jn 2:3-5); Jesus stresses spiritual rather than physical relationship (Mt 12:46-50; Lk 8:20, 21; 11:27, 28).

Masaloth (măs'ȧ-lŏth). See *Mesaloth.*

Maschil (măs'kel, attentive). Word in title of Ps 44, 45, 52—55, 74, 78, 88, 89, 142. May designate nature of poem or music (perh contemplative).

Mash (măsh). Son of Aram (Gn 10:23). Meshech in 1 Ch 1:17.

Mashal (mā'shăl). See *Mishal.*

Masiah, Masias (mȧ-sī'ȧ, mȧ-sī'ăs). Listed in 1 Esd 5:34.

Masman (măs'măn). See *Shemaiah 18.*

mason. See *homes; trade 11.*

Maspha (măs'fȧ). See *Mizpah 5.*

Masrekah (măs'rē-kȧ, vineyard). City in Edom (Gn 36:36; 1 Ch 1:47).

Massa (măs'ȧ). Son of Ishmael (Gn 25:14; 1 Ch 1:30) and tribe descended from him (RSV: Pr 30:1; 31:1).

Massah (măs'ȧ, temptation). Name given to Meribah (Ex 17:7; Dt 6:16; 9:22; 33:8; Ps 95:8 [KJ: temptation]).

Massias (mȧ-sī'ăs). See *Maaseiah 8.*

master. 1. Master of house; husband (Gn 20:3; Mt 10:25). 2. Ruler, owner, posessor, lord (Gn 24:14, 27; 39:20; 2 K 19:4; Mt 24:45; 25:19-26). 3. Teacher (Mt 23: 10; Mk 9:5). See *Rabbi.* 4. Supervisor, superior (Lk 5:5; 8:24).

mat. See *homes 5; trade 2.*

Mathanias (măth-ȧ-nī'ăs). See *Mattaniah 8.*

Mathelas (măth'ē-lăs). See *Maaseiah 6.*

Mathusala (mȧ-thū'sȧ-lȧ). See *Methuselah.*

Matred (mā'trĕd, driving forward). Mother of Mehetabel, wife of Hadad 4 (Gn 36: 39; 1 Ch 1:50).

Matri, Matrites (mā'trī, mā'trīts). Benjaminite family (1 Sm 10:21).

Mattan (măt'ăn, gift). 1. Priest of Baal (2 K 11:18). 2. Father of Shephatiah (Jer 38:1).

Mattanah (măt'ȧ-nȧ, gift). Encampment of Israel in desert (Nm 21:18, 19).

Mattaniah (măt-ȧ-nī'ȧ, LORD's gift). 1. Original name of Zedekiah (2 K 24:17). 2. Son of Heman; leader of 9th division of musicians (1 Ch 25:4, 16). 3. Levite of Asaph family; leader of temple choir after exile (1 Ch 9:15; 2 Ch 20:14; Neh 11: 17; 12:8, 25, 35). 4. Levite of Asaph family; assisted Hezekiah in reformation (2 Ch 29:13). 5. Levite; father of Zaccur (Neh 13:13). 6. Divorced foreign wife (Ez 10:26; 1 Esd 9:27 [KJ, RV: Matthanias]). 7. Divorced foreign wife (Ez 10: 27). Othonias (RSV: Othoniah) in 1 Esd 9:28. 8. Divorced foreign wife (Ez 10: 30). KJ: Mathanias; RV: Matthanias; RSV: Bescaspasmys in 1 Esd 9:31. 9. Divorced foreign wife (Ez 10:37). See *Mamnitanaimus.*

Mattatha (măt'ȧ-thȧ, gift). Grandson of David (Lk 3:31).

Mattathah (măt'ȧ-thȧ). See *Mattattah.*

Mattathiah (măt-ȧ-thī'ȧ). See *Mattithiah 4.*

Mattathias (măt-ȧ-thī'ăs, gift of LORD). 1. 2. Ancestors of Christ (Lk 3:25, 26). 3. See *Mattattah.* 4. See *Mattithiah 4.* 5. Father of the Maccabees (1 Mac 2:1). See also *Maccabees.* 6. Son of Simon Maccabaeus (1 Mac 16:14). 7. A captain (1 Mac 11: 70). 8. An envoy (2 Mac 14:19).

Mattattah (măt'ăt-tȧ, gift). Divorced foreign wife (Ez 10:33 [KJ: Mattathah]; 1 Esd 9:33 [KJ: Matthias; RV: Mattathias]).

Mattenai (măt-ē-nā'ī, generous). 1. Priest of family of Joiarib (Neh 12:19). 2. Divorced foreign wife (Ez 10:33; 1 Esd 9: 33 [KJ: Altaneus. RV: Mattanneus]). 3. Divorced foreign wife (Ez 10:37).

Matthan (măt'thăn, gift. Ancestor of Joseph (Mt 1:15).

Matthanias (măt-thȧ-nī'ăs). See *Mattaniah 6; 8.*

Matthat (măt'thăt). Ancestor of Christ (Lk 3:24, 29).

Matthelas (măt-thē'lăs). See *Maaseiah 6.*

Matthew (măth'ū, H Mattathias, gift of LORD). Son of Alpheus; surnamed Levi; tax collector at Capernaum, where called into discipleship and gave feast for Jesus (Mt 9:9-13; Mk 2:14-17; Lk 5:27-32); appointed apostle (Mt 10:3; Mk 3:18; Lk 6:15; Acts 1:13).

Matthew, Gospel of. Ascribed to Matthew. Papias and Irenaeus hold that he wrote in Hebrew (Aramaic). Gospel written for Jewish converts to show that Jesus is Messiah promised in OT. Outline: 1. Messiah's Birth and Early Years (1:1—4:16). 2. Messiah's Galilean Ministry (4:17—18:35). 3. Messiah's Perean Ministry (19; 20). 4. Messiah Teaches in Jerusalem (21—25). 5. Messiah's Death and Resurrection (26—28). See *Jesus Christ.*

Matthias (mȧ-thī'ăs, gift of LORD). 1. Apostle chosen to fill place of Judas (Acts 1: 15-26). 2. See *Mattattah.*

Mattithiah (măt-ĭ-thī'ȧ, gift of LORD). 1. Korahite Levite in charge of baked food (1 Ch 9:31). 2. Levite; son of Jeduthun; musician (1 Ch 15:18, 21). 3. Divorced foreign wife (Ez 10:43; 1 Esd 9:35 [KJ, RV: Mazitias]). 4. Stood by Ezra at reading of law (Neh 8:4). Mattathias (RSV: Mattathiah) in 1 Esd 9:43.

mattock (măt'uk). See *agriculture 2.*

maul. War club or battle ax (Pr 25:18. RSV: war club).

maxim. See *proverb*.

Mazitias (măz-i-tī'ás). See *Mattithiah 3*.

Mazzaroth (măz'á-rŏth). 12 signs of Zodiac (Jb 38:32).

meadow 1. Pasture land. 2. KJ for H *ahu* (Gn 41:2. RV, RSV: reed grass). 3. KJ: meadows of Gibeah in Ju 20:33 (RV: Maareh-geba. RSV: west of Geba).

Meah (mē´á, hundred). Tower of Jerusalem (Neh 3:1; 12:39. RV: Hammeah; RSV: the Hundred).

meal offering. See *cereal offering*.

Meani (mě-a´ni). See *Meunim*.

Mearah (mě-ā´rá, cave). Place between Tyre and Sidon (Jos 13:4).

measures. 1. *Lineal*. a. *Fingerbreadth*, c ¾ in. b. *Handbreadth*, four fingerbreadths (c 3½ in). c. *Span*, distance from tip of thumb to tip of little finger when outstretched (c 9 in). d. *Cubit*, two spans (c 18 in). e. *Reed* (measuring reed, *calamus*), 6 cubits (c 9 ft). f. *Pace*, distance of step (c 30 in). g. *A little way* (Gn 48:7), the distance one could walk in an hour (c 3 to 4 mi). h. *Day's journey*, distance traveled in a day (c 20 mi). i. *Furlong* (G measure: *stadium*; 600 G ft; 606¾ ft). j. *Fathom*, distance between outstretched hands (5—6 ft). k. *Mile* (L *mille*), 1,000 paces (c 4,854 ft). l. *Sabbath day's journey*, 3,000 ft (see Jos 3:4). In Talmud, 4,500 ft.

2. *Dry*. a. *Handful*, amount held in hand. b. *Kab* (KJ: cab), c 2 qts. c. *Seah* (KJ: measure), 6 kabs (c 10—12 qts). d. *Ephah*, equal to liquid bath (3 pecks and 3 pts). f. *Homer*, 10 ephahs, an ass load (c 8 bushels). f. *Omer*, one-tenth ephah (c 5 pts). g. *Choenix* (KJ: measure; RSV: quart; Rv 6:6), c 1 qt. h. *Modius* (bushel in Mt 5:15; Mk 4:21; Lk 11:33), probably c 1 peck. i. *Saton* (measure in Mt 13:33; Lk 13:21), c 1 peck. j. *Cor* (measure in Lk 16:7), a homer (c 8 bushels).

3. *Liquid*. a. *Log*, amount displaced by 6 hen's eggs (c 1 pt). b. *Hin*, 12 logs (c 6 qts). c. *Bath*, six hins, roughly equal to an ephah (c 8 gals). d. *Firkin*, c 9 gals. e. *Sextarius*, c 1 pt. (Klinck)

meat. See *food 5*.

meat offering. See *cereal offering*.

Mebunnai (mě-bŭn'nī). See *Sibbecai*.

Mecherathite (mě-kē´răth-īt). Perhaps same as Maacathite (1 Ch 11:36; see 2 Sm 23:34).

Meconah (mě-kō´ná, base. KJ: Mekonah). Town near Ziklag (Neh 11:28).

Medaba (měd´á-bá). See *Medeba*.

Medad (mē´dăd). Elder chosen by Moses; prophet (Nm 11:26, 27).

Medan (mē´dăn). Son of Abraham and Keturah (Gn 25:2; 1 Ch 1:32).

Mede (mēd). Person of Median nationality (2 K 17:6; Est 1:19; Is 13:17; Jer 51:11; Dn 5:28). See also *Madai*.

Medeba (měd´ě-bá, quiet water). City 18 mi E of Dead Sea (Nm 21:30; Jos 13:9, 16; 1 Ch 19:7; Is 15:2; 1 Mac 9:36 [KJ, RV: Medaba]).

Media (mē´dī-á). Country NW of Persia, S of Caspian Sea; inhabitants Aryan Indo-Europeans; famous for horses. In 612 BC Medes captured Nineveh. Under Nebuchadnezzar Median kingdom extended from Persian Gulf to Caspian Sea (Est 1:3, 14, 18; 10:2; Is 21:2; Dn 8:20).

mediator (mē´dī-ā-tẽr). Person who acts as go-between (1 Sm 2:25 [KJ, RV: judge]; Jb 33:23 [KJ, RV: interpreter]; Is 43:27 [KJ: teachers; RV: interpreters]). Christ is Mediator of new covenant, through whom God and man are reconciled (1 Ti 2:5; Heb 8:6; 9:15; 12:24). See *Jesus Christ*.

medicine. See *apothecary; disease*.

Mediterranean Sea (měd-i-te-rā'ně-ăn). Referred to as "sea" (Nm 13:29; Acts 10:6), "great sea" (Nm 34:6), "western sea" (Dt 11:24 [RV: hinder sea]; Jl 2:20. KJ: uttermost, utmost sea), or "Sea of Philistines" (Ex 23:31).

medium. See *familiar spirit*.

Meeda, Meedda (mě-ē'dá, -ĕd'á). See *Mehida*.

meek, meekness. Humble, submissive frame of mind; not easily provoked; ready to submit to will and truth of God (Nm 12:3; Ps 10:17; Is 29:19; Mt 5:5; 2 Co 10:1; Eph 4:2; Cl 3:12; Ja 1:21).

Megiddo, Megiddon (mě-gĭd'ō, -ŏn, place of troops). City overlooking plain of Esdraelon; situated on 2 important trade routes (Jos 12:21; 17:11; Ju 1:27; 5:19); fortified by Solomon (1 K 9:15); Ahaziah died there (2 K 9:27); scene of battle between Pharaoh Neco and Josiah (2 K 23:29; 2 Ch 35:22). See also *Armageddon*.

Mehetabeel (mě-hět'á-bēl). See *Mehetabel 2*.

Mehetabel (mě-hět'á-bĕl, God blesses). 1. Wife of Hadad 4 (Gn 36:39; 1 Ch 1:50). 2. Father of Delaiah (Neh 6:10. KJ: Mehetabeel).

Mehida (mě-hī'dá, union). Progenitor of family of Nethinim (Ez 2:52; 1 Esd 5:32 [KJ: Meeda; RV: Meedda]).

Mehir (mē'hẽr, price). Judahite (1 Ch 4:11).

Meholathite (mě-hō'lá-thīt). Native of Meholah (1 Sm 18:19; 2 Sm 21:8), or probably Abel-meholah.

Mehujael (mě-hū'já-ĕl). Grandson of Cain (Gn 4:18).

Mehuman (mě-hū'măn, faithful). Chamberlain of Ahasuerus (Est 1:10).

Mehunim (mě-hū'nĭm). See *Meunim*.

Me-jarkon (mě-jär'kŏn, yellow waters). Town of Dan (Jos 19:46).

Mekonah (mě-kō'ná). See *Meconah*.

Melatiah (měl-á-tī'á, LORD delivered). Gibeonite; helped rebuild Jerusalem's wall (Neh 3:7).

Melchi (měl'kī, my king). Two ancestors of Jesus (Lk 3:24).

Melchiah (měl-kī'á). See *Malchijah 9*.

Melchias (měl-kī'ăs). See *Malchijah 3; 5; 8*.

Melchiel (měl-kī'ĕl, God is king). Father of Charmis, magistrate of Bethulia (Jdth 6:15).

Melchisedec (měl-kĭz'e-děk). See *Melchizedek*.

Melchi-shua (měl-kī-shōō'á). See *Malchishua*.

Melchizedek (měl-kĭz'e-děk, king of righteousness. KJ in NT: Melchisedec). King of Salem (Jerusalem) and priest of God Most High; blessed Abram and received tithes from him (Gn 14:17-20). Symbol of Christ, King-Priest (Ps 110:4; Heb 5:6-10; 6:20; 7).

Melea (mě'lě-á). Ancestor of Jesus (Lk 3:31).

Melech (mē'lěk, king). Son of Micah (1 Ch 8:35; 9:41).

Melicu (měl'ī-kū). See *Malluch 6*.

Melita (měl'ī-tá, honey). Island of Malta (as RSV. Acts 28:1).

melon. See *food 4*.

Melzar (měl'zär). Persian word for steward (RV, RSV, KJ marg: steward. Dn 1: 11, 16).

Memeroth (měm'ĕ-rŏth). See Meraioth 1.

Memmius. See Quintus Memmius.

memorial. Mark or observance to remind of persons or events: stone(s) (Gn 31:45; Jos 4:3-9); Passover (Ex 12:14. See 13:9); written record (Ex 17:14); cereal offering (Lv 2:9); convocation (Lv 23:24); God's name (Is 26:8). Lord's Supper memorial of Christ's death (1 Co 11:24-26).

Memphis (měm'fĭs, place of good. KJ: Noph except Hos 9:6). Ancient Egyptian city on Nile 10 mi N of Cairo. Mentioned negatively in prophets who called it Noph and Moph (Is 19:13; Jer 2:16; 44:1; 46:14, 19; Eze 30:13, 16 [RSV emends text in 16]).

Memucan (mĕ-mū'kăn). Persian prince (Est 1:14-21).

Menahem (měn'à-hěm, comforter). 16th king of Israel; slew Shallum and usurped throne; paid tribute to Pul (Tiglath-pileser); practiced calf worship (2 K 15: 14-22).

Menan (mē'năn). See Menna.

Mene, mene, tekel and parsin (mē'nĕ, mē'nĕ, tĕk'ĕl, ănd pär'sĭn). (KJ, RV: upharsin). Aramaic words (numbered, numbered, weighed, and divisions) which hand wrote on wall at Belshazzar's feast (Dn 5:25-28).

Menelaus (měn-ĕ-lā'us). High priest (2 Mac 4:23).

Menestheus (mĕ-něs'thūs). Father of Apollonius (2 Mac 4:21).

Meni (mē'nī, destiny). Canaanite deity of destiny (Is 65:11. KJ: that number. RV, RSV: Destiny).

Menna (měn'à. KJ: Menan). Ancestor of Jesus (Lk 3:31).

menstealers. Kidnapers (as RSV); stole men, sold them as slaves (1 Ti 1:10. See Ex 21:16; Dt 24:7).

Menuhoth (mě-nū'hŏth, resting places. KJ: Manahethites). Place inhabited by Judahites (1 Ch 2:52). Perhaps same as Manahath.

Meonenim (mě-ŏn'ĕ-nĭm, augurs). Diviners, whose oak (KJ: plain) stood near Shechem (Ju 9:37. RSV: Diviners' Oak).

Meonothai (mě-ŏn'ŏ-thī, my habitations). Judahite (1 Ch 4:14).

Mephaath (měf'à-ăth, beauty). Levitical town of Reuben (Jos 13:18; 21:37; Jer 48:21).

Mephibosheth (mě-fĭb'ŏ-shěth, destroying shame). 1. Son of Saul by Rizpah (2 Sm 21:8). 2. Son of Jonathan; crippled in panic after Saul's death; honored by David and given estates of Saul (2 Sm 4:4; 9: 6-13; 16:1-4; 19:24-30; 21:7). Meribbaal in 1 Ch 8:34; 9:40.

Merab (mē'răb, increase). Daughter of Saul (1 Sm 14:49; 18:17-19; 2 Sm 21:8 [KJ, RV: Michal]).

Meraiah (mě-rā'yà, rebellion). Priest (Neh 12:12).

Meraioth (mě-rā'yŏth, rebellious). 1. Priest; son of Zerahiah (1 Ch 6:6, 7, 52); ancestor of Ezra (2 Esd 1:2. KJ, RV: Marimoth). Memeroth in 1 Esd 8:2 (RSV omits). 2. Priest; son of Ahitub (1 Ch 9:11; Neh 11:11). 3. Priest; head of father's house (Neh 12:15). Meremoth in Neh 2:3.

Meran (mē'răn). See Merran.

Merari (mě-rā'rī, bitter). 1. 3d son of Levi; progenitor of Merarites (Gn 46:11; Ex 6:16; Nm 3:17; 4:29-33; 26:57; Jos 21:7, 34-40). 2. Father of Judith (Jdth 8:1).

Merathaim (měr-à-thā'ĭm, double rebellion). Name given to Babylon (Jer 50:21).

merchant. See commerce.

Mercurius, Mercury (mûr-kū'rĭ-us, mûr'-kū-rĭ). See Hermes 1.

mercy, merciful, show mercy. 1. See steadfast love. 2. H rahamim (bowels), compassion, sympathy (Is 47:6). 3. H hemlah (clemency), pity, clemency (Gn 19:16). 4. H hanan (favorably disposed), show favor (Ps 4:1; 6:2. RSV: be gracious). 3. H kipper (cover), pardon, expiate (Dt 21:8. RV, RSV: forgive). 6. G 'eleos and derivatives (pity), compassion, pity (Mt 5:7; 9:13; Lk 1:50). 7. G 'oiktirmon (feeling pity), compassionate (Ja 5:11. KJ: tender mercy). 8. G 'ilaskomai, 'ileos (incline toward), propitiate, propitious (Heb 8:12). G splanchna (bowels) used to designate feelings of mercy, tenderness, compassion (Cl 3:12. RSV: compassion).

mercy seat. Covering of ark. H kapporeth used especially of "covering" sin (Ex 25: 17-22; 26:34; 37:6-9). On Day of Atonement high priest burned incense before mercy seat, sprinkled blood on it (Lv 16). Blood of Christ is real atonement (Heb 9. G 'ilasterion).

Mered (mē'rěd, rebellion). Son of Ezrah (1 Ch 4:17).

Meremoth (měr'ĕ-mŏth, heights). 1. Divorced foreign wife (Ez 10:36). Carabasion in 1 Esd 9:34. 2. Priest; weighed silver and gold brought by Ezra from Babylon (Ez 8:33; 1 Esd 8:62 [KJ, RV: Marmoth]); repaired wall (Neh 3:4, 21). 3. See Meraioth 3. 4. Priest; sealed covenant with Nehemiah (Neh 10:5).

Meres (mē'rēz). Persian prince (Est 1:14).

Meribah (měr'ĭ-bä, strife). 1. Place near Rephidim where God gave Israel water from rock (Ex 17:1-7). 2. Meribah of Kadesh. See Meribath-kadesh.

Meribath-kadesh (měr'ĭ-băth-kă'děsh, meribah of Kadesh). Place near Kadesh in desert of Zin where Moses struck rock and water flowed (Dt 32:51 [KJ: Meribah-Kadesh]; RV: Meribah of Kadesh]; Eze 47:19 [KJ: strife in Kadesh; RV: Meriboth-kadesh]; Eze 48:28 [KJ: strife in Kadesh]). Meribah in Nm 20:1-24; 27: 14; Ps 81:7; 95:8 (KJ: provocation); 106: 32 (KJ: strife).

Merib-baal (měr'ĭb-bā'ăl, striver against Baal). See Mephibosheth 2.

Meriboth-kadesh (měr'ĭ-bŏth-kā'děsh). See Meribath-kadesh.

Merodach (mě-rō'dăk). Marduk (Bel); chief god of Babylonians (Jer 50:2).

Merodach-baladan (mě-rō'dăk-băl'à-dăn, Marduk gave son). Twice ruler of Babylon (722—710; 703—702 B C. 2 K 20:12 [KJ, RV: Berodach-baladan]; Is 39:1).

Merom (mē'rŏm, height). Place where Joshua defeated N coalition (Jos 11:5-7). Identified with Lake Huleh, Meiron, or Marun.

Meronothite (mě-rŏn'ŏ-thīt). Inhabitant of unidentified Meronoth (1 Ch 27:30; Neh 3:7).

Meroz (mē'rŏz). Town in Esdraelon (Ju 5:23).

Merran (měr'ăn. KJ: Meran). Tribe; sometimes identified with Medan (Bar 3:23).

Meruth (mē'rŭth). See Immer 1.

Mesaloth (měs'à-lŏth. KJ: Masaloth). Place in Arbela (1 Mac 9:2).

Mesech (mē'sěk). See Meshech 1.

Mesha (mē'shà). 1. Place in Arabia (Gn 10: 30). 2. King of Moab (2 K 3:4). 3. Son of Caleb (1 Ch 2:42. RSV: Mareshah). 4. Benjaminite (1 Ch 8:9).

Meshach (mē'shăk). Babylonian name given to Mishael (Dn 1:7; 3).

Meshech (mē'shĕk). 1. Son of Japheth (Gn 10:2; 1 Ch 1:5); descendants lived in SE Asia Minor (Ps 120:5 [KJ: Mesech]; Eze 27:13; 32:26; 38:3; 39:1). 2. See *Mash.*

Meshelemiah (mē-shĕl-ĕ-mī'á, LORD rewards). Kohathite Levite; gatekeeper (1 Ch 9:21; 26:1). Shelemiah in 1 Ch 26: 14. Perhaps same as Meshullam 20 and Shallum 8.

Meshezabel (mē-shĕz'á-bĕl, God frees. KJ: Meshezabeel). 1. Father of Berechiah (Neh 3:4). 2. Sealed covenant with Nehemiah (Neh 10:21). 3. Judahite (Neh 11:24).

Meshillemith (mē-shĭl'ĕ-mĭth). See *Meshillemoth 2.*

Meshillemoth (mē-shĭl'ĕ-mŏth, recompence). 1. Ephraimite (2 Ch 28:12). 2. Priest (Neh 11:13). Meshillemith in 1 Ch 9:12.

Meshobab (mē-shō'băb, restored). Simeonite; migrated with family to Gedor (1 Ch 4:34).

Meshullam (mē-shŭl'ăm, friend). 1. Ancestor of Shaphan (2 K 22:3). 2. Son of Zerubbabel (1 Ch 3:19). 3. Gadite (1 Ch 5:13). 4. Benjaminite; descendant of Elpaal (1 Ch 8:17). 5. Benjaminite; father of Sallu (1 Ch 9:7; Neh 11:7). 6. Benjaminite; son of Shephatiah (1 Ch 9:8). 7. See *Shallum 6.* 8. Priest (1 Ch 9:12). 9. Kohathite Levite; assisted in repairing temple (2 Ch 34:12). 10. Sent by Ezra to obtain Levites for Jerusalem (Ez 8:16; 1 Esd 8:44 [KJ: Mosollamon; RV: Mosollamus]). 11. Active in discussion regarding foreign wives (Ez 10:15; 1 Esd 9:14 [KJ: Mosollam; RV: Mosollamus]). 12. Divorced foreign wife (Ez 10:29; 1 Esd 9:30 [KJ, RV: Olamus]). 13. Son of Berechiah; repaired Jerusalem wall (Neh 3:4, 30; 6:18). 14. Son of Besodeiah; repaired gate (Neh 3:6). 15. Stood by Ezra at reading of Law (Neh 8:4). 16. Priest; sealed covenant with Nehemiah (Neh 10: 7). 17. Chief; signed covenant with Nehemiah (Neh 10:20). 18. 19. Priests (Neh 12:13, 16). 20. Porter (Neh 12:25). Perhaps same as Meshelemiah. 21. Prince (Neh 12:33).

Meshullemeth (mē-shŭl'ĕ-mĕth, friend). Wife of Manasseh; mother of Amon (2 K 21:19).

Mesobaite (mē-sō'bá-ĭt). See *Mezobaite.*

Mesopotamia (mĕs-ō-pō-tā'mĭ-á, between rivers). G translation of Aram-Naharaim, upper part of land between Tigris and Euphrates (Gn 24:10; Dt 23:4; Ju 3:8-11; 1 Ch 19:6; Acts 2:9; 7:2). Modern Iraq.

Messiah, Messias (me-sī'á,-ăs, G *Christos,* anointed one). Christ in NT except Messiah (KJ: Messias) in Jn 1:41; 4:25. High officials were anointed for office. Idea of Kingdom originated with God's promise to Abraham (Gn 12:1-3; 15). King was to be Son of David; Savior (Is 25:9; 63:1-5); Servant (Is 53); Creator of spiritual universal kingdom (Is 60; Jer 33:15-26. Emphasized as political aspirations dimmed). Messiah of Kingdom is anointed with Holy Ghost (Lk 4:18; Acts 4:27; 10:38; Ps 45:7). See also *anoint; Jesus Christ.*

metal. See *copper; gold; iron; lead; silver; tin; trade 7.*

Meterus (mē-tē'rus). See *Baiterus.*

Metheg-ammah (mē'thĕg-ăm'á. RV translates bridle of the mother city). Town taken by David from Philistines (2 Sm 8:1). Probably Gath (1 Ch 18:1).

Methusael (mē-thū'sá-ĕl). See *Methushael.*

Methuselah (mē-thū'ze-lá, man of dart). Son of Enoch; father of Lamech; lived 969 yrs (Gn 5:21-27; 1 Ch 1:3; Lk 3:37 [KJ: Mathusala]).

Methushael (mē-thū'shá-ĕl, man of God. KJ: Methusael). Son of Mehujael; father of Lamech (Gn 4:18).

Meunim (mē-ū'nĭm, from Maon). People who inhabited Mt Seir (1 Ch 4:41 [KJ: habitations]; 2 Ch 20:1 [KJ, RV: Ammonites; RSV: Meunites]; 26:7 [KJ: Mehunims. RSV: Meunites]; Ez 2:50 [KJ: Mehunim]; Neh 7:52). KJ: Meani; RV: Maani; RSV: Meunites in 1 Esd 5:31. Called Maonites (H) and Midian by some LXX mss in Ju 10:12. May have given name to Maon in Judah.

Mezahab (mĕz'á-hăb, water of gold). Grandfather of Mehetabel (Gn 36:39; 1 Ch 1:50).

Mezobaite (mē-zō'bá-ī. KJ: Mesobaite). Designation of Jaasiel (1 Ch 11:47).

Miamin (mī'á-mĭn). See *Mijamin 2; 4.*

Mibhar (mĭb'här). One of David's heroes (1 Ch 11:38).

Mibsam (mĭb'săm, sweet odor). 1. Son of Ishmael (Gn 25:13; 1 Ch 1:29). 2. Simeonite (1 Ch 4:25).

Mibzar (mĭb'zär, stronghold). Chief of Edom (Gn 36:42; 1 Ch 1:53).

Mica (mī'ká, who is like LORD). 1. See *Micah 3.* 2. Levite; signed covenant (Neh 10:11. KJ: Micha). 3. Descendant of Asaph (1 Ch 9:15 [KJ: Micah]; Neh 11: 17, 22 [KJ: Micha]). Micaiah (KJ: Michaiah) in Neh 12:35.

Micah (mī'ká, who is like LORD). 1. Ephraimite; mother made image for which he secured priest (Ju 17; 18). 2. Reubenite (1 Ch 5:5). 3. Jonathan's grandson; Mephibosheth's son (1 Ch 8:34, 35; 9:40, 41). Mica (KJ: Micha) in 2 Sm 9:12. 4. *Mica 3.* 5. Kohathite Levite (1 Ch 23:20; 24:24, 25 [KJ: Michah]). 6. Achbor's father (2 Ch 34:20). Micaiah (KJ: Michaiah) in 2 K 22:12. 7. 6th minor prophet; "of Moresheth" (KJ: Morashtite; RV: Morashtite), probably Moresheth-gath (Mi 1:1, 14); prophesied in reigns of Jotham, Ahaz, Hezekiah (Mi 1:1; Jer 26: 18 [RV: Micaiah]; 2 Esd 1:39 [KJ, RV: Micheas]). 8. Simeonite (Jdth 6:15. KJ: Micha).

Micah, Book of. 6th book of minor prophets. Emphasizes God's judgment on wicked; salvation for all; Bethlehem-born Messiah; worship by justice and love. Outline: 1. Approaching Judgment (1—3). 2. Promises of Deliverance (4, 5). 3. Israel's Failure; God's Faithfulness and Salvation (6, 7).

Micaiah (mī'kā'yá, who is like LORD). 1. See *Maacah 5.* 2. Prophet; son of Imlah; predicted death of Ahab (1 K 22:7-28; 2 Ch 18:6-27). 3. See *Micah 6.* 4. See *Mica 3.* 5. Priest (Neh 12:41. KJ: Michaiah). 6. See *Micah 7.* 7. Reported Jeremiah's prophecies to princes (Jer 36: 11-13. KJ: Michaiah). 8. Prince in Judah (2 Ch 17:7. KJ: Michaiah).

Micha [mī'ká]. See *Mica 2; 3; Micah 3; 5; 8.*

Michael (mī'kĕl, who is like God). 1. Asherite; father of spy Sethur (Nm 13:13). 2. Gadite (1 Ch 5:13). 3. Gadite; ancestor of preceding (1 Ch 5:14). 4. Ancestor of Asaph (1 Ch 6:40). 5. Issacharite (1 Ch 7:3). 6. Benjaminite (1 Ch 8:16). 7. Manassite; joined David at Ziklag (1 Ch 12:20). 8. Omri's father (1 Ch 27:18). 9. Jehoshaphat's son (2 Ch 21:2). 10. Zebadiah's father (Ez 8:8). 11. Archangel (Jude 9; Tob 12:15); fought for

Israel (Dn 10:13, 21; 12:1); disputed with Satan for Moses' body (Jude 9); fought Satan, the dragon (Rv 12:7).

Michah (mī'ka). See *Micah 5.*

Michaiah (mī-kā'a). See *Maacah 5; Mica 3; Micah 6; Micaiah 5; 7; 8.*

Michal (mī'kǎl, Michael). Saul's daughter; David's wife (1 Sm 14:49; 18:20, 27; 19: 11-17; 25:44; 2 Sm 3:13, 14; 6:16-23; 1 Ch 15:29). See also *Merab.*

Micheas (mī-kē'ǎs). See *Micah 7.*

Michmas, Michmash (mĭk'mǎs, mĭk'mǎsh, treasury). Town on E slope of mt ridge of Palestine, 7 mi N of Jerusalem. Strategy of Jonathan at Michmash led to defeat of Philistines (1 Sm 13; 14). Inhabited by Jews after captivity (Neh 11: 31). Michmas in Ez 2:27; Neh 7:31; 1 Esd 5:21 [KJ, RV: Macalon]). Residence of Jonathan Maccabaeus (1 Mac 9:73. KJ: Machmas). Modern Mukhmas.

Michmethah, Michmethath (mĭk'mĕ-thá, -thǎth). Border town of Ephraim and Manasseh (Jos 16:6; 17:7).

Michri (mĭk'rī, precious). Benjaminite (1 Ch 9:8).

Michtam (mĭk'tǎm. RSV: Miktam). Meaning uncertain (title Ps 16; 56—60). KJ marg: a golden Psalm; possibly: "for private meditation"; "covering (for sin)."

Middin (mĭd'ĭn). Town W of Dead Sea (Jos 15:61).

Midian (mĭd'ĭ-ǎn, strife). 1. Son of Abraham and Keturah (Gn 25:2). 2. Midianites and their land (Ex 3:1; Nm 22:4; Ju 7:13). KJ: Madian in Jdth 2:26; Acts 7:29.

Midianites (mĭd'ĭ-ǎn-īts). Race S of Moab and E of Gulf of Aqabah; boundary shifted; merchants (Gn 37:25-36); Moses fled to Midian, married Zipporah (Ex 2—4); opposed and defeated by Israel (Nm 22—25; 31); defeated by Gideon (Ju 6—8).

midwife. Assistant at childbirth (Gn 35:17; 38:28; Ex 1:15-21).

Migdal-el (mĭg'dǎl-ěl', tower of God). Fortified city of Naptali, W of Huleh (Jos 19:38).

Migdal-gad (mĭg'dǎl-gǎd', tower of Gad). Town in Shephelah (Jos 15:37).

Migdol (mĭg'dŏl, tower). 1. Egyptian town near Red Sea (Ex 14:2; Nm 33:7). 2. Egyptian town, 12 mi S of Pelusium (Jer 44:1; 46:14). KJ, RV: tower in Eze 29:10; 30:6.

mighty men. Heroes of David (2 Sm 23:8).

Migron (mĭg'rŏn, precipice). Benjaminite town (1 Sm 14:2; Is 10:28).

Mijamin (mĭj'a-mĭn, on right hand). 1. Head of 6th course of priests (1 Ch 24:9). 2. Divorced foreign wife (Ez 10:25 [KJ: Miamin]; 1 Esd 9:26 [KJ, RV: Maelus]). 3. Priest; sealed covenant with Nehemiah (Neh 10:7). Perhaps same as Miniamin in Neh 12:41. 4. Chief priest; returned with Zerubbabel (Neh 12:5. KJ: Miamin). Father's house called Miniamin (Neh 12:17).

Mikloth (mĭk'lŏth, rods). 1. Benjaminite (1 Ch 8:32; 9:37, 38). 2. Chief officer of David (1 Ch 27:4. RSV omits).

Mikneiah (mĭk-nē'ya, possession of LORD). Temple gatekeeper; musician (1 Ch 15: 18, 21).

Miktam (mĭk'tǎm). See *Michtam.*

Milalai (mĭl-a-lā'ī, eloquent). Levite; musician (Neh 12:36).

Milcah (mĭl'ka, counsel). 1. Haran's daughter; Nahor's wife (Gn 11:29; 22:20-23; 24:15, 24, 47). 2. Daughter of Zelophehad (Nm 26:33; 27:1-8; 36:1-12; Jos 17:3, 4).

Milcom (mĭl'kŏm, their king). National god of Ammonites (1 K 11:5, 33; 2 K 23:13; Jer 49:1, 3 [RV: Malcam; KJ: their king]; Zph 1:5 [RV: Malcam; KJ: Malcham]); worship introduced by Solomon. Sometimes identified with Molech.

mile. See *measures 1k.*

Miletum, Miletus (mī-lē'tum, mī-lē'tus). Ionian coastal city, 36 mi S of Ephesus (Acts 20:15, 17; 2 Ti 4:20 [KJ: Miletum]).

milk. See *food 8.*

mill. See *food 1.*

millennium (L thousand years). Term applied to period when Christ supposedly will appear on earth with saints and rule for 1,000 yrs before or after resurrection and judgment; based on literal interpretation of Rv 20:1-7.

millet. See *food 1.*

Millo (mĭl'ō, filling). 1. Filled-in fortification, probably on N of Davidic Jerusalem (2 Sm 5:9; 1 K 9:15, 24; 11:27; 1 Ch 11:8; 2 Ch 32:5). Probably same in 2 K 12:20). 2. Citadel of Shechem (Ju 9:6, 20. RSV: Beth-millo).

millstone. See *food 1.*

mina (mī'na. KJ, RV: maneh). Babylonian weight used in Palestine (60 shekels). Light mina was c 500 grams; heavy, 1,000 grams (Eze 45:12).

mine. Process of mining described in Jb 28:1-11 (KJ: vein). Iron and copper mined (Dt 8:9). Mines of Spain were famous (1 Mac 8:3).

mineral. See *flint; marble; metal; ornaments.*

Miniamin (mĭn'ya-mĭn, from the right hand). 1. Levite; distributed offerings (2 Ch 31:15). 2. Father's house of priests (Neh 12:17). 3. Priest; blew trumpet at dedication of wall (Neh 12:41). See also *Mijamin 3.*

minister. 1. One who serves or waits on another (Ex 24:13 [RSV: servant]; Jos 1:1. See Mt 27:55). 2. One who is active in special religious service. In OT priests performed ministry (Ex 28:43; Dt 10:8). Prophets and kings also consecrated to sacred service. See *king; prophet; priest.* Usual NT word for ministry is *diakonia* (service). All Christians are ministers of Christ (Jn 12:26) and receive *charisma* (gift. 1 Co 12:4-13; 1 Ptr 4:10). There are, however, special ministries in Word and sacrament (1 Co 12:28-31; 2 Co 6: 3-10; 1 Ti 4:6): apostles (Lk 6:13); evangelists (Acts 21:8; 2 Ti 4:5); pastors (Eph 4:11. See Acts 20:28); teachers (Ro 12:7; Ja 3:1 [KJ: masters]); elders (Acts 14:23; 1 Ti 5:17); bishop (1 Ti 3:1-7); deacons (Ph 1:1; 1 Ti 3:8).

ministration (mĭn-ĭs-trā'shun). See *dispensation.*

Minni (mĭn'ī). People in Armenia (Jer 51: 27).

Minnith (mĭn'ĭth). Town E of Jordan near Rabbath-ammon (Ju 11:33; Eze 27:17 [RSV: olives]).

minstrel. Musician; usually sang to accompaniment (2 K 3:15; Ps 68:25 [KJ: players]; Mt 9:23 [RSV, RV: flute players]; Rv 18:22 [KJ: musicians]).

mint. See *food 4.*

Miphkad (mĭf'kǎd, appointment. RV: Hammiphkad; RSV: Muster). Gate of Jerusalem (Neh 3:31).

miracle. OT: extraordinary manifestation of God's presence (Nm 16:30; Jos 10: 10-14; 2 K 20:8-11); recognized as being from God by faith (Ex 7—12; Ju 6:17-21, 36-40; 1 K 18:38, 39). NT: miracle, or act of power (Acts 19:11); signs

(Lk 21:25; Jn 2:11) whose significance is received by faith (Jn 6:26; 11:25-27, 38-40; 20:30, 31); wonders outside operation of known laws (Jn 4:48; Acts 2:19; 2 Co 12:12).

Miriam (mĭr'ĭ-ăm, rebellion). 1. Sister of Moses and Aaron; led women with timbrels and dancing (Ex 2:4-10); prophetess (Ex 15:20, 21); opposed Moses (Nm 12:1-15); buried at Kadesh (Nm 20:1). 2. Judahite (1 Ch 4:17).

Mirma, Mirmah (mûr'má, deceit). Benjaminite (1 Ch 8:10).

mirror. (KJ in OT: looking glass; in NT: glass.) Of polished metal (Ex 38:8; Jb 37:18; 1 Co 13:12; Ja 1:23; Wis 7:26; Sir 12:11).

Misael (mĭs'ă-ĕl). See *Mishael 2.*

Misgab (mĭs'găb, high. RV marg.: the high fort. RSV: fortress). Possibly, surname for Kir Moab (Jer 48:1).

Mishael (mĭsh'ă-ĕl, who is like God?). 1. Moses' uncle (Ex 6:22; Lv 10:4, 5). 2. Stood by Ezra at reading of Law (Neh 8:4; 1 Esd 9:44 [KJ, RV: Misael]). 3. See *Meshach.*

Mishal (mĭ'shăl, prayer). City of Asher (Jos 19:26. KJ: Misheal); assigned to Levites (Jos 21:30). Mashal in 1 Ch 6:74.

Misham (mĭ'shăm). Benjaminite (1 Ch 8:12).

Misheal (mĭsh'ē-ăl). See *Mishal.*

Mishma (mĭsh'má, hearing). 1. Son of Ishmael; founder of Arabian tribe (Gn 25:14; 1 Ch 1:30). 2. Simeonite (1 Ch 4:25, 26).

Mishmannah (mĭsh-măn'á, fatness). Gadite; joined David at Ziklag (1 Ch 12:10).

Mishraites (mĭsh'rā-īts). Family of Kiriathjearim (1 Ch 2:53).

Mispar (mĭs'pär, narrative). Returned with Zerubbabel (Ez 2:2 [KJ: Mizpar]; 1 Esd 5:8 [KJ, RV: Aspharasus]). Mispereth in Neh 7:7.

Mispereth (mĭs'pē-rĕth). See *Mispar.*

Misrephoth-maim (mĭs'rĕ-fŏth-mā'ĭm, burning waters). Place between Zidon and Mizpah (Jos 11:8; 13:6).

mist (mĭst). 1. Water particles in atmosphere near earth (Gn 2:6; Jer 10:13 [KJ, RV: vapors]). 2. Mist (and cloud) figuratively of transitoriness (2 Ptr 2:17a. KJ: cloud. See Is 44:22; Hos 13:3).

mite (mīt. RSV: copper coin). Coin, c 2 mills (Mk 12:41-44; Lk 21:1-4).

miter (mī'tēr). See *mitre.*

Mithcah, Mithkah (mĭth'kä, sweetness). Desert encampment (Nm 33:28).

Mithnite (mĭth'nīt). Designation of Joshaphat (1 Ch 11:43).

Mithradates (mĭth-rá-dā'tēz). See *Mithredath.*

Mithredath (mĭth'rē-dăth, gift of Mithra). 1. Treasurer of Cyrus (Ez 1:8). Mithridates (RV: Mithradates) in 1 Esd 2:11. 2. Persian officer in Samaria (Ez 4:7). Mithridates (RV: Mithradates) in 1 Esd 2:16.

Mithridates (mĭth-ri-dā'tēz). See *Arsaces; Mithredath.*

mitre (mī'tēr. RSV: turban). Priestly turban; inscribed: Holy (KJ: holiness) to the Lord (Ex 28:4, 36-39; 29:6; 39:28 to 31; Lv 8:9; 16:4).

Mitylene (mĭt-ĭ-lē'nē). City on Lesbos (Acts 20:14, 15).

mixed marriage. See *marriage.*

mixed multitude. Company of non-Israelites, or descendants of mixed marriages (Ex 12:38; Neh 13:3).

Mizar (mī'zär, little). Hill near Hermon (Ps 42:6).

Mizpah, Mizpeh (mĭz'pä, mĭz'pĕ, watchtower). 1. Stone heap erected in Gilead by Jacob as witness of covenant with Laban. Laban called it Jegar-sahadutha; Jacob, Galeed ("cairn of testimony"). Mizpah blessing spoken there (Gn 31:44 to 49). Possibly same as Ramoth-gilead. 2. Region near Mt Hermon (Jos 11:3). 3. Town near Lachish (Jos 15:38). Modern Tell es Safiyeh. 4. See Ramoth-gilead. 5. Territory in Benjamin (Jos 18:26) near Jerusalem (1 Mac 3:46. KJ: Maspha); tribes gathered there (1 Sm 7:5-17); fortified by Asa (1 K 15:16-22); burial place of Gedaliah (2 K 25:23); inhabited after captivity (Neh 3:7). 6. Place in Moab (1 Sm 22:3).

Mizpar (mĭz'pär). See *Mispar.*

Mizpeh (mĭz'pĕ). See *Mizpah.*

Mizraim (mĭz'rā-ĭm). 1. Son of Ham (Gn 10:6, 13, 14; 1 Ch 1:8, 11, 12. RSV: Egypt); ancestor of Egyptians, people of N Africa, Hamitic people of Canaan. 2. H for Egypt (Gn 45:20; Is 11:11).

Mizzah (mĭz'á). Descendant of Esau; chief in Edom (Gn 36:13, 17; 1 Ch 1:37).

Mnason (nā'son). Cyprian disciple (Acts 21:16).

Moab (mō'ăb). 1. Son of Lot by his daughter; ancestor of Moabites (Gn 39:30-38). 2. Moabites and their land, well-watered tableland E of Jordan (Nm 21:13-15); refused passage to Israel (Ju 11:17, 18); sent Balaam to curse Israel (Nm 22—24); held Israel subject (Ju 3:12-14); subdued by David (2 Sm 8:2, 12; 1 Ch 18:2, 11); enemies of Israel (2 K 1:1; 24:2; 2 Ch 20:1-30); denounced by prophets (Is 15; 16; Jer 9:26; 48; Eze 25:8-11; Am 2:1; Zph 2:8-11). Ruth was Moabitess (Ru 1:4).

Moabite Stone (mō'ăb-īt). Black asphalt stele, 2 × 4 ft, inscribed by Mesha of Moab (850 BC) with 34 lines in H characters paralleling events of 2 K 3:4-27.

Moadiah (mō-á-dī'á). See *Maadiah.*

Mochmur (mŏk'mẽr). Brook near Chusi (Jdth 7:18).

Modin (mō'dĭn. RSV: Modein). Ancestral city of Maccabees (1 Mac 2:1, 70; 13:25-29).

Moeth (mō'ĕth). See *Noadiah 1.*

Moladah (mŏl'á-dä). Town c 20 mi S of Judah (Jos 15:26; 19:2; 1 Ch 4:28; Neh 11:26).

mole. 1. H *hapharperah;* burrowing animal, possibly mouse (Is 2:20). 2. See *chameleon 2.*

Molech (mō'lĕk, king). Semitic god worshiped by sacrifice of children, practice forbidden by Jewish law (Lv 18:21; 20:1-5; 2 K 16:3); sanctuary in valley of Hinnom; worship practiced by Manasseh (2 Ch 33:6); abolished by Josiah (2 K 23:10); opposed by prophets (Jer 7:29-34; 19:1-13; Eze 20:26-39; Am 5:26 [RV, RSV: your king; KJ: Moloch]). Moloch in Acts 7:43.

Moli (mō'lī). See *Mahli 1.*

Molid (mō'lĭd). Judahite (1 Ch 2:29).

Moloch (mō'lŏk). See *Molech.*

Momdis (mŏm'dĭs). See *Maadai.*

money. In early times cattle, produce (Gn 13:2; Jb 1:3; 1 K 5:11), weighed metal (Gn 23:16; 1 Ch 21:25) used for exchange. Coins became prominent after exile (Ez 1:4). Coins of conquerors used. In NT coins of various countries used. See *money-changer.*

money-changer. Changed foreign currency into sanctuary coins for fee (Ex 30:13-15; Mt 21:12; Mk 11:15).

monotheism (mŏn'ō-thē-ĭz'm, one God). Belief in one God. See *God; gods, false.*

monster, sea. Large marine animal (Jb 7: 12 [KJ: whale]; Ps 148:7 [KJ, RV: dragons]; Lm 4:3 [RV, RSV: jackals]).

month. See *time.*

Mooli (mōō'lī). See *Mahli 1.*

moon (H *yareah:* pale; *l:bhanah:* white; G *selene:* brightness). Appointed for seasons, days, months, years (Gn 1:14; Ps 104:19. See *time*), and signs (Jl 2:10; Mt 24:29; Lk 21:25). Moon worship forbidden (Dt 4:19; 17:3); practiced during period of kings (2 K 23:5; Jer 8:2); beauty appreciated (Ps 8:3; Jb 31:26).

Moosias, Moossias (mō-ō-sī'ăs, mō-ŏs'ĭ-ăs). See *Maaseiah 9.*

Moph (mŏf). See *Memphis.*

Morashtite, Morasthite (mō-răsh'tīt, mō-răs' thīt). See *Micah 7.*

Mordecai (môr'dĕ-kī). **1.** Benjaminite; cousin and foster father of Esther (Est 2:5-7); saved Ahasuerus from conspirators (Est 2:21-23); saved Jews from Haman's plot and instituted Feast of Purim (Est 3—10). KJ, RV: Mardocheus in Ap Est 10:1; 11:2, 12. **2.** Returned from captivity (Ez 2:2; Neh 7:7; 1 Esd 5:8 [KJ, RV: Mardocheus]).

Moreh (mō'rĕ). **1.** "Oak (KJ: plain) of Moreh," 1½ ml from Shechem (Gn 12:6; Dt 11:30). **2.** Hill in Jezreel (Ju 7:1).

Moresheth-gath (mō'rĕsh-ĕth-găth', possession of Gath). See *Micah 7.*

Moriah (mō-rī'ă). Place to which Abraham went to offer Isaac (Gn 22:2); probably hill in Jerusalem on which Solomon built temple (2 Ch 3:1).

morning. See *time.*

mortar. **1.** Vessel of wood or stone in which grain was crushed with pestle (Nm 11:8; Pr 27:22). **2.** Cement, as sand and lime, bitumen, clay (Ex 1:14; Is 41:25; Jer 43:9 [KJ: clay]; Nah 3:14). See *homes 4.* **3.** See *Maktesh.*

Mosera, Moserah (mō-sē'ră, bond). Encampment of Israel near Mt Hor (Dt 10:6). Moseroth in Nm 33:30, 31.

Moseroth (mō-sē'rŏth, bonds). See *Mosera.*

Moses (mō'zĭz, H drawn out; Egyptian: child). Lawgiver, leader, statesman, prophet. Levite; b in Egypt; saved in basket on Nile; adopted by Pharaoh's daughter (Ex 2:1-10); educated (Acts 7: 22); slew Egyptian, fled to Midian; married Zipporah, priest Jethro's daughter (Ex 2:11-25); called as leader of Israel (Ex 3; 4); with mighty works led Israel out of Egypt and instituted Passover (Ex 5—15); led Israel through Shur (Ex 15: 22-26), Elim (Ex 15:27), Sin (manna given, Ex 16), Rephidim (Ex 17; 18) to Sinai (Ex 19); given law on Sinai (Ex 20—25) and regulations for tabernacle (Ex 26; 27), priests (Ex 28; 29), altars (Ex 30); returned from mt to idolatrous people (Ex 31—33); renewed covenant (Ex 34); made tabernacle (Ex 35—38; 40), apparel for priests (Ex 39); took census (Nm 1; 2); gave diverse regulations (Lv; Nm 3—10); resumed march (Nm 10); opposed by Aaron and Miriam (Nm 12); sent spies (Nm 13—15); opposed by Korah, Dathan, Abiram (Nm 16; 17); sinned at Meribah (Nm 20); erected bronze serpent (Nm 21); named Joshua his successor (Nm 27); d on Mt Nebo (Dt 34).

Moses is great lawgiver (Jn 1:17; Gl 3) with whom Christ is compared (Acts 3: 22; Heb 3) and contrasted (2 Co 3:12-18; Gl 3; 4). Moses wrote numerous documents (Ex 17:14; 20:2-17; 21—23; 24:3,

4; Dt 31:9-11). Pentateuch called "Moses" and attributed to him in NT.

Mosollam, Mosollamon, Mosollamus (mō-sŏl'ăm, -ă-mon, -ă-mus). See *Meshullam 10; 11.*

Most High. See *High, Most.*

mote. Speck of dust, straw, etc. (Mt 7:3-5; Lk 6:41, 42. RSV: speck).

moth. Cloth-eating insect (Jb 13:28; Ps 39:11; Is 50:9; Mt 6:19, 20). Symbol of transitoriness (Jb 4:19; Hos 5:12).

mother. Held in high respect (Ex 20:12). Term used for ancestor (Gn 3:20; 1 K 15:10), benefactress (Ju 5:7). Figuratively: nation (Is 50:1; Jer 50:12; Hos 4:5), city (Gl 4:26; Rv 17:5), New Jerusalem (Gl 4:26-31).

mother-of-pearl. See *alabaster.*

mount of congregation. Mythical mt of gods (Is 14:13. RSV: mount of assembly).

mountain. Lebanon system began at NE corner of Mediterranean and extended NE-SW through Palestine. Mts usually peaks (Zion, Olives, Hermon, Tabor, Sinai). Were places of refuge (Gn 14:10); lookouts (Is 18:3); sites for assemblies (Ju 9:7), camps (1 Sm 17:3), cemeteries (2 K 23:16), false (Nm 33:52; Dt 33:29) and true worship (Dt 33:19; Mt 14:23; Mk 6:46. See Jn 4:20-24), abodes for animals and birds (1 Ch 12:8; Ps 11:1). Sinai (Ex 24:13; Dt 33:2), Zion (Ps 68: 16; 99:9; Is 27:13) were God's mountains. Figuratively: strength (Jer 3:23); authority (Ps 72:3); righteousness (Ps 36:6); pride (Is 2:14); kingdom (Zch 4:7); Messianic reign (Is 2:2).

mountain sheep. Animal with long hair on throat and breast; found in Egypt, Arabia, Sinai (Dt 14:5. KJ, RV: chamois).

mourning. Dead mourned by tearing garments, putting on sackcloth and ashes (Gn 37:34; 2 Sm 1:11; 3:31; Mi 1:10), cutting flesh and shaving head (Lv 19: 27, 28; Dt 14:1), lamenting (Gn 35:8; Ex 12:30; 2 Sm 13:36; Jl 1:8, 13), building fires (2 Ch 16:14; 21:19). Professional mourners hired (2 Ch 35:25; Ec 12:5; Jer 9:17-20; Mt 9:23). Mourning lasted 7 (1 Sm 31:13), 30 (Dt 34:8), or 70 (Gn 50:3) days. Some rites were forbidden (Lv 19:27, 28; Dt 14:1).

mouse. Unclean animal (Lv 11:29); eaten by apostates (Is 66:17); golden mouse trespass offering of Philistines (1 Sm 6: 4-18).

Moza (mō'ză, issue). **1.** Judahite (1 Ch 2: 46). **2.** Descendant of Jonathan (1 Ch 8:36, 37; 9:42, 43).

Mozah (mō'ză). Town of Benjamin (Jos 18:26).

mulberry. **1.** H *baka'* (weeping); tree; identity not established (RSV: balsam tree. 2 Sm 5:23, 24; 1 Ch 14:14, 15). **2.** See *sycamine.*

mule. Imported (Eze 27:14. See Lv 19:19); used already in David's time (2 Sm 13: 29; 18:9; 1 K 1:33, 38, 44; Ez 2:66; Ps 32:9).

Muppim (mŭp'ĭm). See *Shephuphan.*

murder. Forbidden (Ex 20:13; Dt 5:17) on penalty of death (Gn 9:4-6; Ex 21:14; Lv 24:17; Dt 19:11-13). Unintentional slayers freed from death in cities of refuge (Nm 35:9-34; Dt 19:1-10).

murrain (mŭr'ĭn). See *disease.*

Mushi (mū'shī). Levite; son of Merari (Ex 6:19; Nm 3:20).

music. Existed in earliest times of world (Gn 4:21); minstrels mentioned (2 K 3: 15). Folk music commemorated victories

(Ju 5; 1 Sm 18:6, 7); used at special occasions (Gn 31:27; Nm 21:17, 18; 2 Sm 1: 19-27), feasts (2 Sm 19:35), weddings (Jer 7:34), funerals (Ec 12:5; Mt 9:23). David organized sacred choir (1 Ch 6:31 to 48; 2 Ch 29:25) and instrumental musicians (1 Ch 16); continued by Solomon (2 Ch 5:12, 13), Jehoshaphat (2 Ch 20: 21, 28), Joash (2 Ch 23:13, 18), Hezekiah (2 Ch 29:27-30), Josiah (2 Ch 35:15, 25), Ezra and Nehemiah (Ez 2:41; Neh 7:44). David is sweet psalmist of Israel (2 Sm 23:1). Instruments: 1. Stringed (lyre, harp, ten-stringed instrument). 2. Wind (trumpet, pipe, flute, oboe). 3. Percussion (timbrel, sistrum, cymbals). In NT: flute used at funerals (Mt 9:23), for dancing (Mt 11:17; Lk 7:32); harp symbol of praise (Rv 5:8; 14:2; 15:2-4); trumpet used to attract attention (Mt 6:2; 24:31; 1 Co 14:8; 15:52; Rv 8:2-12; 9:1, 13; 11:15). Music and hymnody play important role in worship life (Mt 26:30; Eph 5:19; Cl 3:16).

mustard. See food 4.
Muth-labben (müth-lăb'ĕn). Probably name of melody (Ps 9 title).
Myndos, Myndus (mĭn'dŏs, -dŭs). City of Caria (1 Mac 15:23).
Myra (mĭ'rá). Seaport of Lycia (Acts 27:5).
myrrh (mûr). 1. H mor; G smurna; yellow-brown resin used for perfume, embalming, anointing (Ex 30:23; SS 3:6; Mt 2: 11; Mk 15:23; Jn 19:39; Rv 18:13). 2. H lot; ladanum (Gn 37:25; 43:11).
myrtle. Shrub with white flowers, sweet-smelling berries (Neh 8:15; Is 41:19; 55: 13; Zch 1:8, 10, 11).
Mysia (mĭsh'ĭ-á). Land in NW Asia (Acts 16:7, 8).
mystery. Something unknown until manifested by God through some means (Dn 2. KJ, RV: secrets). Has supernatural element (Mt 13:3-50 [RSV: secrets]; 1 Co 15:51; Eph 3:1-11; 5:28-32; Cl 2:2; 1 Ti 3:16; Rv 17:5). Ministers are stewards of mysteries (1 Co 4:1).
myth. See fable.

N

Naam (nā'ăm, pleasantness). Son of Caleb (1 Ch 4:15).
Naamah (nā'á-má, pleasantness). 1. Sister of Tubal-cain (Gn 4:22). 2. Wife of Solomon; mother of Rehoboam (1 K 14:21, 31; 2 Ch 12:13). 3. City of Judah (Jos 15:41).
Naaman (nā'á-măn, pleasantness). 1. Grandson of Benjamin (Gn 46:21; Nm 26:40; 1 Ch 8:3, 4). 2. Commander of Ben-hadad II; cured of leprosy by Elisha (2 K 5; Lk 4:27).
Naamathite (nā'á-má-thīt). Inhabitant of Naamah (Jb 2:11).
Naamites (nā'á-mīts). Descendants of Naaman 1 (Nm 26:40).
Naarah (nā'á-rá, girl). 1. Wife of Asshur (1 Ch 4:5, 6). 2. Town N of Jericho (Jos 16:7. KJ: Naarath). Naaran in 1 Ch 7:28.
Naarai (nā'á-rī). One of David's heroes (1 Ch 11:37). Paarai in 2 Sm 23:35.
Naaran, Naarath (nā'á-răn, -răth). See Naarah 2.
Naashon, Naasson (nā-ăsh'ŏn, nā-ăs'ŏn). See Nahshon.
Naathus (nā'á-thus). See Adna 2.
Nabal (nā'băl, fool). Rich Carmelite sheep-master; his churlish treatment of David appeased by his wife, Abigail (1 Sm 25).
Nabariah, Nabarias (năb-á-rī'á, -ás). See Hashbadana.
Nabateans, Nabathaeans, Nabathites (năb-á-tē'áns, -thē'áns, năb'á-thīts). See Nebaioth 2.
Naboth (nā'bŏth). Stoned through intrigues of Jezebel so that Ahab obtained his vineyard (1 K 21:1-24; 2 K 9:21-26).
Nabuchodonosor (năb-û-kŏ-dŏn'ŏ-sôr). See Nebuchadnezzar.
Nachon (nā'kŏn). See Nacon.
Nachor (nā'kôr). See Nahor 1.
Nacon (nā'kŏn, ready). Designation of threshing floor where Uzzah died (2 Sm 6:6. KJ: Nachon). Chidon in 1 Ch 13:9. Place thereafter called Perez-uzza(h); see Perez-uzza.
Nadab (nā'dăb, liberal). 1. Son of Aaron; granted near approach to Jehovah; priest; consumed by fire for offering strange fire on altar (Ex 6:23; 24:1, 9-11; 28:1; Lv 10:1-7; Nm 26:60, 61; 1 Ch 6:3; 24:1, 2). 2. Judahite (1 Ch 2:28, 30).

3. Benjaminite; son of Gibeon and Maacah (1 Ch 8:30; 9:36). 4. 2d king of Israel; son and successor of Jeroboam; evil; slain by Baasha (1 K 14:20; 15: 25-31). 5. See Nasbas.
Nadabath, Nadabatha (năd'á-băth, ná-dăb'-á-thá). Place E of Jordan (1 Mac 9:37).
Naggai, Nagge (năg'ī, năg'ē). Ancestor of Christ (Lk 3:25).
Nahalal (nā'há-lăl, pasture). Town of Naphtali; given to Merarite Levites (Jos 19:15 [KJ: Nahallal]; 21:35). Nahalol in Ju 1:30.
Nahaliel (ná-hā'lĭ-ĕl, God's torrent-valley). Encampment of Israel near Pisgah (Nm 21:19).
Nahallal, Nahalol (ná-hăl'ăl, nā'há-lŏl). See Nahalal.
Naham (nā'hăm, solace). Brother of Hodiah's wife (1 Ch 4:19).
Nahamani (nā-há-mā'nī, compassionate). Returned with Zerubbabel (Neh 7:7). KJ: Enenius; RV: Eneneus; RSV: Bigvai in 1 Esd 5:8.
Naharai, Nahari (nā'há-rī, snoring). Joab's armorbearer (2 Sm 23:37 [KJ: Nahari]; 1 Ch 11:39).
Nahash (nā'hăsh, serpent). 1. Ammonite king defeated by Saul at Jabesh-gilead (1 Sm 11:1-11; 12:12). The same or another (2 Sm 10:1, 2; 1 Ch 19:1, 2). 2. Father of Abigail and Zeruiah, David's (half?) sisters (2 Sm 17:25; 1 Ch 2:16). 3. Person at Rabbah in Ammon; father of Shobi (2 Sm 17:27). Possibly same as 1.
Nahath (nā'hăth). 1. Grandson of Esau (Gn 36:13, 17). 2. Kohathite Levite (1 Ch 6:26). Tohu in 1 Sm 1:1. Toah in 1 Ch 6:34. 3. Levite; overseer of offerings (2 Ch 31:13).
Nahbi (nä-bī, comforter). Spy of Naphtali (Nm 13:14).
Nahor (nā'hôr, snoring). 1. Grandfather of Abraham (Gn 11:22-25; 1 Ch 1:26; Lk 3:34 [KJ: Nachor]). 2. Brother of Abraham (Gn 11:26-29; 22:20, 23; 24:10-24; 29:5; 31:53; Jos 24:2).
Nahshon (nä'shŏn. KJ: Naashon in Ex 6:23; Naasson in NT). Prince of Judah (Nm 1:7; 2:3; 7:12, 17; 10:14; Ru 4:20-22; 1 Ch 2:10, 11; Mt 1:4; Lk 3:32); sister married Aaron (Ex 6:23).

Nahum (nā'hŭm, full of consolation). 1. 7th minor prophet; native of Elkosh; prophesied between 663 and 606 BC (Nah 1:1; 3:8-11). 2. See *Johanan 4*.

Nahum, Book of. Announces fall of Nineveh; contrasts justice of Lord of nations, who will enforce judgment, with world power. Outline: 1. God's Majesty (1). 2. Fall of Nineveh (2, 3).

Naidus (nā'ĭ-dŭs). See *Benaiah 9*.

nail. 1. Fingernails of female captives pared (Dt 21:12). 2. Nails of iron, copper, or gold (1 Ch 22:3; 2 Ch 3:9; Is 41:7; Jer 10:4; Jn 20:25). 3. Tent peg (as RSV [RV: tent-pin]. Ju 4:21, 22; 5:26).

Nain (nā'ĭn, beauty). City in Galilee (Lk 7:11). Modern Nein.

Naioth (nā'ŏth, shepherd dwellings). Place in Ramah where Samuel and his prophets dwelt (1 Sm 19:18—20:1).

naked, nakedness. 1. Complete nakedness (Gn 2:25; Jb 1:21). 2. Outer garment removed (Jn 21:7). 3. Poorly clad (Mt 25:36). 4. Figuratively, lack of power or resources (Gn 42:9. RSV: weakness); revealed (Jb 26:6; Mi 1:11); spiritual poverty (Rv 3:17).

name. Consummates reality of being (Gn 2:20; Is 40:26); change of name indicated change in being (Gn 17:5; 35:10). To act in someone's name is to participate in his reality (1 Sm 25:9). Names of God reveal His nature (Ex 3:13-15), will (Ps 22:22; Jn 17:6, 26), attributes (Ex 33:19; Ps 8:1, 9; 1 Ti 6:1). God is present where His name is present (Is 18:7; 30:27).

Nanaea, Nanea (nȧ-nē'ȧ). Fertility goddess worshiped in Syria, Persia, Armenia (2 Mac 1:13, 15).

Naomi (nȧ-ō'mĭ, my pleasantness). Mother-in-law of Ruth (Ru 1; 2; 3:1; 4:3-17).

Naphath (nā'fȧth. KJ: countries; RV: heights). City of Manasseh (Jos 17:11).

Naphath-dor (nā'fȧth-dôr. KJ: coast, region of Dor. RV: height of Dor). Place near Mediterranean (Jos 12:23; 1 K 4:11). See also *Dor*.

Naphish (nā'fĭsh, respiration). Son of Ishmael; founder of tribe (Gn 25:15; 1 Ch 1:31; 5:18-22 [KJ: Nephish]), probably the Nephusheshim.

Naphisi (năf'ĭ-sī). See *Nephusheshim*.

Naphoth-dor (nā'fŏth-dôr). Plural of Naphath-dor (Jos 11:2. KJ: borders of Dor. RV: heights of Dor).

Naphtali (năf'-tȧ-lī, my wrestling). 1. Son of Jacob by Bilhah (Gn 30:8; 46:24). 2. Tribe marched N of tent with Dan and Asher (Nm 2:25-31); territory in N Palestine between Zebulun, Asher, and Manasseh (Jos 19:32-39); Barak was of Naphtali (Ju 4:6); captured by Tiglathpileser (2 K 15:29). KJ: Nephthalim in Mt 4:13, 15; Nepthalim in Rv 7:6, Nephthali in Tob 1:1-5.

naphtha (năf'thȧ). Liquid which consumed sacrifice; called nephthar (KJ: naphthar) by Nehemiah (2 Mac 1:18-36); also called nephi (KJ), nephthai (RV).

Naphtuhim (năf'-tū'hĭm). Tribe of Egypt (Gn 10:13; 1 Ch 1:11).

napkin (G *soudarion*, sweatcloth). Cloth for wiping sweat, etc. (Lk 19:20; Jn 20:7).

Narcissus (när-sĭs'ŭs). Roman friend of Paul (Ro 16:11).

nard (närd. H *nerd*; G *nardos*. KJ, RV: spikenard). Aromatic plant (*Nardostachys jatamansi*) from which fragrant oil is extracted (SS 1:12; 4:13, 14; Mk 14:3; Jn 12:3).

Nasbas (năs'bȧs. RSV: Nadab). Nephew of Tobit (Tob 11:18).

Nasi, Nasith (nä'sē, nä'sĭth). See *Neziah*.

Nasor (nä'sôr. See *Hazor 1*.

Nathan (nā'thăn, He gave). 1. Prophet; told David not to build temple (2 Sm 7:1-17); reproved him (2 Sm 12:1-14); secured succession for Solomon (1 K 1: 8-45); wrote life of David (1 Ch 29:29) and Solomon (2 Ch 9:29). 2. Son of David (1 Ch 3:5; Lk 3:31). 3. Father of Igal (2 Sm 23:36. See 1 Ch 11:38). 4. Judahite (1 Ch 2:36). 5. Leader with Ezra (Ez 8:16). 6. Divorced foreign wife (Ez 10:39). Nathanias (RSV: Nethaniah) in 1 Esd 9:34.

Nathanael (nȧ-thăn'â-ĕl, gift of God). 1. Disciple of Jesus (Jn 1:45-51; 21:2); identified with Bartholomew. 2. Ancestor of Judith (Jdth 8:1). 3. 4. See *Nethanel 7; 8*.

Nathanias (năth-ȧ-nī'ăs). See *Nathan 6*.

Nathan-melech (nā'thăn-mē'lĕk, king's gift). Chamberlain of Josiah (2 K 23:11).

nations. Used in OT for non-Jews (Ex 34:24; Is 43:9; Jer 10:1-25) in addition to ordinary use (Gn 10:5). See also *gentiles*.

Naum (nā'um). See *Johanan 4*.

nave (nā'vē). See *Nun*.

nave (nāv). Holy place of temple (1 K 6: 3, 5, 17, 33 [KJ, RV: temple]; 2 Ch 3: 4, 5, 13 [KJ, RV: house]; Eze 41 [KJ, RV: temple]).

navy. See *boats*.

Nazarene (năz-ȧ-rēn'). 1. Inhabitant of Nazareth (Mt 2:23; Mk 14:67 [KJ: of Nazareth]). 2. A Christian (Acts 24:5).

Nazareth (năz'ȧ-rĕth). Town of Galilee on edge of mts N of Jezreel; home town of Jesus (Mk 1:9; Mt 4:13; Lk 1:26; 2: 4, 51; 4:16-44), who is frequently referred to as "of Nazareth" (Lk 18:37; Jn 1:45, 46; 19:19; Acts 2:22).

Nazarite, Nazirite (năz'ȧ-rīt, -ĭ-īt, separated). Person bound by vows to abstain from intoxicants, not cut hair, avoid contact with dead, abstain from unclean food (Nm 6:1-21; Ju 13; Am 2:11, 12). See Acts 21:20-26.

Neah (nē'ȧ, slope). Border town of Zebulun (Jos 19:13). Perhaps Neiel.

Neapolis (nē-ăp'ō-lĭs, new city). Port city of Philippi (Acts 16:11).

Neariah (nē-ȧ-rī'ȧ, servant of LORD). 1. Judahite (1 Ch 3:22). 2. Simeonite (1 Ch 4:42).

Nebai (nē'bī. RV: Nobai). Sealed covenant with Nehemiah (Neh 10:19).

Nebaioth, Nebajoth (nē-bā'yŏth, -jŏth, high places). 1. Son of Ishmael (Gn 25:13; 28:9; 36:3; 1 Ch 1:29). 2. N Arabian tribe (Is 60:7). RV: Nabathaeans; KJ: Nabathites; RSV: Nabateans in 1 Mac 5:25; 9:35.

Neballat (nē-băl'ăt). Benjaminite town, 4 mi NW of Lydda; inhabited after captivity (Neh 11:34).

Nebat (nē'băt, viewed). Father of Jeroboam I (1 K 11:26).

Nebo (nā'bō, announcer?). Nabu, Babylonian god of learning (Is 46:1).

Nebo (nē'bō, Nabu, or elevated?). 1. 2,643-ft summit of Pisgah of Abarim range in Moab. On it Moses viewed Palestine and died (Dt 32:49, 50; 34:1-5). 2. Reubenite city, E of Jordan (Nm 32:3, 38; 33:47; 1 Ch 5:8). 3. Place repopulated after exile (Ez 2:29; 10:43; Neh 7:33; 1 Esd 9:35 [KJ: Ethma; RV: Nooma]).

Nebuchadnezzar, Nebuchadrezzar (nĕb-û-kăd-nĕz'ẽr, -rĕz'ẽr, Nebo, defend the boundary). 1. Ruler of Old Babylonian Empire (c 1140 BC). 2. Ruler of Neo-

Babylonian empire (605—562 BC); son of Nabopolassar; defeated Pharaoh-necho at Carchemish (605 BC); made Judah vassal (603 BC. Dn 1:1; 2 K 24); carried Jews into captivity (598 BC, 2 K 24: 11-16. 587 BC, 2 K 25:1-21. Probably, c 580 BC, 2 K 25:22-25). Frequently mentioned in OT (1 Ch 6:15; 2 Ch 36; Ez 1:7; 2:1; 5:12, 14; 6:5; Neh 7:6; Est 2:6; Jer 21—52; Dn 1—5). KJ (RV usually): Nabuchodonosor in Apocrypha.

Nebushasban, Nebushazban (nĕb-û-shãs'-băn, -shãz'băn, Nebo save). The Rabsaris, or chief of chamberlains, under Nebuchadnezzar (Jer 39:13).

Nebuzar-adan (nĕb'û-zär-ā'dăn, Nebo gave offspring). Captain of Nebuchadnezzar's bodyguard (2 K 25:8-21; Jer 39:11; 40:1-5).

Necho, Nechoh, Neco (nē'kō). See *Pharaoh 10*.

Necodan (nĕ-kō'dăn). See *Nekoda*.

necromancy (nĕk'rō-măn-sĭ). Consulting dead (Dt 18:11. See 1 Sm 28:1-25).

Nedabiah (nĕd-à-bī'à, LORD impelled). Son of Jeconiah (1 Ch 3:18).

needle. Mentioned in Mt 19:24; Mk 10:25; Lk 18:25.

needlework. See *embroidery*.

Neemias (nē-ĕ-mī'ās). See *Nehemiah 1*.

Negeb (nĕg'ĕb, dry. KJ, RV: south). Grazing region S of Hebron (Gn 12:9; 13:1; 20:1).

Neginah, Neginoth (nē-gē'nä, nĕg'ĭ-nŏth). Stringed instruments (as RV, RSV. Ps 4; 6; 54; 55; 67; 76 titles; Hab 3:19). Neginah (singular) in Ps 61 title.

Nehelamite (nē-hĕl'à-mīt, dreamed. RSV: of Nehelam). Designation of Shemaiah (Jer 29:24, 31, 32).

Nehemiah (nē-hē-mī'à, LORD comforts). **1.** Scn of Hachaliah (Neh 1:1); cupbearer of Artaxerxes Longimanus (Neh 2:1); governor of returned Jews (Neh 2:1-10); rebuilt Jerusalem's walls (Neh 1—4; 6; Sir 49:13 [KJ: Neemias]); instituted reforms (Neh 5; 13); restored worship and Law (Neh 8—13). **2.** Returned with Zerubbabel (Ez 2:2; Neh 7:7; 1 Esd 5:8 [KJ, RV: Nehemias]). **3.** Helped rebuild Jerusalem's walls (Neh 3:16).

Nehemiah, Book of. Describes how God restored Law, worship, government, and physical aspects of Jerusalem through Nehemiah and other leaders after return from captivity. Chs 1—7 and shorter sections in 1st person; referred to as Nehemiah's memoirs. Outline: 1. Restoration of Walls (1—6). 2. Watchmen Appointed, Census Taken (7). 3. Religious and Political Reformation (8—13).

Nehemias (nē-hē-mī'ās). See *Nehemiah 2*.

Nehiloth (nē'hĭ-lŏth. RSV: flutes). Wind instruments (Ps 5 title).

Nehum (nē'hŭm, comforted). See *Rehum 1*.

Nehushta (nē-hŭsh'tà, bronze). Jehoiakim's mother (2 K 24:8).

Nehushtan (nē-hŭsh'tăn, piece of bronze). Name given by Hezekiah to brazen serpent (2 K 18:4).

Neiel (nē-ī'ĕl). Border town of Asher (Jos 19:27). Perhaps Neah.

neighbor. 1. Person who dwells near (Ex 11:2). **2.** OT: fellow member of covenant (Ex 20:16, 17), to whom special considerations were due (Dt 15:1-11). Duty to love neighbor as self included foreigners (Lv 19:18-34). NT: Individual to be neighbor to all men (Lk 10:25-37), extending love to all for whom Christ died (Mt 5:43-48). That done to brother is done to Christ (Mt 25:31-46).

Nekeb (nē'kĕb, pass). Border town of Naphtali near Adami (Jos 19:33. RV, RSV. Adami-nekeb).

Nekoda, Nekodan (nē-kō'dà, -dăn, herdsman). Progenitor of family of Nethinim (Ez 2:48, 60; Neh 7:50, 62; 1 Esd 5:31 [KJ, RV: Noeba], 37 [KJ: Necodan; RV: Nekodan]).

Nemuel (nĕm'û-ĕl). **1.** Brother of Dathan and Abiram (Nm 26:9). **2.** See *Jemuel*.

Nemuelites (nĕm'û-ĕl-īts). Descendants of Nemuel 1.

Nepheg (nē'fĕg, sprout). **1.** Korah's brother (Ex 6:21). **2.** David's son (2 Sm 5:15; 1 Ch 3:7; 14:6).

Nephi (nē'fī). See *naphtha*.

Nephilim (nĕf'i-lĭm. See *giants 1*.

Nephis (nē'fĭs). See *Magbish*.

Nephish (nē'fĭsh). See *Naphish*.

Nephishesim, Nephisim (nē-fĭsh'ĕ-sĭm, nĕf'-ĭ-sĭm). See *Nephusheshim*.

Nephthai (nĕf'thī). See *naphtha*.

Nephthali, Nephthalim (nĕf'thà-lī, -lĭm). See *Naphtali 2*.

Nephthar (nĕf'thär). See *naphtha*.

Nephtoah (nĕf-tō'à, waters of opening). Fountain and town on Judah-Benjamin border 2 mi NW of Jerusalem (Jos 15:9; 18:15).

Nephusheshim, Nephusesim (nē-fū'shĕ-shĭm, -sĭm, expanded ones). Family of Nethinim (Neh 7:52. KJ: Nephishesim; RV: Nephsheshim). Nephisim in Ez 2:50 (KJ: Nephusim); 1 Esd 5:31 (KJ, RV: Naphisi). See also *Naphish*.

Nephusim (nē-fū'sĭm). See *Nephusheshim*.

Nepthalim (nĕp'thà-lĭm). See *Naphtali 2*.

Ner (nûr, lamp). **1.** Son of Abiel; father of Abner; uncle of Saul (1 Sm 14:50, 51; 26:5, 14; 2 Sm 2:8, 12). **2.** Son of Jeiel; grandfather of Saul (1 Ch 8:33; 9:35, 36, 39).

Nereus (nēr'ūs). Paul's Christian friend at Rome (Ro 16:15).

Nergal (nûr'găl). Babylonian man-lion god (2 K 17:30).

Nergal-sharezer (nûr'găl-shà-rē'zĕr, Nergal preserve the king). Babylonian Rabmag (prince) under Nebuchadnezzar (Jer 39: 3, 13).

Neri (nē'rī). Ancestor of Christ (Lk 3:27).

Neriah, Nerias (nē-rī'à, nē-rī'ăs, lamp of LORD). Father of Baruch (Jer 32:12, 16; 36:4, 8; Bar 1:1 [KJ, RV: Nerias]).

Nero (nē'rō). Nero Claudius Caesar Augustus Germanicus; Roman emperor (AD 54 to 68); referred to as "Caesar" (Acts 25:11; Ph 4:22).

nest. Mother bird not to be taken with young or eggs (Dt 22:6, 7).

net. Used in hunting (Is 51:20), fishing (Hab 1:15-17 [RSV: seine]; Mt 4:18; 13:47; Jn 21:6-11), fowling (Pr 1:17). Figuratively, of being caught by intrigues of others (Ps 10:9; 57:6; Pr 29:5; Mi 7:2), by own folly (Jb 18:8; Ps 35:8), by God's justice (Eze 12:13; 17:20; Hos 7:12).

Netaim (nē'tà-ĭm, plantings. KJ: plants). Place in Judah (1 Ch 4:23).

Nethanel, Nethaneel (nē-thăn'ĕl, -ĕ-ĕl, God gave). **1.** Prince of Issachar (Nm 1:8; 2:5; 7:18, 23; 10:15). **2.** David's brother (1 Ch 2:14). **3.** Priest; blew trumpet before ark (1 Ch 15:24). **4.** Levite (1 Ch 24:6). **5.** Son of Obed-edom (1 Ch 26:4). **6.** Prince under Jehoshaphat (2 Ch 17:7). **7.** Levite (2 Ch 35:9; 1 Esd 1:9 [KJ, RV: Nathanael]). **8.** Divorced foreign wife (Ez 10:22). Nathanael in 1 Esd 9:22. **9.** Priest (Neh 12:21). **10.** Levite musician (Neh 12:36).

Nethaniah (nĕth-á-nī'á, Lord gave). 1. Head of 5th course of musicians (1 Ch 25:2, 12). 2. Levite teacher (2 Ch 17:8). 3. Father of Ishmael who assassinated Gedaliah (2 K 25:23, 25; Jer 40:7-16; 41). 4. Jehudi's father (Jer 36:14). 5. See Nathan 6.

Nethinim (nĕth'ĭ-nĭm, dedicated. RSV: temple servants). Servants or slaves who performed menial tasks in temple (1 Ch 9:2; Ez 2:43-58; 8:17-20; Neh 7:46-56). Probably descended from Midianites (Nm 31:47), Gibeonites (Jos 9:23), other captives.

Netophah, Netophas (nĕ-tō'fá, -fãs, dripping). Town SE of Bethlehem (2 Sm 23:28, 29; 1 Ch 11:30; 27:13; Ez 2:22; Neh 7:26; 1 Esd 5:18 [RV: Netophas]).

Netophathi, Netophathite (nĕ-tŏf'á-thī, -thĭt). Inhabitant of Netophah (2 K 25:23; 1 Ch 2:54; 9:16; 27:15; Neh 12:28 [KJ: Netophathi]; Jer 40:8).

nettle. 1. H ḥarul (burning), a thorny shrub (Jb 30:7; Pr 24:31; Zph 2:9). 2. H gimmosh (sting), nettle (Is 34:13; Hos 9:6).

new birth. See conversion.

new commandment. Enjoins love of one another based on love of God manifested in Christ and mediated to heart by Word and Spirit (Jn 13:35; 1 Jn 4:7-21. See 1 Co 13).

new man. Jesus Christ by His resurrection after death brought new man to reality (Ro 5:10; 8:34-39). By faith in Christ man is converted from old man to new man (2 Co 5:17; Gl 6:15) and lives in church (Eph 2:15); this conversion is worked in Baptism (Ro 6:1-4). New life manifested in conduct (Ro 6:5-11; Eph 4:24), constantly renewed in Christ (Cl 3:10, 11).

new moon. Special observances held at time of new moon, which marked beginning of month (Nm 28:11-15).

New Testament. 1. New Covenant (Jer 31:31-34) is work of Christ, by whose life, death, resurrection God's grace is brought to men (2 Co 3; Gl 4; Heb 7:20-22). Holy Spirit brings men into covenant by Word (Jn 3:5; Ro 1:16, 17; 15:16; 1 Co 2:10, 13; 2 Th 2:13). Lord's Supper is embodiment of New Testament (Mt 26:26-28; 1 Co 11:25). See also covenant. 2. Books of Bible from Mt to Rv.

new year. See time 4.

Neziah (nĕ-zī'á, bright). Ancestor of Nethinim who returned from captivity (Ez 2:54; Neh 7:56; 1 Esd 5:32 [KJ: Nasith; RV: Nasi]).

Nezib (nē'zĭb, idol). Town in lowland of Judah (Jos 15:43).

Nibhaz (nĭb'hăz). God of Avites; brought to Samaria from Assyria (2 K 17:31).

Nibshan (nĭb'shăn, soft soil). Town on Dead Sea near En-gedi (Jos 15:62).

Nicanor (nĭ-kā'nôr, conqueror). 1. One of 7 chosen for social work in early church (Acts 6:5). 2. General of Antiochus Epiphanes (1 Mac 3:38; 7:26-32).

Nicodemus (nĭk-ô-dē'mus, victor over people). Pharisee; member of Sanhedrin; held night conversation with Jesus (Jn 3:1-21); indirectly defended Him (Jn 7:50-52); aided at His burial (Jn 19:39-42).

Nicolaitans (nĭk-ô-lā'ĭ-tãns). Gnostic antinomian sect (Rv 2:6, 14, 15).

Nicolas, Nicolaus (nĭk'ô-lăs, nĭk-ô-lā'us, victor over people). Proselyte of Antioch; one of 7 elected for social service in early church (Acts 6:5).

Nicopolis (nĭ-kŏp'ô-lĭs, city of victory). Roman town in Epirus, founded by Caesar Augustus, 31 BC (Tts 3:12).

Niger (nī'jēr, black). Latin surname of Simeon (Acts 13:1).

night. See light and darkness; time 6.

night hag. Demon (Is 34:14. KJ: screech owl. RV: night monster).

nighthawk. H taḥmas, unidentified, unclean bird (Lv 11:16; Dt 14:15).

night monster. See night hag.

Nile (nīl). 4,050-mi river of Egypt; worshiped as god; famous for its fertilizing overflows and many mouths. Moses placed on Nile in papyrus boat (Ex 2:3); waters turned to blood (Ex 7:20, 21); famous for papyrus (Is 19:7). H y:'or (river. Ex 1:22; Is 7:18) and shihor (dark, Jer 2:18. KJ: Sihor. RV: Shihor). RSV: Nile, but Shihor in Jos 13:3; 1 Ch 13:5; Is 23:3, where it is regarded brook of Egypt.

Nimrah (nĭm'rá). See Beth-nimrah.

Nimrim (nĭm'rĭm). Stream of Moab SE of Dead Sea (Is 15:6; Jer 48:34).

Nimrod (nĭm'rŏd). Son of Cush; hunter, builder, founder of kingdoms in Shinar (Gn 10:8-12; 1 Ch 1:10; Mi 5:6). Many places in Mesopotamia had name Nimrod.

Nimshi (nĭm'shī). Father of Jehu (1 K 19:16; 2 K 9:2, 14).

Nineveh (nĭn'e-ve). Assyrian capital on Tigris; founded by Nimrod (Gn 10:9-11); Sargon II (722—705 BC) made it capital of Assyria; Sennacherib, Esarhaddon, and Ashurbanipal strengthened, beautified it (705—626); destroyed (612 BC) by Babylonians, Scythians, Medes. Many ruins excavated (Gn K 19:36; Is 37:37; Jon; Nah; Zph 2:13; Mt 12:41; Lk 11:30, 32 [KJ: Nineve]).

Niphis (nī'fĭs). See Magbish.

Nisan (nī'săn). See time 4.

Nisroch (nĭs'rŏk). God of Nineveh (2 K 19:37; Is 37:18).

nitre (nī'tēr). H nether; sodium carbonates and sulphates found in solution in some desert lakes (Pr 25:20 [RV: soda; RSV: wound]; Jer 2:22 [RV, RSV: lye]). Used to make soap (Jer 2:22; Ml 3:2). H b:bor translated "[make] never so [clean]" (Jb 9:30. RSV, RV marg: "[cleanse] with lye"); KJ: "purely," RV: "thoroughly," RSV, RV margin: "as with lye" in Is 1:25.

No (nō). See Thebes.

Noadiah (nō-á-dī'á, Lord met). 1. Levite; son of Binnui (Ez 8:33). Moeth in 1 Esd 8:63. 2. Evil prophetess (Neh 6:14).

Noah (nō'á, rest). 1. Son of Lamech (Gn 5:28-32); preached 120 yrs against wickedness (Gn 6:1-9; 1 Ptr 3:20; 2 Ptr 2:5); built ark (Gn 6:12-22); saved from flood with wife, sons, their wives, male and female of every kind of beast and fowl (Gn 7; 8); repeopled earth (Gn 9:10); lived 950 yrs. KJ: Noe in Mt 24:37; Lk 3:36; Apocrypha. 2. Daughter of Zelophehad (Nm 26:33; 27:1-8; 36:1-12; Jos 17:3, 4).

No-amon (nō-ā'mŏn). See Thebes.

Nob (nŏb, height). Levitical city in Benjamin near Jerusalem (1 Sm 21:1; 22:9-23; Neh 11:32; Is 10:32).

Nobah (nō'bá). 1. Manassite; took Kenath, renaming it Nobah (Nm 32:42). See Kenath. 2. City near Jogbehah (Ju 8:11). Perhaps same as Nophah.

Nobai (nō'bī). See Nebai.

Nod (nŏd, exile). Region E of Eden (Gn 4:16).

Nodab (nō'dăb, noble). Arabian tribe (1 Ch 5:19).

Noe (nō'ĕ). See *Noah 1.*
Noeba (nō'ĕ-bá). See *Nekoda.*
Nogah (nō'gá, brilliance). Son of David (1 Ch 3:7; 14:6).
Nohah (nō'há, rest). Benjaminite (Ju 20: 43 [KJ: with ease; RV: at their resting place]; 1 Ch 8:2).
Non (nŏn). See *Nun.*
Nooma (nō'ō-má). See *Nebo 3.*
Noph (nŏf). See *Memphis.*
Nophah (nō'fá). Moabite town (Nm 21:30. RSV: fire spread). See also *Nobah 2.*
northeaster. See *Euraquilo.*
nose jewels. Rings worn in nose (Is 3:21. RSV: nose rings).
novice (nŏv'ĭs). Recent convert (as RSV: 1 Ti 3:6).
numbering. See *census.*
numbers. H used letters of alphabet for numbers. Numbers had religious, traditional, or symbolical meaning: 1 (Dt 6:4), 3 (Mt 28:19; 1 Co 13:13), 4 (YHWH, Eze 37:9; Rv 7:1), 7 (Gn 2:2; Rv 1:4, 20; 3:1),

10 (Ex 20:3-17; Mt 25:1-13), 12 (Gn 35: 22; Mk 3:14; Acts 1:26), 40 (Ex 24:18; Mk 1:13), 70 (Mt 18:22; Lk 10:1), 666 (Rv 13:18), 1,000 (Rv 20).
Numbers. 4th book of Pentateuch (H Bible: "In the Wilderness"). Contains various laws, numbering of tribes, journeys of Israelites from Sinai to Palestine. Outline: 1. Events Leading to Departure from Sinai (1:1—10:10). 2. Wandering from Sinai to Moab (10:11—21:35). 3. Events in Moab Preparatory to Entering Canaan (22—36).
Numenius (nū-mē'nĭ-us). Jonathan Maccabee's ambassador to Rome (1 Mac 12:16).
Nun (nŭn, fish). Ephraimite; father of Joshua (Ex 33:11; 13:8; 1 Ch 7:27 [KJ: Non]; Sir 46:1 [KJ: Nave]).
nurse. Position of importance (Gn 24:59; 35:8; 2 Sm 4:4; 2 K 11:2).
nuts. See *orchard 5.*
Nymphas (nĭm'fás, bridegroom). Christian of Laodicea (Cl 4:15).

O

Oabdius (ō-ăb'dĭ-us). See *Abdi 2.*
oak. Translation of a number of H words: *'allon* (Gn 35:8; Is 6:13; 44:14); *'elah* (Gn 35:4; Ju 4:11; 6:11, 19; 2 Sm 18:14). Terebinth in Is 6:13 (KJ: teil); Hos 4:13 (KJ: elm); *'elon* (KJ: plain. Gn 12:6; 13: 18; Dt 11:30); *'el* (Is 1:29; 61:3. KJ, RV: trees); *'allah* (Jos 24:26). Oaks were abundant in Bashan, on Carmel, Tabor, hills of Ephraim, Lebanon. Noted for strength (Is 44:14), associated with important events (Gn 12:6; 13:18; 35:8; Ju 4:11; 9:6, 37), idol worship (Hos 4:13).
oath. A solemn appeal to God (Gn 21: 23; Ex 22:11; 1 Sm 14:39, 44; 20:3; Mt 26:63, 64), person (Gn 42:15; 2 Sm 11: 11), or object (Mt 5:34) as attestation of truth. Oaths of covenants were elaborate (Gn 21:28-31). To swear by God's name shows allegiance (Dt 6:13). Made by lifting hands (Gn 14:22); placing hand under thigh (Gn 24:2); passing between divided sacrificial victim (Gn 15:10, 17; Jer 34: 18, 19); standing before altar (1 K 8:31).
Obadiah (ō-bá-dī'á, worshiper of LORD). 1. Judahite (1 Ch 3:21). 2. Chief of Issachar (1 Ch 7:3). 3. Gadite; joined David at Ziklag (1 Ch 12:9). 4. Son of Azel (1 Ch 8:38; 9:44). 5. Levite; son of Shemaiah (1 Ch 9:16; Neh 12:25). Abda in Neh 11:17. 6. Father of Ishmaiah (1 Ch 27:19). 7. Officer of Ahab; friend of Elijah and prophets (1 K 18: 3-16). 8. Prince; teacher (2 Ch 17:7). 9. Levite; overseer of temple repairs (2 Ch 34:12). 10. Descendant of Joab (Ez 8:9; 1 Esd 8:35 [KJ, RV: Abadias]). 11. Priest; sealed covenant with Nehemiah (Neh 10:5). 12. Prophet (Ob 1:1; 2 Esd 1:39 [KJ, RV: Abdias]).
Obadiah, Book of. 4th of minor prophets. Denunciation of Edomites, who ravaged land of Israel during captivity. Outline: 1. Edom's Sin and Destruction (1-14). 2. Israel's Restoration in Day of the LORD (15-21).
Obal (ō'băl). Son of Joktan; founder of Arabian tribe (Gn 10:28). Ebal in 1 Ch 1:22.
Obdia (ŏb-dī'á). See *Habaiah.*
Obed (ō'bĕd, worshiper, servant). 1. Son of Ruth and Boaz; grandfather of David (Ru 4:17, 21, 22; 1 Ch 2:12; Mt 1:5; Lk 3:32). 2. Jerahmeelite (1 Ch 2:37, 38). 3. One of David's heroes (1 Ch 11:47).

4. Levite; doorkeeper (1 Ch 26:7). 5. Azariah's father (2 Ch 23:1). 6. See *Ebed 2.*
Obed-edom (ō'bĕd-ē'dom, Obed of Edom). 1. Gittite in whose home David placed ark for 3 months (2 Sm 6:10-12; 1 Ch 13:13, 14; 15:25). 2. Levite doorkeeper (1 Ch 15:18, 24). Probably same in 1 Ch 16:38; also Korahite ancestor of doorkeepers (1 Ch 26:4; 2 Ch 25:24). 3. Founder of temple musicians (1 Ch 15:21; 16:5).
obedience. Complete response to God is duty of man (Dt 4:30; Jer 7:23; Zch 6: 15; 1 Jn 5:2); man disobeyed God (Gn 3), and humanity lived in disobedience (Ro 1:24; 5:19). Christ obtained righteousness for mankind by obedience (Ro 5:19; Heb 5:8; Ph 2:8). By faith Christian is obedient (Ro 1:5). Christian is obedient in home (Eph 5:21; 6:1; 1 Ptr 3:6), state (Ro 13:1-7), church (Heb 13: 17), to others (Eph 5:21).
obeisance (ō-bā'sáns). Bow or bodily movement in token of respect or submission (Gn 43:28; Ex 18:7; 2 Sm 1:2).
obelisk (ŏb'e-lĭsk). Four-sided, usually monolithic, tapering pillar, ending in pyramid at top, associated with Egyptian temples (Jer 43:13. KJ: images. RV: pillars).
Obeth (ō'bĕth). See *Ebed 2.*
Obil (ō'bĭl). Ishmaelite; David's camel keeper (1 Ch 27:30).
oblation (ŏb-lā'shun. RSV only in 1 K 18: 29, 36). Ritualistic offering, usually inanimate (Lv 2:3; Nm 18:9-20; Eze 44:30; Dn 2:46).
Oboth (ō'bŏth). Encampment of Israel E of Moab (Nm 21:10, 11; 33:43, 44).
Ochiel, Ochielus (ō-kī'el, ō-kī-ē'lus). See *Jeiel 7.*
Ochran (ŏk'răn, troublesome. KJ: Ocran). Asherite (Nm 1:13; 2:27; 7:72, 77; 10: 26).
Ocidelus (ŏs-ĭ-dē'lus). See *Jozabad 7.*
Ocina (ō-sī'ná). Coast town S of Tyre (Jdth 2:28).
Ocran (ŏk'răn). See *Ochran.*
Oded (ō'dĕd, he restored). 1. Azariah's father (2 Ch 15:1). 2. Prophet of Samaria (2 Ch 28:9-11).
Odollam (ō-dŏl'ăm). See *Adullam.*
Odomera, Odonarkes (ŏd-ō-mē'rá, -när'kēz). Nomad chief (1 Mac 9:66).

odor. 1. Unpleasant smell (Jn 11:39. KJ: stink; RV: decay). 2. Pleasant smell, figuratively, pleasing to God (Gn 8:21; Lv 1:9-17; Nm 15:3-24. KJ, RV usually: savour, savor).

offering. See *sacrifice*.

offices of Christ. See *Jesus Christ*.

Og (ŏg). Amorite; king of Bashan; last of Rephaim (Nm 21:33-35; Dt 3:1-13; Jos 12:4, 5; 13:12; Ps 135:11).

Ohad (ō'hăd). Simeonite (Gn 46:10; Ex 6:15).

Ohel (ō'hĕl, tent). Son of Zerubbabel (1 Ch 3:20).

Oholah (ō-hō'lá, her tent. KJ: Aholah). Personification of Samaria, the kingdom of Israel (Eze 23).

Oholiab (ō-hō'lĭ-ăb, father's tent. KJ: Aholiab). Danite; artificer, prepared furnishings for tabernacle (Ex 31:6; 35:34; 36:1, 2; 38:23).

Oholibah (ō-hŏl'ĭ-bá, my tent is in her. KJ: Aholibah). Personification of Jerusalem and Judah (Eze 23).

Oholibamah (ō-hŏl-ĭ-bä'má). 1. See *Judith 1*. 2. Chief of Edom (Gn 36:41; 1 Ch 1:52. KJ: Aholibamah).

oil. See *orchard 1*.

ointment. Usually perfumed olive oil; used for dressing hair, perfuming skin (Est 2:3-12; SS 1:3; 4:10), anointing (Mt 26:6-13), preparing dead bodies (Lk 23:56). Balm of Gilead and salve were medications (Jer 8:22; Rv 3:18). See *apothecary*.

olamus (ŏl'á-mus). See *Meshullam 12*.

Old Testament. 1. Bible from Gn to Mal. 2. Covenant of Moses. See *covenant*.

olive. See *orchard 1*.

Olives, Mount of; Olivet (ŏl'ĭ-vĕt). Ridge, 1 mi long, E of Jerusalem, beyond Kidron; Gethsemane, Bethphage, Bethany on its slopes (2 Sm 15:30; Zch 14:4; Mt 21:1; 24:3; 26:30; Mk 11:1; 13:3; 14:26; Lk 19:29, 37; 22:39; Jn 8:1; Acts 1:12).

Olympas (ō-lĭm'păs). Roman Christian (Ro 16:15).

Olympius (ō-lĭm'pĭ-us. KJ, RV: Jupiter Olympius. RSV: Olympian Zeus). Title of Zeus (2 Mac 6:2).

Omaerus (ŏm-á-ē'rus). See *Amram 2*.

Omar (ō'mĕr). Descendant of Esau; chief of Edom (Gn 36:11, 15).

omega (ō-mē'gá). See *alpha*.

omer (ō'mĕr). See *measures 2f*.

omnipotence (ŏm-nĭp'ō-tens). Absolute power of God (Gn 17:1; Mt 19:26; Eph 1:21, 22).

omnipresence. Attribute of God according to which He is everywhere (Ps 139:7-10; Pr 15:3; Acts 17:27, 28).

omniscience. Term used to describe God's complete knowledge (1 Sm 2:3; Mt 10:30; Acts 15:18; Eph 1:4). See also *knowledge 2*.

Omri (ŏm'rī). 1. 6th king of Israel; former general of Elah; made king by prophets and army; moved capital to Samaria (1 K 16:16-28). 2. Benjaminite (1 Ch 7:8). 3. Judahite (1 Ch 9:4). 4. Prince of Issachar (1 Ch 27:18).

On (ŏn, strength). Reubenite; participated in Korah's rebellion (Nm 16:1).

On (ŏn). Egyptian city (G Heliopolis), 19 mi N of Memphis; religious center of 1st united Egypt (Gn 41:45, 50; Eze 30:17). Beth-shemesh (RSV: Heliopolis) in Jer 43:13.

Onam (ō'năm, strong). 1. Horite (Gn 36:23; 1 Ch 1:40). 2. Jerahmeelite (1 Ch 2:26, 28).

Onan (ō'năn, strong). Son of Judah; refused to raise heir to brother (Gn 38:4-10; Nm 26:19).

Onesimus (ō-nĕs'ĭ-mus, useful). Slave of Philemon; letter to Philemon written in his behalf (Cl 4:9; Phmn).

Onesiphorus (ŏn-ê-sĭf'ō-rŭs, profit bringing). Ephesian Christian; ministered to Paul in prison (2 Ti 1:16-18; 4:19).

Oniares (ō-nī'á-rēz). See *Onias*.

Onias (ō-nī'ăs, possibly, Coniah). 1. Onias I; Jewish high priest during time of Maccabees (1 Mac 12:7-20). KJ: Oniares (v. 19) is incorrect blending of Onias and Arius. 2. Onias III; high priest (2 Mac 3; 4.)

onion. See *food 4*.

Ono, Onus (ō'nō, ō'nus, strong). Benjaminite town, 7 mi SE of Joppa (1 Ch 8:12; Ez 2:33; Neh 7:37; 1 Esd 5:22 [KJ, RV: Onus]).

onycha (ŏn'ĭ-ká). Incense ingredient; probably from mollusk (Ex 30:34).

onyx (ŏn'ĭks). Stone (H *shoham*); probably cryptocrystalline quartz; fastened to shoulderpieces and breastpiece of high priest (Gn 2:12; Ex 28:9; 35:9, 27; 1 Ch 29:2).

Ophel (ō'fĕl, hill). S end of temple hill (2 Ch 27:3; 33:14; Neh 3:26, 27; 11:21).

Ophir (ō'fêr). 1. Son of Joktan and descendants (Gn 10:29; 1 Ch 1:23). 2. Region centered in SW Arabia, whence algum wood, gold, ivory, peacocks, apes were imported (1 K 9:26-28; 10:11; 22:48; 2 Ch 8:18; 9:10; Jb 22:24; 28:16; Ps 45:9; Is 13:12).

Ophni (ŏf'nī, hill man). Benjaminite village (Jos 18:24).

Ophrah (ŏf'rá, gazelle). 1. Benjaminite town 5 mi NE of Bethel (Jos 18:23; 1 Sm 13:17). 2. Home of Gideon in Manasseh (Ju 6:11, 24; 8:27, 32). 3. Judahite (1 Ch 4:14).

oracle. 1. Shrine, as Holy of Holies (1 K 6. RSV: sanctuary). 2. Message, or word, of God (2 Sm 16:23; Acts 7:38; Ro 3:2; 1 Ptr 4:11). 3. Utterance of prophecy (Is 14:28; 15:1; Eze 12:10; Nah 1:1. KJ, RV: burden).

orchard. 1. Olive planted in form of shoot from cultivated tree, or grown from seed and grafted with fresh twigs from older tree; pruned with saws or pruning hooks. Harvest began in August, when whitish fruit was knocked from trees; oil extracted by placing fruit in stone basin with rolling stone fixed to lever over it, or on concave stone and crushing with stone. Oil used for ceremonial anointing (Ex 29:7; 1 Sm 16:13), fuel for lamps and torches (Ex 27:20), to anoint head and body (Ps 23:5; Lk 7:46), as salve for wounds (Lk 10:34). Symbolized peace and prosperity (Gn 8:11; Ps 52:8).
2. Various kinds of figs common in Palestine (1 K 4:25; Ps 105:33). Fig bore "first-ripe figs" (Is 28:4 [KJ, RV: hasty fruit]; Nah 3:12; Jer 24:2) in May, regular crop in July, August (Am 8:1), sometimes also late in fall; fruit and leaves usually come at same time (Mt 24:32). Sycamore fig had smaller fruit (Am 7:14). Figs were dried for year-round use.
3. Date palms grew wild along Mediterranean, Jordan valley, and in oases of desert. Dates were dried and caked for winter. Branches of palm trees were brought to Passover (Mt 21:8; Mk 11:8; Jn 12:13)

4. Pomegranates often mentioned in OT (Hg 2:19); wine made from their juice (SS 8:2). Apples referred to in number of passages (Pr 25:11; SS 2:3, 5; Jl 1:12). There was undoubtedly also citrus fruit. 5. Almonds plentiful (Gn 43:11; Ex 25: 33; Ec 12:5; Jer 1:11). Walnuts also common in Palestine. (Klinck)

ordination. Act whereby sacred office is conferred. OT priests were ordained (KJ, RV: consecrated) to office (Ex 28:41; 29: 9, 33; Nm 3:3). Ram sacrificed at ordination (Ex 29:22-34; Lv 8:22-33). In NT deacons (Acts 6:6), missionaries (Acts 13:3), elders (Acts 14:23) are ordained ("hands laid on") to office.

Oreb (ō'rĕb, raven, wolf). 1. Midianite prince slain at "rock of Oreb" (Ju 7:25; 8:3; Ps. 83:11; Is 10:26). 2. See *Horeb.*

Oren (ōrĕn, pine). Jerahmeelite (1 Ch 2: 25).

organ. See *pipe.*

Orion (ō-rī'on). Constellation (Jb 9:9; 38: 31; Am 5:8).

ornaments. Worn in large numbers (Gn 24: 22; Is 3:16-24; Jer 2:32; Eze 16:11-19). Ornaments included amulets, anklets, armlets, beads, bracelets, chains, finger and nose rings, mirrors, pendants, and various ornaments of gold, silver, and precious stones.

Ornan (ôr'năn). See *Araunah.*

Orpah (ôr'pä, fawn). Daughter-in-law of Naomi (Ru 1:4-14).

orphan. Protected by law (Ex 22:22); are special care to God (Hos 14:3) and Christians (Ja 1:27).

Orthosia, Orthosias (ôr-thō-sī'á,-ăs). City of N Phoenicia (1 Mac 15:37).

Osaias (ō-zā'yăs). See *Jeshaiah 5.*

Osea (ō-zē'á). See *Hoshea 3.*

Oseas, Osee (ō-zē'ăs, ō'zē). See *Hosea.*

Oshea (ō-shē'á). See *Joshua 1.*

Osnappar (ŏs-năp'ēr. KJ: Asnapper). King (Ez 4:10) usually identified with Ashurbanipal (669—626 BC).

osprey, ospray (ŏs'prĭ). See *vulture 5.*

ossifrage (ŏs'ĭ-frĭj). See *vulture 6.*

ostrich (KJ: owl except Jb 39:13; Lm 4:3). Unclean bird (Lv 11:16; Dt 14:15), cruel (Lm 4:3); mournful (Mi 1:8); dwells in ruins (Is 13:21, 34:13; Jer 50:39); rich in plumage, swift, neglects eggs (Jb 39: 13-18).

Othni (ŏth'nī, powerful). Son of Shemaiah (1 Ch 26:7).

Othniel (ŏth'nĭ-ĕl, God's powerful one). Judge of Israel; son of Kenaz (Jos 15:17; 1 Ch 4:13); captured Kiriath-sepher (Jos 15:15-17; Ju 1:11-13); delivered Israel from Mesopotamians (Ju 3:8-11). Probably same in 1 Ch 27:15.

Othoniah, Othonias (ŏth-ō-nī'á,-nī'ăs). See *Mattaniah 7.*

ouch. Jewel setting (as RV, RSV. Ex 39:6).

oven. See *food 2; furnace 1.*

owl. Unclean bird (Lv 11:17; Dt 14:16). Little owl, great owl (Lv 11:17; Dt 14: 16), horned owl (KJ: swan; RSV: water hen), screech owl (RSV: night hag; RV: night monster) are names in versions. See also *ibis; ostrich.*

Ox (ŏks). Ancestor of Judith (Jdth 8:1).

ox. See *antelope; bull, bullock; wild ox.*

Ozem (ō'zĕm, strength). 1. David's brother (1 Ch 2:15). 2. Jerahmeelite (1 Ch 2:25).

Ozias (ō-zī'ăs). 1. 2. See *Uzziah 1; 6. 3.* See *Uzzi 1. 4.* See *Azariah 7.*

Oziel (ō'zĭ-ĕl). Ancestor of Judith (Jdth 8:1).

Ozni (ŏz'nī). See *Ezbon 1.*

Ozora (ō-zō'rá). See *Ezora.*

P

Paarai (pā'á-rī). See *Naarai.*

pace. See *measures 1f.*

Padan, Paddan (pā'dăn, păd'ăn, plain). See *Padan-Aram.*

Padan-aram, Paddan-aram (pā'dăn-, păd'ănă'răm, plain of Aram). Plain surrounding Haran in Mesopotamia; Abraham's family had settled there; home of Rebecca and Laban (Gn 25:20; 28:2-7; 31: 18; 33:18; 35:9, 26; 46:15). Paddan (KJ: Padan) in Gn 48:7. See also *Aram.*

paddle. Tool for covering excrement (Dt 23:13. RSV: stick).

Padon (pā'dŏn, redemption). Progenitor of Nethinim who returned from captivity (Ez 2:44; Neh 7:47; 1 Esd 5:29 [KJ, RV: Phaleas]).

pagan. See *gentiles.*

pagiel (pā'gĭ-ĕl, meeting with God). Chief of Asher in wilderness (Nm 1:13; 2:27; 7:72, 77; 10:26).

Pahath-moab (pā'hăth-mō'ăb, ruler of Moab). Progenitor of family which returned from captivity (Ez 2:6; 8:4; 10:30; Neh 3:11; 7:11; 10:14; 1 Esd 5:11 [KJ, RV: Phaath Moab]; 1 Esd 8:31 [RV: Phaath Moab]). Addi in 1 Esd 9:31.

Pai (pā'ī). See *Pau.*

paint. Used on houses (Jer 22:14). Painting as fine art mentioned (Eze 23:14-16). Enlarging eyes with black paint was censured (2 K 9:30; Jer 4:30; Eze 23:40). See *colors.*

palace. See *architecture; homes 6.*

Palal (pā'lăl, judge). Helped rebuild walls of Jerusalem (Neh 3:25).

palanquin (păl-ăn-kĕn'. KJ, RV: chariot). Enclosed litter (SS 3:9).

Palestina (păl-es-tī'ná). See *Philistia.*

Palestine (păl'es-tīn). Name derived from Philistia (Ps 60:8); older name: Canaan (Gn 12:5); after conquest: land of Israel (1 Sm 13:19); holy land in Zch 2:12; Judea in Greco-Roman period.

Land (c 70 mi wide, 150 long) S and SW of Lebanon mts, NE of Egypt, N of Sinai Peninsula, E of Arabian Desert; divided into 5 parts: maritime plain on W, Shephelah, central range, Jordan valley, eastern plateau (Bashan, Gilead, Moab). Tablelands of cretaceous limestone.

Climate varied because of diversity of level (Hermon 9,101 ft above sea level; Dead Sea 1,290 below). Mean temperature of Jerusalem c 65 F; Jordan Valley tropical. Plants, animals of many latitudes flourish. Two seasons: winter (Nov—Apr; mild, rainy) summer (May to Oct; dry, hot).

Early inhabitants tall (see *giants*). In days of Abraham inhabited by Canaanites, Amorites, Hittites, Horites, Amalekites; conquered by Israelites under Joshua, judges, kings; 587—166 BC under foreign rule. Maccabees reigned (166—63 BC) until Roman period (63 BC—325 AD). In NT times divided into Judea, Samaria, Galilee.

pallet. See *bed.*

Pallu (păl'ū, famous). Son of Reuben (Gn 46:9 [KJ: Phallu]; Ex 6:14); progenitor of Palluites (Nm 26:5).

palm tree. See *orchard 3.*

palmer-worm. Probably locust in larva stage (Jl 1:4 [RSV: cutting locust]; 2:25 [RSV: cutter]; Am 4:9 [RSV: locust]).

palsy (pôl'zĭ). See *disease.*

Palti (păl'tī, delivered). 1. Spy of Benjamin (Nm 13:9). 2. Man to whom Saul gave Michal, David's wife (1 Sm 25:44. KJ: Phalti). Paltiel (KJ: Phaltiel) in 2 Sm 3:15.

Paltiel (păl'tĭ-ĕl, God delivers). 1. Prince of Issachar (Nm 34:26). 2. See *Palti 2.*

Paltite (păl'tīt, from Beth-pelet). Designation of Helez (2 Sm 23:26). Pelonite in 1 Ch 11:27; 27:10.

Pamphylia (păm-fĭl'ĭ-á, every race). Coastal plain in S Asia Minor (Acts 2:10; 13:13; 14:24; 15:38; 27:5).

pan. Utensil for cooking (Lv 2:5 [RSV: baking pan; RSV: griddle], 7 [KJ, RV: frying pan]; 6:21 [RV: baking pan; RSV: griddle]; 1 Sm 2:14; 2 Sm 13:9).

Pannag (păn'ăg). Perhaps name of a place; but RV: pannag (marg: Perhaps a confection); RSV: early figs (Eze 27:17).

paper. See *papyrus.*

Paphos (pā'fŏs). Capital of Cyprus (Acts 13:6, 13).

papyrus (pá-pī'rŭs). Sedge (8 to 10 ft high), abundant along Nile in ancient times, from which paper was made (Jb 8:11 [KJ, RV: rush]; Is 18:2 [KJ: bulrushes]). Moses' ark (Ex 2:3) probably made of papyrus.

parable. 1. A metaphor or a proverb (Mt 15:14, 15; Mk 13:28; 6:39). 2. A narrative in which things in spiritual sphere are presented by comparison with events that could happen in temporal sphere. Material is serious and true to nature, and teaching centers in important points in parable (Mt 13; Lk 15). Differs from fable, myth, allegory, proverb (which see).

paraclete (păr'á-klēt. KJ, RV: Comforter). LXX uses G *parakletos* (call to one's aid) for restoration of new life to Israel (Is 40:1; 51:3, 12). Designation for Holy Spirit with reference to His mediation of Christ, guidance into truth, judgment of world (Jn 14:16, 26; 15:26; 16:7). Christ is Paraclete (translated Advocate) in 1 Jn 2:1.

Paradise (păr'á-dīs, park). Park (Ec 2:5. KJ: orchard). Garden of Eden was park, or paradise (Gn 2:8-17; Rv 2:7). Paradise is used to describe home of those who die in Christ (Lk 23:43) and of blessed (2 Co 12:4; Rv 2:7). Forest in Neh 2:8; orchard in SS 4:13.

Parah (pā'rá, heifer). Benjaminite town, c 5 mi N of Jerusalem (Jos 18:23).

paralytic (păr-á-lĭt'ĭk). See *disease.*

Paran (pā'răn). "Desert of wanderings" in E central region of Sinai Peninsula (Gn 21:21; Nm 10:12; 12:16; 13:3, 26; Dt 1:1; 1 Sm 25:1). Kadesh 1 (Nm 13:26) and Elath (El-paran in Gn 14:6) situated in it.

Paran, Mount of. Unidentified peak of Sinai wilderness (Dt 33:2; Hab 3:3).

parapet (păr'á-pĕt. KJ, RV: battlement). Required on roofs (Dt 22:8). See *homes 4.*

Parbar (pär'bär, open place). Colonnade or place on W side of outer temple court (1 Ch 26:18).

parched corn. Roasted grains of wheat (sometimes other grains) used for cereal offerings (Lv 2:14) and food (Lv 23:14; Ru 2:14).

parchment. See *leather.*

pardon. See *forgiveness; justification.*

park. See *paradise.*

parlor. Cool upper room (Ju 3:20-25 [RSV: roof chamber]; 1 Sm 9:22 [RV: guest-chamber; RSV: hall]; 1 Ch 28:11 [RV, RSV: chambers]). See also *homes.*

Parmashta (pär-măsh'tá, chief). Son of Haman (Est 9:9).

Parmenas (pär'mē-năs, faithful). One of 7 chosen to perform social service for poor (Acts 6:5).

Parnach (pär'năk). Zebulunite (Nm 34:25).

Parosh (pā'rŏsh, flea). Progenitor of family which returned from captivity (Ez 2:3; 8:3 [KJ: Pharosh]; 10:25; Neh 3:25; 7:8; 10:14; 1 Esd 5:9 [KJ, RV: Phoros]; 8:30 [KJ: Pharez; RV: Phoros]; 9:26 [KJ, RV: Phoros]).

Parousia (pá-rōō'zhĭ-á, presence, coming). 2d coming, or appearing, of Jesus Christ in glory for salvation of church, judgment, overthrow of opposition, consummation of salvation (Mt 24:27-39; 1 Co 15:23; 1 Th 4:15-17; Ja 5:8; 2 Ptr 3:4; 1 Jn 2:28). See also *Advent of Christ; Day of the Lord 2; Jesus Christ; judgment.*

Parshandatha (pär-shăn-dā'thá, given by prayer). Son of Haman (Est 9:7).

Parthians (pär'thĭ-ănz). People of SW Asia (Iran), SE of Caspian Sea; seized Jerusalem (40 BC); large empire in NT times (Acts 2:9).

partridge (pär'trĭj, H *qore'*, crier). Two varieties in Palestine: sand partridge; chukar partridge (1 Sm 26:20; Jer 17:11).

Paruah (pá-rōō'á, flourishing). Father of Jehoshaphat 2 (1 K 4:17).

Parvaim (pär-vā'ĭm, the East?). Place from which gold was obtained (2 Ch 3:6).

Pasach (pā'săk, divide). Asherite (1 Ch 7:33).

Pas-dammim (păs-dăm'ĭm). See *Ephes-dammim.*

Paseah (pá-sē'á, lame). 1. Judahite (1 Ch 4:12). 2. Progenitor of Nethinim who returned from captivity (Ez 2:49; Neh 3:6; 7:51 [KJ: Phaseah]; 1 Esd 5:31 [KJ: Phinees; RV: Phinoe]).

Pashhur, Pashur (păsh'ẽr). 1. Son of Immer; governor of temple; put Jeremiah in stocks (Jer 20:1-6). 2. Son of Malchiah; opposed Jeremiah (Jer 21:1; 38:1, 4). 3. Father of Gedaliah (Jer 38:1). 4. Priest; progenitor of family which returned from captivity (1 Ch 9:12; Ez 2:38; 10:22; Neh 7:41; 10:3; 11:12; 1 Esd 5:25 [KJ: Phassaron; RV: Phassurus]; 9:22 [KJ, RV: Phaisur]).

passion (suffering). Last sufferings and crucifixion of Christ (Acts 1:3). See *Jesus Christ.*

Passover. First of 3 annual festivals (see *feasts 2*) at which Jews were required to come to sanctuary (Ex 23:14-17; Dt 16:16); commemorated "passing over" to Israel when first-born were destroyed in Egypt (Ex 12; 13:3-9); began at sunset on 14th Nisan (Lv 23:5); ritual described (Ex 12:3-20). Called feast of unleavened bread in Ex 23:15; Dt 16:16. Christ (1 Co 5:7. See Jn 19), Lord's Supper is Christian Passover (Lk 22:1-20).

pastor (shepherd). KJ for H *ro'i* (shepherd) in Jer 2:8; 3:15; 10:21 (RV, RSV: ruler, shepherd); leader. G *poimen* is usually for spiritual shepherd of Christ's people (Eph 4:11; see Acts 20:26-32). Christ is chief Shepherd (Heb 13:20; 1 Ptr 2:25; 5:4. See Jn 10).

pastoral epistles. 1, 2 Ti; Tts.

Patara (păt'á-rá). Seaport on SW coast of Lycia (Acts 21:1).

pate (pāt). Top of head (Ps 7:16).
path. Figuratively, way determined by God (Ps 17:5; 25:10). See also *way*.
Patheus (pa-thē'us). See *Pethahiah 2*.
Pathros (păth'rōs, southland). Country of S (Upper) Egypt (Is 11:11; Jer 44:1, 15; Eze 29:14; 30:14).
Pathrusim (păth-rōo'sim). Inhabitants of Pathros (Gn 10:14; 1 Ch 1:12).
patience. Calm fortitude in duties and conflicts with submission to God. Patience exercised with respect to persons (G *makrothumia*. Col 3:12, 13; 1 Th 5:14) or things (G *hupomone*. Ro 5:3, 4; 2 Th 1:4; Ja 5:11).
Patmos (păt'mŏs). Island, 15 mi in circumference, off SW coast of Asia Minor, to which John was banished (Rv 1:9).
patriarch (pa'trĭ-ärk, father-ruler). 1. Fathers of the human race (Gn 4; 5). 2. Fathers of human race after Flood (Gn 11). 3. Fathers of Israelites: Abraham, Isaac, Jacob (1 Ch 1:28, 34; Heb 7:4). 4. Sons of Jacob (Acts 7:8, 9). 5. David (Acts 2:29).
Patrobas (păt'rō-băs, paternal). Roman Christian (Ro 16:14).
Patroclus (pa-trō'klus). Father of Nicanor (2 Mac 8:9).
Pau (pa'ū, bleating). City of Hadad 3 (Gn 36:39). Pai in 1 Ch 1:50.
Paul (pôl, little). Apostle to Gentiles (Acts 18:6; Gl 1:16; 2:2, 8; Eph 3:1-6); Benjaminite Jew (Ph 3:5); native of Tarsus (Acts 21:39; 22:3); father Pharisee from whom he inherited Roman citizenship (Acts 22:28; 23:6); tentmaker (Acts 18:3); student of Gamaliel (Acts 22:3); called Saul until Acts 13:9; sister's son (Acts 23:16), kinsmen (Ro 16:7, 11) mentioned; persecutor of church; present at stoning of Stephen (Acts 7:58; 9:13; 26:10, 11; Gl 1:13); converted on way to Damascus intent on persecuting Christians; baptized by Ananias (Acts 9; 22: 1-16; 26:1-20; 1 Co 15:8-10; Gl 1:12-16; Eph 3:1-8); engaged in evangelistic work at Damascus (Acts 9:15; 26:16-20); forced to flee (Acts 9:23-25) to Arabia (Gl 1:17); visited Jerusalem (Acts 9:26 to 29); went to Tarsus (Acts 9:30. See Acts 15:41); brought to Antioch by Barnabas (Acts 11:25); took famine collection to Jerusalem with Barnabas (Acts 11:29, 30); sent on missionary journey to Asia Minor with Barnabas and Mark (Acts 13; 14); attended council at Jerusalem which reached decision regarding Jewish laws for Gentile converts (Acts 15); made additional missionary journeys to Asia Minor, Macedonia, Greece (Acts 16—20); arrested on visit to Jerusalem and imprisoned (Acts 21:17-40); defense before Jewish people (Acts 21:37—22: 21), Sanhedrin (Acts 22:30—23:10), Felix (Acts 24), Festus (Acts 25:6-12; appeals to emperor), Agrippa and Festus (Acts 26); sent to Rome (Acts 27; 28); probably released at 1st trial, made additional journeys (Ph 2:24; 1 Ti 1:3; 3:14; 2 Ti 4:20; Tts 3:12; Phmn 22); according to tradition, died at Rome c AD 67 (2 Ti 1:8, 15; 4). Author of majority of NT epistles.
Paulus (pô'lus). See *Sergius Paulus*.
pavement. See *Gabbatha*.
pavilion (pa-vĭl'yun). Movable tent or dwelling (1 K 20:12 [RSV: booth]; Jer 43:10 [RSV: canopy]). Figuratively of God's majesty (Jb 36:29 [KJ: tabernacle]; Ps 18:11 [RSV: canopy]) and protection (Ps 27:5 [RSV: shelter]; Is 4:5, 6 [KJ: tabernacle]).

peace. 1. Tranquillity as opposed to war (Mt 5:9; 2 Co 13:11; 1 Ti 2:2). 2. Peace which God gives (Nm 6:26); based on fulfillment of righteousness (Ps 72:3-7). Messianic kingdom is reign of peace (Is 9:5; 11:1-9; Mi 4:1-4). Christ is our Peace with God (Eph 2:14-17) through His death on cross (Cl 1:20); this peace, worked in man by Holy Spirit through faith (Jn 20:19, 22), brings peace to inner self (Gl 5:22), manifests itself in life (Ro 12:18; 14:19; 1 Co 7:15; Eph 4:3; 1 Th 5:13).
peace offering. Animal sacrifice as thank-offering for blessing; as votive offering; or as expression of love for God (Lv 3; Ju 20:26; 2 Sm 24:25). See also *sacrifice*.
peacock 1. Imported from Tarshish (1 K 10:22; 2 Ch 9:21). 2. Ostrich (as RV, RSV, Jb 39:13).
pearls. Formed by secretion of mollusks. Frequently used figuratively (Mt 13:45; 1 Ti 2:9; Rv 17:4; 18:12, 16; 21:21). H *p:ninim* (Jb 28:18; Pr 3:15; 8:11) may refer to pearls (KJ, RV: rubies. RSV: pearls, jewels).
peculiar (RSV: own, special). H *segullah*: 1. Private, personal (1 Ch 29:3). 2. Predicated of Israel to designate it as God's own people to which no one else has a claim; applied to Christians in NT (Ex 19:5 [G *laos eis peripoiesin* in 1 Ptr 2:9]; Dt 7:6; 14:2 [G *laos periousios* in Tts 2:14]; 26:18; Ps 135:4; Ml 3:17).
Pedahel (pĕd'á-hĕl, God saves). Prince of Naphtali (Nm 34:28).
Pedahzur (pĕ-dä'zēr, rock saves). Father of Gamaliel, prince of Manasseh (Nm 1: 10; 2:20; 7:54, 59; 10:23).
Pedaiah (pĕ-dā'yá, Lord saved). 1. Grandfather of Jehoiakim (2 K 23:36). 2. Father of Zerubbabel (1 Ch 3:18, 19). 3. Father of Joel, chief of Manasseh (1 Ch 27:20). 4. Helped rebuild Jerusalem's walls (Neh 3:25). 5. Benjaminite (Neh 11:7). 6. Levite; treasurer (Neh 13:13); stood by Ezra at reading of law (Neh 8:4; 1 Esd 9:44 [KJ: Phaldaius; RV: Phaldeus]).
Pedias (pĕ-dī'ăs). See *Bedeiah*.
Pekah (pē'kä, opening). 18th king of Israel; murdered Pekahiah; conspired with Damascus against Judah; assassinated by Hoshea (2 K 15:25-31; 16; 2 Ch 28:5-15).
Pekahiah (pĕk-á-hī'á, Lord opens). 17th king of Israel; son and successor of Menahem; assassinated by Pekah (2 K 15: 22-26).
Pekod (pē'kŏd). Aramaean tribe E of Tigris (Jer 50:21; Eze 23:23).
Pelaiah (pĕ-lā'yá, Lord distinguished). 1. Judahite (1 Ch 3:24). 2. Levite; stood by Ezra at reading of law; sealed covenant (Neh 8:7; 10:10; 1 Esd 9:48 [KJ: Biatas; RV: Phalias]).
Pelaliah (pĕl-á-lī'á, Lord has judged). Priest (Neh 11:12).
Pelatiah (pĕl-á-tī'á, Lord has saved). 1. Simeonite captain (1 Ch 4:42). 2. Prince of Israel; Ezekiel prophesied against him (Eze 11:1-13). 3. Grandson of Zerubbabel (1 Ch 3:21). 4. Sealed covenant with Nehemiah (Neh 10:22).
Peleg (pē'lĕg, division). Son of Eber; earth divided in his day (Gn 10:25; 11:16-19; 1 Ch 1:19, 25; Lk 3:25 [KJ: Phalec]).
Pelet (pē'lĕt, liberation). 1. Judahite (1 Ch 2:47). 2. Benjaminite; joined David at Ziklag (1 Ch 12:3).
Peleth (pē'lĕth, liberation). 1. Reubenite; his son On joined Korah's rebellion (Nm 16:1). 2. Jerahmeelite (1 Ch 2:33).

Pelethites (pĕl'ē-thīts). Part of David's bodyguard; probably from Philistia (2 Sm 8:18; 15:18; 20:7, 23; 1 K 1:38, 44; 1 Ch 18:17).

Pelias (pē-lī'ăs). See *Bedeiah*.

pelican (pĕl'ĭ-kăn). Unclean bird (Lv 11: 18; Dt 14:17); found in desolate places (Ps 102:6 [RSV: vulture]; Is 34:11 [KJ: cormorant. RSV: hawk]; Zph 2:14 [KJ: cormorant. RSV: vulture]).

Pelonite (pĕl'ō-nīt). Designation of 2 of David's heroes (1 Ch 11:27, 36; 27:10). See also *Paltite*.

Pelusium (pē-lū'shī-um). See *Sin 1.*

pen. 1. Stylus or graving tool (Jb 19:24; Ps 45:1; Jer 8:8; 17:1). 2. Reed pen for writing on papyrus (3 Jn 13. See Jer 36:23).

pencil. Instrument used by carpenter for marking lines (Is 44:13. KJ: line).

pendants. See *Ornaments.*

Peniel (pē-nī'el). See *Penuel.*

penknife. Small knife used to sharpen reed pens (Jer 36:23). See *pen 2.*

Penninah (pē-nīn'ă, coral). Wife of Elkanah (1 Sm 1:2-6).

penny. See *denarius; farthing.*

Pentateuch (pĕn'tă-tūk). 1st five books of Bible; attributed to Moses in Scripture; called Torah by Jews. Greek translators gave books distinctive titles (Genesis, Exodus, Leviticus, Numbers, Deuteronomy).

Pentecost (pĕn'tē-kôst, fiftieth day). 1. Hebrew Feast of Weeks (Ex 34:22; Dt 16: 10), Feast of Harvest (Ex 23:16), day of First Fruits (Nm 28:26), celebrated 50 days after sheaf waving on 16th Nisan. Ritual given in Ex 34:18-26. 2. Christian Pentecost fell on same day as Feast of Harvest and is beginning of Christian church; observed in commemoration of pouring out of Spirit (Acts 2; 1 Co 16:8).

Penuel (pē-nū'el, face of God). 1. Place E of Jordan where Jacob wrestled with God (Gn 32:31; Ju 8:17; 1 K 12:25). Peniel in Gn 32:30. 2. Judahite (1 Ch 4:4). 3. Benjaminite (1 Ch 8:25).

people. 1. Peoples or nations of earth (Dt 32:8; Ps 9:8; Mi 1:2; Lk 2:10). 2. People of covenant, people of Yahveh, of God (Dt 14:2; Ju 5:11; 1 Sm 2:24; 2 Sm 14:13; Is 51:4). 3. Nations as distinguished from people of God (Gn 49:10; Dt 14:2).

Peor (pē'ôr, cleft). Mountain in Moab overlooking Jeshimon, country of Jordan valley (Nm 23:28; 25:3-18; 31:16; Dt 4:3; Jos 22:17; Ps 106:28). RSV: Baal of Peor where KJ, RV: Baal-peor.

Perazim (pĕr'ă-zīm). See *Baal-perazim.*

perdition (pĕr-dīsh'un). See *Gehenna; judgment; punishment.*

Perdition, Son of. 1. Teleological name of Judas (Jn 17:12). 2. Man of sin (2 Th 2:3).

Perea (pe-rē'ă, land beyond). Name given by Josephus to the "beyond Jordan," "land across Jordan" (Mt 4:15; Jn 10:40).

Peres (pē'rĕs, divided). See *mene, mene, tekel and parsin.*

Peresh (pē'rĕsh, distinction). Son of Machir (1 Ch 7:16).

Perez (pē'rĕz, breach). Son of Judah; ancestor of Perezites (Nm 26:20. KJ: Pharzites), of David and Jesus (Gn 38:24-30; Ru 4:12, 18; Mt 1:3; Lk 3:33). KJ: Pharez in OT (except 1 Ch 27:3; Neh 11: 4, 6); Phares in NT.

Perez-uzza, (pĕ'rĕz-ŭz'ă, breach of Uzzah). Later name for threshing floor of Nacon (2 Sm 6:8; 1 Ch 13:11). See *Nacon.*

perfume. Used in incense (Ex 30:34-38); and for personal perfume (Pr 7:17; 27:9; SS 3:6; Is 3:20, 24). See *apothecary; ointment.*

perfumer. See *apothecary.*

Perga (pûr'gă). City of Pamphylia (Acts 13:13; 14:25).

Pergamos, Pergamum (pûr'gă-mos, -mum). City in Mysia in Asia Minor (Rv 1:11; 2:12-17). Modern Bergama.

Perida (pē-rī'dă). See *Peruda.*

Perizzites (pĕr'ĭ-zīts). Aborigines of Canaan (Gn 13:7; Jos 17:15; 1 Esd 8:69 [KJ: Pheresites; RV: Pherezites]; 2 Esd 1:21 [KJ, RV: Pherezites]; Jdth 5:16 [KJ: Pherezite]).

persecution (pûr-sē-kū'shun). 1. Israelites (Ex 1; Ju) and individuals persecuted 1 K 17—19; Jer 38; Am 7). 2. Persecution is mark of belonging to kingdom of Christ (Mt 5:10-12). Every follower of Christ suffers persecution because of discipleship (Mt 10:24, 25; Lk 14:26-33; Acts 14:22; 1 Ptr 4:13, 14).

Persepolis (pēr-sĕp'ō-lĭs, city of Persia). Capital of Persia; established by Darius (2 Mac 9:2).

Perseus (pûr'sūs). King of Macedonia; defeated by Rome (1 Mac 8:5).

Persia (pûr'zhă, land of Aryans). Originally, land around Persian Gulf. Cyrus conquered Media, Babylonia, built Persian empire, which dominated Asia (539 to 331 BC). Cyrus the Great (Is 41:2; 44: 28; 45) authorized return of Jews (2 Ch 36:22, 23; Ez 1); Darius I authorized rebuilding of temple (Ez 6); Xerxes I, probably Ahasuerus (Est 1:1); Artaxerxes I permitted additional exiles to return (Ez 7; 8; Neh 2:1-8).

Persis (pûr'sĭs, Persian). Christian woman at Rome (Ro 16:12).

Peruda (pē-rōō'dă, kernel. Perida in Neh 7:57). Progenitor of family of Solomon's servants who returned from captivity (Ez 2:55; 1 Esd 5:33 [KJ: Pharira; RV: Pharida]).

pestilence. Plague (Ex 5:3; 2 Ch 6:28; Ps 91:3).

Peter (pē'tēr, rock). Simon, son of Jonas (Mt 16:17; Jn 1:42; 21:15-17); lived at Bethsaida (Jn 1:44); fisherman on Sea of Galilee (Mt 4:18; Mk 1:16; Lk 5:1-11); met Jesus through Andrew (Jn 1:40-42); called by Jesus to discipleship at Sea of Galilee (Mt 4:18-22; Mk 1:16-20); called to be apostle (Mt 10:2-4; Mk 3:13-19; Lk 6:13); walked on sea (Mt 14:25-33; declared Jesus' Messiahship and was told: "Thou art Peter, and upon this rock I will build My church" (Mt 16:13-19; Mk 8:27-29; Lk 9:18-20); rebuked Christ's plan to suffer (Mt 16:22; Mk 8: 32); with James and John belonged to inner circle, was leader among apostles (Mt 16:15, 16; 17:1; 19:27; Lk 22:8); present at transfiguration (Mt 17:1; Mk 9: 2; Lk 9:28), in Gethsemane (Mt 26:37; Mk 14:33), at the high priest's palace (Mt 26:69; Mk 14:66; Lk 22:54; Jn 18: 16); denied Jesus (Mt 26:69-75; Mk 14: 70-72; Lk 22:59-62; Jn 18:26, 27); Christ appeared to him 1st of apostles (Lk 24: 34; 1 Co 15:5); preached sermon on Pentecost (Acts 2); leader in early church (Acts 1—12; 15). Tradition holds that he died at Rome under Nero (c AD 65). Called Simon (Mt 4:18; Mk 1:16; Jn 1: 41), Cephas (Jn 1:42; 1 Co 1:12), Simeon (Acts 15:14. RV, RSV: Symeon).

Peter, First Epistle of. Epistle from "Peter, an apostle of Jesus Christ" (1:1) "in Babylon" (5:13), to Christians "in Pontus, Galatia, Cappadocia, Asia, and Bithynia" (1:1). Epistle presents living hope in Christ, who redeemed and will reward His people. Outline: 1. Salutation (1:1, 2). 2. The Christian Hope and Its Effect on Life (1:3—2:10). 3. Christian Life (2:11—3:22). 4. Patience in Adversity (4). 5. Duties of Elders and People (5).

Peter, Second Epistle of. General epistle, warning against false teachings, exhorting to trust promises. Outline: 1. Salutation (1:1, 2). 2. Life and Godliness Through the Word (1:3-21). 3. False Teachers (2). 4. Warnings in View of Judgments (3).

Pethahiah (pĕth-á-hī′á, LORD set free). 1. Head of 19th course of priests (1 Ch 24:16). 2. Levite; divorced foreign wife (Ez 10:23; Neh 9:5; 1 Esd 9:23 [KJ, RV: Patheus]). 3. Counselor of Artaxerxes (Neh 11:24).

Pethor (pē′thôr). Home of Balaam in N Mesopotamia (Nm 22:5; Dt 23:4).

Pethuel (pē-thū′el). Father of Joel (Jl 1:1).

Petra (pē′trá, rock). See *Sela.*

Peullethai, Peulthai (pē-ŭl′lĕ-thī, pē-ŭl′thī, laborious). Levite; gatekeeper (1 Ch 26:5).

Phaath Moab (fā′áth mō′áb). See *Pahath-moab.*

Phacareth (făk′á-rĕth). See *Pochereth-hazzebaim.*

Phaisur (fā′sĕr). See *Pashhur 4.*

Phaldaius, Phaldeus (făl-dā′yus, -dē′us). See *Pedaiah 6.*

Phaleas (fá-lē′ás). See *Padon.*

Phalec (fā′lĕk). See *Peleg.*

Phalias (fá-lī′ás). See *Pelaiah 2.*

Phallu (făl′ōō). See *Pallu.*

Phalti (făl′tī). See *Palti 2.*

Phaltiel (făl′tĭ-ĕl). 1. See *Palti 2.* 2. "Captain of the people" who came to Esdras (2 Esd 5:16. KJ: Salathiel).

Phanuel (fá-nū′ĕl, face of God). Asherite; father of Anna (Lk 2:36).

Pharacim, Pharakim (făr′á-sĭm, -kĭm). Listed in 1 Esd 5:31.

Pharaoh (făr′ō, great house). Title of Egyptian rulers (Gn 12:15; 41:39, 42; Acts 7:10). Individual name given at birth: Pharaoh Neco, Pharaoh Hophra. Pharaohs mentioned: 1, 2. Contemporaries of Abraham (Gn 12:14-20), Joseph (Gn 40; 41). 3. Pharaoh of oppression (Seti I; others Thutmose III). 4. Pharaoh of Exodus (Ramses II; others Amenhotep II). 5. Pharaoh Merneptah, who defeated Canaanites of Gezer; Solomon's father-in-law (1 K 3:1; 7:8; 9:16). 6. Shishak; sacked Jerusalem (1 K 14:25, 26; 2 Ch 12:2-9). 7. Zerah; defeated by Asa (2 Ch 14:9-15; 16:8). 8. So (2 K 17:4. Probably a *tartan,* not a Pharaoh). 9. Tirhakah; fought Sennacherib (2 K 19:9). 10. Neco; killed Josiah; dethroned Jehoahaz; put Jehoiakim on throne; defeated by Nebuchadnezzar (2 K 23:29-35 [KJ: -nechoh; RV: -necoh]; 24:7; 2 Ch 35:20—36:4 [KJ: Necho. RV: Neco]; Jer 46:2 [KJ: -necho; RV: -neco]). 11. Hophra; Jeremiah prophesied of him (Jer 44:30. KJ: -hophra).

Pharaoh's daughter. 1. Reared Moses (Ex 2:5-10). 2. See *Bithiah.* 3. Wife of Solomon (1 K 3:1).

Pharathon, Pharathoni (făr′á-thŏn, făr-á-thō′nī). City of Judea (1 Mac 9:50).

Phares (fā′rēz). See *Perez.*

Pharez (fā′rēz). See *Parosh; Perez.*

Pharida, Pharira (fá-rī′dá, -rá). See *Peruda.*

Pharisee (făr′ĭ-sē, separated). Member of Jewish religious party which originated in time of Maccabees; taught immortality of soul, existence of angels, union of fate and human will, strict adherence to divine law; avoided contact with non-Pharisees; laid great stress on oral law and observances such as washing, tithing, fasting (Mt 9:11-14; 12:1-8; 16:1-12; 23; Lk 11; Acts 15:5; 23:6-8).

Pharosh (fā′rŏsh). See *Parosh.*

Pharpar (făr′pär, swift). River of Damascus (2 K 5:12).

Pharzites (făr′zīts). See *Perez.*

Phaseah (fá-sē′á). See *Paseah 2.*

Phaselis (fá-sē′lĭs). City of Lycia (1 Mac 15:23).

Phasiron (făs′ĭ-rŏn). Nomad chief (1 Mac 9:66).

Phassaron, Phassurus (făs′á-rŏn, fá-sū′rus). See *Pashhur 4.*

Phebe (fē′bē). See *Phoebe.*

Phenice (fē-nī′sē). See *Phoenicia; Phoenix.*

Phenicia (fē-nĭsh′ĭ-á). See *Phoenicia.*

Pheresite, Pherezite (fĕr′ĕ-sīt, -zīt). See *Perizzites.*

Phichol, Phicol (fī′cŏl). Chief of Abimelech's army (Gn 21:22, 32; 26:26).

Philadelphia (fĭl-á-dĕl′fĭ-á, brotherly love). City of Lydia in Asia Minor (Rv 1:11; 3:7-13).

Philarches (fĭ-lär′kĕz. RV: phylarch; RSV: commander). Probably not proper name (2 Mac 8:32).

Philemon (fĭ-lē′mon, friendship). Convert of Paul at Colossae in whose house there was church (Phmn).

Philemon, Epistle to. Addressed by Paul to Philemon in behalf of his runaway slave, Onesimus. Tactful and polite plea to receive Onesimus as brother.

Philetus (fĭ-lē′tus, amiable). Apostate Christian (2 Ti 2:17).

Philip (fĭl′ĭp, lover of horses). 1. Apostle; native of Bethsaida (Jn 1:44; 12:21); called to discipleship (Jn 1:41-43) and apostleship (Mt 10:3; Mk 3:18; Lk 6:14); put to test before feeding of 5,000 (Jn 6:5-7); brought Greeks to Jesus (Jn 12:20-23); asked to see Father (Jn 14:8-12); in upper chamber (Acts 1:13). 2. Native of Caesarea; ministered to poor; preached in Samaria; baptized Ethiopian eunuch (Acts 6:5; 8:4-40; 21:8, 9). 3, 4. See *Herod 4; 5.* 5. King of Macedonia; father of Alexander the Great (1 Mac 1:1). 6. Philip V, king of Macedonia (1 Mac 8:5). 7. Governor of Jerusalem under Antiochus, regent of Syria (2 Mac 5:22).

Philippi (fĭ-lĭp′ī). City of Macedonia; made colony by Octavius, given unique citizenship privileges (Acts 16:12; 20:6; Ph 1:1; 1 Th 2:2).

Philippians, Epistle to. Letter written by Paul in prison to thank Philippians for gift and sending of Epaphroditus. Expresses joy and triumph of faith. Outline: 1. Salutation (1:1-7). 2. The Apostle's Inner Life (1:12-26). 3. Exhortations (1:27—2:18). 4. Commendation of Timothy and Epaphroditus (2:19-30). 5. Exhortations, Warnings (3:1—4:9). 6. Thanks (4:10-20). 7. Close (4:21—23).

Philistia (fĭ-lĭs′tĭ-á. KJ: Palestina in Ex 15:14; Is 24:29, 31; Palestine in Jl 3:4). Country, 50 × 15 mi, from Joppa to S of Gaza. Philistines (non-Semitic, perhaps Aryans) came from Caphtor (Crete. Am 9:7; Jer 47:4) c 1175 BC; gave name (G *Palaistine*) to land; warlike; had monopoly of iron (1 Sm 13:19-22); formed league of 5 cities (Gaza, Ekron, Ashdod, Ashkelon, Gath. See Jos 13:3; 1 Sm 6:17); during period of judges, dominated Israel (Ju 13:1); deliverers: Shamgar (Ju 3:31), Samson (Ju 13—16), Samuel (1 Sm 7:1-14); defeated by Jonathan (1 Sm 13; 14); subjugated by David, made tributary (1 Sm 17; 18); regained power during divided monarchy (1 K 15:27; 2 Ch 21:16; 28:18).

Philistim, Philistines (fĭ-lĭs'tĭm, fĭ-lĭs'tĭnz). People of Philistia (Gn 10:14).

Philologus (fĭ-lŏl'ō-gus, learned). Roman Christian (Ro 16:15).

Philometor (fĭl-ō-mē'tēr). See Ptolemy VI.

philosophy (fĭ-lŏs'ō-fĭ). Epicureans and Stoics mentioned (Acts 17:18). Chief threat to Christianity came from gnostic (Cl 2:8) and syncretistic thought (1 Co 1:18-25; 1 Tim 6:20).

Phineas (fĭn'ē-ăs). See Phinehas 1.

Phinees (fĭn'ē-ĕs). 1. See Paseah 2. 2. 3. See Phinehas 1; 3. 4. Listed in 2 Esd 1:2 (RSV: Phinehas).

Phinehas (fĭn'ē-ăs). 1. Son of Eleazar; ran spear through Israelite and Midianitess; promised lasting priesthood (Nm 25:1-8; 31:6; Jos 22:13; Ju 20:28; 1 Mac 2:26, 54 [KJ: Phinees]; 2 Esd 1:2 [KJ, RV: Phinees]). Phinees (RSV: Phineas) in 1 Esd 8:2. Descendants held high priesthood until AD 70 (except during time of Eli). 2. Wicked son of Eli; killed by Philistines (1 Sm 1:3; 2:34; 4:11-22). 3. Father of Eleazar (Ez 8:33; 1 Esd 8:63 [KJ, RV: Phinees]). 4. See Phinees 4.

Phinoe (fĭn'ō-ē). See Paseah 2.

Phison (fī'son). See Pishon.

Phlegon (flē'gŏn, burning). Roman Christian (Ro 16:14).

Phoebe (fē'bē, pure, radiant. KJ: Phebe). Deaconess at Cenchrea (Ro 16:1, 2).

Phoenicia (fē-nĭsh'ĭ-á, blood-red, purple, or palm. KJ: Phenice, Phenicia). Country c 120 mi long (varying) along coast of Mediterranean from Arvad to Ladder of Tyre (NT, to Dor). People Semitic; distinguished seafarers, founded Carthage, places in Spain, perhaps even reached England; trading center of nations (Is 23:3; Eze 27:25); famous shipbuilders (Eze 27:9) and carpenters (1 K 5:6); spread culture (alphabet, dyes, numbers, weights, measures, architecture); syncretistic, immoral religion (El, Baal, Anath, Astarte, Ashera) brought to Israel by Jezebel (1 K 16:31; 18:19); called Sidonians in Dt 3:9; Jos 13:4; Ju 3:3; 1 K 5:6; Hiram, Phoenician king, was ally of David (2 Sm 5:11; 1 K 5:1) and Solomon (1 K 5:1-12; 2 Ch 2:3-16); another Hiram, craftsman and architect for Solomon (1 K 7:13-47; 2 Ch 2: 13, 14); Elijah fled to Phoenicia (1 K 17:9); Jesus visited its regions (Syrophoenician woman. Mk 7:24-30. See Mt 15:21-28); Paul visited Christians there (Acts 15:3; 21:2-7).

Phoenix (fē'nĭks. KJ: Phenice). Harbor in S Crete (Acts 27:12).

Phoros (fō'rŏs). See Parosh.

Phrurai (frū'rī). See Purim, Letter of.

Phrygia (frĭj'ĭ-á). Province which once included greater part of Asia Minor; obtained by Rome, 133 BC (Acts 2:10; 16:6; 18:23).

Phud (fŭd). See Put.

Phurah (fū'rá). See Purah.

Phurim (fū'rĭm). See Purim, Letter of.

Phut (fŭt). See Put.

Phuvah (fū'vá). See Puvah.

Phygellus, Phygelus (fī-jĕl'us). Apostate of Asia (2 Ti 1:15).

phylactery (fĭ-lăk'tēr-ĭ). See frontlet.

phylarch (fĭ'lärk). See Philarches.

physician (fĭ-zĭsh'ăn). See disease.

Pi-beseth (pĭ-bē'sĕth, abode of Bast, a goddess). City on Egyptian delta (Eze 30:17). Modern Tell Basta.

picture (pĭk'tūr). Jews probably had paintings on walls and wood or carvings on stone (Nm 33:52; Is 2:16; Eze 8:12 [KJ, RV: imagery]).

piece of gold, silver, money. 1. In OT usually supplied by translators where original has "1,000 of silver," etc (Gn 20:16). 2. Drachma (Lk 15:8, 9. RSV: silver coin). 3. Probably shekel. Others denarius (Mt 26:15; 27:3-9. See Ex 21:32).

pigeon. Clean bird used for sacrifice (Gn 15:9; Lv 1:14; 5:7, 11; 12:8; 14:22, 30; 15:14, 29; Nm 6:10; Lk 2:24); sold in temple (Mt 21:12; Mk 11:15; Jn 2:14, 16. KJ, RV: doves).

Pi-hahiroth (pī-há-hī'rŏth). Israelite encampment in Egypt (Ex 14:2-9; Nm 33:7).

Pilate (pī'lát, armed with javelin). Pontius Pilate, 5th procurator of Judea (AD 26—36). Tried Jesus, found Him innocent, delivered Him to soldiers to be crucified (Mt 27; Mk 15; Lk 3:1; 13:1; 23; Jn 18; 19; Acts 3:13; 4:27; 13:28; 1 Ti 6:13).

Pildash (pĭl'dăsh). Son of Nahor (Gn 22:22).

Pileha (pĭl'ē-hä). See Pilha.

pilgrimage. 1. Jews made pilgrimages to sanctuary (see Dt 16:16; Songs of Ascent: Ps 120—134; Acts 2:5-11). 2. Christians are pilgrims to heaven (Heb 11:13; 1 Ptr 2:11. RSV: exiles).

Pilha (pĭl'hä. KJ: Pileha). Sealed covenant with Nehemiah (Neh 10:24).

pillar. 1. Monument marking sacred spot (usually stone or pile of stones), grave, or memorial (Gn 28:18; 31:45; 35:20; 2 Sm 18:18). 2. Architectural pillars (Ju 16:25-30; 1 K 7; 2 K 11:14). 3. Pillar of cloud (fire at night) was God's presence in exodus (Ex 13:21; 14:19-24). Shekinah in targums, early Christian writers. 4. Figuratively, basis (1 Ti 3:15), prominent support (Gl 2:9).

Piltai (pĭl'tī, deliverance). Priest (Neh 12:17).

pim (pĭm. KJ, RV: file). ⅔ shekel (1 Sm 13:21).

pine. Translation disputed, versions varying between plane, pine, box tree, fir, etc (see Neh 8:15; SS 1:17; Is 41:19; 60:13; Eze 27:6).

pinnacle. Part of temple; edge of roof or battlement have been conjectured (Mt 4:5; Lk 4:9).

Pinon (pī'non). Chief of Edom (Gn 36:41; 1 Ch 1:52).

pipe. Woodwind instrument (Gn 4:21; Jb 21:12; 30:31; Ps 150:4. KJ: organ). See also flute; music.

Pira (pī'rá). Perhaps repetition of Caphira (1 Esd 5:19).

Piram (pī'răm). Amorite king (Jos 10: 3-27).

Pirathon (pĭr'á-thŏn, height). Home of Abdon (Ju 12:13-15) and Benaiah (2 Sm 23:30; 1 Ch 11:31) in Ephraim (probably 7½ mi SW of Shechem).

Pisgah, Mount (pĭz'gá). Headland of Abarim mts opposite Jericho (Nm 21:20; 23:14; Dt 3:17, 27; 4:49; 34:1; Jos 12:3; 13:20). See Ashdoth-pisgah.

Pishon (pī'shŏn). River of Eden (Gn 2:11 [KJ: Pison]; Sir 24:25 [KJ: Phison]).

Pisidia (pĭ-sĭd'ĭ-á). Land in S Asia Minor N of Pamphylia (Acts 13:14; 14:24).
Pison (pī'sŏn). See *Pishon*.
Pispa, Pispah (pĭs'pä). Asherite (1 Ch 7:38).
pistachio nut (pĭs-tăsh'ĭ-ō). Tree whose fruit contains greenish seed used in cooking (Gn 43:11. KJ, RV: nuts).
pit. **1.** Hole dug for well or cistern (Gn 37:24); used for prison (Gn 37:24; Is 24:22), burial (Ps 28:1; Is 38:18), trap (2 Sm 23:20; Eze 19:8). **2.** Death, grave, beyond of death (Jb 33:18-30; Ps 28:1; 30:3; Is 14:15, 19). See *abyss; sheol*.
pitch. Asphalt or bitumen (Gn 6:14; Ex 2:3; Is 34:9).
pitcher. See *homes* 5.
Pithom (pī'thŏm, dwelling of Atum, sun-god). Egyptian store-city in Goshen (Ex 1:11).
Pithon (pī'thŏn). Great-grandson of Jonathan (1 Ch 8:35).
pity. Compassion; sorrow over suffering of others. Attribute of God (Ps 103:13; Jon 4:11 [KJ: spare]; Ja 5:11; 1 Ptr 3:8); enjoined on believers (Pr 19:17 [RSV: kind]; Is 1:17; Mt 18:23-35).
plague. **1.** Calamity or affliction (Ex 11:1). **2.** Epidemic (1 Sm 5; 2 Sm 24:13-25). **3.** 10 plagues of Egypt (Ex 7—12).
plain. See *Arabah; oak*.
plane (KJ: chestnut in Gn 30:37; Eze 31:8; pine in Is 41:19; 60:13). Tree which grows along water in Syria and Mesopotamia.
planets. Constellations (as RSV. 2 K 23:5. RV marg: twelve signs).
plaster. Used on walls of houses and palaces (Lv 14:41-48; Dn 5:5); to cover stones before engraving (Dt 27:2, 4).
pledge. **1.** Security for loan (Dt 24:10-13, 17). See also *loan*. **2.** Wager (as RSV. 2 K 18:23; Is 36:8).
Pleiades (plē'yá-dēz, H kimah, cluster). Stars in constellation Taurus (Jb 9:9; 38:31; Am 5:8 [KJ: seven stars]).
plow. See *agriculture 2*.
plowshare. H mahareshah (plowshare), eth (plowbeam, plowshare, mattock). Stone or point of plow (1 Sm 13:20 [KJ, RV: share . . . coulter; RSV: plowshare . . . mattock]; Is 2:4; Jl 3:10; Mi 4:3). See also *agriculture 2*.
plummet. See *trade 5*.
Pochereth-hazzebaim (pŏk'e-rĕth-hă-zē-bā'ĭm). Division of Solomon's servants which returned from Babylon (Ez 2:57; Neh 7:59. KJ: Pochereth of Zebaim). KJ, RV: Phacareth, the sons of Sabi (Sabie) in 1 Esd 5:34.
pods. See *husks*.
poetry. H poetry characterized by rhythm, parallelism, alliteration, rhyme, or other word plays. Job, Psalms, Proverbs, Ecclesiastes, Song of Solomon, sections in prophets are examples of poetry.
poison. Substance which produces morbid or deadly effect; usually venom of serpents (Dt 32:24, 33; Jb 20:16; Ps 140:3). Figuratively, affliction (Jb 6:4); that which causes physical, mental, spiritual pain or ruin (Dt 32:32, 33; Ps 58:4), as wickedness (Jb 20:16; Am 6:12).
police (G 'rabdouchos, staffbearer. L lictor). Petty officer, often attendant of magistrate, roughly equivalent to constable, policeman (Acts 16:35, 38. KJ, RV: serjeants).
Pollux (pŏl'uks). See *Twin Brothers*.
pomegranate (pŏm'grăn-ĭt). See *orchard 4*.
pommel (pŭm'el). Bowl-shaped capital of pillar (2 Ch 4:12, 13. RV, RSV: bowl). Bowl in 1 K 7:41.

Pontius (pŏn'shus). See *Pilate*.
Pontus (pŏn'tus, sea). Region of NE Asia Minor; Roman province in NT times (Acts 2:9; 18:2; 1 Ptr 1:1).
pool. Reservoir for collecting water (2 K 18:17; 20:20; Neh 2:14; Is 7:3; 22:11; 36:2).
poor. See *poverty*.
poplar (H libneh, white). Probably storax, lower surface of whose leaves is white (Gn 30:37; Hos 4:13; 14:5 [KJ, RV: Lebanon]).
Poratha (pŏ-rā'thá, liberal). Son of Haman (Est 9:8).
porch. Veranda-chamber (Ju 3:23. RSV: vestibule); colonnade, portico (Jn 5:2. RSV: portico); vestibule, hall (1 Ch 28:11. RSV: vestibule); passage from street to inner hall (Mt 26:71).
Porcius (pôr'shĭ-us). See *Festus*.
porcupine (pôr'kū-pĭn). See *bittern*.
porphyry (pôr'fĭ-rĭ. KJ, RV: red marble). Rock with dark-red groundmass (Est 1:6).
porpoise (pôr'pus). See *badger*.
porter. See *gatekeeper*.
Posidonius (pŏs-ĭ-dō'nĭ-us). Envoy of Nicanor (2 Mac 14:19).
post. Runner, messenger, courier (Est 8: 10, 14; Jb 9:25).
pot. Clay or metal vessel of varied design (Ju 6:19; 2 K 4:38; Jb 41:20, 31; Lm 4:2 [KJ, RV: pitcher]).
Potiphar (pŏt'ĭ-fêr, who is of the sun). Captain of Pharaoh's guard (Gn 37:36; 39:1).
Potiphera (pŏ-tĭf'ēr-á. who is of the sun. KJ: Potipherah). Egyptian; priest of On; father-in-law of Joseph (Gn 41:45, 50; 46:20).
Potsherd Gate (pŏt'shûrd). See *East Gate*.
pottage. Stew of meat, vegetables (Gn 25: 29, 30, 34; 2 K 4:38-40; Hg 2:12).
potter, potter's field, potter's wheel, pottery. See *trade 6*.
pound. OT: H maneh (50 shekels. 1 K 10: 17; Ez 2:69; Neh 7:71. RSV: mina). NT: G mna (100 drachmas, Lk 19:13-25); G litra (12 ozs. Jn 12:3; 19:39).
poverty. OT took negative view of beggary (Ps 37:25; Pr 20:4). Poverty caused by laziness (Pr 10:4; 14:23; 20: 13), calamities (Ju 10:6-17), oppression (Is 5:8; Mt 23:14). Regulations protected poor: gleaning (Lv 19:9, 10), sabbatical year (Ex 23:11; Lv 25:6), year of jubilee (Lv 25:8-30), prompt wages (Dt 24:14, 15), festivals (Dt 16:11, 14), laws on usury and pledges (Ex 22:25-27); compassionate man extolled (Ps 41:1; Pr 14: 21; 29:7).
praetorian guard. Guard of imperial palace and occupants (Ph 1:13. KJ: all the palace).
praetorium (prē-tō'rĭ-um). **1.** Headquarters of general. **2.** Palace of governor, as of Pilate (Mt 27:27 [KJ: common hall]; Mk 15:16; Jn 18:28 [KJ: hall of judgment, judgment hall]; 18:33 [KJ: judgment hall]; 19:9 [KJ: judgment hall]). Palace of Herod at Caesarea (Acts 23:35. KJ: judgment hall).
praise. Glorify God with jubilation or formal worship, especially worship (Ex 15:1-19; 1 Sm 2:1-10; Ps 24:7-10; 47; 67; 95—100; Ro 1:25; 16:25-27; 2 Co 11:31; Gl 1:5; Eph 3:20, 21; Rv 1:5, 6).
prayer (prâr). Communication with God; prayers of Moses largely intercessory prayers (Ex 32:11-13, 31, 32; Nm 11: 11-15; Dt 9:18-21); psalms are prayers of covenant people to covenant God, usually content of concrete experience seen in

spiritual depth; closely associated with sacrifice (Gn 12:8; 26:25) and hence with temple (1 K 8:30,33; Ps 5:7). In NT prayer is in name of Jesus (Jn 15:16; 14:13) because He is our right to pray (Gl 4:1-7), our new covenant (Mk 14:24; 1 Co 11:25; 2 Co 3:14; Heb 8; 9; 10), author and intercessor (Mt 6:9-13; Lk 11:1-4; Ro 8:34; Heb 4:14-16; 7:25); Holy Spirit through Word of Christ source of prayer (Ro 8:15,16,26,27). Prayers are formal (Ps; Mt 6:9-13; 26:30; Lk 23:46) or spontaneous (Jn 17; Lk 18:13; 1 Th 5:17), community (Acts 1:14) or individual (Mt 6:6; 14:23; Phmn 4), at set times and places (Acts 2:42; 6:4; 16:13), at all times and places (Eph 6:18; 1 Th 5:17; 1 Ti 2:8). Attitudes: uplifted hands (Ps 28:2; 1 Ti 2:8), kneeling (1 K 8:54; Acts 9:40), prostrating (Mt 26:39), standing (Mt 6:5).

preacher, preaching. Prophetic message of OT, whether denunciation, revelation of God's will, or promise (Eze 20:46 [KJ, RV: drop thy word]; Jer 11:6 [KJ, RV, RSV: proclaim]; Is 61:1 [RSV: bring]). Preaching in NT centered in story of Jesus (Acts 2:14-40; 3:11-26). Sermons included Law and Gospel (Mt 4:17; Lk 3:3-14; 4:18; Acts 2:14-40; 17:22-31).

predestination (prē-dĕs-ti-nā'shǔn). God's election concerning children of God whereby He predestinated them to salvation before foundations of world were laid (Eph 1:4,5), namely: (1) to reconcile human race with God; (2) to offer Christ's merits and benefits through Word and sacraments; (3) to be active in hearts with Holy Spirit through Word; (4) to receive by grace as sons and heirs of salvation those who repent and accept Christ by faith; (5) to sanctify them; (6) to lead and protect them against devil, world, and flesh; (7) to preserve them to the end if they cling to and remain active in God's Word; (8) to save them eternally (Mt 20:16; 22:14; Mk 13:20-22; Acts 13:48; Ro 8:28-30; 9:11; 11:15; Eph 1:4,5; 2 Th 2:13; 2 Ti 1:9; 2:10,19; 1 Ptr 1:2).

presbyter (prĕz'bi-tēr). See *elder.*

priest. H *kohen,* G *hieros.* 1. Person who ministered before God; originally individuals (Gn 4:3, 4), fathers of families (Gn 12:7; 13:18; 26:25; 33:20); God through Moses designated Aaron and his sons priests (Ex 28:1); selected according to rigid standards (Lv 21:16-24); consecrated, ministered in special garments in sanctuary, taught people, inquired of divine will (Ex 28; 29); divided into 24 courses, each serving week at time (1 Ch 24:1-19). Kings (2 Sm 6:17; 1 Kgs 3:3, 4), judges (Ju 6:17-21; 13:15-20), prophets (1 Kgs 18:30-38) sacrificed. 2. Chief, or high, priest supervised priests; offered sin offering (Lv 4), sacrifice on Day of Atonement (Lv 16); consulted God by Urim and Thummim (Nm 27:21; 1 Sm 30:7, 8); in addition to priest's garment (breeches, coat, girdle, cap) he wore breastplate (with Urim and Thummim), ephod, girdle, miter (Ex 28). See also *Aaron.* 3. In NT Jesus Christ is only High Priest, in whom Levitical priesthood is abolished (Jn 14:6; 1 Ti 2:5, 6; Heb 5; 7—10). See also *Jesus Christ, Offices.* 4. Believers are priests through participation in Christ and His priestly activity (Eph 2:18; Heb 10:19-25; 13:15; 1 Ptr 2:5, 9; Rv 1:5, 6). 5. Servant of king (2 Sm 8:18. KJ: chief rulers. See 1 Ch 18:17).

priest, high. See *priest 2; 3.*

prince. 1. Head of family or tribe (Gn 25:16; Ju 5:15; 1 Ch 4:38). 2. King (1 Sm 9:16. KJ: captain). 3. In general: ruler, governor, magistrate, satrap, royal descendant (Nm 22:8; 1 Sm 18:30; 2 Ch 12:5, 6; Est 1; 2 K 10:13 [KJ, RV: children of the king]; Dn 6:1 [RV, RSV: satrap]). 4. Spiritual ruler (Is 9:6). 5. Ruler of demons (Mt 9:34).

principality (prĭn-si-pǎl'i-tĭ). 1. Rule, ruler (as RV, RSV. Eph 1:21; Tts 3:1). 2. Order of angels (Ro 8:38; Eph 3:10; Cl 1:16; 2:15).

Prisca, Priscilla (prĭs'kà, prĭ-sĭl'à, little old woman). Wife of Aquila; had church in their house; taught Apollos; helped Paul (Acts 18:2, 18, 26; Ro 16:3; 1 Co 16:19; 2 Ti 4:19).

prison. 1. Oldest prisons were wells or dungeons (Gn 37:24; Jer 38:6-13). During period of kings prison was part of palace (1 K 22:27; Jer 32:2) or private building (Jer 37:15). Herods and Romans had royal prisons (Lk 3:20; Acts 12:4; 23:10, 35). 2. Synonym for abyss, abode of Satan (Rv 20:7; 1 Ptr 3:19. See Jude 6).

Prochorus (prŏk'ō-rus, leader of chorus). One of 7 who performed social service (Acts 6:5).

proconsul (prō-kŏn'sul. KJ: deputy). Governor of Roman province administered by Senate (Acts 13:7; 18:12; 19:38).

profane (H *halal,* open; G *bebeloo,* desecrate). 1. To make common, or defile (Ex 31:14; Lv 19:8, 12; Eze 22:26; Mt 12:5). 2. Common as opposed to holy (Eze 22:26; 42:20. RV, RSV: common).

prognosticator (prŏg-nŏs'ti-kā-tēr). Fortune-teller aided by moon (Is 47:13. RSV: who at new moon predict).

promise. Assertion that God would raise deliverer or Messiah (Gn 3:15; 12:3; Ro 4:13; 9:8; Gl 3:14-19). Promises of OT fulfilled in Christ (Acts 13:23, 32, 33; Ro 1:2, 3; 15:8; Gl 3:14; 2 Co 1:20). Believers are heirs of promise (Ro 4:16; Gl 3:16, 26-29; 4:28). Faith is correlative to promise, brings blessing (Gl 3:1-14).

prophet (H *nabi',* announce; *ro'eh,* seer; *hozeh,* seer. G *prophetes,* speak for). Divinely inspired forthteller (1 Sm 10:6; Jer 1:2; Eze 1:1; Hos 1:1; 1 Ptr 1:11; 2 Ptr 1:21) who rebuked sin (2 Sm 12; Is 58:1; Eze 3:17), showed God's mercy (Is 40; 53), doing this in association with acts of past, present, and future with constant emphasis on God's acts; hence Messiah has prominent place in prophecy. Came from various walks of life (Am 1:1). There were also schools of prophets (1 Sm 19:19, 20; 2 K 2:3, 5; 4:38; 6:1).

propitiation (prō-pĭsh-ĭ-ā'shun, H *kaphar,* cover; G *'ilaskesthai,* incline toward). In OT used in connection with sacrifice, when in some way blood covered sin and effected atonement (Lv 14:18; 17:11; 19:22). God also forgives without sacrifice (Is 6:7; 27:9; Eze 16:63). Jesus by His blood exercised propitiative function and effected atonement between God and men (Ro 3:25; 1 Jn 2:2; 4:10. RSV: expiation).

proselyte (prŏs'e-lĭt). From earliest times there were sojourners (strangers) in Israel who obeyed certain rules (Ex 20:10; Lv 17:10, 15; 18:26; 20:2; 22:18; 24:16). They could become part of Israel by circumcision (Ex 12:48, 49. Exceptions: Dt 23:3, 8). In NT there were people who observed some or all features of Jewish religion (Mt 23:15; Acts 13:43 [KJ: religious proselytes; RV: devout proselytes; RSV: devout converts to Judaism]), or were simply God fearers (Acts 10:2).

prostitution (prŏs-ti-tū'shun). See *harlot.*

proverb. Pithy saying expressing familiar or useful truth; H *mashal*, maxim (Gn 10:9; 1 Sm 10:12; Dt 28:37; Pr).

Proverbs, Book of. Book of Writings (Hagiographa) and Wisdom. Literature attributed to Solomon (1:1; 10:1; 25:1), known for wisdom (1 K 4:29, 32). Wise man recognizes God in all things. Thought of God is reflected everywhere, especially in wise life. Outline: 1. Introduction (1:1-7). 2. Praise of Wisdom (1:7—9:18). 3. Proverbs of Solomon (10.1—22:16). 4. Words of the Wise (22:17—24:22). 5. Sayings of the Wise (24:23-34). 6. Proverbs of Solomon (25—29). 7. Words of Agur (30). 8. Words of Lemuel (31:1-9). 9. Good Wife (31:10—31).

providence (prŏv'ĭ-dens). Activity of God whereby He uninterruptedly upholds, governs, directs entire creation (Jb 9:5, 6; 28:25; Ps 104:10-25; 145:15; 147:9; Mt 4:4; 6:26-28; Lk 12:6, 7; Acts 17:25-28; Heb 1:3).

province. Unit of country, especially of Persian (satrapies) and Roman empires (Ez 2:1; 5:8; Acts 23:34; 25:1).

Psalms, Book of (sämz, H *t:hillim*, songs of praise. G *psalmos*, poem sung to music of stringed instruments). Longest of hagiographa. Authors given in titles: Moses (90), David (3—9, 11—32, 34—41, 51—65, 68—70, 86, 101, 103, 108—110, 122, 124, 131, 133, 138—145), Solomon (72, 127), Asaph (50, 73—83), sons of Korah (42, 44—49, 84, 85, 87, 88), Heman (88), Ethan (89). Meaning of titles is sometimes conjectured; musical directions, instruments, melodies, liturgical instructions, occasions, descriptive. Hebrew Psalter divided into five books: 1. 1—41. 2. 42—72. 3. 73—89. 4. 90 to 106. 5. 107—150. See *music; poetry.*

psaltery (RSV: harp). H *nebel.* Stringed instrument (1 Sm 10:5; Ps 57:8; 71:22; Dn 3:5); at times 10 strings (Ps 33:2; 144:9). See also *music.*

Ptolemais (tŏl-ê-mā'ĭs). See *Accho.*

Ptolemy (tŏl'ê-mĭ). 1. Macedonian dynasty; ruled Egypt (323—31 BC): Ptolemy I; Soter (323—285 BC). Ptolemy II; Philadelphus (285—246 BC; Septuagint translated in his reign. Ptolemy III (c 246—222 BC). Ptolemy IV; Philopator (222—205 BC; 3 Mac 1:1-5). Ptolemy V; Epiphanes (205—181 BC). Ptolemy VI; Philomator(181—145 BC; 1 Mac 10:51 to 58; 11:1-18); showed favor to Jews. Ptolemy VII; Physcon (145—117 BC; 1 Mac 15:16). 2. Ptolemy Marron, a general (2 Mac 4:45; 6:8; 8:8); fought Judas Maccabaeus (1 Mac 3:38; 2 Mac 10:12). 3. Ptolemy, son-in-law of Simon (1 Mac 16:11-23). 4. Father of Lysimachus (Ap Est 11:1).

Pua (pū'á). See *Puvah.*

Puah (pū'á). 1. Egyptian midwife (Ex 1:15). 2. Father of Tola, judge (Ju 10:1). 3. See *Puvah.*

publican (RSV: tax collector). Tax-collector for Romans; used tax-farming system; hated by Jews (Mt 9:10; 18:17; Lk 3:12, 13; 19:2).

Publius (pŭb'lĭ-us, common). Chief man of Melita (Acts 28·7, 8).

Pudens (pū'dĕnz, modest). Roman Christian (2 Ti 4:21).

Puhites (pū'hĭts). See *Puthites.*

Pul (pŭl). 1. African country and people; probably Put. 2. Another name (Babylonian: Pulu) for Tiglath-pileser (2 K 15:19; 1 Ch 5:26).

pulse. Leguminous plants and seeds (peas, beans, etc. Dn 1:12-16. RSV: vegetable).

punishment. Purpose of punishment in OT was to eradicate evil (Dt 13:5), deter crime (Dt 17:13). Law based on justice, punishment matched crime (Ex 21:23-25; Lv 24:17-21; Dt 19:21). Crimes concerned persons, property, morals (Ex 20—23; Lv 5; 19; Dt 19). Capital punishment consisted in stoning (Ex 19:13; Dt 13:10). Romans introduced beheading (Mt 14:10), hanging (practiced already by Babylonians, Est 2:23. Jews hanged body after death, Dt 21:23), crucifixion (Mk 15:21-25). Other punishments: beating (Ex 21:20; Dt 22:18; 25:2, 3; 1 K 12:14), imprisonment (Jer 32:2), fines (Dt 22:19, 29). Crimes considered sins against God (Ps 51:4). Christ procured forgiveness for mankind by bearing punishment for sin (Acts 2:38; 10:38-43; 13:37-39; Eph 1:7; Cl 1:14; Heb 9:22). Eternal punishment for unbeliever (Mt 25:46). See also *eschatology; Gehenna; hell; judgment.*

Punites (pū'nĭts). Descendants of Puvah (Nm 26:23).

Punon (pū'nŏn, darkness?). Encampment of Israel E of Edom (Nm 33:42, 43).

Pur (pûr, lot). Lot cast to destroy Jews (Est 3:7; 9:24, 26). See *Purim.*

Purah (pū'rá, branch. KJ: Phurah). Gideon's servant (Ju 7:10, 11).

purification. Jews endeavored to maintain racial (Dt 23:3, 4; Ez 10), bodily (Mk 7:4; Jn 13:6), ceremonial cleanness. Rites provided for purification of land (Dt 21:1-9), after contact with dead (Lv 5:2, 3; Nm 19), women after childbirth (Lv 12), skin diseases (Lv 14), and others. Christ emphasized that purity comes from heart (Mk 7:18-23).

Purim (pū'rĭm). Name from Pur (Est 9:24-26). Jewish feast, celebrated with hilarity and charity, on 14th and 15th Adar, to commemorate deliverance of Jews by Esther (Est 3:7; 9:24-32).

Purim, Letter of. Letter interpreted by Lysimachus (Ap Est 11:1. KJ: Phurim; RV: Phrural).

purple. Color worn by wealthy and high officials (Ju 8:26; 1 Mac 8:14; Lk 16:19). Included hues between violet and crimson (see Mt 27:28). See *color.*

Put (pŭt). 1. Son of Ham (Gn 10:6 [KJ: Phut]; 1 Ch 1:8). 2. African country and people associated with Egyptians; identified with Libya or Punt (Is 66:19 [KJ, RV: Pul]; Eze 27:10 [KJ: Phut]; 38:5 [KJ: Libya]; Nah 3:9; Jdth 2:23 [KJ: Phud]). See also *Lehabim; Libyans.*

Puteoli (pū-tē'ō-lī), Italian harbor 8 ml W of Naples (Acts 28:13). Modern Pozzuoli.

Puthites (pū'thĭts. KJ: Puhites). Judahite family (1 Ch 2:53).

Putiel (pū'tĭ-ĕl, given by God?). Father-in-law of Eleazar (Ex 6:25).

Puvah (pū'vá). Son of Issachar; founder of family (Gn 46:13 [KJ: Phuvah]; Nm 26:23 [KJ: Pua]). Puah in 1 Ch 7:1.

pygarg (pī'gärg). See *ibex.*

Pyrrhus (pĭr'us). Father of Sopater (Acts 20:4. KJ omits).

Q

quail. Resident in Egypt and Palestine and also migratory, passing Gulf of Aqabah to Sinai (Ex 16:13; Nm 11:31, 32; Ps 105:40).

quarry. See *trade 11.*

quart. See *measures 2; 3.*

Quartus (kwôr'tus, fourth). Corinthian Christian (Ro 16:23).

quaternion (kwa̍-tûr'nĭ-un). Roman guard of 4 soldiers (Acts 12:4. RSV: squad. See Jn 19:23).

queen. 1. H *g:birah,* mistress (i. e., king's woman of power). Influential queen (1 K 11:19; 2 K 10:13), or king's mother (1 K 15:13; 2 Ch 15:16). H *g:bereth,* mistress of kingdoms (Is 47:5, 7. KJ, RV: lady). 2. H *malkah,* queen regnant or king's chief wife (1 K 10:1; Est 1:9; 2:22). 3. H *shegal,* king's wife distinguished from concubine (Neh 2:6). Wives in Dn 5:2, 3.

queen of heaven. Astarte, Semitic deity (Babylonian Ishtar) of female fertility (Jer 7:18; 44:17-25).

queen of the South. Queen of Sheba (Mt 12:42; Lk 11:31. See 1 K 10:1-13; 2 Ch 9:1-12).

quicksands. See *Syrtis.*

Quintus Memmius (kwĭn'tus mĕm'ĭ-us). Roman legate to Jews (2 Mac 11:34).

Quirinius, Publius Sulpicius (kwī-rĭn'ĭ-us, pŭb'lĭ-us sŭl-pĭsh'us. KJ: Cyrenius). Governor of Syria when Caesar Augustus issued decree for census in which Joseph enrolled (Lk 2:2). He was governor of Syria AD 6—10, and historicity of Luke on this point is questioned. Some hold there is textual corruption; others that he was governor 4 BC—AD 1 and also AD 6—10.

quiver. See *archery.*

R

Raama, Raamah (rā'a̍-ma̍). Son of Cush; tribe in SW Arabia (Gn 10:7; 1 Ch 1:9; Eze 27:22).

Raamiah (rā-a̍-mī'a̍, tremble before LORD, or LORD has thundered). Leader of Jews who returned from captivity (Neh 7:7). Reelaiah in Ez 2:2. Resaiah (KJ: Reesaias; RV: Resaias) in 1 Esd 5:8.

Raamses (rā-ăm'sĕz). 1. Store city (and region) in NE Egypt built by Hebrew labor (Ex 1:11); capital of 19th dynasty. Rameses in Gn 47:11; Ex 12:37; Nm 33: 3, 5. 2. See *Pharaoh 4.*

Rabbah (răb'a̍, great). 1. Chief Ammonite city (Dt 3:11 [KJ: Rabbath]; Jos 13:25; 2 Sm 11:1; 12:27-29; 1 Ch 20:1; Jer 49:2, 3; Eze 21:20 [KJ: Rabbath]; 25:5; Am 1:14). Named Philadelphia by Ptolemy Philadelphus. Modern Amman. 2. City of Judah (Jos 15:60).

Rabbath (răb'ăth). See *Rabbah 1.*

Rabbi (răb'ī, my master). Jewish title of respect for spiritual leader and instructor (Mt 23:7, 8; Mk 10:51 [KJ: Lord; RSV: Master]; Jn 1:38, 49; 3:2, 26; 6:25). KJ: Master in Jn 4:31; 9:2; 11:8. Rabboni in Jn 20:16.

Rabbith (răb'ĭth, populous). City of Issachar (Jos 19:20).

Rabboni (ra̍-bō'nī). See *Rabbi.*

Rabmag (răb'măg, chief soothsayer). Title of office (Jer 39:3, 13).

Rabsaces (răb'sa̍-sēz). See *Rabshakeh.*

Rabsaris (răb'sa̍-rĭs, chief eunuch). Assyrian title of high official (2 K 18:17; Jer 39:3, 13).

Rabshakeh (răb'sha̍-kĕ, chief officer). Assyrian title of high official (2 K 18:17-37; 19:4-8; Is 36; 37:4, 8; Sir 48:18 [KJ: Rabsaces]).

raca (ra̍-ka̍', empty, worthless). Aramaic term of contempt (Mt 5:22. RSV: insults).

Racal (rā'kăl. KJ: Rachal). Town in Judah (1 Sm 30:29).

race. Greek, contest (1 Co 9:24; Heb 12:1). See also *games.*

Rachab (rā'kăb). See *Rahab.*

Rachal (rā'kăl). See *Racal.*

Rachel (rā'chel, ewe). Daughter of Laban; favorite wife of Jacob; mother of Joseph, Benjamin (Gn 29—35; Jer 31:15 [KJ: Rahel]).

Raddai (răd'ā-ī, trampling). Brother of David (1 Ch 2:14).

Ragae (rā'jē). See *Rages.*

Ragau (rā'gô). 1. See *Rages.* 2. See *Reu.*

Rages (rā'jēz). City of Media (Tob 1:14). Ragau (RSV: Ragae) in Jdth 1:5, 15.

Raguel (ra̍-gū'el). 1. See *Jethro.* 2. Father-in-law of Tobias (Tob 3:7).

Rahab (rā'hăb, broad). Harlot of Jericho; house on wall; hid Israelite spies (Jos 2: 1-21; 6:17-25; Ru 4:21; Mt 1:5 [KJ: Rachab]).

Rahab (rā'hăb, violent one). Monster representing sea power and violence (Jb 26:12 [KJ: the proud]; Ps 89:10); applied to Egypt (Ps 87:4; Is 30:7 [KJ: strength]; 51:9).

Raham (rā'hăm, pity). Descendant of Caleb (1 Ch 2:44).

Rahel (rā'hĕl). See *Rachel.*

raiment. See *dress.*

rain. Rainy season in Palestine: Oct—Apr; dry season: May—Oct; early rain: Oct, Nov (Ps 84:6; Is 30:23; Jer 5:24; Ja 5:7); later rain: Mar, Apr (Jb 29:23; Pr 16:15; Jer 3:3; 5:24; Zch 10:1; Ja 5:7). Figuratively, teaching and counsel (Dt 32:2; Jb 29:21-25); Word (Is 55:10); righteousness and peace (Ps 72:6), blessings of believers (Ps 84:5, 6); destructive judgments (Jb 20:23; Eze 38:22); nagging (Pr 19:13); oppression (Pr 28:3); favor of king (Pr 16:15).

rainbow. Sign of God's covenant that flood should not again occur (Gn 9:12-17).

raisin, cake of raisins. Dried, pressed grapes (1 Sm 25:18; 1 Ch 16:3 [KJ: flagon of wine]). See also *vineyard 4.*

Rakem (rā'kĕm, variegated). Descendant of Manasseh (1 Ch 7:16).

Rakkath (răk'ăth). Fortified city of Naphtali, probably on Sea of Galilee (Jos 19:35).

Rakkon (răk'ŏn). Town of Dan (Jos 19:46).

ram. Male of sheep; used for food (Gn 31:38), sacrifice (Gn 15:9; 22:13; Lv 1:10; 5:15; 6:6; Nm 7; 28; 29); skins for covering of tabernacle (Ex 26:14); horns for trumpets (Jos 6:4-20).

Ram (răm, high). 1. Judahite (1 Ch 2:9; Ru 4:19; Mt 1:3 [KJ: Aram]). Arni (KJ: Aram) in Lk 3:33. 2. Son of Jerahmeel (1 Ch 2:25, 27). 3. Elihu was "of the family of Ram" (Jb 32:2).

ram, battering. See *armor*.
Rama (rā'mà). See *Ramah 1*.
Ramah (rā'mà, height). **1.** Town of Benjamin 5 mi N of Jerusalem near Deborah's palm tree and Rachel's tomb (Jos 18:25; Ju 4:5; 19:10-15; 1 K 15:17-22; Jer 31:15; 40:1; Mt 2:18 [KJ: Rama]); peopled by Benjaminites after captivity (Ez 2:26; Neh 7:30; 11:33; 1 Esd 5:20 [KJ: Cirama; RV: Kirama]). Modern el-Ram. **2.** Boundary town of Asher (Jos 19:29). **3.** Fortified town of Naphtali (Jos 19:36). **4.** See *Ramoth-gilead*. **5.** Town in Ephraim's mountains; Samuel's birthplace (1 Sm 1:1, 19), residence (1 Sm 7:17; 8:4), burial place (1 Sm 25:1). Ramathaim-zophim in 1 Sm 1:1. Possibly Arimathea of NT. **6.** See *Ramath-negeb*.
Ramath (rā'măth). See *Ramath-negeb*.
Ramathaim (rā-mà-thā'ĭm). See *Ramathem*.
Ramathaim-zophim (rā-mà-thā'ĭm-zō'fĭm, twin heights of watchers or Zophim). See *Ramah 5*.
Ramathem (răm'à-thĕm). Part of Samaria added to Judah (1 Mac 11:34. RV: Ramathaim. RSV: Rathamin). Probably same as Ramathaim-zophim.
Ramathite (rā'măth-īt). Inhabitant of Ramah (1 Ch 27:27).
Ramath-lehi (rā'măth-lē'hī, height of jawbone). See *Lehi*.
Ramath-mizpeh (rā'măth-mĭz'pĕ, height of watchtower). See *Ramoth-gilead*.
Ramath-negeb (rā'măth-nĕg'ĕb. KJ: Ramath of the south; RV: Ramah of the South; RSV: Ramah of the Negeb). Place on S boundary of Simeon (Jos 19:8). KJ: south Ramoth; RV: Ramoth of the South; RSV: Ramoth of the Negeb in 1 Sm 30:27. Identified with Baalath-beer.
Rameses (răm'ĕ-sēz). See *Pharaoh 4*; *Raamses*.
Ramiah (rà-mī'à, high is LORD). Divorced foreign wife after captivity (Ez 10:25; 1 Esd 9:26 [KJ: Hermas; RV: Hiermas]).
Ramoth (rā'mŏth, heights). See *Jeremoth 8*; *Jarmuth 2*; *Ramath-negeb*; *Ramoth-gilead*.
Ramoth-gilead, Ramoth in Gilead (rā'mŏth-gĭl'ē-ăd, heights of Gilead. Ramah in 2 K 8:29; 2 Ch 22:6. Ramath-mizpeh in Jos 13:26. Mizpah or Mizpeh in Ju 10:17; 11:11, 29, 34). Amorite city E of Jordan and Levitical city of refuge in Gad (Dt 4:43; Jos 20:8; 21:38); home of Jephthah (Ju 11:34); residence of taxgatherer of Solomon (1 K 4:13); Ahab slain there (1 K 22:1-38); burned by Judas Maccabaeus (1 Mac 5:35 [KJ: Maspha]).
ransom. Price paid for recovery of person or thing (Ex 21:30; see 1 Co 6:19, 20).
Rapha, rā'fà, he healed). **1.** Son of Benjamin (1 Ch 8:2). **2.** See *Rephaiah 4*.
Raphael (răf'ā-ĕl). Archangel (Tob 3:17; 12:15).
Raphah (rā'fà). See *Rephaiah 4*.
Raphaim (răf'ā-ĭm). Ancestor of Judith (Jdth 8:1).
Raphon (rā'fŏn). City of Gilead (1 Mac 5:37).
Raphu (rā'fū, healed). Benjaminite; father of spy Palti (Nm 13:9).
Rasses (răs'ĕz). Country laid waste by Holofernes (Jdth 2:23).
Rathamin (rà-thā'mĭn). See *Ramathem*.
Rathumus (rà-thū'mus). See *Rehum 2*.
raven. Unclean bird of crow family (Gn 8:7; Lv 11:15; Dt 14:14; Jb 38:41; Ps 147:9; Pr 30:17; SS 5:11; Is 34:11; Zph 2:14 [KJ, RV: desolation]; Lk 12:24); fed Elijah (1 K 17:4-6).

Razis (rā'zĭs). Elder at Jerusalem (2 Mac 14:37-46).
razor. Used for shaving (Ps 52:2; Is 7:20; Eze 5:1); Levites cleansed with razors (Nm 8:7); Nazirites forbidden to shave their heads (Nm 6:5; see Ju 13:5; 16:17; 1 Sm 1:11). See *hair*.
Reaia (rē-ā'yà). See *Reaiah 2*.
Reaiah (rē-ā'yà, LORD has seen). **1.** Judahite (1 Ch 4:2). Haroeh in 1 Ch 2:52. **2.** Reubenite (1 Ch 5:5. KJ: Reaia). **3.** Progenitor of family of Nethinim (Ez 2:47; Neh 7:50; 1 Esd 5:3 [KJ: Airus; RV: Jairus]).
reap. See *agriculture 4*.
Reba (rē'bà, fourth). Midianite king slain by Israel in Moab (Nm 31:8; Jos 13:21).
Rebecca, Rebekah (rē-bĕk'à, noose). Daughter of Bethuel (Gn 22:23); wife of Isaac (Gn 24); mother of Esau and Jacob (Gn 25:21-26).
Recah (rē'kà. KJ: Rechah). Place in Judah (1 Ch 4:12).
Rechab (rē'kăb, rider). **1.** Traitor; with brother slew Ish-bosheth (2 Sm 4:2-12). **2.** Jehonadab's father (2 K 10:15; Jer 35:6-19). **3.** Malchiah's father (Neh 3:14).
Rechabites (rĕk'à-bīts). Sect which sought to return to nomadic life; abstained from wine, lived in tents, abstained from agriculture (Jer 35).
Rechah (rē'kà). See *Recah*.
recompense. See *punishment; reward*.
reconciliation (rĕk-on-sĭl-ĭ-ā'shun). Removal of enmity between God and world by death of Christ; appropriated by sinner through faith (Acts 10:43; 2 Co 5:18, 19; Eph 2:16).
recorder. Official who kept public documents, wrote annals (2 Sm 8:16; 20:24; 1 K 4:3; 2 K 18:18, 37; 1 Ch 18:15; 2 Ch 34:8; Is 36:3, 22).
Redeemer, redemption. Recovery of mankind from sin and death by obedience and sacrifice of Redeemer Christ (Ro 3:24; Gl 3:13; Eph 1:7; 1 Ptr 1:18, 19; 1 Co 6:19, 20).
Red Sea. Body of water 1,350 mi long, extending from Gulf of Suez to Indian Ocean, with two arms: Gulf of Suez and Gulf of Aqabah. "Red Sea" may refer to Gulf of Suez (Nm 33:10, 11), of Aqabah (1 K 9:26), entire Red Sea (Ex 23:31), or nearby lakes. "Sea of Reeds" (H in Ex 10:19; 13:18; 15:4) possibly Papyrus Marsh between Bitter Lake and Suez. Egyptian Sea (RSV: sea of Egypt) in Is 11:15.
reed. 1. Tall grasses, flags, rushes, reeds. Figuratively, uncertain support (2 K 18:21; Is 36:6; Eze 29:6), fickleness (Mt 11:7; Lk 7:24), weakness or helplessness (Is 42:3; Mt 12:20). **2.** See *measures 1e*.
Reelaiah (rē-ĕl-ā'yà). See *Raamiah*.
Reeliah, Reelias, Reelius (rē-ĕl-ī'à, rē-ĕl'ĭ-ăs, -us). See *Raamiah*.
Reesaias (rē-ĕ-sā'yăs). See *Raamiah*.
refiner. Worker in precious metals (Jer 6:29; Mal 3:2, 3). See *trade 7*.
refuge, cities of. Six Levitical cities for temporary escape of involuntary manslayers (Nm 35:6, 11-32; Dt 4:43; 19: 1-13; Jos 20): Kadesh (Naphtali), Shechem (Ephraim), Hebron (Judah), Golan (Manasseh), Ramoth-gilead (Gad), Bezer (Reuben). See also *murder*.
Regem (rē'gĕm, friend). Descendant of Caleb (1 Ch 2:47).
Regem-melech (rē'gĕm-mē'lĕk, friend of king). Sent with Sharezer to pray and ask counsel of priests (Zch 7:2).

regeneration (rĕ-jĕn-ēr-ā'shun). Rebirth, or radical transformation of life worked by Holy Spirit through Word whereby life is changed from self-centered to Christ-centered (Jn 1:13; 3:1-12; 1 Ptr 1:23).

Rehabiah (rē-há-bī'á, LORD has enlarged). Moses' grandson (1 Ch 23:17; 24:21; 26:25).

Rehob (rē'hŏb, open space). 1. Father of Hadadezer of Zobah (2 Sm 8:3, 12). 2. Levite, sealed covenant with Nehemiah (Neh 10:11). 3. N border region searched by Israel's spies (Nm 13:21; 2 Sm 10:8). Beth-rehob in Ju 18:28; 2 Sm 10:6. 4. 5. Two cities in Asher, one a Levitical city (Jos 19:28, 30; 21:31; Ju 1:31; 1 Ch 6:75).

Rehoboam (rē-hō-bō'ăm, enlarger of people). Last king of united kingdom, 1st of Judah; son of Solomon and Naamah (1 K 14:21, 31); lost ten N tribes; Shishak of Egypt captured cities of Judah and Jerusalem (1 K 12; 14; 2 Ch 10—12; Mt 1:7 [KJ: Roboam]).

Rehoboth (rē-hō'bŏth, open places). 1. See Rehoboth-ir. 2. Town at well of Isaac (Gn 26:22). 3. Home of Shaul (Gn 36:37; 1 Ch 1:48).

Rehoboth-ir (rē-hō'bŏth-ēr', open places of the city. KJ: city Rehoboth). Probably suburb of Nineveh (Gn 10:11).

Rehum (rē'hŭm, merciful). 1. Returned with Zerubbabel (Ez 2:2; 1 Esd 5:8 [KJ, RV: Roimus]). Nehum in Neh 7:7. 2. Officer of Persia in Palestine who complained against Jews (Eze 4:8, 9, 17, 23; 1 Esd 2:16 [KJ, RV: Rathumus]). 3. Levite; helped repair Jerusalem's walls (Neh 3:17). 4. Sealed covenant with Nehemiah (Neh 10:25). 5. See Harim 1.

Rei (rē'ī, friendly). David's friend (1 K 1:8).

reins (rānz). 1. Kidneys as seat of emotion (RV, RSV: heart. Ps 7:9; 16:7; 26:2; 73:21; Pr 23:16 [RSV: soul]; Jer 12:2; Rv 2:23 [RSV: mind]). 2. Loins (as RV, RSV: Is 11:5).

Rekem (rē'kĕm, variegation or friendship). 1. Midianite king slain by Israel (Nm 31:8; Jos 13:21). 2. Son of Hebron (1 Ch 2:43, 44). 3. Town in Benjamin (Jos 18:27).

religion. Man's recognition of relationship to God and expression of that relationship; may be correct or perverted (Acts 26:5; Ja 1:26, 27. KJ, RV: godliness in 1 Ti 2:10; 3:16; 2 Ti 3:5. See Acts 17:22; Ro 1; 1 Ti 5:4).

Remaliah (rĕm'á-lī'á, LORD has adorned). Father of Pekah, king of Israel (2 K 15:25-37).

Remeth (rē'mĕth). See Jarmuth 2.

remission, remit. Exemption from guilt and penalties of sin; wrought by Christ; offered in Baptism, Lord's Supper, Gospel (in all forms); received through faith (Mt 26:28; Mk 1:4; Lk 1:77; Acts 2:38; 10:43; Heb 9:22. RSV: forgiveness). RV, RSV: pass over in Ro 3:25. Function of remitting and retaining sin given to church (Jn 20:23. RV, RSV: forgive).

Remmon (rĕm'ŏn). See Rimmon 1.

Remmon-methoar (rĕm'ŏn-mĕth'ō-är). See Rimmon 3.

remnant. 1. People who survived calamity (Jos 12:4; 13:12). 2. Righteous minority in Israel which would survive purging and remain faithful to God; believers added from all peoples to form church (Is 10:20-23; 11:11, 12; Jer 32:38, 39; Zph 3:13; Zch 8:12; Ro 9:27).

Remphan (rĕm'făn). See Rephan.

repentance. Total change of heart and life, worked by God, whereby person is changed from rebellious state to one of harmony with God; embraces contrition and faith (Jer 31:18, 19; Mk 1:4; Lk 3:3, 8; Acts 5:31; 26:29).

Rephael (rē'fā-ĕl, God healed). Levite; sanctuary doorkeeper (1 Ch 26:7).

Rephah (rē'fá, riches). Ancestor of Joshua (1 Ch 7:25).

Rephaiah (rē-fā'yá, LORD has healed). 1. Descendant of David (1 Ch 3:21). 2. Simeonite captain against Amalekites (1 Ch 4:42, 43). 3. Descendant of Issachar (1 Ch 7:2). 4. Descendant of Jonathan (1 Ch 9:43). Raphah (KJ: Rapha) in 1 Ch 8:37. 5. Repairer of Jerusalem wall (Neh 3:9).

Rephaim (rĕf'á-ĭm, giants). 1. See giants 2. 2. Valley running SW of Jerusalem to Bethlehem (Jos 15:8; 18:16 [KJ: giants]; 2 Sm 5:18, 22; 23:13; 1 Ch 11:15; 14:9).

Rephan (rē'făn KJ: Remphan). Star god worshiped by Israelites in desert (Acts 7:43). Identified with Chiun.

Rephidim (rĕf'ĭ-dĭm). Israelite camp between Sin and Sinai (Ex 17:1; 19:2; Nm 33:14, 15).

reprobate (rĕp'rō-bāt). 1. Given to blind wickedness (Ps 15:4 [KJ: vile person]; Ro 1:28 [RSV: base]; Tts 1:16 [RSV: unfit]). 2. Rejected; failed (Jer 6:30 [RV, RSV: refuse]; 2 Co 13:6, 7 [RSV: failed to meet the test]). 3. False (2 Ti 3:8. RSV: counterfeit).

Resaiah, Resaias (rē-sā'yá, -yăs). See Raamiah.

Resen (rē'sĕn). Assyrian city, probably suburb of Nineveh built by Nimrod (Gn 10:11, 12).

Resheph (rē'shĕf, flame). Ephraimite (1 Ch 7:25).

rest. Goal to which God is leading His people; consummation of deliverance (Heb 3:7—4:11).

resurrection (rĕz-u-rĕk'shun). Body sown in corruption, dishonor, weakness as natural body will be raised in incorruption, honor, glory as spiritual body (1 Co 15:42, 43); Christ is 1st to rise (1 Co 15); resurrection will be universal (2 Co 5:10; Rv 20:21). See judgment.

retribution (rĕt-ri-bū'shun). See punishment.

Reu (rē'ū, friend). Son of Peleg (Gn 11: 18-21; 1 Ch 1:25; Lk 3:35 [KJ: Ragau]).

Reuben (rōō'bĕn, see a son). Firstborn son of Jacob and Leah (Gn 29:32); brought mother mandrakes (Gn 30:14-16); immoral with father's concubine (Gn 35:22; 49:3, 4); advised against killing Joseph (Gn 37:22, 29, 30; see Gn 42:16, 21, 22); vouched for safety of Benjamin (Gn 42: 36-38). Tribe settled E of Jordan (Nm 1:20, 21; 32; Jos 13:15-23); pastoral (Nm 32); indifferent in period of judges (Ju 5:15, 16); carried into captivity by Assyrians (1 Ch 5:26).

Reubenites (rōō'bĕn-īts). Descendants of Reuben (Nm 26:7; Jos 1:12).

Reuel (rōō'ĕl, God's friend). 1. Son of Esau; ancestor of Edomite clan (Gn 36: 4, 10, 13, 17; 1 Ch 1:35, 37). 2. See Jethro. 3. See Deuel. 4. Benjaminite (1 Ch 9:8).

Reumah (rōō'má, exalted). Nahor's concubine (Gn 22:24).

revelation (rĕv-e-lā'shun). Act whereby God makes Himself and His ways known to men: by appearing as man (Gn 18;

19), visions (Is 6), phenomena (Ex 3:4; 19:18), dreams (Gn 28:12-16), angels (Gn 16:9), words, prophecies.
Revelation, Book of. Last book of NT; apocalyptic; message in visions, symbols, imagery; written by John on Patmos (1:4,9) to 7 churches in Asia Minor (1—3); deals with past, present, especially future to prepare for tribulation and distress. Outline: 1. Introduction (1). 2. Letters to 7 Churches (2; 3). 3. Seven Seals (4—11). 4. War of Dragon (12—19). 5. Victory (20—23).
revenge. See *avenge.*
reward. 1. Wages (Lk 10:7; 1 Ti 5:18). 2. Divine punishment (Rv 22:12; 2 Ptr 2:12-15). 3. Reward of grace. Man is justified by faith (Ro 3:27-31); through faith, life and salvation is given him (Eph 4:8); this new life shows itself in fruits which are testimonies of faith and whereby God crowns His work in us (Mt 6:4; Mk 9:41; Lk 6:23; 1 Co 3:14; Cl 3:24).
Rezeph (rē'zĕf, glowing stone). Assyrian city (2 K 19:12; Is 37:12).
Rezia (rē-zī'á). See *Rizia.*
Rezin (rē'zĭn). 1. King of Damascus (735 —732 BC); ally of Israel against Judah; defeated and slain by Tiglath-Pileser (2 K 15:37; 16:5, 9; Is 7:1-9; 8:6-8). 2. Progenitor of family of Nethinim (Ez 2:48; Neh 7:50; 1 Esd 5:31 [KJ, RV: Daisan]).
Rezon (rē'zon, prince). General of Hadadezer; king of Damascus (1 K 11:23-25). See also *Hezion.*
Rhegium (rē'jĭ-ŭm, broken off). Greek-founded city on toe of Italy (Acts 28:13). Modern Reggio.
Rhesa (rē'sá). Ancestor of Christ (Lk 3:27).
Rhoda (rō'dá, rose). Maiden in home of Mary, mother of Mark (Acts 12:12-15).
Rhodes (rōdz, roses). Island at SW tip of Asia Minor; center of commerce, literature, art; famous for Colossus (Eze 27:15 [KJ, RV: Dedan]; Acts 21:1; 1 Mac 15:23 [KJ: Rhodus]). Dodanim (Rodanim) probably Rhodians. See also *Javan.*
Rhodocus (rōd'ō-kus). Jewish traitor (2 Mac 13:21).
Rhodus (rō'dus). See *Rhodes.*
Ribai (rī'bī, contention). Benjaminite; father of Ittai (2 Sm 23:29; 1 Ch 11:31).
Riblah (rĭb'lá, fertility). 1. City on boundary of Canaan and Israel between Shepham and Sea of Galilee (Nm 34:11). 2. City on Orontes 50 mi S of Hamath; headquarters of Babylonian kings (2 K 23:33; 25:6, 20, 21; Jer 39:5-7; 52; Eze 6:14 [KJ: Diblath; RV: Diblah]). Modern Ribleh.
riddle. H *hidhah* (dark, or hidden, saying). Enigmatic saying (Dn 8:23; Pr 1:6), proverb (Pr 1:6), musical meditation (Ps 49:4), oracle (Nm 12:8), parable (Eze 17:2), hard question (1 K 10:1; 2 Ch 9:1), riddle (Ju 14:12-19).
rie (rī). See *spelt.*
right hand. Used to show God active in performing His purposes (Ex 15:6; Ps 98:1). Jesus' session at right hand of God shows His power (Acts 2:25; 7:55, 56; Heb 1:3. See Mt 28:18).
righteous. 1. Virtuous, right (Mt 27:19; Ph 1:7; 2 Ptr 1:13). 2. In accord with Law and ceremonies (Mk 2:17; Lk 5:32; Ro 5:7). 3. People righteous when properly related to God (Gn 15:6; Ro 1:17).
righteousness. God's righteousness inherent in His nature; becomes known to men through His activity in their behalf (Jer 23:6; Hos 2:19) to save them from tem-

poral and spiritual foes (Is 40—55). Jesus is our Righteousness, center of right relation to God (Ro 1:16, 17; 3:21-26; 1 Co 1:30; 1 Ptr 2:24).
Rimmon (rĭm'on, pomegranate). 1. Town in S Judah 9 mi N of Beersheba (Jos 15:32; 19:7 [KJ: Remmon; RSV: En-rimmon]; 1 Ch 4:32; Zch 14:10). See also *En-rimmon.* 2. Rock NE of Ai (Ju 20:45-47; 21:13). 3. Levitical city in Zebulun (Jos 19:13 [KJ: Remmon-methoar]; 1 Ch 6:77 [RV, RSV: Rimmono]) N of Nazareth. Dimnah in Jos 21:35. 4. Father of Baanah and Rechab, murderers of Ishbosheth (2 Sm 4:2, 5, 9).
Rimmon (rĭm'on, thunderer). Assyrian storm god (2 K 5:18).
Rimmono (rĭ-mō'nō). See *Rimmon 3.*
Rimmon-parez, Rimmon-perez (rĭm'on-pā'rĕz, -pē'rĕz, pomegranate of the cliff). Camping ground in desert (Nm 33:19, 20).
ring. Jewelry worn as adornment (Ja 2:2; Lk 15:22); when engraved with symbol of owner, used as seal, signet, and symbol of authority (Gn 41:42; Est 3:10, 12; 8:2, 8, 10; Dn 6:17). Gold rings fastened to priest's breastplate and ephod (Ex 28: 26-28).
Rinnah (rĭn'á, shout). Judahite (1 Ch 4:20).
riot, riotous. 1. Abandoned, dissolute, profligate (Lk 15:13; Tts 1:6). 2. Revelry (2 Ptr 2:13. RV, RSV: revel). 3. Gluttonous (as RV, RSV: Pr 23:20).
Riphath (rī'fāth). Son of Gomer; founder of tribe (Gn 10:3; 1 Ch 1:6 [RV, RSV: Diphath]).
Rissah (rĭs'á, ruin?). Camp of Israel in wilderness (Nm 33:21, 22).
Rithmah (rĭth'má, broom plant). Camp of Israel in wilderness (Nm 33:18, 19).
river. Large stream (Gn 2:10-14), channel (Eze 32:6. RV, RSV: water courses), torrent (Am 6:14 [RV, RSV: brook]; Dt 2:37), fountain stream (Ps 119:136. RSV: stream). Used for streams and for beds, ravines, valleys in which streams flow. Figuratively, abundance of good (Jb 20:17; Ps 36:8) or evil (Ps 69:2; Is 43:2). See also *Euphrates; Nile.*
Rizia (rĭz'ĭ-á, delight. KJ: Rezia). Asherite (1 Ch 7:39).
Rizpah (rĭz'pá, hot stone). Concubine of Saul (2 Sm 3:7; 21:8-11).
road. 1. Path; road worn by travel; highway constructed by ruler (Nm 20:17; 21:22) or people (Dt 19:3); Romans built roads in Palestine, used by traders, armies, travelers. Well-known roads: Jerusalem to Jericho and beyond; Jerusalem to Hebron; Jerusalem to Joppa; Damascus to Ptolemais; Ptolemais to Egypt; Galilee to Judea. 2. Raid (as RV, RSV: 1 Sm 27:10).
robbery. Profession among some nomad tribes and predatory peoples (Jb 1:17; 12:6. See Ju 6:3-5; 9:25; 1 Sm 23:1; 2 Co 11:26). Forbidden and condemned (Lv 19:13; Pr 22:22; Is 10:2; 61:8; Eze 22:29; Am 3:10).
robe. See *dress.*
Roboam (rō-bō'ăm). See Rehoboam.
rock. See *Sela.*
Rock of Escape. See *Sela-hammahlekoth.*
rock badger (KJ, RV: coney). *Hyrax Syriacus;* animal, size of rabbit, which lives among rocks (Lv 11:5; Dt 14:7; Pr 30:26).
rod. Branch, stick, staff, shoot; shepherd's rod: stout club for guiding, defending (Ps 23:4), counting (Lv 27:32; Eze 20:37) flock. Figuratively: Messianic ruler (Is 11:1. RV, RSV: shoot), power (Ps 2:9), affliction (Jb 9:34).

Rodanim (rō'dȧ-nĭm). See *Dodanim; Javan; Rhodes.*
roe. See *gazelle; roebuck.*
roebuck (KJ: fallow deer). H *yaḥmur, Cervus capreolus,* small deer (Dt 14:5; 1 K 4:23). See also *gazelle.*
Rogelim (rō'gĕ-lĭm, fullers). Home of Barzillai (2 Sm 17:27; 19:31).
Rohgah (rō'gȧ). Asherite (1 Ch 7:34).
Roimus (rō'ĭ-mŭs). See *Rehum 1.*
roll. See *scroll.*
Romamtiezer (rō-măm-tĭ-ē'zēr, I have raised help). Heman's son (1 Ch 25:4, 31).
Roman (rō'mȧn). 1. See *citizen.* 2. Roman official (Jn 11:48; Acts 28:17).
Roman Empire. See *Rome.*
Romans, Epistle to. Written by Paul during his stay in Greece (Acts 20:2, 3; Ro 1:1; 15:25-27) in view of his intended visit (1:10, 11; 15:14-33); gives detailed exposition of Gospel, revelation of righteousness of God which justifies sinful man by grace through faith. Outline: 1. Introduction (1:1-15). 2. Sinfulness of Man (1:16—3:31). 3. Justification Through Redemption in Christ (4—8). 4. Israel and World Salvation (9—11:36). 5. Justification and Christian Life (12:1—15:13). 6. Concluding Remarks, Greetings (15:14—16:27).
Rome (rōm). City on Tiber, Italy, 17 mi from Mediterranean, founding set at 753 BC; monarchy (753—509); republic (509 —31 BC); empire began 31 BC. First mentioned in Bible in 1 Mac 1:10. Roman empire provided roads, peace, trade, and one Mediterranean world for Gospel. Augustus divided provinces into senatorial (ruled by proconsul, Acts 13:7; 18:12; 19:38) and imperial (ruled by governor, Mt 27:2; Lk 2:2; Acts 23:24). Under Roman rule cities, reservoirs, aqueducts, roads, public buildings built in Palestine. Emperors referred to: Augustus (Lk 2:1), Tiberius (Lk 3:1), Claudius (Acts 11:28), Nero (Acts 25:11, 12).

root. Figuratively: 1. Source or progenitor (Is 11:10; 14:29; Pr 12:3; Ro 15:12; Rv 5:5). 2. Effective, essential cause (1 Ti 6:10; Heb 12:15). 3. That which gives firm foundation and support (2 K 19:30; Jb 5:3; Ps 80:9; Pr 12:12). 4. To tear roots or have decayed roots means loss of life or vitality (Jb 31:12; Is 5:24; 14:30; Hos 9:16; Ml 4:1; Mt 13:6; Lk 3:9).
rose. According to good authorities roses grew in Palestine in Biblical times. Identity of H *ḥabazzeleth* (SS 2:1; Is 35:1 [RSV: crocus]) not established.
Rosh (rōsh, head). 1. Benjaminite (Gn 46:21). 2. RV: prince of Rosh; KJ, RSV: chief prince (Eze 38:1, 2; 39:1).
ruby. 1. Meaning of H *p:ninim* uncertain; probably pearl (Gesenius prefers "red coral." Jb 28:18 [RSV: pearls]; Pr 3:15 [RSV: jewels]; 8:11 [RSV: jewels]; 20:15 [RSV: costly stones]; 31:10 [RSV: jewels]; Lm 4:7 [RSV: coral]. 2. H *kadhkod:* ruby (Is 54:12. RV, RSV: agate).
rudiments (rōō'dĭ-ments). See *elements.*
rue (rōō). Plant, *Ruta graveolens,* cultivated as medicine and condiment (Lk 11:42).
Rufus (rōō'fus, red). Son of Simon of Cyrene (Mk 15:21); possibly same in Ro 16:13.
Ruhamah (rōō-hā'mȧ). "She has received mercy" (Hos 2:1. RSV: She has obtained pity). See 1 Ptr 2:10; Ro 9:25, 26). See also *Lo-ruhamah.*
rule. See *trade 5.*
Rumah (rōō'mȧ, high). City (2 K 23:36), perhaps Arumah (Ju 9:41).
rush. See *reed; papyrus.*
Ruth (rōōth, friendship?). Moabitess; wife of Mahlon, son of Elimelech and Naomi; devoted to Naomi after husbands' deaths; married Boaz; ancestress of David and Jesus (Ru; Mt 1:5).
Ruth, Book of. Placed among Hagiographa. Narrates story of Ruth, Moabitess, ancestress of David and Christ.
rye. See *spelt.*

S

Sabanneus (săb-ȧ-nē'us). See *Zabad 6.*
Sabannus (sȧ-băn'us). See *Binnui 1.*
Sabaoth (săb'ā-ŏth, hosts). See *host 2.*
Sabat (sā'băt). See *Shaphat 6; Shebat.*
Sabateas, Sabateus (săb-ȧ-tē'ȧs, -us). See *Shabbethai.*
Sabathus, Sabatus (săb'ȧ-thus, tus). See *Zabad 5.*
Sabbaias (sȧ-bī'ȧs). See *Shemaiah 20.*
Sabban (săb'ăn). See *Binnui 1.*
Sabbateus (săb-ȧ-tē'us). See *Shabbethai.*
sabbath (săb'ȧth, rest, cessation). Day of rest corresponding to 7th day of rest after creation (Gn 2:3; Ex 20:11; 31:17); Mosaic institution (Ex 16:23-30; 20:8-11; Lv 19:3, 30; 23:3; Dt 5:12-15); observed by cessation from labor (Ex 16:29; 20:10; 35:3; Nm 15:32-36; Am 8:5), holy convocation, increased offerings (Nm 28:9, 10); penalty for breaking Sabbath was death (Ex 31:15). Typical of man's entrance into God's rest which is fulfilled in Christ (Heb 4; Cl 2:16). Day of Atonement also Sabbath (Lv 23:32).
sabbath day's journey. See *measures 11.*
Sabbatheus (săb-ȧ-thē'us). See *Shabbethai.*
sabbatical year (sȧ-băt'ĭ-kȧl yẽr). Observed every 7th year; land rested, poor

received what grew, debtors released (Ex 23:10, 11; Lv 25:2-7; Dt 15:1-18).
Sabbeus (sȧ-bē'us). See *Shemaiah 20.*
Sabeans (sȧ-bē'ȧnz). Possibly descendants of Seba or Sheba 2 or 3. Semitic people; immigrated to S Arabia before 1200 BC, ultimately dwelt primarily in SW (Yemen); power expanded, 1000—700 BC; operated caravans in Middle E. Described as marauders (Jb 1:15), tall (Is 45:14), dealers in slaves (Jl 3:8). Their queen visited Solomon (1 K 10; 2 Ch 9; Mt 12:42; Lk 11:31).
Sabi (sā'bī). 1. See *Shobai.* 2. See *Pochereth-hazzebaim.*
Sabias (sȧ-bī'ȧs). See *Hashabiah 5.*
Sabie (sā'bĭ-ē). See *Pochereth-hazzebaim.*
Sabta, Sabtah (săb'tȧ). Son of Cush (Gn 10:7; 1 Ch 1:9); descendants in S Arabia.
Sabteca, Sabtecha, Sabtechah (săb'tĕ-kȧ). Son of Cush; descendants in S Arabia (Gn 10:7; 1 Ch 1:9).
Sacar, Sachar (sā'kär, hire). 1. See *Sharar.* 2. Son of Obed-edom (1 Ch 26:4).
Sachia (sȧ-kī'ȧ). See *Shachia.*
sackbut (săk'bŭt). See *trigon.*
sackcloth. Coarse cloth of goat's hair worn by mourners (Gn 37:34; 2 Sm 3:31; 2 K

6:30; Neh 9:1; Jb 16:15; Mt 11:21; Rv 11:3). Sacks were made of cloth (Gn 42:25).

sacrament (săk'rá-mĕnt). Ecclesiastical term applied to sacred acts in accordance with limitations set by definition. See *Baptism; Lord's Supper.*

sacrifice (săk'rĭ-fīs). Practiced from ancient times (Gn 4:3, 4; 8:20-22); expressed gratitude of man to God; offered on all occasions: pilgrimage (1 Sm 1:3), time of rejoicing (1 Sm 20:6), making treaty (Gn 31:54), before battle (1 Sm 7:9), after divine manifestations (Gn 12:7). For many purposes; chief: sin offering (Lv 4); trespass offering (Lv 5:15—6:7; 14:12; 19:20-22; Nm 6:12); burnt offering, whole burnt offering, holocaust (Lv 1; 6:8-13), offered morning, evening, each Sabbath, new moon, at 3 leading festivals (Ex 29:38-42; Nm 28; 29); peace offering (Lv 7:11-34); meal and drink offerings (Lv 5:11, 12; 6); heave and wave offering (Lv 22:12; Nm 5:9; 18:8; 31: 28, 29); red heifer (Nm 19). All sacrifices point to, and merge in, Christ (Heb 9:10).

Sadamias (săd-á-mī'ăs). See *Shallum 6.*

Sadas (sā'dăs). See *Azgad.*

Saddeus (să-dē'us). See *Iddo 8.*

Sadduc (săd'ŭk). See *Zadok 2.*

Sadducees (săd'ū-sēz). Jewish sect at time of Christ; held beliefs found in written law; denied resurrection, angels, spirits (Mk 12:18; Lk 20:27; Acts 23:8); opposed tradition; stressed moral freedom; supported Hasmonaeans; small influential group; denounced by John Baptist (Mt 3:7, 8) and Jesus (Mt 16:6, 11, 12).

Sadduk (săd'ŭk). See *Zadok 2.*

Sadoc (sā'dŏk). See *Zadok 2; 6.*

saffron (săf'run). Aromatic crocus used for flavoring and perfume (SS 4:14).

saint. 1. Pious Israelite (2 Ch 6:41; Ps 16:3). 2. Person (priest, etc) consecrated to God (Ps 106:16; 1 Ptr 2:5). 3. Members of Jerusalem congregation (Acts 9:13; 1 Co 16:1). 4. Believers (Ro 1:7; 1 Co 1:2; 2 Co 1:1).

Sakkuth (săk'ŭth). False god worshiped by Israel (Am 5:26. KJ: tabernacle; RSV: Siccuth).

Sala, Salah (sā'lá). 1. See first *Shelah 1.* 2. See *Salmon 2.*

Salamiel (sá-lā'mĭ-ĕl). See *Shelumiel.*

Salamis (săl'á-mĭs). City on Cyprus visited by Paul (Acts 13:5).

Salasadai (săl-á-săd'á-ī). See *Zurishaddai.*

Salathiel (sá-lā'thĭ-ĕl). 1. See *Phaltiel 2.* 2. See *Shealtiel.* 3. Another name of Esdras (2 Esd 3:1. KJ omits).

Salcah, Salchah, Salecah (săl'ká, săl'ê-ká). City of Bashan (Dt 3:10; Jos 12:5; 13:11; 1 Ch 5:11). Modern Salkhad.

Salem (sā'lĕm, peace). 1. City of Melchizedek; probably Jerusalem (Gn 14:18; Ps 76:2; Heb 7:1, 2). 2. See *Shallum 6.*

Salemas (săl'ê-măs). See *Shallum 6.*

Salim (sā'lĭm, peace). Place near Aenon W of Jordan (Jn 3:23).

Salimoth (săl'ĭ-mōth). See *Shelomith 6.*

Sallai (săl'á-ī). 1. Benjaminite family (Neh 11:8). 2. Chief of priests (Neh 12:20).

Sallu in Neh 12:7.

Sallu (săl'ū, exaltation). 1. Benjaminite (1 Ch 9:7; Neh 11:7). 2. See *Sallai 2.*

Sallumus (să-lū'mus). See *Shallum 11.*

Salma (săl'má). 1. See *Salmon 2.* 2. Descendant of Caleb (1 Ch 2:51, 54).

Salmai (săl'mī). See *Shalmai.*

Salmanasar (săl-má-nā'sĕr). See *Shalmaneser 2.*

Salmon (săl'mon). 1. See *Zalmon 2.* 2. Father of Boaz (Ru 4:21; Mt 1:4; Lk 3:32 [RSV: Sala]). Salma in 1 Ch 2:11.

Salmone (săl-mō'nē). Promontory of E Crete (Acts 27:7).

Saloas (sá-lō'ăs). See *Elasah 1.*

Salom (sā'lŏm). 1. Ancestor of Jehoiakim, high priest (Bar 1:7. RSV: Shallum). 2. See *Salu.*

Salome (sá-lō'mĕ, of Solomon). 1. Wife of Zebedee (Mk 15:40); witnessed crucifixion (Mt 27:56); anointed Jesus' body (Mk 16:1). 2. Daughter of Herodias (Mt 14:6; Mk 6:22). Josephus (*Ant* XVIII, v, 4) supplies her name.

salt. Used as condiment and preservative (Jb 6:6; Is 30:24; Mt 5:13); for sacrifices (Lv 2:13; Nm 18:19); token of indissoluble union (Lv 2:13; Nm 18:19; 2 Ch 13:5). Lot's wife turned to salt (Gn 19:26). Shechem's site sown with salt to keep it fruitless (Eze 47:11; Ju 9:45). Disciples of Jesus are salt of earth (Mt 5:13; Mk 9:50; Lk 14:34).

Salt, City of. Town on Salt Sea near Engedi (Jos 15:62).

Salt Sea. 46 × 9½ mi; fed by Jordan; 1,292 ft below sea level; 1,300 ft deep; no outlet, so water bitter and buoyant (Gn 14:3; Nm 34:3; Jos 15:2). Sea of Arabah (KJ: plain) in Jos 3:16; 12:3. East (eastern) sea in Eze 47:18; Jl 2:20. Sea in Eze 47:8. Former (eastern) sea in Zch 14:8.

Salt, Valley of. Ravine S of Salt Sea (2 Sm 8:13; 2 K 14:7; 1 Ch 18:12; 2 Ch 25:11).

saltwort (sôlt'wûrt). See *mallow.*

Salu (sā'lū). Father of Zimri (Nm 25:14; 1 Mac 2:26 [KJ: Salom]).

Salum (sā'lum). See *Shallum 6; 8.*

salvation. 1. Temporal deliverance (Ex 14: 13, 30; Dt 28:29; Jb 22:29; Is 49:25). 2. Deliverance from sin (Mt 1:21; Acts 4:12; Heb 2:10), death (Ro 6:9; 8:2; 1 Co 15:54-57), evil (Gl 1:4; 2 Ti 4:18), power of darkness (Cl 1:13); is gift of grace through faith in Christ (Acts 16:31; Ro 5:1), entrance into life (Jn 5:24; Cl 3: 9, 10) through sonship (Gl 4:1-7).

salve. See *ointment.*

Samael (săm'á-ĕl). See *Shelumiel.*

Samaias (sá-mā'yăs). See *Shemaiah 16; 17; 18; 27.*

Samaria (sá-mâr'ĭ-á, watch-mountain). 1. Capital of N kingdom built by Omri on tableland 5½ mi NW of Shechem; rebuked for luxury and corruption (1 K 17—19; 21; 2 K 3:3-9; Is 7:9; Jer 31:5; Eze 23:33; Hos 8:5, 6; Am 3:1-12); excavated 1908—10; 1931—35. Modern Sebastiyeh. 2. Area of N kingdom of Israel, or Ten Tribes (1 K 13:32). 3. Inhabited by Samaritans after captivity. See *Samaritans.*

Samaria, Mountains of. See *Ephraim, Mount.*

Samaritans (sá-măr'ĭ-tăns). Ten tribes (2 K 17:29); after captivity, colonists from Babylonia, Syria, Elam, other Assyrian territories (2 K 17:24-34) mingled with remnants of Jews in Samaria; despised by Jews (Neh 4:1-3; Mt 10:5; Jn 4:9-26; 8:48).

Samatus (săm'á-tus. RSV: Shemaiah). Listed in 1 Esd 9:34.

Sameius (sá-mē'yus). See *Shemaiah 19.*

Samellius (sá-mĕl'ĭ-us). See *Shimshai.*

Sameus (sá-mē'us). See *Shemaiah 19.*

Samgar-nebo (săm'gär-nē'bō, Nebo, be gracious). Officer of Nebuchadnezzar (Jer 39:3).

Sami (sā'mī). See *Shobai.*

Samis (sā'mĭs). See *Shimei 16.*

Samlah (săm'lä, garment). Edomite king (Gn 36:36, 37; 1 Ch 1:47, 48).

Sammus (săm'ŭs). See *Shema 5.*

Samos (sā'mŏs, height). Mountainous island off coast of Lydia (Acts 20:15).

Samothrace, Samothracia (săm'ŏ-thrās, săm-ō-thrā'shá, Thracian Samos). Island between Troas and Neapolis (Acts 16:11).

Sampsames (sămp'sá-mēz). Place of uncertain location (1 Mac 15:23).

Samson (săm's'n, sunlike). Danite; son of Minoah; Nazarite; married Philistine Timnath who was later given to another; burned Philistine fields; slew great numbers; performed feats of strength; betrayed by Delilah; died by pulling down pillars of house of Dagon; judge of Israel 20 yrs (Ju 13—16; Heb 11:32).

Samuel (săm'û-el, God has heard). Levite; son of Elkanah and Hannah (1 Sm 1: 19, 20); educated by Eli (1 Sm 3); prophet and judge (1 Sm 3—7; Acts 3:24); anointed Saul (1 Sm 10), David (1 Sm 16:13) as kings; died at Ramah (1 Sm 25:1).

Samuel, 1st and 2d Book of. Historical books named after one of chief characters. Samuel not author (1 Sm 25:1; 28:3). History of Israel from Eli to David's old age. Outline: 1. Samuel as Judge (1 Sm 1—7). 2. Saul as King (1 Sm 8—2 Sm 1). 3. David as King (2 Sm 2 —24).

Sanaas (săn'á-ăs). See *Hassenaah.*

Sanabassar, Sanabassarus (săn-á-băs'ẽr, -á-rŭs). See *Sheshbazzar.*

Sanasib (săn'á-sĭb). RSV: Anasib). Listed in 1 Esd 5:24.

Sanballat (săn-băl'ăt, Sin [moon-god] has given life). Persian officer; opposed Ezra and Nehemiah (Neh 2:10; 4:1-9; 6:1-14; 13:28).

sanctification (săngk-ti-fĭ-kā'shun). H *qadash,* separation from secular and sinful and consecration to sacred purpose (1 Ch 15:14; 2 Ch 5:11; 29:15) by LORD (Ex 31:13; Lv 20:8). G *'agiasmos;* in wider sense: entire process whereby man through Word is reborn from spiritual death to life and is made perfect in life eternal (Acts 26:18; Eph 5:26; 2 Th 2:13; Heb 10:14); in narrow sense: spiritual growth which follows justification (Ro 6:15-23; 2 Ptr 3:18); worked by God (Gl 5:22, 23; Ph 2:13).

sanctuary (săngk'tū-ẽr-ĭ). 1. Sacred place where God's presence is signalized. Promised Land to be God's sanctuary (Ex 15:17). 2. See *tabernacle.* 3. Inner sanctuary (1 K 6. KJ, RV: oracle) or whole temple (2 Ch 20:8; Neh 10:39). 4. Judah (Ps 114:2). 5. Preceding sanctuaries symbolic of access to God in Christ (Heb 8:1-5; 9:1-8).

sand. Dunes on Mediterranean and in wilderness. Figuratively, innumerable number; abundance (Gn 22:17; 32:12; 41:49; Ju 7:12; Ps 78:27); hiding place (Ex 2:12); poor foundation (Mt 7:26).

sand lizard. See *snail 1.*

sandal. See *shoe.*

sandal-thong. Cord or strap for fastening shoes to feet (KJ, RV: shoe-latchet. Gn 14:23; Is 5:27; Mk 1:7; Lk 3:16; Jn 1:27).

Sanhedrin (săn'hē-drĭn, council). Mentioned 3d c BC; supreme native court for enforcing Mosaic civic and religious law; composed of high priests, elders, scribes; high priest presided; 71 maximum membership; in time of Christ had jurisdiction in Judea; G *sunedrion* (KJ,

RV, RSV: council. Mt 5:22; 26:59; Mk 14:55; 15:1; Lk 22:66; Jn 11:47; Acts 4:15; 6:12; 22:30; 23:1; 24:20). Elders (*presbuterion*) in Lk 22:66; Acts 22:5; senate (*gerousia*) in Acts 5:21 (see 2 Mac 1:10; 4:44; 11:27).

Sansannah (săn-săn'á, palm branch). Town N of Beer-sheba (Jos 15:31). Modern Khirbet esh-Shamsaniyat.

Saph (săf). Philistine giant (2 Sm 21:18). Sippai in 1 Ch 20:4.

Saphat (sā'făt). See *Shaphat 6; Shephatiah 7.*

Saphatias (săf-á-tī'ăs). See *Shephatiah 7.*

Sapheth (sā'fĕth). See *Shephatiah 9.*

Saphir (sā'fẽr). See *Shaphir.*

Saphuthi (sā-fū'thī). See *Shephatiah 9.*

Sapphira (să-fī'rá, beautiful). Wife of Ananias; fell dead at Peter's feet after lying (Acts 5:7-10).

sapphire (săf'īr). Blue stone (*lapis lazuli,* blue chalcedony, etc. Ex 24:10; 28:18; Jb 28:16; Lm 4:7; Eze 1:26; Rv 21:19).

Sara (sā'rá). See *Sarah 1; 3.*

Sarabias (săr-á-bī'ăs). See *Sherebiah.*

Sarah (sā'rá, princess). 1. Wife of Abraham; mother of Isaac (Gn 11:29; 21:2, 3); name Sarai changed to Sarah (Gn 17: 15, 16); cruel toward Hagar, whom she banished (Gn 16:5-16; 21:9-21); buried at Machpelah (Gn 23); praised for faith (Heb 11:11. KJ: Sara) and obedience (1 Ptr 3:6). See also *Abraham.* 2. See *Serah.* 3. Raguel's daughter (Tob 3:7. KJ: Sara).

Sarai (sā'rī). See *Sarah 1.*

Saraias (sá-rā'yás). See *Seraiah 4.*

Saramel (săr'á-mĕl). See *Asaramel.*

Saraph (sā'răf, noble). Judahite (1 Ch 4:22).

Sarasadai (săr-á-săd'á-ī). See *Zurishaddai.*

Sarchedonus (săr-kĕd'ŏ-nus). See *Esarhaddon.*

Sardeus (săr-dē'us). See *Aziza.*

Sardis (săr'dĭs). City of W Asia Minor 50 mi E of Smyrna; manufactured textiles, gold jewelry; minted coins; patron of mystery cults (Rv 1:11; 3:1-6).

sardius (săr'dĭ-us). Deep-red or brownish-red carnelian (Ex 28:17; 39:10).

Sardites (săr'dĭts). See *Seredites.*

sardonyx (săr'dŏ-nĭks. RSV: onyx). Variety of onyx containing layers of red carnelian (Rv 21:20).

Sarea (sá-rē'á). Scribe (2 Esd 14:24).

Sarepta (sá-rĕp'tá). See *Zarephath.*

Sargon II (săr'gŏn). Assyrian king; lived 772—705 BC; successor of Shalmaneser; father of Sennacherib; completed conquest of Samaria (2 K 17:5; Is 20:1).

Sarid (sā'rĭd). Border town of Zebulun SW of Nazareth (Jos 19:10, 12). Modern Tell Shadud.

Saron (sā'rŏn). See *Sharon.*

Sarothie (sá-rō'thī-ē). Listed in 1 Esd 5:34.

Sarsechim (săr'sē-kĭm). Prince of Nebuchadnezzar (Jer 39:3).

Saruch (sā'ruk). See *Serug.*

Satan (sā'tăn, adversary). 1. H *satan* as common noun: enemy or adversary (1 Sm 29:4; 1 K 5:4; 11:14; Ps 38:20; 17:13). 2. As proper noun: the adversary hostile to good and enemy of God and man (Jb 1:6, 12; 2:1; Zch 3:1); head of evil angels (Mt 8:28; 9:34 Lk 11:18), beings of great power (Mt 8:29); enemy (Mt 13:39; 1 Ptr 5:8); murderer and liar (Jn 8:44); conquered by Christ (Lk 10:18; Ro 16:20). Called Abaddon, angel of bottomless pit (abyss), Apollyon (Rv 9:11), adversary (1 Ptr 5:8), Beelzebul (Mt 12:27), Belial (2 Co 6:15), devil (Mt 25:41; 1 Ptr 5:8), dragon (Rv 12), evil (wicked) one (Eph 6:16; 1 Jn 2:13), prince of this world (Jn 16:11), prince of power of the air (Eph 2:2), serpent (Rv 12:9).

Sathrabuzanes (săth-rȧ-bū'zȧ-nēz). See *Shethar-bozenai.*

satrap (sā'trăp). Viceroy who exercised military and civil authority in combined provinces (satrapies). KJ: lieutenant in Ez 8:36; Est 3:12; 8:9; 9:3; prince in Dn 3:2, 3, 27; 6:1-7.

satyr (săt'ẽr). Mythical creature, half man, half goat (Is 34:14).

Saul (sôl, asked). **1.** See *Shaul 1.* **2.** 1st king of Israel; Benjaminite; son of Kish (1 Sm 8; 9); anointed by Samuel (1 Sm 9:27; 10:1-13); chosen by lot (1 Sm 10: 17-27); defeated Ammonites, Philistines, Moabites, Zobah, Amalekites (1 Sm 11 —14); disobeyed; rejected by Samuel (1 Sm 13:1-14; 15); jealous of David as his power declines (1 Sm 16—31); killed self after wounded in battle (1 Sm 31). **3.** Hebrew name for Paul (Acts 13:9).

Savaran (săv'ȧ-răn). See *Avaran.*

save. See *salvation.*

Savias (să'vī-ȧs). See *Uzzi 1.*

savior (săv'yẽr). **1.** Human deliverer (2 K 13:5). **2.** Jehovah (Ps 106:21). Jesus (Lk 2:11; Jn 4:42; 1 Ti 1:1; 2 Ptr 1:1). See *Jesus Christ; salvation.*

savor, savour. See *odor 2.*

saw. See *trade 5; 11.*

saying. See *proverb.*

scab. See *diseases.*

scales. See *diseases; weight.*

scapegoat. See *Azazel.*

scarlet. See *color.*

scepter, sceptre (sĕp'tẽr). Symbol of royal power (Gn 49:10; Nm 24:17; Ps 45:6).

Sceva (sē'vȧ). Ephesian priest (Acts 19: 14-16).

schism (sĭz'm). See *heresy.*

scorpion. **1.** Animal of arachnid class (spiders, etc) with elongated body, sting in tail (Dt 8:15; Lk 10:19; Rv 9:5, 10). **2.** Scourge, probably tipped with spikes (1 K 12:11, 14; 2 Ch 10:11, 14).

scourging. **1.** Punishment with whip of cords or thongs (Jos 23:13; Mt 23:34; 27:26; Mk 15:15; Jn 19:1; Heb 11:36); stripes limited to 40 (2 Co 11:24. See Dt 25:1-3); unlawful for Roman citizen (Acts 22:24, 25). **2.** Calamity, plague, catastrophe (Jb 9:23; Ps 91:10 [KJ, RV] plague]; Is 10:26), tongue lashing (Jb 5:21).

screech owl. See *night hag.*

scribe. Penman or copyist; served as secretary, recorder, clerk (1 Ch 24:6; 27:32). After exile scribes became copyists of Scripture, interpreters, powerful leaders (Ez 7:6, 11; Neh 8:1-13; 13:13; Mt 16:21; 26:3; Acts 4:5).

scrip. **1.** Shepherd bag (as RSV. 1 Sm 17:40). **2.** Small traveling bag (Mt 10:10; Lk 9:3; 10:4; 22:35, 36. RV: wallet. RSV: bag).

scripture. The Bible (OT and NT).

scroll. Sheets of skin, papyrus, parchment sewed together to make strip c 11 in wide, many ft long, rolled on sticks to make book, roll, or scroll (Is 34:4; Jer 36; Eze 3:1-3; Rv 5; 10:1-10).

scrolls, Dead Sea. Ancient mss of parts of OT, commentaries, other writings found in caves around Dead Sea; 1st discovery 1947.

scurvy. See *diseases.*

Scythian (sĭth'ĭ-ăn). One of a nomadic people N and E of Black Sea (Cl 3:11).

Scythopolis (sī-thŏp'ŏ-lĭs). Beth-shan, so called when held by Scythians (2 Mac 12:29).

sea. **1.** Large, deep body of water (Gn 1:26; Ex 10:19; Dt 30:13; Jb 12:8). **2.** See *Salt Sea.* **3.** See *Mediterranean Sea.* **4.** See *Galilee, Sea of.* **5.** See *Merom.* **6.** See *Red Sea.*

sea, bronze or brazen. Great laver of Solomon's temple (2 K 25:13; 2 Ch 4:2).

sea gull. See *cuckoo.*

seal. **1.** Instrument used to authenticate and secure packages, doors, etc (Jb 38:14; Mt 27:66). **2.** See *badger.*

sea mew (sē mū). See *cuckoo.*

sea monster. See *monster, sea.*

Seba (sē'bȧ). **1.** Son of Cush (Gn 10:7; 1 Ch 1:9). **2.** Nation (Ps 72:10; Is 43:3). See also *Sabeans.*

Sebam (sē'băm). See *Sibmah.*

Sebat (se-băt'). See *Shebat.*

Secacah (sē-kā'kȧ, thicket). Town of Judah (Jos 15:61).

Sechenias (sĕk-ē-nī'ȧs). See *Shecaniah 4; 6.*

Sechu (sē'kū). See *Secu.*

second coming of Christ. See *advent; eschatology; parousia.*

sect. Religious party, group with distinctive doctrine: Pharisees (Acts 15:5. RSV: party), Sadducees (Acts 5:17. RSV: party). Applied to Christians (Acts 24: 5, 14 [KJ: way]; 28:22).

Secu (sē'kū, watchtower. KJ: Sechu). Place between Ramah and Gibeah (1 Sm 19:22).

Secundus (sē-kŭn'dus, second). Thessalonian Christian (Acts 20:4).

Sedecias, Sedekias (sĕd-ē-sī'ȧs, -kī'ȧs). See *Zedekiah 4; 6.*

seed. **1.** Unit of reproduction in plants and animals (Gn 1:11, 12; 38:9). See *agriculture.* **2.** Progeny (Gn 3:15; 4:25). **3.** Seed or progeny of Abraham is reckoned by descent (Ro 9:7), also by faith (Ro 4:16). **4.** Christ used seed figuratively (Mt 13:3-39; Mk 4:26-29; Lk 8:5-15). Paul used seed to explain resurrection (1 Co 15:36-38).

seer (sẽr). See *prophet.*

Segub (sē'gŭb, exalted). **1.** Son of Hiel; died when father rebuilt Jericho's gates (1 K 16:34). **2.** Hezron's son (1 Ch 2: 21, 22).

seine. See *net.*

Seir (sē'ĭr, shaggy). **1.** Horite chief (Gn 36:20; 1 Ch 1:38). **2.** Mt Seir, or land of Seir: hilly region of Edom S of Dead Sea, extending toward Arabah (Gn 14:6; 32:3; 33: 14-16); originally occupied by Horites (Gn 14:16); later by Edomites (Gn 36:8, 9). **3.** Landmark on boundary of Judah (Jos 15:10).

Seirah, Seirath (sē-ī'rȧ, -răth, hairy animal). Town in Ephraim (Ju 3:26).

Sela, Selah (sē'lȧ, rock). Edomite city called Petra by Greeks (Ju 1:36 [KJ, RV: rock]; 2 K 14:7; Is 16:1; 42:11 [KJ: rock]).

Selah (sē'lȧ, lift up?). Found frequently in Psalms (Ps 9:16) and in Hab 3:3, 9, 13. Possibly instruction to singers or musicians.

Sela-hammahlekoth (sē'lȧ-hă-mä'lĕ-kŏth, rock of escape. RSV: Rock of Escape). Cliff in wilderness of Maon (1 Sm 23:28).

Seled (sē'lĕd, exultation). Judahite (1 Ch 2:30).

Selemia (sĕl-ē-mī'ȧ). Scribe (2 Esd 14:24).

Selemias (sĕl-ē-mī'ȧs). See *Shelemiah 2.*

Seleucia (sē-lū'shĭ-ȧ). Seaport of Syrian Antioch, 16 mi W of Antioch, founded by Seleucus Nicator (Acts 13:4).

Seleucids (sĕ-lū'cĭds). Rulers of Babylonia, Bactria, Persia, Syria, part of Asia Minor (312—64 BC); descended from Seleucus I, general of Alexander the Great (1 Mac 7:1; 2 Mac 3:3).

Sem (sĕm). See *Shem.*

Semachiah (sĕm-à-kī'à). Levite gatekeeper (1 Ch 26:7).

Semei (sĕm'ē-ī). See *Semein; Shimei 13; 15.*

Semeias (sē-mē-ī'ăs). See *Shimei 13.*

Semein (sĕ-mē'ĭn. KJ: Semei). Ancestor of Christ (Lk 3:26).

Semeis (sĕm'ē-ĭs). See *Shimei 14.*

Semellius (sē-mĕl'ĭ-us). See *Shimshai.*

Semis (sē'mĭs). See *Shimei 14.*

Senaah (sĕn-ā'à). See *Hassenaah.*

senate. See *Sanhedrin.*

Seneh (sē'nĕ). See *Bozez.*

Senir (sē'nĭr). See *Hermon.*

Sennacherib (se-năk'ēr-ĭb, Sin [moon-god] has increased brothers). King of Assyria (705—681 BC); son of Sargon II; extended conquests to Mediterranean; invaded Judah in time of Hezekiah; army miraculously destroyed (2 K 18; 19; Is 36; 37); his annals describe victories in Judah.

Senuah (sē-nū'à). See *Hassenuah.*

Seorim (sē-ō'rĭm). Head of 4th course of priests (1 Ch 24:8).

Sephar (sē'fär, numbering). Border of Joktan in S Arabia (Gn 10:30).

Sepharad (sē-fä'răd). Place to which Jews were deported (Ob 20).

Sepharvaim (sĕf-är-vā'ĭm). Place near Riblah whence Assyrians brought people to Samaria (2 K 17:24-34; 18:34; 19:13; Is 37:13). Perh same as Sibraim and Ziphron.

Sepharvites (sē'fär-vīts). Inhabitants of Sepharvaim (2 K 17:31).

Septuagint (sĕp'tū-à-jĭnt). Greek translation of OT prepared at Alexandria, Egypt, in 3d c BC.

sepulcher, sepulchre (sĕp'ul-kēr). See *burial.*

Serah (sē'rà, abundance). Asher's daughter (Gn 46:17; Nm 26:46 [KJ: Sarah]; 1 Ch 7:30).

Seraiah (sĕ-rā'yà, soldier of Lord). 1. See *Shavsha.* 2. Son of Kenaz (1 Ch 4:13). 3. Simeonite (1 Ch 4:35). 4. Chief priest; slain by Nebuchadnezzar at Riblah (2 K 25:18-21); ancestor of Ezra (1 Ch 6:14, 15; Ez 7:1; 1 Esd 5:5 [KJ, RV: Saraias]; 8:1 [KJ: Saraias; RV: Azaraias]; 2 Esd 1:1 [KJ, RV: Saraias]). 5. Submitted to Gedaliah (2 K 25:23; Jer 40:8). 6. Sent to arrest Jeremiah and Baruch (Jer 36:26). 7. Prince carried into captivity (Jer 51:59-64). 8. Returned with Zerubbabel (Ez 2:2; 1 Esd 5:8 [KJ: Zacharias; RV: Zaraias]). Azariah in Neh 7:7. 9. Priest (Neh 12:1, 12); sealed covenant with Nehemiah (Neh 10:2). 10. See *Azariah 8.*

seraphim (sĕr'à-fĭm). Order of angels around God's throne (Is 6:2-7).

Serar (sē'rär). See *Sisera 2.*

Sered (sē'rĕd, fear). Zebulun's son (Gn 46:14; Nm 26:26).

Seredites (sē'rĕ-dīts. KJ: Sardites). Descendants of Sered (Nm 26:26).

Sergius Paulus (sûr'jĭ-us pô'lus). Proconsul of Cyprus (Acts 13:7-12).

serjeant. See *police.*

Seron (sē'rŏn). Syrian general (1 Mac 3:13, 23).

serpent. Eight H words designate type of serpent. *Naḥash* is generic term. Asp (Dt 32:33), perhaps cobra. Others: adder (Gn 49:17. RSV: viper), probably horned cerastes of desert; cockatrice (Jer 8:17. RSV: adder); viper (Jb 20:16). Symbol of evil, malignity, and poison (Gn 49:17; Ps 58:4; Pr 23:32; Mt 23:33). Subtle

Gn 3:1), wise (Mt 10:16). Serpent deceived Eve (Gn 3). Brazen (RSV: bronze) serpent type of Christ (Nm 21:4-9; Jn 3:14).

Serpent's Stone. See *Zoheleth.*

Serug (sē'rŭg, branch). Father of Nahor; ancestor of Abraham (Gn 11:20, 23; 1 Ch 1:26; Lk 3:35 [KJ: Saruch]).

servant. H *'ebhedh, 'amah, shiphah* used of slave; *na'ar* of young person who toiled; *sakhar* of wage servant; G *doulos* of slave; *misthios* of hired servant. Israelites had slaves through purchase (Lv 25:44, 45), war (Nm 31:25-47). Children of slaves remained slaves (Gn 14:14; Ec 2:7). Fellow Israelites became slaves through poverty (Ex 21:1-11; Lv 25:39, 47; 2 K 4:1), theft (Ex 22:3), birth (Ex 21:4). Servants protected by OT laws (Ex 20:10; Lv 25:55), usually treated as members of household (Gn 24; 30; 32:16; 1 Sm 9:5, 8. See Gn 15:2, 3; 1 Ch 2:35). Slaves and servants common in NT times (Mk 1:20; 14:66; Jn 18:10-18; Acts 12:13-15). Jesus was kind to servants (Mt 8:5-13), refers to them in parables (Mt 18:23-35; 24:45-51; Mk 13:34-37; Lk 20:9-16). Faith in Christ removes barriers between master and servant (Gl 3:28; Phmn).

servant of the LORD (Jehovah), of Christ, of Church. 1. Adherent or agent of the Lord (Ex 4:10; 1 K 1:26; Ps 105:42), Christ (Ro 1:1; 2 Co 11:23; Cl 4:12; Tts 1:1; 2 Ptr 1:1; Rv 1:1). 2. Ministers in church (Cl 4:7; 1 Th 3:2).

Servant, Suffering. Jesus is fulfillment (Mt 12:18; Lk 22:37) of suffering servant depicted in OT (Is 42:1-4; Is 52:13—53:12).

Sesis (sē'sĭs). See *Shashai.*

Sesthel (sĕs'thĕl). See *Bezaleel 2.*

Seth (sĕth). 1. 3d son of Adam (Gn 4:25, 26; 5:3-8; 1 Ch 1:1 [KJ: Sheth]; Lk 3:38). 2. Unknown king or race (Nm 24:17).

Sethur (sē'thēr, hidden). Asherite spy (Nm 13:13).

seven. Used of abundance, completeness (Gn 4:15, 24; Mt 18:21, 22); as round number (1 Sm 2:5; Mt 12:45); simply and in multiple for religious cycles (Gn 2:2). See *jubilee; numbers; Sabbath.*

Seveneh (sē-vĕn'ĕ). See *Syene.*

Seventy, The. Disciples sent on special mission by Jesus (Lk 10).

Shaalabbin (shā-à-lăb'ĭn, fox-holes). Town between Jerusalem and Lydda (Jos 19:42). Shaalbim in Ju 1:35; 1 K 4:9. Modern Selbit.

Shaalbim (shā-ăl'bĭm). See *Shaalabbin.*

Shaalbonite (shā-ăl-bō'nīt). Inhabitant of unknown Shaalbon or of Shaalbim (2 Sm 23:32; 1 Ch 11:33. RSV: of Shaalbon).

Shaalim (shā'à-lĭm, foxes. KJ: Shalim). District in Ephraim (1 Sm 9:4).

Shaaph (shā'ăf, balsam). 1. Son of Jahdai (1 Ch 2:47). 2. Caleb's son (1 Ch 2:49).

Shaaraim (shā-à-rā'ĭm, two gates). 1. Town in Shephelah on border of Judah and Dan (Jos 15:36 [KJ: Sharaim]; 1 Sm 17:52). 2. Simeonite town in Judah (1 Ch 4:31). Sharuhen in Jos 19:6; Shilhim in Jos 15:32. Modern Tell el Far'ah.

Shaashgaz (shā-ăsh'găz). Chamberlain in charge of concubines of Ahasuerus (Est 2:14).

Shabbethai (shăb'ē-thī, of the Sabbath). Favored divorcing foreign wives (Ez 10:15; 1 Esd 9:14 [KJ: Sabbatheus; RV: Sabbateus]); prominent at rebuilding of walls and reading of law (Neh 8:7; 1 Esd 9:48 [KJ: Sabateas; RV: Sabateus]).

Shachia (shá-kī'á. RSV: Sachia). Benjaminite (1 Ch 8:10).
Shadrach (shā'drăk). Babylonian name given to Hananiah (Dn 1:7; 3).
shades (H repha'im, silent ones. KJ: dead, deceased; RSV at times: dead). Those in beyond of death, Sheol (Jb 26:5; Ps 88: 10; Pr 2:18; 9:18; 21:16; Is 14:9; 26: 14, 19).
Shage, Shagee (shā'gē, wandering). Father of David's hero Jonathan (1 Ch 11:34). Probably same as Shammah (2 Sm 23:33).
Shaharaim (shā-há-rā'im, double dawning). Benjaminite (1 Ch 8:8).
Shahazimah, Shahazumah (shā-há-zī'má, -zū'má, lofty places). Border town of Issachar (Jos 19:22).
Shalem (shā'lĕm, safe. RV: in peace. RSV: safely). Town near Shechem (Gn 33: 18, 20).
Shalim (shā'lĭm). See Shalim.
Shalisha (shá-lī'shá). Region near Mt Ephraim (1 Sm 9:4).
Shallecheth (shăl'ĕ-kĕth, casting out). W gate of temple (1 Ch 26:16).
Shallum (shăl'um, pacified). 1. 15th king of Israel for 1 month (2 K 15:10-15). 2. Husband of prophetess Hulda (2 K 22:14; 2 Ch 34:22). Probably Jeremiah's uncle (Jer 32:7). 3. Descendant of Sheshan (1 Ch 2:40, 41). 4. See Jehoahaz 2. 5. Simeonite (1 Ch 4:25). 6. High priest; Zadok's son (1 Ch 6:12, 13); ancestor of Ezra (Ez 7:2; 1 Esd 8:1 [KJ: Salum; RV: Salem]; 2 Esd 1:1 [KJ: Sadamias. RV: Salemas]). Meshullam in 1 Ch 9:11; Neh 11:11. 7. Naphtali's son (1 Ch 7:13). 8. Chief gatekeeper; descendant of Kore (1 Ch 9: 17, 19, 31; Ez 2:42; Neh 7:45; 1 Esd 5:28 [KJ, RV: Salum]). Perhaps same as Meshelemiah. 9. Father of Jehizkiah (2 Ch 28:12). 10. Divorced foreign wife (Ez 10:42). 11. Temple gatekeeper; divorced foreign wife (Ez 10:24; 1 Esd 9:25 [KJ, RV: Sallumus]). 12. Ruler of half Jerusalem; repaired wall (Neh 3:12). 13. See Salom 1. 14. See Shallun.
Shallun (shăl'un). Repaired Fountain Gate; governor of Mizpah (Neh 3:15. RSV: Shallum).
Shalmai (shăl'mī). Ancestor of Nethinim (Ez 2:46 [RV, RSV: Shamlai]; Neh 7:48 [RV: Salmai]). Subai (RSV: Shamlai) in 1 Esd 5:30.
Shalman (shăl'măn). See Shalmaneser 2.
Shalmaneser (shăl-măn-ē'zĕr). 1. Shalmaneser III, king of Assyria (859—824 BC); conquered Hittites to Mediterranean; opposed by Benhadad of Damascus, Ahab of Israel, others; defeated Hazael, Benhadad's successor, and made Israel tributary (extra-Biblical sources). 2. Shalmaneser V, king of Assyria (727—722 BC); besieged Samaria and (or his successor Sargon) carried N tribes into captivity (2 K 17:3; 18:9; 2 Esd 13:40 [KJ, RV: Salmanasar]; Tob 1:2-16 [KJ, RV: Enemessar]). Shalman in Hos 10:14.
Shama (shā'má, hearing). One of David's heroes (1 Ch 11:44).
Shamariah (shăm-á-rī'á). See Shemariah 2.
shame. Sensation wrought by sense of guilt (Ez 9:7 [KJ, RV: confusion]; Ro 6:21), impropriety (Ex 32:25 [RV: derision]; 1 Co 11:6 [RSV: disgraceful]; Rv 3:18), adversity (Ps 69:19; Eze 16:52), or disillusionment through false confidence (Ps 97:7 [KJ: confounded]; Ro 5:5 [RSV: disappoint]). Crucifixion shameful death (Heb 12:2). See also conscience.
Shamed (shā'mĕd). See Shemed.

Shamer (shā'mĕr). See Shemer 2; 3.
Shamgar (shăm'gär). Son of Anath; slew 600 Philistines with ox-goad (Ju 3:31).
Shamhuth (shăm'hŭth). David's commander (KJ, RV: captain) for 5th month (1 Ch 27:8). Perh Shammah 4.
Shamir (shā'mĕr, thorns). 1. Town in highlands of Judah (Jos 15:48). 2. Home of Tola, judge, in Ephraim (Ju 10:1, 2). 3. Levite (1 Ch 24:24).
Shamlai (shăm'lī). See Shalmai.
Shamma (shăm'á, desolation). Asherite (1 Ch 7:37).
Shammah (shăm'á). 1. Grandson of Esau; Edomite leader (Gn 36:13, 17). 2. See Shimea 3. 3. Hararite; one of David's heroes (2 Sm 23:11). Perhaps same in 2 Sm 23:33. See also Shage. 4. Harodite; one of David's heroes (2 Sm 23:25). Shammoth in 1 Ch 11:27. Perh same as Shamhuth.
Shammai (shăm'ā-ī, waste). 1. Descendant of Jerahmeel (1 Ch 2:28, 32). 2. Son of Rekem (1 Ch 2:44, 45). 3. Judahite (1 Ch 4:17).
Shammoth (shăm'ōth). See Shammah 4.
Shammua, Shammuah (shā-mū'á, fame). 1. Reubenite spy (Nm 13:4). 2. Son of David and Bathsheba (2 Sm 5:14; 1 Ch 14:4). Shimea in 1 Ch 3:5. 3. See Shemaiah 9. 4. Priest (Neh 12:18).
Shamsherai (shăm'shĕ-rī). Benjaminite (1 Ch 8:26).
Shapham (shā'făm). Gadite chief (1 Ch 5:12).
Shaphan (shā'făn, rock badger). Son of Azaliah (2 K 22:3); father of Ahikam (Jer 26:24), Elasah 2 (Jer 29:3), Gemariah 2 (Jer 36:10-25), and Jaazaniah (Eze 8:11); state scribe and secretary under Josiah (2 K 22:3-14).
Shaphat (shā'făt, he has judged). 1. Simeonite spy (Nm 13:5). 2. Father of prophet Elisha (1 K 19:16; 2 K 3:11). 3. Descendant of David (1 Ch 3:22). 4. Gadite (1 Ch 5:12). 5. Herdsman of David (1 Ch 27:29). 6. Listed in 1 Esd 5:34 [KJ: Sabat; RV: Saphat].
Shapher (shā'fĕr). See Shepher.
Shaphir (shā'fĕr, beautiful. KJ: Saphir). Town in Judah (Mi 1:11).
Sharai (shá-rā'ī). Divorced foreign wife (Ez 10:40).
Sharaim (shá-rā'im). See Shaaraim 1.
Sharar (shā'rĕr, firm). Father of one of David's warriors (2 Sm 23:33). Sacar (RSV: Sachar) in 1 Ch 11:35.
Sharezer (shá-rē'zĕr, protect king). 1. Son and murderer of Sennacherib (2 K 19:37; Is 37:38). 2. Sent by Bethel to inquire about fasts (Zch 7:2. KJ: Sherezer).
Sharon (shăr'un, plain). 1. Coastal plain c 50 mi long, 6—12 mi wide, between Joppa and Carmel (1 Ch 27:29; Is 33:9; 35:2; 65:10; Acts 9:35 [KJ: Saron]). 2. Pasture region E of Jordan (1 Ch 5:16).
Sharonite (shăr'un-īt). Designation of Shitrai, David's herdsman (1 Ch 27:29).
Sharuhen (shá-rōō'hĕn). See Shaaraim 2.
Shashai (shā'shī, whitish). Divorced foreign wife (Ez 10:40; 1 Esd 9:34 [KJ, RV: Sesis]).
Shashak (shā'shăk). Benjaminite (1 Ch 8:14,25).
Shaul (shā'ŭl, wished). 1. Edomite king (Gn 36:37, 38 [KJ: Saul]; 1 Ch 1:48, 49). 2. Son of Simeon; founder of clan (Gn 46:10; Nm 26:13). 3. Kohathite Levite (1 Ch 6:24).
Shaveh (shā'vĕ, plain). Place, probably near Jerusalem, where Melchizedek met Abraham (Gn 14:17).

Shaveh-kiriathaim (shā'vĕ-kĭr-yá-thā'ĭm).
See *Kiriathaim 1.*
shaving (shăv'ĭng). See *beard; razor.*
Shavsha (shăv'shá). Scribe of David and
Solomon (1 Ch 18:16). Seraiah in 2 Sm
8:17; Sheva in 2 Sm 20:25; Shisha in
1 K 4:3.
Sheal (shē'ăl, asking). Divorced foreign
wife (Ez 10:29; 1 Esd 9:30 [KJ: Jasael;
RV: Jasaelus]).
Shealtiel (shĕ-ăl'tǐ-ĕl, I have asked God).
Son of Jeconiah (1 Ch 3:17; Mt 1:12.
KJ: Salathiel), or of Neri (Lk 3:27. KJ:
Salathiel). Probably in line of succession
between Jaconiah and Zerubbabel (Ez
3:2; 1 Ch 3:17-19). KJ, RV: Salathiel
in 1 Esd 5:6.
Sheariah (shē-á-rī'á, LORD prized). Descendant of Jonathan (1 Ch 8:38; 9:44).
shearing house. Place between Jezreel and
Samaria where Jehu slew 42 of royal
family (2 K 10:12, 14. RSV: Beth-eked
of the Shepherds).
Shear-jashub (shē'är-jā'shŭb, remnant shall
return). Symbolical name given by Isaiah
to his son (Is 7:3. See Is 10:21).
Sheba (shē'bá). 1. Descendant of Ham (Gn
10:7; 1 Ch 1:9). 2. Joktan's son (Gn 10:
28; 1 Ch 1:22). 3. Jokshan's son (Gn
25:3; 1 Ch 1:32). 4. Benjaminite; revolted from David; beheaded (2 Sm 20:
1-22). 5. Gadite (1 Ch 5:13). 6. Town
near, or identical with, Beer-sheba (Jos
19:2). 7. See *Sabeans.*
Shebah (shē'bá). See *Shibah.*
Shebam (shē'băm). See *Sibmah.*
Shebaniah (shĕb-á-nī'á, grown by LORD).
1. Priest; trumpeter (1 Ch 15:24). 2.
Priest (Neh 10:4; 12:14). Probably same
as Shecaniah 3. 3. Levite; assisted at
feast of covenant (Neh 9:4, 5); sealed
covenant (Neh 10:10). 4. Levite; sealed
covenant (Neh 10:12).
Shebarim (shĕb'á-rĭm, ruins). Place near
Ai (Jos 7:5).
Shebat (she-băt'). 11th month (Zch 1:7
[KJ: Sebat]; 1 Mac 16:14 [KJ: Sabat.
RV: Sebat]). See *time.*
Sheber (shē'bĕr, breaking). Caleb's son
(1 Ch 2:48).
Shebna, Shebnah (shĕb'ná, tenderness).
Steward and secretary of Hezekiah; re-
buked by Isaiah (2 K 18:18-26 [RV, RSV:
Shebnah], 37; 19:2; Is 22:15-25; 36:3,
11, 22; 37:2).
Shebuel (shē-bū'ĕl, return, O God). 1.
Grandson of Moses (1 Ch 23:16; 26:24).
Shubael in 1 Ch 24:20. 2. Musician;
Heman's son (1 Ch 25:4). Shubael in
1 Ch 25:20.
Shecaniah, Shechaniah (shĕk-á-nī'á, LORD
has dwelt). 1. Head of 10th course of
priests (1 Ch 24:11). 2. Levite (2 Ch
31:15). 3. Chief priest; returned with
Zerubbabel (Neh 12:3). Probably same
as Shebaniah 2. 4. Descendant of David
(1 Ch 3:21; Ez 8:3; 1 Esd 8:29 [KJ, RV:
Sechenias]). 5. Divorced foreign wife
(Ez 10:2; 1 Esd 8:92 [KJ, RV: Jecho-
nias]). 6. Returned with Ezra (Ez 8:5;
1 Esd 8:32 [KJ, RV: Sechenias]). 7.
Father of Shemaiah (Neh 3:29). 8.
Father-in-law of Tobiah (Neh 6:18).
Shechem (shē'kĕm, shoulder). 1. Town of
Ephraim, Levitical city of refuge, in pass
between Mt Ebal and Mt Gerizim (Gn
12:6 [KJ: Sichem]; 35:4; Jos 20:7; Ju
9:7; Acts 7:16 [KJ: Sychem]), where
Abraham halted (Gn 12:6), Jacob bought
ground (Gn 33:18-20), Joseph was buried
(Jos 24:32). Modern Tell Balatah, near

later Neapolis and Nablus. 2. Seduced
Dinah; slain by Simeon and Levi (Gn
34). 3. Manassite (Nm 26:31; Jos 17:2).
4. Gileadite (1 Ch 7:19).
Shechemites (shē'kĕm-īts). Descendants of
Shechem 3 (Nm 26:31; Jos 17:2).
Shedeur (shĕd'ē-ēr, light sender). Reubenite; father of Elizur (Nm 1:5; 2:10;
7:30, 35; 10:18).
sheep. Early domesticated (Gn 4:2); patriarchs and descendants herded flocks
(Gn 12:16; Ex 10:9; 12:32, 38; 1 Ch
27:31); used for sacrifices (Ex 20:24; Lv
9:3), food (1 Sm 14:32); wool for clothing
(Lv 13:47) and tribute (2 K 3:4); rams'
horns for flasks (1 Sm 16:1), trumpets
(Jos 6:4); shearing time was time of
festivity (1 Sm 25:4, 11, 36). Sheep.
shepherd often used figuratively (2 Ch
18:16; Ps 23; 119:176; Mt 9:36; Jn 10).
Palestinian sheep broad-tailed variety.
sheepfold. Enclosure for protection (especially at night) and shearing of sheep
(Nm 32:16; Ju 5:16; 1 Sm 24:3; Ps
78:70; Zph 2:6; Jn 10:1).
Sheep Gate. Gate of Jerusalem (Neh 3:
1, 32; 12:39).
sheep-market. RV, RSV: sheep gate (Jn
5:2).
Sheerah (shē'ê-rá, female relative. KJ:
Sherah). Daughter of Ephraim; descendants built Beth-horon and Uzzen-
sheerah (1 Ch 7:24).
Shehariah (shē-há-rī'á, LORD dawned).
Benjaminite; Jeroham's son (1 Ch 8:26).
shekel (shĕk'el, weight). 1. Weight for
metal, c ½ oz (Ex 30:13; 2 Sm 14:26).
2. Coin (Mt 17:27. KJ: piece of money).
Shelah (shē'lá). 1. Son of Arphaxad (Gn
10:24 [KJ: Salah]; 11:12-15 [KJ: Salah];
1 Ch 1:18, 24; Lk 3:35 [KJ: Sala]).
2. See *Siloam.*
Shelah (shē'lá, prayer). Judah's son; progenitor of Shelanites (Gn 38:2-26; Nm
26:20).
Shelemiah (shĕl-ē-mī'á, LORD repays). 1.
See *Meshelmiah.* 2. Divorced foreign
wife (Ez 10:39; 1 Esd 9:34 [KJ, RV:
Selemias]). 3. Divorced foreign wife (Ez
10:41). 4. Father of Hananiah (Neh 3:30).
5. Priest; treasurer (Neh 13:13). 6.
Cushi's son (Jer 36:14). 7. Abdeel's son
(Jer 36:26). 8. Hananiah's son (Jer 37:
13). 9. Jehucal's father (Jer 37:3; 38:1).
Sheleph (shē'lĕf, ancestor). Joktan's son
(Gn 10:26; 1 Ch 1:20).
Shelesh (shē'lĕsh, triad). Asherite (1 Ch
7:35).
Shelomi (shē-lō'mī, my peace). Asherite
(Nm 34:27).
Shelomith (shē-lō'mĭth, peaceful). 1.
Daughter of Dibri; son stoned for blasphemy (Lv 24:11). 2. Kohathite Levite
(1 Ch 23:18). Shelomoth in 1 Ch 24:22.
3. Descendant of Eliezer; treasurer (1 Ch
26:25, 26, 28. RV, RSV: Shelomoth). 4.
Gershonite Levite (1 Ch 23:9. RV, RSV:
Shelomoth). 5. Rehoboam's child (2 Ch
11:20). 6. Son of Josiphiah (Ez 8:10;
1 Esd 8:36 [KJ: Assalimoth; RV: Sali-
moth]). 7. Zerubbabel's daughter (1 Ch
3:19).
Shelomoth (shē-lō'mŏth). See *Shelomith
2; 3; 4.*
Shelumiel (shē-lū'mĭ-ĕl, God is friend).
Simeonite prince (Nm 1:6; 2:12; 7:36, 41;
10:19). Salamiel (KJ: Samael) in Jdth
8:1.
Shem (shĕm). Son of Noah (Gn 5:32; 10:1;
Lk 3:36 [KJ: Sem]). Worshipers of true
God descended from him (Gn 9:21-27).
Ancestor of Hebrews, Aramaeans, Arabs.

Shema (shē'má, rumor, fame). **1.** Town in S Judah (Jos 15:26). **2.** Hebron's son (1 Ch 2:43, 44). **3.** Benjaminite (1 Ch 8:13). Shimei (KJ: Shimhi) in 1 Ch 8:21. **4.** Reubenite; Joel's son (1 Ch 5:8). Probably Shemaiah in 1 Ch 5:4. **5.** Assisted Ezra at reading of law (Neh 8:4; 1 Esd 9:43 [KJ, RV: Sammus]).

Shemaah (shē-mā'á, report). Father of Ahiezer and Joash, David's warriors (1 Ch 12:3).

Shemaiah (shē-mā'yá, LORD has heard). **1.** Prophet; counseled Rehoboam (1 K 12:22; 2 Ch 11:2; 12:5, 7, 15). **2.** Father of prophet Uriah (Jer 26:20). **3.** False prophet; opposed Jeremiah (Jer 29: 24:32). **4.** Delaiah's father (Jer 36:12). **5.** Shecaniah's son (1 Ch 3:22). Perh same as 21. **6.** Simeonite (1 Ch 4:37). **7.** Reubenite; Joel's son (1 Ch 5:4). See *Shema* **4** **8.** Levite (1 Ch 9:14; Neh 11:15). **9.** Levite (1 Ch 9:16). Shammua in Neh 11:17. **10.** Kohathite leader (1 Ch 15:8, 11). **11.** Levite; listed priestly offices (1 Ch 24:6). **12.** Son of Obededom (1 Ch 26:4, 6, 7). **13.** Levite; taught Law in Judah (2 Ch 17:8). **14.** Levite; helped cleanse temple (2 Ch 29:14). **15.** Levite; distributed freewill offerings (2 Ch 31:15). **16.** Levite (2 Ch 35:9; 1 Esd 1:9 [KJ, RV: Samaias]). **17.** Levite; returned with Ezra (Ez 8:13; 1 Esd 8:39 [KJ, RV: Samaias]). **18.** Sent by Ezra to Iddo to ask for Levites and temple ministers (Ez 8:16; 1 Esd 8:43 [KJ: Mamaias; RV: Samaias]). Maasmas (KJ: Masman) in 1 Esd 8:43. **19.** Priest; divorced foreign wife (Ez 10:21; 1 Esd 9:21 [KJ: Sameius; RV: Sameus]). **20.** Layman; divorced foreign wife (Ez 10:31). Sabbeus (RSV: Sabbaias) in 1 Esd 9:32. **21.** Helped rebuild Jerusalem's walls (Neh 3:29). **22.** Son of Delaiah; prophet; tried to intimidate Nehemiah (Neh 6: 10-14). **23.** Priest; sealed covenant (Neh 10:8; 12:6, 18, 35). **24.** Prince (Neh 12:34). **25.** Musician (Neh 12:36). **26.** Priest (Neh 12:42). **27.** Kinsman of Tobit (Tob 5:13. KJ: Samaias). **28.** See *Samatus.*

Shemariah (shĕm-á-rī'á, LORD has kept). **1.** Benjaminite; joined David at Ziklag (1 Ch 12:5). **2.** Rehoboam's son (2 Ch 11:19. KJ: Shamariah). **3.** Son of Harim; divorced foreign wife (Ez 10:32). **4.** Son of Bani; divorced foreign wife (Ez 10:41).

Shemeber (shĕm-ē'bēr). King of Zeboiim (Gn 14:2).

Shemed (shē'mĕd). Benjaminite; rebuilt Ono and Lod (1 Ch 8:12. KJ: Shamed).

Shemer (shē'mēr, guardian). **1.** Sold hill of Samaria to Omri (1 K 16:24). **2.** Merarite Levite (1 Ch 6:46. KJ: Shamer). **3.** Asherite (1 Ch 7:34. KJ: Shamer). Shomer in 1 Ch 7:32.

Shemida, Shemidah (shĕ-mī'dá). Founder of Shemidaites (Nm 26:32; Jos 17:2; 1 Ch 7:19).

Sheminith (shĕm'ĭ-nĭth, eighth). Musical term; perhaps octave, scale, or strings of instrument (1 Ch 15:21; Ps 6; 12 titles).

Shemiramoth (shē-mĭr'á-mŏth, lofty name). **1.** Levite; singer (1 Ch 15:18, 20; 16:5). **2.** Levite (2 Ch 17:8).

Shemuel (shē-mū'el, heard of God). **1.** Simeonite; assisted in land division (Nm 34:20). **2.** Samuel (as RV, RSV. 1 Ch 6:33). **3.** Prince of Issachar (1 Ch 7:2).

Shen (shĕn, tooth). See *Jeshanah.*

Shenazar, Shenazzar (shĕ-nā'zär, -năz'ẽr, Sin [moon-god] protect). Jeconiah's son (1 Ch 3:18).

Shenir (shē'nēr). See *Hermon.*

Sheol (shē'ōl, from H *sha'al*, dig? ask?). **1.** Grave (Jb 17:16 [KJ: pit]; Is 38:10 [KJ: grave]). **2.** Realm of the dead, described as place full of darkness where dead dwell (Dt 32:22 [KJ: hell]; Jb 7:9 [KJ: grave]; 11:8 [KJ: hell]; Ps 89:48 [KJ: grave]. See Jb 10:20-22). Occasionally negative connotation (Nm 16:30 [KJ: pit]; Pr 5:5 [KJ: hell]. See also Ps 94:17; 115:17). **3.** Inhabitants of Sheol (Is 14:9 [KJ: hell]; 38:18 [KJ: grave]). See also *eschatology; eternal life; Gehenna; grave; Hades; hell.*

Shepham (shē'făm). Place on N border of Canaan (Nm 34:11).

Shephathiah (shĕf-á-thī'á). See *Shephatiah* **4.**

Shephatiah (shĕf-á-tī'á, LORD has judged). **1.** David's son (2 Sm 3:4; 1 Ch 3:3). **2.** Haruphite; joined David at Ziklag (1 Ch 12:5). **3.** Simeonite chief (1 Ch 27:16). **4.** Benjaminite (1 Ch 9:8. KJ: Shephathiah). **5.** Jehoshaphat's son (2 Ch 21:2). **6.** Prince; advised death of Jeremiah (Jer 38). **7.** Progenitor of family which returned with Zerubbabel (Ez 2:4; Neh 7:9; 1 Esd 5:9 [KJ, RV: Saphat]) and Ezra (Ez 8:8; 1 Esd 8:34 [KJ, RV: Saphatias]). **8.** Judahite (Neh 11:4). **9.** Progenitor of family of Solomon's servants (Ez 2:57; Neh 7:59; 1 Esd 5:33 [KJ, RV: Saphuthi]).

Shephelah, The (shē-fē'lá, low. KJ: low country, plain, vale, valley. RV: lowland). Land between central highlands of Palestine and Mediterranean plain (1 K 10:27; 1 Ch 27:28; 2 Ch 1:15; 9:27; 26:10; Jer 17:26; 32:44; Ob 19).

Shepher (shē'fēr, beauty. KJ: Shapher). Mountain where Israel camped in wilderness (Nm 33:23, 24).

shepherd. Honorable profession (Gn 29:6, 7; 30:29, 30; Ex 2:16-22). Led sheep to pasture (Ps 23; Jn 10:4), water (Gn 29:7; Ex 2:16; Ps 23:2); tended them (Ps 23; Jn 10); protected them (1 Sm 17:34; Jn 10); sought lost (Ps 119:176; Is 53:6; Eze 34:11, 12; Mt 10:6; Lk 15:1-7); brought sheep home at night, counted them by passing them under rod (Lv 27:32; Eze 20:37). Equipment: sheepskin mantle, bag, sling, crook. Assisted by dog (Jb 30:1). Often dangerous employment (Gn 31:40; 1 Sm 17:34; Jn 10: 11-13). Overseers, chief shepherds, often overshepherds (1 Ch 27:31; 1 Ptr 5:4). Figuratively: Jehovah (Ps 77:20; 80:1; Jer 31:10); king (Is 44:28; Eze 34:10); ministers (Is 56:11; Jer 23:4; Acts 20: 28-30); Christ (Jn 10:14; Heb 13:20; 1 Ptr 5:4).

Shephi, Shepho (shē'fī, -fō, barren?). Grandson of Seir (1 Ch 1:40). Shepho in Gn 36:23.

Shephupham, Shephuphan (shē-fū'făm, -făn). Son of Bela (1 Ch 8:5; 26:39 [KJ: Shupham]). Shuppim in 1 Ch 7:12, 15. Muppim in Gn 46:21.

Sherah (shē'rá). See *Sheerah.*

Sherebiah (shĕr-ē-bī'á, LORD has sent heat). Levite; joined Ezra at Ahava; sealed covenant with Nehemiah (Ez 8:18, 24; Neh 8:7; 9:4, 5; 10:12; 12:8, 24; 1 Esd 8:47 [KJ: Asebebia; RV: Asebebias], 54 [KJ: Esebrias; RV: Eserebias]; 9:48 [KJ, RV: Sarabias]).

Sheresh (shē'rĕsh, root). Machir's son (1 Ch 7:16).

Sherezer (shē-rē'zẽr). See *Sharezer* **2.**

sheriff. Babylonian official (Dn 3:2, 3. RSV: magistrate).

Sheshach (shē'shăk). Perhaps cryptic spelling for Babel, or Babylon (Jer 25:26; 51:41).

Sheshai (shē'shī, whitish). Son of Anak; slain by Caleb (Nm 13:22; Jos 15:14; Ju 1:10).

Sheshan (shē'shăn). Jerahmeelite; daughter married Egyptian (1 Ch 2:31-35).

Sheshbazzar (shĕsh-băz'ẽr, sun god, guard lord?). Entrusted with sacred vessels by Cyrus; usually identified with Zerubbabel (Ez 1:8; 5:14, 16; 1 Esd 2:12-15 [KJ, RV: Sanabassar]; 6:18-20 [KJ, RV: Sanabassarus]).

Sheth (shĕth). 1. See *Seth*. 2. Designation for Moab (Nm 24:17. RV: tumult).

Shethar (shē'thär). Persian prince (Est 1:14).

Shethar-bozenai, Shethar-boznai (shē'thär-bŏz'e-nī, -bŏz'nī). Persian official in Syria (Ez 5:3, 6; 6:6, 13). Sathrabuzanes in 1 Esd 6:3, 7, 27.

Sheva (shē'vá). See *Shavsha*.

shewbread (shō'brĕd). See *showbread*.

Shibah (shī'bá, seven, oath. KJ: Shebah). Well dug by Isaac's servants at Beersheba (Gn 26:31-33).

Shibboleth (shĭb'ō-lĕth, ear of grain; stream). Pronounced sĭb'ō-lĕth by Ephraimites, hence used to distinguish them (Ju 12:6).

Shibmah (shĭb'má). See *Sibmah*.

Shicron (shĭk'rŏn). See *Shikkeron*.

shield. See *armor*.

Shiggaion, Shigionoth (shĭ-gā'yŏn, pl shĭg-ī-ō'nŏth, wandering). Musical term; perh indicates music or meter (Ps 7 title; Hab 3:1).

Shihon (shī'hŏn). See *Shion*.

Shihor (shī'hôr, black). See *Nile*.

Shihor-libnath (shī'hôr-lĭb'năth, turbid stream of Libnath). Small river on SW corner of Asher (Jos 19:26). Perh modern Nahr-zerka.

Shikkeron (shĭk'e-rŏn, drunkenness. KJ: Shicron). Town on N boundary of Judah (Jos 15:11).

Shilhi (shĭl'hī). Grandfather of Jehoshaphat (1 K 22:42; 2 Ch 20:31).

Shilhim (shĭl'hĭm). See *Shaaraim* 2.

Shillem (shĭl'ĕm). See *Shallum* 7.

Shillemites (shĭl'ĕm-īts). Descendants of *Shallum* 7.

Shiloah (shĭ-lō'á). See *Siloam*.

Shiloh (shī'lō, peace). 1. Site of Israel's early sanctuary, 9 mi N of Bethel; ark there about 300 yrs (Jos 18:1, 8-10; Ju 21:19-23); residence of Eli and Samuel (1 Sam 3); home of Ahijah (1 K 14: 1-18); desolate in Jeremiah's times (Jer 7:12-14; 26:6-9). 2. Disputed word regarded as reference to Messiah by ancient Jews and later Christians (Gn 49:10).

Shiloni (shĭ-lō'nī). See *Shilonite 2*.

Shilonite (shī'lō-nīt). 1. Dweller in Shiloh; title of Ahijah (1 K 11:29; 12:15; 2 Ch 9:29). 2. Descendant of Shelah (1 Ch 9:5; Neh 11:5 [KJ: Shiloni]).

Shilshah (shĭl'shä, triad). Descendant of Asher (1 Ch 7:37).

Shimea (shĭm'ē-á, fame). 1. Merarite Levite (1 Ch 6:30). 2. Gershonite Levite (1 Ch 6:39). 3. Brother of David (1 Ch 2:13 [KJ: Shimma]; 20:7). Shimeah in 2 Sm 13:3, 32; 21:21 (RV, RSV: Shimei), Shammah in 1 Sm 16:9; 17:13. 4. See *Shammua 2*.

Shimeah (shĭm'ē-á). See *Shimea 3*; *Shimeam*.

Shimeam (shĭm'ē-ăm). Benjaminite (1 Ch 9:38). Shimeah in 1 Ch 8:32.

Shimeath (shĭm'ē-ăth, rumor). Ammonitess; mother of one of Josiah's assassins (2 K 12:21; 2 Ch 24:26).

Shimeathites (shĭm'ē-ăth-īts). Kenite family of scribes (1 Ch 2:55).

Shimei (shĭm'ē-ī, famous). 1. Gershon's son (Ex 6:17 [KJ: Shimi]; Nm 3:18; 1 Ch 23:7, 10; Zch 12:13). 2. Merarite Levite (1 Ch 6:29). 3. Simeonite (1 Ch 4:26, 27). 4. Descendant of Gershom (1 Ch 6:42). 5. See *Shema 3*. 6. Descendant of Gershon (1 Ch 23:9. 7. Levite; head of 10th course of singers (1 Ch 25:17). 8. Overseer of David's vineyards (1 Ch 27:27). 9. Benjaminite; cursed David (2 Sm 16:5-13; 1 K 2: 44-46). 10. Adherent of David (1 K 1:8; 4:18). 11. Reubenite (1 Ch 5:4). 12. Levite; purified temple (2 Ch 29:14-16). Perhaps same in 2 Ch 31:12. 13. Ancestor of Mordecai (Est 2:5; Ap Est 11:2 [KJ: Semei; RV: Semeias]). 14. Divorced foreign wife (Ez 10:23; 1 Esd 9:23 [KJ: Semis; RV: Semeis]). 15. Divorced foreign wife (Ez 10:33; 1 Esd 9:33 [KJ, RV: Semei]). 16. Divorced foreign wife (Ez 10:38; 1 Esd 9:34 [KJ: Samis; RV: Someis]). 17. Brother of Zerubbabel (1 Ch 3:19). 18. See *Shimea 3*.

Shimeon (shĭm'ē-un, hearing). Divorced foreign wife (Ez 10:31). Simon Chosamaeus (Chosameus) in 1 Esd 9:32.

Shimhi (shĭm'hī). See *Shema 3*.

Shimi (shĭm'ī). See *Shimei 1*.

Shimites (shĭm'īts). Descendants of Shimei 1 (Nm 3:21).

Shimma (shĭm'á). See *Shimea 3*.

Shimon (shī'mŏn). Judahite (1 Ch 4:20).

Shimrath (shĭm'răth, watching). Benjaminite (1 Ch 8:21).

Shimri (shĭm'rī, vigilant). 1. Simeonite (1 Ch 4:37). 2. Father of Jediael, David's guard (1 Ch 11:45). 3. Levite (2 Ch 29:13). 4. Merarite Levite (1 Ch 26:10. KJ: Simri).

Shimrith (shĭm'rĭth, vigilant). See *Shomer*.

Shimrom (shĭm'rŏm). See *Shimron 1*.

Shimron (shĭm'rŏn, watching). 1. Son of Issachar; founder of family (Gn 46:13; Nm 26:24; 1 Ch 7:1 [KJ: Shimrom]). 2. Border town of Zebulun (Jos 11:1; 19:15). Probably same as Shimron-Meron (Jos 12:20).

Shimronites (shĭm'rŏn-īts). Descendants of Shimron 1.

Shimron-meron (shĭm'rŏn-mē'rŏn). See *Shimron 2*.

Shimshai (shĭm'shī). Scribe and leader in Samaria; wrote against Jews to Artaxerxes (Ez 4:8, 9, 17, 23; 1 Esd 2:16 [KJ: Semellius; RV: Samellius]).

Shinab (shī'năb). King of Admah (Gn 14:2).

Shinar (shī'nẽr). Alluvial plain of S Babylonia in which were Babel, Erech, Accad, Calneh (Gn 10:10; 11:2; Dn 1:2); ruled by Amraphel (Gn 14:1, 9); Jews carried captive thither (Is 11:11; Zch 5:11).

Shion (shī'ŏn, destruction. KJ: Shihon). City of Issachar (Jos 19:19). Perh 'Ayun esh-Sh'ian, 3 mi NW of Mt Tabor.

ship. See *boats*.

Shiphi (shī'fī). Simeonite prince (1 Ch 4:37).

Shiphmite (shĭf'mīt). Probably native of Siphmoth (1 Ch 27:27).

Shiphrah (shĭf'rá, beauty). Hebrew midwife (Ex 1:15).

Shiphtan (shĭf'tăn, judicial). Ephraimite; father of Kemuel (Nm 34:24).

Shisha (shī'shá). See *Shavsa*.

Shishak (shī'shăk). See *Pharaoh 6*.

Shitrai (shĭt'rī). David's herdsman in Sharon (1 Ch 27:29).

shittah, shittim (shĭt'ă, -ĭm. RV, RSV: acacia). Tree in Jordan valley, Sinai, around Dead Sea; acacia. Wood hard, fine-grained, insect-repelling; used for tabernacle, altars, tables, bars and pillars (Ex 25:5-28; 26:15-37; Is 41:19).

Shittim (shĭt'ĭm, acacias). 1. Last encampment of Israel before entering Palestine; thence Joshua sent spies (Nm 25:1; Jos 2:1; Mi 6:5). Abel-shittim in Nm 33:49. 2. Barren valley N of Dead Sea (Jl 3:18).

Shiza (shī'ză). Reubenite; father of one of David's warriors (1 Ch 11:42).

Shoa (shō'ă). People connected with Babylonians, Chaldeans, and Assyrians (Eze 23:23). Probably Sutu.

Shobab (shō'băb, rebellious). 1. David's son (2 Sm 5:14). 2. Calebite (1 Ch 2:18).

Shobach (shō'băk, one who pours out). General of Hadadezer; defeated by David (2 Sm 10:16). Shophach in 1 Ch 19: 16, 18.

Shobai (shō'bī). Levite; progenitor of family of doorkeepers (Ez 2:42; Neh 7:45; 1 Esd 5:28 [KJ: Sami; RV: Sabi]).

Shobal (shō'băl). 1. Son of Seir; Horite chief (Gn 36:20-30; 1 Ch 1:38). 2. Son of Hur; founder of Kiriath-jearim (1 Ch 2:50; 4:1, 2).

Shobek (shō'běk, one who forsakes). Sealed covenant with Nehemiah (Neh 10:24).

Shobi (shō'bī, one who leads captive). Ammonite; brought provisions to David (2 Sm 17:27).

Shocho, Shochoh, Shoco (shō'kō). See Soco.

shoe. Sole of leather fastened under foot by various devices. RSV: shoe 11 times (as Ex 3:5; Jos 5:15; Is 20:2; Eze 24:17; Ps 60:8); sandal 21 times (as Ex 12:11; Dt 29:5; Am 8:6; Mt 3:11).

Shoham (shō'hăm, beryl). Levite (1 Ch 24:27).

Shomer (shō'mĕr, keeper). 1. See Shemer 3. 2. Jehozabad's mother (2 K 12:21). Shimrith in 2 Ch 24:26.

shoot. See rod.

Shophach (shō'făk). See Shobach.

Shophan (shō'făn). See Atroth-shophan.

Shoshannim (shō-shăn'ĭm, lilies). Symbolical of content, musical instrument, or melody (Ps. 45; 69 titles. RSV: according to Lilies).

shovel. Used to take ashes from altar (Ex 27:3; 38:3; Nm 4:14; Jer 52:18).

showbread. H lehem panim: bread of presence (Ex 25:30; 35:13; 39:36); lehem hattamidh: continual bread (Nm 4:7); lehem ma'arekheth: bread piled or arranged (1 Ch 9:32). 12 loaves of unleavened bread placed fresh every Sabbath in 2 stacks on table of acacia wood in Holy Place; old loaves eaten by priests (Ex 25:30; 1 Sm 21:1-6; Mt 12:3, 4).

Shua (shoo'ă, wealth). 1. Canaanite; Judah's father-in-law (Gn 38:2, 12 [KJ: Shuah]; 1 Ch 2:3). 2. Heber's daughter (1 Ch 7:32).

Shuah (shoo'ă, depression). 1. Abraham's son by Keturah (Gn 25:2); ancestor of Arab tribe. 2. See Shua. 3. See Shuhah.

Shual (shoo'ăl, fox, jackal). 1. Asherite (1 Ch 7:36). 2. District near Michmash (1 Sm 13:17).

Shubael (shoo'bā-ĕl). See Shebuel.

Shuham (shoo'hăm). See Hushim.

Shuhah (shoo'hă, depression). Judahite (1 Ch 4:11. KJ: Shuah).

Shuhite (shoo'hīt). Descendant of Shuah 1 (Jb 2:11).

Shulamite, Shulammite (shoo'lăm-īt). Probably native of Shunem (SS 6:13).

Shumathites (shoo'măth-īts). Family of Kiriath-jearim (1 Ch 2:53).

Shunammite (shoo'năm-īt). Native of Shunem (1 K 1:3; 2 K 4:8, 12; 8:1).

Shunem (shoo'něm, two sleeping places). City of Issachar 3½ mi N of Jezreel; site of Philistine encampment (Jos 19:18; 1 Sm 28:4); home of Abishag (1 K 1:3) and Shunammite woman (2 K 4:8-37). Modern Solam.

Shuni (shoo'nī). Son of Gad; progenitor of Shunites (Gn 46:16; Nm 26:15).

Shupham (shoo'făm). See Shephupham.

Shuppim (shŭp'ĭm). 1. Levite gatekeeper (1 Ch 26:16). 2. See Shephupham.

Shur (shoor, wall). Region in wilderness, S of Palestine, E of Egypt (Gn 16:7; 25: 18; Ex 15:22).

Shushan (shoo'shăn, lily. RSV: Susa). Capital of Elam and Persian Empire (Neh 1: 1; Est 1:2; Dn 8:2). Susa in Ap Est 11:3. Code of Hammurabi found there. Modern Shush.

Shushanchites (shoo'shăn-kīts). See Susanchites.

Shushan-eduth (shoo'shăn-ē'dŭth, lilies of the Testimony). Musical term, perh melody (Ps 60 title).

Shuthelah (shoo-thē'lă). 1. Son of Ephraim; founder of family (Nm 26:35, 36; 1 Ch 7:20). 2. Ephraimite (1 Ch 7:21).

shuttle. See trade 4.

Sia, Siaha (sī'ă, sī'ă-hă, assembly). Nethinim (Ez 2:44; Neh 7:47; 1 Esd 5:29 [KJ: Sud; RV: Sua]).

Sibbecai, Sibbechai (sĭb'ē-kī, entangling). One of David's heroes; Hushathite; slew Saph, giant's son (2 Sm 21:18; 1 Ch 11: 29; 20:4; 27:11). Mebunnai in 2 Sm 23:27.

Sibboleth (sĭb'ō-lěth). See Shibboleth.

Sibmah (sĭb'mă). Town E of Jordan; assigned to Reuben (Nm 32:38 [KJ: Shibmah]; Jos 13:19; Is 16:8, 9; Jer 48:32). Sebam (KJ: Shebam) in Nm 32:3. Probably near Heshbon.

Sibraim (sĭb-rā'ĭm). Place on N boundary of Palestine (Eze 47:16). Perh Sepharvaim.

Siccuth (sĭk'ŭth). See Sakkuth.

Sichem (sī'kěm). See Shechem 1.

sickle. See agriculture 4.

Sicyon (sĭsh'ĭ-on). City on Gulf of Corinth near isthmus (1 Mac 15:23).

Siddim (sĭd'ĭm, valley of fields). Territory E of Dead Sea on S end (Gn 14:3, 8, 10).

Side (sī'dē). Coastal town of Pamphylia (1 Mac 15:23).

Sidon (sī'd'n, fishery. KJ, RV often: Zidon). Ancient Canaanite (Gn 10:19) city situated on Mediterranean promontory about 22 mi N of Tyre; assigned to Asher but never conquered (Ju 1:31; 10:12; 18:7, 28); assisted in building temple (1 K 5:6; 1 Ch 22:4. See Ez 3:7): its religion corrupted Israel (1 K 11:5); native city of Jezebel (1 K 16:31); denounced by prophets (Jer 27:3; Jl 3:4-6); region visited by Christ (Mt 15:21); Paul touched there (Acts 27:3). Modern Saida. 2. Canaan's son (Gn 10:15; 1 Ch 1:13).

siege, siegework. In early Israel sieges of short duration (Ju 9: 46-55; 2 Sm 20:15). Later siege engines (protected ladders, battering rams) constructed (2 Ch 26:15. See Eze 21:22). See also armor; army; war.

sieve (H k:bharah, netted; naphah, shake). Made of rushes; probably also of horsehair or string (Is 30:28; Am 9:9).

signet. See ring.

Sihon (sī'hŏn, sweeping out). Amorite king; defeated by Israelites (Nm 21:21-31; Dt 1:4; 2:24-37; Jos 13:15-28).

Sihor (sī'hôr). See *Nile*.

Silas (sī'lăs, sylvan). Jerusalem Christian; accompanied Paul to Antioch (Acts 15:22, 27, 32) and on 2d missionary journey (Acts 16—18). Silvanus in 2 Co 1:19; 1 Th 1:1; 2 Th 1:1; 1 Ptr 5:12.

silk. Phoenicians imported silk. Probably referred to in OT (Pr 31:22 [RV, RSV: fine linen]; Eze 16:10, 13; Am 3:12 [KJ: in Damascus in a couch; RV: silken cushions of a bed; RSV: part of a bed]); referred to in Rv 18:12.

Silla (sĭl'á, twig). Place near Milla (2 K 12:20).

Siloah, Siloam (sĭ-lō'á, -ăm, shooting forth, sent). Pool on S side of temple mt which received waters through 1,780-ft tunnel from En-rogel (Jn 9:7). Shiloah in Is 8:6. Shelah (KJ: Siloah) in Neh 3:15. Modern Birket Silwan.

Silvanus (sĭl-vā'nŭs). See *Silas*.

silver. Used from earliest times for money (Gn 23:16; Jb 28:15), ornaments (Gn 24:53), crowns (Zch 6:11), trumpets (Nm 10:2), vessels (Gn 44:2), furnishings of tabernacle (Ex 26:19; 27:10; 38:19), idols (Ps 115:4).

silversmith. See *trade* 7.

Simalcue (sĭ-măl-kū'ĕ). See *Imalcue*.

Simeon (sĭm'ē-un, hearing). 1. Son of Jacob and Leah (Gn 29:33); with Levi massacred inhabitants of Shechem (Gn 34:24-31); kept as hostage by Joseph in Egypt (Gn 42:24); destined to be scattered in Israel (Gn 49:5-7). 2. Tribe of Simeon (Nm 1:23); received cities and villages in Judah (Jos 19:1-9; 1 Ch 4:28-33) in neighborhood of Beer-sheba. 3. Ancestor of Christ (Lk 3:30 [RV: Symeon]). 4. Righteous and devout Jew who blessed Christ Child (Lk 2:25-35). 5. Simeon Niger, Christian at Antioch (Acts 13:1 [RV: Symeon]). 6. See *Peter*. 7. Great-grandfather of Judas Maccabaeus (1 Mac 2:1).

Simon (sī'mun, hearing). 1. Sorcerer of Samaria (Acts 8:9-24). 2. Simon the Canaanite, or Simon Zelotes (the Zealot), apostle (Mt 10:4). 3. Brother of Jesus (Mt 13:55; Mk 6:3). 4. Leper of Bethany (Mt 26:6). 5. Simon of Cyrene; compelled to bear Christ's cross (Mt 27:32; Mk 15:21; Lk 23:26). 6. Pharisee in whose house woman anointed Jesus' feet (Lk 7:36-50). 7. Tanner at Joppa (Acts 9:43). 8. Father of Judas Iscariot (Jn 6:71; 13:2, 26). 9. See *Peter*. 10. See *Shimeon*. 11. 12. 13. Three Maccabean high priests: Simon Thassi, Simon I, Simon II (1 Mac; Josephus, *Ant XII*). 14. Benjaminite; opponent of Onias III (2 Mac 3:4; 4:23).

Simri (sĭm'rī). See *Shimri* 4.

Sin (sĭn). 1. Strategic Egyptian city in Nile delta (Eze 30:15, 16. RSV: Pelusium). 2. Wilderness of Sin; desert plain lying inland from Red Sea (Ex 16:1; 17:1; Nm 33:11, 12).

sin. By fall of Adam sin came to entire human race (Gn 3; Ps 51:5; Ro 3:9-23; 5:21; 6:6-17; 7:21-23). Original sin is hereditary guilt (Ro 5:12) and corruption of man's nature. Corruption consists in alienation from God (Ro 1:18-24; 8:7), inclination to evil (Ro 1; 7:14), expresses itself in actual sinful deeds contrary to God's will expressed in Law (Ro 3:20; 4:15; 7:7; Ja 4:12-17; 1 Jn 3:4). Sin is against God (Gn 39:9; 2 Sm 12:13; Ps

51:4), puts self in place of God (Ro 15:3; 1 Co 13:5; 2 Th 2:3, 4) and opposite to love (1 Jn).

sin offering. See *sacrifices*; *atonement*, *day of*.

sin, unpardonable. Conscious, stubborn, malicious opposition and blasphemous hostility to divine truth once recognized as such (Mt 12:31; Mk 3:29; Lk 12:10; 1 Jn 5:16).

Sina, Sinai (sī'ná, -nī, thorny, *or* Sin [moon-goddess]). Mt on which Law was given; Horeb (Ex 3:1; 17:6; Dt 1:6; 4:10) is probably general range and Sinai (Ex 16:1; 19:11; 24:16; Lv 25:1) peak. Identification disputed (Seir, Jebel Musa or Ras es Sufsafeh, Serbal, Jebel, Hellal); favored: Jebel Musa, 7,363 ft. Decalog given from peak, covenant ratified at base (Ex 20:1—24:8; Acts 3:38 [KJ: Sina]); Israel organized; legislation of Ex 20—Nm 10 enacted (Ex 24:12; Lv 1:1; 27:34; Nm 9:1). Sinai peninsula between Red Sea, Gulf of Aqaba, Gulf of Suez.

singing. See *music*.

Sinim (sī'nĭm). Remote unidentified people (Is 49:12).

Sinites (sī'nĭts). Canaan people (Gn 10:17; 1 Ch 1:15).

Sion (sī'un). See *Hermon*; *Zion*.

Siphmoth (sĭf'mŏth). Place in S Judah (1 Sm 30:28).

Sippai (sĭp'ī). See *Saph*.

Sirach (sī'răk). Father of the Jesus who wrote Sirach (Ecclesiasticus).

Sirah (sī'rá, recession). Well; mi N of Hebron; there Joab killed Abner (2 Sm 3:26).

Sirion (sĭr'ĭ-ŏn). See *Hermon*.

Sisamai (sĭs'á-mī). See *Sismai*.

Sisera (sĭs'ē-rá). 1. Canaanite; commander of Jabin's army; defeated by Barak; slain by Jael (Ju 4; 5; 1 Sm 12:9; Ps 83:9). 2. Ancestor of Nethinim (Ez 2:53; Neh 7:55; 1 Esd 5:32 [KJ: Aserer; RV: Serar]).

Sisinnes (sĭ-sĭn'ēz). See *Tatnai*.

Sismai (sĭs'mī). KJ: Sisamai). Jerahmeelite (1 Ch 2:40).

sister. 1. Full or half sister (Gn 20:12; Dt 27:22). 2. Wife (SS 4:9). 3. Woman of same tribe (Nm 25:18). 4. Female fellow Christian (Ro 16:1).

Sithri (sĭth'rī, hiding place. KJ: Zithri). Kohathite Levite (Ex 6:22).

Sitnah (sĭt'ná, hostility). 2d well dug by Isaac at Gerar (Gn 26:21).

Sivan (sĕ-vän'). See *time*.

skull. See *Calvary*.

slander. See *backbite*.

slave. See *servant*.

sleep. 1. Repose of body (Ps. 4:8; Pr 24:33; Jn 11:13). 2. Death (1 K 1:21; Ps 13:3; Jer 51:39; Jn 11:11). 3. Spiritual indolence, stupidity (Ro 13:11; 1 Th 5:6).

slime. See *bitumen*.

sling. Pair of leather thongs or cords of hair or sinews of animals with leather pouch in middle for missile; whirled around head, then one end released; used in war (2 Ch 26:14), by shepherds (1 Sm 17:40), hunters (Jb 41:28).

slothfulness, sluggard. Indolence, laziness; sluggard censured (Pr 6:6-9; 12:24-27; 21:25; 22:13; Mt 25:26). See *labor*.

smelter. See *trade* 7.

smith. See *trade* 7.

Smyrna (smûr'ná, myrrh). Ancient Ionian city 40 mi N of Ephesus; rebuilt by Alexander the Great, 320 BC (Rv 1:11; 2:8-11).

snail. 1. Lizard (H *ḥomet.* Lv 11:30. RV, RSV: sand lizard). **2.** Snail (H *shabb:lul,* slimy one. Ps 58:8).

snow. Fell in hilly country of Palestine (2 Sm 23:20; Is 55:10). Frequently mentioned in poetry (Jb 37:6; 38:22; Ps 51: 7; 147:16), in metaphor (Is 1:18; Mt 28:3).

snuff-dish. Tray for wick snuff from tabernacle lamps (Ex 25:38. RSV: tray).

snuffers. Instruments for snuffing tabernacle lamps (Ex 37:23).

So (sō). See *Pharaoh 8.*

soap. H *borith:* cleanser (Jer 2:22; Ml 3:2). See also *nitre.*

Soco, Socoh, Sochoh, Shocho, Shocho, Shochoh (sō'kō, shō'kō, thorn). Town in lowland of Judah (Jos 15:35) 14 mi SW of Jerusalem; fortified by Rehoboam (2 Ch 11:7); captured in reign of Ahaz (2 Ch 28:18). Modern Khirbet es-Shuweikeh. **2.** Town in hill country of Judah (Jos 15: 48).

Sodi (sō'dī, my secret council). Zebulunite; father of spy Gaddiel (Nm 13:10).

Sodom, Sodoma (sŏd'-um, -ŏ-má). Located with Gomorrah, Admah, Zeboiim, Zoar in plain of Siddim (Gn 13:12), regarded as SE end of Dead Sea. Royal city (Gn 14: 2); Lot lived there (Gn 13:11-13); destroyed because of its wickedness (Gn 19). Used as example of sin (Dt 29:23; Is 1:9; 3:9; Jer 50:40; Eze 16:46; Mt 10:15; Ro 9:29 [KJ: Sodoma]; 2 Ptr 2:6). "City of sin" called Sodom and Egypt (Rv 11:8).

Sodomites (sŏd'um-īts). Those who practiced unnatural vice of Sodom (Gn 19:5; Dt 23:17. See 1 K 14:24; Ro 1:27).

sojourner (sō-jûr'nēr). See *foreigner; proselyte.*

soldier (sōl'jēr). See *army.*

Solomon (sŏl'ō-mun, peaceable). David's son (2 Sm 12:24; 1 Ch 3:5); Nathan called him Jedidiah (2 Sm 12:25); proclaimed king (1 K 1:5-40); executed Abiathar, Shimei, Adonijah, Joab (1 K 2); married Pharaoh's daughter (1 K 3:1); prayed and noted for wisdom (1 K 3:5-28; 10:1-10; 2 Ch 1:3-12); with Tyrian help built temple in 7 years and palace (1 K 5—8; 2 Ch 2—7); showed wisdom in government (1 K 4:2-19) and commerce (1 K 10:11-29; 2 Ch 9:10-22). Naturalist (1 K 4:33); proverbs and psalms (72, 127) attributed to him. Established harem; wives caused him to apostatize; only fragment of kingdom left to descendants (1 K 11:1-13).

Solomon, Song of. See *Song of Songs.*

Solomon's Porch. 1. Portico attached to Solomon's palace (1 K 7:7). **2.** Colonnade on E side of Herod's temple (Jn 10:23; Acts 3:11; 5:12).

Solomon's servants, children of. Returned from captivity; probably descendants of servants assigned to temple duties by Solomon (Ez 2:55, 58; Neh 7:57, 60. See 1 K 9:20, 21).

Someis (sō-mē'is). See *Shimei 16.*

son. 1. Male child; immediate descendant (Gn 27:1). **2.** Remote descendant (2 K 9:20; Ml 3:6). **3.** Spiritual son (2 K 2:3; 1 Ti 1:18; 2 Ti 2:1). **4.** Address to younger person (1 Sm 3:6). **5.** Member of profession (Neh 12:28). **6.** Devotee or follower (Nm 21:29). **7.** Adopted son (Ex 2:10). **8.** Inhabitant or native (Lm 4:2). Children in Ez 2; Neh 7. **9.** Possessor of quality (1 Sm 25:17; Lk 10:6). **10.** See *Jesus Christ.*

Son of God. 1. Adam (Lk 3:38). **2.** Angels (Jb 38:7). **3.** Believers (Ro 8:14; 2 Co 6:18; Gl 4:1-7). See also *adoption.* **4.** See *Jesus Christ.*

Son of man. 1. Human being (Nm 23:19; Jb 25:6; Ps 8:4; Eze 2:1; Dn 8:17). **2.** See *Jesus Christ.*

song. See *music; psalms.*

song of ascents (degrees). See *degrees, song of.*

Song of Songs, Which Is Solomon's. Also called Canticles from Latin *Canticum Canticorum* (Song of Songs). Given allegorical interpretation by (1) Jews: Shulammite, bride, is Jewish people, bridegroom (Solomon) is God, and poem embraces history of Jews from Exodus to Messiah; (2) Christians: Christ is Bridegroom, church is bride. View developed in 18th c: dramatic poem (Solomon woos country girl from Shulam who prefers shepherd lover) with ethical significance. God or Christ as Bridegroom is frequent (Is 54:5; 62:5; Jer 2:2; Hos 2: 19,20; Mt 9:15; Jn 3:29; 2 Co 11:2; Eph 5:25-32; Rv 19:7; 21:2).

sonship. See *adoption; Son of God.*

soothsayer. One who pretends to foretell future (Dt 18:10, 14 [KJ: observer of times; RV: one that practiseth augury]; Dn 2:27 [RSV: astrologer]).

sop. Morsel dipped in soup, milk, or other liquid (Jn 13:26. RSV: morsel).

Sopater (sō'pá-tēr, father saved). Berean companion of Paul (Acts 20:4).

sope (sōp). See *nitre.*

Sophereth (sō-fē'rĕth, secretariat). Name (probably title) given to some of Solomon's servants (Ez 2:55 [RV, RSV: Hassophereth]; Neh 7:55. Hassophereth (KJ: Azaphion; RV: Assaphioth) in 1 Esd 5:33.

Sophonias (sŏf-ō-nī'ás). See *Zephaniah 1.*

sorcerer. See *magic.*

Sorek (sō'rĕk, vine). Valley of Philistia (Ju 16:4).

Sosipater (sō-sĭp'á-tēr, savior of father). **1.** Christian (Ro 16:21). **2.** General of Judas Maccabeus (2 Mac 12:19-24).

Sosthenes (sŏs'thē-nēz, savior). **1.** Ruler of synagog at Corinth (Acts 18:17). Possibly same as Paul's co-worker (1 Co 1:1).

Sostratus (sŏs'trá-tus). Syrian general (2 Mac 4:28).

Sotai (sō'tī, fickle). Descendants returned from captivity (Ez 2:55; Neh 7:57).

soul, spirit (translations vary; at times also life, ghost). H *nephesh,* G *psuche,* soul: that which breathes, inner man as distinguished from flesh (Jb 14:22); departs at death (Gn 35:18; Lk 12:20); becomes living being through breath of God (Gn 2:7; animals: Gn 2:19); described as living (Gn 12:13) and dying (Eze 18:4; Ju 16:30; Is 53:12); life itself (Gn 44:30; Acts 20:10; animals: Dt 12:23; Rv 8:9); man himself (Gn 49:6); seat of appetites, emotions, passions (Dt 12:20; Ps 107:9; Mt 22:37; Lk 1:46; 12:19; Jn 12:27); can be lost and saved (Mk 8:35, 36). H *ruah,* G *pneuma,* spirit: breath (Jb 15: 30; 2 Th 2:8); spirit of life created (Jb 27:3; Zch 12:1), preserved (Jb 10:12) by God; inner aspects of personality (1 Cor 5:3-5); seat of moral character (Eze 11:19; 18:31; 36:26; Mk 2:8); returns to God at death (Ec 12:7; Mt 27:50; Jn 19: 30). Spirit of God imparts special gifts (Ex 31:3; Nm 24:2; Jb 32:8).

Soul, spirit synonymous (Lk 1:46, 47), contrasted (1 Cor 15:44, 45). Both designate one life principle from two points of view (though not consistently): *nephesh, psuche* views it as subjective life in world; carnal animation; emphasizes individuality, worldly existence, self-centeredness (Lk 12:18, 19; 1 Co 15:44, 45; 2 Ptr 2: 14). *Ruah, pneuma* is life principle from God (Ec 12:7; see Gn 2:7); describes God-related life (Ro 1:9; 1 Co 2:14; Eph 4:23, 24; 2 Ti 1:7). See also *death; eschatology; eternal life; Holy Spirit.*

South. See *Negeb.*

South, Queen of. See *Sabeans.*

south Ramoth (south rāmoth). See *Ramath-negeb.*

Spain (spān). Peninsula now Spain and Portugal (Ro 15:24, 28).

span. See *measures 1 c.*

sparrow. H *tsippor* (chirper); usually: bird, but: sparrow in Ps 84:3; 102:7 (RSV: bird); Pr 26:2 (KJ: bird). G *strouthion* probably Eurasian house sparrow (Mt 10: 29; Lk 12:6, 7).

Spartan (spär'tăn). See *Lacedemonians.*

spear. See *armor.*

speckled bird. Bird of prey (Jer 12:9).

spelt. H *kussemeth,* inferior kind of wheat (Ex 9:32 [KJ: rie]; Is 28:25 [KJ: rie]; Eze 4:9 [KJ: fitches]). See *food 1.*

spices. Fragrant gums, barks, etc, used for ceremonies, medicine, toilet, embalming, anointing (Gn 37:25; 43:11; SS 4:14; Mk 16:1; Jn 19:39, 40).

spider. Spider's web emblematic of vanity of wickedness (Jb 8:14; Is 59:5). Should be lizard (RV, RSV) in Pr 30:28.

spikenard (spĭk'nērd). See *nard.*

spinning. See *trade 3.*

spirit. See *soul, spirit; Holy Spirit.*

Spirit, Holy. See *Holy Spirit.*

spiritual gifts. Special capabilities given to Christians by Holy Spirit (1 Co 12).

spoil. See *booty.*

sponge. Elastic, porous mass produced in sea (Mt 27:48; Mk 15:36; Jn 19:29).

spot. 1. Mark or blot (Gn 30:32-39; Lv 13: 2-39). 2. Physical or moral blemish (Lv 13; 21:17-24; Dt 32:5).

spouse. See *marriage.*

sprinkling. With blood, water (Ex 29:21; Lv 14; Nm 8:7) as expiation (see Heb 9:13, 14).

Stachys (stā'kĭs, ear of corn). Roman Christian (Ro 16:9).

stacte (stăk'tē). Aromatic gum or spice used in incense (Ex 30:34; Sir 24:15 [KJ: storax]).

stadium (stā'dĭ-um). See *measures 1 i.*

staff. See *rod.*

stairs, stairway. See *homes 4.*

standard. See *ensign.*

star. Any heavenly body except sun and moon; observed from patriarchical times (Gn 37:9). Figuratively, brightness (Ps 148:3; Dn 12:3), multitudes (Gn 22:17; Ps 147:4), important persons (Gn 37:9; Nm 24:17; Dn 8:10; Rv 6:13). Star of the East led Wise Men to Bethlehem (Mt 2:2-10). See also *astronomy.*

steadfast love (H *hesed*). Act of kindness by which God chooses Israel, promises salvation, is persistent in love and devotion; through covenant God binds Himself to duty of love. Person in this love relation to God is also in that relation to fellow men (Gn 24:12-27 [KJ, RV: kindness]; Ex 20:6 [KJ, RV: mercy]; Ps 5:7 [KJ: mercy; RV: lovingkindness]; 17:7; 26:3; 36:7; 48:9; 92:2; Jer 16:5. KJ, RV, usually: lovingkindness). See also *love; grace; mercy.*

steel. Bronze (2 Sm 22:35; Jb 20:24; Ps 18:34; Jer 15:12. RV: brass. RSV: bronze).

Stephanas (stĕf'á-năs, crown). Corinthian Christian (1 Co 1:16; 16:15-18).

Stephen (stē'ven, crown). Probably Hellenist; one of 7 ministers; man of faith, wisdom, power; disputed with Hellenistic Jews; charged with blasphemy, stoned after remarkable defense. Paul favored execution (Acts 6:5—8:2).

stocks. 1. Wooden frame in which head, hands, feet were fastened (2 Ch 16:10 [KJ: prison; RV: prison house]; Jer 20: 2). 2. Wooden frame or block to which feet were fastened (Jb 13:27; 33:11). 3. Wooden idols (Jer 2:27. RSV: tree).

Stoics (stō'iks, porch scholars). Greek philosophical school founded by Zeno; held that virtue, by which action is brought into harmony with nature and universal reason, is highest good. Religion pantheistic; God formative force in universe. Austere ethics; unmoved by pleasure or pain (Acts 17:18-32).

stones. Used for building (1 K 5:17; Am 5:11), markers (Gn 28:18; 35:14), agricultural tools (see *agriculture*), various instruments (see *trade*). Symbol of hardness (1 Sm 25:37), firmness (Gn 49:24).

stoning. See *punishment.*

storax (stō'răks). See *poplar; stacte.*

storehouse. See *Asuppim.*

stork. Unclean bird (Lv 11:19; Dt 14:18), dwelt in fir trees (Ps 104:17), migratory (Jer 8:7). Black and white storks in Palestine.

Straight street. Street of Damascus (Acts 9:11).

strange fire. Burning of incense not compounded according to Law (Lv 10:1; Nm 3:4).

stranger. See *foreigner; gentile; proselyte.*

straw. Wheat and barley straw used as fodder (Gn 24:25; 1 K 4:28; Is 11:7; 65:25). Mixed with clay for making bricks by Egyptians (Ex 5:7-18).

strong drink (H *shekar,* strong drink). Intoxicating liquor (Nm 28:7) from grapes, barley, honey, dates. Forbidden to priests entering sanctuary (Lv 10:9), Nazirites (Nm 6:3; Ju 13:4, 7; Lk 1:15). Perverted judgment (Pr 31:4, 5).

stumbling block. 1. OT: obstacle which causes person to fall (Lv 19:14). Figuratively, offense (Is 8:14; Jer 6:21). See also *3.* 2. NT: Jesus and cross are stumbling block (1 Co 1:23) and stumbling stone. He stands as antithesis to all egocentric achievement, Jewish or Gentile, and brings reality accessible only to faith. 3. Occasion for inner conflict or sin (Ro 14:13; 1 Co 8:9).

Sua (sū'á). See *Sia.*

Suah (sū'á, sweepings). Asherite (1 Ch 7: 36).

Suba (sū'bá). See *Subas.*

Subai (sū'bā-ī). See *Shalmai.*

Subas (sū'băs). Listed in 1 Esd 5:34 (KJ: Suba).

Sucathites (sū'kăth-īts. KJ: Suchathites). Designation of scribes at Jabez (1 Ch 2: 55).

Succoth (sŭk'ŏth, booths). 1. Place E of Jordan, near Damiyeh; Jacob built booths there (Gn 33:17); assigned to Gadites (Jos 13:27); refused Gideon aid (Ju 8:5-16); site of bronze foundries (1 K 7:46; 2 Ch 4:17). 2. 1st encampment of Israel after leaving Rameses (Ex 12:37; 13:20; Nm 33:5, 6).

Succoth-benoth (sŭk'ŏth-bē'nŏth). Babylonian idol set up in Samaria (2 K 17:30).

Suchathites (sū'kăth-īts). See *Sucathites.*

Sud (sŭd). 1. River of Sura (Bar 1:4). 2. See *Sia.*

Sudias (sū'dĭ-ăs). See *Hodaviah 4.*

suffering. Physical (Gn 3:16; Jb 7:5; Mt 27:27-30) and moral (Jb; Mt 27:39-44) culminate in spiritual suffering through realization that man suffers because of alienation from God (Jb 10:2; Ps 51:4). Christ bore depth of suffering (Ps 22; Mt 27:45, 46) as expiation of sin. Suffering of righteous understood by faith in Christ (Ro 8:24; 2 Co 1:5-14). Suffering is destiny of ungodly. See *punishment.*

Sukkiim (sŭk'ĭ-ĭm). People in army of Shishak; perhaps Arabian tent-dwellers (2 Ch 12:3).

sun. Greater light created (Gn 1:16; Ps 74:16) and preserved (Jer 31:35; Mt 5:45; Ps 104:19) by God; promotes vegetation (Dt 33:14); burns it (Jon 4:8). Worshiped by Hebrews (2 K 21:3, 5; 23:5) and others (Jb 31:26, 27). Metaphorically: glory of Christ (Mt 17:2; Rv 1:16), heavenly beings (Rv 10:1; 12:1), saints (Mt 13:43). Death in prime, loss compared to sun setting at midday (Jer 15:9; Am 8:9; Mi 3:6); darkened sun symbolic of calamity (Eze 32:7; Jl 2:10, 31).

Sunday. Later name of pagan origin for Biblical "first day of the week." See *Lord's day.*

Suph (sōof, reeds). Possibly abbreviation of Yam-suph, Reed Sea (Dt 1:1. KJ: Red Sea).

Suphah (sōo'fà). Probably region of Red Sea (Nm 21:14. KJ: Red Sea).

Sur (sûr). Place on seacoast of Palestine (Jdth 2:28).

supplication (sup'lǐ-kā'shun). Prayer for mercy or favor in special need (1 K 8:28-54; Jb 8:5; Ps 6:9; Eph 6:18; 1 Ti 5:5). See also *prayer.*

surety. Liability assumed for obligation of another (Gn 44:32), especially in trade and finance (Pr 6:1; 22:26); risks warned against (Pr 11:15; 17:18; 20:16).

Susa (sū'zà). See *Shushan.*

Susanchites (sū-săn'kĭts. RSV: men of Susa. RV: Shushanchites). Natives of Susa (Ez 4:9).

Susanna (sū-zăn'à, lily). 1. Ministered to Christ (Lk 8:3). 2. Heroine of apocryphal book History of Susanna.

Susi (sū'sī, horseman). Manassite; father of spy Gaddi (Nm 13:11).

swallow. H *d:ror,* shooting straight out (Ps 84:3; Pr 26:2) and *sus,* leap for joy (Is 38:14; Jer 8:7. KJ: crane). Swifts, swallows, martins abound in Palestine.

swan. See *water hen.*

swearing. See *oath.*

swine. Jews forbidden to eat pork (Lv 11:7; Dt 14:8. See Pr 11:22; Is 65:4; 66:3, 17; Mt 7:6).

sword. See *armor.*

sycamine (sĭk'à-mĭn). Black mulberry (Lk 17:6; 1 Mac 6:34).

sycamore (sĭk'à-mòr). Tree of fig species valued for small, edible fruit, light, durable wood (1 K 10:27; 1 Ch 27:28; Ps 78:47; Lk 19:4). See also *orchard 2.*

Sychar (sī'kär). Village ½ mi N of Jacob's well, 1 mi SE of Shechem (Jn 4:5). Modern Askar.

Sychem (sī'kĕm). See *Shechem 1.*

Syelus (sī-ē'lŭs). See *Jehiel 6.*

Syene (sī-ē'nē. RV: Seveneh). Town on border of Egypt and Ethiopia (Eze 29:10; 30:6). Modern Aswan.

Symeon (sĭm'ê-un). See *Peter; Simeon 3; 5.*

synagog (sĭn'à-gŏg, led together). Jewish assembly for religious and social purposes; undoubtedly originated during captivity (Ez 8:15; Neh 8:2; 9:1). Building erected where ten men of leisure could look after its affairs (elders). Furnishings: 1. Chest for sacred books. 2. Reading platform with lectern. 3. Seats for congregation. 4. Lamps and trumpets. Officers: ruler of synagog, attendant, almoner. Order of service: 1. Shema. 2. Prayer. 3. Reading Law. 4. Reading Prophets. 5. Benediction. See *education.*

Syntyche (sĭn'tĭ-kē, fortunate). Woman Christian at Philippi (Ph 4:2).

Syracuse (sĭr'à-kūs). Leading city on E coast of Sicily (Acts 28:12).

Syria (sĭr'ĭ-à). Aram in OT; territory bounded by Taurus Mts, Euphrates, Arabian Desert, Mediterranean; conquered by David (2 Sm 8; 10); became independent under Solomon (1 K 11:23-25); persistent enemy of Jews (1 K 15:18-20; 20; 22; 2 K 6:8-33; 7; 9:14, 15; 10:32, 33; 13). See also *Aram 5.*

Syriac (sĭr'ĭ-ăk). Language of Syria; Aramaic (as RSV. Dn 2:4).

Syria-maachah (sĭr'ĭ-à-mā'à-kà). See *Maacah 3.*

Syrophenician, Syrophoenician (sī-rô-fê-nĭsh'ăn). Inhabitant of N Phoenicia, absorbed into Syrian kingdom (Mk 7:26).

Syrtis (sûr'tĭs. KJ: quicksands). Sandbanks off shores of N Africa S of Crete (Acts 27:17).

T

Taanach (tā'à-năk). Canaanite city 5 mi SE of Megiddo; conquered by Joshua; assigned to Manasseh and Kohathite Levites (Jos 12:21; 17:11; 21:25 [KJ: Tanach]; Ju 1:27; 1 K 4:12). Probably Aner in 1 Ch 6:70. Modern Taanak.

Taanath-shiloh (tā'à-năth-shī'lō, approach to Shiloh). Town on NE boundary of Ephraim (Jos 16:6) 7 mi SE of Shechem.

Tabaoth, Tabbaoth (tà-bā'ōth, tă-bā'ōth, signets). Nethinim family (Ez 2:43; Neh 7:46; 1 Esd 5:29).

Tabbath (tăb'ăth. Place in Jordan Valley (Ju 7:22). Modern Ras Abu Tabat.

Tabeal (tā'bē-ăl). See *Tabeel 1.*

Tabeel (tā'bē-ĕl, God is good). 1. Rezin of Syria and Pekah of Israel proposed to put his son on throne of Judah (Is 7:6. KJ: Tabeal). 2. Persian official in Samaria (Ez 4:7; 1 Esd 2:16 [KJ, RV: Tabellius]).

Tabellius (tà-bĕl'ĭ-us). See *Tabeel 2.*

taber (tā'bēr. RSV: beat). Beat as one strikes cymbal (Nah 2:7).

Taberah (tăb'ê-rà, burning). Encampment of Israel in wilderness of Paran where fire consumed murmurers; also called Kibroth-hattaavah (Nm 11:3, 34; Dt 9:22).

tabernacle (tăb'ēr-năk-'l). 1. See *tent of meeting.* 2. Movable sanctuary in form of tent where God dwelt as King among His people (Ex 25: 8, 9). Called: *'ohel mo'ed* (RV, RSV: tent of meeting; KJ: tabernacle of congregation. Ex 29:42, 44; Nm 17:4); *'ohel ha'eduth* (tent [tabernacle] of witness [testimony], because it contained ark and 2 tables. Ex 38:21; Nm 9:15; 17:7; 18:2); *mishkan* (dwelling, Ex 25:9); *bayith* (house, Ex 23:19; 34:26); *miqdash* (sanctuary, Ex 25:8); temple (1 Sm 1:9; 3:3). Described in Ex 25:10—27:19: Court was space (100 by 50 cu) inclosed by acacia pillars 5 cu high with silver bands and hooks connected at top by silver-covered rods (KJ: fillets) on which hung sheets of fine linen, embroidered on E entrance. Frame of tabernacle (30×10×10 cu) was gold-covered acacia, covered on outside with double blankets of skin, on inside with embroidered linen tapestry. Tabernacle divided into holy (20×10×10 cu) and most holy (10×10×10 cu) place by linen veil embroidered with cherubim. Altar of burnt offering in court between entrance and tabernacle; laver halfway between altar and tabernacle. In holy place: table of showbread, golden candlestick, altar of incense. Ark of covenant in Holy of Holies. Tabernacle stationed at Gilgal (Jos 4:19) and Ebal (Jos 8: 30-35) during conquest; later at Shiloh (Jos 18:1; 1 Sm 4:17, 22), Nob (1 Sm 21:1), Gibeon (1 Ch 16:39; 21:29). Ark moved to new (Davidic) tabernacle in Jerusalem, finally placed in temple (2 Sm 6:17; 1 Ch 15:1).

tabernacles, feast of. 3d annual festival (15—22 Tisri); commemorated tent life of Israel; celebrated by constructing booths of fruit and palm trees (Ex 23:16; Lv 23:34-43; Dt 16:13-15; 31:10-13; Neh 8). Called feast of ingathering (Ex 23:16), feast of the LORD (Lv 23:39).

Tabitha (tăb'ĭ-thá, gazelle). Christian woman of Joppa, friend of poor, restored to life by Peter (Acts 9:36-42).

table. 1. See showbread; tabernacle. 2. Table spread with food (Ju 1:7; 1 K 2:7; Mt 15:27; Mk 7:28; Lk 16:21). 3. See Lord's Supper. 4. Stand of money-changers (Mt 21:12). 5. Stone tablets on which Law was written (Ex 24:12; 31:18).

tablet. See armlet.

Tabor (tā'bẽr). 1. Limestone mt (Jebel et-Tor), 1,843 ft above sea level, 6 mi E of Nazareth (Jos 19:22); gathering place of Barak (Ju 4:6-14); Gideon's brothers murdered there (Ju 8:21). 2. Levitical town in Zebulun (1 Ch 6:77). 3. Oak (KJ: plain) of Tabor in Benjamin (1 Sm 10:3).

tabret. Timbrel (1 Sm 10:5).

Tabrimon, Tabrimmon (tăb'rĭm-ŏn, Rimmon is good). Father of Ben-hadad I (1 K 15:18).

taches. See clasps.

Tachmonite (tăk'mō-nīt). See Hachmoni.

Tadmor (tăd'môr, palm tree). Desert city (later Palmyra) built by Solomon, probably to control caravan route; magnificent ruins excavated (2 Ch 8:4). Tamar in 1 K 9:18, 19 (see Eze 47:19; 48:28).

Tahan (tā'hăn). Ephraimite (Nm 26:35; 1 Ch 7:25).

Tahapanes (tá-hăp'á-nēz). See Tahpanes.

Tahash (tā'hăsh, fishlike animal. KJ: Thahash). Son of Nahor and Reumah (Gn 22:24).

Tahath (tā'hăth, porpoise). 1. Encampment of Israel in desert (Nm 33:26, 27). 2. Kohathite Levite (1 Ch 6:24, 37). 3. 4. Two Ephraimites (1 Ch 7:20).

Tahchemonite (tä'kĕ-mŏn-īt). See Hachmoni.

Tahpanhes (tä'păn-hĕz). Egyptian city at E mouth of Nile to which Jews fled after murder of Gedaliah (Jer 2:16 [KJ: Tahapanes]; 43:7-9; 44:1; 46:14; Jdth 1:9 [KJ: Taphnes]). Tehaphnehes in Eze 30:18. Modern Tell Defenneh.

Tahpenes (tä'pĕ-nĕz). Egyptian queen (1 K 11:19, 20).

Tahrea (tä'rĕ-á, cunning. Tarea in 1 Ch 8:35). Descendant of Saul (1 Ch 9:41).

Tahtim-hodshi (tä'tĭm-hŏd'shī). See Kadesh 2.

talent. Largest H metal weight. Talent of gold c $30,000; of silver, c $2,000 (Mt 25: 14-30).

talitha cumi (tá-lī'thá koō'mī). Aramaic: "maiden, arise" (Mk 5:41).

Talmai (tăl'mī). 1. Son of Anak (Nm 13:22; Jos 15:14; Ju 1:10). 2. King of Geshur; father-in-law of David (2 Sm 3:3; 13:37).

Talmon (tăl'mŏn, oppressed). Temple porter (1 Ch 9:17) whose descendants returned from captivity (Ez 2:42; Neh 7:45; 11:19; 12:25; 1 Esd 5:28 [RV: Tolman]).

Talsas (tăl'săs). See Elasah 1.

Tamah (tā'má). See Temah.

Tamar (tā'mēr, palm tree). 1. Wife of Er; mother by Judah of Perez and Zerah (Gn 38:6-26; Nm 26:20, 21; Mt 1:3 [KJ: Thamar]). 2. Absalom's sister; abused by Amnon (2 Sm 13; 1 Ch 3:9). 3. Daughter of Absalom; mother of Maacah (2 Sm 14:27; 2 Ch 13:2). 4. See Tadmor.

tamarisk (tăm'á-rĭsk). Bush tree with pinkish flowers (Gn 21:33; 1 Sm 22:6; 31:13. KJ: grove or tree).

tambourine (tăm-boō-rēn'). See timbrel.

Tammuz (tăm'ūz). 1. Semitic god corresponding to G Adonis; brother of Ishtar (Eze 8:14). 2. See time.

Tanach (tā'năk). See Taanach.

Tanhumeth (tăn-hū'mĕth, consolation). Netophathite (2 K 25:23; Jer 40:8).

Tanis (tā'nĭs). See Zoan.

tanner. See trade 8.

Taphath (tā'făth, drop). Solomon's daughter (1 K 4:11).

Taphnes (tăf'nēz). See Tahpanhes.

Taphon (tā'fŏn). See Beth-tappuah.

Tappuah (tă-pū'á, apple). 1. Judahite (1 Ch 2:43). 2. Town in Shephelah of Judah (Jos 15:34). 3. Ephraimite town 8 mi S of Shechem (Jos 16:8; 17:8; 2 K 15: 16 [KJ, RV: Tiphsah]).

Tarah (tā'rá). See Terah 2.

Taralah (tăr'á-lä, staggering). Town of Benjamin (Jos 17:27).

Tarea (tā'rĕ-á). See Tahrea.

tares (G zizanion. RSV: weeds). Probably bearded darnel, poisonous plant; looks like wheat until grown (Mt 13:25-30).

target. 1. Javelin (as RV, RSV. 1 Sm 17:6). 2. Shield (1 K 10:16; 2 Ch 9:15. RSV: shield). See also armor.

Tarpelites (tär'pel-īts. RSV: officials). Colonists of Samaria (Ez 4:9).

Tarshish (tär'shĭsh, foundry, refinery. KJ often: Tharshish). 1. Place on Mediterranean, perhaps in Spain or Tunisia (2 Ch 9:21; 20:36, 37; Ps 72:10). 2. "Ships of Tarshish": large, seagoing ships which carried refined ore or other cargo (1 K 9:26; 10:22; 22:48; 2 Ch 9:21). 3. Son of Javan (Gn 10:4). 4. Benjaminite (1 Ch 7:10). 5. Persian prince (Est 1:14).

Tarsus (tär'sus). Chief city of Cilicia on Cydnus river; free city; noted for education; home of Paul (Acts 9:11, 30; 11:25; 21:39; 22:3; 2 Mac 3:5 [KJ: Thraseas. RV: Thrasaeus]).

Tartak (tär'tăk). Idol introduced into Samaria by Avvites (2 K 17:31).

Tartan (tär'tăn). Title of Assyrian commander-in-chief (2 K 18:17; Is 20:1 [RSV: commander in chief]).

tassel. See fringes.

Tatnai, Tattenai (tăt'nī, -ĕ-nī). Persian governor W of Euphrates; opposed rebuilding of temple (Ez 5:3; 6:6). Sisinnes in 1 Esd 6; 7:1.

tattoo. Prohibited by Levitical law (Lv 19:28. KJ, RV: print).

taxes. Under judges taxes were for support of priests and tabernacles. Under kings: 1. Taxes in kind (1 K 4:7-28). 2. Military service (1 Sm 8:12; 1 Ch 27:1). 3. Special gifts (1 Sm 10:27; 16:20). 4. Duties (1 K 10:15). 5. Tribute and service (Ju 1:28-36; 2 Sm 8:6, 14; 1 K 9:20, 21; 10:15) from subject people. 6. Monopoly of certain commerce (1 K 9:28; 22:48).
Under Persians satraps paid fixed sum (Neh 5:14, 15) collected by tribute, customs, toll (Ez 4:13, 20. See Neh 5:4; 9:37). Priests, Levites, Nethinim, etc exempt (Ez 7:24). Egyptians and Syrians sold right to tax at auction (see 1 Mac 10:29-31; 11:34, 35; 13:37, 39). Romans practiced tax farming (see Mt 17:24; 22:17). See also *census*; *publican*.

Tebah (tē'bà, slaughter). Nahor's son (Gn 22:24).

Tebaliah (tĕb-à-lī'à, LORD has immersed). Merarite Levite (1 Ch 26:11).

Tebeth (tā-vāth'). See *time* 4.

Tehaphnehes (tĕ-hăf'nĕ-hēz). See *Tahpanhes.*

Tehinnah (tĕ-hin'à, grace). Son of Eshton (1 Ch 4:12).

teil tree (tēl. RV, RSV: terebinth). Oak (Is 6:13).

Tekoa, Tekoah (tĕ-kō'à). Town in Judah 6 mi S of Bethlehem (2 Sm 14:2, 4, 9; 1 Mac 9:33 [KJ: Thecoe]); fortified by Rehoboam (2 Ch 11:6); home of Amos (Am 1:1). Modern Tekuʻa.

Tekoite (tĕ-kō'īt). Inhabitant of Tekoa (2 Sm 23:26; Neh 3:5, 27).

Tel-abib (tĕl-ā'bĭb, grain heap). Residence of Ezekiel on Chebar canal (Eze 3:15).

Telah (tē'là). Ephraimite (1 Ch 1:25).

Telaim (tĕ-lā'ĭm, lambs). Probably *Telem 1.*

Tel-assar (tĕl-ăs'ẽr, hill of Asshur). City (Tell Afer?) in upper Mesopotamia (2 K 19:12 [KJ: Thelasar]; Is 37:12).

Telem (tē'lĕm). 1. Town in S Judah (Jos 15:24). Probably same as Telaim (1 Sm 15:4). 2. Divorced foreign wife (Ez 10:24; 1 Esd 9:25 [KJ, RV: Tolbanes]).

Tel-haresha, Tel-harsa, Tel-harsha (tĕl-hà-rē'shà, -hãr'sà, -shà, hill of wood). Place in Babylon (Ez 2:59; Neh 7:6; 1 Esd 5:36 [KJ, RV: Thelersas]).

Tel-melah (tĕl-mē'là, hill of salt). Place in Babylon (Ez 2:59; Neh 7:61; 1 Esd 5:36 [KJ, RV: Thermeleth]).

Tema (tē'mà, south). Son of Ishmael and tribe (lived between Damascus and Medina) descended from him (Gn 25:15; 1 Ch 1:30; Jb 6:19; Is 21:14; Jer 25:23).

Temah (tē'mà). Progenitor of family of Nethinim (Ez 2:53 [KJ: Thamah]; Neh 7:55 [KJ: Tamah]; 1 Esd 5:32 [KJ: Thomoi; RV: Thomei]).

Teman (tē'màn, south). 1. Grandson of Esau; prince of Edom (Gn 36:11, 15, 42; 1 Ch 1:36). 2. District in N Edom inhabited by Teman's descendants (Eze 25:13; Am 1:12; Bar 3:22 [KJ: Theman]); its people noted for wisdom (Jb 2:11; Jer 49:7).

Temani, Temanite (tē'-mà-nī, tē'mǎn-īt). Member of tribe of Teman (Gn 36:34 [KJ: Temani]; Jb 2:11).

Temeni (tĕm'ĕ-nī). Son of Asshur (1 Ch 4:5, 6).

temple. David conceived of building temple (2 Sm 7; 1 Ch 17; 28:12-19); collected material for it (1 Ch 22; 29:1-9). Solomon built temple on Mt Moriah with assistance of Hiram of Tyre. Temple proper was 60 cubits long, 20 broad, 30 high. Built of stone; roofed with cedar; floor covered with cypress overlaid with gold; walls carved cedar overlaid with gold. Holy of Holies was 20 cu cube. Contained: 2 olive wood cherubim (10 cu high; 5 cu wings) overlaid with gold; ark with mercy seat. Holy place was 40 cu long, 20 broad, 30 high. Contained: cedar altar overlaid with gold for incense; 10 golden 7-lamp candlesticks, 10 tables for showbread. Separated from Holy of Holies by cedar doors and veil. On W, E, S were 3 stories of rooms for officials and storage; on N was portico 10 cu wide with pillars (Jachin, Boaz). Next around temple was inner or upper court for priests. Contained: altar of burnt offering (brazen altar, $20 \times 20 \times 10$ cu); brazen or molten sea. Around inner court was outer court for Israel (1 K 6—8; 2 Ch 3—7).
Solomon's temple burned by Chaldeans (2 K 25:8-17; Jer 52:12-23). Zerubbabel's temple larger but less magnificent (Ez 3—6; 2 Mac 10:1-9). Herod rebuilt, enlarged, beautified Zerubbabel's temple. It had outer court (frequented by Gentiles), court of women, inner court. Beautiful Gate on E side (Acts 3:2). See also *nave.*

temple servants. See *Nethinim.*

temptation. Tension between good and evil, duty and desire, in which all live but which is climaxed in specific situations (Gn 3:5; 22:1-19; Mt 6:13). See also *trial.*

Ten Commandments. See *Decalog.*

tent. See *homes* 3; *tabernacle*; *trade* 10.

tent of meeting (KJ: tent or tabernacle of the congregation). Provisional tent where Jehovah met His people (Ex 33:7-11; 34: 34, 35).

tent pin. See *homes* 3.

Tephon (tē'fŏn). See *Beth-tappuah.*

Terah (tē'rà, ibex). 1. Father of Abraham, Nahor, Haran (Gn 11:26; 1 Ch 1:26; Lk 3:34 [KJ: Thara]); served idols (Jos 24:2); moved from Ur to Haran (Gn 11: 24-32). 2. Israelite encampment in wilderness (Nm 33:27, 28. KJ: Tarah).

teraphim (tĕr'à-fĭm. KJ: images). Household deities; figurines in human form (Gn 31:19, 32-35; 1 Sm 19:13; Eze 21:21; Zch 10:2).

terebinth (tĕr'ē-bĭnth). See *oak*; *teil tree.*

Teresh (tē'rĕsh). Chamberlain of Ahasuerus (Est 2:21-23). Tharra in Ap Est 12:1.

Tertius (tûr'shĭ-us, third). Paul's scribe (Ro 16:22).

Tertullus (tẽr-tŭl'us, little third). Roman lawyer hired by Jewish authorities to prosecute Paul before Felix (Acts 24: 1-8).

testament. 1. Will (Heb 9:16, 17). 2. Covenant (Heb 8:6-10; 9:1, 4). 3. Books of Bible pertaining to Old (Gn—Mal) and New (Mt—Rv) covenants. See also *covenant.*

testimony. 1. H *'edhah*, divine commands (Dt 4:45; 6:17). 2. H *'edhuth*, decalog as found in ark (Ex 25:16; 27:21); divine commands (2 K 11:12). 3. H *t:'udhah*, legal evidence; witness (Ru 4:7).

Teta (tē'tà). See *Hatita.*

tetrarch (tē'trärk, ruler of ¼). Prince of small territory (Mt 14:1; Lk 3:1; 9:7; Acts 13:1).

Thaddaeus (thă-dē'us, wise). See *Judas 5*.

Thahash (thā'hăsh). See *Tahash*.

Thamah (thā'mä). See *Temah*.

Thamar (thā'mär). See *Tamar 1*.

Thamnatha (thăm'nä-thä). See *Timnah 3*.

Thara (thā'rä). See *Terah 1*.

Tharra (thăr'ä). See *Teresh*.

Tharshish (thär'shĭsh). See *Tarshish*.

Thassi (thăs'ī). Surname of Simon Maccabaeus (1 Mac 2:3).

theater (place for seeing). Place where games and dramatic productions were exhibited (Acts 19:29, 31).

Thebes (thēbz). Ancient metropolis of Upper Egypt; built on both sides of Nile; famous for temples (Karnak), other ruins (Jer 46:25 [KJ: multitude of No; RV: Amon of No; RSV: Amon of Thebes]; Eze 30:14, 15, 16 [KJ, RV: No]; Nah 3:8 [KJ: populous No. RV No-amon]).

Thebez (thē'bĕz). Village near Shechem; Abimelech slain there (Ju 9:50-55; 2 Sm 11:21). Modern Tubas.

Thecoe (thē-kō'ē). See *Tekoa*.

theft. Punishment severe; 4- and 5-fold restitution; thief could also be sold (Ex 22:1-4).

Thelasar (thĕ-lā'sĕr). See *Tel-assar*.

Thelersas (thĕ-lûr'săs). See *Tel-haresha*.

Theman (thē'măn). See *Teman 2*.

Theocanus (thē-ŏk'ä'nus). See *Tikvah 2*.

theocracy (thē-ŏk'rä-sĭ, ruled by God). Government as existed in OT (1 Sm 8:4-9; 12) with power and authority attributed to God.

Theodotus (thē-ŏd'ō-tus, God-given). Messenger of Nicanor (2 Mac 14:19).

Theophilus (thē-ŏf'ĭ-lus, friend of God). Unknown person, possibly official to whom Lk and Acts are addressed (Lk 1:3; Acts 1:1).

Theras (thē'răs). See *Ahava*.

Thermeleth (thûr'mĕ-lĕth). See *Tel-melah*.

Thessalonians, Epistles to (thĕs-ä-lō'nĭ-anz). 1st epistle written from Corinth to stimulate Thessalonians to good conduct and comfort them concerning those who had died. Outline: 1. Commendation of the Church (1). 2. Paul's Ministry at Thessalonica (2). 3. Paul's Concern and Intercession for Thessalonians (3). 4. Specific Instructions (4, 5). 2d epistle written to correct misconceptions concerning return of Christ. Outline: 1. Comfort in Suffering (1). 2. Apostasy and Man of Sin Precede Coming of Lord (2:1-12). 3. Confidence in Election and Fidelity (2:13-17). 4. Exhortations (3).

Thessalonica (thĕs-ä-lō-nī'kä, victory of Thessaly). Free commercial city on Thermaic Gulf in Macedonia; ruled by politarchs (Acts 17:1-8). Modern Salonika.

Theudas (thū'dăs). Insurgent Jew (Acts 5:36).

thief. See *theft*.

thigh. Placing hand under thigh form of adjuration (Gn 24:2; 47:29).

Thimnathah (thĭm'nä-thä). See *Timnah 1*.

Thisbe (thĭz'bē). Boeotian city (Tob 1:2).

thistles. See *thorns and thistles*.

Thocanus (thō-kā'nŭs). See *Tikvah 2*.

Thomas (tŏm'ăs, twin). One of 12 disciples; surnamed Didymus (G for twin); showed great love for Jesus; doubted resurrection; with apostles after ascension (Mt 10:3; Mk 3:18; Lk 6:15; Jn 11:16; 14:5, 6; 20:24-29; Acts 1:13). Tradition holds he preached in Parthia.

Thomei, Thomoi (thŏm'ē-ī, -ō-ī). See *Temah*.

thorns and thistles. In most passages generic. There are 22 H words for thistle, thorn, brier, bramble; prolific in.Palestine (Gn 3:18). Figuratively: desolation (Pr 24:31; Is 5:6); wickedness (2 Sm 23:6; Nah 1:10); divine visitation (Nm 33:55); messenger of Satan (2 Co 12:7); neglect (Pr 15:19); troubles (Pr 22:5); mockery (Mt 27:29).

Thracia (thrā'shĭ-ä). Classic name for N Turkey (2 Mac 12:35).

Thrasaeus, Thraseas (thrä-sē'us, -ăs). See *Tarsus*.

Three Taverns. Station on Appian way, 30 mi from Rome (Acts 28:15).

threshing, threshing floor. See *agriculture 6*.

throne. Elevated seat of person in authority: king (2 Sm 3:10; 1 K 2:12; Acts 12:21); high priest (1 Sm 1:9); judge (Ps 122:5); military leader (Jer 1:15).

Thummim (thŭm'ĭm). See *Urim and Thummim*.

thunder. Natural (Jb 28:26); rare in Palestine (1 Sm 12:17); accompanied hail in Egypt (Ex 9:22-29); accompanied giving of law (Ex 19:16; 20:18). Symbol of Jehovah's voice (Jb 37:2; Ps 18:13; Is 30:30), glory, power (Ex 19:16; 1 Sm 2:10; 2 Sm 22:14; Is 29:6; Rv 8:5).

Thyatira (thī-ä-tī'rä, burning incense). City on Lycus river, N Lydia, Asia Minor; noted for purple dyeing and weaving (Acts 16:14; Rv 2:18-29).

thyine wood (thī'ĭn. RSV: scented wood). Hard, fragrant, reddish-brown, ornamental wood of tree of cypress family (Rv 18:12).

Tiberias (tĭ-bēr'ĭ-ăs). City on W shore of Sea of Galilee; built by Herod Antipas; named for emperor Tiberius; after AD 70 center of Jewish learning; later Sanhedrin there (Jn 6:1, 23; 21:1). Modern Tabariyeh.

Tiberias, Sea of. See *Galilee, Sea of*.

Tiberius (tĭ-bēr'ĭ-us). Tiberius Claudius Nero; 2d Roman emperor (Lk 3:1. See Mk 12:14; Jn 19:12, 15).

Tibhath (tĭb'hăth, slaughter). See *Betah*.

Tibni (tĭb'nī). Competed with Omri for throne of Israel (1 K 16:21, 22).

Tidal (tī'dăl). King of Goiim; Chedorlaomer's confederate (Gn 14:1, 9).

Tiglath-pileser (tĭg'lăth-pī-lē'zĕr, trust is [Ninip] son of E-Sarra). Assyrian king (Pul); extended Assyrian empire; broke coalition of Uzziah; put Hoshea on throne of Israel; aided Ahaz against Pekah and Rezon (2 K 15:29; 1 Ch 5:26; 2 K 16:7-10). Tilgath-pilneser in 1 Ch 5:6; 2 Ch 28:20.

Tigris (tī'grĭs). Twin stream of Babylonia with Euphrates (Tob 6:1; Jdth 1:6; Sir 24:25). See also *Hiddekel*.

Tikvah (tĭk'vä, expectation). 1. Father of Shallum; father-in-law of Huldah (2 K 22:14). Tokhath (KJ: Tikvath) in 2 Ch 34:22. 2. Father of Jahaziah (Ez 10:15; 1 Esd 9:14 [KJ: Theocanus; RV: Thocanus]).

Tikvath (tĭk'văth). See *Tikvah 1*.

tile (tīl). Thin slab of burnt clay (Eze 4:1 [RSV: brick]; Lk 5:19).

Tilgath-pilneser (tĭl'găth-pĭl-nē'zĕr). See *Tiglath-pileser*.

Tilon (tī'lon). Judahite (1 Ch 4:20).

Timaeus (tĭ-mē'us, honored). Bartimaeus' father (Mk 10:46).

timbrel (tĭm'brel. H *toph, taphah,* beat, strike. Percussion instrument used to mark time (Gn 31:27; Ex 15:20; Ju 11:34; Jb 21:12; Ps 81:2). Also called tabret (KJ, RV), tambourine (RSV).

time. 1. Time and seasons (Gn 1:5,14-16; 8:22; Ex 34:21; Lv 26:5; Ps 74:17; Zch 14:8) mentioned early. G *kairos* often used for set time, *chronos* for period of time, *'aion* (aeon) for perpetuity of time, unbroken age (Mt 12:32); eternity (Lk 1:33; Jn 6:51). **2.** Time dated by important events (Ex 12:40; 1 K 6:1; Eze 33:21); reign of kings (2 K 3:1); rulers (Lk 3:1, 2); phenomena (Am 1:1). **3.** Year was lunar (354 days, 8 hrs, 38 sec), divided into 12 lunar months. 7 intercalary months added over 19 yrs. **4.** Hebrew month began with new moon. Before exile designated by number; named after exile: 1. Abib, Bab, Nisan (Mar—Apr). 2. Iyyar, Zif, or Ziv (Apr—May). 3. Sivan (May—June). 4. Tammuz (June—July). 5. Ab (July—Aug). 6. Elul (Aug—Sept). 7. Tishri, Ethanim (Sept—Oct). 8. Marchesvan, Bul (Oct—Nov). 9. Chislev (KJ: Chislev, Ap Casleu, Nov—Dec.). 10. Tebeth (Dec—Jan). 11. Sebat (Jan—Feb). 12. Adar (Feb—Mar). Abib, Ziv (Zif), Ethanim, Bul of Canaanite origin. Sacred year began with Nisan; secular with Tishri. **5.** Months divided into weeks of seven days ending with Sabbath (Ex 20:11; Dt 5:14, 15). **6.** Day was sunset to sunset (Gn 1:5; Lv 23:32; Ex 12:18); also dawn to darkness (Gn 8:22; Jn 11:9); divided into morning, noon, evening (Ps 55:17). Period of action or condition (Jb 20:28; Ps 20:1; Is 2:12; Jn 8:56; 1 Co 5:5; 2 Ptr 3:10). Sundials used to divide day (2 K 20:11; Is 38:8). Hours first mentioned in Daniel (3:6; 5:5. See Mt 27:45; Jn 11:9). **7.** Night is time of darkness. Divided into periods called watches (Ju 7:19; Ex 14: 24; Mk 13:35; Lk 12:38).

Timna (tĭm'nà, restraint). **1.** Daughter of Seir; sister of Lotan; mother of Amalek (Gn 36:12, 22; 1 Ch 1:39). **2.** Prince of Edom (Gn 36:40; 1 Ch 1:51. KJ: Timnah).

Timnah (tĭm'nà, assigned portion). **1.** Town on N boundary of Judah 3 mi SW of Beth-shemesh (Jos 15:10; 19:43 [KJ: Thimnathah]); occupied by Philistines (Ju 14:1-5 [KJ: Timnath]; 2 Ch 28:18). Modern Tibnah. **2.** Town in hill country of Judah (Gn 38:12-14 [KJ: Timnath]; Jos 15:57). **3.** Town of Judah, possibly same as 1 (1 Mac 9:50. KJ: Thamnatha). **4.** See *Timna 2.*

Timnath (tĭm'năth). See *Timnah 1; 2.*

Timnath-heres (tĭm'năth-hē'rĕz). See *Timnath-serah.*

Timnath-serah (tĭm'năth-sē'rà, double portion). City given Joshua; his home and burial place (Jos 19:50; 24:30). Timnath-heres in Ju 2:9.

Timnite (tĭm'nīt). Designation of Samson's father-in-law (Ju 15:6).

Timon (tī'mon). One of 7 ministers (Acts 6:5).

Timotheus (tĭ-mō'thē-*us*). See *Timothy.*

Timothy (tĭm'ô-thĭ. KJ: usually Timotheus, venerating God). **1.** Son of Jewess and Greek (Acts 16:1-3); religious training by mother and grandmother (2 Ti 1:5; 3:15); converted by Paul (1 Co 4:17; 1 Ti 1:2); active at Lystra, Iconium (Acts 16:1, 2);

set apart for church work by laying on of hands (1 Ti 4:14; 2 Ti 1:6); circumcised (Acts 16:3); companion of Paul (Acts 16: 12; 17:14; 19:22; 20:3-6; 2 Co 1:1; Ph 1:1; Cl 1:1; 1 Th 3:2; 2 Th 1:1; Phlm 1). Tradition makes him bishop at Ephesus. **2.** Leader of Ammonites; opponent of Judas Maccabaeus (1 Mac 5:6, 40; 2 Mac 12:2. KJ, RV: Timotheus).

Timothy, Epistles to. 1st Timothy written by Paul to Timothy at Ephesus to give him manual of instruction for office as head of church at Ephesus (1) and warn against false teachers. Outline: 1. False Doctrine at Ephesus (1). 2. Rules for Worship (2). 3. Presbyters and Deacons (3). 4. False Teachers (4). 5. Attitude Toward Members (5). Social Questions (6).

2d Timothy written to admonish Timothy to be faithful and urge him to come to Rome with Mark. Outline: 1. Christian Ministers (1). 2. Instruction for Various Classes in Church (2). 3. Non-Christians and False Teachers (3).

tin. Well known to ancients; used in manufacture of bronze; probably imported by Phoenicians from Britain. H *b.dil,* tin or lead (Nm 31:22; Is 1:25 [RSV: alloy]; Eze 22:18, 20; 27:12).

Tiphsah (tĭf'sá, ford). **1.** City on Euphrates (1 K 4:24). Modern Thapsacus. **2.** See *Tappuah 3.*

Tiras (tī'răs). Youngest son of Japheth (Gn 10:2; 1 Ch 1:5).

Tirathites (tī'răth-īts). Designation of scribes at Jabez (1 Ch 2:55).

tire. See *bonnet; dress.*

Tirhakah (tûr'há-kä). See *Pharaoh 9.*

Tirhanah (tûr'há-nä). Son of Caleb and Maacah (1 Ch 2:48).

Tiria (tĭr'ĭ-à, fear). Judahite (1 Ch 4:16).

Tirshatha (tûr-shä'thá, revered). Title of Judean governors under Persians (Ez 2: 63; Neh 7:65, 70; 8:9; 10:1. RSV: governor). Attharates in 1 Esd 9:49. Attharias (KJ: Atharias) in 1 Esd 5:40.

Tirzah (tûr'zá, delightfulness). **1.** Youngest daughter of Zelophehad (Nm 26:33; 27: 1-8; 36:1-12; Jos 17:3, 4). **2.** Canaanite city (Jos 12:24); capital of kings of Israel to Omri (1 K 14:17; 15:21, 33; 16:6); 5 mi E of Samaria; seat of Menahem's conspiracy (2 K 15:14, 16). Modern Tell el-Far'ah.

Tishbe (tĭsh'bê, settler. KJ: inhabitants; RV: sojourners). Place in Gilead (1 K 17:1).

Tishbite (tĭsh'bīt). Designation for Elijah (1 K 17:1; 21:17, 28; 2 K 1:3, 8; 9:36). Place unknown.

Tishri (tĭsh'rē). See *time.*

Titans (tī'tănz). Early Palestinian race of giants (Jdth 16:7).

tithe (tĭth). One tenth; Abram gave tithes to Melchizedek (Gn 14:20; Heb 7:2, 6); Jacob to God (Gn 28:22). Mosaic law made tenth of all produce of land and herds sacred to Jehovah (Lv 27:30-33); used for support of Levites (Nm 18: 21-24); tenth of this tithe for priests (Nm 18:25-32). Probably additional tithes used for festivals and poor (Dt 12: 5-18; 14:22-29). Pharisees tithed mint, anise, cummin, rue (Mt 23:23).

Titius (tĭsh'ĭ-*us.* KJ omits; RV: Titus). Pious man of Corinth, surnamed Justus (Acts 18:7).

tittle. Small line, dot, or projection of Hebrew letters (Mt 5:18; Lk 16:17. RSV: dot).

Titus (tī'tŭs). 1. Gentile (Gl 2:3); accompanied Paul, Barnabas to Jerusalem; uncircumcised (Gl 2:3-5); sent to Corinth (2 Co 2:13; 8:6, 16; 12:18); rejoined Paul in Macedonia (2 Co 7:6, 13, 14); went to Dalmatia (2 Ti 4:10). Tradition makes him bishop of Crete. 2. Titus Manius; Roman legate to Jews (2 Mac 11:34. KJ: Manlius). 3. See *Titius*.

Titus, Epistle to. Written by Paul to Titus as manual for ministers and congregation. Outline: 1. Christian Ministers (1). 2. Instructions for Church Members (2). 3. Non-Christians and False Teachers (3).

Tizite (tī'zīt). Designation of Joha (1 Ch 11:45).

Toah (tō'à, child). See *Nahath 2*.

Tob (tŏb, good). Region, perhaps in Hauran, E of Jordan, to which Jephthah fled (Ju 11:3-5; 2 Sm 10:6-14 [KJ: Ish-tob]). See also *Tubias*.

Tob-adonijah (tŏb-ăd-ō-nī'jà, good is Lord Lord). Levite sent by Jehoshaphat to teach Law to people (2 Ch 17:8).

Tobiah (tō-bī'à, good is Lord). 1. Progenitor of family which returned with Zerubbabel (Ez 2:60; Neh 7:62; 1 Esd 5:37 [KJ, RV: Ban]). 2. Ammonite; opposed Nehemiah (Neh 2:10-20).

Tobias (tō-bī'às). 1. Tobit's son (Tob 4; 5). 2. Father of Hyrcanus (2 Mac 3:11).

Tobie (tō'bī). See *Tubias*.

Tobiel (tō-bī'el). Father of Tobit (Tob 1:1).

Tobijah (tō-bī'jà, good is Lord). 1. Levite; taught Law to people (2 Ch 17:8). 2. Jew; brought gold and silver offerings of Jews in exile for crown for Joshua, high priest (Zch 6:10-14).

Tobit (tō'bĭt, goodness). Father of Tobias; author of apocryphal book (Tob).

Tochen (tō'kĕn, weight). Town of Simeon (1 Ch 4:32).

Togarmah (tō-gär'mà). Descendant of Japheth (Gn 10:3; 1 Ch 1:6). See also *Bethtogarmah*.

Tohu (tō'hū, low). See *Nahath 2*.

Toi (tō'ī). See *Tou*.

Tokhath (tŏk'hăth). See *Tikvah 1*.

Tola (tō'là, crimson worm). 1. Son of Issachar; progenitor of Tolaites (Gn 46:13; Nm 26:23; 1 Ch 7:1). 2. Judge; son of Puah (Ju 10:1, 2).

Tolad (tō'lăd). See *Eltolad*.

Tolaites (tō'là-īts). See *Tola 1*.

Tolbanes (tŏl'bà-nēz). See *Telem 2*.

toll. Revenue on bridges, fords, highways (Ez 4:13; 7:24). See also *taxes*.

Tolman (tŏl'măn). See *Talmon*.

tomb. See *burial*.

tooth. Used to illustrate law of retaliation (Ex 21:24; Mt 5:38). Figuratively: plenty (Gn 49:12); teeth of beasts: cruelty, rapacity (Dt 32:24; Jb 4:10); cleanness of teeth: famine (Am 4:6); gnashing teeth: rage, despair (Jb 16:9; Ps 37:12; Mt 8:12); oppression (Pr 30:14).

topaz (tō'păz). Variously hued gem corresponding to chrysolite (Ex 28:17; Jb 28:19; Rv 21:20).

Tophel (tō'fĕl). Place on boundary of desert of Paran (Dt 1:1). Perhaps modern Tafileh.

Tophet, Topheth (tō'fĕt). Place E or SE of Jerusalem in Valley of Hinnom, polluted by worship of Moloch; dumping and burning place for refuse (2 K 23:10; Jer 7:31; 19:6-14).

torch (KJ usually: lamp). Portable light of unknown construction (Ju 7:16; Eze 1:13; Dn 10:6; Neh 2:3, 4; Zch 12:6; Jn 18:3).

Tormah (tôr'mà, fraud). See *Arumah*.

tortoise (tôr'tŭs). See *lizard, great*.

Tou (tō'ŏō). King of Hamath; congratulated David (2 Sm 8:9, 10 [KJ, RV: Toi]; 1 Ch 18:9, 10).

Toubiani (tū-bĭ-ā'nī). See *Tubieni*.

tower. For observation or defense at exposed places (Gn 35:21; 2 Ch 26:10; Is 21:5, 8, 11), in vineyards (Mt 21:33), for shepherds (Mi 4:8).

Tower of Babel. See *Babel*.

town clerk. Official in Ephesus; ranked next to president of council (Acts 19:35-41).

Trachonitis (trăk-ō-nī'tĭs, rough). Rugged region, 370 sq mi, S of Damascus (Lk 3:1).

trade. 1. In Palestine trades were often carried on in home.

2. Weaving of mats and baskets. Mats woven by braiding straws into cords, winding into spiral or oblong design, sewing together. Another method: lay straw or pliable rushes on floor, weave other strands over and under. Or fiber laid so that it crossed at center, radiated uniformly in all directions. Weaver then worked over and under these ribs in ever-increasing circles. Baskets woven same way as mats, but material pulled tighter as each circle was completed. Strong baskets woven from pliable branches of willow, dogwood, etc.

3. Spinning. Wool washed and combed to straighten fiber, then tuft of wool twisted into yarn between fingers while continually pulling in other strands to keep yarn of uniform thickness; done more rapidly and uniformly by using distaff. Flax, cotton spun in same way.

4. Weaving. Loom was rectangular framework of wooden slats with small nails or pegs around edges; yarn tied to peg at one edge, then passed back and forth to corresponding pegs until framework was covered with parallel strands; shuttle then passed vertically over and under strands.

5. Carpentry. Tools: saw (Is 10:15), axe (Jer 10:3), adze, chisels, hammer, nails (Jer 10:4), mallet, awl (Ex 21:6), drill (worked with bow like Indian fire bow), chalk line, plummet, rule. Carpenter made agricultural machinery, woodwork for house, furniture, wooden utensils. Because of scarcity of good timber, Palestinian carpenter was handicapped in competition with carpenters from some other countries (2 Sm 5:11; 1 K 5:2-8).

6. Pottery and Brickmaking. Palestine has good supply of clay; many items made from it (Gn 24:14-20; Ec 12:6; 1 K 17:12; Lv 6:28; 11:33). Place where potter's clay was dug was called "potter's field" (Mt 27:7). Pottery was roughly shaped by hand or worked on potter's wheel (Jer 18:3-6), dried and baked in kiln. Brick was molded in wooden molds, baked in loosely built stacks or in kiln (Ex 9:8-10. KJ, RV: furnace).

7. Metal Casting and Forging. Well-equipped metalworker's shop contained smelter in which rough chunks of iron or copper, or bits of scrap metal, could be melted down in charcoal flame brought to white heat by blast of air from bellows (Jer 6:29. See Ps 12:6; Eze 22:18). After metal was formed it was heated in smaller furnace, beaten into shape on anvil (Is 41:7) with hammer (Gn 4:22; 1 Sm 13:19-21). Molten copper was poured into sheets as thin as possible, hammered into vessels or other desired forms (Ex 27:3;

2 Sm 8:10; **2 Ch** 4:16). Gold and silver were worked similarly though much more carefully. Smelters, hammers, tongs, chisels, or "graving tools" (**Ex** 32:4) were smaller.

8. Tanning. After all loose matter was scraped off, hide was soaked in solution of lime or lye to loosen hair and fatty matter; then scraped clean, washed, soaked in tanning solution (made of oak bark). Leather could be softened with oil (**Ex** 25:5; 26:14; **Acts** 10:6).

9. Leatherwork. Leatherworker used low bench, awls of various sizes, knives, needles, waxed linen thread; made sandals, parts of armor, aprons, belts, shoes, purses, etc (**Gn** 3:21; **2 K** 1:8; **Eze** 16:10; **Mt** 3:4).

10. Tentmaking. Tentmaker used knives, shears, awl, needle, thread. Best tents woven of goats' hair, usually dark in color (**Ex** 25:4; **Acts** 18:3).

11. Stonecutting. Stonecutter quarried stone with pickaxe, crowbar, chisel, mallet, hammer, saw, drill; with chisel and mallet dressed stone to desired shape and smoothness.

12. Gem cutter used hammers, chisels, files, drills to cut, grind precious, semiprecious stones into ornaments (Klinck). See also *commerce*.

tradition (trå-dĭsh'un). 1. Interpretations of OT Law (**Mt** 15:1-9; **Gl** 1:14). 2. Apostolic testimony; teaching handed down by witnesses to Christ (**Lk** 1:2; **Ro** 6:17; 1 **Co** 11:2; 15:3-9; 2 **Ptr** 2:21).

transfiguration (trăns-fĭg-û-rā'shun). Glorified manifestation of Jesus to 3 disciples on mount, probably Hermon (**Mt** 17:1-13; **Mk** 9:2-13; **Lk** 9:28-36).

treasure. Anything (grain, wine, gold, silver) collected in storehouses (1 **K** 14:26; 15:18; **Mt** 2:11; 6:19). Figuratively: God's resources in nature (**Dt** 28:12; **Jb** 38:22); God's peculiar people (**Ex** 19:5); piety (**Is** 33:6); Gospel (2 **Co** 4:7); Christ-centered wisdom and knowledge (**Cl** 2:3).

treasury. Place in temple where gifts were received (1 **Ch** 9:26; **Mk** 12:41; **Lk** 21:1; **Jn** 8:20).

trespass. See *sin*.

trial. Testing, usually by painful process, for purpose of purifying or achieving good (**Ps** 7:9; **Zch** 13:9; 1 **Ptr** 1:6, 7).

tribe. H tribes sprang from 12 sons of Jacob with Joseph's sons (Ephraim, Manasseh) forming 2 (**Gn** 48:5; **Nm** 26: 5-51; **Jos** 13:7-33; 15—19); no tribal territory allotted to Levi. Heads or elders of tribe had great influence (1 **Sm** 8; 2 **Sm** 3:17; 2 **K** 23:1). Tribes waged war separately (**Ju** 1:2-4; 2 **Sm** 2:4-9; 1 **Ch** 5:18-22).

tribulation (trĭb-û-lā'shun). See *persecution; suffering*.

tribute. 1. See *taxes*. 2. Temple tax (**Mt** 17:24. RSV: half-shekel tax).

trigon (trī'gŏn. KJ, RV: sackbut). Triangular stringed instrument (**Dn** 3:5, 7, 10, 15).

Trinity (trĭn'ĭ-tĭ). Ecclesiastical term for eternal, infinite Spirit, subsisting in three Persons: Father, Son, Holy Spirit (**Is** 48: 16; 63:9, 10; **Mt** 3:13-17; 28:19), in one undivided, indivisible essence (**Dt** 6:4; **Is** 44:6; **Jn** 10:30; 1 **Ti** 2:5).

Tripolis (trĭp'ô-lĭs, 3 cities). Aradus, Tyre, Sidon (2 **Mac** 14:1).

triumph (trī'ŭmf). Celebration of victory (**Ex** 15:1-21; **Ju** 5; 11:34-37; 1 **Sm** 18: 6-8).

Troas (trō'ăs). City in Mysia 6 mi S of Hellespont entrance near site of ancient Troy; founded by Alexander the Great (**Acts** 16:8-11; 20:5-10; 2 **Ti** 4:13).

Trogyllium (trô-jĭl'ĭ-um). Town and promontory on W coast of Asia Minor opposite Samos (**Acts** 20:15).

troop. 1. Band of marauders, or raiders (**Gn** 49:19; 2 **Sm** 22:30; **Jer** 18:22). 2. See *Gad* 4.

Trophimus (trŏf'ĭ'mus, nourishing). Christian at Ephesus (**Acts** 20:4; 21:29; 2 **Ti** 4:20).

trumpet. Wind instrument of ram's or goat's horn or metal (**Nm** 10:2); used for music or battle and other signals (**Ju** 3:27; 1 **K** 1:39; **Is** 18:3; **Hos** 8:1; **Am** 3:6; 1 **Th** 4:6 [KJ, RV: trump]).

trumpets, feast of. New Year's Day festival of Jewish civil year. Feast of new moon on 1st of Tisri (**Nm** 29:1-6; **Lv** 23: 24, 25).

truth. That which is eternal, ultimate, secure, steadfast. God is truth in contradistinction to all that is relative and derived (**Ps** 31:5; **Is** 65:16; **Jn** 17:3; 1 **Jn** 5:20); cannot be lie (2 **Ti** 2:13; **Heb** 6:18). All that comes from God is true (**Ps** 33:4 [RV, RSV: faithfulness]). Truth is manifested in Christ (**Jn** 1:14, 17; 14:6). Spirit imparts truth of Christ (1 **Jn** 2:20-22), through whom truth is known (**Jn** 8:31, 32) and whose Word is truth (**Jn** 17:17-19; 2 **Co** 4:2; **Gl** 5:7; **Eph** 1:13; **Ja** 1:18). Truth is known in sanctified life (**Jn** 17:7-19; 1 **Jn** 2:4-6).

Tryphaena, Tryphena (trī-fē'nå, delicate). Christian woman at Rome (**Ro** 16:12).

Trypho, Tryphon (trī'fô, -fŏn. Surname of Diodotus, Syrian king (1 **Mac** 12:39).

Tryphosa (trī-fō'så, delicate). Christian woman at Rome (**Ro** 16:12).

Tubal (tū'bål). Son of Japheth (**Gn** 10:2; 1 **Ch** 1:5); tribe associated with Javan (**Is** 66:19) and Meshech (**Eze** 32:26).

Tubal-cain (tū'bål-kān, Tubal the smith). Son of Lamech; worker in brass (RSV: bronze) and iron (**Gn** 4:22).

Tubias (tū'bĭ-ås. KJ: Tobie. RSV: Tob). District E of Jordan; probably Tob (1 **Mac** 5:13).

Tubieni (tū-bĭ-ē'nī. RSV: Toubiani). Inhabitants of Tob (2 **Mac** 12:17).

tumor (tū'mēr). See *disease, emerod*.

turban. See *bonnet; diadem; dress; mitre*.

turtle, turtledove. Common, collared, and palm turtledoves in Palestine (**Gn** 15:9; **Ps** 74:19); used for sacrifice by poor people (**Lv** 12:6-8; **Lk** 2:24).

Twin Brothers. Dioscuri, Roman divinities (Castor and Pollux), sons of Leda, protectors of sailors (**Acts** 28:11. KJ: Castor and Pollux).

Tychicus (tĭk'ĭ-kus, fortune). Disciple, messenger, spokesman of Paul (**Acts** 20:4; **Eph** 6:21, 22; **Cl** 4:7, 8).

type. See *antitype*.

Tyrannus (tĭ-răn'us, tyrant). Greek rhetorician; Paul carried on his work in Tyrannus' school (**Acts** 19:9).

Tyre, Tyrus (tīr, tī'rus, rock. KJ: Tyrus in OT prophets, apocrypha). Phoenician city on Mediterranean; built partly on rocky coast, partly on island; Alexander the Great built causeway to island. David formed alliance with it (2 **Sm** 5:11; 1 **K** 5:1; 2 **Ch** 2:3); its merchants powerful (**Is** 23:8); denounced by prophets (**Is** 23:1-17; **Jer** 27:3; **Eze** 26—28). Jesus visited its region (**Mt** 15:21; **Mk** 7:24. See **Mt** 11:21, 22). Paul stayed there 7 days (**Acts** 21:3, 4).

U

Ucal (ū'kăl, I am strong). Obscure word; usually taken as name of pupil of Agur (Pr 30:1).

Uel (ū'ĕl, will of God). Divorced foreign wife (Ez 10:34). Juel (RSV: Joel) in 1 Esd 9:34.

Ulai (ū'lī). River near Susa in Persia on whose bank Daniel saw vision of ram and he-goat (Dn 8).

Ulam (ū'lăm, first). 1. Manassite (1 Ch 7: 16, 17). 2. Descendant of Jonathan (1 Ch 8:39, 40).

ulcer. See *disease.*

Ulla (ŭl'á, yoke). Asherite (1 Ch 7:39).

Ummah (ŭm'á). City of Asher (Jos 19:30).

umpire. See *daysman.*

unbelief. Lack of faith; rejection of promises and threats of God's Word (Heb 3: 19); especially refusal to accept Christ (Jn 3:36; Ro 11:20).

uncircumcised. 1. Gentiles (Gn 34:14; Ju 14:3; 1 Sm 14:6; Ro 4:9). 2. Tree under 3 yrs old (Lv 19:23). 3. Ears which do not hear truth (Jer 6:10; Acts 7:51). 4. Hearts not open to God (Lv 26:41; Jer 4:4; Acts 7:51). See also *circumcision.*

uncle. 1. Father's brother (2 K 24:17). 2. Kinsman on father's side (Lv 10:4; Am 6:10).

unclean. 1. Food: animals which do not part hoof and chew cud; animals and birds which eat blood or carrion; insects which lack hind legs for jumping; water creatures without scales and fins (Lv 11—15; Nm 19; Dt 14). 2. Contact with dead rendered unclean (Lv 11:24-40; 17:15; Nm 19:16-22; 31:19). 3. Leprosy (Lv 13; 14; Nm 5:2), sexual discharge (Lv 15) rendered unclean.

unction (ŭngk'shŭn). See *anoint.*

understanding. See *knowledge; wisdom.*

ungodly. 1. Worthless (2 Sm 22:5; Ps 18:4. RV: ungodliness. RSV: perdition). 2. Unjust; evil (Jb 16:11). 3. Wicked (as RV, RSV. 2 Ch 19:2; Ps 1:1; 3:7; 73:12). 4. Impious (Ps. 43:1; Ro 4:5; 5:6; 1 Ti 1:9; 1 Ptr 4:18 [RSV: impious]; 2 Ptr 2:5, 6; 3:7; Jude 4, 15).

unicorn (ū'ni-kôrn). See *wild ox.*

unknown god. Altars erected to unknown gods, to appease deities which might have been overlooked (Acts 17:23).

unleavened. Bread without yeast (Gn 19:3); eaten at Passover (Ex 12:8; 13:3-10).

Unni (ŭn'ī, oppressed). 1. Levite; musician (1 Ch 15:18, 20). 2. See *Unno.*

Unno (ŭn'ō, oppressed. KJ: Unni). Levite (Neh 12:9).

unquenchable fire. See *hell.*

unrighteous. See *justice; righteous; unbelief; ungodly.*

Uphaz (ū'făz). Region rich in gold (Jer 10:9; Dn 10:5).

upper chamber, room. See *homes* 4.

upright (H *yashar,* straight, right, level). Impartial, righteous, just, possessing integrity (2 Ch 29:34; Jb 17:8; Ps 25:8; 92:15).

Ur (ûr). 1. City in S Babylonia near Uruk; called Ur of Chaldees; Abraham's native city (Gn 11:28, 31; 15:7; Neh 9:7). Modern Tell Mugheir. 2. Father of Eliphal (1 Ch 11:35); identified with Ahasbai (2 Sm 23:34).

Urbane, Urbanus (ûr-bān', -bā'nus, urbane). Roman Christian (Ro 16:9).

Uri (ū'rī, fiery). 1. Father of Bezalel (Ex 31:2). 2. Father of Geber (1 K 4:19). 3. Divorced foreign wife (Ez 10:24).

Uriah (û-rī'á, flame of LORD). 1. Hittite; made victim to David's infatuation for Bathsheba, his wife (2 Sm 11; Mt 1:6 [KJ: Urias]). 2. Chief priest in Ahaz' reign; witnessed tablet by Isaiah (Is 8:2). Urijah in 2 K 16:10-16. 3. Father of Meremoth (Ez 8:33; 1 Esd 8:62 [KJ: Iri; RV: Urias]; Neh 3:4, 21 [KJ: Urijah]). 4. Priest; stood by Ezra as he read Law (Neh 8:4 [KJ: Urijah]; 1 Esd 9:43 [KJ, RV: Urias]). 5. Prophet; slain by Jehoiakim after he predicted destruction of Judah (Jer 26:20-23. KJ: Urijah).

Urias (û-rī'ăs). See *Uriah 1; 3; 4.*

Uriel (ū'rī-el, light of God). 1. Kohathite Levite (1 Ch 6:24). Probably same as Zephaniah 3. 2. Kohathite Levite chief; helped bring ark from house of Obededom (1 Ch 15:5, 11). 3. Maternal grandfather of Abijah 1 (2 Ch 13:2). 4. Angel (2 Esd 4:1). RV, RSV: Jeremiel in v 36.

Urijah (û-rī'já). See *Uriah 2; 3; 4; 5.*

Urim and Thummim (ū'rĭm and thŭm'ĭm, lights and perfections). Exact nature unknown; placed in breastpiece of high priest; used in determining will of Jehovah (Ex 28:30; Lv 8:8; Nm 27:21); mentioned once during kings (1 Sm 28:6); missing after captivity (Ez 2:63; Neh 7: 65).

usury (RSV: interest). See *loans.*

Uta (ū'tá). See *Uthai* 3.

utensil. See *homes* 5; *trade* 7.

Uthai (ū'thī). 1. Son of Ammihud (1 Ch 9:4). 2. Sons returned from captivity (Ez 8:14; 1 Esd 8:40 [KJ, RV: Uthi]). 3. Listed in 1 Esd 5:30 (KJ, RV: Uta).

Uthi (ū'thī). See *Uthai* 2.

uttermost, utmost sea. See *Mediterranean Sea.*

Uz (ŭz). 1. Land of Job; usually located in Arabian desert adjacent to Edom (Jb 1:1; Jer 25:20; Lm 4:21). 2. Son of Aram; grandson of Shem (Gn 10:23; 1 Ch 1:17). 3. Son of Dishan; grandson of Seir (Gn 36:28). 4. Son of Nahor (Gn 22:21. KJ: Huz).

Uzai (ū'zī). Father of Palal (Neh 3:25).

Uzal (ū'zăl). Son of Joktan; founder of tribe which lived in Yemen with Uzal (later Sana) as capital (Gn 10:27; 1 Ch 1:21; Eze 27:19 [RSV]).

Uzza (ŭz'á, strength). 1. Benjaminite (1 Ch 8:7). 2. Progenitor of Nethinim (Ez 2:49; Neh 7:51; 1 Esd 5:31 [KJ: Azia; RV: Ozias]). 3. Owned garden near Jerusalem in which Manasseh and Amon were buried (2 K 21:18, 26). 4. 5. See *Uzzah.*

Uzzah (ŭz'á, strength). 1. Son of Abinadab; slain by Lord for putting hand to cart bearing ark when oxen stumbled (2 Sm 6:3-11; 1 Ch 13:7-11 [KJ, RV: Uzza]). 2. Merarite Levite (1 Ch 6:29. KJ: Uzza).

Uzzen-sheerah, Uzzen-sherah (ŭz'en-shē'ê-rá, -shē'rá). Village near Beth-horon built by Sheerah (1 Ch 7:24).

Uzzi (ŭz'ī, strength). 1. Son of Bukki; father of Zerahiah; ancestor of Ezra (1 Ch 6:5, 6; Ez 7:4; 1 Esd 8:2 [KJ, RV: Savias]; 2 Esd 1:2 [KJ, RV: Ozias]). 2. Issachar's grandson (1 Ch 7:2, 3). 3. Benjaminite; son of Bela (1 Ch 7:7). 4. Ancestor of a Benjaminite house (1 Ch 9:8, 9). 5. Overseer of Levites after captivity (Neh 11:22). 6. Priest (Neh 12:19). 7. Priest; participated at dedication of Jerusalem's walls (Neh 12:42).

Uzzia (ŭ-zī'å, might of LORD). One of David's heroes (1 Ch 11:44).

Uzziah (ŭ-zī'å, LORD is strength). **1.** 10th king of Judah; also called Azariah (see *Azariah 3*); son of Amaziah; fought successfully against Mehunim, Arabs, Philistines; developed agriculture; strengthened Jerusalem; raised army; died of leprosy (2 K 14:21, 22; 15; 1 Ch 3:12; 2 Ch 26; Is 7:1; Hos 1:1; Am 1:1; Zch 14:5; Mt 1:8, 9 [KJ: Ozias]). **2.** Ancestor of Samuel (1 Ch 6:24). Azariah in 1 Ch 6:36. **3.** Father of Jehonathan, overseer of David's storehouses (1 Ch 27:25). **4.**

Divorced foreign wife (Ez 10:21). Azarias (RSV; Azariah) in 1 Esd 9:21. **5.** Judahite (Neh 11:4). **6.** Magistrate of Bethulia (Jdth 6:15. KJ, RV: Ozias).

Uzziel (ŭ-zī'el, might of God). **1.** Levite; son of Kohath (Ex 6:18, 22; Nm 3:19, 30; Lv 10:4); ancestor of Uzzielites (Nm 3: 27. See 1 Ch 15:10). **2.** Simeonite captain (1 Ch 4:42). **3.** Benjaminite (1 Ch 7:7). **4.** See *Azarel 2*. **5.** Levite; helped cleanse temple (2 Ch 29:14-19). **6.** Priest in charge of sacred vessels; helped repair walls (Neh 3:8).

Uzzielites (ŭ-zī'el-īts). See *Uzziel 1*.

V

Vaheb (vā'hĕb). See *Waheb*.

vail. See *dress; veil*.

Vaizatha, Vajezatha (vī'zå-thå, vå-jĕz'å-thå). Haman's son (Est 9:9).

vale, valley. Plain (Dt 8:7; Is 40:4), valley (Jos 7:24), ravine (Jos 15:8). See *Shephelah*.

Vaniah (vå-nī'å). Son of Bani; divorced foreign wife (Ez 10:36); 1 Esd 9:34 [KJ, RV: Anos]).

vanity. 1. Unprofitableness (Ec 1:2). **2.** Nothingness, emptiness; as idols (2 K 17: 15; Is 41:29), lies (Ps 4:2). **3.** Human help is vain (Ps 60:11). **4.** Iniquity and sin (Ps 119:37; Ro 8:20. RSV: futility).

Vashni (văsh'nī). See *Joel 2*.

Vashti (văsh'tī). Wife of Ahasuerus; queen of Persia (Est 1:9-22).

Vedan (vē'dån. KJ: Dan also; RSV: wine). Perhaps place name (Eze 27:19).

vegetable. See *food 3*.

veil. 1. See *dress*. **2.** Screen separating Holy Place and Most Holy Place in tabernacle and temple (Ex 26:31-35; 2 Ch 3:14; Mt 27:51).

vermilion (vēr-mĭl'yun). See *color*.

versions of the Bible (vûr'shunz). Translations of Bible. Greek: Septuagint (LXX, OT) started c 250 BC, completed over long period of time. Aquila, Theodotion, Symmachus (OT 2d century AD). Latin: Old Latin (160—200 AD); Vulgate of Jerome (c 382) long standard. Syriac date from 2d century; Peshitta of OT in use by 3d century. Aramaic: Targums (Babylonian, Jerusalem, Palestinian) are Aramaic paraphrases of OT begun before time of Christ. Coptic: Sahidic (3d century); Bohairic (c 6th century). Ethiopic date from 4th, 5th century. Gothic prepared by Ulfilas c 350. Armenian c 400. Georgian from 5th, 6th century. Slavonic by Cyril, Methodius in 9th century. Arabic version made in 10th century. Some English versions: Wyclifite (1382—1384); Tyndale (NT, c 1526); Coverdale (1535); Matthew's Bible (1537); Great Bible (1539); Taverner (1539); Geneva Bible (1560); Bishops' Bible (1568); King James (KJ), or Authorized Version (AV, 1611); Revised Version (RV, 1881, 1884); American Standard Version (ASV, 1901); Revised Standard Version (RSV, 1946, 1952). Many private versions. German translations from Vulgate as early as 14th century. Luther translated OT from Hebrew (1534) and NT from Greek (1522).

vine. See *vineyard*. Figuratively: Israel (Ps 80:8); happiness and contentment (1 K 4:25; Ps 128:3; Mi 4:4); apostate Israel wild grapes, strange vine (Is 5:2; Jer 2:21); empty vine: spiritual unfruitfulness (Hos 10:1); vine of Sodom: god-

less people (Dt 32:28-33); vine and branches: Christ and believers (Jn 15: 1-6).

vinegar. See *vineyard 3*.

vineyard. 1. Israelites expanded industry they found in Canaan (Nm 13:23-27). Land cleared of stones, terraced (Is 5:1, 2; Mi 1:6); choicest shoots planted, carefully cultivated, trained (1 K 4:25; Hos 2:12). Wall often built around vineyard, watchtower erected (Is 5:1-7; SS 2:15).

2. Harvest began in June; bunches of grapes gathered in baskets (Jer 6:9; Rv 14:14-20), taken to winepress. Winepress usually cut from solid rock, 6 to 12 ft in diameter, 1 to 2 ft deep, with trench leading to deeper receptacle. Grapes tramped by men until juice flowed into lower receptacle. Other methods of pressing undoubtedly used.

3. Grape juice was taken to homes, allowed to ferment, poured off lees, or dregs (Is 25:6), stored in large jars of stone or bottles of goatskins (Mt 9:17). Pulp might be placed in vat covered with water, allowed to ferment to make vinegar or poor grade of wine (Ps 69:21; Mt 27:48).

4. Fresh grape juice might also be boiled down to make "grape honey." Grapes eaten raw in season and dried to make raisins (1 Sm 25:18). (Klinck)

vineyards, plain of. See *Abelcheramim*.

vintage (vin'tij). Time of joy (Ju 9:27; Is 16:10; Jer 25:30). See also *vineyard*.

viol (vī'ul). See *music*.

viper. See *serpent*.

Virgin Mary (vûr'jĭn mâr'ĭ). See *Mary, Mother of Jesus*.

vision. Inspired dream phantasy or apparition (Nm 24:4; Is 6; Eze 1; 8—10; Dn 7; 8; Acts 10:9-16; 26:13-19; 2 Co 12:1-4).

vocation. Act of Spirit of God in Christ whereby He, according to His purpose and grace, calls people through Word and sacraments out of darkness to light, places them into special relationship to Himself by participation in Christ through faith (Is 41:8, 9; Mt 22:1-14; Ro 1:6, 7, 16; 6:1-11; 8:28-30; 1 Co 1:9; 10:16, 17; Gl 5:8; Cl 3:15; 2 Ti 1:9; 1 Ptr 2:9). People called to be holy (Ro 1:7; 1 Co 1:2) in the body of Christ (Cl 3:15). Call of God becomes vocation of individual in life, namely, to build body of Christ (Eph 4:11, 12) by serving God and man in circumstances of environment (1 Co 7:17-24; Ph 1:27; 1 Th 2:12). While various gifts of Christians are used for common good (1 Co 12), God also calls to special service (Ex 3:4; 1 Sm 3:10-14; Mt 4:21; Ro 1:1).

Vophsi (vŏf'sī). Father of spy Nahbi (Nm 13:14).

vow. Expression of religious character pledging either to do something or abstain from something. OT did not require vows but regulated them (Lv 27; Nm 30; Dt 23:18-23).

vulture. 1. See *eagle*. 2. Gier eagle is soaring bird of prey. KJ: gier eagle for H *raham* (Lv 11:18 [RV, RSV: vulture]; Dt 14:12 [RSV: vulture]). 3. RV, RSV: kite

for H *da'ah* and *dayyah* (Lv 11:14; Dt 14: 13; Is 34:15. KJ: vulture); KJ: kite for *'ayyah* in Lv 11:14 (RV, RSV: falcon) and Dt 14:13 (also RSV. RV: falcon). 4. RV, RSV: falcon in Jb 28:7 (KJ: vulture). 5. Osprey (ospray) is unclean bird of the eagle family (Lv 11:13; Dt 14:12). 6. Ossifrage (H *peres*) largest of vultures of Palestine (Lv 11:13 [RV: gier eagle]; Dt 14:12 [RV: gier eagle; RSV: vulture]).

W

wafer. Thin meal cake. Offering wafers were unleavened wheat wafers spread with oil (Ex 16:31; 29:2; Lv 2:4; 7:12; Nm 6:15; 1 Ch 23:29 [KJ: cakes]).

wages. In early times often paid in kind (Gn 29:15, 20; 30:28-34). Mosaic law demanded daily payment of wages (Lv 19:13; Dt 24:14, 15; Mt 20:8). Withholding wages condemned (Jer 22:13; Ml 3:5; Jas 5:4). See also *labor; servant*.

wagon. Planks fixed on 2 circular solid block wheels (Gn 45:19-27; 46:5; Nm 7: 3-8; Eze 23:24; 26:10 [KJ: wheels]). See also *cart; chariot*.

Waheb (wā'hĕb). Place near Arnon (Nm 21:14, 15. KJ: what she did; RV: Vaheb).

walk. 1. Hebrews frequently journeyed on foot. 2. Conduct, behavior, spiritual character (Gn 17:1; Ex 16:4; Lv 18:3, 4; Ro 8:1, 4; 2 Co 5:7; Gl 5:16; 2 Ptr 2:10; 1 Jn 1:6, 7).

wall. 1. See *homes*. 2. City walls often of clay (Ps 62:3; Is 30:13). Stone walls around fortified cities (Neh 4:3; Is 2:15; Zph 1:16). 3. Symbol of truth and strength (Jer 15:20), protection (Zch 2:5), salvation (Is 26:1). See also *fort*.

wall of partition. Separated Holy Place from Most Holy Place (1 K 6:31, 35; figuratively in Eph 2:14).

wallet. See *scrip* 2.

wanderings of Israel. See *Moses*.

war. Contest often preceded by sacred acts (Ju 1:1; 20:2; 1 Sm 7:9; 14:37; 1 K 22: 6); battle signal (1 Sm 17:52; Is 42:13); combat hand-to-hand engagements (2 Sm 1:23; 2:18; 1 Ch 12:8); strategies employed: double attack (Gn 14:15), ambush (Jos 8:12), surprise (Ju 7), false retreat (Ju 20:36), night attack (2 K 7:12). Wars sometimes settled by single combat (1 Sm 17). After battle slain countrymen (1 K 11:15) and enemies (if on own soil, Eze 39:11-16) buried, lamentation held (2 Sm 3:31-39), triumph expressed (1 Sm 31:9; Jos 10:24), captives slain (Dt 20:16-18; 2 Ch 25:12) or sold into slavery (Am 1: 6, 9), booty equally divided (1 Sm 30:24, 25). See also *armor; army*.

Wars of the Lord (Jehovah). Source book quoted in Nm 21:14.

washing. Cleanliness emphasized in Bible; hands washed before meals, feet after journey (Gn 18:4; Ex 30:19, 21; Ju 19: 21; Mt 15:2; Mk 7:3; Lk 7:37-44; 11:38; Jn 13:5-14). See also *purification*.

wasp. Common wasp, *Vespa vulgaris*, abundant in E (Wis 12:8. RV, RSV margin: hornets).

watch. 1. Guard (Ju 7:19; 2 K 11:5; Neh 4:9; Mt 27:62-66). 2. Lookout (1 Sm 14: 16; 2 Sm 13:34; 2 K 9:17; Is 21:8). 3. Hebrew night divided into 3 watches (Ex 14:24; Ju 7:19; 1 Sm 11:11; Lm 2:19); Roman into 4 (Mt 14:25; Mk 13:35; Lk 12:38).

watchtower. See *tower; vineyard 1*.

water. Highly valued (Is 3:1; 33:16); finding water important (Gn 16:7; Ex 15:22; Nm 21:16-18); failure of water a calamity (Dt 28:12; 1 K 17:1). Figuratively: Messianic age (Is 30:25; 35:6, 7; Jer 31:9), good news (Pr 25:25), wife (SS 4:15), grace (Ps 23:2; Is 32:2; 41:17, 18; Jn 4: 7-15); negatively: trouble, misfortune (Ps 66:12; 69:1; 88:17; Is 8:7; 17:13).

water hen. Gallinule, bird of rail family (Lv 11:18; Dt 14:16. KJ: swan; RV: horned owl).

water of separation, impurity. Water prepared with ashes of red heifer for removal of sin (Nm 19).

waterspout. Cataract (as RSV, Ps 42:7).

wave offering. Sacrificial portion waved before the Lord: 1. Breast of peace offering (Lv 7:30, 34; 9:21). 2. Sheaf of first ripe grain (Lv 23:10, 11). 3. Two loaves, two lambs at Pentecost (Lv 23:15, 20). 4. Guilt offering of leper (Lv 14:12, 21). 5. Meal offering of jealousy (Nm 5:25).

wax. Beeswax. Melting wax used as simile (Ps 22:14; 68:2; 97:5; Mi 1:4).

way. 1. Path, road (Gn 38:16; Is 30:11; Mt 2:12). 2. Trip (Gn 28:20; Acts 8:36). 3. Attitude, conduct, habit (Ex 32:8; Dt 5: 33; Ps 119:9). 4. God's plan of salvation, which through Gospel involves believer's thought and life (Mt 3:3; Jn 14:6; Acts 9:2; 19:9; 22:4; 2 Ptr 2:2).

weasel. Animal of genus *Mustela* (Lv 11: 29).

weaving. See *trade 4*.

wedding. See *marriage*.

weeks, feast of. See *Pentecost*.

weeping. See *Baca; mourning*.

weight. Stones used for weights (Lv 19:36; Dt 25:15; Mi 6:11), balances for scales (Lv 19:36; Pr 16:11). Hebrews used Babylonian system (though at times with Phoenician or Aeginetan values): 60 shekels (light: .36; heavy: .72 oz) equals 1 mina (light: 1 1/12 lb: heavy 2 1/6 lb). 60 minas equal 1 talent (light: 65 lbs; heavy: 130). In Phoenician-Greek system 50 shekels (light: .33 oz; heavy .66 oz) equal 1 mina; 60 mina equal 1 talent. In the Syrian system 50 shekels (light: .457 oz; heavy: .914 oz) equal 1 mina. In Aeginetan system shekel was .554 oz, gerah 1/20 shekel; beka 1/2 shekel.

well. Water supply important in Palestine (Gn 24:11; Nm 20:17-19; Ju 7:1); at times cause of strife (Gn 21:25); deep (Jn 4:11); owned in common (Gn 29: 2, 3); covered (Gn 29:2-8); stopped by enemies (Gn 26:15, 16). H *b:'er, bor* (dug, G *phrear*): well, cistern; *'ayin, ma'yan, maqor* (G *pege*): spring. See also *water*.

wen (wĕn). See *disease*.

western sea. See *Mediterranean Sea*.

whale. 1. H *tannin* (monster): any large marine animal (Gn 1:21; Eze 32:2). 2.

H *dagh gadhol* (G *ketos*): large fish, sea monster; at times regarded as sperm whale or shark (Mt 12:40). Great fish in Jon 1:17.

wheat. See *agriculture; food; grain.*

whirlwind. Proper H word is *galgal* (wheel. Ps 77:18 [KJ: heaven]; 83:13 [KJ: wheel; RV, RSV: whirling dust]; Is 17:13 [KJ: rolling thing; RV, RSV: whirling dust]). Frequently for H *suphah* (storm wind), *sa'ar, s:'arah* (storm; tempest). Figuratively: swift destruction (Pr 1:27; Is 5: 28; Jer 4:13); God's way in whirlwind (Jb 38:1; 40:6; Nah 1:3).

white of egg. Meaning uncertain (Jb 6:6. RSV: slime of purslane).

wickedness. See *sin.*

widow. Law protected widows (Ex 22:22; Dt 27:19; Ps 94:6; Eze 22:7; Ml 3:5); shared in triennial tithe (Dt 14:29; 26: 12), feasts (Dt 16:11, 14), rights of gleaning (Dt 24:19-21). If man died without son, his brother obligated to marry widow (Dt 25:5, 6; Mt 22:23-30). See *levirate marriage*. In NT widows cared for (Acts 6:1-6; 1 Ti 5:3-16); older pious widows enrolled, probably for special service (1 Ti 5:9, 10).

wife. See *marriage.*

wilderness. Wild, thinly populated, uncultivated region used for pasturage; described as abode of wild asses (Jb 24:5), ostriches (Lm 4:3), jackals (Ml 1:3). H *midhbar* (place for driving cattle, Jb 24: 5), *'arabah* (barren, Is 33:9), *y:shimon* (dry, Ps 68:7), *tsiyyah* (arid desert, Hos 2:3), *tohu* (waste, as RSV: Jb 12:24). Chief wildernesses: of wandering in Sinai peninsula (Nm 14:33; Dt 1:1; Jos 5:6; Neh 9:19, 21; Ps 78:40, 52); of Judah (Ju 1:16); of Moab (Dt 2:8).

wild ox. Now extinct animal known for ferocity, strength, speed (Nm 23:22; 24: 8; Dt 33:17; Jb 39:9, 10; Ps 29:6. KJ: unicorn; had more than 1 horn.

will. Inclination or choice. God's will is that which He determines (Eph 1:11), as revealed in His acts, Law, especially in Christ (Mt 6:10; Acts 22:14; Ro 2:18; 12: 2; Cl 1:9). Man's fallen (natural) will cannot will good (Ro 8:7). God's grace alone inclines will to good (Ph 2:13). See also *election; predestination; sin.*

will. See *testament.*

willow. Several species in Palestine; originally symbol of joy (Lv 23:40; Jb 40: 22; Is 44:4). Weeping willow of Babylon symbol of sorrow (Ps 137:2).

willows, brook of the. Brook in Moab (Is 15:7).

wimple. Article of woman's dress (Is 3:22. RV: shawl; RSV: cloak).

wind. Hebrews recognized 4 winds (Eze 37:9; Dn 8:8; Zch 2:6; Mt 24:31): east, violent (Gn 41:6; Ex 14:21; Jb 1:19; Jer 13:24); north, cold (Jb 37:22; SS 4:16); south, heat (Lk 12:55); west, rain (1 K 18:43-45; Ps 148:8).

window. See *homes 4.*

wine, winepress, wineskin. See *vineyard.*

winnow, winnowing fork. See *agriculture 6.*

winter. Winters proper are short (Dec—Feb), but autumn and seasons of seedtime included (Gn 8:22; Ps 74:17; Zch 14:8; Mt 24:20); though mild, usually bring snow, hail to higher regions.

wisdom. Skill, intelligence, judgment, understanding (Ex 31:6; Pr 10:1; 1 K 3:28; 5:12; Dn 5:11). God's wisdom is completeness and perfection of His knowledge (Jb 10:4; 26:6; Pr 5:21; Is 31:2) and is shown in creation (Jb 38; 39; Pr 3:19, 20), especially of man (Jb 12; Ps 139:14).

God's wisdom is far above man (Jb 11: 6-9; Is 40:14, 28). God gives wisdom to man (Pr 2:6). Fear of God is beginning of wisdom (Pr 9:10). In Christ God's ultimate purposes in history are revealed, hence Jesus is wisdom (1 Co 1:30; Cl 2:2, 3). This wisdom is man's by faith and expressed in life (1 Co 1:19-24; Eph 5:15). Contrasted with this wisdom is worldly orientated understanding (1 Co 1:19-26; Mt 11:25).

Wisdom of Jesus. See *apocrypha.*

Wisdom of Solomon. See *apocrypha.*

Wise Men. See *Magi.*

witch, witchcraft. See *divination; magic.*

witness. 1. Witness in court (Dt 17:6, 7; Nm 35:30) and church (2 Co 13:1; 1 Ti 5:19). 2. Memorial (Gn 21:30). 3. People who believed God and proclaimed him (Is 43: 10-12; Heb 11; 12). 4. Those who associated with Jesus, believed Him, proclaimed Him (Mt 28:18-20; Lk 24:48; Acts 1:21, 22; 2:32); Paul included (1 Co 15:1-11). 5. Believers who risked or gave life to witness for Christ (Rv 6:9). 6. God is witness for truth (2 Co 1:23; Ph 1:8; Heb 2:4). 7. Jesus is faithful witness who reveals God (Jn 3:11-36; Rv 1:5). 8. Holy Spirit witnesses to our adoption (Ro 8:16; Gl 4:6). 9. See *Ed; martyr.*

wizard. See *divination; magic.*

wolf. Enemy of sheep (Mt 7:15; 10:16; Jn 10:12; Acts 20:29), ferocious (Gn 49:27; Eze 22:27; Hab 1:8), nocturnal in habit (Jer 5:6; Zph 3:3). Figuratively, wicked (Eze 22:27; Mt 10:16; Lk 10:3), false teachers (Mt 7:15; Acts 20:29), ferocious enemies (Jer 5:6; Jn 10:12). In Messianic kingdom wolf lives with lamb (Is 11:6; 65:25). See also *hyena.*

woman. Helpmeet of man; together with man forms unity, created in image of God, rules over creation (Gn 1:26-28; 2:18-23). See also *family; marriage.*

wool. See *dress; trade 3; 4.* Mixing wool and linen forbidden (Lv 19:19; Dt 22:11).

word. By Word God created heaven, earth (Gn 1); Word is revelation of God to men (1 K 6:11; 13:20; Jer 1:4, 11); by Word faith is created, church built (Jn 14:26; Acts 4:29, 31). Word comes to man in various forms: oral (2 Ti 4:2), written (Jn 20:31), vision (Jer 1:11), symbol (Jn 3:14, 15), etc. Word is dynamic (Is 55:10, 11; Ro 1:16), creative (Ps 147: 15-18), functional (Mt 8:24-27). Christ is Word giving knowledge (see *wisdom*), creative, dynamic (Jn 1; Cl 1:16, 17). This Word is preached and written by apostles and prophets; dwells in believers (Cl 3:16. See 2 Co 3:3). See *inspiration.*

works. 1. Works of God: creation, preservation, redemption (Gn 1; Jb 37:14-16; Ps 104:24; 107; Jn 5:20-36; 10:25-38; 14: 10-12). 2. Man's works good or bad dependent on relationship to God; good works fruit of faith (Jn 6:28, 29; Ro 6; 14:23; Gl 2:20, 21; Cl 1:21-23). See also *faith; justification; sanctification.*

world. 1. Universe (Jn 1:10). 2. Human race (Jn 3:16; 2 Co 5:19). 3. The wicked, unregenerated; egotistically, antigodly orientated (Jn 15:18; 1 Jn 2:15). Devil is prince of world (Jn 12:31). 4. Earth (1 Sm 2:8; Jb 37:12; Is 18:3). 5. Roman Empire (Lk 2:1).

worm. Creeping, boneless animal (generically: H *tola'ath, tole'ah*; G *skolex.* Dt 28:39; Is 14:11; Jon 4:7; Mk 9:48); especially maggot (Jb 21:26; Is 14:11. RSV: maggot), larva (Is 51:8). Crawling things (KJ: worms) in Mi 7:17.

wormwood. Bitter plant which grows in desert places (Pr 5:4; Jer 9:15; 23:15; Lm 3:15, 19; Am 5:7; 6:12 [KJ: hemlock]; Rv 8:11).

worship. H *shaḥah* (bow down), G *proskuneo* (kiss hand to), *sebomai* (revere), regard worship as expression of reverence for deity. H *'atsab* (work, form), G *latreuo*, *therapeuo* (serve), perform services, worship by performing rites. Patriarchs worshiped by building altars and sacrificing (Gn 12:7, 8; 13:4). Mosaic regulations established place of worship, times, forms. Prophets condemn ceremonies which do not express conviction or cover ungodly life (Is 1:11-17). NT worship is activity in Word: reading OT; psalms, hymns, songs; teaching, message; prayer; Lord's Supper (Lk 4:16-22; Acts 2:42; Ro 12:7, 8; 1 Co 11:23-34; 14:26; Eph 5:19).

wrath. 1. Anger of men (Gn 30:2; 1 Sm 17:28; 20:30); evil (2 Co 12:20) work of flesh (Gl 5:20), step removed from murder (Gn 4:5-8; Mt 5:21, 22; Eph 4:26); may be reaction to evil (1 Sm 20:34; Jn 2:15). 2. Reaction of righteous God to evil (Dt 9:7, 22; Is 13:9; Ro 1:18; Eph 5:6; Rv 14:10, 19).

writing. Sumerians wrote in pictograms (c 3,000 BC), which led to cuneiform (wedge-shaped) letters written on clay. Hebrews obtained alphabet from Phoenicians. Semitic script from 1500 BC discovered at Serabit el Khadem. First mentioned in Ex 17:14. Tables of Sinai written by finger of God (Ex 31:18; 32: 15, 16; 34:1) on stone. Writing among Hebrews attributed to men of learning (Dt 17:18; 24:1; Is 29:11, 12). Materials: clay, wax, wood, metal, plaster (Dt 27:2, 3; Jos 8:32; Lk 1:63); later vellum, parchment (2 Ti 4:13), papyrus (2 Jn 12) in long rolls (Ps 40:7; Is 29:11; Dn 12:4; Rv 5:1). Stylus used on hard material (Ex 32:4; Jb 19:24; Is 8:1), reed pen on parchment, papyrus (2 Co 3:3; 2 Jn 12). Ink made of lampblack or soot.

X

Xanthicus (zăn'thĭ-kus). Name for month Nisan in 2 Mac 11:30, 33, 38.

Xerxes (zûrk'sēz). See *Ahasuerus*.

Y

year. See *time*.

yeast. See *leaven*.

yoke. Bar or frame held on neck of draft animal by thongs around neck; attached to wagon tongue, plow beam, or other burden by another thong (Nm 19:2; Dt 21:3). Figuratively: subjection (1 K 12: 4, 9-11; Is 9:4); iron yoke: hard servitude (Dt 28:48; Jer 28:12-14); removal of yoke: deliverance (Gn 27:40; Jer 2:20; Mt 11:29, 30); yokefellow: co-laborer at difficult task (Ph 4:3).

Z

Zaanaim (zā-á-nā'ĭm). See *Zaanannim*.

Zaanan (zā'á-năn, place of flocks). Place in lowlands of Judah (Mi 1:11).

Zaanannim (zā-á-năn'ĭm, departures. KJ: Zaanaim). Place NW of Lake Huleh (Jos 19:33; Ju 4:11, 17-22).

Zaavan (zā'á-văn, unquiet. KJ: Zavan). Son of Ezer (Gn 36:27; 1 Ch 1:42).

Zabad (zā'băd, he has given). 1. Jerahmeelite; son of Nathan (1 Ch 2:36, 37). 2. Ephraimite; slain by Gathites (1 Ch 7:21). 3. Son of Ahlai; one of David's heroes (1 Ch 11:41). 4. See *Jozacar*. 5. Divorced foreign wife (Ez 10:27; 1 Esd 9:28 [KJ: Sabatus; RV: Sabathus]). 6. Divorced foreign wife (Ez 10:33; 1 Esd 9:33 [KJ: Bannaia; RV: Sabanneus]). 7. Divorced foreign wife (Ez 10:43; 1 Esd 9:35 [KJ: Zabadaias; RV: Zabadeas]).

Zabadaeans, Zabadeans (zăb-á-dē'ănz). Arab tribe in region of Damascus (1 Mac 12:30-32).

Zabadaias (zăb-á-dā'yás). See *Zabad 7*.

Zabadeas (zăb-á-dē'ás). See *Zabad 7*.

Zabbai (zăb'ā-ī). 1. Divorced foreign wife (Ez 10:28; 1 Esd 9:29 [KJ: Josabad; RV: Josabdus]). 2. Repaired wall of Jerusalem (Neh 3:20). Perhaps same as Zaccai.

Zabbud (zăb'ŭd, endowed). Head of family which returned with Ezra (Ez 8:14. RSV: Zakkur). Istalcurus in 1 Esd 8:40.

Zabdeus (zăb-dē'us). See *Zebadiah 9*.

Zabdi (zăb'dī, gift of LORD). 1. Judahite (Jos 7:1). Zimri in 1 Ch 2:6. 2. Benjaminite (1 Ch 8:19). 3. Overseer of David's vineyards (1 Ch 27:27). 4. Asaph's son; head of family of singers (Neh 11:17). Zichri in 1 Ch 9:15.

Zabdiel (zăb'dĭ-ĕl, gift of God). 1. Father of Jashobeam (1 Ch 27:2). 2. Temple overseer (Neh 11:14). 3. Arabian prince; killed Alexander Balas (1 Mac 11:17).

Zabud (zā'bŭd, given). Nathan's son; minister of Solomon (1 K 4:5).

Zabulon (zăb-û-lon). See *Zebulun 2*.

Zaccai (zăk'ā-ī, pure). Founder of family which returned with Zerubbabel (Ez 2:9; Neh 7:14). Chorbe (KJ: Corbe) in 1 Esd 5:12.

Zacchaeus (ză-kē'us, pure). 1. Chief tax-collector; climbed sycamore tree to see Jesus; converted (Lk 19:1-10). 2. Officer of Judas Maccabaeus (2 Mac 10:19. KJ: Zaccheus).

Zaccheus (ză-kē'us). See *Zacchaeus 2*.

Zacchur (zăk'ûr). See *Zaccur 2*.

Zaccur (zăk'ûr, mindful). 1. Reubenite; father of spy Shammua (Nm 13:4). 2. Simeonite (1 Ch 4:26. KJ: Zacchur). 3. Merarite Levite (1 Ch 24:27). 4. Son of Asaph; head of musicians (1 Ch 25:2, 10; Neh 12:35). Probably Zabdi. 5. Son of Imri; helped rebuild Jerusalem's walls (Neh 3:2). 6. Levite; sealed covenant (Neh 10:12). 7. Father of Hanan (Neh 13:13). 8. See *Bacchurus*.

Zachariah (zăk-á-rī'á). See *Zechariah*.

Zacharias (zăk-á-rī'ás). See *Heman 3*; *Seraiah 8*; *Zechariah*.

Zachary (zăk'á-rī). See *Zechariah*.

Zacher (zā'kēr). See *Zechariah 1*.

Zadok (zā'dŏk, righteous). 1. Descendant of Eleazar (1 Ch 24:3); son of Ahitub (2 Sm 8:17); supported David (1 Ch 12: 27, 28); high priest with Abiathar (2 Sm 8:17); supported David against Absalom (2 Sm 15:24-29); remained faithful to David (2 Sm 19:11; 1 K 1:7, 8, 32, 45). 2. Priest (1 Ch 6:12; 9:11; Ez 7:2; Neh 11: 11; 1 Esd 8:2 [KJ: Sadduc; RV: Sadduk]; 2 Esd 1:1 [KJ, RV: Sadoc]). 3. Uzziah's grandfather (2 K 15:33). 4. Repaired wall (Neh 3:4); sealed covenant (10:21). 5. Priest; repaired wall; treasurer (Neh 3:29; 13:13). 6. Ancestor of Christ (Mt 1:14. KJ, RV: Sadoc).

Zaham (zā'hăm, loathing). Rehoboam's son (2 Ch 11:19).

Zair (zā'ĭr, little). Place in Idumea, E of Dead Sea (2 K 8:21).

Zakkur (zăk'ûr). See Zabbud.

Zalaph (zā'lăf, fracture). Father of Hanun (Neh 3:30).

Zalmon (zăl'mŏn, shady). 1. See Ilai. 2. Mt near Shechem (Ju 9:48; Ps 68:14 [KJ: Salmon]).

Zalmonah (zăl-mō'nà, shady). Encampment of Israel SE of Edom (Nm 33:41, 42).

Zalmunna (zăl-mŭn'à, shade denied). One of two kings of Midian; slain by Gideon Ju 8:5-21; Ps 83:11).

Zambis (zăm'bĭs). See Amariah 5.

Zambri (zăm'brī). See Amariah 5; Zimri 1.

Zamoth (zā'mŏth). See Zattu.

Zamzummim (zăm-zŭm'ĭm). See giants 5.

Zanoah (zá-nō'à, marsh?). 1. Town in lowland of Judah (Jos 15:34; Neh 3:13; 11:30). Modern Khirbet Zanu'. 2. Town of Judah, c 10 mi SW of Hebron (Jos 15:56; 1 Ch 4:18). Perhaps modern Zanuta.

Zaphenath-paneah, Zaphnath-paaneah (zăf'-ĕ-năth-pá-nē'à, zăf'năth-pā-á-nē'à, the god speaks and he lives, or revealer of secrets). Name given Joseph by Pharaoh (Gn 41:45).

Zaphon (zā'fŏn, north). Canaanite city in lower Jordan valley (Jos 13:27; Jn 12:1 [KJ: northward]). Perhaps modern Tell el Qos.

Zara (zā'rá). See Zerah 3.

Zaraces (zăr'á-sēz. RV: Zarakes. RSV: Zarius). Brother of Jehoiakim (1 Esd 1:38).

Zarah (zā'rá). See Zerah 3.

Zaraias (zá-rā'yás). See Seraiah 8; Zerahiah 1; 2; Zebadiah 8.

Zarakes (zăr'á-kēz). See Zaraces.

Zardeus (zär-dē'us). See Aziza.

Zareah (zā'rē-á). See Zorah.

Zareathites (zā'rē-ăth-īts). See Zorathites.

Zared (zā'rĕd). See Zered.

Zarephath (zăr'ē-făth). Phoenician town (Sarafand) 8 mi S of Sidon (1 K 17:9, 10; Ob 20; Lk 4:26 [KJ: Sarepta]).

Zaretan, Zarethan (zăr'ē-tăn, -thăn). City in Jordan valley near Adamahand Succoth; bronze cast in its vicinity (Jos 3:16 |KJ: Zaretan]; 1 K 4:12 [KJ: Zartanah]; 7:46 [KJ: Zarthan]). Zeredathah (KJ: Zeredathath) in 2 Ch 4:17. Zererah (KJ: Zererath) in Ju 7:22.

Zareth-shahar (zā'rĕth-shā'här). See Zereth-shahar.

Zarhites (zär'hīts). See Zerahites.

Zarius (zá-rī'us). See Zaraces.

Zartanah, Zarthan (zär-tā'nà, zär'thăn). See Zaretan.

Zathoe, Zathoes, Zathui, Zatthu (zăth'ō-ē, ēz, zá-thū'ī, zăt'thū). See Zattu.

Zattu (zăt' û). Founder of family which returned from exile; some descendants divorced foreign wives; representative sealed covenant (Ez 2:8; 8:5 [KJ, RV

omit]; 10:27; Neh 7:13; 10:14 [KJ: Zatthu]; 1 Esd 5:12 [KJ, RV: Zathui]; 8:32 [KJ: Zathoe; RV: Zathoes]; 9:28 [KJ, RV: Zamoth]).

Zavan (zā'văn). See Zaavan.

Zaza (zā'zá, abundance). Jerahmeelite (1 Ch 2:33).

zealots (zĕl'utz). Party organized by Judas of Gamala in opposition to census of Quirinius, AD 6; increasing fanaticism provoked Roman war (Josephus, Wars, II, viii, 1; IV, iii, 9; VII, viii, 1). Apostle Simon called Zealot (Lk 6:15; Acts 1:13. KJ: Zelotes). Cananaean (Aramaic for Zealot. KJ: Canaanite) in Mt 10:4; Mk 3:18.

Zebadiah (zĕb-á-dī'á, LORD has given). 1. Son of Beriah (1 Ch 8:15). 2. Son of Elpaal (1 Ch 8:17). 3. Benjaminite; joined David at Ziklag (1 Ch 12:7). 4. Korahite; temple gatekeeper (1 Ch 26:2). 5. Asahel's son; David's commander of 4th division (1 Ch 27:7). 6. Levite; taught people Law (2 Ch 17:8). 7. Son of Ishmael; in charge of king's matters under Jehoshaphat (2 Ch 19:11). 8. Returned with Ezra from captivity (Ez 8:8). Zeraiah (KJ, RV: Zaraias) in 1 Esd 8:34. 9. Priest; divorced foreign wife (Ez 10:20; 1 Esd 9:21 [KJ, RV: Zabdeus]).

Zebah (zē'bá, sacrifice). One of two Midianite kings slain by Gideon (Ju 8:5-21; Ps 83:11).

Zebaim (zē-bā'ĭm). See Pochereth-hazzebaim.

Zebedee (zĕb'ē-dē, LORD has endowed). Husband of Salome; father of James, John; fisherman (Mt 4:21, 22; 27:56; Mk 1:19, 20; Lk 5:10; Jn 21:2).

Zebidah (zē-bī'dá, given. KJ: Zebudah). Mother of Jehoiakim (2 K 23:36).

Zebina (zē-bī'ná, acquired). Divorced foreign wife (Ez 10:43).

Zeboiim (zē-boi-ĭm, gazelles). One of 5 cities in plain defeated by Chedorlaomer (Gn 14:2); destroyed with Sodom and Gomorrah (Gn 10:19 [KJ: Zeboim]; 14:2, 8; Dt 29:23 [KJ: Zeboim]; Hos 11:8 [KJ, RV: Zeboim]).

Zeboim (zē-bō'ĭm, hyenas). 1. Valley E of Michmash (1 Sm 13:16-18). 2. Town inhabited by Benjaminites after exile (Neh 11:34). 3. See Zeboiim.

Zebudah (zē-bū'dá). See Zebidah.

Zebul (zē'bŭl, habitation). Governor of city of Shechem; loyal to Abimelech (Ju 9: 28-41).

Zebulun (zĕb'û-lun, dwelling). 1. 10th son of Jacob, 6th of Leah (Gn 30:20; 35:23; Gn 46:14); in his blessing Jacob describes him as dwelling by sea (Gn 49:13). 2. Tribe stood on Ebal and pronounced curses (Dt 27:13); territory between Sea of Galilee and Mediterranean included Nazareth (Jos 19:10-16; Is 9:1; Mt 4: 12-16 [KJ: Zabulon]); idolatrous (2 Ch 30:10-18); carried into captivity (2 K 15:29). KJ: Zabulon in Rv 7:8.

Zechariah (zĕk-á-rī'á, LORD has remembered. KJ, RV: Zachariah, Zacharias, or Zachary in Apocr, NT). 1. Benjaminite (1 Ch 9:37). Zecher (KJ: Zacher) in 1 Ch 8:31. 2. 14th king of Israel; son of Jeroboam II; assassinated by Shallum (2 K 14:29; 15:8, 11. KJ: Zachariah]). 3. Grandfather of Hezekiah (2 K 18:2 [KJ: Zachariah]; 2 Ch 29:1). 4. Reubenite (1 Ch 5:7). 5. Levite; gatekeeper (1 Ch 9:21; 26:2, 14). 6. Levite; musician (1 Ch 15:18, 20; 16:5). 7. Priest (1 Ch 15:24). 8. Kohathite Levite (1 Ch 24:25). 9. Merarite Levite (1 Ch 26:11). 10.

Manassite (1 Ch 27:21). **11.** Deputy of Jehoshaphat (2 Ch 17:7). **12.** Descendant of Asaph; encouraged Jehoshaphat against Moab (2 Ch 20:14). **13.** Son of Jehoshaphat (2 Ch 21:2). **14.** Priest; son of Jehoida; reformer, slain in temple by order of King Joash (2 Ch 24:20-22). Probably referred to in Mt 23:35; Lk 11:51. **15.** Prophet; adviser of Uzziah (2 Ch 26:5). **16.** Descendant of Asaph (2 Ch 29:13). **17.** Kohathite Levite; overseer of temple repairs (2 Ch 34:12). **18.** Ruler in God's house in Josiah's times (2 Ch 35:8). **19.** Son of Parosh; returned with Ezra (Ez 8:3; 1 Esd 8:30). **20.** Son of Bebai; returned with Ezra (Ez 8:11; 1 Esd 8:37). **21.** Chief; sent by Ezra to get servants for temple (Ez 8:16; 1 Esd 8:44. Probably same as 19 or 20. **22.** Divorced foreign wife (Ez 10:26; 1 Esd 9:27). **23.** Stood by Ezra when he read Law (Neh 8:4; 1 Esd 9:44). Probably same as 21. **24.** Judahite (Neh 11:4). **25.** Judahite (Neh 11:5). **26.** Priest; son of Passhur (Neh 11:12). **27.** Priest; descendant of Asaph (Neh 12:35, 41). **28.** Contemporary of Isaiah (Is 8:2). **29.** Father of captain Joseph (1 Mac 5:18). **30.** Minor prophet; son of Berechiah; grandson of Iddo (Zch 1:1); contemporary of Zerubbabel, Jeshua, Haggai (Zch 3:1; 4:6; 6:11; Ez 5:1, 2; 6:14; 2 Esd 1:40); exhorted Jews to resume work on temple; probably priest (Neh 12:16). **31.** Father of John the Baptist; husband of Elizabeth; priest of course of Abijah (Lk 1:5). See 1 Ch 24:10; lived in hill country (Lk 1:5-25, 39-80).

Zechariah, Book of. Postexilic minor prophet (see *Zechariah 30*). Deals with destiny of God's people. Outline: 1. Visions of People of God Under New Covenant (1—6). 2. Two Addresses of Exhortations and Warnings (7; 8). 3. Future of God's People and Kingdom; Coming of Messiah (9—14.)

Zecher (zē'kēr). See *Zechariah 1*.

Zechrias (zēk'rǐ-ăs). See *Azariah 8*.

Zedad (zē'dăd). City on N boundary of Palestine (Nm 34:8; Eze 47:15).

Zedechias (zĕd-ė-kī'ǎs). See *Zedekiah 4*.

Zedekiah (zĕd-ė-kī'ă, righteousness of LORD). **1.** Son of Chenaanah; head of prophetic school (1 K 22: 11, 24; 2 Ch 18:10, 23). **2.** Son of Maaseiah; lying prophet (Jer 29:21-23). **3.** Son of Hananiah; prince (Jer 36:12). **4.** Last king of Judah, son of Josiah; appointed by Nebuchadnezzar, who changed name from Mattaniah to Zedekiah; revolted and occasioned final captivity (2 K 24:17-20; 25:1-21; 2 Ch 36:10-21; Jer 21—39; Eze 17:15-21; 1 Esd 1:46 [KJ: Zedechias. RV: Sedekias]; Bar 1:8 [KJ: Sedecias. RV: Sedekias]). **5.** Sealed covenant with Nehemiah (Neh 10:1; KJ: Zidkijah). **6.** Ancestor of Baruch (Bar 1:1. KJ: Sedecias. RV: Sedekias).

Zeeb (zē'ĕb, wolf). Midianite prince slain at "winepress of Zeeb" (Ju 7:25; 8:3; Ps 83:11).

Zela, Zelah (zē'lă, rib side). Town in Benjamin; site of family tomb of Kish (Jos 18:28; 2 Sm 21:14).

Zelek (zē'lĕk, cleft). Ammonite; one of David's heroes (2 Sm 23:37; 1 Ch 11:39).

Zelophehad (zė-lō'fė-hăd). Manassite; had no sons but 5 daughters, which led to law of female inheritance (Nm 26:33; 27: 1-11; 36:1-12; Jos 17:3; 1 Ch 7:15).

Zelotes (zė-lō'tēz). See *Zealots*.

Zelzah (zĕl'ză). Place on Ephraimite-Benjaminite border near Rachel's tomb (1 Sm 10:2).

Zemaraim (zĕm-á-rā'ĭm, two fleeces?) **1.** Town between Beth-arabah and Bethel (Jos 18:22). Perhaps modern Ras ez Zemara. **2.** Mt near town (2 Ch 13:4).

Zemarite (zĕm'á-rīt). Descendant of Canaan (Gn 10:18; 1 Ch 1:16).

Zemer (zē'mēr. KJ, RV: Tyre). Town of Zemarites (Eze 27:8).

Zemira, Zemirah (zē-mī'rá, music). Grandson of Benjamin (1 Ch 7:8).

Zenan (zē'năn, point). Town of Judah (Jos 15:37). Perhaps Zaanan.

Zenas (zē'năs). Christian lawyer of Crete (Tts 3:13).

Zephaniah (zĕf-á-nī'á, LORD hides). **1.** 9th minor prophet; son of Cushi; descendant of Hezekiah; contemporary of Josiah (Zph 1:1; 2 Esd 1:40 [KJ, RV: Sophonias]). **2.** Priest under Zedekiah (2 K 25:18; Jer 52:24); arbiter of true and false prophets (Jer 29:25); emissary to Jeremiah (Jer 21:1; 37:3); carried captive to Riblah (Jer 52:24, 25). **3.** Kohathite Levite (1 Ch 6:36). Probably same as Uriel 1. **4.** Father of Josiah (Zch 6:10) and Hen (RSV: Josiah. Zch 6:14).

Zephaniah, Book of. 9th minor prophet; written in days of Josiah. Outline: 1. Coming of Day of Jehovah (1). 2. Fall of Philistia, Moab, Ammon, Assyria (2). 3. Sins of Jerusalem; Admonitions (3: 1-8). 4. God-Fearing, Unscathed Remnant (3:9-13). 5. Restored Daughter of Zion (3:14-20).

Zephath (zē'făth, watchtower). See *Hormah*.

Zephathah (zĕf'á-thá, watchtower). Valley near Mareshah (2 Ch 14:9, 10).

Zephi, Zepho (zē'fī, -fō, watch). Grandson of Esau; chief of Edom (Gn 36:11-15). Zephi in 1 Ch 1:36.

Zephon (zē'fŏn, watching). Son of Gad; founder of Zephonite family (Nm 26:15). Ziphion in Gn 46:15.

Zer (zûr, flint). City of Naphtali (Jos 19:35).

Zerah (zē'rá, dawn). **1.** Descendant of Esau; chief of Edom (Gn 36:13, 17; 1 Ch 1:37). **2.** Father of Jobal; perhaps same as 1 (Gn 36:33; 1 Ch 1:44). **3.** Son of Judah; ancestor of Zerahites (Gn 38:30; 46:12; Nm 26:20; Jos 7:1. KJ: Zarah in Gn; Zara in Mt 1:3). **4.** Son of Simeon; ancestor of Zerahites (Nm 26:13; 1 Ch 4:24). Zohar in Gn 46:10; Ex 6:15. **5.** Levites (1 Ch 6:21, 41). **7.** See *Pharaoh 7*.

Zerahiah (zĕr-á-hī'á, LORD is risen). **1.** High priest (1 Ch 6:6, 51; Ez 7:4). Zaraias in 1 Esd 8:2. Arna in 2 Esd 1:2. **2.** Leader of returned captives from Pahath-moab (Ez 8:4; 1 Esd 8:31 [KJ, RV: Zaraias]).

Zerahites (zĕr'á-īts. KJ: Zarhites). **1.** Descendants of Zerah 3 (Nm 26:20; Jos 7:17; 1 Ch 27:11, 13). **2.** Descendants of Zerah 4 (Nm 26:13).

Zeraiah (zē-rā'yá). See *Zebadiah 8*.

Zerdaiah (zĕr-dā'yá). See *Aziza*.

Zered (zē'rĕd, exuberant growth). Valley between Edom and Moab; encampment of Israel (Nm 21:12 [KJ: Zared]; Dt 2: 13, 14). Perhaps modern wadi el Hesa.

Zereda, Zeredah (zĕr'ė-dá). **1.** Town in Mt Ephraim; birthplace of Jeroboam (1 K 11:26). **2.** See *Zaretan*.

Zeredathah, Zererah, Zererath (zĕr-ė-dā'thá, zĕr'ė-rá, -răth). See *Zaretan*.

Zeresh (zē'rĕsh). Haman's wife (Est 5: 10-14).

Zereth (zē'rĕth, brightness). Ashhur's son (1 Ch 4:7).

Zereth-shahar (zē'rĕth-shā'här, brightness of dawn. KJ: Zareth-shahar). Perhaps modern Zara.

Zeri (zē'rī). See Izri.

Zeror (zē'rôr). Ancestor of Saul (1 Sm 9:1).

Zeruah (zē-rōō'ȧ, leprous). Jeroboam's mother (1 K 11:26).

Zerubbabel (ze-rŭb'ȧ-bel, born in Babylon). Son of Shealtiel (Ez 3:2, 8; 5:2; Neh 12: 1; Hg 1:1, 12, 14); led 1st colony of captives to Jerusalem (Ez 2; Neh 7:7); rebuilt temple despite Samaritan opposition (Ez 3—6) with support of Haggai and Zechariah (Hg 1:12, 15; 2:2-4; Zch 4:6-10); restored courses of priests (Ez 6:18; Neh 12:47); observed Passover (Ez 6:19). KJ: Zorobabel in Mt 1:12, 13; Lk 3:27.

Zeruiah (zĕr-ōō-ī'ȧ). David's sister (1 Ch 2:16), perhaps by earlier marriage of mother (2 Sm 17:25); mother of Abishai, Joab, Asahel (2 Sm 2:18).

Zetham (zē'thăm). Gershonite Levite (1 Ch 23:8; 26:22).

Zethan (zē'thăn, olive). Benjaminite (1 Ch 7:10).

Zethar (zē'thär). Chamberlain of Ahasuerus (Est 1:10).

Zeus (zūs. KJ, RV: Jupiter). Supreme god of Greeks corresponding to Roman Jupiter (Acts 14:12, 13).

Zia (zī'ȧ, trembling movement). Gadite (1 Ch 5:13).

Ziba (zī'bȧ). Servant of Saul; assigned by David to cultivate Mephibosheth's land; slandered Mephibosheth (2 Sm 9; 16:1-4; 19:17, 24-30).

Zibeon (zīb'ē-ŭn). Horite; son of Seir (Gn 36:20, 24, 29; 1 Ch 1:38, 40). Called Hivite in Gn 36:2.

Zibia (zīb'ĭ-ȧ, gazelle). Benjaminite (1 Ch 8:9).

Zibiah (zīb'ĭ-ȧ, gazelle). Mother of Jehoash (2 K 12:1; 2 Ch 24:1).

Zichri (zīk'rī, mindful). 1. Levite; Izhar's son (Ex 6:21. KJ: Zithri). 2. Benjaminite; son of Shimhi (1 Ch 8:19). 3. Benjaminite; son of Shashak (1 Ch 8:23). 4. Benjaminite; son of Jeroham (1 Ch 8:27). 5. See Zabdi 4. 6. Levite; descendant of Eliezer (1 Ch 26:25). 7. Reubenite (1 Ch 27:16). 8. Amasiah's father (2 Ch 27:16). 9. Elishaphat's father (2 Ch 23:1). 10. Mighty man in army of Pekah (2 Ch 28: 7). 11. Joel's father (Neh 11:9). 12. Priest (Neh 12:17).

Ziddim (zĭd'ĭm, sides). Fortified city of Naphtali 5½ mi NW of Tiberias (Jos 19: 35).

Zidkijah (zĭd-kī'jȧ). See Zedekiah 5.

Zidon (zī'd'n). See Sidon.

Ziha (zī'hȧ). 1. Ancestor of Nethinim (Ez 2:43; Neh 7:46; 1 Esd 5:29 [KJ, RV: Esau]). 2. Leader of Nethinim (Neh 11: 21).

Ziklag (zīk'lăg). City in S Judah between Beer-sheba and Gath (Jos 15:31; 19:5); given by Achish of Gath to exiled David (1 Sm 27:6; 30:1, 2; 2 Sm 1:1; 4:10). Probably modern Tell el-Khuweiefeh.

Zillah (zīl'ȧ, shadow). Lamech's wife (Gn 4:19, 22, 23).

Zillethai (zīl'ē-thī, shadow. KJ: Zilthai). 1. Benjaminite (1 Ch 8:20). 2. Manassite captain; joined David at Ziklag (1 Ch 12:20).

Zilpah (zīl'pȧ, dropping). Syrian woman; Jacob's concubine (Gn 29:24; 30:9-13; 35:26; 37:2, 46:18).

Zilthai (zīl'thī). See Zillethai.

Zimmah (zīm'ȧ, purpose). 1. Gershonite Levite (1 Ch 6:20). 2. Gershonite Levite; father of Ethan (1 Ch 6:42). 3. Gershonite Levite; father of Joah (2 Ch 29:12).

Zimran (zĭm'răn). Son of Abraham and Keturah (Gn 25:2; 1 Ch 1:32).

Zimri (zĭm'rī, mountain sheep). 1. Prince of Simeon; slain at Shittim by Phinehas for participating in licentious idolatry with Midianites (Nm 25:14; 1 Mac 2:26 [KJ: Zambri]). 2. 5th king of Israel; general; murdered and succeeded Elah; overthrown by Omri (1 K 16:9-20; 2 K 9:31). 3. See Zabdi 1. 4. Descendant of Saul (1 Ch 8:36; 9:42). 5. Unknown locality (Jer 25:25).

Zin (zĭn). Wilderness S of Judah (Nm 34: 3; Jos 15:1); Kadesh on boundary of Zin (Nm 20:1) and Paran (Nm 13:26).

Zina (zī'nȧ). See Zizah.

Zion (zī-ŭn. KJ: Sion in Ps 65:1 and NT). 1. Jebusite city on S spur of E ridge of Jerusalem, S of Haram esh Sherif, on which Herod's temple later stood; water received from Gihon Spring (Virgin Fountain) through aqueduct; captured by David, renamed "City of David," made capital (Jos 15:63; 2 Sm 5:6-9; 1 Ch 11: 5-8). 2. After temple was built on Moriah, name Zion extended to include it (Is 8:18; 18:7; 24: 23; Jl 3:17; Mi 4:7). 3. David began extension of city (2 Sm 5:9) and name extended to whole city (2 K 19:21; Ps 48; 69:35; Is 1:8). 4. Temple hill (1 Mac 7:32, 33). 5. Symbol of God's kingdom (Ps 76:2; Is 1:27; 2:3; 4:1-6; Jl 3:16; Zch 1:16, 17; 2:3-8; Ro 11:26). 6. New heavenly Jerusalem (Heb 12:22-24; Rv 14:1; 21; 22).

Zior (zī-ôr, smallness). Town of Judah near Hebron (Jos 15:54).

Ziph (zīf). 1. Grandson of Caleb (1 Ch 2: 42). 2. Judahite (1 Ch 4:16). 3. City (Tell Zif) 5 mi SE of Hebron (Jos 15:55) where David hid (1 Sm 23:14-24; 26:1, 2; Ps 54 title). 4. Place in Judah (Jos 15: 24).

Ziphah (zī'fȧ). Brother of Ziph 2 (1 Ch 4: 16).

Ziphims (zīf'ĭmz). See Ziphites.

Ziphion (zīf'ĭ-ŏn). See Zephon.

Ziphites (zīf'īts). Inhabitants of Ziph (1 Sm 23:19; 26:1; Ps 54 title [KJ: Ziphims]).

Ziphron (zīf'rŏn, fragrance). Place on N boundary of promised land (Nm 34:9). Perhaps Sepharvaim.

Zippor (zīp'ôr, bird). Balak's father (Nm 22:2-16; 23:18).

Zipporah (zĭ-pō-rȧ, sparrow). Moses' wife; daughter of priest of Midian (Ex 2:16-22; 4:25; 18:2-4).

Zithri (zĭth'rī). See Sithri; Zichri 1.

Ziz (zĭz, bright thing). Ascent from Dead Sea to Tekoa (2 Ch 20:16).

Ziza (zī'zȧ). 1. Son of Shiphi; prince of Simeon (1 Ch 4:37). 2. Rehoboam's son (2 Ch 11:20).

Zizah (zī'zȧ, plenty). Gershonite Levite (1 Ch 23:11). Zina in 1 Ch 23:10.

Zoan (zō'ăn). City on E side of Tanitic branch of Nile (Nm 13:22; Ps 78:12, 43; Is 19:11, 13; 30:4; Eze 30:14). Tanis in Jdth 1:10.

Zoar (zō'ẽr). City of plain with Sodom and Gomorrah (Gn 13:10); spared from destruction; refuge of Lot (Gn 19: 20-30. See Is 15:5; Jer 48:4 [RSV], 34). Bela in Gn 14:2, 8.

Zoba, Zobah (zō'bȧ). Aramaean principality N of Damascus which, under Hadadezer, had extended sway to Euphrates; conquered by David (1 Sm 14:47; 2 Sm 8: 3-8; 10:6-19; 1 Ch 18:3-8; 19:6; 2 Ch 8:3).

Zobebah (zŏ-bē'bá, gentle movement). Judahite (1 Ch 4:8).

Zohar (zō'här, whiteness). **1.** Hittite; father of Ephron (Gn 23:8; 25:9). **2.** See *Zerah 4.*

Zoheleth (zō'hĕ-lĕth, serpent. RSV: Serpent's Stone). Stone or ledge of En-rogel (1 K 1:9).

Zoheth (zō'hĕth). Judahite (1 Ch 4:20).

Zophah (zō'fá, expanded flask). Asherite (1 Ch 7:35, 36).

Zophai (zō'fī). See *Zuph 1.*

Zophar (zō'fĕr, chirper). Job's counselor and friend; called Naamathite, from an unidentified town (Jb 2:11; 11:1; 20:1; 42:9).

Zophim (zō'fĭm, watchers). High point on Pisgah (Nm 23:14).

Zorah (zō'rá, hornet, scourge). Canaanite city at highest point of Shephelah, c 5 mi NW of Beth-shemesh; home of Samson (Jos 15:33 [KJ: Zoreah]; 19:41; Ju 13:2;

16:31; 18:2, 8, 11; 2 Ch 11:10; Neh 11; 29 [KJ: Zareah]). Modern Sar'a.

Zorathites (zō'răth-īts). Calebite family at Zorah (1 Ch 2:53 [KJ: Zareathites]; 4:2).

Zoreah (zō'rē-á). See *Zorah.*

Zorites (zō-'rīts). Judahite family (1 Ch 2: 54).

Zorobabel (zŏ-rŏb'á-bel). See *Zerubbabel.*

Zorzelleus (zôr-zĕl'yũs). See *Barzillai 1.*

Zuar (zū'ĕr, smallness). Prince of Issachar (Nm 1:8; 2:5; 7:18, 23; 10:15).

Zuph (zŭf, honeycomb). **1.** Kohathite Levite; ancestor of Samuel (1 Sm 1:1; 1 Ch 6:35). Zophai in 1 Ch 6:26. **2.** Region to which Saul came in search of his father's asses (1 Sm 9:5-15).

Zur (zûr, rock). **1.** Midianite king; slain by Israel (Nm 25:15; 31:8; Jos 13:21). **2.** Founder of Gibeon (1 Ch 8:30; 9:36).

Zuriel (zū'rĭ-ĕl, God is my rock). Abihail's son (Nm 3:35).

Zurishaddai (zū-rĭ-shăd'á-ī, my rock the Almighty). Shelumiel's father (Nm 1:6; 2:12; 7:36, 41; 10:19). Salasadai (RSV: Sarasadai) in Jdth 8:1.

Zuzim (zū'zĭm). See *giants 5.*